THE AMERICAN CONSTITUTION
ITS ORIGINS AND DEVELOPMENT

THE AMERICAN CONSTITUTION ITS ORIGINS AND DEVELOPMENT

Volume I

by
Alfred H. Kelly, Winfred A. Harbison,
and
Herman Belz

SEVENTH EDITION

W · W · NORTON & COMPANY

NEW YORK · LONDON

PRINTED IN THE UNITED STATES OF AMERICA.

The text of this book is composed in Times Roman with the display set in Janson.
Composition by Com Com. Manufacturing by Maple-Vail.

Library of Congress Cataloging-in-Publication Data

Kelly, Alfred Hinsey, 1907-
    The American Constitution: its origins and development/by
Alfred H. Kelly, Winfred A. Harbison, and Herman Belz. -- 7th ed.
      p. cm.
    Includes index.
    1. United States--Constitutional history. I. Harbison, Winfred
Audif, 1904-. II. Belz, Herman. III. Title.
JK31.K4 1991
342.73'029--dc20
[347.30229]   90-25619

ISBN: 0-393-96056-0 (paper)

W. W. Norton & Company, Inc.,
500 Fifth Avenue, New York, N.Y. 10110

W. W. Norton & Company, Ltd.,
10 Coptic Street, London WCIA 1PU

1 2 3 4 5 6 7 8 9 0

FOR KRISTIN AND AARON

Contents

Volumes I (Chapters 1–18) and II (Chapters 17–33)

Preface to the Seventh Edition   xv

Preface to the Sixth Edition   xvii

Introduction   xix

Members of the Supreme Court   xxvi

VOLUME I

1. *The Founding of English Colonies in North America*   1

   THE CORPORATION COLONIES: VIRGINIA AND MASSACHUSETTS BAY •
   GOVERNMENT BY COMPACT: PLYMOUTH, RHODE ISLAND, CONNECTICUT, AND
   NEW HAVEN • THE PROPRIETARY PRINCIPLE

2. *The Formation of the Colonial Constitution: 1640–1700*   12

   COLONIAL AUTONOMY DURING THE ENGLISH CIVIL WAR • THE SECOND WAVE
   OF COLONIZATION IN ENGLISH NORTH AMERICA • IMPERIAL
   CENTRALIZATION • THE GLORIOUS REVOLUTION IN AMERICA •
   SIGNIFICANCE OF THE REVOLUTIONARY SETTLEMENT

3. *The Colonial Constitution in the Eighteenth Century*   27

   THE THEORY OF MIXED GOVERNMENT • THE GROWTH OF ASSEMBLY POWER
   • THE GOVERNOR AND COUNCIL • POLITICAL INSTABILITY IN AMERICA •
   PRE-REVOLUTIONARY POLITICAL THOUGHT • COLONIAL COURTS • LOCAL
   GOVERNMENT

4. *The American Revolution*   43

   IMPERIAL REORGANIZATION • THE FEDERAL THEORY OF EMPIRE • THE
   FORMATION OF AN AMERICAN RESISTANCE MOVEMENT • THE DOMINION
   THEORY OF EMPIRE • THE FIRST CONTINENTAL CONGRESS • THE COMING
   OF INDEPENDENCE • THE AMERICAN CONCEPTION OF CONSTITUTIONALISM

5. *Revolutionary Constitutionalism: The States and the Articles of Confederation*   65

REPUBLICANISM AS A REVOLUTIONARY PHILOSOPHY • THE STATE CONSTITUTIONS • THE SEPARATION OF POWERS AND THE STATE CONSTITUTIONS • THE PROBLEM OF REPRESENTATION • THE ARTICLES OF CONFEDERATION

6. *Constitutional Reform and the Federal Convention of 1787*   82

THE PROBLEM OF EXCESSIVE STATE POWER • REPUBLICANISM AND THE CONSTITUTION • THE NEW JERSEY PLAN • THE GREAT COMPROMISE • THE EXECUTIVE • FEDERAL SUPREMACY AND THE JUDICIARY • THE LOCUS OF SOVEREIGNTY • THE CONSTITUTION COMPLETED

7. *Ratification of the Constitution*   103

ANTIFEDERALIST PRINCIPLES • FEDERALIST CONSTITUTIONAL THEORY • THE TRIUMPH OF THE FEDERALISTS • THE CONSTITUTION AND THE REVOLUTION

8. *Establishing the New Government: Federalist Constitutionalism*   117

THE BILL OF RIGHTS • ORGANIZATION OF THE EXECUTIVE DEPARTMENT • FOREIGN POLICY AND EXECUTIVE PREROGATIVE • HAMILTONIAN BROAD CONSTRUCTION • THE RISE OF POLITICAL PARTIES • THE SEDITION ACT CRISIS • THE VIRGINIA AND KENTUCKY RESOLUTIONS

9. *Republican Constitutionalism: 1801–1828*   138

REPUBLICAN CONSTITUTIONAL IDEAS • THE JEFFERSONIAN EXECUTIVE • THE LOUISIANA PURCHASE • THE EMBARGO • THE WAR OF 1812 AND NATIONAL REPUBLICAN MERCANTILISM • REPUBLICAN CONSTITUTIONAL INTERPRETATION

10. *The Place of the Judiciary in the Constitutional System and the Origins of Judicial Review*   156

THE JUDICIARY ACT OF 1789 • THE FEDERAL JUDICIARY IN THE 1790s • JUDICIAL REFORM: THE JUDICIARY ACT OF 1801 • FEDERAL COMMON LAW • THE REVOLUTION OF 1800 AND THE JUDICIARY • IMPEACHMENT OF FEDERAL JUDGES • JUDICIAL REVIEW • *Marbury* v. *Madison* • THE BURR TRIAL AND JUDICIAL INDEPENDENCE

11. *John Marshall and Constitutional Nationalism*   178

JUDICIAL NATIONALISM • MARSHALL'S THEORY OF FEDERALISM • VESTED RIGHTS AND THE CONTRACT CLAUSE • THE CORPORATION IN CONSTITUTIONAL LAW • THE CONTRACT CLAUSE AND BANKRUPTCY LAWS • THE COMMERCE CLAUSE • MARSHALL'S CONTRIBUTION TO AMERICAN CONSTITUTIONALISM

12. *Jacksonian Democracy and Dual Federalism*   200

JACKSONIAN CONSTITUTIONALISM • GEORGIA AND FEDERAL INDIAN POLICY

• THE BANK WAR • NULLIFICATION: CALHOUN'S THEORY • THE
NULLIFICATION CRISIS: FEDERAL SOVEREIGNTY VINDICATED • THE MODERN
TWO-PARTY SYSTEM • JACKSON AND EXECUTIVE POWER • STATE
CONSTITUTIONAL CHANGE • POPULAR SOVEREIGNTY

13. *Jacksonian Jurisprudence: The Taney Court and Constitutional Law*
    222
    THE NEW ERA IN CONSTITUTIONAL LAW • THE *Charles River Bridge* CASE •
    THE SANCTITY OF CONTRACT • THE LEGAL STATUS OF CORPORATIONS •
    THE COMMERCE POWER AND DUAL FEDERALISM • THE TANEY COURT AND
    JUDICIAL NATIONALISM • STATE MERCANTILISM

14. *Slavery and the Constitution*   241
    SLAVERY AND REPUBLICAN GOVERNMENT • THE PROBLEM OF FUGITIVE
    SLAVES • THE NATIONALIZATION OF THE SLAVERY QUESTION • SLAVERY
    IN THE TERRITORIES • THE COMPROMISE OF 1850

15. *Slavery and the Crisis of the American Republic*   263
    THE POLITICAL REALIGNMENT OF THE 1850S • THE KANSAS-NEBRASKA BILL •
    THE *Dred Scott* CASE • THE LINCOLN-DOUGLAS DEBATES • STATE
    SOVEREIGNTY VINDICATED: *Ableman* V. *Booth* • SECESSION • ATTEMPTS
    AT COMPROMISE • FORMATION OF THE CONFEDERACY • LINCOLN AND THE
    SECESSION CRISIS

16. *The Civil War*   291
    LINCOLN AND THE CONSTITUTION • THE LEGAL NATURE OF THE WAR • THE
    PROBLEM OF INTERNAL SECURITY • THE HABEAS CORPUS ACT OF 1863 •
    FEDERAL CENTRALIZATION OF AUTHORITY • COMPULSORY MILITARY
    SERVICE • UNION WAR AIMS • EMANCIPATION • CONSTITUTIONAL
    SIGNIFICANCE OF THE CIVIL WAR

BEGIN VOLUME II

17. *Reconstruction: The Nationalization of Civil Rights*   319
    WARTIME RECONSTRUCTION • THEORIES OF RECONSTRUCTION • JOHNSON'S
    POLICY OF RECONSTRUCTION • FEDERAL FREEDMEN'S POLICY IN 1865 •
    THE MODERATE REPUBLICAN POLICY OF 1866 • THE FOURTEENTH
    AMENDMENT

18. *Congressional Reconstruction*   336
    THE MILITARY RECONSTRUCTION ACTS OF 1867 • THE IMPEACHMENT OF
    JOHNSON • NATIONAL ENFORCEMENT OF CIVIL RIGHTS • THE ELECTION OF
    1876 • RECONSTRUCTION AND THE JUDICIARY • THE CONSTITUTIONAL
    SIGNIFICANCE OF RECONSTRUCTION

    Appendix 1: Declaration of Independence   A1

    Appendix 2: Articles of Confederation   A5

    Appendix 3: The Constitution of the United States   A13

Bibliography   *A34*
Table of Cases   *A115*
Index   *A133*

END VOLUME I

19. *Constitutional Change in the Era of the Industrial Revolution*   *362*
CONGRESSIONAL GOVERNMENT • THE NATURE AND TENDENCY OF FEDERAL
GOVERNANCE • POLITICAL PARTIES IN THE GILDED AGE • CIVIL SERVICE
REFORM • TOWARD NATIONAL ECONOMIC REGULATION • RAILROAD
REGULATION: THE INTERSTATE COMMERCE ACT OF 1887 • THE SHERMAN
ANTITRUST ACT OF 1890 • IMPERIALISM AND FEDERAL INDIAN POLICY •
OVERSEAS IMPERIALISM

20. *The Supreme Court and Entrepreneurial Liberty*   *386*
STATES' RIGHTS AND ECONOMIC REGULATION • JUDICIAL PROTECTION OF THE
NATIONAL MARKET • TOWARD A CONSERVATIVE JURISPRUDENCE •
CONSERVATIVE CONSTITUTIONALISM: THE COURTS AND LABOR •
CONSERVATIVE CONSTITUTIONALISM: THE INCOME TAX CASES • JUDICIAL
SUPREMACY • THE ELECTION OF 1896

21. *Progressive Constitutionalism*   *408*
TOWARD THE MODERN PRESIDENCY • ORIGINS OF THE BUREAUCRATIC STATE
• NATIONAL REGULATION AND CONSTITUTIONAL LAW • PROGRESSIVE
REGULATION: THE TRUST QUESTION • PROGRESSIVE REGULATION: THE
RAILROADS • GOVERNMENT REGULATION OF POLITICS: RESTORING
GOVERNMENT TO THE PEOPLE

22. *The Constitution and World War I*   *433*
FEDERAL POWER IN WARTIME • WILSON'S WAR LEADERSHIP

23. *The Constitution in Transition: 1900–1933*   *442*
CONFLICTING TENDENCIES IN CONSTITUTIONAL LAW • PRESERVING THE
FUNDAMENTALS • LABOR AND THE SUPREME COURT • SUBSTANTIVE DUE
PROCESS AND STATE SOCIAL LEGISLATION • CONFLICTING THEORIES OF
JURISPRUDENCE • TOWARD POSITIVE GOVERNMENT AND THE REGULATORY
STATE • NATIONAL PROHIBITION • THE HOOVER ADMINISTRATION AND
THE DEPRESSION

24. *The New Deal*   *467*
NEW DEAL CONSTITUTIONAL POLITICS: THE ANALOGUE OF WAR •
COORDINATING THE NATIONAL ECONOMY • THE SUPREME COURT AND THE
NEW DEAL • THE COURT-PACKING CRISIS OF 1937

25. *The New Deal and the Emergence of a Centralized Bureaucratic State* 487

THE COURT ACCEPTS THE NEW DEAL • THE NEW CONSTITUTIONAL LAW: THE FEDERAL REGULATORY STATE • STATE REGULATION AND THE COMMERCE POWER • THE REJECTION OF ECONOMIC DUE PROCESS • BUILDING THE BUREAUCRATIC STATE: EXECUTIVE REORGANIZATION • FEDERALISM AND THE NEW DEAL • CONSTITUTIONAL SIGNIFICANCE OF THE NEW DEAL

26. *The Development of Modern Civil Liberties Law: 1919–1950* 508

CIVIL LIBERTIES LAW BEFORE WORLD WAR I • THE WAR AND THE BILL OF RIGHTS • CIVIL LIBERTIES IN THE 1920s • CIVIL LIBERTIES IN THE NEW DEAL ERA • THE NEW MEANING OF FREEDOM OF SPEECH: PICKETING • FREEDOM OF SPEECH: PUBLIC MEETINGS, PARADES, PAMPHLET PEDDLING • DISSIDENT MINORITIES: REVIVAL OF THE CLEAR-AND-PRESENT-DANGER DOCTRINE

27. *The Constitution and World War II* 533

PRESIDENTIAL PREROGATIVE AND THE CRISIS IN FOREIGN POLICY, 1939–1941 • THE FEDERAL GOVERNMENT IN WORLD WAR II • ROOSEVELT'S EXERCISE OF EXECUTIVE POWER • THE WAR POWER AND THE JAPANESE-AMERICAN MINORITY • MILITARY TRIAL OF ENEMY WAR CRIMINALS • THE CRAMER AND HAUPT TREASON CASES: WHAT IS AN OVERT ACT? • OTHER WARTIME CIVIL LIBERTIES ISSUES: DENATURALIZATION AND ESPIONAGE CASES • THE SIGNIFICANCE OF WORLD WAR II FOR CONSTITUTIONAL GOVERNMENT

28. *The Constitution and the Cold War: Collective Security and Individual Rights* 553

THE STEEL SEIZURE CASE: A CHECK TO PRESIDENTIAL EMERGENCY POWER • THE UNITED NATIONS AND FEDERAL-STATE RELATIONS • INTERNAL SECURITY AND CIVIL LIBERTIES • THE FEDERAL LOYALTY PROGRAM • CONGRESSIONAL INVESTIGATIONS • INTERNAL SECURITY LEGISLATION • JUDICIAL REACTION TO INTERNAL SECURITY POLICY • THE *Dennis* CASE • JUDICIAL REACTION TO INTERNAL SECURITY MEASURES • THE TRIUMPH OF LIBERTARIANISM IN INTERNAL SECURITY MATTERS • THE HISTORICAL SIGNIFICANCE OF LIBERTARIANISM

29. *Civil Rights and the Constitution* 581

DESEGREGATION IN HOUSING AND TRANSPORTATION • THE CONSTITUTIONAL BATTLE OVER SCHOOL SEGREGATION • ENFORCEMENT OF SCHOOL DESEGREGATION • THE COLLAPSE OF SEGREGATION IN SOUTHERN SOCIETY • THE DRIVE FOR FEDERAL CIVIL RIGHTS LEGISLATION • THE CIVIL RIGHTS ACT OF 1964 • TOWARD THE NEW EQUALITY: AFFIRMATIVE ACTION • SCHOOL INTEGRATION • AFFIRMATIVE ACTION IN VOTING AND EMPLOYMENT • CONSTITUTIONAL SIGNIFICANCE OF THE NEW EQUALITY

30. *The Warren Court and the Culmination of New Deal Liberalism* 612

THE APPORTIONMENT REVOLUTION • THE REFORM OF CRIMINAL PROCEDURE:

THE NATIONALIZATION OF THE BILL OF RIGHTS • FREEDOM OF EXPRESSION: THE LAW OF LIBEL • THE RIGHT OF PRIVACY • FREEDOM OF EXPRESSION: OBSCENITY • THE ESTABLISHMENT AND THE FREE EXERCISE OF RELIGION • THE WARREN COURT AND SUBSTANTIVE EQUAL PROTECTION • THE NATURE OF ACTIVIST DECISION-MAKING

31. *Liberal Constitutionalism in a Bureaucratic Age: The Post–New Deal American Polity*   639

POSITIVE GOVERNMENT: CONFIRMING THE MODERN PRESIDENCY • THE REGULATORY STATE: INTEREST-GROUP LIBERALISM • GOVERNMENT UNDER INTEREST-GROUP LIBERALISM • THE NEW FRONTIER AND INTEREST-GROUP LIBERALISM • THE CRISIS OF PUBLIC AUTHORITY IN THE 1960s • THE LIBERAL RESPONSE TO THE CRISIS OF PUBLIC AUTHORITY • THE NEW WAVE OF FEDERAL REGULATION

32. *The Watergate Scandal and the Crisis of the Modern Presidency*   657

GROWTH OF THE MODERN PRESIDENCY • NIXON AND THE CULMINATION OF THE LIBERAL ACTIVIST PRESIDENCY • TOWARD THE PLEBISCITARY PRESIDENCY • THE WATERGATE AFFAIR • THE SIGNIFICANCE OF WATERGATE • THE POST-WATERGATE PRESIDENCY

33. *The Burger Court and the Transition to Conservative Constitutionalism*   678

JUDICIAL RESISTANCE TO SOCIAL EGALITARIANISM • AFFIRMATIVE ACTION AND SUBSTANTIVE EQUAL PROTECTION • EQUAL PROTECTION AND WOMEN'S RIGHTS • THE BURGER COURT AND CRIMINAL PROCEDURE • THE ABORTION CASES • FIRST AMENDMENT FREE-SPEECH PROBLEMS • FREEDOM OF THE PRESS IN THE 1970s • THE BURGER COURT AND THE JUDICIAL FUNCTION

34. *Divided Government and the Separation of Powers in the 1980s*   705

POLITICAL SOURCES OF DIVIDED GOVERNMENT • THE PROBLEM OF LIMITED GOVERNMENT IN THE 1980s • THE STRUGGLE FOR CONTROL OF THE ADMINISTRATIVE STATE • CONGRESSIONAL POWER AND THE PROBLEM OF LEGISLATIVE SUPREMACY • THE INDEPENDENT COUNSEL • THE IRAN-CONTRA AFFAIR: DIVIDED GOVERNMENT IN FOREIGN POLICY • THE CONSTITUTIONAL SIGNIFICANCE OF DIVIDED GOVERNMENT

35. *The Supreme Court and the Constitution in the Era of Divided Government*   729

CIVIL LIBERTIES IN THE 1980s • THE ESTABLISHMENT CLAUSE AND THE FREE EXERCISE OF RELIGION • SUSPECT CLASSIFICATIONS, FUNDAMENTAL RIGHTS, AND GOVERNMENT REGULATION • AFFIRMATIVE ACTION AND GROUP RIGHTS • THE REVIVAL OF ECONOMIC LIBERTY AND PROPERTY RIGHTS • FEDERALISM AND THE SEPARATION OF POWERS

36. *Judicial Review and Constitutionalism: A Bicentennial Perspective*
   754

THE REVIVAL OF JUDICIAL RESTRAINT AS A JUDICIAL MODEL • THE
CONTROVERSY OVER ORIGINAL-INTENT JURISPRUDENCE • THE BORK
NOMINATION FIGHT • CONSTITUTIONAL AMENDMENT VERSUS
CONSTITUTIONAL CHANGE

Appendix 1: Declaration of Independence   A1

Appendix 2: Articles of Confederation   A5

Appendix 3: The Constitution of the United States   A13

Bibliography   A34

Table of Cases   A115

Index   A133

Preface to the Seventh Edition

The sixth edition of *The American Constitution* recognized the revival of the decentralist, individual-rights, laissez-faire tradition in American politics as a powerful constitutional influence in the late 1960s and the 1970s. Events in the 1980s confirmed the strength of this political outlook as the Republican party won three presidential elections and maintained control of the executive branch. Contrary to the expectations of many political observers and electoral theorists, however, the tradition of centralizing economic and social welfare regulation continued to have wide appeal and enabled the Democratic party to control the legislative branch. The result was the emergence of divided government as the central constitutional development of the decade. This development, which placed a premium on political compromise and constitutional statesmanship even as it paradoxically encouraged partisan tendencies, forms the central organizing theme in the new chapters of this seventh edition.

I wish to acknowledge the patient and perceptive editorial guidance provided by Steven Forman of W. W. Norton & Co., and the helpful criticism offered by three anonymous readers of the manuscript.

HERMAN BELZ
UNIVERSITY OF MARYLAND
AUGUST 1990

Preface to the Sixth Edition

IN THE YEARS SINCE its original publication Alfred H. Kelly and Winfred A. Harbison's *The American Constitution* has become recognized as the standard work in the field of American constitutional history. Valuable as a reference work, textbook, and single-volume account of the American constitutional experience, it was distinguished by a judicious blend of specialized constitutional knowledge and perceptive understanding of the broad political and social forces that have shaped constitutional institutions in the United States. In recent years, however, widespread interest in and willingness to reconsider basic constitutional issues—stimulated by the constitutional crisis through which the nation passed a decade and more ago—have produced important new findings in history, law, and political science dealing with the subject of constitutional change. In significant ways these findings have altered the contour and content of American constitutional history. Accordingly, in preparing this edition of *The American Constitution* I have undertaken a thorough and comprehensive revision of both narrative and interpretation. The result is a substantially new book based on the extensive body of scholarship that in the past generation has altered our understanding of virtually every aspect of the American constitutional experience.

Written from the perspective of progressive historiography and the liberal nationalist reform tradition, Kelly and Harbison's work reflected the acceptance of and confidence in federal centralization and activist, interventionist government that achieved political and intellectual ascendancy in the New Deal era. That era has come to an end, however, and events in the 1960s and 1970s have revealed a deep-seated and continuing skepticism about whether centralized bureaucratic institutions can fulfill the ideals of liberty, equality, and democratic self-government that historically have defined American nationality. We have been forcefully reminded—by movements on both the left and the right—of the strength and persistence of decentralist, democratic-participatory, and antigovernmental values in the American constitutional order. Without rejecting the valuable insights offered by the liberal nationalist perspective, I have perforce recognized the enduring legitimacy and influence of the alternative decentralist, individualist, laissez-faire tradition in American constitutionalism. Furthermore, I have tried to incorporate in this book an awareness, greater perhaps than was available in the scholarship of a generation ago, of the centrality in American thought of constitutionalism as a basic ideology and approach to political life, rather than, as the progressive generation of historians was wont to regard it, as an expedient method of promoting class and economic interests.

Numerous colleagues and friends have helped me in writing this book. I owe special thanks to Professors Maxwell Bloomfield of the Catholic University of America, George M. Dennison of Colorado State University, Phillip S. Paludan of the University of Kansas, Stanley I. Kutler of the University of Wisconsin, R. T. Miller of Baylor University, Michael Les Benedict of Ohio State University, and Harold M. Hyman of Rice University, all of whom offered perceptive and extremely helpful criticism at various stages of the preparation of the manuscript.

HERMAN BELZ

Introduction

IN BROADEST PERSPECTIVE, American constitutional history is concerned with the interaction between law and politics in American government. Its most obvious focus is the federal Constitution of 1787, which marked the founding of the nation's principal political institutions and after more than two hundred years continues to serve as its preeminent symbol and source of legitimate governmental authority. Yet American constitutional history is more than an account of the written Constitution, important as that instrument has been in the nation's political life. Constitutional history goes beyond the history of constitutional law because the actual constitution of government has consisted in practices and understandings shaped as much by political exigency and constitutional theory as by the prescriptions of the documentary text.

As in physiology the word *constitution* refers to the makeup of the human body, so in politics it describes the framework and parts of government or the overall composition of the polity. In ancient Greek political thought a constitution was the principles, institutions, laws, practices, and traditions by which a people carried on their political and governmental life. The term carries the same broad meaning today. From one standpoint it is descriptive, referring to existing governmental arrangements. In this descriptive sense it may be said that every country has a constitution. But like law itself, a constitution also has a normative content which is intended to guide and control political and governmental action—to state what ought to be rather than what is. In this sense a constitution prescribes official conduct and provides a standard of legitimacy for assessing the validity of governmental action. In the ancient and medieval world this normative function derived from the belief that the way a people traditionally organized and conducted their political life, in accordance with human nature and their distinctive character, was the most reliable indication of what was reasonable and just. In the modern era, beginning with the American Revolution, nations have adopted the practice of fixing in a written constitution the basic principles and procedures that express their sense of political right and justice.

The purpose of a constitution, then, is not merely to create, organize, and distribute governmental power, but also to assure that governmental power is exercised legitimately. Inherent in the concept of legitimacy is the idea of imposing restraints on government, lest it degenerate into tyranny. Indeed, the very notion of defining institutions of government implies placing limits on them. Accordingly, constitutional government has usually been described as limited government. Constitutionalism, in turn, is the theory and practice of conducting politics in accordance with a constitution.

An essential component of constitutionalism is legalism, the belief that right conduct consists in following rules. This is especially so in the United States, where the Constitution is expressly declared to be "the supreme Law of the Land." Yet constitutionalism cannot be exclusively or excessively legalistic. Lest it become arid formalism, divorced from the forces of social change which it is intended to modulate and channel, constitutionalism must accommodate—without being overwhelmed by—purposive political action.

Without diminishing the importance of mobilizing governmental power for the accomplishment of positive social goals, it would be accurate to say that the major challenge to constitutionalism throughout history has been to make constitutional limitations effective against rulers to whom they have theoretically applied. In general there have been two basic approaches to this problem. One is the rule-of-law tradition, in which the legitimacy of governmental action is judged against the standard of a higher or fundamental law. The second basic technique of constitutionalism is to structure and balance the institutions of government so that power is limited as a result.

The rule-of-law tradition derives from ancient Rome and medieval England. In the writings of the Roman jurists the law of nature provided a standard of justice and equity whereby the validity of the positive laws enacted by government could be judged. Roman constitutionalism, however, was unable to evolve effective sanctions for holding government to account under natural law norms. In medieval England, by contrast, the rule of law acquired a greater degree of practical effectiveness as a restraint on royal power. Like other feudal lords, the king was bound by a web of contractual rights and obligations under the common law deriving from ownership of the land. These mutual obligations created a sphere of personal liberty and individual right protected by the courts, which placed the king under the law. On the other hand, in matters of war, diplomacy, and commerce the king had unlimited power.

The immediate origins of American constitutionalism lay in the English Civil War and the Glorious Revolution of the seventeenth century. Parliament, supported by the common law courts, significantly strengthened the rule of law by extending legal limitations into the sphere of government previously under the exclusive control of the royal prerogative. A struggle for sovereignty occurred between the king and Parliament in which the latter prevailed. The power of Parliament, however, though supreme in relation to the crown, was not unlimited. It was considered to be subject to the basic principles of the common law, or what was also referred to as fundamental law. Moreover, Parliament identified itself with the people as the source of legimate authority, and this identification imposed a further restraint on its sovereignty. In constitutional theory, then, English government after the Glorious Revolution was subject to fundamental law and was accountable to the people. The first essential of constitutional government was in place.

In their struggle against the crown seventeenth-century Englishmen also employed the second basic method of constitutionalism. They attempted to devise an institutional structure to balance and correlate the major forces in society and government. Ancient political thought had taught that there were three elements in society which had to be recognized in the structure of government: monarchy, aristocracy, and democracy. If any one of these elements controlled the government, the result would be despotism, oligarchy, or mobocracy. But if they were properly balanced, tyranny and corruption would be prevented.

English constitutionalism in the late medieval and early modern period adhered to this theory of mixed government. As the royal prerogative was steadily circumscribed, king, lords, and commons shared in the tasks of government. During the Civil War, however, Parliament claimed exclusive sovereignty under the new theory of the separation of powers. Instead of combining the social orders in a system of fused or mixed powers, this theory sharply differentiated between government and society. Whereas in mixed government king, lords, and commons were seen as jointly engaged in one essential activity—to declare through legislation what the law was—the separation-of-powers theory held that government consisted of two basic functions: making law and enforcing it. The new theory further provided that the lawmaking power, tantamount to sovereignty, belonged exlusively to Parliament. The king was to be confined to a strictly administrative function. Although with the restoration of the monarchy the forms of mixed government were revived, the essential feature of the separation-of-powers theory persisted—namely, Parliamentary control over lawmaking.

These constitutional changes of the seventeenth century, illustrating both the rule-of-law or juridical approach to constitutionalism and the institutional balance or forms-of-government technique, occurred during the time of the founding of the American colonies. English government itself was to develop along the lines of the second of these two constitutional methods, with the rise of cabinet government in the eighteenth century. In the American colonies, however, both approaches to limited government took root. Out of them a distinctive American theory of constitutionalism evolved.

As even this brief survey suggests, the legal and governmental substance of constitutional history cannot be understood apart from a broad knowledge of political and social history. In a sense, constitutional history may be thought of as an extension of social history, inasmuch as constitutional problems originate in and reflect substantive conflicts in the society. Yet the relationship between a constitution and the society in which it exists is reciprocal. If social change affects the constitution, the constitution has an equally important impact on political and social events. The very structure of politics and the course that political events take depend on the shaping power of constitutional principles, rules, and understandings.

A constitution shapes political reality in a variety of ways. Constitutional principles, like political ideas in general, can be adhered to as matters of philosophical understanding and commitment that motivate political action. Moreover, when citizens and governing officials internalize constitutional principles and procedures, acting on the basis of the intrinsic validity rather than simply the expedient or instrumental value of these principles, their constitutionalist convictions give direction to political action. The constitution thus has a configurative effect. This effect is seen further insofar as the Constitution provides the institutional forms, procedures, rhetoric, and symbols by which politics is carried on in the United States. Groups and individuals choose courses of action that are consistent with or required by the Constitution. They do so not because they are in each instance irrevocably committed to the constitutional rule or principle at issue; on the contrary, in different circumstances they may adhere to a conflicting principle or rule. Political actors and government officials in any event recognize the preeminent status accorded the Constitution as a document. They know that the American people regard the Constitution as paramount and binding law, and believe it embodies fundamental principles and prescribes forms and procedures that define governmental legitimacy. Indeed, Americans venerate the Constitution; as a result, political actors and government officers are constrained to act in conformity with its provisions. In this way the Constitution shapes the form and content of American politics.

Although modern constitutional politics dates from the adoption of the federal Constitution in 1787–88, the founding of the colonies in the seventeenth century marks the proximate beginning of American constitutional history. For a century and a half the American colonists exercised broad powers of self-government within the British Empire. From diverse origins they evolved similar institutional structures, legal doctrines, and political assumptions which in effect formed a colonial constitution. The Declaration of Independence transformed the colonies into independent states, and these states created republican governments based on written constitutions of liberty. At the same time the states were loosely organized into a continental union under the Articles of Confederation, a constitutional framework intended to secure cooperation for diplomatic and military purposes which expressed a nascent sense of American nationality. Subsequently, the necessity of strengthening the Confederation and reforming the state governments led to the Constitutional Convention of 1787 and the formation of a republican government for the entire nation. The successful establishment of this new republican regime by 1801 closed the first period of American constitutional development.

Between 1800 and 1877 the central constitutional issue facing the American people concerned the nature of the Union. At the outset the federal government combined features of both a unitary state and a confederation. Sovereign in the authority it derived directly from the people as constituent power, it was nevertheless limited in the range of its powers by the existence of the states. As American culture and society became more nationally uniform in the first half of the nineteenth century, the constitutional system paradoxically became more decentralized. The westward movement had centrifugal consequences as the number of states increased. Jacksonian democracy, based on the constitutional philosophy of dual federalism, was even more important in causing a shift of power from the national government to the states. After 1840 the struggle over slavery between North and South exacerbated these decentralizing tendencies.

In order to defend slavery, Southerners used the doctrine of state sovereignty to deny sovereign authority to the federal government. When this constitutional theory failed to give the slaveholding states the security they desired within the Union, they seceded and formed the Confederate States of America. The Civil War ensued, a crisis of constitutionalism and the rule of law as well as of national unity. The outcome of the war vindicated the Union government's claim to sovereignty as a legitimate nation-state without denying a legitimate, albeit reduced, sphere of states' rights. The Reconstruction period ended with the authority of the federal government greatly expanded in consequence of the Thirteenth, Fourteenth, and Fifteenth Amendments, but with the states still exercising preponderant power in the regulation of civil society.

In the third phase of constitutional development, from 1877 to 1933, the social transformations wrought by industrialization and urbanization imposed severe strains on the political order. Principles of limited government and entrepreneurial liberty which in the preindustrial era had encouraged broadly democratic economic progress now permitted disparities of wealth and power that challenged republican liberty and equality. Reformers began to demand that government not merely allocate economic resources as it had traditionally done, but also regulate the economic market with a view toward restricting the power of private corporations and redistributing social goods. Considering the powerful appeal of localism, minimal government, and laissez-faire economic theory, public policy in the late nineteenth and early twentieth centuries to a surprising extent adjusted to the requirements of the new age. Yet classical liberal constitutionalism remained dominant on the whole.

The New Deal of the 1930s opened the fourth major phase of American constitutional development. In a governmental system that was designed to give wide scope to executive authority, Franklin D. Roosevelt went further than any of his predecessors in making the presidency constitutionally dominant. Presidential government has remained the constitutional norm since the New Deal, irrespective of the personal inclinations of the incumbent and even when political circumstances have weakened executive influence. This has been well illustrated in the post-Watergate period, when despite repudiation of the concept of the imperial presidency and congressional resurgence leading to substantial legislative supervision of administrative agencies, the presidency continues to be the focus of policy-making responsibility and action in American government.

Furthermore, as entrepreneurial capitalism evolved into government-regulated capitalism, blurring the distinction between public and private power, the New Deal inaugurated an American version of bureaucratic centralization. Intended to provide social and economic security against the perilous forces of modern industrial organization, the New Deal established federal authority in areas previously the preserve of the states. It created a regulatory welfare state that altered the federal system and possibly transformed the spirit of American constitutionalism by inducing groups and individuals to turn to the federal government to guarantee their basic needs. In the 1960s and 1970s another wave of reform carried the transformation further by extending affirmative government into new areas of social activity, including environmental protection, consumer welfare, occupational health and safety, and civil rights.

To be sure, elements of continuity persisted as the old constitutional order gave way to the new. Foremost among them was the power of the federal judiciary, which after 1937 was used to uphold the civil rights and civil liberties of individuals rather than to protect business and property interests. The development of judicial activism as an adjunct of liberal reform in the 1960s provoked strong opposition among conservative critics, who questioned whether judicial review had not become primarily a policy-making institution employing essentially legislative power, contrary to the design of the Constitution. As the nation commemorated the bicentennial of the Constitution in the late 1980s, controversy over the nature of judicial review and constitutional adjudication, provoked by the urging of the Republican Reagan administration for a jurisprudence of original intent, ensured that in one form or another the Constitution as fundamental law would continue to play a pivotal role in the conduct of American politics.

THE AMERICAN CONSTITUTION
ITS ORIGINS AND DEVELOPMENT

1790			
★ JOHN JAY 1789-1795	JOHN RUTLEDGE 1789-1791		
★ JOHN RUTLEDGE 1795 (UNCONFIRMED)	THOMAS JOHNSON 1791–1793		JAMES WILSON 1789-1798
★ OLIVER ELLSWORTH 1796-1800	WILLIAM PATERSON 1793-1806	WILLIAM CUSHING 1789-1810	

1790

1800

1810

1820

1830

1840

1850

1860

1870

1880

★ JOHN JAY
1789-1795

★ JOHN RUTLEDGE
1795
(UNCONFIRMED)

★ OLIVER ELLSWORTH
1796-1800

★ JOHN MARSHALL
1801-1835

★ ROGER B. TANEY
1836-1864

★ SALMON P. CHASE
1864-1873

★ MORRISON R. WAITE
1874-1888

JOHN RUTLEDGE
1789-1791

THOMAS JOHNSON
1791–1793

WILLIAM
PATERSON
1793-1806

H. BROCKHOLST
LIVINGSTON
1806-1823

SMITH THOMPSON
1823-1843

SAMUEL NELSON
1845-1872

WARD HUNT
1872-1882

SAMUEL
BLATCHFORD
1882-1893

WILLIAM CUSHING
1789-1810

JOSEPH STORY
1811-1845

LEVI WOODBURY
1845-1851

BENJAMIN R.
CURTIS
1851-1857

NATHAN CLIFFORD
1858-1881

HORACE GRAY
1881-1902

JAMES WILSON
1789-1798

BUSHROD
WASHINGTON
1798-1829

HENRY BALDWIN
1830-1844

ROBERT C. GRIER
1846-1870

WILLIAM STRONG
1870-1880

WILLIAM B.
WOODS
1880-1887

MEMBERS OF THE UNITED STATES SUPREME COURT

1789–1990

★ DENOTES CHIEF JUSTICE

JOHN BLAIR
1789-1796

JAMES IREDELL
1790-1799

SAMUEL CHASE
1796-1811

ALFRED MOORE
1799-1804

WILLIAM JOHNSON
1804-1834

THOMAS TODD
1807-1826

GABRIEL DUVAL
1811-1835

ROBERT TRIMBLE
1826-1828

PHILIP P. BARBOUR
1836-1841

JOHN McLEAN
1829-1861

JOHN McKINLEY
1837-1852

PETER V. DANIEL
1841-1860

JAMES M. WAYNE
1835-1867

JOHN CATRON
1837-1865

JOHN A. CAMPBELL
1853-1861

DAVID DAVIS
1862-1877

STEPHEN J. FIELD
1863-1897

SAMUEL F. MILLER
1862-1890

NOAH H. SWAYNE
1862-1881

JOSEPH P. BRADLEY
1870-1892

STANLEY MATTHEWS
1881-1889

JOHN MARSHALL HARLAN
1877-1911

Year	(Chief Justices ★)			
	★ MORRISON R. WAITE 1874-1888			WILLIAM B. WOODS 1880-1887
1890		SAMUEL BLATCHFORD 1882-1893	HORACE GRAY 1881-1902	LUCIUS Q. C. LAMAR 1888-1893
				HOWELL JACKSON 1893-1895
1900	★ MELVILLE W. FULLER 1888-1910	EDWARD D. WHITE 1894-1910		RUFUS W. PECKHAM 1895-1909
1910				HORACE H. LURTON 1909-1914
	★ EDWARD D. WHITE 1910-1921		OLIVER WENDELL HOLMES 1902-1932	
1920		WILLIS VAN DEVANTER 1910-1937		
	★ WILLIAM H. TAFT 1921-1930			JAMES C. McREYNOLDS 1914-1941
1930				
	★ CHARLES E. HUGHES 1930-1941		BENJAMIN N. CARDOZO 1932-1938	
1940				JAMES F. BYRNES 1941-1942
	★ HARLAN F. STONE 1941-1946			WILEY B. RUTLEDGE 1943-1949
1950	★ FRED M. VINSON 1946-1953		FELIX FRANKFURTER 1939-1962	SHERMAN MINTON 1949-1956
		HUGO L. BLACK 1937-1971		
1960	★ EARL WARREN 1953-1969		ARTHUR J. GOLDBERG 1962-1965	
			ABE FORTAS 1965-1969	WILLIAM J. BRENNAN, JR. 1956-1990
1970			HARRY A. BLACKMUN 1970-	
	★ WARREN E. BURGER 1969-1986	LEWIS F. POWELL, JR. 1972-1986		
1980				
	★ WILLIAM H. REHNQUIST 1986-	ANTHONY KENNEDY 1988-		DAVID H. SOUTER 1990-
1990				

Seat 1	Seat 2	Seat 3	Seat 4	Seat 5	Seat 6
SAMUEL F. MILLER 1862-1890	JOSEPH P. BRADLEY 1870-1892	STANLEY MATTHEWS 1881-1889		JOHN MARSHALL HARLAN 1877-1911	STEPHEN J. FIELD 1863-1897
HENRY B. BROWN 1890-1906	GEORGE SHIRAS, JR. 1892-1903	DAVID J. BREWER 1889-1910			JOSEPH McKENNA 1898-1925
WILLIAM H. MOODY 1906-1910					
JOSEPH R. LAMAR 1910-1916	WILLIAM R. DAY 1903-1922	CHARLES E. HUGHES 1910-1916		MAHLON PITNEY 1912-1922	
		JOHN H. CLARKE 1916-1922			
LOUIS D. BRANDEIS 1916-1939	PIERCE BUTLER 1922-1939	GEORGE SUTHERLAND 1922-1938	HARLAN F. STONE 1925-1941	EDWARD T. SANFORD 1923-1930	
				OWEN J. ROBERTS 1930-1945	
	FRANK MURPHY 1940-1949	STANLEY F. REED 1938-1957	ROBERT H. JACKSON 1941-1954		
WILLIAM O. DOUGLAS 1939-1975	TOM C. CLARK 1949-1967			HAROLD H. BURTON 1945-1958	
		CHARLES E. WHITTAKER 1957-1962	JOHN M. HARLAN 1955-1971		
				POTTER STEWART 1958-1981	
	THURGOOD MARSHALL 1967-	BYRON R. WHITE 1962-	WILLIAM H. REHNQUIST 1972-1986		
JOHN PAUL STEVENS 1975-				SANDRA DAY O'CONNOR 1981-	
			ANTONIN SCALIA 1986-		

ONE

The Founding of English Colonies in North America

IN CONTRAST TO the governments of most European countries, American government began at an identifiable historical moment as an instrument for accomplishing specific and limited purposes. Its character was, therefore, in a sense artificial rather than natural and organic in the manner of governments rooted in the immemorial past. Government in the United States has, moreover, rested on a broadly popular base. Because the ruling authorities have been limited in their powers, ordinary citizens have borne a larger share of the responsibility of government than have their counterparts in European nations. These defining characteristics of American constitutionalism derived from the circumstances of English colonization in North America in the early seventeenth century.

The English colonies in the New World gave broader scope to private initiative than did the colonies of European states such as France or Spain. Nevertheless, English colonization was not the almost exclusively private enterprise sometimes described. Although the English government did not aggressively initiate and control settlement like the Spanish crown, English colonization had a distinctive public and national character. At the start of the seventeenth century the English monarchy was immeasurably stronger than it had been a hundred years earlier; the existence of a powerful centralized government was indeed a precondition of the overseas expansion of which colonization was an integral part. Yet in comparison with the monarchies of Spain and France, the English crown was weak and its financial resources limited. Accordingly, although the English government was vitally interested in competition for trade and overseas dominion, it was forced to rely on private adventurers, merchants, and members of the aristocracy to carry out English ambitions in the world. For their part, the sponsors of overseas settlement had personal reasons for undertaking colonization, but they were also conscious of extending English influence, including the religious purpose of promoting the Protestant faith against Roman Catholics.

The specific constitutional problem presented by the settlements of the early seventeenth century was the founding of government in new territory. It would be a recurrent one in American constitutional history for over two centuries. After the nation gained its independence, Americans typically sent a governor and council to organize unsettled lands. But while the Spanish and French employed this method in their seventeenth-century colonizing efforts, the English government, unable to commit the resources required by this approach, did not. Instead it used two governmental instruments that had been historically relevant to the problems posed by colonization. These were the feudal proprietary grant and the corporation charter. Another method of organizing government in unsettled territory derived from the religious principle of the covenant.

The Corporation Colonies: Virginia and Massachusetts Bay

Virginia and Massachusetts Bay were founded on the joint-stock principle, an instrument of early English commercial expansion that lay ready to hand as a means of overseas settlement at the start of the seventeenth century. We tend to regard the joint-stock company as an economic institution, for it was only through this form of associated endeavor that the capital needed to initiate English colonization could be raised. For present purposes, however, the political and governmental aspect of the joint-stock company commands our attention.

The joint-stock company was a type of corporation, and corporations in an important sense had been used in England since the fourteenth century as an instrument of government. A corporation was a body or association of persons upon whom the crown conferred rights and powers appropriate for the carrying out of specific public purposes or functions. Guilds, boroughs, ecclesiastical bodies, and educational institutions, for example, benefited from the privilege of incorporation. Through the grant of corporate status, expressed in a legal charter which imposed duties and responsibilities as well as bestowing powers, the crown could adjust relations among and within social groups and exercise greater control over the internal affairs of the realm. In this sense incorporation served the purpose of centralized royal administration. On the other hand, incorporated groups received the power to regulate their own affairs—that is, to govern themselves. Incorporation thus extended governmental powers to private groups that in consequence assumed the character of public, or quasi-public, organizations. According to the understanding of the time, the idea of a private corporation was a contradiction in terms.

The joint-stock company, the form of incorporation that was used in planting colonies in English North America, had its origins in the Middle Ages. The merchants of fifteenth-century Italy developed the business technique of pooling capital resources to expand operations and distribute risk, and English merchants no doubt borrowed from the Italian idea. The English joint-stock companies, however, also evolved directly out of the medieval guild merchant. Since the twelfth century it had been customary for the merchants of a community to organize guilds for the purpose of carrying on trade. The guild often became a kind of closed corporation—that is, one to which admission was necessary if a merchant wished to trade within the area over which the guild had control. Very often it sought and obtained from the crown a charter giving legal recognition to the trade rights it claimed, a step particularly important to the guild when it had secured a monopoly over some segment of foreign trade.

In the commercial development of the sixteenth century, the principle of the "company of merchant-adventurers," a corporate entity licensed by the crown and having certain trade privileges, was combined with the continental device of pooling the capital of investors to share both risk and profits in a common enterprise. The result was the emergence of the great English trading companies of the late sixteenth and early seventeenth centuries as the principal media of English commercial and colonial expansion.

It became the practice for various groups of traders to petition the crown for charters affording commercial favors, prescribing their form of organization, and granting the right to raise money by selling stock. A typical joint-stock charter of this time gave the company a name and a formally recognized legal position, and specified the terms of organization. The charter usually vested control in a council, the original members of which were customarily named in the document. Generally, the membership of this body varied from six to more than twenty, and the direction of the affairs of the company was in its hands. Sometimes the charter provided for a governor as the head of the company, in which case he was chosen by the council, usually from its own membership. Membership in the company was secured through stock ownership. The smaller stockholders had little to say about general policy; however, they met periodically in a general court to elect members to vacancies in the council and occasionally to express their opinion upon some major question of policy.

The typical charter also granted a number of privileges thought to be of some financial advantage. These might include a grant of land, the right to convey title to any portion of its domains, and the title to all precious metals discovered within the specified region. A monopoly of trade within the area was an almost invariable provision.

Finally, the charter sometimes conferred upon the company extensive governing powers. This was necessary either because the contemplated region to be exploited was unsettled wilderness, as in America, or because the company was to be the actual instrument of English conquest in an already civilized region, as in India. In either case the company needed authority to establish law and order within its domains, and, therefore, the charter commonly bestowed the right to set up some local governing body, to maintain defense, to coin money, to establish courts, and to enact ordinances for local government. Thus certain of the companies took on a quasi-sovereign character.

Virginia, the earliest successful English colony, was founded in 1607 by the Virginia Company of London under a grant from the crown which gave it the right to found a colony anywhere between the 34th and 41st parallels on the North American continent. The company's charter provided for a governor, who with an advisory council of thirteen was empowered to direct the general affairs of the organization. The stockholders were also instructed to assemble from time to time in a general court. Concurrently, a second group of merchants from Plymouth was authorized by the crown to form the Virginia Company of Plymouth and to settle in the area between the 38th and 45th parallels. Taking a strong interest in the overseas venture, the crown also established a Royal Council in London, separate from the company's council, with power to supervise matters that affected the government's interests. The original plan for Virginia thus provided for dual control by royal and company authority in England. Local matters within the colony would be in the hands of a governor and council appointed from London. Ordinary settlers were given no part in the government.

The Plymouth group failed in its efforts to establish a colony in Maine, and economic and political difficulties led the London Company to secure a new charter in 1609. The company now became a regular joint-stock concern, with some seven hundred permanent stockholders. The separate Royal Council in London was abolished, control being vested in the company's treasurer and the London council. The crown also extended the company's lands to include all the lands from sea to sea for two hundred miles on either side of its settlement. A supplementary charter of 1612 strengthened the stockholders' control of company affairs by providing for four "great courts" or stockholders' meetings each year to dispose of matters of great importance. The 1612 charter also extended the company's boundaries three hundred leagues seaward to include Bermuda.

In 1610 the reorganized company resorted to outright military rule in Virginia. The treasurer and council revoked the authority of the local governor and council and vested absolute authority in a "lord-governor and captain-general" who was given full military, executive, and lawmaking power. By this experiment in autocracy the company hoped to end the indolence and petty wrangling which had so far crippled the colony's life.

The enterprise nonetheless did not prosper, mainly because it lacked an adequate economic base. The settlers had attempted more or less unsuccessfully to raise corn, produce wine and silk, and mine gold. Although the cultivation of tobacco, begun in 1612, brought some prosperity, the significance of the new crop was not appreciated, and the company still failed to pay dividends. Furthermore, the despotic local government gave the settlement a bad name and discouraged immigration.

In 1618 the company, in an effort to encourage immigration and to promote a better spirit among the colonists, attempted a general reorganization of local government in Virginia. The governor's instructions for 1619 contained an order for the establishment of a local representative assembly. This body, patterned after the company's general court or stockholders' meeting in London, was the beginning of the Virginia colonial legislature. The local council, which at first sat with the assembly to compose one chamber, was a counterpart of the company's council in London.

Thus, through the establishment of a local governor, a council, and a representative assembly, the Virginia Company of London evolved a colonial government for Virginia modeled upon its own charter provisions. Substantially the same pattern of government eventually appeared in all the English colonies.

The Virginia Company of London, beset by financial failure and internal dissension, lost its charter in 1624. The king now named a royal governor and, the following year, formally incorporated Virginia in the royal domain. Virginia thereby became the first royal colony in America. The assembly, a mere creature of the company, might well have expired at this time, and in fact no regular assemblies met in Virginia from 1623 to 1628. Thereafter the legislature met annually, although it was not until 1639 that the king recognized the right of the assembly to permanent existence.

The alteration of government that occurred in Virginia in 1619 was constitutionally significant as the first instance in which the corporation principle provided the basis for a self-governing polity. Nor was the governmental change merely formal. Before 1618 Virginia had been, in a strict sense, a business enterprise in which governmental and political considerations were subordinate. The abandonment of military government and the adaptation of the corporation for the purposes of local self-government signified the transformation of the business into a political society. It was constitutionally appropriate, therefore, that the joint-stock company should be dissolved a few years later. The formation of a representative assembly by the company in 1619 accordingly was not a conscious borrowing of English political institutions. The Virginia House of Burgesses resembled Parliament insofar as it embodied the principle of representation, and in later years local lawmakers argued the comparability of their assembly with the House of Commons. But the impetus for creating a body of elected representatives came from practical necessities that stimulated the adaptation of a business instrument to the purpose of organizing political relationships.

Like Virginia, Massachusetts Bay was founded by a trading company, but in its case the company's charter straightaway became the actual constitution of the colony. The company's founders were for the most part Puritans who desired to found a Calvinist religious refuge in the wilderness. Many of the stockholders had mercantile backgrounds, however, and some were interested primarily in the venture's commercial possibilities. Hence it was not unnatural for the interested parties to organize as a joint-stock company.

The charter of the Massachusetts Bay Company, secured in 1629, provided for a governor, a deputy governor, and eighteen assistants, who together were to constitute the council. Provision was made for four "great and general courts" each year, to be attended by the freemen of the company. The power to make laws and ordinances not contrary to the laws of England was bestowed in a somewhat ambiguous fashion upon the governor, the deputy governor, the assistants, and the General Court. The charter granted also the right to establish all necessary offices and to appoint appropriate magistrates. Included also was a grant of all the land lying between a point three miles south of the Charles River and three miles north of the Merrimac River, extending to the "Westerne Sea."

While the foregoing provisions were not unusual, the charter in one important respect differed vitally from others of the period in that it failed to specify where the seat of government was to be located. The omission may have been an inadvertent one, for it was only reasonable to assume that the governor and assistants would normally reside in London; or it may have been intentional, at least on the part of some of the grantees. In either case, the absence of any such stipulation opened the way for the eventual transfer, in 1630, of the seat of government of the colony from London to Massachusetts.

At this time most of the influential members of the Massachusetts Bay Company belonged to the faction interested in a religious colony rather than a commercial enterprise. Many of them preferred to migrate to Massachusetts along with other religious dissidents and direct company affairs on the scene rather than stay in England. The mercantile group still had some influence, however, and they would not concur in a move which might foreclose the possibility of future profits from the venture. The result was a compromise, arrived at in the famous Cambridge Agreement of 1629. The mercantile group assented to the removal of the company to Massachusetts Bay, and in return the merchants were given certain exclusive trading concessions with the colony. This made possible the transfer of the seat of government to Massachusetts Bay, a move that was symbolized by the actual transfer of the charter to the new colony. The company's connection with any superior governing body in England within the corporation forthwith ceased.

Although Massachusetts Bay provides the clearest illustration of the adaptation of the corporation charter to the purposes of a political constitution, it is impossible to understand the distinctive character of this most important colony without taking into account its religious dimension. Central to the Puritan world view was the idea of the covenant. Puritans believed that God had formed a covenant or contract with them which, though not dictating a particular form of government, made them a distinct people. Belief in the covenant held the community together and was a source of energy for political action that was given shape and direction by the use of the corporate form. Within the body of the Puritan community another kind of agreement or contract existed between the rulers and the ruled. Believing themselves blessed by God and commanded to rule, leaders such as Governor John Winthrop espoused the aristocratic view that the people should unquestioningly obey them.

As designated officers of the trading company, Winthrop and the few corporation members who came to New England could have governed entirely by themselves in the General Court. They chose to broaden the base of their new political society, however, by admitting 116 men to freemanship status in 1631. These freemen, who became members of the General Court, agreed to confine their role to that of electing the assistants (called magistrates) in the government; the magistrates would elect the governor and deputy governor, who together with the magistrates would make the laws, levy taxes, and run things generally. To assure that the proper religious perspective would be maintained, freemanship was restricted to church members.

The same political logic that led to the transformation of Virginia government produced in 1634 a significant broadening of the base of Massachusetts government. Dissatisfied with the tax levies imposed by Winthrop and the magistrates, a number of freemen protested and were allowed to consult with the governor about taxation. Encouraged, they next made their famous demand to see the charter, with a view toward exercising the rights that were legally theirs as members of the General Court. With some reluctance, the governor and his assistants produced the charter, and by it, the freeholders were able to demonstrate that the lawmaking powers of the corporation were vested in the General Court. The governor and assistants were forced to consent to the calling of the General Court at regular intervals to function as a legislature, and from that time on, the supremacy of the General Court was never questioned.

The metamorphosis of a trading-company charter into the constitution of an English colony thus determined the outlines of the government of Massachusetts. The governor, the deputy governor, and the eighteen assistants, who together had constituted the board of directors of the trading corporation, functioned almost from the start as the executive council which handled day-to-day affairs of the colony. The "Great and General Court," formerly the quarterly meeting of the stockholders, now became the legislature, and each town was authorized to send two representatives to its annual meetings. The only important subsequent change in the structure of the General Court was the introduction of bicameralism in 1644.

In Virginia the dissolution of the joint-stock company was followed by the imposition of royal-colony status. In Massachusetts Bay the business corporation that founded the colony also ceased to exist in a political and constitutional sense, but the Puritan leaders successfully resisted English attempts to bring them under royal administration. The rights of self-government which the charter granted the company, symbolized in the physical transfer of the charter itself, enabled Massachusetts Bay to flourish for fifty years as a virtually autonomous commonwealth only nominally accountable to English authority.

Government by Compact: Plymouth, Rhode Island, Connecticut, and New Haven

Just as voluntary association for business purposes became the basis for political society in the corporate colonies, so association for religious reasons formed the foundation for self-governing polities in Plymouth, Rhode Island, Connecticut, and New Haven. These colonies never acquired the political importance that Massachusetts Bay did, and they were constitutionally derivative insofar as they borrowed the governmental forms of their larger New England neighbor. Nevertheless, they were constitutionally significant because they illustrated the idea of government based on a social compact.

In Protestant theory every individual was ultimately his or her own source of authority in religious matters, and it followed logically from this that mere agreement among individuals was all that was necessary for church organization. Applying this idea, a Calvinist sect known as separatists in the late sixteenth century advocated separation from the Church of England and the formation of churches by covenant or compact among the body of believers. Rejecting any connection with the Church of England, the separatists came into direct conflict with established Anglican authorities and with the English government itself. Since the church was still regarded as an arm of the state and the king was the personal head of the church, to deny the authority of the church government was to attack the authority of the state itself. Mild persecution under the reign of Elizabeth became more serious under James I, with the result that various separatist groups in search of greater religious freedom migrated shortly after 1600 to the Netherlands, a country already practicing almost complete religious toleration.

Intent upon creating a wilderness Zion, a number of separatist families resident in Holland decided to migrate to America. After some negotiation they secured consent from the Virginia Company of London to settle within its domain. There followed the voyage on the *Mayflower* and the founding of Plymouth Colony in November 1620.

The Plymouth colonists thus found themselves presented with a unique opportunity to apply the compact doctrine, hitherto used by the separatists only for church organization, to the organization of a body politic. In the Mayflower Compact, they translated abstract theory into practice. Their grant from the Virginia Company of London proved meaningless, since the portion of the New England coast upon which they were to settle lay entirely outside the company's domains, and hence they were without any recognized political authority. Before landing, therefore, the adult males of the little body of separatists gathered in the cabin of the *Mayflower,* and there set their hands to a covenant intended to provide the basis for civil government:

We whose names are underwritten . . . Do by these Presents, solemnly and mutually in the Presence of God and one another, covenant and combine ourselves together into a civil Body Politick . . .

Here for the first time the compact theory of the state found expression in America. Plymouth Colony, in fact, had no other formal basis for its political order throughout its seventy-one years of existence.

The Mayflower Compact was only the first of many such covenants by which civil authority was established within the various New England settlements. When Roger Williams and his followers fled from Massachusetts to Rhode Island in the winter of 1636 and founded the town of Providence, they also found themselves outside all organized government. They solved their problem as the settlers at Plymouth had, binding themselves by a compact very similar to that executed aboard the *Mayflower.* The other principal Rhode Island towns founded within the next few years, notably Newport and Portsmouth, established governments in the same fashion.

The Puritan followers of John Davenport and Theophilus Eaton, who founded New Haven Colony, likewise organized their body politic through compact. They first met at New Haven in 1639, and with the declaration that the Bible offered perfect guidance for establishing government, they covenanted together in a body politic to enforce the laws of God. Seven men, known as the "seven Pillars," were chosen to constitute the government; and to them was granted virtual dictatorial power to make laws, administer affairs, and admit new freemen to the colony.

Eventually, a number of towns grew up around New Haven, and in 1643 they united to form the colony of New Haven. Under this compact the freemen of the colony elected a governor, deputy governor, and magistrates, while the several towns each sent two delegates to a General Court. The governor, deputy governor, and magistrates sat with the delegates to compose a one-house legislature with general lawmaking and taxing powers and supreme judicial authority.

The most famous of all early covenants after the Mayflower Compact was the Fundamental Orders of Connecticut, executed in 1639 among the settlers in the Connecticut River towns of Hartford, Windsor, and Wethersfield. The covenant created a government patterned after the joint-stock company organization. Once a year all freemen in the colony were to assemble in a "Courte of Election" to choose a governor and a board of magistrates. In addition, each of the three towns elected four deputies to meet with the governor and magistrates in a General Court or legislature. The General Court possessed all lawmaking authority for the colony, including the power to raise taxes, admit freemen, make grants of undisposed lands, and call the magistrates to account for misconduct. The General Court was more powerful than the governor; it could meet and adjourn without the consent of the governor and magistrates, while the governor possessed no veto but only a casting vote in case of a tie.

The Fundamental Orders of Connecticut have been described as the first modern written constitution because they were a written compact of the people by which a fundamental frame of government was erected. This is an exaggeration which gives Connecticut more credit than it deserves and unfairly diminishes the significance of the other early colonies. Although the Connecticut scheme was more elaborate, it was not essentially different from the formal written compacts that provided the basis of government in Plymouth, Rhode Island, and New Haven. Moreover, if one is concerned with the functional equivalent of a modern written constitution, one finds it more conspicuously in the corporation charters, which, though granted by the crown rather than formed by the mutual consent of the people, supplied frames of government. In point here is the evident copying in the Fundamental Orders of Connecticut from the Massachusetts Bay charter. The Fundamental Orders of Connecticut furthermore differed from a modern constitution in failing to make a distinction between organic supreme law and ordinary enactments of the legislature; that distinction, unknown also to the corporation charters, would not appear until the late eighteenth century. Nevertheless, compacts such as the Fundamental Orders, like the corporation charters, were enormously important in the development of American constitutionalism because they expressed the idea that government could be created in a deliberate and purposeful way, with definite, circumscribed powers.

The Proprietary Principle

A third method of establishing overseas settlement in the seventeenth century employed the feudal proprietary principle. It consisted in the grant of a feudal patent which gave the recipient vast land holdings and endowed him virtually with the powers of a king to rule new territory. Initially used to settle parts of northern England in the Middle Ages, the feudal patent legitimized the abortive colonization efforts of Sir Humphrey Gilbert and Sir Walter Raleigh in the late sixteenth century. The proprietary principle continued to have political and social relevance in the seventeenth century. Despite the growing power of the English mercantile classes, the landed aristocracy retained its influence at court, and many nobles looked on overseas settlement, carried out under a feudal patent, as a way of acquiring wealth and power. For this reason the proprietary principle became the favored means of promoting English colonization in the latter part of the seventeenth century. It also formed the basis of the colony founded by George Calvert, the first Lord Baltimore, in the 1630s.

The proprietary grant for Maryland came close to erecting an autonomous feudal principality in America. In the patent issued in 1632, Charles I as overlord granted Lord Baltimore all the rights, privileges, and immunities possessed then or in the past by the bishop of Durham. Between the years 1300 and 1500 the palatinate of Durham in England had been little less than an independent feudal state, and thus, by implication, reference to Durham's past status made Baltimore a virtually independent feudal lord, with but very slight obligation to the crown. The Maryland charter also gave the proprietor complete control over local administration, lawmaking, and military matters in his province. He could establish an assembly, but was not required to do so. All writs ran in his name, and no appeals could be taken to England from his courts. He possessed the right of subinfeudation, and the charter provided further that grantees owed allegiance only to Baltimore and not directly to the king. In short, Baltimore enjoyed a status not unlike that of a king except that he had no crown.

Nevertheless, political institutions developed in Maryland along the lines already marked out in Virginia, albeit more slowly. Cecilius Calvert, the second Lord Baltimore, in 1638 called an assembly of freemen to consult with the proprietary governor, and within a few years the assembly became an established body which began to demand a share of the legislative power. Indeed, as the proprietor was in effect a king in the new territory, the assembly soon identified itself as a little Parliament. In that sense Maryland and the later proprietary colonies offer an example of the transfer of English political institutions. In a more practical political sense, however, the model for Maryland's constitutional development was neighboring Virginia, with its elected assembly. Experience there, as well as in Massachusetts Bay, made it clear that successful colonization required giving to those whose labor was essential to the prosperity of the community a share in its government.

By 1640 the first wave of colonization in North America had ended, with settlements established in Virginia, Massachusetts Bay, Plymouth, New Haven, the Rhode Island and Connecticut River towns, and Maryland. The corporation, the covenant, and the feudal patent provided the means of founding governments in the new territory, and of these the corporate principle was the most important. Virginia and Massachusetts Bay were politically dominant in their regions and served as a model for governmental development in nearby colonies. To be sure, the covenant colonies were significant for the social-compact theory of government that became so influential during the American Revolution. Yet governments founded as corporations also expressed the idea of creating political authority out of voluntary association. Moreover, the corporation was important in supplying a structure of governmental authority to colonies founded on covenant or feudal patent. Although power relationships differed in the several colonies, in each a governor, council, and assembly shared the functions of government. Having their origin in written charters that served as a source of authority and prescribed an institutional structure, the corporate colonies foreshadowed the central theme in American constitutional history: the idea of limited government under a positive fundamental law.

TWO

The Formation of the Colonial Constitution: 1640-1700

Two FUNDAMENTAL ISSUES have given shape and direction to American constitutional history. The first has concerned the structure of government, the distribution of power among its parts, the relationship of individual citizens to the government. Although the colonists differed in their approach to these matters, by 1700 a general pattern of institutional practice had taken shape which in effect created a colonial constitution. The second fundamental issue in American constitutional development has been the relationship of several smaller governments to a central authority. In the seventeenth and eighteenth centuries this issue took the form of the imperial question. Because of domestic political turmoil and limited resources, the earliest English colonization efforts lacked coherent overall direction. The relationship of the parts to the whole was implicit in the founding of the colonies, however, and in the middle of the seventeenth century it became a matter of conscious concern. By the end of the century attempts to coordinate colonial affairs had evolved into an imperial constitutional system. As far as Americans were concerned, the critical question that was resolved in the sixty years after the initial period of settlement was whether they would achieve a distinct constitutional order of their own or remain entirely subservient to English governmental control.

Events favored the first of these alternatives. From 1640 to 1700 the central theme in constitutional development was the extension and confirmation of local self-government through the instrumentality of elected assemblies. In some colonies the assemblies achieved considerable powers, especially in the period of the English Civil War and Interregnum. Indeed, while the English were preoccupied with internal politics, the assemblies in Massachusetts Bay, Virginia, and Maryland aggrandized power to such an extent that these colonies for a time enjoyed virtual autonomy. After 1660 the idea of self-governing representative institutions found expression in the founding of several new colonies, all but one of which from the outset had elected assemblies that struggled with the executive for a greater share of governmental power.

In imperial affairs the chief development in the latter half of the seventeenth century was the formation of a coherent policy drawing the colonies more closely into the orbit of English government and asserting greater control over them. Heightened consciousness of imperial administration was evident in the period 1640 to 1660, even though little was accomplished in the way of structural reform because of internal political upheaval. In the Restoration era after 1660 the English extended their overseas influence through the founding of several additional colonies and the adoption of systematic policies not only for commercial regulation, but also for the internal political administration of the colonies.

Because the American Revolution in the most general sense resulted from the conflict between the American demand for self-government and the English insistence on imperial control, it appears paradoxical to say that events of the seventeenth century advanced both of these themes simultaneously. As yet, however, the contradiction between these ideas was not apparent. The interests of Englishmen in North America and Englishmen at home could be compatibly pursued within evolving constitutional arrangements that recognized the legitimacy of both the power of the colonial assemblies and the imperial authority.

Colonial Autonomy during the English Civil War

In the period of the Civil War and Interregnum the General Court of Massachusetts Bay became the dominant political institution in a virtually independent state. Internally a key structural development in this period was the division of the General Court into two distinct bodies. This change resulted from political conflict between the wealthier and more socially prominent men who served as magistrates on the governor's council and the men of lesser property who asserted their interests as elected delegates in the General Court.

The governor and magistrates at first held preponderant power and were fearful that too large a role for the elected members of the General Court would jeopardize authority and order. Accordingly, the magistrates reserved to themselves the right to approve any action taken by the General Court. Moreover, they constituted a standing council which exercised executive powers when the legislature was not in session. For their part the elected delegates expressed fear of arbitrary government and tried to curb the magistrates' power. In 1644 the two groups resolved the conflict by agreeing to an institutional separation. Henceforth the magistrates and the elected delegates, though together continuing to form the General Court, would sit separately and each would possess a veto over legislation. This change marked an apparent victory for the deputies, since they acquired a power that had not previously been theirs. In a more significant sense it was a victory for the magistrates, who retained a power that had been under attack for several years. This bicameral legislative structure reflected the differentiation of interests in the new society, and in the eyes of both deputies and magistrates kept a proper balance between stability and order on the one hand and the rights and liberties of the people on the other.

More constitutionally significant than this internal development was the fact that Massachusetts Bay gained an autonomous position in imperial affairs in the troubled decades from 1640 to 1660. As early as 1637 royal authorities, mainly out of hostility to Puritanism, had tried to invalidate the Massachusetts charter. As the power of English Puritanism rose and became ascendant in the 1640s and 1650s, the English government persisted in the endeavor to subject Massachusetts Bay to English authority. But continued political unrest at home prevented the Commonwealth government from doing more than sending a commission to secure the subordination of the remote settlement on Massachusetts Bay (as well as of the other colonies in North America). Though religiously sympathetic to the Cromwellian regime, the Puritans of New England were uncompromising in their insistence on maintaining their independence. In 1645 the General Court denied any subordination to the English government and declared that the laws of Parliament and the king's writ did not affect them. As though to express this autonomy, the General Court adopted a code of laws in 1648 (the *Laws and Liberties of Massachusetts*), and in 1652 required all inhabitants to subscribe an oath of loyalty to the laws of the colony. In the same year Massachusetts took control of settlements that had been undertaken under proprietary grants in Maine and New Hampshire. These were acts of sovereignty that for all practical purposes identified Massachusetts Bay as an independent state. The General Court at no point disavowed allegiance to England, but this loyalty was merely an empty formality.

In these same years Virginia, though continuing to be a royal colony, acquired a more substantial measure of autonomy under an increasingly assertive elected assembly. A creature of the joint-stock company, the House of Burgesses met only intermittently after the crown took control of the colony in 1625. In 1639, however, on royal instructions, the elected assembly achieved a fixed position in the constitution of the colony. This was principally because it had become an essential means of securing the support and cooperation of the varied political and economic interests that appeared as settlement spread. In the 1640s the House of Burgesses professed loyalty to the crown, and after the abolition of the monarchy in 1649, it resisted the demand of the Commonwealth government for subordination to English authority.

Virginia eventually yielded where the Bay colony did not, the fact of twenty-five years of royal rule and the absence of a charter having an evident effect. But the outcome of negotiations between Virginia's political leaders and the commissioners whom the Commonwealth government sent to the colony in 1652 was a significant shift in constitutional power from the governor and council, previously the main source of law and policy, to the House of Burgesses. The elected deputies now chose the governor and council, appointed justices of the peace (the chief officers in the politically and administratively important county courts), and in general controlled the government in the 1650s. After the restoration of the Stuart monarchy, William Berkeley returned to power as governor, the choice of both imperial authorities and local political leaders. But the House of Burgesses, though it ceased to be the dominant force in the government, occupied a stronger position than it had prior to the Commonwealth period. Having made Berkeley's appointment contingent on its approval, the Burgesses successfully insisted on their right to meet regularly in biennial session, to be dissolved by the governor only with their consent, and to approve appointments to the governor's council. In 1663, as a sign of its institutional maturity and political influence, the House of Burgesses began to sit separately. Virginia, of course, never ceased to be a royal colony, but in the mid-seventeenth century it attained, and under the locally popular Governor Berkeley continued to enjoy, a considerable autonomy.

In still a third colony, proprietary Maryland, the assembly played a more conspicuous governmental role in the Interregnum period. Although the proprietor permitted an assembly to be formed in 1637, he was for all intents and purposes the government. Small in number (about twenty members) and serving strictly as a consultative body, the assembly throughout the 1640s sought the right to initiate legislation and sit separately. Aided by the fact that they comprised a large Protestant interest and that the proprietor, a Catholic, was the object of antiproprietary pressure from the Puritan Commonwealth government in England, the assembly in 1650 secured these goals. Through the ensuing decade the government of Maryland was in turmoil as Catholics and Protestants, looking to the powers of the proprietor and the assembly, respectively, tried to establish control. From 1655 to 1658 the Puritan-dominated assembly repudiated the proprietor and governed the colony. In 1660 the proprietor regained political control and relegated the assembly again to a subordinate role. Retaining its legislative initiative and bicameral status, however, the assembly adopted an opposition stance and attacked the exercise of power by the proprietary governor and council for the next thirty years.

Massachusetts Bay, Virginia, and Maryland thus secured a broad degree of assembly-based autonomy, despite the imperial ambitions of both royalist and parliamentary English authorities. Because of their necessary preoccupation with domestic politics, neither crown nor Commonwealth officials could do much to promote imperial control. The restoration of the monarchy in 1660, however, provided that opportunity. For the next thirty years the founding of additional colonies and the formulation of a commercial policy for the overseas settlements gave substance to the imperial vision.

The Second Wave of Colonization in English North America

From 1607 to 1641 about 70,000 English men and women migrated to the colonies in New England and the Chesapeake region. From 1664 to 1681 a second wave of emigration produced colonies in New York, New Jersey, Carolina, and Pennsylvania. All of these colonies were founded on the proprietary principle. Nevertheless, despite the theoretically autocratic nature of this governing instrument, their constitutional development, with one exception, reinforced the theory and practice of local self-government under an elected assembly.

The revival of aristocratic influence under Charles II made the feudal patent an appropriate means of colonization in the Restoration era. The crown had political obligations that could be repaid with land grants in North America, and ambitious members of the nobility were eager to seek power and wealth as feudal lords in the New World. At the same time the joint-stock corporation no longer appealed as a colonizing device since settlements based on this approach had not rewarded their investors, however successful they had become as political communities. Accordingly, in 1662 Charles II granted extensive lands along the Atlantic coast south of Virginia to eight court favorites who were empowered to rule, as Maryland's proprietor had been, with all the rights and privileges of the bishop of Durham. Named Carolina after the king, the colony consisted of three widely scattered settlements. When the English conquered New Netherlands in 1664, Charles II granted it to his brother James, duke of York, through a proprietary charter that gave him absolute power; James in turn made a grant of part of the land to John Berkeley and George Carteret as proprietors of New Jersey. Finally, in 1681 the Quaker gentleman William Penn secured a proprietary grant to found a colony to the west of New Jersey, along the Delaware River.

What was constitutionally significant about these colonies, with the exception of New York, was that their original design provided for an elected assembly. Earlier in the seventeenth century the assembly was a political expedient needed to make settlement more attractive, as in Virginia. Later, in Massachusetts Bay, Maryland, and the New England covenant colonies, the assembly served the purpose of coordinating and achieving a proper balance between the interests of rulers and ruled. By the 1660s the planners of new settlements saw the assembly as a necessary part of a colony's political institutions. Along with the promise of religious toleration and the availability of cheap land, the promise of political participation through an elected assembly was an important inducement for settlers. The assembly thus became the basic American constitutional institution.

In order to appeal especially to New England Puritans accustomed to representation in an assembly, the proprietors of Carolina and New Jersey, in the Concessions and Agreement of 1665, provided for elected assemblies in the two colonies. Together with a governor and council, these bodies would possess the lawmaking power. In Carolina each of the three dispersed settlements (Charlestown, Albemarle, and Port Royal) was to have an assembly. Subsequently, the Fundamental Constitutions of Carolina, an elaborate governmental plan drawn up in 1669 to regulate the aristocratic and democratic elements of society, proposed to create a parliament in which elected freeholders would share legislative power with a governor and deputies of the proprietors and the nobility. Farther north the Quakers, who bought part of the New Jersey grant and founded the colony of West Jersey, in their Concessions and Agreement of 1677 projected a representative body having exclusive lawmaking power. And in 1682 William Penn included an assembly in the first of several frames of government designed to serve as the constitutional foundation for Pennsylvania.

From the proprietors' standpoint the promise of representative institutions was a promotional device more than an expression of philosophical commitment. It was only with difficulty that settlers succeeded in translating the promise into institutional reality. Expecting deference, the sponsors of the later proprietary colonies assumed that government would remain the exclusive affair of the landed elite. The freeholder-dominated assemblies did constant battle, however, seeking to go beyond a merely consultative role and win the right to initiate legislation. In 1671, for example, the Carolina assembly at Charlestown refused to accept the Fundamental Constitutions of Carolina because that document did not concede such a right. The assembly in West Jersey gained the right to initiate legislation and other powers in relation to the colony executive in 1681. And in 1682 the Pennsylvania assembly, protesting William Penn's paternalistic, council-dominated scheme of government, began a fourteen-year struggle to attain genuine legislative power. New York had no assembly, but it too witnessed a drive for popular participation in government, led by Puritan settlers from New England who agitated for the creation of an elective lawmaking body. In 1683 the duke of York, proprietor of the colony, relented and allowed an elected assembly to convene. Subsequent political changes in the colony and the empire, however, prevented it from continuing. Nevertheless, throughout the colonies people were coming to regard the existence of an assembly as a matter of right and a necessary part of the colonial constitution.

By achieving self-government through representative institutions despite their proprietors' reluctance, the Restoration era colonies gave promise of becoming practically autonomous, like the earlier corporate colonies. This autonomy was in large part based on the fact that they were the personal property of recipients of feudal patents. Yet colonial independence conflicted with the desire of many of the king's advisers for more systematic imperial control. By 1680, when William Penn sought his charter, the inconsistency inherent in trying to create a centralized empire while giving away vast territories to men with virtually independent powers of government led imperial officials to impose limitations on the Pennsylvania charter. Penn had to agree to send the colony's laws to England for acceptance or disallowance, allow appeals from the colony's courts, and recognize the king's reserved right to levy taxes on the colony. Furthermore, he promised to obey the series of laws governing imperial trade enacted by Parliament over the previous two decades as an expression of the new quest for empire.

Imperial Centralization

International rivalry with the Netherlands, Spain, and France led English statesmen to seek a more centralized administration of the colonies and to coordinate colonial economic affairs with those of England. Between 1661 and 1675 Parliament passed a series of Navigation Acts, embodying the fundamental principles of mercantilism. All trade with the colonies was required to be carried in English or colonial ships, and the colonies were to have a monopoly in the English market for their leading products, the so-called enumerated commodities including tobacco, sugar, indigo, rice, cotton, ginger, and naval stores. These could be sent only to England, and except for a few products such as wine and salt, the colonies were obliged in turn to get all their imports from England. The colonies also had to pay duties on their products, meaning that trade within the empire was not free but preferential.

The acts implementing this commercial design affected the American colonists not only in an obvious economic sense, but also politically and constitutionally. In this respect the Plantation Duties Act of 1673 was the most important of the new measures. Obliged to carry their enumerated products to English or other colonial ports, American merchants at first evaded the rule by landing their cargo in a colonial port before reshipping it outside the empire. The act of 1673 stopped this practice by requiring merchants to pay export duties on enumerated products at the point of departure, and it provided for the appointment of customs collectors assigned from London. Previously, customs collection had been a responsibility of the colonial governors, only one of whom—in Virginia—was a royal officer. Now English customs officials were placed in North America and expected to assume a role in the administration of a colony's internal affairs. Although historians have traditionally drawn a sharp distinction between the British commercial system of the seventeenth century and the internal colonial administration undertaken after 1763, there was both a logical and historical connection between the two phases of imperial control.

Indeed, after 1660 crown officials set in motion a process of systematizing and tightening the relationship of the colonies to England which, in conjunction with the requirements of the Navigation Acts, in the 1680s culminated in the establishment of centralized imperial rule over most of the American colonies. Imperial power expanded in the 1660s and 1670s through the imposition of royal governments, under the command of military officers, in Jamaica (formerly a Spanish colony) and Barbados and the Leeward Islands (formerly proprietaries); the conquest of New Netherlands from the Dutch; and the reassertion of royal influence in Virginia. In 1662 and 1663 the crown granted charters to Connecticut and Rhode Island, covenant colonies which feared that Charles II might refuse to recognize their existing governments. Except for a parliamentary grant to Rhode Island in 1644, these colonies had possessed no official sanction or legitimacy. Their new charters in effect confirmed the existing governments in each colony, which in Connecticut was enlarged by the absorption of New Haven. But the charters also required that Rhode Island and Connecticut submit to royal customs control and agree not to enact laws contrary to the laws of England. Connecticut and Rhode Island welcomed the protection of royal charters because they feared being taken over by Massachusetts, a not unreasonable apprehension considering the Bay colony's willingness to challenge even the authority of England.

On several counts Massachusetts Bay stood as an affront to the emerging imperial policy. Controlled by an entrenched Puritan oligarchy, Massachusetts refused to permit Anglican or other kinds of worship outside the state-established Congregational church. It also restricted suffrage to church members. To complaints about the colony's long-standing religious intolerance was added growing impatience with its equally long-standing insistence on its constitutional autonomy. Only in the most general sense did Massachusetts profess allegiance to Charles II in 1662, when the crown demanded expressions of subordination from the colonies. Most of the time, as when it was charged with violating the Navigation Acts, the Bay colony declared itself beyond the scope of parliamentary law. In the late 1670s English authorities began a concerted effort to bring Massachusetts into line by appointing Edward Randolph collector of customs, the first royal official resident in the colonies charged with enforcing the trade acts. Massachusetts' leaders remained obdurate, however. They declared the Navigation Acts in force by the authority of the General Court and appointed the colony's own customs collectors. Supremely uncompromising, the colony kept the customs revenues for itself. These actions presented the English government with a challenge to its sovereignty that it could not avoid. Accordingly, imperial officials inaugurated legal proceedings against Massachusetts Bay in the royal courts and in 1684 secured the desired result: revocation of the colony's charter.

This momentous step prepared the way for the creation of centralized imperial control over the northern colonies. Concurrently with the campaign against Massachusetts, crown officials in the early 1680s tightened the administration of the Navigation Acts and initiated legal action against the proprietary grants in Maryland, New Jersey, and Carolina, with a view toward making them royal colonies. The death of Charles II in 1685 and the accession of James II, a Catholic with even more pronounced imperial ambitions, brought plans for the subordination of the colonies rapidly to fruition.

To begin with, James was the proprietor of New York, which meant that upon his accession it became a royal colony. Politically and strategically, however, Massachusetts was the critical problem. In place of the deposed charter-based Puritan oligarchy, James and his advisers decided that an English governor-general should rule, assisted by a council but without a locally elected assembly. Instead of governing themselves, the colonists should pay taxes and obediently accept the laws given to them by the governor-general, on the theory that the colonies were the personal possession of the king.[1] In the view of imperial officials, the very existence of the colonies and whatever representative institutions they possessed depended on royal grace and favor, not on any right of political participation or self-government that the colonists might claim.

To carry out this conception of empire, as well as to enforce England's commercial policy and strengthen English military power against the Indians and the French in North America, James II appointed Edmund Andros governor-general of a new imperial administrative structure, the Dominion of New England. In 1687 Andros went to Boston as a military officer charged with the conduct of government and civil administration.[2] Aided by internal opposition to the Puritan establishment, Andros took control of Massachusetts Bay, appointed a council from among the anti-Puritan element, and in due course forced the submission of Plymouth, New Hampshire, Maine, Rhode Island, and Connecticut to imperial rule. In 1688 the crown added New York and East and West Jersey to the Dominion's jurisdiction.

In destroying the elected assemblies in eight colonies the Dominion of new England had a profound constitutional impact. Indeed, the new imperial structure denied the very idea of a colonial constitution, resting instead on the theory that there was only an imperial constitution in which the colonies were utter dependencies of the crown. In Massachusetts the consequences of imperial reorganization transcended the governmental sphere and affected the religio-social order that had existed for fifty years. It was bad enough to legislate and levy taxes without the consent of the inhabitants in the General Court. What was even more objectionable, Andros insisted on religious toleration, introduced Anglican worship, and prohibited the government from paying ministers' salaries. The consequence was the disestablishment of the Congregational church. Furthermore, on the theory that all land should be held

---

1. In technical legal terms the colonies were *dominions* of the king, subject to his personal rule, as distinguished from the *realm* of England where the king's rule was limited by the common law.

2. Reliance on military officers in politico-administrative positions was characteristic of the British Empire from the outset. Approximately 90 percent of the 206 commanders in chief of royal colonies who were appointed between 1660 and 1727 were English army officers. This fact is evidence that imperial officials sought to promote the traditional social values of order, obedience, and military security, all of which at times conflicted with the more modern commercial values that overseas trade encouraged.

from the king, Andros negated land titles, required owners of real property to petition for royal patents, and forced them to pay a quitrent to the crown. When people used town meetings (the basic form of local government) to protest the collection of taxes without their consent, Andros restricted the towns to one meeting a year. He also changed the judicial system by permitting nonchurch members to sit on juries. The other colonies that came under Dominion rule suffered the loss of their assemblies, but they were not subjected to the same treatment as Massachusetts because they were less important. They were also far enough away from Boston to make direct imperial control impractical.

The Glorious Revolution in America

The Dominion of New England lasted only as long as the government that had created it. The Revolution of 1688, which deposed James II and brought William of Orange to the throne, had an American phase that overthrew the Dominion government in Boston and New York. The Glorious Revolution in America also included the removal of the proprietary government in Maryland. These colonial uprisings expressed Americans' opposition to imperial centralization, led to a redefinition of the status of the colonies in the empire, and in effect revised both the colonial and imperial constitutions. But the rebellions of 1689 also reflected internal political and social pressures within the colonies that had developed in the context of the new imperial order. For this reason it is necessary to consider the nature of American politics in the late seventeenth century.

In most colonies politics consisted of a struggle between an established oligarchy that was secure in the governor's council and new groups of ambitious men who used the assembly to seek political power appropriate to their economic position. Turbulent enough without outside influences, political conflict became even more intense and destabilizing when imperial policy intruded into the local situation. The uprising in Virginia in the 1670s known as Bacon's Rebellion provides apt illustration.

Impatient with the governor's lenient Indian policy as well as frustrated by a declining tobacco market for which the Navigation Acts were partly responsible, lesser landowners and gentry in 1676 rebelled against Governor William Berkeley. Their rebellion mainly took the form of a vigilante expedition, led by Nathaniel Bacon, against neighboring Indians. Bacon's followers showed no inclination to repudiate their English allegiance; their grievances were directed at specific policies and at the council-dominated political establishment rather than at royal authority as such. Nevertheless, the uprising was regarded in England as a challenge to imperial authority, and it was met by a show of imperial strength. The crown dispatched 1,100 troops to maintain the government, thus for the first time establishing a military garrison in North

America. As it happened, the troops were not needed, for the rebellion quickly collapsed when Bacon died in late 1676. In the aftermath of the uprising a series of laws was adopted limiting the privileges of the council, extending the suffrage, and broadening opportunities for participation in local government. But these reforms were soon repealed. The local elite maintained its hold on politics and society, and imperial control was strengthened, although the garrison was disbanded. With the appointment of a new royal governor, the House of Burgesses agreed to grant the crown a permanent revenue and to surrender its right to sit as the highest court of appeals in the colony.

In other colonies internal political tensions, exacerbated by the imperial policy of the 1680s, erupted in the rebellions of 1689. In Massachusetts and Connecticut merchants hostile to the Puritan ruling group at first supported the Dominion of New England with a view toward advancing their own political and economic interests. Opposition to the Andros regime became so widespread, however, that when news of the English Revolution reached Massachusetts Bay in 1689 it touched off an armed uprising that immediately destroyed the authority of the Dominion government. Local leaders formed a provisional government and, significantly deciding against restoration of the old charter government, began negotiations with the new monarch, William III, to determine the nature of the colony's government and its constitutional status in the empire.

In the other New England colonies the fall of the Dominion government was quietly followed by the resumption of the old governments, but in New York political upheaval ensued and important changes took place. Local merchants and gentry, many of them Puritan immigrants from New England who had long criticized the concentration of power in the governor's council and demanded an assembly, seized on the news of Andros's fall to overthrow the lieutenant governor of the Dominion, stationed in New York. Claiming authority under the neglected Charter of Liberties of 1683, they organized a provisional government under the leadership of Captain Jacob Leisler, held elections for an assembly, and proclaimed the new king.

In Maryland imperial authority was not involved in the political struggle, but word of the Glorious Revolution was a signal for the Protestant-dominated assembly, after years of contesting the special privilege and power belonging to the governor and council, to cast off proprietary rule itself. Seizing control of the government, the assembly proclaimed William and Mary the new sovereigns and sent delegates to England requesting that the colony be made a royal province. There was governmental turmoil also at this time in Carolina and Pennsylvania. A revolt in Albemarle County, in northern Carolina, resulted in the dispatch of an agent to England seeking aid in resolving the local conflict, and Pennsylvania continued to witness conflict between the council and the assembly. Meanwhile in England William Penn tried to keep hold of his colony against strong antiproprietary sentiment in imperial circles.

The extent to which political and constitutional instability was a general characteristic of the colonies at this time can be seen in the fact that in 1689 ten colonies—Massachusetts, New Hampshire, Rhode Island, Connecticut, East and West Jersey, North and South Carolina,[3] Maryland, and New York— had agents in England negotiating the status if not the very existence of their local governments in the empire. Conditions were more unsettled in some of these colonies than in others, but all of them sought a sanction—in the form of a charter from the English government—that would guarantee their right to exist as something more than mere dependencies of the crown. In the most literal sense they were going through a crisis of legitimacy as self-governing polities. For their part the officials and advisers under William III, though seeking to avoid the excesses of the imperial system of James II, were little inclined to yield where questions of English sovereignty were involved. Both colonists and imperialists, however, had learned something from the disastrous experiment in centralized imperial administration. The constitutional settlement that was worked out in the decade following the Glorious Revolution secured the basic goals of each group.

Significance of the Revolutionary Settlement

The most conspicuous feature of the constitutional settlement was the extension of royal authority into new spheres. Massachusetts was the prize example in this respect: The only colony able to secure a charter, nevertheless it now became a royal colony. Its governor was to be appointed by the crown, and it was required to send its laws to England for approval. The autonomy of the old Puritan Commonwealth was plainly ended. In neighboring New Hampshire, which the crown had removed from the jurisdiction of Massachusetts Bay in 1679 only to lose it again in the aftermath of the rebellion in 1689, royal authority was restored. Elsewhere, in a significant change, Maryland became a royal colony, although the proprietor was permitted to keep the land and the revenues from it. New York had been a royal colony since 1685, but it now received a typical royal government for the first time. Pennsylvania and the Carolinas remained proprietaries, though from 1692 to 1694 the former came under the jurisdiction of the royal government in New York, and as of 1696 the governors of both proprietary colonies had to be approved by the crown. An antiproprietary drive continued to characterize imperial policy, and East Jersey and West Jersey maintained separate existences only until 1702, when they were united as a single royal colony. Connecticut and Rhode Island, regarded as politically insignificant, resumed their charter governments in 1689 and were pretty much left alone. Finally Plymouth Plantation was absorbed into Massachusetts.

3. Carolina had in reality become two colonies by this time. In 1691 this distinction was formally recognized by the proprietors.

Accompanying the increase in the number of royal colonies was the extension and strengthening of the imperial commercial system. In the Navigation Act of 1696 Parliament placed the customs service on a more solid legal basis, enlarged the collection bureaucracy, and authorized the creation of twelve vice-admiralty courts for enforcing the Navigation Acts. Vice-admiralty courts operated directly under crown authority and, unlike common law courts, lacked juries. Colonial common law courts in the colonies, which had previously tried violations of the trade acts, were permitted under the act of 1696 to have concurrent jurisdiction with the new courts. But the royal governor had the power to determine which tribunal would be used to enforce the commercial regulations. The crown also expressed its seriousness of imperial purpose by creating in 1696 the Board of Trade. A body of salaried officials, many of them merchants, the board replaced the subcommittee of the Privy Council known as the Lords of Trade that had existed since 1675. The Board of Trade prepared instructions for colonial governors, reviewed colonial legislation, and in general advised the crown and Parliament on colonial matters.

If the settlement achieved at the end of the seventeenth century strengthened the authority of the English government in North America, it also underscored the importance of the assembly as the fundamental feature of the colonial constitution and confirmed it as an element in the imperial constitution. Continuous as the growth of representative institutions had been since the original settlements, the Dominion of New England showed how vulnerable the assemblies were. In the Glorious Revolution and its aftermath the colonists restored the assemblies and extended their powers. Connecticut and Rhode Island revived their assemblies without incident. In Massachusetts the new charter of 1691 provided for a General Court. Although its powers were more circumscribed than they had been in the period of independence, it enjoyed a privileged position relative to the governor unlike that found in any other royal colony. The elected deputies in the General Court chose the governor's council, created new courts, and held annual sessions under a guarantee contained in the charter.

In Maryland the assembly gained control over taxation, the judicial system, and the determination of its membership and internal organization, issues over which it had struggled for decades with the proprietary council. Especially notable was the establishment of a representative assembly in New York. Promised in the Charter of Liberties of 1683 but never realized, the creation of an assembly was the first work of the Leisler rebels in 1689. The New York assembly straightaway assumed an important governmental role as it settled land titles, passed tax measures, and reorganized the judicial system.

With the exception of New England, the role of the assembly in the seventeenth century had been more consultative than decisive or determinative. By 1700, however, each colony had an assembly, and everywhere, with the ironic exception of Massachusetts, it played a more forceful and significant role than it had previously. All the assemblies had won the right to initiate legislation, to sit separately, and to participate in the shaping of fiscal policy. Increasingly, the assemblies gave up the judicial functions that they had shared with the council and the courts, and confined themselves to legislation (which function they continued to share with the governor and council). Assemblies at this time also cultivated the habit of referring to Parliament as a legislative model, as they tried to wrest from the governor privileges which the House of Commons had won against the crown throughout the seventeenth century.

The clearest expression of the enhanced position of the lower houses of assembly appeared in the Pennsylvania Charter of Privileges of 1701. The last in a series of constitutional instruments in Pennsylvania's founding period, this frame of government ended two decades of struggle between council and assembly by excluding the former from lawmaking and placing the legislative function entirely in the latter's hands. Possessing the power to choose its own speaker and to pass on the qualifications of its members, as well as to hold fixed meetings and control its adjournment, the Pennsylvania deputies asserted their right to "all other powers and privileges of an assembly, according to the rights of the free born subjects of England." More successful than their counterparts in other colonies, the Pennsylvania assembly pointed out the direction of constitutional change in the eighteenth century.

The assembly was the key institution in the colonial constitution, and by 1700 it had become in practice and experience a fixed part of the constitution of the empire. English officials, however, held theories about the imperial constitution which clashed with colonial reality. They regarded the colonies as dominions of the king, subject to his personal rule and outside the scope of the common law except insofar as he might choose to apply it there. In 1689–91 many colonists disputed this view, arguing that they possessed all the rights of English subjects under the common law, such as the right to representation and the guarantee of protection against arbitrary deprivation of their liberty and property. Pursuing this constitutional position, the assemblies in New York and Maryland in the 1690s passed resolutions stating that representation in an elected assembly was a right based on Magna Charta or the fundamental laws of England. English officials rejected these declarations, insisting on the contrary that such representative institutions as existed in the colonies flowed from royal favor rather than constitutional right. Yet the more important fact was that, despite its own theories, the English government after 1690 acted as though representation in an assembly, and a substantial degree of assembly self-government in local affairs, existed by right. Never thereafter did the English found a colony without an elected assembly. In American eyes the perpetuation of this political practice created a constitutional right of representation and local self-government.

Nowhere in the colonies did political leaders in the late seventeenth century seek or even contemplate an independent existence for their provincial governments outside the empire and completely detached from the English nation. For that reason, despite some similarity in the arguments presented, the historical situation that the colonists faced in the 1680s differed fundamentally from that which existed on the eve of the Revolution in the eighteenth century. Indeed, as a result of the changes in the late seventeenth century the colonists became more self-consciously English in their constitutional outlook. This tendency was evident in Massachusetts. In the long dispute over the status of Massachusetts Bay that lasted from 1660 to 1684, the colony's spokesmen had relied on the charter and the covenant to defend their position. Once the charter was abrogated, however, they turned elsewhere. In resisting the Dominion of New England and in demanding the restoration of local liberties after the Glorious Revolution, the representatives of Massachusetts argued from the constitution and laws of England. These instruments, they contended, guaranteed them fundamental rights of representation, consent to taxation, and protection of their person and property. In other colonies, especially New York and Maryland, where rebellions took place, colonists made the same argument.

The English denied that the principles of the Glorious Revolution applied to the colonies. The colonists insisted that they did, and in the course of the eighteenth century they built a constitutional tradition of resistance to arbitrary executive power on this foundation. Though at the end of the seventeenth century they were hardly equals within the empire—that is, possessed of the same liberties as subjects of the king within the realm of England—the logic of their rights-of-Englishmen argument suggested that equality was the goal toward which they were moving.

THREE

The Colonial Constitution
in the Eighteenth Century

IN THE FIRST HALF OF THE EIGHTEENTH CENTURY the American colonies evolved constitutionally along the paths marked out in the aftermath of the Glorious Revolution of 1689. It is clear in retrospect that the colonists continued to prepare the institutional and philosophical foundations on which republican government was later established. The steady increase in colonial population, wealth, and prosperity suggests a growing organism whose differentiation and eventual separation from England were natural and irresistible. Yet in this period Americans consciously tried to emulate their English superiors, like any intelligent colonial people. This was true in society and culture, where increasing stratification and concentration of wealth made the colonies more nearly resemble England in the eighteenth century than they had in the seventeenth. It was true also in government and politics, where, employing the concepts and practices of English constitutionalism, the American colonists extended the powers of their provincial assemblies and achieved a broader degree of autonomy within the empire. Until events revealed the different direction they had actually taken, colonial American government was a variation of English constitutionalism.

The expansion of colonial political power in the eighteenth century took place within the framework of—indeed, it was encouraged by—the British imperial system. From 1700 to about 1720 military-executive control of imperial affairs in London operated in effective balance with the management of local affairs in America by the several provincial assemblies. As a practical arrangement rather than a formal legal enactment, a division of power and responsibility existed which adumbrated the division of sovereignty later provided for in American federalism. During Queen Anne's War (1702–13) the crown made territorial gains in French Canada, while the colonial assemblies played a pivotal role in shaping local defense and finance policies. As a matter of conscious policy, England assigned the task of raising and equipping a fighting force to the colonies, who in the process were able to expand the powers of the assembly vis-à-vis the governor.

In England after 1720 Whig views of empire favoring commercial interests and tolerant of local assembly autonomy prevailed over the more centralized, land-oriented and military-dominated approach to imperial administration urged by the Tories. A period of "salutary neglect" ensued during which the assemblies strengthened their position in relation to the royal governor, the influence of the Board of Trade declined, and imperial affairs lacked systematic direction and control. Responsibility for the government of the empire was shared among the Privy Council, Secretary of State, Treasury, Admiralty, and Parliament, along with the Board of Trade; the result was often confusion and mismanagement. In order to keep abreast of imperial politics and defend colonial interests, the colonies were authorized to send agents to England in a kind of diplomatic capacity. Although imperial officials approved of this practice, by 1750 the assemblies had gained the power to appoint the colonial agents, another step in their assumption of a larger governmental role.

The Theory of Mixed Government

Within this loose imperial framework the American colonists managed local affairs according to English precepts. As they looked to the common law for guidance in settling private disputes, so they regarded the English constitution as their model in public law and governance. What distinguished the English constitution as the colonists considered it was the balance that existed among the component parts of the government, a balance intended to preserve liberty while providing the necessary degree of authority to maintain social order. This concern with balance, which was to remain a central theme in American constitutionalism, is usually associated with the separation of powers and checks and balances. In the eighteenth century, however, the separation of powers and checks and balances. In the eighteenth century, however, the separation of powers was a new doctrine not widely accepted. A different and much older concept—the theory of mixed government—served as the principal means of reconciling liberty and authority. This doctrine provided the intellectual framework for Anglo-American thinking about government.

The basic point of mixed-government theory was to give a distinct role in the governmental structure to the constituent elements of society. Modern constitutional theory, since the ascendancy of the rival doctrine of separation of powers, is premised on the division of government into three essential functions—the legislative, executive, and judicial. In the theory of mixed government, however, no such functional distinction existed. Rather, government power was conceived of as generalized, undifferentiated, unspecialized.

Writers on government referred mainly to the tasks of government, such as levying and collecting taxes, regulating trade, controlling the militia, conducting diplomacy, and so on—matters that we would regard as policy questions. Insofar as the making and executing of law were discussed, people thought these powers were shared by all the parts of a government. The key distinction was not between separate governmental functions, but rather, as in medieval theory, between the sphere of government power (or *gubernaculum*) on the one hand and the rights and liberties of subjects (or *jurisdictio*) on the other.

Focusing on the estates or orders of society, the theory of mixed government was intended to maintain equilibrium among them, lest government come under the exclusive control of any single social class. This theory was rooted in the ancient notion, central to classical political thought, that if not checked, the monarchical element in society would degenerate into tyranny, the aristocratic element into oligarchy, and the democratic element into mob rule. Mixed-government theory in England tried to accomplish this purpose by bringing king, lords, and commons together in Parliament, where each body, representing a distinct social order, would share in the exercise of governmental power. Mixed together in the structure of government, each order would balance and restrain the others by assuming particular tasks of government, as in the practice by which money bills originated in the House of Commons. Finally, mixed-government doctrine identified basic political values with the different social orders. The king was thought to provide energy and dispatch in government; the House of Lords, wisdom; the House of Commons, a special concern for liberty and virtue.

Despite the assertion of parliamentary sovereignty in the seventeenth century, English government in the eighteenth century conformed to mixed-government theory. In the aftermath of the Glorious Revolution, English politics became stabilized under the rule of a Whig oligarchy. Parliament was theoretically supreme as the lawmaking power and the king a mere executive, but in practice a strong executive institution emerged. This occurred through the development of cabinet government under a prime minister. During the administration of Robert Walpole (1721–42), usually regarded as the first prime minister, Parliament was effectively controlled by the king's officers, through methods of patronage disposition and electoral manipulation that came under the heading of "influence." The key to the system was the actual presence in Parliament of the cabinet ministers, including the prime minister, which represented an adaptation of the older mixed-government idea that English government consisted of the king in Parliament.

American colonial government as it had evolved by the eighteenth century adhered to the theory of mixed government. Its chief structural characteristic was that the governor, council, and elected deputies together formed the legislature and shared many governmental tasks. The governor performed what we would consider to be executive functions, but he was not confined to an executive role; sitting with the council, he possessed lawmaking power as a member of the upper house of the legislature. In the proprietary colonies the proprietor or his appointed governor initially controlled lawmaking, but in time came to share this power with the deputies in the lower house. In the royal colonies that began as corporations, elected representatives earlier acquired lawmaking power which they shared with the governor and council. By the same token the lower houses of assembly joined in what we would define as executive functions, such as the appointment of administrative officers. Frequently, the deputies in the lower house acted in a judicial capacity, settling disputes, punishing offenders, and hearing cases on appeal from the colony's common law courts, although it was more usual for the governor and council to serve in an appellate judicial capacity.

The Growth of Assembly Power

Despite a superficial resemblance based on common acceptance of the theory of mixed government, American constitutionalism in the eighteenth century differed significantly from the English pattern. The chief difference appeared in the imbalance that arose between the assembly and the royal governor. The lower houses of assembly steadily gained power, until on the eve of the American Revolution they formed not merely a counterweight to the executive, but a preponderant force that signaled a shift in the center of constitutional gravity from the executive to the popular element in government. Socially, this expansion of authority reflected the emergence in the colonies of a prosperous class of merchants, lawyers, and planters ambitious for a political role. In the seventeenth century elected deputies had typically come from the ranks of smaller property owners, while the governor's council comprised men of greater wealth. Social and economic change in the eighteenth century, however, produced elite groups too numerous to be accommodated in the council, which ordinarily numbered only about a dozen men. The lower houses of assembly, whose membership ranged from fifty to one hundred, offered opportunities for political careers congruent with the aspirations of emergent elites.

The rise of the assembly in part resulted from the colonists' application of English constitutional principles—in particular those identified with the Glorious Revolution—to problems in their local communities. Underlying it was the colonists' belief that they were entitled to the same rights enjoyed by Englishmen at home, under the protection of the common law and the English constitution. Moreover, the view sometimes expressed by royal officials—that the assembly existed only at the sufferance of the crown and possessed the powers merely of a local corporation—stimulated colonial self-consciousness about the colonies' constitutional status. But often what appears in retrospect as the assemblies' quest for power proceeded on an expedient basis, from one pedestrian issue to another without regard to or seeming awareness of constitutional theory. The building of roads, ferries, and wharves; the formulation of land policy; the issuance of paper currency; defense against Indians and promotion of the Indian trade; the regulation of immigration into the colony; boundary disputes between colonies—all of these matters supplied the content of everyday politics. And most of the time in dealing with them, assembly delegates were primarily concerned with achieving a particular result. Nevertheless, whether by forcing concessions from the governor or by cooperating with him, the lower houses enhanced their institutional stature and established precedents that in time assumed constitutional significance.

Having acquired the right to sit separately, elect a speaker, and initiate legislation, the assemblies in the first half of the eighteenth century further defined their identity and maintained their integrity as a legislative body. Consciously imitating Parliament, they requested and secured freedom of speech on the floor of the assembly; immunity from arrest and molestation; access to the governor; the right to fix the qualifications for membership and to judge the elections and returns of deputies in the lower house; the right to try and punish outsiders who abused, insulted, or committed violence against a member; and the right to organize internal proceedings and discipline members who violated the rules of procedure. Together these rights were known as parliamentary privilege, and although certain privileges that Parliament enjoyed remained beyond the grasp of the assemblies—for example, the right to hold regular meetings irrespective of the will of the governor—the elected deputies in the colonies were highly successful in establishing the analogy between themselves and the House of Commons in relation to the executive power.

To these legislative attainments the lower houses of assembly added substantial powers over administration and policy-making. Gaining control over finance was the single most important step in the process. Drawing on the parliamentary tradition by which elected representatives consented to and later came to control taxation, the lower houses acquired exclusive power to initiate all revenue and appropriations measures and to exercise administrative oversight concerning the expenditures of funds. In most colonies the assembly appointed the treasurer, or finance minister. Equipped with these powers, the deputies were able to resist the repeated demands of royal governors, acting on instructions from London, for permanent revenue acts that would make annual appropriations unnecessary. Victory in the struggle for the purse strings was of tremendous importance in the growth of colonial internal autonomy. Governors could not very well maintain royal or proprietary prerogative against assemblies which could specify the expenditure of every penny and withhold money from any governmental function, however vital. Hardly less important was the power the assemblies gained in the years before 1756 in regard to Indian policy, defense, and intercolonial relations, matters that in theory belonged to imperial authorities but that in practice were left to local governments. In establishing policy in these spheres the lower houses of assembly appointed subordinate officials and created committees to supervise their administrative performance.

The Governor and Council

The lower houses of assembly gained power at the expense of the colonial governor, who, with the exception of proprietary Maryland, Pennsylvania, and Delaware and the covenant-charter colonies of Connecticut and Rhode Island, was appointed by the crown. As the king's representative in lands deemed his personal dominions, the governor in legal theory exercised virtually all the traditional prerogatives of the English monarchy. He was empowered to summon the assembly; make laws with the assent of the elected deputies; exercise an absolute veto over legislation and nominal control over appropriations and expenditures; administer and enforce laws; appoint subordinate officers; command military and naval forces; act as head of the established church; create courts and appoint judges; and serve in a judicial capacity as a chancery court (with equity powers) and, with the council, as a court of appeals.

Great as these powers were in theory, they amounted to something less in practice because of the tenuous position the governor occupied in the structure of colonial politics. Often caught in a cross fire between imperial authorities and provincial leaders, royal governors lacked political experience—or at least the kind of experience needed in the more democratic politics that colonial conditions encouraged. At the same time royal instructions restricted the governors' political latitude. Uncertain of the discretion available to them, they might be recalled if they showed too much flexibility in responding to local pressures. But the governors' principal weakness stemmed from their inability to control finance and administration. A governor who tried to execute locally disagreeable instructions from London was likely to become embroiled in a long struggle with the assembly, which he would probably lose. For effective political power lay in the hands of those who controlled taxes and expenditures. Although the lower houses of assembly did so infrequently, the fact that they could withhold the governor's salary dramatically illustrates the weakness of his position. Far more common, however, and more effective in demonstrating executive weakness, were the deputies' threats to withhold appropriations for the implementation of imperial policies. The Board of Trade's failure to obtain a permanent civil list—that is, a budgetary supply line for the support of royal officers independent of assembly appropriations—was a continuing reminder of the political disadvantage under which the governor labored.

Nevertheless, the royal governor was hardly an abject prisoner or mere puppet of the assembly. In an age when deference to established rulers and elites was still the norm and democratic sentiments sparked fear, the governor's office carried great prestige and authority. The rise of the assembly notwithstanding, the governor remained a formidable constitutional force. Try as they might, the elected deputies could not wrest from him a number of key powers, especially those that permitted him to veto legislation, prorogue and dissolve the assembly, create new electoral districts, and appoint judges. The assemblies were also unable to secure the right to hold guaranteed regular meetings and to have their choice of a speaker automatically accepted by the governor.

The colonial council, supposedly the voice of the aristocratic element in society, was an anomalous institution that failed to give the governor the support that theoretically he was entitled to. Appointed by the crown, the council was chiefly an advisory body to the governor. In conjunction with him, it also formed the upper house of the assembly and sat as an appellate court. Intended to balance the democratic element represented by the elected deputies, the council was unsuccessful in fulfilling its role of buttressing royal authority because it did not in fact represent interests basically different from those found in the lower house. American society lacked a hereditary aristocracy on the English model, which meant that the council could hardly become the analogue of the English House of Lords. Drawn from the same planter-merchant-lawyer elite that populated the lower houses of assembly, the council usually sided with the deputies in their struggles with the governor.

Political Instability in America

Although in formal terms the structure of colonial government was similar to that of the mother country, it failed to produce the political stability that characterized English constitutionalism in the age of Walpole. American politics was volatile and disputatious, in part because no settled and cooperative relationship between governor and assembly existed. Political instability was rooted also in anxieties provoked by perceived discrepancies between the colonial and the English constitution. These anxieties were in turn shaped and reinforced by the writings of critics of the ruling Whig oligarchy in England, which found a ready audience in the colonies. Directed against schemes of executive influence which were thought to corrupt the legislature, their main effect was to teach Americans to be vigilant about the loss of local liberty through the undermining of assembly power. American politics furthermore reflected the democratizing tendencies released by the Great Awakening of the 1740s. Sensitive and responsive to conflict, the colonial constitution thus provided a milieu in which Americans were disposed scrupulously and skeptically to examine the changes in imperial policy that occurred after 1763.

Beyond the inability of the governor to control the assembly, an important cause of political instability in the colonies was the openness and expendability of the electoral system. It contrasted markedly with the closed system controlled by the executive in England. Property ownership was a prerequisite for colonial voting, but the typical qualifications—possession of land returning an income of 40 shillings per year or land or other property valued at 50 to 300 pounds—were easy to meet. As population increased, the franchise was broadened until about three-fourths of adult white males could vote. The result was the continual expansion of the assembly's political base and the source of its power.

The colonial system of representation further limited executive influence. With population growth new towns and counties were created. As these were the constituent units in the assembly, the size of that institution—and its political power—accordingly increased. Although newly settled areas were sometimes underrepresented, representation, on the whole, was equitably apportioned. Moreover, seats in the colonial assembly were not regarded as the personal property of the incumbent, nor were there "rotten boroughs"—that is, districts without population that were nevertheless entitled to representation, as in England—which the royal executive could control to his advantage. The decentralized and localist nature of representation in the colonies also helped to curb executive influence. Members of the assembly usually lived in the town or county that they represented, giving rise to a residency requirement that still exists. They were viewed as attorneys for the people who elected them rather than as independent-minded statesmen representing some broader interest or concern. Frequently, voters bound their deputies' actions in the assembly by express instructions. Because more people in the colonies, in comparison to England, actually voted for deputies, and because the deputies tended to represent the views actually held by the local electorate, American representation was *actual* representation. In England, by contrast, *virtual* representation existed. Subjects were said to be virtually represented, regardless of whether they had actually voted for a member of Parliament, so long as there were members whose interests were similar to theirs.

The chronic instability of American politics in the eighteenth century was an expression not only of differences between English and colonial constitutionalism, but also of the character of American society. As the medieval world gave way to modernity, the advancement of economic interests replaced the quest for religious truth and the aristocratic pursuit of military glory and virtue as the principal ends of political life. In England this historical transformation was modulated by established institutions and social orders. By the middle of the eighteenth century the interests that dominated English politics were few in number, clearly defined in identity, and relatively stable in their functional relationships. Land, commerce, the church, the army, and the professions were represented in the mixed and balanced constitution. In the fragment of English society that had been flung off into North America, however, no such historical stabilization or rationalization had taken place. Consequently, the interests that entered the arena of colonial politics, interests that more often than not were motivated by bourgeois economic aspirations, produced an often turbulent factionalism.

Although immigration from non-English countries gave rise to ethnic, cultural, and religious factionalism, the major source of conflict among interests was the economic rewards that control of government offered in a rapidly expanding society. Wealth and power inevitably attach to political office, but the American environment gave a special urgency to the struggle for power because government necessarily had a more active role to play than it did in the more settled society of England. Moreover, the mercantilist assumptions of the age called for government promotion and regulation of economic activity. Accordingly, questions concerning land distribution, paper money, the Indian trade, and internal improvements lay at the heart of colonial political factionalism. In a constitutional order that encouraged institutional conflict between governor and assembly, and that lacked the mediating influence of an established class structure, the development of an interest-group mentality contributed to political and constitutional instability.

Pre-Revolutionary Political Thought

As Americans considered their constitutional arrangements in the light of mixed-government theory and the tenets of English constitutionalism, they found perplexing and disturbing discrepancies. Unable to appreciate the advantage the assembly enjoyed in its dealings with the royal governor, they focused attention on the extensive powers that the colonial executive retained—powers greater indeed than those possessed by the monarchy in the English constitution. Believing their assemblies stood in a direct line of descent from Parliament's triumph over executive tyranny in the Revolution of 1689, the colonials formed a body of principles and ideas that shaped not only their struggles against the governor, but also their actions in controversies over imperial policy from 1765 to 1776.

Colonial political thought in general was concerned with the origins and nature of government, and the proper combination of the parts of government in a sound constitution. In addressing the former issue Americans drew on the tradition of natural law and natural rights that derived from antiquity through the medieval era to early modern times. In their quest for a proper governmental balance they turned to eighteenth-century English political writers who criticized the British system of mixed government.

Natural law theory held that certain eternal principles were inherent in the very structure of the universe which the positive law of a state, in order to be regarded as true law worthy of being obeyed, must embody or affirm. Perhaps the greatest classical advocate of this point of view was the Roman legist Cicero, who argued that the binding quality of civil law depended on its being in harmony with the principles of right and justice found in the law of nature. Important in the medieval period, this theory became even more prominent in the seventeenth century, when it was joined with the idea of the social compact as expressed in Calvinist covenantal theology. In this form it provided sanction and legitimacy for the modern nation-state.

Natural law theory, as Americans received it from seventeenth-century English writers such as John Locke, James Harrington, and Algernon Sidney, posited a state of nature which preceded the creation of society and government. According to Locke's second *Treatise on Civil Government,* the most famous explication of the theory, human nature was essentially good. For the better protection of the principles of right and justice inherent in the natural order, however, men and women, through a social compact, formed a government and agreed on rules for its operation. Government created in this manner rested on the consent of the governed: The people surrendered the unfettered liberty of the state of nature and gave allegiance to government in return for protection of their natural rights. The most important of these rights were life, liberty, and property, which were to be given broad application so long as their exercise did not threaten the common good or bring injury to others. Indeed, the purpose of government was to preserve the natural law, including fundamental natural rights, and to promote peace, security, and the public good. In pursuing these ends rulers were granted powers which they were to exercise as a public trust. But the whole emphasis of natural law theory was on limiting governmental power. If government violated the purposes and rules contained in the social compact, if it denied natural rights and abused public trust, the people were justified in resisting and overthrowing it.

In America natural law ideas figured prominently in the writings of John Winthrop, Thomas Hooker, and Roger Williams, theorists and architects of covenant communities in the founding period. In the eighteenth century outstanding clerical exponents of natural law were John Wise, who argued that the people had a right to determine their own form of ecclesiastical and civil government, and Jonathan Mayhew, who counseled resistance to tyranny in church and state. Natural law reasoning and rhetoric appeared in the opposition to the Dominion of New England in the 1680s, and even more conspicuously in the resistance to British imperialism in the 1760s and 1770s. The natural law tradition was thus central to American political thought.

In the eighteenth century, however, until the eve of the Revolution, Americans were chiefly concerned with maintaining a proper relationship between the parts of government in order to preserve local autonomy and individual liberty. For instruction in these matters they consulted English critics of the ruling Whig oligarchy such as Viscount Bolingbroke, and John Trenchard and Thomas Gordon, authors of the widely circulated *Cato's Letters* (1720–23). These men, who have been labeled opposition writers, provided a body of ideas that appealed to Americans in their conflicts with the royal governors and that influenced their understanding of British imperial policy after 1763.

The English opposition writers and the colonial pamphleteers and essayists who applied their teachings regarded the preservation of liberty through a properly mixed and balanced constitution as the basic purpose of political life. Unlike modern constitutional critics, they did not seek to *change* the constitution, but rather to *prevent* change from occurring. For it was axiomatic that constitutional change meant degeneration and decline, resulting in the destruction of liberty. Especially to be feared was the consolidation of power by a single part of the government representing only one of the component elements of society. Of course, considered abstractly, social order and the active exercise of governmental power were as important to a sound constitutional structure as was liberty. Opposition writers and their American adherents believed, however, that in actuality government power constantly threatened to undermine liberty.

The preservation of liberty depended not only on a properly balanced constitution, but also on civic and personal virtue. As conceived of in eighteenth-century opposition ideology, virtue had its foundation in the social independence that resulted from the ownership of property. Only a person who was independent in this sense, who could transcend selfish considerations and resist manipulation by men ambitious for power, was truly free politically to act for the good of the commonwealth. The great enemy of virtue was corruption. This term carried the ordinary meaning of immoral conduct based on dishonesty, profligacy, luxury, and other forms of vice. But it also possessed a technical constitutional meaning. It referred to the subversion of civic virtue through the ability of the executive to influence the elected representatives of the people.

In England the crown and the ministries, in the colonies the royal or proprietary governor, were believed to threaten the proper balance of the constitution by controlling the assembly, thus undermining civic virtue and liberty. An aggrandizing executive could work corruption by placing officeholders in the legislature, as was the practice in England; by creating a numerous and supine bureaucracy to carry the government's point of view to the public; by buying votes and otherwise trying to rig the outcome of elections; by incurring large debts and then levying taxes requiring the appointment of still more officials; and by encouraging luxury, wealth, credit, and speculation at the expense of habits of frugality and honest labor that were the basis of civic and personal virtue.

To preserve liberty, believed to be the special interest of the people's elected representatives, opposition writers argued for the complete exclusion of executive officials from the legislature. Instead of a *sharing* of power, there should be a *separation* of powers. The lawmaking power ought to be given to the people's deputies; the executive power, for strictly administrative, nondiscretionary tasks, assigned to the king's ministers or the royal governor. The separation of powers had first been advanced by parliamentary opponents of the crown in the seventeenth-century Civil War. The opposition writers of the eighteenth century popularized the theory as a means of achieving the desired balance between liberty and power.

Americans found the idea of a separation of powers suitable to their needs. The reason was not, as has sometimes been suggested, that it confirmed already existing institutional practice; on the contrary, in their actual constitutional arrangements they followed conventional mixed-government theory. Since the establishment of the imperial system in the late seventeenth century, however, the colonists had often acted from a point of view so different from that of the colonial governor as to constitute a separate interest or outlook. In this sense their political experience disposed them toward the separation of powers as an alternative to mixed government. Accordingly, departing from mixed-government theory, they tried to make the assembly more independent of the governor. This could be achieved by securing a guarantee of regular elections and meetings of the assembly; by denying the governor the right to reject the speaker and prorogue the assembly; and by passing laws, known as place acts, which prohibited executive and administrative officials from sitting in the assembly. Only in regard to the last issue were the assembly leaders successful; on the other two counts the governors retained their accustomed powers. Despite their effectiveness in dealing with the governor, therefore, colonial political leaders continued to fear the broad legal powers of the royal governor. Their familiarity with the opposition literature sharpened their sensitivity to questions of authority and inclined them, when changes in imperial policy in the 1760s gave royal officials new powers, to understand the changes as a threat to their rights and liberties. When American interests eventually demanded independence from England, the doctrine of the separation of powers, which had become intellectually popular in the colonies through the dissemination of Montesquieu's *The Spirit of the Laws* (1748), stood ready to hand as a basis for constitutional organization in a time of revolutionary crisis.

Lest the development of American political thought be seen as excessively dependent on or derivative of external sources, it is important to remember that doctrines of natural rights and republicanism were received into substantially self-governing political communities founded on religious covenants and social compacts in the seventeenth-century American colonies. Through mutual agreements and voluntary associations that made explicit popular consent the basis of political authority, the founders of these communities defined themselves as a people and asserted basic principles and values prescribing a way of life. Although the exigencies of adaptation to the wilderness environment stand out in the history of the early settlements, the continuous process of constituting political communities was broadly guided by the biblical doctrine of the covenant and the practices of the commercial corporation. When the colonies declared their independence in 1776, this history provided a constitutional tradition that formed the basis of revolutionary state making.

Colonial Courts

In their concern for constitutional balance and the preservation of liberty, Americans relied principally on the assembly rather than courts of law. Nevertheless, colonial courts formed an important if subordinate part of the structure of local government that had evolved by the middle of the eighteenth century.

In understanding the place of courts and the legal system in the colonial constitution it is necessary to keep in mind that judicial tasks were not confined to a segregated corps of judges, as under the modern theory of the separation of powers. Mixed government, of course, provided for judicial officers, but they frequently exercised nonjuridical powers. By the same token, executive and legislative officers often performed judicial tasks. This sharing of power, as we have seen, was characteristic of mixed government. Conceptually, it was rooted in the medieval belief that the purpose of government was essentially judicial—to declare and carry out the word of God. Thus law was not made by human agency, but was discovered. Before Parliament acquired supreme lawmaking power in the seventeenth century, it was viewed as a court; in the traditional expression, it was "the High Court of Parliament." During the Civil War the common law courts sided with Parliament in resisting royal power. Moreover, in establishing its supremacy over the crown Parliament removed the courts from royal influence (though not from parliamentary oversight). This was accomplished by the Act of Settlement of 1701, which provided that judges should serve during good behavior rather than at the pleasure of the crown. In the colonies, however, no such condition of judicial independence existed.

In creating their legal institutions the colonists understandably relied from the beginning on their experience with English law. There was, however, no unified system of English law to be appropriated, but rather several different systems of law, including the common law, admiralty, equity, ecclesiastical and mercantile law, and the local and customary law of towns, boroughs, and counties. In addition to fashioning entirely new law to deal with their special circumstances, the colonists in the earlier phases of settlement borrowed most heavily from English local law and from what they knew of the common law doctrines formulated by the king's courts at Westminster. The presence of English judges and lawyers in the colonies after 1660 facilitated the reception of the common law as the most important source of colonial law. What the common law provided was not so much a body of technical legal precedents as a set of fundamental principles of public law that placed limitations on government and hence were constitutional in nature. In the eighteenth century the common law became more widely accepted in the colonies, although imperial authorities never officially conceded its rightful application in America since to do so would imply restrictions on royal power.

A variety of officials carried on judicial business. In most of the colonies in the founding period the governor and council settled disputes at law. The assembly also took part in the administration of justice, although by the end of the seventeenth century the deputies confined themselves more exclusively to legislative and administrative matters. As population spread, a more highly articulated judicial system came into existence. Local courts of original jurisdiction were created, usually at the county level by executive order. County courts had jurisdiction of most civil and criminal matters; the individual magistrates or justices of the peace who sat on the county court in turn resolved petty legal conflicts in the towns where they lived. From the county courts cases were taken on appeal to the governor and council, who in most colonies sat as a kind of supreme court. The Privy Council in England could also act as an appeals or reviewing court, although it in fact did little in this regard. In comparison to England's courts, the rudimentary judicial systems in the colonies were fairly unified and hierarchical because the appellate principle received more recognition than it did in the home country.

Courts became the object of struggle between the governor and assembly in the eighteenth century. One source of conflict was the creation of new courts. The governor's commission charged him with this responsibility, but assemblies asserted their power in the matter. By about 1760 it was generally accepted that the governor would not create new tribunals without the approval of the assembly. On the other hand, the governor controlled judicial tenure, another contentious issue in several colonies. Assemblies wanted judges to serve during good behavior, as provided in the Act of Settlement of 1701, rather than at the pleasure of the crown. Because this arrangement would place judges beyond the influence of the executive, however, imperial officers regarded it as subversive of royal authority. Hence they refused to permit "good-behavior" appointments.

Disputes over admiralty and chancery courts also assumed political importance. Introduced into the colonies by the Navigation Act of 1696, nine vice-admiralty courts dealt with enforcement of trade acts and other maritime matters. These courts aroused opposition because, lacking juries, they operated beyond the reach of public opinion. Chancery courts, which also lacked juries, dealt with special or emergency situations by the application of equity principles and rules. They provided remedies that were not available in common law courts. Chancery courts were unpopular among the colonists not on principle, but as a vehicle of executive power. In some colonies the county courts possessed both common law and equity powers. In others, however, the chancery courts were composed of the governor alone, or the governor and council. It was the latter situation that provoked opposition. Fearful of executive power, the colonists objected to royal authority as the source of equity jurisdiction. They looked instead to the assembly, and ultimately to the people, as the source of this special branch of law, which they would assign to the local courts in addition to their common law jurisdiction.

Local Government

The interest in colonial autonomy evinced at the provincial level in matters such as judicial tenure and chancery courts was evident also in the development of governmental institutions at the local level. In founding local institutions the colonists adopted the forms they had known in England—namely, county, church parish, and municipal corporation. In the southern and middle colonies the county was the basic governmental unit as well as the constituent unit in the assembly (that is, representation was apportioned by counties as corporate entities rather than according to the population of the county). In New England, counties and townships were the relevant form of government, the towns being the constituent element in the assembly, and in all the colonies a number of municipal corporations governed themselves under charters granted by the provincial assembly.

If mixed government characterized constitutional arrangements at the provincial level, it was all the more evident at the local level, where a single agency performed a wide variety of governmental tasks embracing what we now describe as executive, legislative, and judicial functions. The county court provides the clearest illustration. Composed of justices of the peace nominally appointed by the governor but actually self-selected by the magistrates themselves, the county court exercised judicial responsibilities, as previously noted. But it also wielded a wide array of executive, administrative, and legislative powers in dispatching the numerous duties it acquired over the course of a century. The county court supervised the construction and maintenance of roads, bridges, docks, and ferries; levied taxes; adopted local ordinances concerning trade and industry; issued licenses to inns and taverns; cared for the indigent (in conjunction with the parish vestry); acted as a probate court and orphan's court; enforced the laws of the assembly; and in general managed local affairs.

In New England the township, formed in conjunction with the creation of Congregational churches, was the principal unit that attended to the general range of executive and administrative tasks. The town assembly, or meeting, which by about 1700 permitted all adult male residents to vote, was the local legislative authority. A popularly elected body of selectmen carried out executive and administrative duties between town meetings. County courts in New England confined themselves more to judicial matters than elsewhere, though they too had some administrative duties. By 1750, moreover, the chartered municipal corporation, under the direction of a mayor and council, provided local government in fourteen cities scattered along the Atlantic coast. Unlike the towns and counties of New England and elsewhere, the main purpose of local government in these municipalities, as specified in their charters, was to promote and regulate commercial and industrial development.

Local government early assumed an importance in American political culture that in modified form it retains to the present day. In studying it historians have analyzed the political sociology of the county courts, the degree of popular participation in the New England town meeting, and the nature and extent of the social control wielded by that institution. These studies, conducted with a view toward determining whether democracy existed in early America, show that local government provided significant opportunities for political activity and experience. Under the hierarchical and deferential attitudes of the day, however, local officeholding was largely confined to a narrow segment of colonial society.

Though hardly democratic in a modern sense, local institutions were important in the development of republican government in America because they reinforced the decentralist tendencies in colonial government. In England local government, like the common law linked to the national monarchy, promoted the centralization of power. In the colonies local government was connected to provincial authority rather than to the empire. As a result it strengthened the movement toward autonomy that flourished in the assembly. When this concern for local autonomy eventuated in the American Revolution, institutions of local government served as focal points for organizing resistance to English rule. They also acted as a stabilizing force and provided a basis for the creation of new state governments.

FOUR

The American Revolution

REVOLUTIONS BY DEFINITION HAVE CONSTITUTIONAL SIGNIFICANCE, for if they accomplish nothing else they remove the existing regime and install another one—in theory different—in its place. This fact notwithstanding, modern revolutions are usually thought of as social and economic rather than constitutional in nature, their purpose being to overthrow an oppressive ruling class and create a new order of society. The American Revolution differed from the stereotype of modern revolution. It produced significant constitutional change—the creation of thirteen republican state governments organized in a continental union—and the issues that provoked it were preeminently constitutional. It was not the purpose of the Revolution, moreover, to construct a new social order. Furthermore, while the American Revolution led to the creation of an independent people and a new nation, it differed from twentieth-century colonial uprisings and national liberation movements by virtue of the fact that the American colonists living under English rule had long enjoyed substantial political autonomy. They rebelled against England in order to preserve their local governing establishments rather than to acquire political liberty after decades of acute subordination.

Two fundamental constitutional issues lay at the heart of the imperial conflict that led to the American Revolution. The first and more conspicuous, a source of contention as early as the seventeenth century, concerned the place of the colonies in the British empire. What powers did the colonies possess in relation to the English government, and what was the status of the American colonists under the laws and constitution of England? These were essentially questions of intergovernmental or interstate relations. They led to a series of attempts to formulate theories of imperial organization, which, though unsuccessful in resolving Americans' conflict with Britain, significantly foreshadowed the development of American federalism. The rights of individual subjects or citizens were also involved in the imperial controversy, giving rise to the second major constitutional issue of the Revolution: the proper organization and distribution of governmental power in the polity. More so than the matter of relations among states, this question raised the basic problem of constitutionalism—namely, how to create a structure of authority and rules of public law that gave government sufficient power to maintain order while limiting that power in the interest of individual liberty and political and social freedom.

In struggling with this issue in the revolutionary era, Americans embarked on a reconsideration of the very nature of constitutionalism and fundamental law as the English had understood them. In England the constitution was the general structure of principles, laws, and institutions by which government was carried on. Government was not separate from the constitution, so that Parliament, for example, could change the constitution through its legislation. The Americans, in contrast, conceived of a constitution as anterior to and separate from government. For them a constitution was a paramount and binding law that fixed the principles, forms, and procedures necessary for achieving a proper balance between power and liberty.

Imperial Reorganization

Constitutional controversy erupted when England introduced major changes in imperial policy following the Seven Years' War (1756–63). To deal with the territorial gains and financial burden that resulted from the war, the ministry determined to tighten the administration of the now sprawling British Empire. Accordingly, the loosely fitting commercial, civilian-legislative rule that prevailed after 1720 gave way to a more highly centralized military-executive style of government that looked to closer supervision of colonial affairs, including for the first time direct taxation of the colonists. Although this policy plainly differed from the casually enforced mercantilism that preceded it, it would be a mistake to regard it wholly as innovation. A degree of internal administrative control had always been implicit in the Navigation Acts, and for a brief period under the Dominion of New England had become oppressively explicit. One reason Americans reacted so swiftly to the imposition of political controls after 1763 is that their earlier experience had alerted them to its dangers.

The immediate crisis in imperial affairs was precipitated by the attempt of the ministry of George Grenville to impose certain reforms upon the administration of the colonies. Colonial military cooperation with Britain, based upon voluntary appropriations by the colonial assemblies, had all but collapsed in the Seven Years' War. Grenville and his associates therefore concluded, with much justice, that since the colonies would not voluntarily defend either themselves or the empire, regular British troops must be sent to the colonies. As Britain had already incurred a heavy indebtedness in defense of the empire, and since her tax burden was considered already too heavy, the ministry determined to levy taxes on the colonies to pay for the new army. In addition, Grenville decided to tighten enforcement of the customs laws, a step that might be made to yield still further revenue.

The ministry was also concerned with the problem of the trans-Allegheny West. Extensive colonial migration into this region appeared to be imminent, and such a development might injure British speculative landholdings on the seaboard, prejudice imperial relations with the Indian tribes controlling the valuable fur trade, and ultimately build a new colonial world too remove for effective British control. Grenville, therefore, determined to check western settlement for the moment.

The ministry resorted to three principal measures to accomplish these ends: the Proclamation of 1763, the Sugar Act of 1764, and the Stamp Act of 1765. The Proclamation of 1763 closed the frontier west of the Alleghenies to further settlement and forbade further land purchases or patents in the region. Although the decree was of slight constitutional significance, it greatly annoyed colonial land speculators and western settlers.

The Sugar Act, however, provoked powerful constitutional objections in the colonies. The statute levied a duty of threepence per gallon on molasses imported into the colonies, and it also levied small duties on a variety of other imports, among them sugar, indigo, coffee, wines, calicoes, and linens. On the surface there was nothing revolutionary in the character of these duties, for England had long imposed small tariffs upon the colonies for the regulation of trade, and under the Molasses Act of 1733 Britain had levied a duty of sixpence per gallon on molasses imported into the colonies from other than the British West Indies.

What was revolutionary in the Sugar Act was the statement in the preamble of the statute that the proceeds were to be applied toward "defraying the expenses of defending, protecting, and securing the colonies." In other words, the Sugar Act was a revenue measure, not a regulation of trade, and thus it raised the whole question of the power of Britain to tax the colonies.

In February 1765 Parliament passed the Stamp Act, the second revenue measure in Grenville's series of imperial reforms. This law provided for excise duties, to be paid by affixing revenue stamps upon a variety of legal documents, bills of sale, liquor licenses, playing cards, newspapers, and so on. The duties, which ranged from one halfpenny to six pounds and were required to be paid in specie, touched nearly every aspect of commercial and industrial life in the colonies. The power of Parliament to lay taxes of this sort immediately became of vital concern.

At the suggestion of Massachusetts, delegates from nine colonies gathered in New York in October 1765 to protest against the law. The Stamp Act Congress objected to the parliamentary measure on the ground that it violated the rights of the colonists as Englishmen under the constitution and laws of England, and the rights of the colonies as member states in the empire. The former of these positions provided the first line of protest against the act.

Resolutions emanating from the Stamp Act Congress stated: "It is inseparably essential to the freedom of a people, and the undoubted right of Englishmen, that no taxes be imposed on them, but with their own consent, given personally or by their representatives." In the Virginia House of Burgesses Patrick Henry advanced the same view. By the original corporate charter, he declared, Virginians possessed all the rights, privileges, and immunities of Englishmen. He reasoned that "taxation of the people by themselves" was "the distinguishing characteristic of British freedom, without which the ancient Constitution cannot exist." The colonists furthermore made clear their belief that local circumstances prevented their ever being represented in the House of Commons. Asserting the need for actual representation, they rejected the idea that they were virtually represented in the English legislature.

Almost imperceptibly the rights-of-Englishmen argument passed into the very different theoretical proposition that the Stamp Act was unconstitutional because it violated the rights of the colonies in the empire. After denying the validity of virtual representation, the Stamp Act Congress declared that "the only Representatives of the people of these Colonies are people chosen therein by themselves, and that no taxes ever have been, or can be constitutionally imposed on them, but by their respective Legislature." As Patrick Henry expressed it: "the General Assembly of this Colony have the only and sole exclusive right and power to lay taxes and impositions upon the inhabitants of this Colony." But while insisting that the whole subject of taxation belonged to the colonial assembly, the colonists agreed that other matters came under the purview of Parliament. It was not simply a desire to be diplomatic that led the Stamp Act Congress to profess "the same Allegiance to the Crown of Great Britain, that is owing from his Subjects born within the Realm, and all due Subordination to that August Body the Parliament of Great Britain." As numerous contemporary documents make clear, the colonists regarded the power of Parliament as controlling in trade and other matters of general concern throughout the empire.

The Federal Theory of Empire

Implicit in the protest against the Stamp Act was a conception of the relationship between the colonies and England that can be described as a federal theory of empire. The essence of federalism is the division of sovereignty, or governmental authority, among several states. For over a century this circumstance had characterized the actual operation of the empire. Through their assemblies the colonists had managed their own internal affairs, including taxation, trade, and the administration of justice; had paid for the support of civil administration; and had even shared responsibility in matters reaching beyond strictly local concern such as Indian affairs and the currency. On the other hand the king and Parliament governed in matters of interest to the empire as a whole, namely, commerce, foreign affairs including war and peace, the control of military and naval forces, the post office, and the money supply. To these responsibilities imperial officials, after the Seven Years' War, added territorial administration of the western lands and defense against the Indians. Occasionally, parliamentary legislation bore directly on internal affairs in the colonies, as in the Woolen Act (1699), the Hat Act (1733), the Iron Act (1750), the act fixing the value of foreign coins in the colonies (1708), and the act forbidding the issuance of paper money in New England (1751). These measures were concerned with policy for the entire empire, however, rather than with strictly local concerns. Finally, although the crown was the more heavily involved in imperial government, Parliament had plainly legislated in matters of import to the empire as a whole, and the colonies had just as plainly accepted this legislation as legitimate.

In the years immediately after the Stamp Act several American political leaders propounded a federal theory of empire. Governor Stephen Hopkins of Rhode Island wrote that "each of the colonies hath a legislature within itself, to take care of its Interests . . . yet there are things of a more general nature, quite out of reach of these particular legislatures, which it is necessary should be regulated, ordered, and governed." These general concerns, including commerce, money, and credit, were properly in the keeping of Parliament. Daniel Dulany of Maryland acknowledged the dependence of the colonies on England and their subordination to Parliament in matters of general significance for the empire. But though subordinate, the colonies had the rightful power to deal with local subjects not pertinent to the empire as a whole. Dulany alluded to the division of power that was taking shape in American minds when he distinguished between legislation that imposed a tax for the purpose of revenue and legislation to regulate trade that might incidentally produce revenue. The former was properly within the power of the colonial assembly, the latter within the power of Parliament.

The clearest exposition of federal imperial theory came from John Dickinson in *The Letters from a Pennsylvania Farmer* (1768). Dickinson began with an attack on the supposed distinction between internal and external taxes which Benjamin Franklin had conspicuously referred to in his famous examination before the House of Commons in 1766, but which had almost no standing in America. No such difference could be admitted, Dickinson reasoned; Parliament in fact had no authority "to lay upon these colonies any tax whatever." He admitted that Parliament had in the past levied certain charges incident to the regulation of trade. These were in no way taxes, however, for their main purpose was the regulation of commerce, and the duties were purely incidental to that end. To Dickinson, there was a profound difference between the power to regulate commerce and the power to tax. That Parliament properly could regulate the trade of the colonies no one denied; that it could tax the colonies in any guise, Dickinson utterly denied.

This statement clearly implied that two types of governmental powers were exercised within the empire, those properly exercised by Parliament, and those properly exercised by the local or colonial governments. Here was plainly a federal conception of the British Empire. Dickinson went on to describe the empire as it had in fact existed for a century—a great federal state with a practical distribution of authority between local and central governments.

Protest against the Stamp Act proceeded on the level of direct political action as well as constitutional theory. Popular mobbing, which sometimes ran to excess but was on the whole kept under restraint, intimidated appointed stamp collectors into resigning and effectively nullified the act. Concurrently, American leaders organized nonimportation agreements directed against English products. London merchants, their trade badly injured, clamored for repeal. All this had its effect upon the government in London. The ministry of the Marquis of Rockingham, which succeeded that of Grenville in 1766, determined upon repeal of the law.

Before the act was repealed, however, an extensive debate in both houses of Parliament revealed how profoundly English thinking differed from American on the question of imperial relations. Almost without exception English leaders insisted that sovereignty was unitary and indivisible, that it lay in Parliament, and that Parliament was the supreme legislative body not only for the realm of England but also for the empire as a whole, including the colonies. This conclusion was the result of periodic attempts since the late seventeenth century to rationalize the relationship of the colonies to the mother country and their place in the empire.

Initially the colonies had been regarded as vacant, discovered territories rather than as conquered kingdoms to be ruled by force rather than law.[1] According to this discovery theory of imperial expansion, the American emigrant-settlers were English subjects, entitled to claim the protection of the common law and so much of parliamentary statute as was applicable to their local situation. The American colonists thus enjoyed a privileged status. But the corollary of the status was an obligation to accept the ultimate authority of Parliament. Later, in the mid-eighteenth century, imperial officials justified parliamentary control over the colonies by reference to orthodox Lockean social compact theory. They held that the colonists, like all English subjects, had entered into the original compact that formed the basis of legitimate governmental authority. Having given their consent, the colonists received the protection of government and law. In return, as natural-born subjects, they

---

1. English constitutional theory at the end of the seventeenth century distinguished between infidel and Christian conquered territory. In the former, all law and governmental authority ceased to exist upon conquest, the land being subject to the will of the king. In Christian territory existing law continued until the king chose to alter it or create new law. In either case, however, the rule of the king was subject to the ultimate supervisory authority of Parliament, in accordance with the theory of parliamentary sovereignty.

owed perpetual allegiance to the English nation. The American colonists thus were seen as members of a unified political community—the empire—governed by a single sovereign, Parliament, in which they, like all English subjects, were represented.

Accordingly, the English rejected the American contention that there were limits to the authority of Parliament over the colonies, that the colonists' right of representation could be exercised only in their provincial assemblies, and that these assemblies had exclusive power over legislation in local affairs. Lord Mansfield, for example, held that the British legislature "represents the whole British Empire, and has authority to bind every part and every subject without the least distinction." Lord Lyttleton stated the case for the unlimited authority of Parliament with the remark that "in all states . . . the government must rest somewhere, and that must be fixed, or otherwise there is an end of all government. . . . The only question before your lordships is, whether the American colonies are a part of the dominions of the crown of Great Britain? If not, Parliament has no jurisdiction, if they are, as many statutes have declared them to be, they must be proper subjects of our legislation."

The English rejection of federalism as incomprehensible was eminently reasonable from the standpoint of conventional political science, for no doctrine seemed more certain than that within the state there must be one supreme authority. If sovereignty was supreme authority, it was by definition destroyed when divided. It was illogical and irrational to contemplate a government within a government—an *imperium in imperio*—as Americans did in suggesting that within the empire, side by side with Parliament's power over commerce and other general matters, the colonial assemblies possessed sovereignty in local affairs. The English had for so long clung to the idea of the colonies as local corporations, dependent on royal grace and favor for their very existence, that they were unable to grasp the historical reality that the empire had become a federal state.

In the debate in Commons, most members were also unwilling to accept the American doctrine of actual representation. George Grenville, author of the Stamp Act, declared for the complete sovereignty of Parliament and added that "taxation is a part of the sovereign power." Another member stated that "enacting laws and laying taxes so intirely go together that if we surrender the one we lose the others." However, America was not without friends in Parliament. In the Commons the great William Pitt lent the weight of his immense prestige to the American cause. He upheld the supremacy of Parliament, but almost alone among Englishmen he insisted at the same time that "taxation is no part of the governing or legislating power." He followed this assertion with a direct attack upon the whole theory of virtual representation, which he called "the most contemptible idea that ever entered the head of man."

A shrewd commentary upon the conflict was made by Edmund Burke, who pointed out that "some of the Charters declare the Right, others suppose it, none deny it." But he saw "a real Distinction in every Country between the speculative and practical constitution of that country. . . . The British empire must be governed on a plan of freedom, for it will be governed by no other." The colonies, he continued, "were mere Corporations, Fishermen and Furriers, they are now commonwealths." Burke was issuing a warning that if archaic constitutional theories were allowed to blind Parliament to the fact that the colonies were rapidly becoming great and powerful states, then the empire was headed for disaster. The colonies were not corporations, but great states whose population, commerce, and industry were thriving and whose economic and social order was now powerful enough to stand alone, even if British politicians were unaware of it. American requests for freedom from taxation and for internal autonomy were demands that this situation be recognized.

Parliament at length repealed the Stamp Act, but not before asserting the very principle of parliamentary supremacy and unitary sovereignty that Americans had called into question. It affirmed this constitutional position, at least to its own satisfaction, in the Declaratory Act of 1766, which stated simply that Parliament had full power to make laws and statutes binding the colonies "in all cases whatsoever." Although the act carefully avoided any reference to taxation, debate in Parliament made it clear that it was intended to comprehend that issue, the main source of conflict. But Americans, not knowing the legislative history of the measure and observing its omission of any mention of taxation, could plausibly regard it as not inconsistent with their federal conception of empire.

The Formation of an American Resistance Movement

England persisted in its determination to tax the colonies in 1767 under Pitt as prime minister and Charles Townshend as Chancellor of the Exchequer. Acting on the distinction between internal and external taxes misleadingly laid down by Benjamin Franklin, Townshend proposed a revenue act in June 1767 that levied a series of duties upon glass, red and white lead, painters' colors, tea, and paper imported into the colonies. While the manner of collection was not different from those older duties incident to the enforcement of the Navigation Laws, the law's preamble specifically stated that it was a revenue measure for "the support of civil government, in such provinces as it shall be found necessary." The law was an undisguised tax measure, not a commercial regulation.

The Americans were particularly alarmed by Townshend's proposal to use the proceeds of the law to create a colonial civil list, from which colonial governors and judges would receive their salaries. This struck directly at the hard-won control that the assemblies had come to exercise over the colonial governors. If the governors were given independent salaries and a civil list independent of assembly control, much of colonial autonomy would be destroyed. The colonists also objected to another statute of Townshend's which created a separate board of customs commissioners for the American colonies. They viewed the board as merely another instrument of sharpened British control and unconstitutional taxation. Still another Townshend statute created new admiralty courts and specifically authorized the hated writs of assistance permitting open-ended searches in customs cases.

The direct political action that had met the Stamp Act resumed in response to the Townshend Acts. Nonimportation associations, backed by petition campaigns and Sons of Liberty organizations, applied economic pressure. Again Parliament undertook a tactical retreat. In 1769 it repealed all the duties except the tax on tea, with the result that colonial boycotts for the most part collapsed. By 1770 the crisis precipitated by the Townshend measures was at an end.

The years 1770–73 were superficially a period of quiescence. But the suspicion of the English government that Americans harbored and their heightened political awareness made further conflict highly probable, if not inevitable, so long as England insisted on a unitary theory of sovereignty in its imperial policy. Now the years of exposure to the opposition ideology, with its stress on the continual struggle between power and liberty, had a telling effect on the colonists. Matters which when considered in isolation would seem of minor importance took on ominous significance as part of an apparent attack on American liberty. In addition to their protest against taxation without actual representation, Americans criticized British reliance on juryless vice-admiralty courts for enforcement of the Navigation Acts, and prosecution in common law courts by the use of informations rather than through grand-jury proceedings. Both practices eliminated the influence of public opinion in the administration of justice and added to Americans' fear of executive control of the government. A threat to liberty also appeared in the Quartering Act of 1765, which required any colony in which English troops were stationed to supply them with provisions. Regarded as tantamount to a tax, the act in colonial minds augured the imposition of a standing army, one of the most persistent themes in the opposition literature. Another provocative measure emanating from Parliament was the Restraining Act of 1767. Less well known than the revenue laws but perhaps even more threatening, it suspended the power of the New York assembly until it should comply with the Quartering Act. But even without such bluntly repressive legislation the power of the assemblies seemed in jeopardy, and with it the colonists' treasured local autonomy.

John Dickinson's *Letters from a Pennsylvania Farmer* captured the sense of apprehension that eroded American trust in British intentions even before critical events in the mid-1770s precipitated armed struggle. Describing the substance of local sovereignty, Dickinson observed that the assembly had been responsible for the defense of society, the administration of justice, and the support of civil government in general. But the expected consequence of the

Townshend revenue act, with its establishment of a colonial civil list, would be the superseding of the assembly in its governing function. "Why should these trusts be wrested out of their hands?" Dickinson asked. "Why should they not be permitted to enjoy the authority, which they have exercised from the first settlement of these colonies?" To conduct government at the expense of the people, Dickinson averred, but independently of their opinions and judgment, was slavery. The reaction to imperial centralization also had a personal, psychological dimension. Assemblymen whose authority had been comparable to Roman senators, Dickinson wrote, would have no more importance than local constables making rules for the yoking of hogs or the impounding of stray cattle! In the very terms employed in the opposition writings which Americans had read for decades, Dickinson warned against the extension of ministerial influence through the appointment of revenue collectors, customs officers, postal agents, and sundry government officials. He reminded his readers that perpetual vigilance about liberty was essential in all free states, especially in a mixed constitution where domination by any single part of the government forecast tyranny.

In an atmosphere tense not only with the resentment at specific imperial policies but also with pervasive distrust of British authority in general, the Tea Act of 1773 triggered a series of events that swiftly transformed colonial resistance into incipient revolution. The act granted a bounty to the East India Company on its tea exports to America, thereby enabling it to undersell all other competitors, including colonial merchants. In response to the act Massachusetts patriots destroyed several cargoes of tea in the famous Boston Tea Party. The English government retaliated with the so-called Intolerable Acts, which in colonial eyes conclusively demonstrated the English intention to subject the colonists to political slavery.

The Boston Port Act, March 31, 1774, closed the port of Boston until the town should make restitution to the East India Company. The Massachusetts Government Act, May 20, 1774, altered the charter of Massachusetts in an attempt to bring the colony more directly under the control of the English government. The assistants were no longer to be elected by the General Court but appointed by the crown. The governor was also given the power to appoint, without consent of the council, all judges of inferior courts, and to nominate all judges of superior courts. In the future, also, no town was to call any meeting of its selectmen other than the annual meeting without the consent of the governor.

The Administration of Justice Act, May 20, 1774, provided that in case of alleged felonies committed by crown officers, magistrates, and so on, in pursuit of their duties in Massachusetts Bay, trial was, upon order of the governor, to be moved to some other colony or to Great Britain. The act was intended to protect officials in the discharge of their duties by guaranteeing them against the wrath of colonial juries. The Quartering Act, June 2, 1774, permitted officials in any colony to quarter royal troops upon the inhabitants of a town when necessary. This law was intended to force the colonists to make adequate provision for housing soldiers wherever they might be needed; yet clearly it violated one of the traditional guarantees of the Petition of Right.

The Quebec Act, passed June 22, 1774, although not intended as a punitive measure, was so regarded in America. The law extended the boundaries of the Province of Quebec to include the area north of the Ohio River and west of the Proclamation Line of 1763, and it thus appeared to violate several colonial charters by stripping the colonies of their trans-Allegheny possessions. The law also extended religious liberty to the Catholics of Quebec. While this provision was of no constitutional or social significance to the seaboard colonies, it was nonetheless represented as an attempt to impose the hated Church of Rome upon Protestant America.

The Dominion Theory of Empire

As the rift between the colonies and the mother country grew wider and the possibility of independence was bruited about, colonial leaders altered their conception of empire accordingly. They now brought forward a commonwealth or dominion theory of empire, holding that each colony, like England itself, had a sovereign and independent legislature and was connected to Great Britain only through the king. English history and law—as Americans interpreted it—offered solid support for such a view. The relevant historical example was Scotland. An independent kingdom before the accession of James VI to the English throne, Scotland afterward remained a separate political jurisdiction, not subject to parliamentary rule. Yet, as laid down in *Calvin's Case* (1608), the historic decision that defined the nature of the union between Scotland and England, the Scots were English subjects, loyal to the king.[2] This was precisely the situation that the American colonists desired: political autonomy within a single community of allegiance to the English crown. Accordingly, the colonists made frequent reference to *Calvin's Case* in their arguments of the 1770s.

The dominion theory of empire aptly served American purposes. It pre-

---

2. A contrived suit brought for the purpose of settling the constitutional dispute over the relationship between Scotland and England caused by the accession of James VI, Calvin's case concerned the right of Robert Calvin, a Scots infant born in 1606 after the accession, to inherit property in England. If, in addition to being a subject of Scotland, Robert Calvin was in the eyes of English law also an English subject, he could inherit property. If not, he was an alien and could not own property in England. Edward Coke, chief justice of common pleas, whose opinion of the several rendered was accepted as authoritative, held that Calvin was a subject of the king of England and, therefore, eligible to inherit property. Insofar as Scots and English subjects were bound in a common allegiance to the king, the two countries were united. Yet the union was a limited one, for Coke declared Scotland and England to be separate jurisdictions, with distinct legal systems and political institutions.

served internal autonomy while enabling the colonists to maintain their loyalty to the king and their connection to the empire. The constitutional significance of the theory was its categorical denial of parliamentary authority over the colonies, including commercial regulation. The original domain of North America, wrote Samuel Adams in 1773, was not part of the realm of England but adhered to the crown alone, as the king's personal property. Through the prerogative, the king could dispose of his domains as he wished. Adams and others contended that royal grants, in the form of seventeenth-century corporate and proprietary charters, established a direct link between the colonies and the crown which lay outside the sphere of parliamentary competence.

The dominion theory reflected the colonists' seemingly paradoxical desire to assume a position of equality with England, while remaining within the empire and hence in some sense in a dependent status. Like the thesis of imperial centralization and parliamentary supremacy maintained by the English, the dominion theory was doctrinaire in its failure to recognize the actual division of sovereignty that existed in the empire. Aside from the psychological benefit of enabling the colonists still to profess loyalty to Great Britain, it was hard to see the practical significance of the imperial tie in the theory as formally presented; apparently there was none, the king as the common sovereign of the colonies possessing merely a nominal authority. Yet even as they denied any legitimate parliamentary power in the dominion theory, Americans were in fact prepared to acknowledge parliamentary legislation for imperial purposes on a pragmatic basis. In the words of John Adams: "Parliament has no authority over the colonies, except to regulate their trade, and this not by any principle of common law, but merely by the consent of the colonies, founded on the obvious necessities of the case." James Madison said that commercial regulation by Parliament was "a practice without a right, and contrary to the true theory of the constitution." But it was nevertheless convenient and necessary, and hence permissible as a measure that might preserve imperial unity.

While the colonists clung, albeit in attenuated fashion, to the imperial tie, their protest against taxation and other imperial innovations by 1774 directly challenged English rule and led to the formation of a revolutionary governing authority. Rioting in response to the Stamp Act, though controlled and discriminating in its application, forced many English officers to resign and encouraged more systematic American efforts at political organization. One result was the spread of nonimportation associations that made and enforced rules of economic boycott. Acting like authentic governments, they inspected merchants' activities, judged persons accused of violating the agreements, and imposed sanctions on the guilty. The non-importation associations also received reinforcement from established local institutions like the town meeting. Further significant steps toward revolutionary government came with the formation of committees of correspondence in New England and Virginia in 1772–73, and throughout the rest of the colonies in 1774 in reaction to the

Intolerable Acts. Like the economic boycott groups, the committees assumed duties commonly vested only in sovereign political bodies. Most important was their attempt to give colonial boycott agreements the force of law by means of publicity, intimidation, and resolutions against offenders. In reality the committees were revolutionary bodies, taking the lead in concerted resistance to British authority.

These committees soon gave rise to colonywide revolutionary governments. Thus in Massachusetts, General Thomas Gage, now governor of the colony, dissolved the regularly constituted General Court in June, and the Boston committee of correspondence thereupon demanded the election of a provincial congress to take charge of the government of Massachusetts until Parliament and the crown should accept their constitutional functions. The provincial congress met in October 1774, and henceforth the effective government of Massachusetts Bay was no longer in the hands of the governor and the other regularly constituted crown officers, but in the hands of the provincial congress.

Events took a similar turn in the other colonies. In Virginia, the royal governor dissolved the assembly in May because of its rebellious temper. Thereupon a portion of the House of Burgesses under the leadership of Patrick Henry, Thomas Jefferson, and others issued a call for an election of members of a provincial congress to meet in Williamsburg on August 1. By the close of 1774, all the royal and proprietary colonies except New York, Pennsylvania, and Georgia had established provincial congresses, and these three colonies took this step the following year. In the two charter colonies of Connecticut and Rhode Island, the legal governments were so nearly autonomous that no such move was necessary. The existing governments simply accepted the patriot cause.

In most of the colonies the governor's dissolution of the regularly constituted legislature or his refusal to call it into session was the immediate occasion for the erection of the provincial congress. In some cases, a congress was a rump of the regular assembly, composed of delegates in sympathy with the popular cause. This was true in Massachusetts, New Hampshire, Delaware, Virginia, and North Carolina. In New Jersey, Maryland, and South Carolina, delegates to the congresses were chosen by means of elections held at popular meetings throughout the colonies.

As noted, the provincial congresses were in fact revolutionary state governments. Although the members protested their loyalty to the crown, they engaged in steady suppression of the remnants of royal authority in the colonies. Thus the Massachusetts congress, late in 1774, took over the tax machinery and the operation of the courts, and began raising an army for the field. Much the same seizure of power occurred in all the colonies. The American colonies were now in the process of becoming the American states, a metamorphosis completed by 1776, some time before the Declaration of Independence was signed.

The First Continental Congress

While this revolution was going on within the various colonies, the pyramid of revolutionary government was completed by the establishment of an intercolonial congress. In September 1774 the First Continental Congress, called at the suggestion of several of the provincial congresses, met in Philadelphia. All the colonies except Georgia were represented, and some of the most distinguished men in America were present, among them Samuel and John Adams of Massachusetts; Stephen Hopkins of Rhode Island; Roger Sherman of Connecticut; John Jay and Philip Livingston of New York; John Dickinson and Joseph Galloway of Pennsylvania; George Washington, Richard Henry Lee, and Patrick Henry of Virginia; and John Rutledge of South Carolina.

Although the delegations varied in size and represented colonies of different territorial extent and population, it was nevertheless shortly decided that the vote would be taken by states, each state present having one vote. Thus the principle of state equality was established, a principle soon to be incorporated in the Articles of Confederation and later to gain recognition in the Constitution of the United States.

For a time the delegates considered a plan of union submitted by Joseph Galloway of Pennsylvania. This plan proposed the establishment of an intercolonial legislature or "grand council" composed of delegates chosen for three years by the respective colonial assemblies. A president-general appointed by the king would preside. The grand council would be "an inferior and distinct branch of the British Legislature," and would have authority over the general affairs of the colonies. Either the British Parliament or the grand council would enact legislation for intercolonial matters, but the assent of both legislatures would be necessary before any statute became invalid.

In a calmer day the plan might have been adopted and might have paved the way for dominion status for America, but the trend was against conciliatory measures. After some indecision the plan was tabled by a majority of one vote, and the congress turned toward more radical proposals.

The first evidence that the extremist faction was obtaining the upper hand came with the introduction of the Suffolk Resolves, a series of resolutions of a popular convention in Suffolk County, Massachusetts. The resolves asserted that no obedience was due the Intolerable Acts and that no taxes should be paid into the provincial treasury until constitutional government was restored in the colony. Their introduction was in reality a successful stratagem to force the congress toward a more radical position. Although the congress took no positive action upon the resolves, the reaction toward the measures nonetheless indicated the steady growth of radical opinion among the delegates.

The Declaration and Resolves of the First Continental Congress, a series of resolutions adopted by the congress on October 14, showed how far radical sentiment had progressed in the gathering. This document, though conciliatory in tone, virtually reiterated the dominion conception of colonial status, which had become extremely popular among the colonial radicals. The Declaration and Resolves held the colonists to be "entitled to a free and exclusive power of legislation in their several provincial legislatures . . . in all cases of taxation and internal polity, subject only to the negative of their sovereign." The only concession to parliamentary authority was a provision that "from the necessity of the case, and a regard to the mutual interest of both countries, we cheerfully consent to the operation of such acts of the British parliament, as are bona fide restrained to the regulation of our external commerce." This expressed not only a desire to win moderate support, but also the continuing appeal of a federal division of sovereignty.

Other provisions of the resolutions amounted essentially to an assertion of a colonial bill of rights as against even royal authority. The colonists were declared entitled to "life, liberty, and property," and to "all the rights, liberties, and immunities of free and natural-born subjects within the realm of England." They were further declared entitled to the common law of England, to the benefits of such English statutes as had existed at the time of their colonization and that had been found applicable to American circumstances, and to all the privileges and immunities granted by the several royal charters or secured by their own legal systems. The resolutions affirmed further the colonists' right to assemble peaceably, consider their grievances, and petition the king. They denounced as "against law" the maintenance of a standing army in any colony in time of peace without the consent of the legislature of that colony. Finally, they condemned appointment of colonial councils by the crown as "unconstitutional, dangerous, and destructive to the freedom of American legislation."

Six days after the adoption of the Declaration and Resolves came the formation of the Continental Association, the first positive measure of resistance to British authority taken by the colonies acting in their united capacity. Through this organization the congress laid down an intercolonial nonimportation agreement against all British goods, effective December 1, 1774. The slave trade as well was banned as of the same date. The congress also threatened to invoke nonexportation to Britain, to be effective September 1, 1775, unless the obnoxious acts of Parliament were repealed. The boycott was given sanctions by recommending the formation of local committees "whose business it shall be attentively to observe the conduct of all persons touching this association."

With the creation of the Continental Congress, the formation of local, state, and federal revolutionary governments was complete. However, neither the local committees of correspondence, the provincial assemblies, nor the Continental Congress before January 1776 laid claim to any permanent sovereign political authority. Nor, at first, was it their overt intention to engage in armed rebellion against England. Actually, however, they not only steadily carried out the seizure of authority from agents of the crown, but in April 1775 they began an armed rebellion against British troops.

The Coming of Independence

When the Second Continental Congress met in May 1775, the battle of Lexington and Concord had been fought, armed clashes had occurred in Virginia, and the major battle of Bunker Hill was in the offing. The congress responded to the challenge by raising and appointing an army and naming Washington to command it. In July, the congress issued a Declaration of the Causes and Necessity of Taking Up Arms, a document prepared by Dickinson and Jefferson. It disavowed any intention of seeking independence, but pledged resistance until Parliament abandoned its unconstitutional rule in America. The estrangement between England and America was now complete, though there was a general reluctance in the colonies to admit the fact. The king's Proclamation of Rebellion in August 1775, the Prohibitory Act of December 1775, by which Parliament declared the colonies outside Britain's protection and proclaimed a blockade of all colonial ports, and the steady extension of military engagements made reconciliation impossible. Throughout 1775 most colonials denounced the idea of independence, but early in 1776 there developed a marked increase in the sentiment for formal separation from the mother country.

In January 1776 Thomas Paine's pamphlet *Common Sense* gave a powerful impetus to both the movement for independence and the idea of republican government as an alternative to monarchy. After nine months of actual warfare, Paine's tract answered Americans' need for convincing reasons for complete separation. In a vivid and emotional style that made the work immediately accessible and popular (it sold 120,000 copies in three months), Paine said that further dependence on England would be ruinous for it would mean involvement in European wars and the destruction of American commerce. It was politically absurd moreover, he observed, for a continent to be governed by an island. More significant in a constitutional sense and equally important in stimulating sentiment for independence was Paine's attack on monarchy and the English mixed constitution. Employing the analysis made familiar in the opposition literature of the eighteenth century, Paine condemned the corruption and despotism inherent in a government that gave special powers, transmitted by hereditary right, to monarchy and aristocracy. It was farcical, he charged, to suppose that the different parts of the English constitution checked and balanced each other when the same people—the king's ministers and appointees—both advised and carried out as the executive part of the government what they enacted as law in Parliament. Arguing for the abolition of crown and nobility, Paine urged a republican conception of the state that would derive government exclusively from the people.

Paine's pamphlet hastened an imminent separation. By 1776 the rebellious colonists had carried their movement too far to turn back without abandoning the whole cause and placing their very lives in danger. They had organized *de facto* state and national governments and had shot the king's troops, ousted his officials, and destroyed his trade. Conciliation was impossible. Independence was already a fact, and it remained only to make it true in theory and law as well.

In the spring of 1776 events moved swiftly toward the establishment of formal independence. On April 6 the congress declared all colonial ports open to foreign trade, thus repudiating imperial trade laws. On May 10 it adopted a resolution calling upon the several colonies to create regular state governments. A preamble to this resolution, adopted on May 15, went even further; it stated that since Great Britain had placed the colonies outside her protection and made war upon them, it was now necessary that every kind of authority under the crown be totally suppressed and all governmental powers transferred to the people of the several colonies.

On June 7, Richard Henry Lee, acting in accordance with instructions from the state of Virginia, laid the following resolution before the congress:

Resolved, that these United Colonies are, and of right ought to be, free and independent States, and that they are absolved from all allegiance to the British Crown, and that all connection between them and the State of Great Britain is, and ought to be, totally dissolved.

On June 11, the congress referred Lee's resolution to a committee of five men, Thomas Jefferson, John Adams, Benjamin Franklin, Roger Sherman, and Robert Livingston, who were assigned the task of drafting a "declaration to the effect of the said resolution." The result was the Declaration of Independence.

Although Americans frequently appealed to natural law in their protest against British policies, their chief reliance had been on the rights of Englishmen under the constitution and laws of England, and on the federal and dominion theories of empire. In throwing off English authority, however, they appealed primarily to the law of nature. Jefferson's opening paragraph in the Declaration of Independence signaled the necessary shift in perspective:

When in the course of human events, it becomes necessary for one people to dissolve the political bands which have connected them with another, and to assume among the powers of the earth the separate and equal station to which the Laws of Nature and of Nature's God entitle them, a decent respect to the opinions of mankind requires that they should declare the causes which impel them to the separation.

Jefferson next proposed a condensed statement of the natural law–compact philosophy then prevalent in America:

We hold these truths to be self-evident, that all men are created equal, that they are endowed by their Creator with certain unalienable rights, that among these are life, liberty, and the pursuit of happiness. That to secure these rights, governments are instituted among men, deriving their just powers from the consent of the governed. That whenever any form of government becomes destructive of these ends, it is the right of the people to alter or to abolish it, and to institute new government. . . . Prudence, indeed, will dictate that governments long established should not be changed for light and transient causes; . . . But when a long train of abuses and usurpations, pursuing invariably the same object, evinces a design to reduce them under absolute despotism, it is their right, it is their duty, to throw off such government, and to provide new guards for their future security.

There are four fundamental political ideas here: the doctrine of natural law and natural rights, the compact theory of the state, the doctrine of popular sover-eignty, and the right of revolution. These conceptions were common to nearly all seventeenth- and eighteenth-century natural law theorists, but Jefferson's phraseology was closely modeled on John Locke's *Second Treatise*.

The Declaration of Independence proclaimed a series of truths that be-came the first principles of American political life. First in importance was the assertion that "all men are created equal." In the revolutionary era, it served at a minimum to condemn hereditary legal and political privilege. This tend-ency reached fruition in the concept of democratic opportunity and careers open to talent in the Jacksonian period. In the Civil War era controversy focused on whether Jefferson's appeal to equality was intended to apply univer-sally—to blacks as well as whites—or encompassed only those who were already members of the political community. Lincoln showed the former to be the correct meaning. In the twentieth century the Declaration's language of equality has taken on even broader import as American society has become increasingly sensitive to inequality in all its forms. Jefferson did not, however, intend to lay down any broad premise of extreme democratic equality. He did not mean that all people were equal in moral, spiritual, or intellectual ability, or that government should try to create equality of condition for all people. Natural law theory held that in a state of nature all men were equal in the possession of certain inalienable rights—"life, liberty, and the pursuit of happi-ness," in Jefferson's words. Government was instituted to protect those rights and could not impair them; it must, in other words, regard all men as equal in the eyes of the law. It is in this sense that all men are created equal.

Twentieth-century supporters of bureaucratic and socially responsive government have made much of Jefferson's substitution of "happiness" for "property" in his description of natural, inalienable rights. In conventional natural law theory the happiness of society, or public happiness, was the first end of government. This was not understood in contradistinction to property, however, but as complementary to and even contingent upon it. Property meant preeminently land or access to land, ownership of which enabled a person to become truly independent. It was the basis of civic virtue on which republican government depended. Property and liberty were thus inextricably related, and were considered necessary for the attainment of happiness. It is inaccurate, therefore, to see in the Declaration of Independence a distinction between property rights and human rights.

Jefferson presented an indictment of George III to illustrate "the long train of abuses" that had spurred the colonies to revolt. Most of the alleged offenses had grown out of issues that had arisen since 1763, involving acts of Parliament asserting authority over the colonies. Yet the Declaration attacked the crown and said virtually nothing of Parliament. This rhetorical strategy was necessary because Jefferson and the congress accepted the dominion theory of empire, which presented the colonies as united to England only through the person of the king and denied all parliamentary authority over the colonies.

The American Conception of Constitutionalism

Although the colonists objected to imperial policy as a violation of their rights under the constitution and laws of England, their protest led them to question not only the authority of the English government, but also the English conception of constitutionalism. In the prerevolutionary era they began to formulate a new approach to constitutionalism that ultimately caused American political development to differ basically from that of England.

In England the constitution was the complex of institutions, laws, customs, practices, and principles by which the people conducted their political and governmental life. In theory the constitution derived from established principles of reason and justice, its purpose being to promote the common good and achieve a proper balance between liberty and order. Although certain historic documents such as Magna Charta possessed special significance, the constitution was not a written instrument but an organically evolving assemblage of statute, belief, and institutional practice.

The ability of the constitution to limit governmental power came from three sources: common law guarantees of private rights and individual liberty (jurisdictio) enforced by the courts against government (gubernaculum); balanced institutional arrangements according to the theory of mixed government; and fundamental law. Although usually equated with natural law, fundamental law had a more explicit content in the principles of reason used in interpreting and applying the common law. It was in this sense that Sir Edward Coke, the great seventeenth-century jurist, had pursued the idea of constitutional limitations on government in the famous case of Dr. Bonham in 1610. Dr. Bonham was charged with violating an act of Parliament that authorized the London College of Physicians to license the practice of medicine in the city, and that empowered the college to punish physicians practicing without the required license. Coke found Dr. Bonham innocent on the ground that the law in question was void. The common law, Coke said, will control acts of Parliament and sometimes adjudge them to be void when an act is against common right or reason, repugnant, or impossible to be performed.

Coke did not mean that English courts could declare acts of Parliament unconstitutional, as American courts were to do under the doctrine of judicial review. The separation of powers did not yet exist; Parliament was a court as well as a legislative body and formed part of the constitution. Nor did Coke mean that the entire body of the common law stood as a restraint on Parliament's lawmaking power. The London College of Physicians, however, by charging Dr. Bonham, by finding him guilty, and by collecting half the fine he was assessed as punishment, had in effect decided a matter in which it had an interest. And this violated the common law principle that no man should be a judge in his own case. Coke's opinion nevertheless contained the idea of a fundamental or higher law restraining governmental acts.

In the seventeenth century Parliament established its legislative supremacy. By the mid-eighteenth century the doctrine of fundamental law had lost much of its intellectual appeal and delimiting force in English political life. Considering Parliament's claim to sovereignty, and the fact that its enactments were by definition part of the constitution, how could there be any limits on its power? Although theorists might say that Parliament was obliged to follow principles of right reason and natural justice in its actions, it was difficult to see how the English constitution restrained government in the interest of liberty.

This at any rate was the way it appeared to Americans as they contemplated imperial affairs. If Parliament was sovereign, then the constitution was not really a constitution at all. In protesting parliamentary statutes Americans argued that a constitution, in order to accomplish its purpose of controlling the government, must be fixed. Moreover, it must be separate from and antecedent to government so as to be unalterable by the legislature or other agencies. Americans reasoned that the essential principles of reason and justice, and the rules for the proper arrangement and distribution of governmental power, must be abstracted from actual institutions and given fixed form. Eventually, after the blow for independence was struck, they concluded that these principles and rules must be given positive, written, documentary expression as a fixed standard—a higher law—against which to hold the government accountable.

In 1761 James Otis pointed toward the new American conception of constitutionalism in his attack on parliamentary authorized writs of assistance, recently employed in Massachusetts to enforce the Navigation Laws. Citing Coke's opinion in *Dr. Bonham's Case,* Otis said the writs violated fundamental principles of law which guaranteed a man security in his own home. An act of Parliament against natural equity was void, Otis reasoned, and so too was an act against the constitution. In 1768 the *Circular Letter* of the Massachusetts General Court to the assemblies of the other colonies argued that the constitution consisted in fundamental rules which neither the legislature nor the executive could alter. "In all free states," the Massachusetts deputies declared in protest against the Townshend Acts, "the constitution is fixed, and the supreme legislative power of the nation, from thence derives its authority." The *Circular Letter* stated that the constitution ascertains and limits sovereignty, and that the legislature could not "overleap the bounds of the constitution without subverting its own foundation." John Dickinson apprehended the new conception of constitutionalism when he wrote, in *Letters from a Pennsylvania Farmer*, that a free people are "Not those over whom government is reasonably and equitably exercised, but those, who live under a government so constitutionally checked and controlled, that proper provision is made against its being otherwise exercised."

The idea of a fixed, normative constitution existing outside of and superior to government represented a significant theoretical innovation. Yet in the American context it was not altogether unfamiliar. On the contrary, the seventeenth-century experience in founding new governments had prepared the way for this conceptual development. The joint-stock corporation charters, proprietary concessions and agreements, and fundamental orders of the covenant-compact colonies resembled fixed constitutional instruments. Although they never assumed the extra-institutional status that constitutions in the revolutionary era did, they were antecedent to government and were later appealed to as a restraint on imperial authority. In Bernard Bailyn's apt expression, the new American conception of constitutionalism represented experience elevated to principle.

Revolutionary constitutionalism also drew upon the Western tradition of natural law and English notions of fundamental law, both of which contained the idea of protecting legal rights by placing limitations on legislative power. But, though occasionally invoked by common law courts, these traditions suffered distinct institutional weakness because their implementation essentially depended on their being internalized by governing officials. Americans tried to remedy this defect by giving fundamental law positive expression in written constitutions. At the same time they regarded written constitutions as embodying moral values derived from natural law.

There were philosophical difficulties in this attempt to combine positive law and natural law. Legal positivism—the belief that law rests on the command of the superior power—separates law from morality, or holds that morality and justice are whatever the ruling authority posits them to be. It stands at the opposite pole from natural law, which appeals to eternal principles of justice and right as the basis of the rules of action in civil society and insists on an identification between law and morality. The new American constitutionalism was intended not only to use natural law as a standard for judging the wisdom and morality of government actions, but also to give natural law a fixed, objective form as a standard for assessing the legality of government actions. American constitutionalism thus contained within it a theoretical tension, which began to manifest itself as Americans formed revolutionary state governments following the separation from England. Constitutions that were intended to embody higher law or natural rights principles appeared in practice mainly to express the expedient demands of ruling groups in the society. Considerable experimentation in the practice of republican government would be required before Americans effectively institutionalized the new conception of constitutionalism.

FIVE

Revolutionary Constitutionalism: The States and the Articles of Confederation

In its initial phase the American Revolution was an attempt to protect the rights and liberties of the colonists as individual subjects and of the colonies as states or units in the empire under the laws and constitution of England. When Americans realized the impossibility of this task and forcibly rejected English authority, however, they were concerned with achieving not only home rule as a separate people, but also a particular kind of home rule. English imperial policy had threatened to impose what Americans regarded as an outside or alien presence. It also threatened to destroy institutions of local liberty, rooted in the very founding of the colonies, which to a significant extent were based on the democratic element in society. With the collapse of English authority, Americans of necessity organized new governments. But in restoring law and order they did not simply maintain their old political establishments. They seized the opportunity which the struggle for national liberation presented to create constitutions of liberty that expressed even more cogently than the Declaration of Independence the "spirit of '76."

The essence of that spirit was republican constitutionalism. The governments that Americans now projected for their independent states rested in theory on the new conception of constitutionalism and fundamental law formulated during the imperial controversy. Equally significant was the assertion of republicanism as the philosophical foundation of the American political order. Until the eve of the Revolution most colonists could scarcely conceive of a political framework other than mixed government and constitutional monarchy. The English constitution and their own provincial constitutions contained a democratic component, but a government based entirely on the popular element was practically unthinkable. In the received wisdom of the day republics were disdained as small, weak, and ineffective; the word *republican* was derisive, a term of opprobrium. With the abolition of monarchy in America, however, the perception of republican government changed.

Americans espoused the idea of republicanism with conviction, even fervor. In a sense it was familiar to them from their history, for colonial government manifested many of the characteristics of local liberty and responsiveness to public opinion identified with republican government. And considering the absence in America of a titled aristocracy, the elimination of the crown left the popular element as the only basis of government. Yet if republican constitutionalism was the product of history, and even in some sense historically necessary, the fact is incontrovertible that in making republicanism the foundation of their polity Americans acted with a self-conscious sense of purpose, deliberation, and choice. Furthermore, for all the practical anticipation of republican politics evident in the colonial period, Americans made significant constitutional innovations in creating state governments. Rejecting mixed government as an organizing principle, they structured their republican state constitutions on the doctrine of the separation of powers.

Republicanism as a Revolutionary Philosophy

Republican theory dealt mainly with the nature and sources of political and legal authority rather than with the internal constitutional structure of the polity. Derived from the Latin *res publica,* or "public thing," republicanism defined government as a public matter, the people's affair conducted for their interest and well-being rather than for the benefit of the ruler. Accordingly, republican government had its origin in and derived its authority from the people. The precise forms that popular action might take in creating government could, of course, vary, although the theory of the social contract supplied the intellectual rationale of the process. Eventually, the constitutional convention, superseding *ad hoc* interventions of state legislatures, became the accepted mode by which the people as constituent power formed their government.

Americans' rapid conversion to republicanism after the Declaration of Independence so thoroughly established it as the theoretical basis of the new order that it is difficult to grasp the radicalism of the undertaking as it appeared to contemporaries. It was radical chiefly because it abolished monarchy and aristocracy, two of the three components of mixed government, and proposed to base government exclusively on the democratic element in society. Yet at the same time republicanism was a traditional doctrine insofar as, in the manner of premodern political philosophy in general, it emphasized pursuit of the common good over and against individualism.

In the writings of Harrington, Sidney, and other seventeenth-century theorists of republicanism, the interest and welfare of society as a whole transcended the interests of particular groups or individuals. Corporatist in outlook, republicanism held that the purpose of political action and of government was to transcend individual interests and promote the common good. A corporatist or commonwealth spirit was expressed in the revolutionary period in America in the strict control of markets, price fixing, restriction of consumption by sumptuary legislation, and general economic regulation undertaken by the state governments. These policies were consistent, moreover, with contemporary doctrines of mercantilism, which assigned government broad responsibility for the promotion and regulation of economic life. Economic individualism and free trade stood at the opposite pole from mercantilism.

Alongside the corporatist tendency in revolutionary republicanism, however, powerful individualistic strains were apparent. Until recently historians treated the Revolution as a vindication of life, liberty, and the pursuit of happiness understood in the classic laissez-faire sense of property accumulation by self-seeking individuals. The discovery of a corporatist dimension to revolutionary thought has provided an important corrective to the earlier view of a primeval Lockean liberalism dominating American politics and society. Yet individualism, which was supported for civic and moral as well as economic reasons, was a potent force in revolutionary politics. At the height of the revolutionary crisis the corporatist outlook was stronger, especially in areas touched by the war; otherwise, it was on the wane. Colonial politics was interest- and faction-dominated, and despite the appeal of revolutionary leaders to patriotism and the common good, the individualism that stimulated interest-group politics was widely evident in state politics during and after the Revolution.

This tension within republicanism may also be considered in terms of positive and negative conceptions of liberty. Central to the opposition ideology that influenced American thinking in the prerevolutionary period was the idea that true liberty consisted in political action. Liberty as political participation was thought to be the key to personal and civic virtue, the essence of which was to act for the good of the whole rather than for individual ends. Derived from ancient political philosophy by way of Florentine civic humanism of the fifteenth century and the English republican theorists of the seventeenth century, this positive conception of liberty offered one approach to revolutionary republicanism. Looked at in this light, the pursuit of happiness referred to in the Declaration of Independence meant *public* happiness, in which individuals devoted themselves to the commonwealth rather than to narrow personal ends.

The alternative conception of liberty and republican government emphasized limitations on government in the interest of individual freedom. Negative in the sense that it sought to curtail government, this conception of liberty depended on common law property rights, privileges and immunities, guarantees of due process, and fundamental law. Rooted in ancient and medieval natural law doctrines, it lay at the heart of English constitutionalism and was conspicuous in the seventeenth-century struggle against the monarchy. The animus of negative liberty also played a central part in the American struggle against British imperialism.

In the American Revolution these two traditions of liberty fused in republican constitutionalism. The exigencies of the revolutionary crisis required decisive political action, which usually was justified under the ideal of positive liberty and civic virtue. At the same time, a sober regard for the propensities of ordinary human nature, in the context of the natural rights, social contract, and fundamental law traditions, led Americans to base their constitutions more on the negative than the positive conception of liberty. Liberty as participation and political action was by no means foreclosed; on the contrary, it remained a fundamental requirement of American constitutionalism. But guarantees of property rights and protection of individual liberty against arbitrary power acquired precedence in constitution writing and in the conduct of American politics.

The State Constitutions

Whatever the exact relationship between negative and positive liberty in revolutionary constitutionalism, it was axiomatic in the 1770s that republican government could exist only in small geographical areas. This belief, which reflected and confirmed the historical development of the colonies as autonomous units of government, caused the spirit of '76 to be expressed principally in the formation of constitutions and codes of law in the states.

It was of the utmost importance for American constitutional development that the political events by which Americans first defined themselves as a national people occurred at the state level. The Continental Congress, first convened in 1774, was a kind of continuing emergency meeting of representatives from the states. Its very name signified an assembly of ambassadors from independent states, which was precisely what the Declaration of Independence proclaimed the former colonies to be ("these United Colonies are, and of Right ought to be Free and Independent States"). The common cause was to secure the independence of thirteen separate states. No one doubted that the work of forming governments and establishing civil order—work that would determine the nature of the new nation's political institutions—would take place in the states. For that reason many revolutionary leaders spent most of the war years engaged in state constitution making. Americans were aware, moreover, of having a decisive opportunity to act as lawgivers and founders of new commonwealths. "In no age did man ever possess an election of the kind of government under which he would choose to live," observed the physician-historian David Ramsay of South Carolina. "In America alone," he wrote, "reason and liberty concurred in the formation of constitutions."

After the break from England—and in a few colonies even before then—constitution writing was the first objective of revolutionary political action. The purpose of the Revolution became the founding of constitutions of liberty. Revolutionary councils and committees of public safety governed from October 1774 through 1775, following the collapse of British authority. All things considered, the period of emergency government was of short duration because many colonial leaders feared that protest against authority might get out of hand. In fact, as early as six months before the Declaration of Independence, the process of regularizing and legitimizing revolutionary government by making constitutions had begun. In January 1776 New Hampshire adopted a brief, temporary constitution; South Carolina did the same in March. In June a convention of members of the Virginia House of Burgesses wrote a constitution for that state, and after the Declaration seven other states placed their government on a new foundation by approving constitutions. New York and Georgia wrote charters of fundamental law in 1777, and Massachusetts, after one unsuccessful attempt, adopted a constitution in 1780. Rhode Island and Connecticut retained their corporate charters from colonial days as state constitutions.

Although Americans had begun to think of a constitution as a higher law separate from legislative institutions, the first state constitutions reflected this view in an imperfect way. For the most part they were written and adopted by provincial congresses or state legislatures that also dealt with routine legislative matters and thus were not truly distinctive in function. In New Jersey, Virginia, and South Carolina the revolutionary provincial congresses drafted permanent constitutions without seeking any new authority from the people. New Hampshire, New York, Pennsylvania, Delaware, Maryland, North Carolina, and Georgia all held special elections for new congresses to write constitutions, but these bodies also legislated. In none of the states acting in 1776–77 did the constitution-writing assemblies submit their work to the people for popular approval; they merely proclaimed the new constitution to be in effect.

In the early period of constitution making there was confusion concerning the source of constitutional enactments. The constitution must derive from the people, but the state legislatures might be considered as fulfilling this requirement. As a result of factional struggles provoked by constitution making in the legislature, however, the practice arose of holding popular conventions to draft constitutions, which were subsequently submitted to the people for ratification. The Massachusetts constitution of 1780, drafted by a special convention after the constitution written by the state legislature was rejected in part because it emanated from the General Court, illustrated what eventually became orthodox constitutional procedure.

Constitution making proceeded under the moral sanction provided by social-contract theory—the first principle of republican philosophy. Indeed, it was by considering the framing of the first constitutions in light of the requirement of popular consent that critics were able to gain acceptance for the convention-and-ratification method of adopting or changing the fundamental law. In this sense social-contract theory stimulated change. In other respects, however, the use of social-contract theory reflected the limits of revolutionary constitutional change.

A key result of the galvanizing of political awareness that the Revolution produced was the emergence of new men in local politics. Frequently critical of the colonial political establishment, these men sought to extend the principle of self-government to its logical conclusion by making town and county government more independent of state authority. Leaders at the state level, however, successfully resisted these efforts. Denying that all the bonds of government had been dissolved in the movement for independence, they rejected the application of social-contract theory to justify changes in local government. Throughout the revolutionary era, accordingly, institutions of local government tended to serve as a stabilizing force. They were able to do so in part because state constitution making absorbed the political energies that the struggle for independence released.

The new state constitutions offer a body of evidence for addressing the time-honored but still important question of the radicalism of the American Revolution. Did the Revolution promote radical change, or did it merely consummate and confirm tendencies long evident in the colonial period? Two basic responses to this question have usually been given, one progressive or radical, the other conservative. The former holds that the Revolution, though initiated by the merchant-lawyer-planter elite that controlled colonial politics, became a truly radical movement of the middle and lower classes for political, social, and economic democracy. According to the progressive interpretation, this democratization can be seen in the assertion of legislative supremacy in the state constitutions and Articles of Confederation. The conservative interpretation contends that in a society that was already in social and economic terms broadly democratic, the purpose of the Revolution was to preserve the institutions of political democracy that imperial policy threatened. In separating from England, historians of this persuasion argue, the most radical change was the founding of a new nation and eventually a strong central government expressing the sense of American nationality.

The evidence of the state constitutions suggests that although there was little authentic class conflict in the sense of pitched battle between distinctly higher and lower social groups, republican principles had a potentially radical effect on American politics. State politics showed that the language of equality, consent, and individual liberty quickly acquired a persuasiveness and legitimacy that conferred an advantage on those who could employ it most effectively. At best, republican principles became ideals guiding political action by groups seeking to eliminate injustice and improve society. At worst they became shibboleths that obscured self-seeking political expediency and the quest for power.

In any event, it was not simply a nation, but a *republican* nation that the

Revolution created. This republican identity was at once old and new. Historically, it rested on what were in effect republican tendencies in colonial politics, even though they were not so regarded at the time. The elevation of these tendencies and practices to the level of republican theory and philosophical commitment, however, was new. A blend of institutional continuity and theoretical innovation thus stands out as characteristic of revolutionary constitutionalism.

The Separation of Powers and the State Constitutions

Continuity and change are evident in the most important result of state constitution making, the ascendancy of the legislative and the reduction of the executive power. This dual development culminated trends of long duration in the colonial period, yet it occurred within a new constitutional framework. This framework was the doctrine of the separation of powers.

In repudiating English authority Americans also repudiated the organizing principle of English constitutionalism, the theory of mixed government. In its place they substituted the theory of the separation of powers. Because both of these doctrines aimed at achieving balance in government, they are often seen as similar, if not interchangeable. In fact they differed profoundly. Mixed government, as noted previously, recognized and gave a place in the structure of government to the several orders of society. In the hierarchical, feudal society in which it developed it expressed the assumption that social and political authority were identical, that government and society were organically linked and overlapping. The separation of powers, by contrast, rested on recognition of distinct and clearly differentiated functions of government. It held that governmental powers, not social classes, must be kept in balance in order to preserve liberty. Separation theory was not in a formal sense concerned with sociology or class structure, although historically it developed in the distinctive social setting created by the rise of the bourgeoisie. The first to argue for the separation of powers, the leaders of Parliament in their struggle against the crown in the seventeenth century, professed to speak for the entire people, whom they regarded as the basis of each distinct branch or function of government. As mixed government was appropriate in hierarchical premodern society, separation of powers was appropriate in America—a society so thoroughly middle class and open that compared to England it was a classless society.

The constitutions adopted in 1776 showed the swift conversion of Americans to the separation of powers as an organizing principle of government. Republican teaching did not logically require the separation-of-powers structure. Yet given the abolition of monarchy and the absence of aristocracy and inherited legal privilege, the theory of separation was the only available doctrine on which to base constitutions of liberty. Thus the Virginia constitution of 1776 stated that "The legislative, executive and judiciary departments shall be separate and distinct, so that neither exercises the powers properly belonging to the other: nor shall any person exercise the powers of more than one of them at the same time." Five other states established governments on this basis, all of them for the most part rejecting the idea of checks and balances, or *sharing of power,* required by the theory of mixed government. In its theoretically pure or radical form the separation principle placed all legislative power in a single body—a unicameral legislature. (Bicameralism, characteristic of mixed government, provided for sharing of the lawmaking power by two legislative houses, each drawn from a distinct social order.) In its pure form, too, the separation doctrine denied any lawmaking power to the executive, who was simply to enforce and administer the law. In revolutionary America actual experience with the separation of powers ranged from radical or pure application with a unicameral legislature and plural executive (Pennsylvania) to substantial though not complete acceptance in most of the states that employed the principle (Virginia, North Carolina, Georgia, Maryland, New York, Massachusetts, New Hampshire, South Carolina, Delaware) to no acceptance at all (Rhode Island, Connecticut, and New Jersey, which retained their colonial constitutional structures).

The separation-of-powers principle served much the same purpose in revolutionary America as it had in the English Civil War: to assert the supremacy of the people's representatives in lawmaking and, by denying the executive any share in this highest and most important power of government, to confine him to a merely administrative function. Republican government was to be grounded in the action and consent of the people, and the separation theory was a means of establishing this popular control. It was a democratizing instrument which carried to completion the drive of the colonial assembly for legislative hegemony. Moreover, in conjunction with the fear of executive power inculcated by the eighteenth-century opposition writers, it resulted in the transformation of the executive office.

Instead of possessing a wide range of prerogative powers that placed him at the very center of the government, as in the colonial mixed constitution, the governor (or president or executive council) under the separation of powers merely enforced the rules made by the legislature. Accordingly, the state constitutions either denied the executive a veto power outright (eleven states) or permitted him to exercise it in restricted form; where the veto was provided for, it was reversible by a simple majority of the legislature. The method of appointing the governor was a second key issue in defining the executive office. Where the separation principle was more thoroughly applied, the executive was chosen by the people, with a view toward making the office independent of the legislature. In some states, however, fear that the executive office might become more than merely administrative caused constitution makers to entrust election of the governor to the legislature. The same fear led to either a categorical denial or severe restriction of the governor's appointive power. In accordance with the long-standing belief that the greatest danger to liberty lay in executive corruption—that is, the undermining of civic virtue and the independence of the people's deputies through the distribution of patronage, emoluments, bribes, etc.—many state constitutions gave the power of appointment to the legislature exclusively. In some states the governor had limited appointment powers, but in none did he possess the power exclusively. The state constitutions also made provision for impeachment of the governor, although this was a checks-and-balances device not strictly consistent with the separation principle. Its inclusion further expressed fear of a strong executive, as did the provision for short terms in office and restrictions on the reelection of the executive. The only element of the prerogative substantially retained by the governor was the power of pardon and reprieve.

Related to the transformation of the governor's office was the abolition of the governor's council. Its lawmaking powers were assumed by the upper house of the legislature, leaving it a strictly advisory body in the executive branch. So diminished was the role of the governor that he was viewed essentially as first among equals on the executive council. The council, moreover, was elected by the people or the legislature rather than appointed by the governor, as in the colonial constitution.

The redistribution of power resulting from the transformation of the governor's office located the constitutional center of gravity in the new state governments in the legislative branch. After decades of struggle against the royal governor, the colonial assemblies, like Parliament in the seventeenth century, seized the opportunity that a revolutionary situation presented to assert their supremacy in lawmaking. This highest power in government now belonged exclusively, or nearly so, to the people's representatives. Along with it went technical parliamentary powers that the colonial assemblies had long struggled to acquire, such as the right to establish regular meetings, determine their own membership by judging the elections and qualifications of members, and control their own internal organization. Under the separation of powers the executive was denied the power to prorogue and dissolve the legislature and to reject the speaker, important prerogatives of the colonial governor.

In the first few years of government based on the separation of powers, it was not clear what the limits of legislative authority were. The purpose of the separation theory was to prevent any single branch of government from controlling the other two. Legislative supremacy in lawmaking was not to be a warrant for supremacy over government in general, as though the state legislatures inherited the sovereignty of Parliament. Yet in practice, under the pressure of political events, there proved to be few effective limitations on the state legislatures. In the volatile setting of interest-group and factional politics, legislative power was used in ways that many people considered improper—for example, to set aside judicial decisions in disputes over property. It soon became apparent that a proper separation of powers required certain institutional checks and balances, and this need to curtail state legislative power became a central issue of constitutional reform in the 1780s. These facts do not justify the conclusion, however, that the separation of powers was not taken seriously in the first state constitutions. In fact the state legislatures' bold exercise of power and their eclipse of the executive were evidence of the impact the separation-of-powers theory had on revolutionary constitutionalism.

The Problem of Representation

In addition to the distribution of power between the legislature and executive, the traditional colonial system of representation underwent change during the Revolution. In the colonial period towns and counties were the constituent units in the assembly. Population did not affect the apportionment of deputies, since representation was conceived of in corporate rather than individualistic terms. In a few states after 1776, however, the constituent basis of representation shifted to population and property. In Massachusetts, for example, commercial interests from coastal Essex County resented their lack of political power relative to the agrarian counties in the western part of the state. The proportion of taxes the county paid was greater than the share of power it enjoyed in the General Court under the system of equal town representation. Accordingly, in the Massachusetts constitution of 1780, Essex County delegates obtained the representation of numbers and property. Each town would still receive a minimal number of deputies, but more populous towns would have more representatives in the lower house. In the state senate, on the other hand, property was recognized. Counties were the basic unit of representation here, but they were awarded representatives according to the taxes paid. These changes expressed the idea that the constituent elements of government were people and property, considered in a liberal individualist rather than corporatist sense.

This conjunction of values reflected the connection that existed in republican philosophy between liberty and property: The latter was the necessary basis of the former. Population was a rational basis for representation because it was considered an accurate indication of the wealth and economic power of an area. If property interests were to be recognized in the structure of government, it made sense to give a more prominent place to the principle of the numerical majority.

American representation also changed during the Revolution as a result of suffrage reform. As noted previously, because of the broad-based character of the electorate, actual rather than virtual representation tended to exist in the colonies. Yet as long as suffrage was restricted, an element of virtual representation persisted. Only persons with a sufficient property interest were permitted to vote, on the theory that only in this way could there be assurance of the personal and civic virtue needed to sustain political independence and concern for the common good. Yet such an arrangement resembled English representation: Those who did not vote were thought to be virtually represented by those who did. Once the principle of no taxation without actual representation gained currency in the prerevolutionary years, however, it was inevitable—given the factional nature of American politics—that it should be introduced into local politics.

Accordingly, in several states the process of constitution making included attempts to extend actual representation by broadening the suffrage. If all men were created equal, and if government rested on public opinion and the consent of the governed, then it followed that the implicit consent of virtual representation was inadequate. Reformers argued that all men, or at least more than were presently permitted to do so, ought actually to vote. Under this natural rights rationale, reinforced by political pressure to extend rights to men being called on to fight a war, suffrage reform proceeded in Pennsylvania, New Hampshire, New Jersey, Georgia, and Maryland. In general the change consisted in substituting a taxpayer qualification for the freehold qualification of colonial times. Although liberalization of the suffrage resulted in only a modest increase in the number of voters (because widespread distribution of property already created a broad electorate), and although property was not altogether rejected as a relevant consideration, the reforms that took place were a significant step toward universal manhood suffrage.

The changes that occurred in American representation make it clear that republican constitutionalism had genuine, if limited, democratizing effects. The struggle against imperial policy, carried on in the pluralistic arena of colonial politics, stimulated political awareness and drew new men into public life who challenged the traditional colonial elite. The protest against England also provoked a degree of hostility toward authority in general, which to some extent undermined the spirit of deference that prevailed in colonial politics. Furthermore, the principles of equality and natural rights employed in the struggle against England could be and were used to seek changes in American society. Yet this is not to say, as some historians have argued, that deep-seated class conflict characterized the American Revolution.

Interest groups—merchants, lawyers, planters, farmers, artisans, and others—disagreed in their views of sound public policy and, in their disagreement, hurled charges of "aristocracy" and "democracy" against each other with deceptive certainty. In fact, however, no objective social and economic reality, such as would warrant describing the struggle as a class conflict, divided them. On the contrary, once the restraining influence of British authority was removed, there occurred a proliferation and intensification of group conflict. Intended to influence public opinion, it not only drew new men into politics, but also spread throughout the society ideas such as equality, natural rights, and popular sovereignty that appealed to a large and continually expanding electorate. Conflict there undeniably was in American politics, but it occurred in an open and materially abundant social order. Moreover—and this is the point of significance for constitutional history—conflict ran in channels marked out by agreed-upon principles of government. Republicanism based on the natural rights philosophy and the separation of powers were the central ideas, and despite disagreement about their application, almost all Americans supported them as the basis of the new political order.

The chief significance of revolutionary constitutionalism, then, was to create limited governments that would safeguard individual liberty and property as well as promote the common good. Particularly expressive of this purpose were the bills of rights that revolutionary leaders included in most of the state constitutions. Drawn from English history and the colonial experience, the bills of rights protected jury trial, moderate bail, fair procedure in criminal cases, and freedom of speech, press, and religious worship; prohibited unreasonable searches and seizures; forbade taxation without the consent and representation of the people; espoused the principle of a free militia; and upheld the right of resistance to arbitrary rule and oppression. Of special interest in the bills of rights was the assertion of the doctrine of natural rights and the social-contract origins of the state, in contrast to the customary basis of rights in English law. It is important to note that the bills of rights were not judicially enforceable legal guarantees, in the nature of twentieth-century civil liberties law. Possessing the status of political principle rather than legally obligatory rules of action limiting government, bills of rights could be suspended by the state legislature when the public safety required it. Nevertheless, they expressed the idea of protecting individual liberty against government encroachment.

The Articles of Confederation

While revolutionary leaders dealt with the problems of constitutionalism in the states, the necessity of conducting the war against England led them to create a continental union that received definite form in the Articles of Confederation. Although the Declaration of Independence stated that the colonies were free and independent states, it also described them as "the united States of America," and referred to Americans as "one people." The Articles of Confederation accordingly reflected the idea that in joining together for the purpose of achieving their independence as individual sovereignties, the states created a new political unit which expressed a nascent sense of American nationality. It is also true that the Confederation in many respects acted like a government in coordinating the states' united effort against England. Nevertheless, the Confederation was not in any systematic or comprehensive sense an authentic government possessing the sanction of law and the power of command; it was at best a quasi-government. Moreover, the spirit of nationality it embodied was expressed constitutionally in the dispersal of power that the establishment of state governments signified, rather than in any provision for unitary sovereignty such as is usually identified with the modern nation-state.

The Articles of Confederation are often described as the first constitution of the United States. Insofar as they set forth a plan of federal organization that divided sovereignty between the states and a central authority, thus anticipating the Constitution of 1787, the description is apt. Yet, recalling the republican spirit of '76, it cannot be said that the Articles were truly or primarily an attempt to implement revolutionary constitutionalism. In a broad political sense the United States may have been a republic from 1776 to 1787, considering that public opinion and sectional and interest-group pressures influenced the actions of Congress. In a legal and constitutional sense, however, the Confederation did not possess a republican form of government—that is, a government based on the people as constituent power and organized and conducted according to the principles of revolutionary constitutionalism. The Articles were concerned with relations among states rather than with the proper balance between power and liberty in the constitutional structure.

The proximate origins of the Confederation lay in the formation of the First Continental Congress in 1774. The ambivalence concerning the true nature of the Confederation that characterized it throughout its fifteen-year history—its status as a quasi-government—was evident at the outset of the revolutionary crisis. Congress exercised real political power but, carefully respecting the fact that it represented autonomous colonies or states, it left to them the performance of authentic acts of sovereignty in relation to individual citizens. Congress clearly directed military and diplomatic efforts pointing to independence, for example, and in May 1776, declaring British authority at an end, instructed the colonies to form regular constitutional governments. But it did all of this as a kind of superintending advisory body communicating the consensus of patriotic opinion and recommending governmental action. It was for the states to enact laws punishing treason, exacting loyalty oaths, levying taxes, regulating trade, and so on.

Pertinent in this connection is the question of citizenship. If we regard determination of the qualifications and admission to citizenship as a test of governmental sovereignty, it is apparent that Congress was not sovereign. The Confederation did not naturalize aliens, nor was it the object of loyalty oaths and affirmations. In June 1776 Congress adopted a resolution providing a general definition of citizenship, but that definition specified only state citizenship. It proposed that all free persons residing in a state be regarded as citizens of that state. The states accordingly naturalized aliens, and it was to the states that allegiance was due. An idea of national citizenship existed, but it was shadowy and amorphous at best.[1]

---

1. The comity clause of the Articles of Confederation (Article IV, Section I) expressed the idea of national citizenship. It stated that "the free inhabitants of each of these states . . . shall be entitled to all privileges and immunities of free citizens in the several states; and the people of each state shall have free ingress and regress to and from any other state, and shall enjoy therein all the privileges of trade and commerce, subject to the same duties, impositions, and restrictions,

The nature of the Confederation was established in 1774, when the First Continental Congress decided that each colony would have one vote in the conduct of congressional affairs. This action resolved the question of how the Confederation should be constituted; and although the matter was raised again in subsequent years, no different approach was ever agreed on. In 1774 delegates from some of the larger states proposed to base representation on the population, wealth, and general weight or importance of the several states as measured by various economic criteria. That this approach would have placed the Confederation on a direct popular basis—that is, the people of the United States considered as a single national entity—cannot be assumed, for the people represented in Congress could be merely the people of the several states. Congress rejected this method of representation, however, principally because in the crisis that existed in 1774 it was not feasible to determine the relative weight of each state before taking action. Moreover, the data for making this kind of determination were not available. Needless to say, the decision for state equality, which made it difficult to ratify the Articles and impossible to amend them, was profoundly important.

At the same time that it issued the Declaration of Independence, the congress began to draft Articles of Confederation, a set of rules for the cooperation of the states in matters of common concern. A proposed version of the Articles was debated in July 1776, in the spring of 1777, and still further in November 1777, when, amid pressing war matters, it was adopted by Congress and sent to the states for approval. In March 1781 endorsement of the Articles by the Maryland legislature fulfilled the requirement of unanimity in the ratification process and enabled the Articles formally to go into effect.

Congress early acquired certain functions and responsibilities in relation to the states. In the opening months of 1776, for example, it seized the political initiative in urging the colonial assemblies to repudiate British authority and organize state governments. Subsequently, it defined treason and citizenship, and supervised the military and diplomatic phases of the war for independence. So far from projecting a new relationship between Congress and the states, the Articles of Confederation confirmed the existing *ad hoc* pattern and translated the political power of Congress into formal terms. By the time the Articles assumed final form, however, Congress possessed less influence than during the crisis of 1776.

The first version of the Articles of Confederation, known as the Dickinson draft, reflected the stronger political position Congress enjoyed at the moment of separation from England. It gave the Confederation exclusive power to settle disputes concerning boundaries, jurisdictions, and other matters between

---

as the inhabitants thereof respectively." However, the precise legal effect of this language was highly uncertain. It appeared to provide that a noncitizen (inhabitant) in a state could acquire in another state rights of citizenship not available to him in his state of residence.

the states, and said the states could retain their local laws and regulate internal police in all matters that did not interfere with the Articles. This language suggested that the Articles might become a standard against which the exercise of state powers would be measured, and implied the existence of an undefined, residual sphere of power in Congress that could be used to encroach on state jurisdiction. Nevertheless, because the Dickinson draft fully recognized state equality in representation and voting, and because it denied Congress taxing and commerce powers, it can hardly be regarded as a centralizing instrument. So widespread and pronounced was the belief in state sovereignty, however, and so keen the apprehension that one section would use a stronger Confederation to impose its own political and social views on the others, that a reaction set in against the modestly integrating tendency of the Dickinson draft. The provisions alluded to were struck out and a ringing assertion of state sovereignty added. Article II now announced: "Each state retains its sovereignty, freedom and independence, and every Power, Jurisdiction, and right, which is not by this confederation expressly delegated to the United States, in Congress assembled."

The inclusion of this language in the Articles of Confederation did not guarantee that the states would actually qualify as fully sovereign and independent governments in the sense of international law. In fact they did not, despite an inclination in this direction based on the assumption that the collapse of British authority had resulted in a transfer of sovereignty to them. Yet if the sovereign power of the states was incomplete, that of Congress was far more so. If not entirely chimerical, its formal sovereignty was insufficiently developed to permit it effectively to fulfill the responsibilities assigned to it by events themselves or by the formal plan of union. The central fact of constitutional history in this period, accordingly, is a division of sovereignty between the states and the Confederation, according to an as yet imperfectly realized federal principle. This division of power can be seen in express provisions of the Articles and in the actions of Congress during and after the war.

The distribution of specific powers between the states and the Confederation presented little difficulty. Since the Confederation was to be a league or alliance rather than a government, there was no thought of giving it powers of taxation and commercial regulation, except in relation to Indian tribes. It is often said that Americans denied these critical powers to the Confederation in a fit of irrational pique that reflected their hostility to England rather than sober judgment. Certainly, anti-English sentiment abounded, but the point is that with the British presence removed Americans could organize the empire as all along they thought it should be. And their preference clearly excluded the exercise of taxing and local commercial regulation bearing on individual citizens. More than that, the American conception of imperial organization categorically denied the central authority any legislative power. Here language is revealing. Congress, according to the Articles, could make resolutions, determinations, and regulations, but not laws. Only the states, in which the people as constituent power were represented, had legislatures—and executive and judicial establishments as well.

As a superintending authority in matters that concerned all the states, Congress had an array of powers similar to those of Parliament and the crown under the old empire. Thus it was given authority to make war and peace, send and receive ambassadors, enter into treaties and alliances, coin money, fix the standard of weights and measures throughout the United States, establish a post office, regulate Indian affairs, and appoint officers and make rules for military forces in the service of the United States. Congress could also establish rules for captures on land or water, grant letters of marque and reprisal, appoint courts for the trial of piracies, and settle on appeal disputes between the states. On the other hand, despite the affirmation of state sovereignty, the states were expressly prohibited from declaring war, making treaties, and so on. And they were enjoined to abide by the determinations of Congress and observe the Articles of Confederation.

The division of authority and responsibility evident in the Articles can be seen also in the political history of the Confederation. It is apparent that in many respects the states shaped policy as sovereign governments, though not in a comprehensive way. By the same token, for all its institutional weaknesses, the Confederation in some respects acted like a real government. Most conspicuous was its conduct of the war and diplomacy. But it also vindicated its authority in a keenly disputed nonmilitary sphere—the problem of the western lands. This question was of great importance because it involved fixing the boundaries of states with claims to the west, forming a policy of land distribution, and determining the principles of settlement that would shape the future of civil society in a large part of the country. In a larger political sense the West had a potentially nationalizing influence that could hold the Confederation together.

The Dickinson draft of the Articles gave Congress power to settle the states' conflicting western claims, dispose of lands not held by any state or purchased from the Indians, and create territories for the formation of new states. The objections of states with land claims—Virginia, Pennsylvania, Massachusetts, New York, Connecticut—caused the elimination of these provisions, however, and the Articles as approved by Congress in 1777 merely stated that no state shall be deprived of territory for the benefit of the United States. Yet this stipulation proved unacceptable to states without land claims, and eventually they were able to force a change. In 1779 Congress passed a resolution asking states with western claims to suspend land sales and transfer title to all trans-Allegheny lands to the Confederation. A more far-reaching resolution was adopted in 1780, which proposed that all lands that were ceded to Congress should be disposed of for the common benefit of the United States and settled and formed into republican states and admitted to the Union. Opinion having shifted against them, the landed states ceded their claims, and Maryland, which had withheld its approval of the Articles over this issue, finally ratified the plan of confederation in March 1781. Subsequently, Congress adopted the Ordinance of 1785 and the Northwest Ordinance of 1787, establishing a territorial policy based on the principle of national supervision of state making with guaranteed admission to the Union.

Congress not only acted in some matters like a real government, but it also served as a forum for the expression of opinions and interests that to some extent achieved the effect of a republican government. With the New England, middle, and southern states voting in blocs, the clearest source of political identity in Congress was sectionalism. Economic interests that were dependent on geographical as well as social and demographic differences gave specific content to sectionalism, as did variations in the way puritanical New Englanders, commercial-minded middle-states men, and slavery-protecting Southerners viewed republicanism. States also acted on the basis of their size, population, and wealth—that is, as large or small states.

Yet if republican tendencies found expression in congressional politics, the organization of the Confederation on the principle of state equality ignored the forms and procedures of republicanism in a way that presented insuperable obstacles to the successful conduct of continental affairs. It may be conceded that the Articles were adequate as a framework for cooperation among the states. They even contained provisions of a genuinely nationalizing, integrating tendency, such as the comity clause guaranteeing the inhabitants of each state all privileges and immunities of citizens in the several states, and the provision requiring each state to give full faith and credit to the judicial proceedings of the other states. But the Confederation did not—and probably could not— overcome the structural defects that denied it the formal attributes of a republican government. Constituted as it was, it could not transcend its nature as an alliance.

James Madison accurately summarized the difficulty when he observed that the Confederation suffered not from a want of specific powers, but of power in general. Congress lacked power—the legal sanction of command— because it did not rest on the people as constituent power. Nor did its organization conform to the separation of powers, the new structural principle of American constitutionalism. Embodying the separation-of-powers doctrine and based on direct popular consent, the state governments were both republican in their political character and legally authoritative. The problem with the Confederation thus was not an insufficiently national outlook where its responsibilities were concerned, but a lack of republican power and authority in its formal constitution.

SIX

Constitutional Reform and the Federal Convention of 1787

THE WEAKNESS OF THE CONFEDERATION stimulated numerous reform efforts in the 1780s. That it might more effectively discharge its responsibilities, it seemed necessary, at a minimum, to strengthen Congress by giving it a source of revenue independent of the states. Continental-minded statesmen with an interest in commercial development, such as Alexander Hamilton and Robert Morris, led the way in proposing such reforms, but most state-based politicians agreed that reinforcement of Confederate authority was imperative. Nevertheless, by itself the problem of a weak central authority could not command the attention and support needed to bring about change. Only when the prospect of a stronger Union served the additional purpose of improving, if not actually preserving, republican government in the states did national constitutional reform succeed. In an atmosphere marked by apprehension over the instability of the state governments, as well as by discouragement at the commercial, diplomatic, and military weakness of the Confederation, the Constitutional Convention met at Philadelphia in May 1787.

There was no denying that Congress was embarrassingly weak. Most of Congress's difficulties between 1776 band 1787 were connected in some degree with its financial incompetence, in turn ascribable to its lack of taxing power and the habitual failure of the states to meet their assessments promptly. During the Revolutionary War, the army went chronically unpaid, while in 1783 the officers encamped at Newburg, New York, threatened mutiny in attempt to recover back salaries. In despair the Continental Congress resorted to the printing presses to finance itself, issuing, by 1780, some $40,000,000 in paper money, the entire issue ultimately being virtually repudiated. Also Congress borrowed several million between 1778 and 1783 from the French and Dutch governments; during the Confederation period it was unable even to

meet the interest on these loans, and interest and principal accumulated until
the national debt was refunded under the Constitution. Financial weakness
after 1783 also made it difficult to protect the great trans-Allegheny wilderness
region acquired in the Peace of 1783, for Congress was utterly without the
resources to garrison the West properly in order to protect settlers, keep out
British and Spanish intruders, and control the Indian tribes. As a result,
Britain, contrary to the provisions of peace, retained her forts in the Northwest
Territory, both Spain and England intrigued to separate the West from the new
republic, and Indians ravaged the settlements in Kentucky and Tennessee.

Another important series of difficulties arose out of congressional impo-
tence in the field of foreign and interstate commerce. It was almost impossible
for Congress to negotiate commercial treaties with foreign states, in part
because they realized that Congress could not guarantee compliance by the
states with any commercial policy agreed to. When John Adams, American
minister to England, sought a commercial treaty with Britain, Foreign Secretary Charles James Fox contemptuously suggested that ambassadors from the
thirteen states ought to be present, since Congress had no authority over the
subject. Recognizing that Congress was impotent to impose a retaliatory commercial policy, Britain closed the West Indies to American trade, and discriminated against Yankee merchantmen in her own ports. Within the Confederation, the various states carried on retaliatory trade wars against one
another, Congress being powerless to interfere. New York, for example, prof-
iting by her port of entry, laid duties upon incoming commerce destined for
New Jersey and Connecticut, while these states in return taxed interstate
commerce with New York.

Further numerous difficulties arose out of the inability of Congress to
compel obedience by the states and individuals to acts of Congress and treaties.
The weakness of Confederation foreign policy was in part due to this fact.
Congress was unable to compel the states to execute the provisions in the treaty
of peace with respect to the return of Tory property and the payment of
merchant debts, and Britain used this as an excuse to retain control of the
Northwest forts. France and Holland also hesitated to negotiate treaties with
a nation that could not meet its commitments.

The Problem of Excessive State Power

While Congress conducted continental affairs in a fitful manner, the
actions of the state legislatures raised doubts in the minds of many about the
future of republican government in America. In the flush of revolutionary
enthusiasm Americans gave their elected deputies virtually exclusive control
over lawmaking under the separation-of-powers doctrine. In effect they regarded the state legislatures as inheritors of the sovereignty that Parliament
had attempted to exercise. At the same time, however, the potentially conflict-

ing idea of popular sovereignty took hold. This was derived from belief in the people as constituent power not only capable of creating government *de novo,* but also justified in acting outside of established institutions should government prove repressive or irresponsible. From both sources came political tensions and anxieties that spurred the movement for constitutional reform in the 1780s.

On the eve of the Federal Convention a popular uprising in Massachusetts known as Shays's Rebellion caused alarm that unruly mobs, falsely acting in the name of popular sovereignty, might bring republican government to ruin. Demanding inflationary legislation, armed bands of farmers closed the courts in western Massachusetts and even threatened to lay siege to Boston to force the General Court to grant credit relief. State officials dealt with the crisis without Confederation assistance, but not because they did not desire it; Congress simply lacked the ability to respond to a crisis of this sort. The event made many people aware of the need for a stronger central authority to support state governments against internal subversion, and was directly responsible for the inclusion in the Constitution of a guarantee of republican government to each state in the Union. More vexing than the people acting "out of doors" in defiance of established authority, however, was the tendency toward unlimited legislative power in the states.

Although at first the scope of legislative power was understandably imprecise under the separation-of-powers doctrine, by the mid-1780s much of this uncertainty was gone. Men professed to know the limits of legislative power, and concluded with equal certainty that those limits had been breached. In several states lawmakers usurped power thought properly to belong to the executive or judicial branch of the government. Legislatures vacated judicial proceedings, modified court judgments, authorized appeals, reopened controversies, expounded the law, and granted exemptions from the standing law. They also passed legislation authorizing the emission of paper money, suspending actions on debts or permitting them to be paid in kind, and declaring paper money a legal tender. Supported by agrarian majorities, these measures reflected the vigorous factionalism of American political life. To unsympathetic contemporaries, however, they threatened individual property rights and public virtue. Troublesome, too, was the variability of state legislation. State legislatures passed laws one year which they repealed the next, thereby producing political instability and undermining public confidence in republican government. Added to more familiar grievances such as the failure of the states to meet their financial quotas, their mutual hostility in matters of trade and taxation, and their encroachment on congressional authority, state legislative excesses gave Confederation reform the practical significance it needed to enable it to succeed.

The movement for constitutional reform that culminated in the Philadelphia Convention in 1787 began with changes in state government during the later stages of the Revolution. Experience showed that the separation of powers in its pure or radical form did not effectively limit legislative power. The solution to this problem was to give the executive and judicial branches greater leverage vis-à-vis the legislature by instituting checks and balances derived from the older theory of mixed government. Most apparent was the need to strengthen the executive by giving him a share of the lawmaking power in the form of a qualified veto; by placing his election directly in the hands of the people so as to make him independent of the legislature; and by restoring the power to appoint subordinate administrators which had belonged to the royal governor. The New York constitution of 1777 and the Massachusetts constitution of 1780 contained these provisions for checks and balances. *The Essex Result,* a political pamphlet written in support of the Massachusetts constitution, expressed the rationale of the separation of powers, modified by the addition of checks and balances: "Each branch is to be independent, and further, to be so balanced, and be able to exert such check upon the others, as will preserve it from a dependence on, or a union with them." By the time of the Philadelphia convention widespread agreement existed on the need for checks and balances within the framework of the separation of powers.

Bicameralism, in most states a relic of mixed government that reflected the force of institutional habit more than rational design, assumed new importance in the 1780s as a further restraint on legislative power. In the radical version of the separation of powers a single-chamber legislature was seen as the appropriate forum for the expression of the homogeneous public opinion that republican theory posited. Although only Pennsylvania had a unicameral assembly, republican theory in the early stages of the Revolution offered no rationale for the two-chamber arrangement that the other states retained from their colonial constitution. As the pressure of factional politics grew more intense, however, and legislatures aggrandized power, bicameralism recommended itself as a barrier to precipitate action.

An additional reason for bicameralism lay in the distinction between property and numbers that was coming to characterize American representation. No one doubted that in a republican society it was essential for the people to express their views in the legislature. But given the danger of popular majorities overriding minority rights, there was reason to give property interests representation also. A solution lay in representing population in the lower chamber and property in the upper, as in the Massachusetts constitution of 1780. As checks and balances were derived from the theory of mixed government, so the introduction of property and numbers as constitutional considerations represented an adaptation in the American setting of the older mixed-government idea that the distinct orders of society ought to have formal recognition in the structure of government.

Still another change in state constitutionalism that anticipated reform at the continental level concerned the judiciary. At the height of the Revolution the chief constitutional difficulty lay in redefining the relationship between the executive and legislature. Beyond the settlement of private disputes, the role of the judiciary under the separation of powers was as yet unclear. As legislatures extended their power, however, their political opponents turned to the courts as a means of restricting them. The basic purpose of the new American conception of constitutionalism was to limit legislative power. Given a written constitution as supreme law, an independent judiciary as posited in the separation of powers, and the traditional assumption that courts had a responsibility to declare the law, a rational basis existed for judicial review. It was plausible to argue, in other words, that courts ought to declare the meaning of the constitution and determine when legislation transgressed constitutional limits.

Although the earliest state cases involving judicial review contained technical ambiguities, they reflected a tendency to seek limits on legislative power by holding lawmakers accountable to the fundamental law. *Holmes* v. *Walton,* a New Jersey case of 1780, involved an appeal to the Supreme Court from a trial under a state law of 1778 for forfeiture of property taken in trade with the enemy. The law in question provided for trial of small causes (those involving less than £10) by six-man juries in apparent violation of the guarantee of twelve-man jury trial in the Constitution of 1776. The difficulty with the precedent was that the *Walton* case itself was not a "small cause," and the Court apparently reversed the trial court because the latter had violated the law itself as much as because six-man juries violated the Constitution. The New Jersey assembly, however, in a strenuous protest indicated that it considered the Court actually to have declared the law void.

In the more famous case of *Trevett* v. *Weeden* (1786), the Rhode Island Superior Court went to the verge of specifically declaring unconstitutional the state's recently enacted paper-money force act. Technically, however, the judges merely refused to entertain an action for damages under the law on the ground that the act was "internally repugnant," in that it contradicted itself in providing for trials without jury "according to the law of the land." It is quite clear, nonetheless, that they took this position because they thought the law violated the property guarantees of the old charter. *Bayard* v. *Singleton,* a North Carolina case of 1787, was an even clearer instance of judicial review. Here the Supreme Court held unconstitutional a law of 1785 requiring a trial court to dismiss forthwith any action for the recovery of property under an earlier Tory confiscation law, on the ground that the statute in question violated the constitutional guarantee that "every citizen had undoubtedly a right to a decision of his property by trial by jury."

We must be careful not to exaggerate the extent to which these exercises of judicial power anticipated the institution of judicial review as it developed in the late nineteenth and twentieth centuries. A few judges and constitutional thinkers, realizing the implications of the new constitutionalism conceived of in the Revolution, were seeking to establish only that courts could legitimately refuse to enforce concededly unconstitutional acts of the legislature. The idea that courts could "interpret" the Constitution, the essence of the modern theory of judicial review, formed no part of this judicial action. Although viewed as fundamental law, the Constitution was conceived more as a body of fixed political principles, in the nature of a social contract, rather than as an ordinary legal instrument. Nevertheless, judicial nonenforcement of clearly unconstitutional acts was a significant limit on the tendency toward legislative supremacy that emerged in the states in the 1780s.

Republicanism and the Constitution

Like constitutional reformers in the states, the members of the Constitutional Convention sought to limit state legislative power. It is often said that the framers' great achievement was to create a truly national government in place of the decentralized Confederation. Clearly, the Constitution adjusted and improved the relationship between the states and the central government, creating "a more perfect Union." The more significant change, however, concerned not the scope of the new government—on that score the Confederation was satisfactorily national—but rather the legal sanction and power of command that it acquired as an authentic sovereign government. This sovereign capability depended on the fact that the federal government derived its authority from the people as constituent power. It was, in short, a genuine republican government. And although the political values of the Revolution may seem to have precluded any other outcome, the creation of an effective republican system depended heavily on constitutional changes that had taken place in the states.

The framers of the Constitution resolved the crisis of republicanism which had its source in state legislative excesses by erecting a new layer of republican government at the continental level. This new government formed a counterweight to and in a relative sense restricted the power of the states. The framers accomplished this end by denying certain powers to the states and by giving the federal government broad powers to encourage national economic unity and integration. The guiding principle of the convention, in Madison's words, was to provide a republican remedy for the diseases most incident to republican government.

Proximate steps leading to the Federal Convention began in 1785, when Virginia and Maryland signed an agreement settling a long-standing dispute over commercial regulation of the Potomac. The Maryland legislature subsequently proposed a general commercial convention to include Delaware and Pennsylvania, and Virginia suggested that the invitation be extended to all the states for the purpose of considering a common interstate policy. The convention met at Annapolis, Maryland, in September 1786. Although delegates from only five states were present, Alexander Hamilton and James Madison used the occasion to call for a new convention to be held at Philadelphia in May of the following year, "to render the constitution of the Federal Government adequate to the exigencies of the Union." Congress was initially too jealous of its power to endorse the call, but eventually did so after every state except Rhode Island approved it.

The convention met at Philadelphia in May 1787 with fifty-five delegates from seven states in attendance. (By July twelve states were represented.) It was decided at the outset that voting would be by states, and that a majority of the states present must decide any question. The Virginia delegation had prepared a plan of government that served as the starting point for the convention's deliberations. Referred to the committee of the whole in order to permit informal discussion of its provisions, the plan was debated from May 31 to June 19, during which time the committee examined it point by point, voting to accept, reject, or modify each item it contained. From June 19 to July 26 the full convention debated the report of the committee of the whole, and then gave twenty-three resolutions on which agreement had been reached to a five-man committee on detail. This committee on August 6 reported a draft constitution of twenty-three articles, which was the subject of discussion for several weeks. Early in August a committee on unfinished business settled certain matters, including the method of choosing the president, and on September 8 a committee of style was named to prepare the final draft of the Constitution.

The Virginia Plan provided for a legislative body of two chambers, the lower house to be elected by the people of the respective states, and the upper house to be chosen by the lower house from nominations submitted by the state legislatures. The powers of Congress were to be those enjoyed under the Articles of Confederation, with the important addition of the right "to legislate in all cases in which the separate States are incompetent." The executive was to be chosen by the legislature for an unspecified term and was to be ineligible for reelection. The executive, together with a portion of the national judiciary, was to constitute a Council of Revision, with an absolute veto over acts of the legislature. A national judiciary was to be established, consisting of one or more supreme courts and such inferior tribunals as the legislature might determine upon. Federal judicial authority was to extend to all cases involving piracies and felonies on the high seas, captures from an enemy, foreigners or citizens of different states, collection of the national revenue, impeachment of national officers, and questions involving national peace and harmony.

The Virginia Plan offered a plainly centralist solution to the problem of federalism created under the Articles of Confederation. What was needed was some arrangement by which the central and state governments would each exercise effective jurisdiction unhampered within their respective spheres without intruding upon the functions entrusted to the other, and which would settle any disputes that might arise as to the extent of state or national power.

The Virginia Plan principally attempted to solve this problem by giving Congress a negative over state legislation. In language drafted and supported by Madison in particular, the plan empowered Congress "to negative all laws passed by the several States, contravening in the opinion of the National

Legislature the articles of Union." To reinforce the authority of the central government, the succeeding clause contemplated the coercion of a state, by force if necessary. Congress was authorized "to call forth the force of the Union against any member of the Union failing to fulfill its duty under the articles thereof." The negative over state legislation was similar to the power exercised by the Board of Trade over the colonial assemblies before the Revolution. But whereas the latter had operated as a subsequent check, Madison's negative was to occur previous to the legislation's taking effect. Its purpose was to make the national legislature in effect a supervisory branch of the state legislatures.

The Virginia Plan also gave Congress a broad and indefinite grant of legislative authority in all cases where the states were "incompetent." It is not clear from the phraseology whether the plan intended to give Congress the power to alter at will the extent of its authority and that of the states; at the very least, however, the plan would solve the problem of federalism by giving Congress the power to define the extent of its own authority and that of the states. There was to be but one check upon this power: The Council of Revision was authorized to examine "every act of a particular legislature before a negative thereon shall be final."

With the Virginia Plan before it, the convention went into a committee of the whole house. Immediately thereafter, the centralizers scored an important victory when, at the suggestion of Gouverneur Morris, Edmund Randolph moved the postponement of the first point in his plan in order to present a new resolution. This asserted that no "Union of the States merely federal" nor any "treaty or treaties among the whole or part of the States" would be sufficient. It concluded:

That a *national* government ought to be established consisting of a *supreme* Legislative, Executive and Judiciary.

The meaning of this resolution was clear. It went beyond any proposal to establish a federal state with limited powers in the central government. In the discussion that followed, Morris contended "that in all Communities there must be one supreme power, and one only," and proposed that this supreme power be lodged unequivocally in the national government. Several delegates objected to the proposal as meaning that state sovereignty was to be obliterated and replaced by a powerful national government. The resolution was nevertheless adopted, only Connecticut voting in the negative.

This was an astounding victory for centralization in a convention that had been commissioned merely to modify the Articles of Confederation. It put to rout at the very beginning proponents of state sovereignty and those who wished merely to patch up the Articles. Later the localists were to rally sufficiently to secure the formation of a government based upon the principles of divided sovereignty. But for the moment it appeared that the proponents of national sovereignty were in complete control and that any suggestions for preserving state autonomy would be swept aside.

The committee of the whole now took up the provisions of the Virginia Plan point by point. The composition of the legislature involved the most fundamental question the convention faced—namely, the basis on which the new government would be constituted. Would the constituent units be the states, represented equally by delegates chosen by the state legislatures, as the small-state group desired? Or would the constituent element be the people of the United States, choosing the members of both houses of the legislature through direct election and with representation in both chambers apportioned according to population, as the large-state group wished? The former method would retain the essential plan of the Confederation and imply state sovereignty; the latter would signify that the central government rested directly upon individuals rather than states and was truly sovereign in character.

The mode of election of national lawmakers was a subordinate issue in the composition of the legislature on which both sides showed a willingness to compromise. The small states accepted the proposal in the Virginia Plan for direct popular election of the lower house. But almost no one thought that the lower house should elect members of the upper, and a resolution to that effect was voted down 7 to 3 when it was first considered. John Dickinson of Delaware then moved on June 7 that the Senate be elected by the various state legislatures. In the debate that followed, Madison and James Wilson contended that authority in a truly national government ought to flow directly from the people, while Roger Sherman, speaking for the small-state faction, argued that representation of the states as such would maintain balance and harmony between the states and the national government. It was clear that the small states were prepared to insist upon representation of the states as such in at least one chamber, and at the end of the discussion, the convention adopted Dickinson's resolution unanimously.

Meanwhile, the convention attacked the more vital issue of whether representation in the two houses should be apportioned according to population or based upon state equality. Debate continued for some days, and at times became very heated. Madison and Wilson repeatedly insisted that in a proportional system, the people as such, rather than states, would be represented, and that on this basis the people of Delaware would have the same representation in Congress as would those of Pennsylvania or Virginia. They were nonetheless unable to quiet the apprehensions of the small-state faction that proportional representation would swallow up the existence of the small states, and Paterson proclaimed that his state would "rather submit to a monarch, to a despot, than to such a fate." Wilson impatiently struck back with the warning that "if New Jersey will not part with her Sovereignty, it is in vain to talk of government."

Many moderates in the small-state faction were in reality prepared to compromise on the issue of proportional versus equal representation, and to concede proportional representation in the lower house, insisting only upon state equality in the Senate. Sherman suggested this solution on June 11, at the opening of an important debate on the question.

However, the centralizers were at the moment in control of affairs, and they carried the day without compromise. Sherman's proposal was silently rejected, and immediately thereafter Rufus King moved that suffrage in the lower house ought to be "according to some equitable ration of representation." After some debate, the resolution was carried, 7 to 3, only New York, New Jersey, and Delaware opposing, with Maryland divided. Sherman thereupon moved that each state have one vote in the upper house. "Everything," he said, "depended upon this," since "the smaller states would never agree to the plan on any other principle than an equality of suffrage in this branch." In spite of this warning, the convention rejected his motion, 6 to 5, and then adopted by the same vote a resolution of Wilson and Hamilton that representation in the upper house be apportioned "according to the same rule as in the 1st branch."

Thus as the committee of the whole neared completion of its work, the centralizers had scored victories on three out of four points. They had won proportional representation in both chambers and popular election in the lower house, and had conceded only that state legislatures might still elect the Senate. Whether they could retain their gains, however, remained to be seen.

The New Jersey Plan

On June 15, the committee of the whole finished its discussion of the Virginia Plan and prepared to report the revised draft out upon the floor of the convention; but at this point the small-state party counterattacked powerfully. Their ranks had been augmented by the arrival of additional delegates from the small states, among them Luther Martin of Maryland, Gunning Bedford of Delaware, and John Lansing of New York, and they evidently felt that if the drift toward complete centralization was to be checked at all, it must be done then and there. Accordingly, William Paterson of New Jersey now asked permission to introduce an alternate plan, of which the small states approved and which was "purely federal" in principle as opposed to the centralizing Randolph Plan.

The New Jersey Plan was a modification of the Articles of Confederation. It would have expanded the powers of Congress by adding the right to tax and to regulate commerce. Curiously, the Virginia Plan failed to make specific provision for these two critically important powers, and their inclusion in the small-state proposal indicates that the key issue was not how strong the general government ought to be, but who would control it. Ultimately, the question was whether the existence of an authentic government at the continental level would jeopardize the continued vitality of the states. The small-state or states'-

rights delegates clearly supported a stronger central authority, but they insisted that institutional changes resulting in a stronger Union should rest on an affirmation of states' rights. Unless protected against congressional encroachment, the powers of the states, they believed, would be eroded and superseded through a consolidation of power in the central authority. To provide the necessary guarantee against this eventuality, the New Jersey Plan retained state equality in the legislature and created an executive directly subject to state control. It also granted the federal government the right to coerce recalcitrant states, a further indication of the small-state interest in creating a more potent central authority.

The New Jersey Plan showed that the basic division in the convention was not between centralizers and localists, but between centralizers like Madison, who at best thought the states might be retained merely as subordinate administrative units, and states'-rights men, who supported both state sovereignty and a stronger central government. The supremacy clause in the New Jersey Plan, which has often seemed a curious if not paradoxical part of the states'-rights counteroffensive, further illustrates the dual emphasis of the small-state outlook. The clause declared that all acts of Congress and treaties made under the authority of the United States "shall be the Supreme law of the respective States," so far as they relate to the states or their citizens. It also said that the state courts shall be bound by acts of Congress and U.S. treaties in their decisions. This provision subsequently proved to be the solution to the problem of federalism, an ironic outcome if one sees the small-states men merely as localists, yet appropriate if one considers their desire both to strengthen national authority and to guarantee the integrity of the states.

After sharp debate in the committee of the whole, the New Jersey Plan was voted down 7 to 3. Again the proponents of centralization had triumphed. Yet the small states, realizing that no plan could succeed without their support, were now determined to force a compromise between centralization and state sovereignty.

The modified Virginia Plan was reported from the committee of the whole on June 19. By large majorities the convention accepted popular election of the lower house and election of the upper chamber by state legislatures. But when on June 27 the convention touched upon the question of proportional representation versus state equality in the two chambers, all the differences between the large-state and small-state factions flared up again. Two days later the convention once again voted, six states to four, for proportional representation in the lower house. The moderates on both sides at once saw in this vote the possibility of compromise: The small-state faction would accept proportional representation in the lower house in return for state equality in the upper. Arguing for this solution, Oliver Ellsworth pointed out that "we were partly federal, partly national." The compromise would recognize both the unitary and federal elements and would mutually protect the large and small states against one another. The convention was not yet ready to accept this solution, however, but neither was it prepared to adopt the large-state view. On July 2 the question of proportional representation in the upper house was put, and the small-state faction deadlocked the vote, 5 to 5 (one state split its vote and hence was not counted).

The Great Compromise

At this point the convention appointed a committee of eleven, one man from each state, to devise a compromise. The committee consisted entirely of moderates or defenders of state sovereignty, and their report on July 5 was regarded by the centralizers as a setback. The committee recommended that in the lower house each state be allowed one member for every 40,000 inhabitants; that all bills for raising or appropriating money originate in the lower house without amendment by the upper; and that each state have an equal vote in the upper house. (It had already been decided that the Senate was to be elected by the legislatures of the several states.)

Up to this time the principal line of division in the convention was between large-state and small-state blocs, or centralizers and defenders of state sovereignty. Now, however, the politics of the convention became sectional, and it was sectional interests that led the delegates finally to accept the compromise recommended by the committee of eleven.

Important as the perception of large-state and small-state differences was with respect to population and area, the distinction also contained a sectional coloration. Although the large-state bloc included Massachusetts and Pennsylvania, four states in this group were southern: Virginia, North Carolina, South Carolina, and Georgia. The small-state group on the other hand was principally northern: Maryland, Delaware, New Jersey, New York, Connecticut, and New Hampshire. Furthermore, the average population of the large states, exclusive of heavily populated Virginia, was 307,000; of the small states, excluding tiny Delaware, it was 278,000, a relatively small difference. That sectional interests should lie barely below the surface of the large- versus small-state distinction is hardly surprising, moreover, when one considers that Confederation politics usually rested on conflicting regional interests.

In the convention debate over representation in the upper house of the national legislature, the large-state delegates had rested their case on the correctness of the republican principle of representation of individual citizens rather than states. Toward the end of June, however, sectional considerations emerged as a crucial factor in the delegates' thinking. The disposition and development of the western lands as part of the Union provided the focal point for this sectional concern.

Southerners looked to the West in an expansionist way. Led by Virginia, which had a long history of involvement in the Northwest and claimed large land holdings in what later became Kentucky, Southerners anticipated migration across the Appalachians and north of the Ohio, where they would build a society based on agrarian republican principles and preserving slavery. Delegates from the mid-Atlantic and New England states, however, representing commercial and professional interests, were hostile toward the prospect of western development, especially under southern auspices. They opposed the creation of new states in the West and the admission of these states to the Union on an equal basis with the original ones. Gouverneur Morris of Pennsylvania and Elbridge Gerry of Massachusetts, for example, argued that the Atlantic states ought to maintain control over the interior of the continent lest populous new western states undermine their power. Evidence of sectional thinking was apparent, too, in the delegates' reaction to a report in early July assigning representatives in the lower house on the basis of population. Suddenly, instead of seeing their states as large or small, members of the convention saw them as belonging to regional blocs.

The emergence of sectional attitudes did not by itself resolve the deadlock over representation in the upper legislative house. What assisted in preparing the way for the Great Compromise was action taken by the Confederation Congress, which was simultaneously in session in New York. Addressing itself to the issue that had provoked sectional deadlock at the convention—the disposition of the western lands—Congress effected a sectional compromise that pointed the way toward a solution of the problem in Philadelphia. It did so by adopting the Northwest Ordinance.

Although the Northwest Ordinance contained an anti-slavery provision that later figured prominently in abolitionist rhetoric and strategy, it represented a southern policy-making initiative. Its main effect was to integrate the West into the Union on terms beneficial to the South. Expansionist in outlook, Southerners hoped to people the West rapidly, create a number of states, and secure their admission to the Union on terms of equality with the original states. Southerners also desired to organize territorial government in the West to assist diplomatically in gaining access to the Ohio and Mississippi rivers as an outlet for commercial agriculture. In order to secure these objectives they were willing to permit the prohibition of slavery in territory north of the Ohio River, provided that a fugitive slave law operated in the area and provided further that slavery be permitted to expand into unorganized territory lying south of the Ohio. Southerners gave up their hope of creating ten new states in the Northwest, but they succeeded in reducing the length of the territorial period preceding statehood. The required population for statehood was set at 60,000, rather than one-thirteenth of the population of the original states, as previously agreed. For their part, Northerners gave up the idea of retaining permanent control over the West, which would have been difficult to do in any case, given the national commitment to republicanism. What the North got out of the compromise, besides the prohibition of slavery, was a limit on the number of states that could be formed in the old Northwest (no fewer than three nor more than five). And although Southerners were regarded as more expansionist, Northerners, too, could set their sights on the West and send emigrants there to replicate their own social institutions.

The accomplishment chiefly of southern delegates (with northern land speculators outside Congress also supplying much impetus), the Northwest Ordinance was a sectional compromise that went far toward resolving the thorny question of the disposition of the western lands that had emerged as a source of contention in Philadelphia. Given final form in Congress on July 11, with the help of four southern delegates who left the convention and traveled to New York so Congress would have a quorum, the ordinance was at once reported to the Philadelphia assemblage, where it appears to have assisted in settling the North-South conflict over the composition of the legislature. On July 16 the convention approved the Connecticut or Great Compromise by a 5–4–1 vote. Two states that had previously supported proportional representation in the Senate now did not. North Carolina voted for the compromise and for state equality in the Senate, while Massachusetts, some of whose delegates feared western influence, split its vote and hence was counted as an abstention.

The Great Compromise was acceptable because it met the needs of both sections. Although at the time the North had a larger population, it expected in the future to be outnumbered by the South and it, therefore, looked on equal state representation in the Senate as providing needed long-range protection. In the meantime, proportional representation in the House of Representatives would register its existing population superiority. The South, on the other hand, for the time being had protection against northern numbers in the Senate and could look forward to proportional representation in the lower house as a guarantee of its interests.

A series of other North-South compromises, based on the views and votes of mid-Atlantic states which held the balance of power, followed the critical mid-July accommodation over the composition of the legislature. Fearful that Northerners would use a centralized commerce power against them, Southerners had initially demanded a two-thirds majority for the enactment of commerce or navigation laws. Eventually, they accepted simple majority approval of exercises of the commerce power, however, in return for a constitutional prohibition of taxes on exports. Three provisions concerning slavery also reflected sectional adjustment: the fugitive slave clause, declaring that persons held to service or labor under the laws of a state shall be returned to the person claiming service; the denial of congressional power to prohibit the slave trade for a twenty-year period; and the three-fifths clause, which included slaves in the reckoning of population for the purposes of representation and direct taxation. The third of these measures further illustrated the sectional conflict between North and South that had the West as its focal point.

The idea of counting five slaves as three free persons was first suggested in Congress in 1783 as part of a plan for basing taxation on population. Although the plan was not adopted, the three-fifths ratio aroused no sectional antagonism, and it was introduced without incident in the Constitutional Convention and approved as part of a plan for proportional representation in the early stages of proceedings. When sectional hostility crystallized in early July, however, the three-fifths clause was identified as a sectional issue. It was connected with another sectional problem—whether the apportionment of representatives in the national legislature should be determined by Congress or by a constitutionally required decennial census. Several northern delegates, fearing the rapid development of the West, sought to keep control over apportionment in the national legislature. Although they did not repudiate the three-fifths clause, they now labeled it a pro-southern instrument and opposed its adoption either as a constitutional provision or subsequently in the form of a national statute. Southerners protested that if Congress controlled representation, it might reject the three-fifths idea. Accordingly, with the help of a few strongly committed ideological republicans like James Wilson of Pennsylvania, who saw the three-fifths clause as a means of gaining southern support for the principle of representation of persons rather than property, they succeeded in writing both the requirement of a decennial census and the three-fifths clause into the Constitution. Two key issues of interest to the pro-slavery South were thus removed from a potentially hostile national legislature.

The Executive

Throughout the convention, as different issues were dealt with, coalitions formed on the basis of sectional division or large-state versus small-state identification. The latter was especially prominent in discussions of the executive. Fearful of being overwhelmed by the large states, the small states insisted that the election of the president—the major point of contention in shaping the executive branch—should in certain crucial respects be on their terms.

Two schools of thought existed concerning the executive. The first, represented by Sherman of Connecticut, Dickinson of Delaware, and Martin of Maryland, argued for a weak executive, chosen by and responsible to the legislature. The second point of view, represented by James Wilson, James Madison, Gouverneur Morris, and Alexander Hamilton, proposed a strong, independent executive, preferably chosen by direct popular election. These two conceptions of the presidency came into conflict the moment the committee of the whole took up the matter. The strong-executive men attacked the Virginia Plan provision for an executive elected by Congress, and Wilson suggested direct popular election as an alternative. This idea received little favor with most of the delegates, in part because it was too democratic, in part because the idea of a popularly elected executive was as yet largely foreign to American experience. Wilson then offered as a compromise that the people of the states should choose presidential electors, who should meet and choose the executive. This was defeated, eight states to two. The convention proceeded to ratify the plan for the election of the president by Congress, and there matters stood when the committee of the whole reported on June 15.

Proponents of a strong executive in debates throughout July hammered away at the idea that an executive chosen by the legislature would be corrupt and incompetent. They scored a temporary success when on July 19 the convention voted 6 to 3 to accept the electoral college idea. But on July 26 the delegates reversed themselves by adopting legislative election once again. A month later, on August 31, the convention appointed a committee of eleven to consider parts of the Constitution that had been postponed.

Comprising one delegate from each state, the committee on postponed parts was dominated by a group of small northern and middle states—New Hampshire, Connecticut, New Jersey, Delaware, and Maryland—who together with Massachusetts and Georgia formed a controlling coalition. The committee recommended the electoral college method of choosing the president. Each state was to choose its own electors in a manner prescribed by its legislature. This provision recognized the states, yet allowed for the possibility of popular choice of the electors. The electors were to vote by ballot for two persons, the one receiving the greatest number of votes to be president, providing that the number of votes cast for him was a majority of all the electors. If no candidate won a majority, the Senate was to elect the president, providing that the number of votes cast for him was a majority of electoral votes.

Debate revealed, however, a widely shared belief that in most elections no candidate would receive a majority in the electoral college for want of systematic coordination of the voting process from state to state. Yet the committee's proposal in that circumstance to shift the election of the president to the Senate was opposed by a minority of large and southern states— Virginia, Pennsylvania, North Carolina, and South Carolina—who feared that the Senate as a bastion of aristocracy would become too powerful. The solution offered by the committee was to place the choice in the House of Representatives, with voting by the states equally. The convention accepted this proposal. The small states thus gained satisfaction in the thought that they would have final control over the selection of the president most of the time, while the large-state minority kept the choice out of the Senate. The convention also followed the recommendations of the committee on unfinished parts by giving the treaty-making power and the power to appoint ambassadors and public ministers to the president with the advice and consent of the Senate, and by giving the Senate the power of trial in impeachment. Like the method of electing the president, these decisions were intended to satisfy the small-state point of view in particular.

On balance the convention created a strong, unitary executive, rejecting both the plural executive found at the time in most of the states and the British concept of a ministerial executive responsible to the legislature. In transforming the Confederation into a genuine government it was necessary to give it not only legislative power, but also executive power capable of acting directly upon individual citizens to enforce or give sanction to the laws. Although republican theory up to this time preferred a weak executive out of fear that a strong one would undermine liberty, in the reassessment of republicanism that took place in the 1780s an executive possessed of energy, dispatch, and responsibility came to be seen as necessary. Accordingly, the convention gave the president the power to act as commander in chief of the army and navy, to make treaties and conduct foreign relations, and to appoint judges and subordinate officers for the internal administration of the government. The executive was authorized to recommend measures to Congress and was given an express role in the legislative process in the form of a veto. The president was also eligible for reelection. Finally, the language of Article II of the Constitution creating the executive suggested an undefined, residual authority in stating that "The executive Power shall be vested in a President of the United States." The powers of Congress, by contrast, were carefully enumerated.

Federal Supremacy and the Judiciary

Intermittently, the convention returned to the two related problems that had plagued the Confederation in the 1780s: the use of the states as agencies of the central government, and the demarcation of the spheres of state and federal power. As it became clear that the federal government would act directly on individuals rather than states, the proposal in the Virginia Plan for coercion of states deficient in their obligations to the Union came to appear irrelevant. The central government would possess its own agents—executive officers, courts, attorneys, marshals, revenue officers, and the like—to carry out its functions and impose its will. Viewed in this light, the idea of coercing states implied that the Union was still a league or confederation dependent on the will of the various sovereign states. Coercion of a state would then, as Madison observed, "look more like a declaration of war, than an infliction of punishment, and would probably be considered by the party attacked as a dissolution of the union."

Coercion was dropped, but the problem of safeguarding and defining the spheres of state and central governments—the problem of federalism—remained. Madison's congressional negative in the Virginia Plan, in conjunction with the grant of power in Congress to legislate in all cases in which the states were incompetent or in which individual state legislation might be disruptive of unity, offered a highly centralist solution. At first the negative found favor, but by mid-July its weaknesses stood out. Because it would in effect have made Congress an integral part of the state legislatures, many delegates saw it as a genuine menace to the states and thought the people would never accept it. The congressional negative also presented grave practical difficulties. In order to review all state legislation Congress would have to be in session continuously and would have little time for anything else. Moreover if Congress did not veto a law that was unconstitutional (the negative had been amended to apply only to unconstitutional state acts), it would by implication remain operative even though contrary to the fundamental law. Such a circumstance, as Sherman of Connecticut said, involved a "wrong principle." Whatever the force of these difficulties, the decision in mid-July to create a partly confederate and partly unitary government eliminated the negative from serious consideration. Intended to consolidate a confederate system, it was out of place in the mixed regime that the Great Compromise produced.

Having rejected the congressional negative, the convention accepted a judicial veto as the solution to the federal problem. The key maneuver here was Luther Martin's introduction of a provision from the New Jersey Plan declaring federal law supreme and making state courts the agency by which the states and the federal government would be kept within their respective spheres. Martin's resolution stated that national legislation and treaties were to be the supreme law of the states, with state courts bound thereby, anything in their state laws to the contrary notwithstanding. Subsequent changes made judges "in the states," rather than "of the states," the enforcing authority; announced "This Constitution," as well as laws and treaties, as the supreme law of the land; and declared all of these instruments superior to state constitutions as well as state laws. The result was the all-important supremacy clause (Article VI, Section 2), which in express terms gave the Constitution the force of law. As Edward S. Corwin observed many years ago, it was not the aspect of supremacy that was so critical or distinctive in the new Constitution, but rather its character as law, enforceable in ordinary courts throughout the land. The Constitution was not, in other words, mere political exhortation.

Although the supremacy clause seems plainly to imply judicial review, it does not specifically provide for appeals from state to federal courts. Nevertheless, there is evidence that many delegates assumed the existence of such a power. The original Virginia Plan, for example, provided for one or more supreme and lower federal tribunals. States'-rights men, believing lower federal courts would undercut the state courts, objected and argued that the latter could act as courts of first instance for federal cases. They also said that uniformity of decision could be secured by granting a right of appeal to the supreme national tribunal. Although the convention rejected the proposal for establishing inferior national courts, preferring to leave that issue for Congress, it is clear that the delegates contemplated the possibility of appeals from state courts to the Supreme Court. Yet it is equally true that the convention did not regard the right of appeal as involving or creating a general power in the federal judiciary to interpret in a comprehensive way the extent of state authority under the Constitution.

Similarly, many delegates seem to have thought that the federal judiciary would have the right to refuse to recognize an unconstitutional federal law without attributing to it an ultimate power to fix the meaning of the Constitution. Probably most members of the convention would have agreed with Gouverneur Morris that the judiciary should not be bound "to say that a direct violation of the constitution was law." Yet this did not mean that the Supreme Court had a general power to interpret the Constitution. In point here was debate over extending the jurisdiction of the Supreme Court to "all cases arising under this Constitution" and the laws passed by Congress. According to Madison:

[there was doubt] whether it was not going too far to extend the jurisdiction of the Court generally to cases arising under the Constitution & whether it ought not to be limited to cases of a Judiciary Nature. The right of expounding the Constitution in cases not of this nature ought not to be given to that Department . . . it being generally supposed that the jurisdiction given was constructively limited to cases of a Judiciary nature.

If the import of this passage is correct, the delegates were generally agreed that the federal judiciary was not to possess the general power of expounding the Constitution.

Regardless of where the final power to interpret the Constitution was to be lodged, there is no doubt that the convention intended the federal sphere of sovereignty to be a limited one. As previously noted, in the Virginia Plan the scope of federal power was defined in broad and general terms to include power over all matters in which the states were incompetent, as well as those over which power was exercised by the Confederation Congress. This proposal would have given Congress vast authority of a vague and undefined character, inconsistent with the nature of a federal state. Although two or three delegates expressed alarm at the sweeping grant of power it implied, the convention took no positive action until the committee on detail produced a draft constitution early in August.

In this draft the committee had abandoned the original vague statement of congressional authority, and incorporated a series of specific delegated powers. This was done partly out of fear of an indefinite grant of legislative authority to the general government. Another reason lay in the necessity of separating and assigning to different branches of the new government powers that had been exercised by Congress under the Confederation. By the same token, some powers that were traditionally executive, such as the power to declare war or to create government offices, were to be given to Congress. In order to make clear this reassignment of powers, enumeration was necessary. Although there is little documentary evidence explaining enumeration, its constitutional significance proved to be profound. For it expressed in unmistakable terms the central theme of American constitutionalism: the limitation of legislative power by fundamental law. That the new government had only the powers assigned to it meant that other powers were kept by the states or the people, the constituent elements of the new government.

The Locus of Sovereignty

The enumeration of congressional powers throws light on the founding fathers' disposition of the question that lay at the root of the imperial controversy—the problem of sovereignty. In English and European constitutional theory sovereignty was unitary and indivisible. In the dispute over the imperial constitution, Americans rejected this notion and argued for divided sovereignty. Subsequently, however, some of them embraced the orthodox theory in their assertions of state sovereignty during the Revolution. Yet this situation proved unsatisfactory, not only because it encouraged legislative excesses in the states, but also because it contradicted the republican principle of the people as constituent power possessing ultimate authority. The solution was to recognize the sovereignty of the people, who could then allocate it in appropriate measure to the central and state governments. The first phase of this process took place in state constitution making during the Revolution. The second phase occurred at the Constitutional Convention and in the campaign for ratification that followed it.

Regarding the people as sovereign, the convention denied ultimate sovereignty to both state and federal governments. This denial of sovereignty was implicit in the very act of framing a government of defined and hence limited powers, and it was expressed documentarily—albeit in a negative way—by the omission from the Constitution of any reference to sovereignty. It proved virtually impossible in the future to conduct government without reference to the language of sovereignty. Hence in the debates over ratification and in the political struggles of the 1790s, and indeed throughout the nineteenth century, the locus of sovereignty in the states or the federal government formed a major theme of constitutional discourse. Yet the division of power between the states and the federal government had changed the meaning of sovereignty in the American constitutional order.

That two authentic governments could exist in the same geographic area, resting on the same constituent basis, was impossible to conceive of under the old theory of sovereignty. Critics dismissed it as illogical, an *imperium in imperio* (a government within a government) which denied all reason. But this was precisely what American federalism provided for, and the doctrine of popular sovereignty made it possible. Created by the people, state and federal governments could legislate and govern concurrently over the same population in the same territory. The difference between the two kinds of government, the one general, the other local, lay in the purposes assigned to each. Thus a federal republic—a compound scheme embodying the characteristics of both a confederation and a unitary government—was the American answer to the problem of sovereignty.

In early September, with substantive matters disposed of, the convention appointed a committee of style to produce a finished document. The actual task of drafting the final version was performed by Gouverneur Morris, assisted by

Alexander Hamilton, William Samuel Johnson, and Rufus King. The committee's draft was accepted almost as it stood, the only substantial change being a reduction of the ratio of representation for members of the House of Representatives from 40,000 to 30,000.

The convention had previously decided upon ratification by state conventions, favorable action by any nine states to be sufficient to establish the Constitution among those states so acting. This plan violated the method of amendment in the Articles of Confederation, which stipulated that proposed amendments must be submitted by Congress and ratified by all the states before becoming effective. But an alternative suggestion that the Constitution be submitted and approved in this manner was rejected on the ground that it would endanger the chances of adoption. Forty-two of the fifty-five delegates were still present, and on September 17, 1787, thirty-nine of them signed the new instrument of government. The convention then adjourned. Ten days later Congress submitted the Constitution to the states, which proceeded to set convention dates and issue calls for the election of delegates. The Rhode Island legislature refused to cooperate, but in the other states attempts to block the calling of conventions were defeated. Accordingly, starting in late 1787 delegates met in twelve states to consider the question of entry into the new union.

SEVEN

Ratification of the Constitution

Ratification of the Constitution, decided by popularly elected state conventions, provided the occasion for the new nation's first organized political struggle. Characterized by excursions into political theory and the rhetoric of social conflict, ratification inaugurated a new type of constitutional politics. Although the purpose of the contest was to decide whether to adopt the document emanating from the Philadelphia convention, the very nature of the process caused it to be a sustained exercise in constitutional interpretation—an attempt to ascertain the meaning of the Constitution. The opponents of the Constitution were in the ironic position of legitimizing the new instrument of government even as they sought to prevent its acceptance. Moreover, interest groups played a major role in the ratification contest, foreshadowing a key feature of the developing American political system. Of increasing importance in the late colonial period, interest groups now began to assume a legitimate place in the constitutional order. In still another way the ratification struggle anticipated modern American politics. Federalists and Antifederalists fought bitterly over the Constitution, but once the issue was resolved, they cooperated in implementing the new system of government. Shared political values permitted this cooperation. Yet in 1787–88 the most important principles on which the American national consensus was based—unionism and republicanism—received sharply conflicting interpretations from the opposing sides in the ratification fight.

In discussing ratification a word on nomenclature is necessary at the outset. In the late eighteenth century federalism referred to a confederation, league, or alliance—the opposite of a unitary sovereign government. Although the critics of the Constitution desired a stronger central government, in arguing to retain the Articles of Confederation they were closer to this position than were the advocates of the new government. Yet the latter appropriated the term "federalism" for themselves and pinned the label "Antifederalist" on their opponents. This gave them an important tactical advantage. Proposing a formidable new central authority that was sure to arouse fear of consolidation, they sought to disarm their adversary and allay states'-rights apprehension by identifying their cause—through their choice of rhetoric in calling themselves "Federalists"—with the values of decentralization which had a presumptive legitimacy in American political culture.

The Antifederalist leader Abraham Yates believed a more accurate description of the division over ratification would have been "republican" versus "antirepublican." This would have been misleading in implying that the supporters of the Constitution were not republican in outlook. Nevertheless, their republicanism differed considerably from that of their opponents. Yates's suggestion would have appealed to many contemporaries who saw the Antifederalist position as being more consistent with the spirit of revolutionary republicanism than was the Federalist position.

Antifederalist Principles

The geographical area appropriate to republican government was the most obvious problem in republican theory on which Antifederalists based their opposition to the Constitution. In accordance with conventional political science, Antifederalists insisted that republican government could succeed only in smaller nations possessing a high degree of social harmony and homogeneity. This proposition rested more on history than on logic: Large republics had failed, and the American colonies, considered to be relatively small, had flourished as the embryo of republican self-government. Small as they were, it was difficult in the states to transcend conflicting interests and legislate for the common good. Antifederalists argued that in the geographically extensive government projected in the Constitution it would be impossible to do so. The result would be the disintegration of republicanism into warring factions.

Antifederalists further objected that only in a small republic could full and equal representation be achieved. Republican government required close contact between electors and deputies. In order to represent their interests effectively, elected delegates must be familiar with their constituents' opinions and outlook. This familiarity was possible only in compact jurisdictions. It followed that full and equal representation required numerous representatives. Inasmuch as there were 200 state senators in the thirteen states, reasoned Antifederalist leader Richard Henry Lee of Virginia, to have fewer than that number in the national legislature would be inadequate. Yet the framers of the Constitution had provided for only 65 members in the House of Representatives—one for every 30,000 people. It was inconceivable to the Antifederalists that this arrangement could satisfactorily represent the people or create in them the reciprocal interest in supporting the new government that its success required. Noting the differences that separated the states, critics of the Constitution denied that a single national policy could or should be applied to such a variety of interests and conditions. Antifederalists warned that the new government, distant from the people because of its vast size, would maintain itself by standing armies and military coercion rather than by winning the affection and consent of its constituents.

Antifederalists further contended that the government envisioned in the Constitution would centralize and consolidate power, thus destroying republican government in the states. Behind this fear of consolidation lay the Antifederalists' adherence to the orthodox view of sovereignty as unitary and indivisible. Seeing only the alternatives of autonomous states joined in a confederation or a unitary government, they placed the new government in the latter category. Although Richard Henry Lee and other Antifederalist leaders professed to desire a plan of union that would create a unitary power for certain general purposes while leaving local matters to the states, they rejected the Federalist contention that the new government, by combining confederate and unitary features, satisfied this criterion. Guided by the unitary theory of sovereignty, the Antifederalists said it was impossible to have two governments exercising sovereign power within the same territory over the same population. To suggest such a scheme was a contradiction in terms—an *imperium in imperio*—which would result in the larger and stronger government aggrandizing power at the expense of the smaller and weaker. In short, the very existence of a central government with legislative, executive, and judicial powers threatened the states, and hence American republicanism.

Among the powers conferred by the Constitution Antifederalists especially objected to those assigned to the executive. In this they expressed the traditional republican fear of corruption or executive influence in the form of patronage distribution and electoral manipulation which undermined the independence of the legislature. The relationship between the executive and the Senate, whose members enjoyed six-year terms and who possessed special powers in treaty making and administrative appointments, was a particular source of apprehension. Fearing that the president and the Senate would form a conspiracy of power, many critics called for a more complete separation of powers.

But it was not simply the specter of executive corruption that stirred Antifederalist suspicion toward the new Constitution. Their ingrained republican hostility to government in general was reflected in opposition to national legislative powers as a threat to republican liberty. The power to tax and appropriate money; to declare war, raise armies, and command the state militia; to make laws necessary and proper for carrying into execution the enumerated powers of Congress and "all other powers vested . . . in the Government of the United States, or in any Department or Officer thereof"— all seemed to augur consolidation of legislative power in derogation of the states. Finally, the supremacy clause, declaring the Constitution and laws and treaties passed in pursuance of it superior to state constitutions and laws, expressed in Antifederalist eyes a centralizing purpose.

Still another Antifederalist objection to the Constitution concerned the absence of a bill of rights. The convention had briefly considered a proposal for a bill of rights, but decided against it on the ground that if the general government had only the powers delegated to it, a bill of rights reserving powers to the people was superfluous. The state constitutions, which did contain bills of rights, were thought to be a sufficient protection of individual liberty. In the state ratifying conventions, however, the Antifederalists seized on the absence of a bill of rights with telling effect. Reflecting orthodox republican theory, they viewed politics as a struggle between power and liberty, and the Constitution as a contract between rulers and ruled. Hence they insisted on a bill of rights as an additional guarantee of individual liberty. The argument was effective. Unwilling to appear less solicitous of liberty than their opponents, Federalists in several states informally agreed to accept subsequent inclusion of a bill of rights as a condition of ratification.

Federalist Constitutional Theory

As advocates of a stronger Union, the Federalists have gone down in history preeminently as nationalists. It would be a mistake to place too much emphasis on this fact, however, first, because it implies that opponents of the Constitution did not care about strengthening the Union—a point that is manifestly untrue—and second, because it obscures the significant contribution the Federalists made to the theory and practice of republicanism. The founding of republican governments in the states was the quintessential expression of the spirit of '76, and the Federalist authors of the Constitution brought the Revolution to completion by establishing a republican government for the Union as a whole. In doing so they modified republican theory and infused federalism with a republican content that enabled the central authority, in consequence of the identification that it now enjoyed with the sovereign people, to become a national government.

Federalists modified republican theory most significantly by extending the sphere of government. According to the conventional teaching, as noted previously, republican principles were considered appropriate in a circumscribed territory with basically homogeneous interests. The experience of the states since the Revolution, however, showed the impossibility of permanently subordinating interest-group conflict to the general good. Accordingly, the Federalists proposed an extended sphere of government that would be large enough to accommodate interest-group conflict, while preventing any single interest from gaining control of the government.

The best exposition of Federalist ideas appeared in *The Federalist,* a series of eighty-five newspaper essays written by James Madison, Alexander Hamilton, and John Jay to support ratification in New York and published in 1787–88 under the pseudonym of Publius. The most famous of the essays,

which subsequently were accepted as an authoritative treatise on the meaning
of the Constitution, was Madison's No. 10, setting forth the classic exposition
of the doctrine of the extended republic.

In *The Federalist* No. 10 Madison lamented the frequent conflict that
existed between the factions into which American society was divided and the
public good. Nevertheless, he regarded landed, mercantile, manufacturing,
creditor, and monied interests as necessarily involved in the operations of
government. Ordinarily, he explained, legislation could control the spirit of
faction through the operation of majority rule. Where the controlling faction
was a majority, however, the rights and interests of minorities had no protection. In this situation, which Madison said existed in several states, constitutional forms concealed the fact that the actions of the majority were based on
narrow factional concerns rather than on the general welfare. The proper
remedy—a republican remedy, Madison pointedly observed—was to enlarge
the sphere of government in which factions might compete. Coming together
in the legislature of the new federal republic, interest groups would seek to
influence the government, but they would be too numerous and varied to allow
any one faction to gain control of the government.

Instead of arguing that the purpose of politics was to deny or transcend
the differences between interest groups, as conventional republican theory
held, Madison reasoned that republican government should give expression to
the various interests in society. Abandoning the traditional republican belief
in the necessity of social homogeneity, Madison and his Federalist colleagues
adopted a positive, though not uncritical, view of interest groups which
pointed toward pluralistic conflict as the norm in American politics. Madison
did not entirely reject the notion of a general good existing apart from competing groups. But he suggested that most of the time, for most purposes, factional
struggle would *ipso facto* promote the good of the whole.

In the Federalists' extended republic representation served a modulating,
restraining purpose that set it apart from the more locally oriented view of
attorneyship representation favored by the Antifederalists. The extensive public space created by the Constitution would impede but could not by itself
provide an absolute guarantee against factional domination of the government.
Wisdom and virtue were also needed, and these qualities would be supplied
by the men of learning, ability, and standing in the community whom Madison
and his fellow Federalists counted on to support the new Constitution. Aware
of the social dimension of politics, Federalists entered the ratification debate
with the expectation that men of distinction would be chosen as representatives
in the new government. Larger electoral districts—one representative for every
30,000 people—would place elected lawmakers at a certain remove from the
people and enable them to refine, filter, and enlarge public opinion while
discouraging demagoguery. Originating in discussions of the House of Representatives, this argument applied with special force to the Senate, elected as
it was by the state legislatures, and to the president, chosen by the electoral

college. It is pertinent to note also that although the framers of the Constitution did not in express terms require a property qualification to vote in elections for U.S. representatives, in effect they did so by accepting as criteria in national elections state qualifications for electors of the more numerous branch of the state legislature. Representation in the Federalist view would thus be republican, but it would be modified in ways that would restrain the tendency in the states toward a more volatile and potentially despotic populist rule.

The Federalists' appeal for moderation and stability in state affairs could be appreciated by many Antifederalist leaders, who also opposed paper money and other economic measures that in effect threatened to alter property values. What was more difficult for the Federalists to deal with, what they had especially to overcome, was the charge that the new Constitution would consolidate power in the general government. To counter this charge they offered the theory of federalism as divided sovereignty.

Once again it was Madison, in *The Federalist* No. 39, who provided the most cogent argument in behalf of the proposed Constitution. A few specific powers were to be withdrawn from the states, he explained, but in general they would retain their sovereign authority. On the other hand, the central government would blend characteristics of a unitary national government with those of a confederation so as to give the states a distinct role in the new constitutional order. Seeking to allay the apprehensions of state-minded men, Madison said the new government would be a confederation as far as the source of its power was concerned. The act establishing it—ratification of the Constitution—would rest on "the people of America," which Madison said meant the people as citizens of separate states rather than of a unitary nation. With respect to enumerated powers, those possessed by the House of Representatives rested directly on popular election and derived their legitimacy from the unitary model, while those of the Senate derived authority from the confederation model. In view of the electoral college method of choosing a president, executive powers derived from both sources. In the scope of its powers, too, the new government would be both unitary and confederate. Insofar as its powers were enumerated and restricted to certain spheres it was a confederation, all other powers by implication being reserved for the states or the people. Insofar as its powers were supreme, as stated in the supremacy clause of the Constitution, it was a unitary nation.

Conventional political science classified governments as either unitary or federal (that is, a confederation). The proposed new government combined the characteristics of both types, yet its supporters called it a federal plan. They thus gave a new meaning to the term *federal.* Because of the novelty of the plan no one knew the effect it would have on the states, or how conflicts between the states and the federal government would be resolved. All that was certain was that within a single constitutional system both central and state governments would act directly on individuals, exercising a dual, and hence qualified, sovereignty. The Federalists' outstanding achievement, necessitated by the existence of the states as powerful sovereignties, was to employ the principle of duality and the language of coordinate or co-equal status to define federalism as divided sovereignty and to project it as the constitutional structure of the new nation.

The third major element in Federalist ratification strategy was popular sovereignty. Like the doctrine of divided sovereignty, this, too, had a lasting effect on American constitutionalism. Although the Antifederalists saw themselves as closer to the people and more sympathetic with democratic tendencies than their opponents, it was the Federalists who more perceptively understood popular sovereignty to be the distinguishing feature of the new government. In Federalist theory the sovereign people, standing outside the government, expressed their will in the form of a written Constitution which placed absolute limits on elected officials. Furthermore, it was the people who divided governmental power between the states and the central government. Indeed, popular sovereignty rendered intelligible the definition of federalism as divided sovereignty and enabled the Federalists to answer the Antifederalist charge that the Constitution created an *imperium in imperio.* For if the people possessed and were the source of power to begin with, they could give some of it to the central government and some to the states without internal contradiction. Assigning sovereignty to the people thus meant the rejection of sovereignty in anything like its traditional sense. This relocation of sovereignty also underscored the limited nature of federal authority as a delegated, enumerated power and explained the absence of a bill of rights in the Constitution. If the new government had only the powers given to it and the people retained all the rest, reasoned the Federalists, a bill of rights, denying the government powers that no one pretended it had, was superfluous.

That stability-seeking Federalists should appeal to popular sovereignty in the ratification debates has seemed to some historians a disingenuous tactic aimed at reversing the democratic course of the Revolution. According to this point of view, the Constitution was a conservative, centralizing reaction to the states'-rights democracy sanctioned by the Declaration of Independence and the Articles of Confederation. This argument is unconvincing, however, because there is no warranty for concluding either that the essence of the Revolution was a spirit of radical populistic democracy or that the Antifederalists represented more genuinely popular tendencies than the Federalists. Although the Federalists were critical of the popularly elected state legislatures in the 1780s, their commitment to republican self-government was no less genuine than that of their opponents. The support that the Constitution received from a majority of the electorate in the ratification elections and conventions is evidence of its democratic character.

Indeed, it was the broad base of popular support on which the new government rested, a concrete expression of the sovereignty of the people, that enabled the Federalists to counter the Antifederalists' attack on the illegality of the Constitution. It was true, as the Antifederalists argued, that the Philadelphia convention exceeded its powers and "new modeled" the Confederation government against the express instructions of Congress. Moreover, the convention bypassed Congress and devised rules for ratification—approval by nine states rather than unanimity in order to commence the government—that disregarded the requirement concerning amendment of the Articles of Confederation. The charge of illegality was a serious one, and Federalists answered it by declaring that the exigencies of union demanded substantive changes in disregard of established forms. Federalists furthermore appealed to the sovereignty of the people, the first principle of the regime as asserted in the Declaration of Independence. The Constitution was written by a special convention called for the purpose—the means by which, according to republican constitutional theory, the voice of the people was heard apart from ordinary governmental institutions. And it was ratified by state conventions elected by the people. Popular ratification above all overcame the charge of illegality and conferred legitimacy on the Constitution.

The Triumph of the Federalists

Ratification occurred over a ten-month period in eleven states. In smaller states which were less capable of maintaining an independent sovereign existence or which stood in special need of a strong central government, the Constitution received rapid and broad popular endorsement. Delaware, New Jersey, Connecticut, and Maryland were in the former category, while Georgia, with her fear of Indian attacks, was in the latter. States that had been more successful, but in which factionalism had been a disruptive element, ratified with greater difficulty and by smaller margins. These states were Pennsylvania, South Carolina, New Hampshire, and Massachusetts. In Virginia and New York, two politically important states, ratification succeeded by very slim margins, and two states that thought they could go it alone, North Carolina and Rhode Island, at first rejected the Constitution and then adopted it in 1789 and 1790, respectively. Where the struggle was close, the Federalists won decisive votes by promising to add amendments to the Constitution incorporating Antifederalist demands for a bill of rights.

Inequalities in the apportionment of delegates to the state ratifying conventions, which was based on the system employed in the state legislatures, gave an advantage to the Antifederalists in six states that approved the Constitution by wide margins, and to the Federalists in two states of strategic importance, where the contest was close. To this limited extent ratification was influenced by less than fully democratic procedures. In South Carolina, the eighth state to ratify, delegates voting for the Constitution represented only 39 percent of the population; in New York, whose ratification as the eleventh state was politically though not legally necessary to launch the new government, pro-Constitution delegates represented 33 percent of the population. Nevertheless, in the first nine states that ratified, delegates representing 65 percent of the population voted for the Constitution. By July 1788, after eleven states had given their approval, pro-Constitution delegates represented a majority of the total United States population. When the process of ratification was completed in 1790, the proportion of the entire population represented by pro-Constitution delegates stood at 59 percent. Thus in actual practice as well as in republican theory, the Constitution expressed the people's will. Nor does the disfranchisement of landless and propertyless persons gainsay the accuracy of this conclusion. Certainly, in formal terms the Constitution rested on a more complete expression of public opinion than either the Declaration of Independence or the Articles of Confederation.

It is possible to analyze the controversy over ratification along socioeconomic lines, following Charles A. Beard's famous work, *An Economic Interpretation of the Constitution of the United States* (1913). Beard argued that the framers of the Constitution, through their possession of public securities and paper assets, had a personal economic interest in the establishment of a strong central government that would aid the mercantile and creditor classes. The opponents of the Constitution, he contended, were agrarian and debtor classes whose economic interest lay in land. Although more numerous than their rival, the Antifederalists were politically outmaneuvered by the Federalists. Beard's thesis in its original formulation has long since been disproved. But in attenuated form it persists in studies that show that the Constitution was supported by occupational groups—in rural as well as urban areas—which were involved in the market economy, and that it was opposed by groups whose economic outlook and needs were oriented toward subsistence and hence were strictly local. In other words, commercial-cosmopolitan interests struggled against agrarian-localist interests.

If one assumes that decisions on political questions follow an underlying and often obscure economic calculus, then the market-orientation analysis of ratification is convincing. But to reach this conclusion requires ignoring or discounting a vast body of evidence that on its face suggests that constitutional concerns—especially Unionism and republicanism—disposed people for and against the Constitution. This is not to deny that economic issues were related to political-constitutional considerations or that governmental decisions had economic consequences. It is to deny that constitutional choices can be reduced to economic interest as the chief motivating element.

It is true that some on the pro-Constitution side started from the premise that the country's most pressing need was economic reforms—funding of the national debt, establishment of a sound currency, the creation of a national bank and a free market for internal commerce—and that constitutional reform was necessary to achieve these results. The more common perception, however, was that the Union needed to be strengthened and republicanism improved, and that as a corollary of these changes certain economic consequences would follow. After the new government came into existence, Hamilton's policies as secretary of the Treasury introduced changes in public finance and taxation, but these consequences prove nothing about the intention of the framers and ratifiers of the Constitution. The Constitution, in other words, was preeminently a political, not an economic, document.

Even when we consider ratification from an economic perspective, it is attitudes toward the constitutional issue of centralization that stand out as decisive. It is obvious that economic problems such as tariffs, currency, and regulation of markets commanded the attention of political leaders and that governmental control in this sphere appealed widely to Americans. Most people were mercantilist rather than laissez-faire in outlook. Yet though the Constitution addressed many of these issues by direct and indirect means, the participants in the ratification debate showed no inclination to seek support on this basis. The Antifederalists criticized the Constitution out of opposition to centralized control of economic life; the Federalists denied that ratification would lead to any such centralized result. Both sides thus respected the value of decentralization of state control of economic affairs. They differed principally in their views of the kind or degree of Union needed to promote what Hamilton, in *The Federalist* No. 1, called the "political prosperity" of the nation and in their understanding of the effect of the Constitution on republican government.

If the ratification debates provide little support for an economic interpretation of the Constitution, they nevertheless contain much extreme language that appears to express class hostility. Antifederalists charged their opponents with an aristocratic ambition to control the new government in the interest of the wealthy few, while Federalists attacked critics of the Constitution as irresponsible and unprincipled demagogues, preoccupied with the pursuit of selfish local interests. Rhetoric of this sort obviously has significance, but that it can be taken as evidence of deep-seated class conflict is doubtful. Although some Antifederalist leaders were of socially modest background and means, too many of them possessed generally the same educational, cultural, and social qualifications as their opponents to permit the conclusion that ratification was at bottom a question of class struggle.

Rather than taken literally, the rhetoric of aristocracy versus democracy ought to be seen as an expression of a struggle between competing groups who were trying to appeal to fundamental values in the political order. The republican spirit of equality stimulated by the Revolution condemned aristocratic special privilege, and Antifederalists traded on this theme heavily—and with exaggeration—in their campaign against the Constitution. It is important to note, however, that the Antifederalists did not seek to promote political democracy by extending the franchise to the propertyless classes. Popular sovereignty notwithstanding, the spirit of the Revolution also condemned excessive reliance on the popular element in the actual conduct of government. On the other hand, the Federalists were reckless in accusing their opponents of desiring a mobocracy. What the ratification struggle reveals, then, is differently situated but not basically dissimilar social groups seeking to influence public opinion by appealing to different strands in the doctrine of revolutionary republicanism.

The Constitution and the Revolution

If republicanism were a static system of ideas and institutional practices with a fixed content, it would perhaps be possible to say that one side or the other in the ratification debate was more faithful to the essential meaning of the Revolution. The spirit of '76 was not a rigid theoretical construct, however, but a dynamic philosophy that changed in response to actual events. If the Antifederalists had reason to be apprehensive about their opponents' high-toned style, the Federalists spoke truly when they identified their cause with the constitutional limitations that lay at the heart of the Revolution. When the actions of the state legislatures in the 1780s forced a greater appreciation of this aspect of republicanism, those who prescribed remedies in the new Constitution were completing the Revolution, not diverting it from its true course. Madison was not being disingenuous when he said that the objective of the framers was to preserve the public good and private rights while retaining the form and spirit of popular government. If local self-government was the goal of the Revolution, and if union among the states was a means of establishing republican rule, then to strengthen the Union in order to improve republicanism in the states, as the Federalists did, was a proper culmination of the Revolution.

To call attention to the narrow range of disagreement in this first organized national political controversy does not rob the conflict of its essential meaning. On the contrary, it enables us to understand how the Federalists were able to present their plan for a centralized government—something that most Americans opposed when considered in the abstract—as a *national* government endorsed by the people of the states. Republican values characterized American society, but the Confederation did not reflect or embody republican values in ways that would lead the people to develop a sustained interest in or attachment to it. Hence its weakness and ineptness. Recognizing and appealing to interests in an essentially modern way, yet at the same time trying to restrain them out of concern for the general good, the Federalists used the idea of popular sovereignty and republican representation and citizenship to legitimize the central government that they believed necessary to limit state power.

At bottom the dispute between the Federalists and Antifederalists was over the nature of the Union, not over whether there ought to be a union or whether republican government ought to be the political system of America. As the Civil War would show, in other historical circumstances controversy over the nature of the Union was capable of generating the most profound and rending conflict. But in this formative era of nation and constitution making, union was a means of achieving republican self-government rather than an end in itself. Federalists and Antifederalists disagreed about the kind of union that should be created to give expression to American nationality. But their commitment to republicanism, despite different emphases in their approach to it, explains how the new central government acquired legitimacy as a national government.

Antifederalists preferred a decentralized state system in the belief that the success of republican government depended on homogeneous political communities that could inculcate public virtue and happiness in individual citizens. Self-governing communities acting through legislative power under majority rule, organized to promote the common good and to subordinate the rights of individuals to the public interest, defined the constitutional ideal in Antifederalist republicanism. In contrast the Federalists, reacting against state encroachments on liberty and property, pursued a conception of union that emphasized protection of individual rights rather than the promotion of virtue and community consensus as the purpose of government. Rather than an unattainable ideal of public virtue in ordinary citizens, they appealed to enlightened self-interest as the social reality on which the Constitution would rest. This is not to say that mere private enrichment at the expense of the common good was the end of the Constitution. The concepts of virtue and the public interest remained integral to American political thought. But virtue assumed a new meaning as the prudent and rational pursuit of private commercial activity. Instead of professing to tell people how to live in accordance with particular conceptions of political justice or religious truth, the Federalist framers promoted ends beneficial to all members of free society—peace, economic growth, intellectual advancement—by accommodating social competition and upholding citizens' natural rights against invasion by the organized power of the community, whether local, state, or national.

As the creation of republican governments in the states gave rise to national consciousness at the start of the Revolution, so the Constitution identified American nationality with republican forms and values. American nationality derived from practical, utilitarian considerations, rather than from religion, race, culture, and an immemorial past as in Europe. What Americans had in common was citizenship in republican state governments; it was this that gave them a distinct national character. By providing for republican government at the continental level, the Constitution strengthened American nationality. Accordingly, the national idea in America was defined not simply by identifying it with sovereign governmental powers—the taxing and commerce powers, for example, or the power of legal sanction and command—but by establishing a *republican* government. In this sense the Constitution pointed ahead to the correlation between nationalism and liberalism that existed in the nineteenth century and that characterized the defense of the Union during the Civil War.

The framers fulfilled the Revolution, furthermore, in perfecting and giving institutional expression to the idea that a constitution, in order to function as a limiting grant of power, must be higher as well as fundamental law. In addition to originating or organizing power, it must be maintained separate from and paramount to government. The Constitution as a formal document was superficially similar to the state constitutions. A preamble explained the reasons for the instrument, proclaimed the existence of a people and political community, defined specific purposes, and ordained a framework of government. In reality, however, the framers departed from the model of the state constitutions more than they adhered to it. On the whole, they believed it unnecessary to return to the fundamentals of the social compact and the purposes of republican government, as state constitution writers were inclined to do. The authors of the Constitution observed that they were not addressing the natural rights of man apart from society, but natural rights modified by society and interwoven with the rights of the states. They recognized that the American nation was amorphous, loosely related in its constituent parts, and united by few principles and interests. It was far from being the kind of cohesive, integrated community that the states by contrast seemed to be, and very unlike the nation-state communities of Europe. Hence the framers addressed in the Preamble only briefly those few basic unifying purposes and values—liberty, justice, domestic peace, military defense, the general welfare—and gave virtually the entire document to stipulating the forms, institutions, and procedures of government. As fundamental law the Constitution was less a social compact for a coherent, homogeneous, like-minded community and more a contract-like specification of the powers, duties, rights, and responsibilities among the diverse polities and peoples that constituted the American Union.

Modern scholarship so readily assumes that constitutions reflect or are determined by social forces that it fails to recognize that the historical significance of the Constitution was to demonstrate, as Alexander Hamilton wrote in *The Federalist* No. 1, that "societies of men are really capable . . . of establishing good government from reflection and choice," and are not "forever destined to depend for their political constitutions on accident and force." At a superficial level it is accurate to say, for example, that the idea of a constitution as a higher, fixed law appealed to Americans as an effective means of protesting colonial policy. Historical analysis may hesitate to reach the more normative conclusion that the constitutionalism of 1787 was based on a sound understanding of human nature, that it propounded valid principles of government, and that it possessed intrinsic and not merely instrumental value. Yet if history is reluctant to judge whether the framers formulated a valid science of politics, it can employ as an evaluative criterion the requirement that a constitution must recognize and conform to a people's principal characteristics and nature.

Considered from this point of view, the achievement of the founding fathers is undeniable. They created a complex government of delegated and dispersed, yet articulated and balanced powers based on the principle of consent. Confirmation of that principle was in turn required by the Constitution in the cooperation and concurrence among the branches of government that were necessary for the conduct of public business. Made for an open, acquisitive, individualistic, competitive, and pluralistic society, the Constitution ordered the diverse constituent elements of American politics. Among these elements were the political communities in which Americans organized themselves in the states, and where with very little restriction from the new national authority, under constitutions that may be considered a completion of the Constitution of the United States, they would continue to pursue ends and objects that properly belonged to local communities, such as religion and education. More than merely a neutral procedural instrument for registering the play of social forces, the Constitution was a statement of ends and means for maintaining the principles that defined Americans as a national people. The framers made a liberal constitution for a liberal society.

The powers granted the new government reflected in part American experience with federalism under the British Empire and the Articles of Confederation. The scope of federal authority was essentially the same as that of the central governments under the old British Empire and under the Articles of Confederation. Experience had taught the statesmen of the Revolutionary era that a central government could not function effectively without the right to tax and to regulate commerce, and they now added these items to the grant of federal authority. Yet the federal government was still conceived of as having few other functions than the maintenance of peace against external and internal disturbance, though for this purpose it was thought that it must also be financially sound and efficient. Even the power over interstate commerce, eventually to become so potent an arm of federal authority, was apparently granted for negative rather than positive reasons—to protect trade from the manifold abuses of state control rather than to make possible extensive regulation by the central government.

As America's middle-class social order was basically similar to English society yet different in the emphasis it placed on individualism, competition, and mobility, so government and politics in the United States shared the general purposes and aspirations of English constitutionalism while employing different institutional means. Like the English, Americans sought to create and maintain balanced and limited government in the interest of individual and local liberty. But whereas English constitutionalism developed for the most part incrementally and organically by essentially political means, Americans dealt with constitutional change in a more deliberative and rationally self-conscious way. The adoption of a written constitution as the fundamental law and framework of government, while it brought to completion tendencies deeply rooted in the colonial experience, signified the beginning of a distinctive approach to constitutional politics which carried American constitutionalism in the future ever further from the English model.

EIGHT

Establishing the New Government:
Federalist Constitutionalism

ATHOUGH THE CONSTITUTIONAL CONVENTION determined the basic character of the new government, ratification by no means completed the task of constitutional formation. Defining the nature of the executive, legislative, and judicial branches through institutional practice was the most important, if also the most perduring, of the problems facing American political leaders. Other issues dealt with in the 1790s included the place of an organized political opposition in the constitutional system, the manner of settling disputes about the meaning of the Constitution, and the proper relationship between the states and the federal government. Yet underlying these questions was the issue of the legitimacy of the new central government.

Legitimacy in the sense in which it is used here meant political acceptance of the new government by the states and the people—the constituent elements in the new order. Because the political culture of America was republican, the popular base on which the government rested was an asset. Yet the value of this asset was limited by the fact that conflicting approaches to republicanism were possible that could provoke disruptive opposition threatening to the government. Unionism was another source of legitimacy, for all Americans believed that some degree of cooperation among the states was necessary. This might also be problematic, however, inasmuch as the Antifederalists saw the new government as tending toward a centralized unitary state. Needless to say, no government in America could claim legitimacy if perceived in that light. Thus, although in a general sense the new government was consistent with American political values, that fact alone would not win it acceptance. Legitimacy would depend more on specific policies adopted by the government than on what it represented in an abstract or theoretical sense.

An important source of legitimacy on which the new government drew was the character and personality of George Washington, the first president.

Handsome in appearance, renowned for his military accomplishments, possessing a reputation for integrity, dignity, and republican virtue that made him trusted and revered among all segments of the population, Washington was a charismatic figure to Americans of the Revolutionary generation. More to the point, he was a symbol of Unionism and republicanism without whom it is possible that the presidential office as conceived by the Constitutional Convention would never have been agreed on. Unquestionably, Washington's presence helped establish the authority of the new government.

The Bill of Rights

The recommendation by the first Congress of a bill of rights was an important step in winning acceptance for the general government. It will be recalled that during the contest over ratification, Federalists had won in several states by promising a series of constitutional amendments embodying a bill of rights. Many members of the first Congress now felt a moral obligation to fulfill these promises. They believed, moreover, that persons lukewarm or unfriendly to the new government could be enlisted in support of it should such amendments be adopted. Accordingly, James Madison, now a representative from Virginia, took the initiative in coordinating the suggestions of the state ratifying conventions, formulating amendments, and introducing them into the House.

A few Federalists continued to oppose a bill of rights on the ground that since the government possessed only delegated powers, it was superfluous to enumerate the things it could not do. Opponents of the Constitution, however, had announced their intention to seek a second constitutional convention for the ostensible purpose of adding a bill of rights, but actually with a view toward undoing the work of the convention. Politically, therefore, it was of the utmost importance to carry through the project for a bill of rights.

As prepared by Madison and approved by the House of Representatives, the Bill of Rights restricted both the federal and state governments. In the Senate, however, the states'-rights point of view prevailed, and the seventeen amendments under consideration were altered to apply only to the federal government. This was, of course, a momentous change which showed that federalism—rather than a desire to protect individual liberty against government encroachment from whatever source—was the chief concern of Congress in approving the Bill of Rights. Madison and his colleagues had sought to appease states'-rights sentiment by offering general guarantees of individual liberty, but the states'-rights men exacted a higher price by turning the amendments exclusively into restrictions on the federal government.

By the proposed amendments, Congress was to be prohibited from abridging the freedom of religion, speech, the press, assembly, petition, or the right to bear arms; federal authority was closely restricted in quartering troops, prosecuting citizens for crimes, and inflicting punishments. Out of these proposals grew the first five amendments and the Eighth Amendment. Extensive changes designed to guarantee the citizen a fair trial by a jury in his own district as well as the benefits of the common law were also proposed; these eventually became the Sixth and Seventh Amendments. The Ninth Amendment, stating that "The enumeration in the Constitution, of certain rights, shall not be construed to deny or disparage others retained by the people," responded to the contention that it might be dangerous to make only a partial listing of the basic rights guaranteed in the Constitution.

One of the most significant events in framing the Bill of Rights was the failure of states'-rights advocates, in what became the Tenth Amendment, to limit the federal government to those powers "expressly" enumerated in the Constitution. This move was blocked by Madison and others, who believed that in any effective government some powers "must necessarily be admitted by implication." In its final form the Tenth Amendment stated that "The powers not delegated to the United States by the Constitution, nor prohibited by it to the States, are reserved to the States respectively, or to the people." Even without restrictive language negating the possibility of implied federal powers, however, the Tenth Amendment provided a textual basis for striking down federal legislation as an encroachment on states' rights. It proved to be a kind of supremacy clause for the states.

In September 1789 Congress submitted twelve proposed amendments to the states. Two proposals, one providing that there should be not less than one representative in the lower house for every 50,000 persons and another postponing the effect of any alteration in the compensation of senators and representatives until an election had intervened, failed to secure acceptance. The ten amendments, which were approved by the requisite number of states in November 1791, worked no real alteration in federal power and thus may be described as declaratory of the existing Constitution. They gave formal recognition to certain traditionally accepted natural rights, hitherto incorporated in the English charters, colonial grants, and state bills of rights. They took no substantive powers from Congress that could reasonably have been implied before the amendments had been passed, and most of the procedural limitations probably would have been taken for granted in any event.

Organization of the Executive Department

In September 1788, after eleven states had ratified the Constitution, the Confederation Congress designated the first Wednesday of the following January for the selection of presidential electors, the first Wednesday in February for the casting of the electoral vote, and the first Wednesday in March (March 4) for the inauguration of the new government. The Constitution had left the method of selecting presidential electors to the state legislatures. In the first election the states accordingly chose their electors in a variety of ways, some by popular election on a general ticket, some by popular district election, and some by legislative vote. This lack of uniform electoral procedure was to continue for several elections, and it was not until after 1860 that the choice of electors on a general ticket became universal.

When the electoral vote was counted, George Washington was found to have received one of the two votes cast by every elector. John Adams received the second highest number of electoral votes and thereby became vice-president. Meanwhile the various states held elections for members of the House of Representatives, and the state legislatures chose their senators. A large majority of the successful candidates for both houses had actively supported ratification of the new Constitution, although a few opponents of ratification won seats. The success of the Federalists was due in part to the prestige these men had gained through sponsorship of the Constitution and to the discomfiture of the Constitution's opponents, and in part to the fact that the Constitution's champions were vitally interested in the successful operation of the new government and hence sought office in greater numbers than did the Antifederalists.

Congress, meeting in New York by direction of the Confederation Congress, obtained a quorum and began to do business in April 1789. Among the first statutes it enacted were laws providing for the establishment of three executive departments—the State, Treasury, and War Departments. The Constitution made no direct provision for administrative departments. Congress thus had a large measure of discretion in the matter, though the system of administrative departments evolved in the later Confederation period was available as a precedent.

Madison's proposal of May 1789 to create a Department of Foreign Affairs precipitated a prolonged debate on the president's removal power. The bill expressly granted the president the right to remove the head of the prospective department. The Constitution was silent on the removal power, an omission which was to open the way for two centuries of intermittent controversy on the question. Some congressmen now opposed the provision in Madison's bill on the grounds that the Senate, being associated with the president in appointments, was by implication properly associated with him in removals as well. Others contended that the removal power was an inherent part of the executive prerogative and a proper means of implementing the president's duty to take care that the laws be faithfully executed; hence, they held, the president could properly make removals without the Senate's consent. Still others argued that the Constitution permitted Congress to locate the removal power according to its judgment. The bill in question was finally phrased so as to imply that the power of removal had already been lodged in the president by the convention. While this precedent was for a time generally followed in subsequent legislation, the question of the removal power arose again during the administrations of Jackson and Johnson in the nineteenth century.

In creating a Treasury Department Congress took deliberate steps to make the secretary of the Treasury responsible to Congress as well as to the president. The secretary was required from time to time to make reports and "give information to either branch of the legislature, in person or in writing (as may be required), respecting all matters referred to him by the Senate or the House of Representatives, or which shall appertain to his office; and generally shall perform all such services relative to the finances, as he shall be directed to perform." Thus, while Congress made the heads of other departments subordinates of the president, it made the secretary of the Treasury, primarily at least, its own agent to execute its constitutional powers in the field of finance.

Here was an important move toward ministerial responsibility and parliamentary government. The basic proposition implied in the Treasury Act was that Congress could constitutionally make an executive department responsible to itself rather than to the president. Subsequent developments, however, were to arrest the trend toward ministerial responsibility.

The creation of other departments involved no major controversies. The War Department received supervision over both military and naval affairs, an arrangement continued until 1798, when the quasi-war with France led to the establishment of a separate Navy Department. The Judiciary Act of 1789 provided for an attorney general, whose chief duties were to prosecute cases for the United States before the Supreme Court and to give legal advice to the president and the heads of departments. Although he did not become the official head of a department until 1870, he became immediately a principal executive officer and presidential adviser. The post office was organized on an annual basis until 1794, when it was given permanent standing; not until 1829, however, did the postmaster general become a regular cabinet member.

A proposal of August 1789 to create a Home Department failed because of the implied invasion of state authority; instead, Congress altered the name of the Department of Foreign Affairs to the Department of State, a title general enough to cover a variety of small additional duties then assigned to the department—among them the custody of public records and correspondence with the states.

The Constitutional Convention had contemplated a strong executive, who would not only execute federal laws but would also take a prominent part in the formulation of legislation. The Constitution provided several possible instruments for executive leadership in Congress, among them the president's duty to advise Congress on the state of the Union and to "recommend to their Consideration such Measures as he shall judge necessary and expedient," and his veto power. Eventually, also, the appointive power was to become an important device for the control of policy, although it did not develop as such during Washington's time.

In advising Congress on the state of the Union, Washington early adopted the practice of appearing in person before Congress at the opening of each session to review the developments of the preceding year and to recommend matters for congressional consideration. During sessions also he sent special messages, chiefly to provide Congress with information as occasion arose. Although early Congresses followed an elaborate ceremonial in making formal response to the president's annual messages, they did not always accept his recommendations. The annual message was in fact not destined to become a major instrument of executive leadership in Congress.

The veto was also potentially an important instrument for the control of legislative policy, but it, too, did not become significant in the early national period. Federalist leaders favored the exercise of the veto power as a part of a desirable strong executive. Their opponents, on the other hand, conscious of the unpopularity of the governor's veto power in the colonial era and aware of the weak veto given most state governors, believed that the power should be used very sparingly.

Washington first used the veto in 1791, when he refused his assent to a bill apportioning representation in the House in such a manner that some states would have more than the one representative for every 30,000 inhabitants permissible under the Constitution. The president sympathized with Jefferson's argument that he ought not to refuse his assent to any bill unless he was certain that it was unauthorized by the Constitution. However, in his opinion the bill under consideration was unquestionably unconstitutional, and he finally vetoed it on that ground. While use of the veto in this case aroused little opposition, the veto power was to be used very rarely for a long time. Neither Adams nor Jefferson vetoed a single law, and not until Jackson's time was the veto used to defeat any measure that the president considered objectionable for reasons of policy.

During Washington's first administration, department heads took an active part in advising Congress upon legislative policy, even to the extent of drafting legislation. Alexander Hamilton, secretary of the Treasury, in particular considered himself to be a kind of prime minister, a coordinator between Congress and the president. Washington, other department heads, and many members of Congress were at first inclined to accept him as such. The House refused to allow Hamilton to appear before it in person; but by means of written reports, the domination of party caucuses, and the control of congressional committee personnel, the secretary of the Treasury became for a time the most important person in the government in the determination of legislative policy.

This trend toward executive leadership in Congress was sharply checked during Washington's second term and the Adams administration. The change was due not to an altered conception of the presidency by either incumbent, but to a less favorable response to such leadership from Congress. With the rapid growth and crystallization of the Republican opposition in Congress, Hamilton and his colleagues were faced by 1793 with a hostile majority in the House. Not only did Hamilton's hopes for a premiership disappear but also he was subjected to various attacks in both houses, charging him with intruding upon congressional authority and with certain improprieties and actual violations of law.

Through the rest of the decade, under the impetus provided by the nascent Republican party, Congress asserted its institutional autonomy and resisted executive domination. A principal reason for this development was the fear, central to the Anglo-American republican tradition, of undue executive influence or corruption. Insisting on the importance of the separation of powers, Republicans held that reliance on the executive departments for proposals and advice allowed those officers to usurp the lawmaking function of Congress. In accordance with this view, they formed standing committees that could gather information and expertise needed for legislation. Ways and Means, Manufactures, and Commerce were among the earliest important committees by which Congress avoided dependence on the executive departments. Republicans did not, however, aim at a complete or extreme separation of powers. Rather they looked on standing committees as a way of maintaining the necessary degree of legislative autonomy, while making it possible occasionally to call on the executive branch for guidance.

Although the Constitutional Convention had made no specific provision for an advisory council to the president, to some extent the finished Constitution implied that the Senate was to serve in this capacity. It was given two specific advisory functions: treaty making, and the appointment of diplomatic, judicial, and administrative officers. The Senate's small size and the fact that since colonial times the upper house had constituted an executive council strengthened the concept of the Senate as a presidential advisory body. The upper house did not, however, fulfill this expectation. Washington's initial request for senatorial advice led to misunderstanding and irritation, and caused the president subsequently to submit finished treaties to the Senate merely for their acceptance or rejection.

The development of a cabinet of department heads was both a cause and a result of the failure of the Senate to become an advisory body. Washington early requested written opinions from department heads, and by 1793 regular meetings of these officers as an executive cabinet were taking place. Soon, too, the cabinet came to be made up exclusively of men who were personally loyal to the president and in agreement with him on policies of the administration. Washington's attempt to draw on men of differing outlook, as when Hamilton and Jefferson were in the cabinet, proved unsatisfactory. The president's power to remove principal policy-making subordinates, first confirmed by Congress in 1789, became an additional factor in establishing cabinet unity. Under President John Adams a partial and temporary disintegration of executive unity occurred, largely because Adams retained Washington's cabinet, several members of which were loyal to Hamilton. But when Jefferson became president, he formed a cabinet of men who accepted his leadership and strove to carry out his program. Only rarely thereafter were cabinet officers to be much more than the president's subordinates and agents.

Foreign Policy and Executive Prerogative

The idea of the president as a powerful independent executive capable of initiating policy and controlling events on his own responsibility was strongly reinforced by the exercise of executive policy in foreign affairs during Washington's administration.

At the outbreak of war between France and Britain in 1793, France sent a new minister to the United States, one Edmond Genêt, to obtain this country's cooperation with the French war effort. Genêt came as emissary from the new French republic, the monarchy having been overturned in 1792 by revolution. His reception by the United States would under international law constitute formal recognition of the new French government, and the question, therefore, arose as to whether under the Constitution the president was authorized to take this step. The cabinet nonetheless agreed that Washington should receive Genêt, an action which set a precedent for the absorption by the executive of the right to extend recognition to a foreign government.

Though the United States had signed a treaty of alliance with monarchist France in 1778, Washington's cabinet was unanimously of the opinion that the nation ought to remain neutral in the current war. It was accordingly agreed that Washington should issue a proclamation of neutrality, a step shortly taken.

The administration's opponents immediately charged that Washington's proclamation of neutrality had infringed upon the province of Congress, to which the Constitution had assigned the authority to declare war. Hamilton replied by publishing in the press, under the pseudonym of "Pacificus," an elaborate statement of his theory of the strong executive. "If, on the one hand," he concluded, "the Legislature have a right to declare war, it is on the other, the duty of the executive to preserve peace till the declaration is made."

Hamilton then contended that the president possessed an inherent body of executive prerogative, above and beyond those rights and duties specifically mentioned in the Constitution. "The general doctrine of our Constitution, then, is," he asserted, "that the *executive power* of the nation is vested in the President; subject only to the *exceptions* and *qualifications* which are expressed in the instrument." To put it differently, the clause in the Constitution vesting executive authority in the president was itself a general grant of executive power, and the subsequent enumeration of functions was not in any sense all-inclusive. Part of the inherent executive prerogative, Hamilton added, was the general authority to conduct foreign relations and to interpret treaties in their nonjudicial aspects.

This broad claim of inherent executive prerogative caused Jefferson and Madison to believe with some reason that Hamilton was contriving to attach to the president powers approximating the royal prerogatives of the British crown. To Jefferson and his colleagues the executive authority was limited by the specific grants of the Constitution and of laws, and in domestic affairs this concept has since largely prevailed. The Hamiltonian doctrine, however, strongly supported by the hard fact that the executive department is always available and has superior sources of information regarding foreign affairs, has succeeded in giving the president very broad powers in the conduct of foreign relations.

The phase of the foreign policy of the Washington administration that aroused the bitterest opposition was the treaty drawn up by John Jay with Great Britain in 1794. It provided for the clarification of commercial relationships as well as for an amicable settlement of outstanding differences growing out of the misunderstanding and nonfulfillment of the Treaty of Peace of 1783. Since Britain now occupied an advantageous diplomatic position, most of the terms of the Jay Treaty were more favorable to her than to the United States. The treaty was, therefore, unpopular in many parts of the country, but the Federalist-dominated Senate in 1795 agreed to all of it except one clause.

Certain provisions in the treaty required appropriations of money before they could be put into effect. This necessitated action by the House of Representatives, where the opponents of the treaty were especially strong. By a considerable majority the House requested the president to furnish that body with a copy of the instructions to Jay and of other documents relative to the treaty. Washington, with the approval of his cabinet, refused to comply with this request on the ground that the papers demanded had no relation to the functions of the House. He also reminded the representatives that the Constitutional Convention had very deliberately assigned the power of making treaties to the president and the Senate, and he insisted that "the boundaries fixed by the Constitution between the different departments should be preserved." The House then disclaimed any part in the treaty-making power but insisted upon its rights to originate all appropriations, even those for treaties, and, therefore, upon its inherent right to deliberate upon the expediency of carrying the treaty into effect. Washington held to his position and finally, by a very narrow margin, the House acquiesced and voted the necessary appropriation.

Hamiltonian Broad Construction

Simultaneous with these institutional developments, Alexander Hamilton, the first secretary of the Treasury, formulated an economic program aimed at building up the political support needed to assure the legitimacy of the new government. In a series of reports to Congress in 1790–91 dealing with the public credit, Hamilton proposed to fund the outstanding Confederation debt at face value, assume the unpaid debts of the states contracted during the Revolutionary War, and charter a national bank to assist in handling the government's monetary and financial problems. He intended thereby to create a network of influence connecting creditors, men of property, and the commercial classes in general with the federal government. Appealing to motives of economic self-interest, which he believed could be made to serve the public good, Hamilton hoped to draw mercantile groups away from a primary attachment to the state governments and link their interest to that of the general government. The result would be a mutually beneficial relationship that would at once promote commercial growth and assure the stability and success of the new republic.

There was comparatively little opposition to the refunding of the national debt, which was guaranteed by the Constitution itself. However, certain congressmen did object to paying the old obligations off at face value, a step which they argued would redound to the advantage of the speculator class. And the states'-rights faction attacked the assumption of state debts by the federal government as a scheme to consolidate national authority at the expense of the states. The Virginia legislature adopted a resolution declaring assumption to be both dangerous to the states and repugnant to the Constitution. Representatives from states that had already paid off a large part of their debts also objected to assumption as inequitable. Hamilton nonetheless carried his proposal through Congress with the aid of a political bargain by which certain southern members voted for assumption in return for some northern support for a bill to locate the future national capital on the Potomac River.

Hamilton's proposal to charter a national bank was severely attacked in Congress on constitutional grounds. The opposition was led by Madison, who was becoming increasingly hostile to Hamilton's program. Although the two men had supported strong national government in the convention and had worked together to secure ratification of the Constitution, neither their constitutional philosophies nor their economic interests were harmonious. Hamilton wished to push still further in the direction of a powerful central government, while Madison, now conscious of the economic implications of Hamilton's program and aware of the hostility which the drift toward nationalism had aroused in his own section of the country, favored a middle course between centralization and states' rights.

In the Constitutional Convention Madison had proposed that Congress be empowered to "grant charters of incorporation," but the delegates had rejected his suggestion. In view of this action, he now believed that to assume that the power of incorporation could rightfully be implied either from the power to borrow money or from the "necessary-and-proper" clause in Article I, Section 8, would be an unwarranted and dangerous precedent.

In February 1791, the bank bill was passed by Congress, but President Washington, who still considered himself a sort of mediator between conflicting factions, wished to be certain of its constitutionality before signing it. Among others, Jefferson was asked for his view, which in turn was submitted to Hamilton for rebuttal.

In a strong argument Jefferson advocated the doctrine of strict construction and maintained that the bank bill was unconstitutional. Taking as his premise the Tenth Amendment (which had not yet become a part of the Constitution), he contended that the incorporation of a bank was neither an enumerated power of Congress nor a part of any granted power and that implied powers were inadmissible. He further denied that authority to establish a bank could be derived from either the "general-welfare" or the "necessary-and-proper" clause. The constitutional clause granting Congress power to impose taxes for the "general welfare" was not of all-inclusive scope, he said, but was merely a general statement to indicate the sum of the enumerated powers of Congress. In short, the "general-welfare" clause did not even convey the power to appropriate for the general welfare but merely the right to appropriate pursuant to the enumerated powers of Congress.

With reference to the clause empowering Congress to make all laws necessary and proper for carrying into execution the enumerated powers, Jefferson emphasized the word "necessary," and argued that the means employed to carry out the delegated powers must be indispensable and not merely "convenient." Consequently, the Constitution, he said, restrained Congress "to those means without which the grant of power would be nugatory."

In rebuttal Hamilton presented what was to become the classic exposition of the doctrine of the broad construction of federal powers under the Constitution. He claimed for Congress, in addition to expressly enumerated powers, resultant and implied powers. Resultant powers were those resulting from the powers that had been granted to the government, such as the right of the United States to possess sovereign jurisdiction over conquered territory. Implied powers, upon which Hamilton placed his chief reliance, were those derived from the "necessary-and-proper" clause. He rejected the doctrine that the Constitution restricted Congress to those means that are absolutely indispensable. According to his interpretation, "necessary often means no more than needful, requisite, incidental, useful, or conducive to. . . . The degree in which a measure is necessary, can never be a test of the legal right to adopt it; that must be a matter of opinion, and can only be a test of expediency."

Then followed Hamilton's famous test for determining the constitutionality of a proposed act of Congress: "This criterion is the *end,* to which the measure relates as a *mean.* If the *end* be clearly comprehended within any of the specified powers, and if the measure have an obvious relation to that *end,* and is not forbidden by any particular provision of the Constitution, it may safely be deemed to come within the compass of the national authority." This conception of implied powers was later to be adopted by John Marshall and incorporated in the Supreme Court's opinion in *McCulloch* v. *Maryland* on the constitutionality of the second national bank.

In his report on manufactures, Hamilton presented a powerful argument for a protective tariff for certain industries as a means of attaining a proper balance between agriculture, commerce, and manufacturing, and a prosperous and expanding economy. Since the protection of industry was not an enumerated power of Congress, the authority for such action had to rest again upon the doctrine of implied powers. Although Hamilton's recommendation to Congress was adopted in only a modified form, the opposition to the protective tariff was based more upon policy than upon alleged unconstitutionality.

Distinctly unsympathetic to the states, Hamilton used the doctrine of implied powers to advance a centralizing conception of federalism. At the Constitutional Convention Hamilton had supported a general legislative power for Congress; in interpreting the Constitution in the 1790s he fashioned virtually a plenary power out of the taxing, spending, and commerce powers of Congress. The taxing power, he held, was limited only by the restrictions contained in the Constitution that duties be uniform throughout the United States and that direct taxes be levied in proportion to population. The power to promote the general welfare through appropriations was limited only by the requirement that the objects sought be general rather than local. And the commerce power in Hamilton's view extended to all commercial activity in the United States, whether crossing state lines or confined within the borders of a single state. Although never formally disavowing the divided sovereignty of federalist theory, Hamilton came close to asserting exclusive sovereignty in the general government.

Hamilton's constitutional program secured for the federal government the support it needed to achieve legitimacy in the public mind. Confirmation of this fact came in the Whisky Rebellion of 1794, when farmers in Pennsylvania protested and threatened to block execution of the excise tax on whisky contained in Hamilton's fiscal program. Alarmed by frontier unrest and eager to assert national authority, Congress in May 1792 enacted a law authorizing the president to call out the militia in case an insurrection occurred against federal authority or in case a state, threatened by internal disorder beyond its control, called for federal aid. Based on the idea that the employment of military power should be unequivocally subordinated to the processes of civil government, the act provided that the militia was to be employed only when "the laws of the United States shall be opposed, or the execution thereof obstructed, in any state, by combinations too powerful to be suppressed by the ordinary course of judicial proceedings, or by the powers vested in the marshals." Even then the president was required first to issue a proclamation warning the insurrectionists to disperse peaceably.

In 1794 resistance to the whisky tax in western Pennsylvania took on an organized character and threatened to result in a serious breakdown of the federal revenue laws. In August 1794, therefore, Washington issued a proclamation in accordance with the Act of 1792, commanding all insurgents to submit to federal authority within three weeks. When they failed to do so, he proceeded to call out 13,000 militiamen from Pennsylvania and nearby states to suppress the insurrection. The uprising quickly disintegrated, a few of the leading rebels being arrested and tried for treason. The episode demonstrated conclusively that the new federal government possessed ample power to enforce its authority over individuals, even recalcitrant ones.

The Rise of Political Parties

Hamilton's program depended for its success on systematic political support in the national legislature. This, in turn, provoked a rival constellation of interests and ideas that led to an unforeseen constitutional development: the formation of political parties. Previously in the states a system of factional politics had existed in which alignments changed from one issue to the next in a fitful and episodic way. Within a few years of the launching of the new government, however, something very like modern political parties—voluntary associations identified by a distinctive political philosophy and possessing a permanent organization that extended from the general government to the local level—became a principal force in American political life.

The requirements of organizing public opinion and directing the activity of the new continental government provided the occasion for organizing political parties. The starting point was Congress. Supporters of Hamilton's mercantilist program, most of whom had been Federalists in the ratification campaign, coordinated their votes in adopting his recommendations. Led by the Virginians James Madison and Thomas Jefferson, the latter the secretary of state in Washington's administration, critics of Hamilton's policies reacted by forming a southern-oriented and agrarian-based opposition—the Republican party. Foreign policy questions, especially those arising out of the necessity of adopting a position on the French Revolution, presented additional issues in relation to which the nascent party groups formed distinct identities.

Sympathetic to the French republic, the party of Madison and Jefferson adhered to classic agrarian republicanism. In the political context of the 1790s the chief tenets of Republican ideology were the moral and social necessity of a virtuous and economically independent yeomanry; fear of mercantilist-designed schemes of executive influence or corruption; resistance to centralizing broad construction of federal legislative power; and support of state powers and local sovereignty. The Federalist party, in contrast, was less confident of the collective wisdom of the people and hence more elitist in its political style. Federalists promoted mercantile capitalist economic development through a broad construction of federal power, a strong and unitary executive branch, subordination of state powers to a centralizing federalism, and a foreign policy openly oriented toward British interests.

From a constitutional perspective the formation of political parties was a surprising innovation, for the framers of the Constitution had anticipated no such development. Even as political leaders conformed to the dictates of party behavior and constructed a party system in the 1790s, they persisted in the ancient belief that a permanent organized opposition was a danger to the body politic and inherently seditious. Yet ancient beliefs notwithstanding, in the expanded republic it was necessary to organize and transmit public opinion to elected officials as a guide to policy-making. It was further necessary to com-

bine, coordinate, and mobilize the welter of competing interests that characterized American society. And it was necessary also to bring together in some
manner the branches of government that were disjoined under the doctrine of
the separation of powers. All of these constitutional purposes were served by
political parties, which accordingly may be described as having a constituent
or constitutional function. In the broadest sense, then, parties were an extension and refinement of republican representation.

The emergence of political parties had still further significance related to
the concern for constitutional fidelity that early came to characterize American politics. The rapid acceptance of the Constitution as a test of political
legitimacy, despite conflicting interpretations of the basic document, has often
been noted. In a general way the practice can be explained as a consequence
of the new theory of constitutionalism which Americans adopted during the
Revolution. Political circumstances in the 1790s, however, supplied the decisive impetus that committed Americans to Constitution worship as a political
method and style.

Ironically, principal credit for insisting on literal fidelity to the Constitution as a test of political action belongs to Antifederalist critics of the Constitution, many of whom formed the Republican party in the early 1790s. Imbued
with eighteenth-century republican opposition ideas, the party of Madison and
Jefferson feared arbitrary executive power, broad construction leading to consolidation of legislative power in the federal government, and corruption in the
form of "government by debt" as in Hamilton's fiscal policies. More to the
point, these several threats stimulated a general fear of constitutional degeneration and decline that was an essential element in classical republican thought.
Indeed, it was axiomatic in the republican tradition that the tendency of any
constitution was toward degeneration. Vigilance in its defense was necessary,
therefore, lest liberty be destroyed. Accordingly, although many Republicans
had opposed ratification, once the Constitution was adopted, they insisted in
a highly literal way that its provisions be maintained. As classical eighteenth-
century republicans had venerated the ancient constitution of England, so
Republicans worshiped America's new Constitution as though it were old.
Functionally and effectively, the Constitution became the ancient constitution,
to be venerated for the sake of preserving republican liberty. The movement
toward party identification in the early 1790s thus stimulated Constitution
worship, which in turn provided a further rationale for promoting party organization.

The Sedition Act Crisis

At the end of the decade, deteriorating relations between the United
States and France resulted in an undeclared naval war which provided the
occasion for the new nation's first constitutional crisis. In 1798 the Federalist

majority in Congress, responding to the intense excitement generated by the war, enacted the Alien and Sedition Acts. Based generally on the conventional view that equated organized political opposition with treason, these measures, of which there were four, were intended to suppress the partisan activities of the Republican opposition.

Least open to constitutional attack was a new Naturalization Act, which stipulated that an alien, to be eligible for citizenship, must prove fourteen years of residence within the United States. Far more controversial were the Alien Act, the Alien Enemies Act, and the Sedition Act. The Alien Act authorized the president to order the deportation of an alien whom he deemed dangerous to the peace and safety of the United States. The Alien Enemies Act empowered the president in case of war to deport aliens of an enemy country or to subject them to important restraints if they were permitted to remain in this country. The Sedition Act not only made it a high misdemeanor for any person to conspire to oppose any measure or to impede the operation of any law of the United States but also made it illegal for any person to write, print, or publish "any false, scandalous and malicious writing . . . against the government of the United States, or either house of the Congress . . . , or the President . . . , with intent to defame . . . , or to bring them, or either of them, into contempt or disrepute; or to excite against them, or either or any of them, the hatred of the good people of the United States."

The two Alien Acts were aimed at French and pro-French foreigners in the United States, who were virtually unanimous in their support of the Republican party. Jefferson's followers at once attacked the laws as grossly unconstitutional. They argued, first, that the acts would deprive persons of their liberty without due process of law in violation of the Fifth Amendment and, second, that they contemplated the imposition of penalties without judicial process upon persons not convicted of any offense.

The Sedition Act posed a far more difficult constitutional problem. The sponsors of the law admittedly had intended virtually to reenact the English common law of seditious libel as a congressional statute. The First Amendment, the Federalists contended, had merely incorporated the English common law guarantee of "no prior restraint," which prohibited censorship before publication but which permitted very broad prosecution for seditious libel subsequent to the publication of anything unfriendly to the government. The truth of the published matter at issue did not constitute a defense, and the judge had sole power to decide whether or not it was libelous. English freedom of the press thus meant little more than a prior right to publish, or a prohibition of prior censorship. The present law softened the traditional law of seditious libel, for it permitted truth as a defense and allowed the jury to decide whether an utterance was libelous—two reforms for which the champions of free speech had long contended.

Federalists held to the existence of a federal criminal common law, received into American law from the English courts and enforceable by the federal judiciary. Under this law Federalists reasoned that it would be constitutional to institute prosecutions in the federal courts for seditious libel without benefit of any statute, and in 1797 they began two common law prosecutions of Republican newspaper editors for seditious libel in lower federal courts. To provide a more secure political basis for dealing with the opposition, however, and because there was doubt in some circles about the existence of federal criminal common law, the Federalists enacted antisedition legislation. Their constitutional argument was that the First Amendment accepted and was compatible with the English view of freedom of speech as no prior restraint. The Sedition Act imposed no prior restraint, and thus in no way interfered with freedom of the press. The act did interfere with the licentiousness of the press, but Federalists believed that this merely maintained true liberty of the press.

The Adams administration enforced the Sedition Act with vigor, securing some fifteen indictments and ten convictions. The hope entertained by some Republicans that the federal courts might declare the law unconstitutional proved false; Federalist judges refused to allow counsel to challenge its constitutionality. Technically, most presiding judges allowed defense counsel to plead the truth of alleged libel, but in their charges to the jury refused to admit proof of libel, so this defense invariably failed. In addition, Federalist judges conducted Sedition Act trials in a partisan manner, browbeating counsel and witnesses and delivering partisan harangues to the jury.

The Virginia and Kentucky Resolutions

Republicans strenuously protested the Sedition Act. Given the risks that now attended published criticism of the government, and the refusal of the Federalist-dominated judiciary to permit the constitutionality of the measure to be tested in court, the Republicans' immediate problem was to find an appropriate forum in which to argue for repeal of the act. Their choice was the state legislatures. Accordingly, Thomas Jefferson and James Madison anonymously prepared resolutions denouncing the Sedition Act and its companion measures, which they caused to be introduced into the legislatures of Kentucky and Virginia. Framed for the practical purpose of removing what Republicans considered obnoxious legislation, the Kentucky and Virginia Resolutions also were documents of seminal importance in the development of American constitutional theory.

The Virginia legislature expressed "a warm attachment to the union of the states" and a firm resolve to support the government of the United States in all of its legitimate powers. But it viewed "the powers of the Federal Government as resulting from the compact to which the states are parties, as limited by the plain sense and intention of the instrument constituting that compact; as no further valid than they are authorized by the grants enumerated in that compact." The Kentucky legislature also subscribed to the idea of the Constitution as a compact, and both states condemned the Sedition Act as unconstitutional. Each also appealed to the other states for support in sustaining this judgment and in bringing about the repeal of the measure.

In the Kentucky and Virginia Resolutions and in related protest writings, Republicans raised four fundamental constitutional issues: the scope of federal legislative power; the settlement of constitutional disputes and the role of the states therein; the nature of the Union; and the meaning of freedom of speech and of the press and its bearing on the question of legitimate political opposition.

Republicans held the Sedition Act to be a violation of the First Amendment prohibition against congressional legislation abridging freedom of speech and of the press. But this transgression of constitutional limitations was objectionable, according to Jefferson's Kentucky Resolutions, not because it was wrong for government in general to restrict the freedom of the press, but because regulation of the press lay in the sphere of state power. "No power over the freedom of religion, speech, press being delegated to the United States by the Constitution, nor prohibited by it to the states," Jefferson wrote, "all lawful powers respecting the same did of right remain, and were reserved to the states, or to the people." The states and the people thus retained "the right of judging how far the licentiousness of speech and of the press may be abridged without lessening their useful freedom." Deference to state power—or a concern for federalism—was thus the principal reason for limiting the scope of federal legislative authority.

A related consideration, pertinent to limiting not only federal legislative but also judicial power, was the Republican rejection of a federal common law of crimes. According to the Republican view, Congress could punish as crimes only those matters enumerated as such in the Constitution; seditious libel not having been so enumerated, Congress lacked the power to enact a sedition law. Repudiation of the idea of a federal common law of crimes, and by extension a general common law, was important for the implications it contained for the scope of federal legislative power. In England, a common law country, Parliament was empowered to legislate on any subject dealt with in the common law. If the common law were regarded as federal law and liable to revision and alteration by Congress, Madison wrote in 1800,

it then follows that the authority of Congress is coextensive with the objects of common law; that is to say, with every object of legislation; for to every such object does some branch or other of the common law extend. The authority of Congress would, therefore, be no longer under the limitations marked out by the Constitution. They would be authorized to legislate in all cases whatever.

Congress would in effect have a general legislative power, as in a unitary state, contrary to the federal requirement of divided sovereignty.

Federal judicial authority would, of course, also expand enormously if a federal common law were recognized. Jefferson warned against this danger in attacking as most "novel" and "formidable" the Federalist argument for "a system of law for the United States without the adoption of their legislature [that is, the common law]." "If this assumption be yielded to," Jefferson predicted, "the state courts may be shut up, as there will be nothing to hinder citizens of the same state suing each other in the federal courts in every case."

A second issue in the Sedition Act crisis concerned the settlement of constitutional disputes in general, and those involving the exercise of federal powers in particular. Eventually the Supreme Court was to assume the power to resolve questions about the meaning of the Constitution, but in the early years of the republic the federal judiciary played no such role. Either the separate branches of the government presumed to exercise this power or, as in the Sedition Act episode, the states tried to determine the meaning of the Constitution and keep the federal government from transgressing constitutional limitations. Denying that the federal government had the exclusive power to judge the extent of its own powers, the legislatures of Kentucky and Virginia declared that "in case of a deliberate, palpable, and dangerous exercise of other powers not granted by the said compact, the states, who are parties thereto, have the right and are in duty bound to interpose for arresting the progress of the evil, and for maintaining within their respective limits the authorities, rights, and liberties appertaining to them." Kentucky and Virginia also expressed confidence that the other states would join in declaring the Sedition Act and the other Federalist measures unconstitutional.

Reliance on the states to decide constitutional controversies grew out of the Republican theory of the Union, the third major constitutional issue in the Sedition Act crisis. Seizing on the confederation aspect of the mixed system created by the Constitutional Convention, Jefferson and Madison declared the Union to be a compact among sovereign states, rather than the constituent act of the people of the United States considered as a single polity. In the language of the Kentucky Resolutions, the Constitution was a compact to which "each State acceded as a State, and is an integral party, its co-States forming, as to itself, the other party."

The precise meaning of the compact theory as presented in the Virginia and Kentucky Resolutions was and remains problematic even today. It may have been nothing more than a statement of political philosophy derived from the Revolution asserting the compact theory of the state and the limited character of federal sovereignty. Probably it did not signify rejection of the divided sovereignty of federalism. Nevertheless, as John C. Calhoun and a later generation of southern political leaders showed, the language of the Kentucky and Virginia Resolutions lent itself to an interpretation denying federal sovereignty altogether. Although Madison in his last years disavowed any legitimate connection between the Virginia Resolutions and Calhoun's doctrine of state sovereignty, nullification, and secession, Madison and Jefferson prepared the way for, if they did not fully anticipate, the South Carolina theory.

More pertinent perhaps than the subsequent application of Madison and Jefferson's theory of the Union are the questions of what the Republican leaders hoped to achieve in 1798 and how they expected to accomplish their goal. The Kentucky Resolves declared that the Alien and Sedition laws exceeded the constitutional power of Congress and hence were "not law" but were "altogether void and of no force." The legislature said further that the states would not tamely submit to such extension of congressional authority beyond the constitutional limits, and it added ominously that "these and successive acts of the same character, unless arrested on the threshold, may tend to drive these States into revolution and blood."

Jefferson's original draft had declared that "where powers are assumed which have not been delegated, a nullification of the act is the right remedy," and had expressed hope that the "co-States . . . will concur in declaring these [Alien and Sedition] acts void and of no force, and will each take measures of its own for providing that neither of these acts . . . shall be exercised within their respective territories." For expediency or other reasons this section was replaced by an appeal to the other states and by instructions to Kentucky's congressional representatives "to use their best endeavors to procure, at the next session of Congress, a repeal of the . . . unconstitutional and obnoxious acts."

In 1799 Kentucky issued a second set of resolves reasserting the view that if the general government was the exclusive judge of its own delegated powers, the result would be despotism. Now Jefferson stated "That the several States who formed that instrument [the Constitution] being sovereign and independent, have the unquestionable right to judge of the infraction; and, that a nullification of those sovereignties, of all unauthorized acts done under color of that instrument is the rightful remedy."

In the antebellum period "interposition" and "nullification" became terms to conjure with, and it is an intriguing question to ask what Madison and Jefferson meant in using this language in 1798. These were strong words which conceivably implied the use of force. Yet it is likely that Madison and Jefferson had something else in mind—a coordinated and peaceful state response, employing the convention method of political action in preference to state legislative decision.

Madison and Jefferson's success in protesting the Sedition Act depended on the cooperation of the other states. On this score the results were not encouraging. The other southern states made no official response, sentiment being fairly evenly divided in their legislatures, and the northern states, controlled by Federalists, endorsed the Alien and Sedition measures. The northern states also held that the federal courts, not the state legislatures, were the proper tribunal for settling constitutional disputes. The Sedition Act was thus not repealed, but expired according to its original terms at the end of the Adams administration in March 1801.

Behind the controversy over state interposition and the settlement of constitutional disputes lay the fact that there was no general agreement on the precise nature of the Union. Everybody agreed that the powers of the government were divided between the states and the central government. It was also evident that the Constitution had made no explicit provision for the settlement of disputes over power between the two units of government. Article VI, which provides for the supremacy of the Constitution and federal laws, might be balanced against the Tenth Amendment, which provides for the reservation of undelegated powers to the states, without producing a conclusive answer. The government established under the Constitution was essentially a compromise between a confederation and a unitary state. In limited and varying degrees the political leaders realized that in the long run such a compromise might prove unworkable and that the federal system might evolve either into modified confederation or into a strongly centralized national government. The Republicans claimed that if a branch of the federal government had the final power to judge of the extent of federal authority, the states would ultimately and inevitably be reduced to a subordinate position. On the other hand, the Federalists asserted that the recognition of the right of each state to act as final judge in case of vital disputes would lead to utter confusion and probably to "an interruption of the peace of the states by civil discord." No decision on this all-important issue was reached in 1799, and in one form or another the question was to crop up almost continuously through the years until it was finally settled on the battlefield.

The Sedition Act gave rise to a fourth constitutional issue: the meaning of freedom of speech and of the press and the relevance of these First Amendment freedoms to the legitimacy of an organized political opposition. From the Republican standpoint the reforms that the Federalists had put into the Sedition Act were inconsequential: The very idea that freedom of the press existed so long as there was no prior restraint of publication suddenly appeared inadequate. Punishment after publication, Republicans argued, was every bit as inhibiting as prior censorship. Accordingly, they repudiated the whole idea of seditious libel and drew a modern libertarian distinction between critical, even inflammatory words, which they believed should be permitted, and overt actions injurious to the state, which they believed government could properly prevent. Republicans furthermore rejected the notion that political opinions could be subjected to tests of truth and falsehood, as the existing law on seditious libel assumed. On the contrary, it now began to appear that political opinions were subjective and relative, and thus not capable of evaluation according to objective criteria. Moreover, Republicans turned their new libertarian view of the First Amendment to the legitimation of party activity. In a republican constitutional order, they reasoned, a free press was an essential means of shaping the public opinion needed to control and direct government. An organized political opposition was but a refinement of this process of forming and expressing the public opinion on which republican government rested.

The Republican argument for a modern view of freedom of the press and a legitimate opposition was by no means conclusive or decisive. For one thing, despite the existence of the rule that defined freedom of the press as no prior restraint, in the American colonies there had been relatively little punishment after publication and hence much that we would recognize as freedom of the press in a modern sense. Second, when the Republicans came to power after 1800 they violated the standards of free speech and a free press which they had invoked against the Federalists in 1798. On several occasions they prosecuted Federalist editors in the state courts for seditious libel against state governments. Nor did the Republican justification of an organized political opposition compel an abandonment of earlier views denying the legitimacy of party. Nevertheless, despite the persistence of rhetoric suggesting otherwise, political opposition in the United States was not subsequently to be treated as subversive.

Although constitutional theory lagged behind events, in a practical sense political parties were recognized as legitimate in the election of 1800. With Jefferson's election as president, power was transferred peacefully from the party that had written and implemented the Constitution to the organized opposition, whose protests of government policy only a few months earlier had been branded seditious. The "Revolution of 1800" ended the period of constitutional formation and inaugurated an era of Republican constitutionalism.

NINE

Republican Constitutionalism: 1801–1828

THE ELECTION OF 1800 brought to power a party whose character and identity were shaped by eighteenth-century English opposition thought, and whose constitutional principles were set forth in the Virginia and Kentucky Resolutions. At the core of Republican philosophy of government lay a cluster of constitutional ideas: the separation of powers and legislative independence, resistance to executive influence, strict construction of federal powers, and states' rights and the compact theory of the Union. In the first Jefferson administration Republicans adopted policies that were both consistent with these constitutional precepts and politically effective. Starting with the Embargo of 1807, however, Republican constitutionalism underwent profound change, until by the 1820s it evinced the same centralizing, consolidating tendency that it had originally opposed.

The causes of this transformation were diplomatic and military events beyond the power of Americans to control, and the inevitable requirement that theory yield to practice in the actual conduct of government. The changes in Republican constitutionalism also reflected the irresistible tendency in modernizing countries, of which the United States was an early example, toward integration and centralization in government, law, and administration. Yet because decentralist, antigovernmental values were deeply embedded in the political culture, the trend toward constitutional centralization was soon arrested. Although largely abandoned by the Republican party after the War of 1812, these principles reappeared as the constitutional basis of a new opposition party in the 1820s, the Jacksonian Democrats.

Republican Constitutional Ideas

Both Federalists and Republicans referred to the election of 1800 as a revolution because it portended the introduction of political and constitutional values entirely different from those that prevailed in the first decade of the new government. Instead of anticipating a new order in the manner of modern revolution, however, the Republicans saw their victory as signaling a return to an earlier condition of liberty and civic virtue. Regarding Federalist rule as a threat to republicanism, the triumphant Jeffersonian party proposed to restore the true principles of the American Revolution.

Republicans took as their point of departure the eighteenth-century agrarian philosophy, which regarded land as the source of all political, social, and economic values. Ownership of land enabled men to become personally and politically independent and hence capable of civic virtue and patriotism. In the Republican theory of society, therefore, agriculture was the preeminent concern; commerce was a useful and necessary adjunct to it. This was not true, however, of banks, credit, paper money, and the related instruments of capitalist expansion that had developed in England and, under the auspices of the Federalist party, were spreading with dangerous effect in the United States. These mercantilist devices, seen in Hamilton's funding, assumption, national bank, and protective tariff schemes, not only lacked the moral sanction bestowed by productive enterprise on the soil, but they also created social and political distinctions and privileges that threatened the liberty and equality of republican self-government. This agrarian philosophy naturally appealed to the principal constituent elements in the Jeffersonian party—southern planters and yeoman farmers, both North and South. But its vision of a natural social order in which individual liberty was reconciled with social justice, and in which a general equality of condition could result from the rule of equal opportunity and individual initiative in a materially abundant environment, held attraction also for urban merchants, artisans, and craftsmen whose original loyalty to the Federalist party was eroded by Hamilton's high-toned and elitist policies. When Jefferson in his inaugural address said "We are all Republicans, we are all Federalists," he was expressing his belief that his election demonstrated the appeal of his party's ideals to all groups in the society.

Legislative independence based on the separation of powers provided the foundation principle of Republican constitutionalism. The separation of powers was important chiefly as a means of resisting British-style ministerial government—emanating from the executive branch and undermining legislative autonomy through patronage, a national bank and national debt, a standing army and navy, and monopolistic corporate privileges. This, of course, was what Hamilton's policies represented in the eyes of Republicans, and, as noted previously, it was to prevent this kind of ministerial manipulation that Republicans formed standing committees in Congress in the later 1790s. Recalling parliamentary spokesmen in the seventeenth century and American revolutionary leaders in 1776, Republicans appealed to the separation-of-powers theory in its radical form in an attempt to make the lawmaking branch paramount. In contrast to the Federalists, the Republicans came to power as the party of the legislature and hence of the people.

This legislative identification notwithstanding, Republicans also endorsed strict construction of congressional power and—its logical corollary under federal theory—states' rights. The strict-construction–states'-rights equation was not basic to Republican philosophy in the same way that the separation of powers or opposition to executive influence were. This was because the problem of federal-state relations was not part of the body of classical republican thought transmitted by the opposition writers of the eighteenth century. Republican theory was concerned with the essential problems of constitutionalism: the relationship between citizens and the government, the distribution of powers among the parts of government, the proper limits on governmental power in the interest of individual liberty. By contrast, federalism, rooted in the peculiar history of the American colonies and intended to satisfy conflicting tendencies toward centralization and local autonomy in American society, was a deliberately ambiguous institutional arrangement which invited a more flexible, expedient response.

This is not to say that the Republican party did not embrace federalism as a principle of union expressing the American people's sense of nationality. Within the framework of federal theory, however, a number of approaches were possible, one of which was summed up in the strict-construction–states'-rights formula. As an opposition party challenging Federalist rule, the Republicans necessarily were attracted to and employed theories that would deny the constitutional basis of Federalist policies. When under the pressure of subsequent events they adopted a more centralizing stance and favored the exercise of national power, they were not being cynical and opportunistic, but rather were obeying the imperative of constitutional politics within a federal framework. Groups or parties involved in public policy-making could be expected to shift their position on the grid of federal-state relations as their needs and circumstances altered. More important than consistency in adhering to a particular view of the federal-state balance was the commitment to the Union implied in the different approaches to federalism adopted in the nineteenth century.

The compact theory of the Union, the third major element of Republican constitutionalism, was, of course, the foundation of the strict-construction–states'-rights idea. Here, too, however, it would be a mistake to exaggerate the importance of this doctrine in the Jeffersonian outlook or to read back into the period of Federalist-Republican struggle theories about the nature of the Union that were not developed in a systematic way until the 1820s and 1830s. When Virginia and Kentucky protested the Sedition Act, no other state supported them. But all the states except one accepted the compact theory; only

Vermont argued in contrast that the Union was formed by the people of the United States. The compact theory was thus not specially identified with the Republican party, despite its conspicuous recognition in the events of 1798. Its widespread acceptance was perhaps a further reason why upon taking office Jefferson felt able to emphasize the elements of consensus between Republicans and Federalists.

Jefferson's inaugural address pronounced good government to be "a wise and frugal Government, which shall restrain men from injuring one another [and] shall leave them otherwise free to regulate their own pursuits of industry and improvement." To a considerable extent Republican policies during Jefferson's first term were able to implement this laissez-faire, republican ideal. The Hamilton national bank and funding system was left in place, but internal excise taxes were repealed, government expenditures were reduced by the elimination of certain civil offices, and the regular army and navy were drastically cut back. Using revenues from customs duties and public land sales, Republicans also went far toward retiring the public debt, the hated engine of corruption according to their opposition republican philosophy.

The Jeffersonian Executive

Successful as these reform efforts were in fulfilling the promise of the Revolution of 1800, in several respects Republicans departed from the constitutional position they professed in their opposition period. Despite their earlier appeal to the strict separation of powers, for example, Republican practice rapidly evolved a system of coordination between the executive and legislative branches that depended heavily on presidential leadership and influence. Like their Federalist predecessors, the Jeffersonians had to figure out a way to make Congress an effective policy-making body. Hamilton had tried to do so by creating a ministerial system on the British model. Without formally abjuring the separation of powers, the Republicans fashioned their own system of executive influence.

Jefferson solved the problem of coordinating the political branches within the separation-of-powers framework through the great prestige and unquestioned ascendancy he possessed as party leader. Nominally, he accepted the theory of congressional ascendancy in legislation. Unlike Washington and Adams, he sent his messages to Congress by a clerk rather than reading them in person, and he was uniformly deferential in his messages and in his other relationships with Congress. He did not veto a single bill.

At the same time, Jefferson used a variety of methods to assert a strong executive leadership in Congress. Although his practice varied, depending upon conditions, he often had his political lieutenants placed in key legislative and political positions and worked through them to effect his legislative program. Also, Treasury Secretary Gallatin served as an effective and valuable liaison officer between the president and Congress. Although the Republicans had earlier condemned the Federalist practice of referring legislative matters to Hamilton as secretary of the Treasury, they now revived the practice by asking Gallatin to make reports and proposals to the House. He attended committee meetings and assisted in the preparation of reports to be presented to the House. In general he became a sort of executive manager who cooperated with the congressional leaders in steering measures through Congress.

This unofficial fusion of the executive and legislative departments would have been very difficult if not impossible without the employment of another extraconstitutional device, the party caucus. From time to time the president, cabinet officers, and party members in Congress met in caucus and discussed proposed legislation fully and came to a conclusion upon policy before specific measures reached the floor of either house. It was alleged that Jefferson himself upon occasion presided at these secret meetings. By holding doubtful members in line, the caucus increased party solidarity in Congress and facilitated enactment of important measures.

Before Jefferson became president, Hamilton said of him that he would be no enemy to executive power, while John Marshall, in a contrary estimate, predicted that Jefferson would weaken the presidency by embodying himself in the legislature. In different ways both of these judgments proved accurate. To be sure, Jefferson vigorously employed executive power, in particular by relying on skills of persuasion but also occasionally by using the power of legal compulsion and even military coercion. At the same time, however, Jefferson's exercise of power caused no immediate or permanent alteration in the contours of the office. Rather the result was, as Marshall had feared, the cultivation of lines of influence into Congress through which power could and did run in the opposite direction when presidents lacking Jefferson's enormous prestige and instinct for power occupied the White House. Such was the case with the successor Republican presidents James Madison, James Monroe, and John Quincy Adams. Indeed, their tenure in office can be described as a period of congressional government, when Congress formulated policy, involved itself deeply in the administration of the government, and, through a system of standing committees, used the power of investigation to hold the executive closely accountable for the conduct of public business. Further evidence of a decline in executive power was the fact that cabinet offices were frequently continuous from one administration to the next, with the president acting as head of a directory or first among equals.

Nevertheless, Jefferson changed the presidential office, or showed a previously unrealized dimension, by making it a popular institution. The founding fathers, and Washington and Adams as the first chief executives, viewed the presidency as a counterweight to the popularly elected legislature, and thus in some sense as an anti- or a nonrepublican institution. Jefferson, however, as head of government and head of state who was also the leader of a political party, politicized the office in an unprecedented way. Under the separation-of-powers doctrine the legislative branch could always claim to be in a special sense the voice of the people, but starting with Jefferson, presidents could make the same claim by virtue of their identification with a political party. Although the personality and political skills and persuasiveness of the incumbent would always do much to determine the actual power of the executive office at any given time, Jefferson made American government in some permanent sense presidential government.

Finally, the republicanization of the executive office associated with the rise of political parties was related to a formal constitutional change in the method of electing the president. Under the framers' plan for filtering and refining public opinion, the Constitution required electors in the states to vote for two persons, the one with the most votes to become president, the runner-up vice-president. The emergence of political parties in the 1790s politicized the operation of the electoral college, however, and in 1796 resulted in the election of a president, Adams, and vice-president, Jefferson, who belonged to different parties. Further difficulty occurred in 1800 when a tie vote between Jefferson and Aaron Burr threw the election into the House of Representatives. To avoid a repetition of this situation and to assure a unified executive, and fearing machinations between Burr and the Federalists that might enable the latter to win the vice-presidency,[1] the Republicans proposed a constitutional amendment providing for separate ballots for president and vice-president. Ratified in September 1804, the Twelfth Amendment reflected the politicization of the presidency and Republican determination to unify the executive branch under their control.

The Louisiana Purchase

Paralleling the spread of republican influence in the constitutional order was the expansion of the republic itself through territorial annexation. The acquisition of Louisiana from France provided the occasion for this constitutional development.

Expansion was inherent in the very founding of the colonies in the seventeenth century. After more than a century and a half of social and demographic growth, the founding fathers transposed this expansionist tendency into a constitutional key in the expanded republic of 1787. The Constitution left territorial matters rather vague, principally because of sectional disagreement over the character and disposition of the western lands as a national resource. With the launching of the new government, however, expansion became a more urgent issue as southern and western landed and commercial interests

1. Republicans feared that Federalist votes would be cast for Burr, forcing them to scatter their second votes to ensure the election of Jefferson as president and allowing their opponents to secure the vice-presidency.

pressed the federal government to take control of the Mississippi River from Spain and later France. In 1803 the Jefferson administration, seeking to satisfy the land hunger of its agrarian constituents, purchased and proposed to annex to the Union the vast area of Louisiana. This bold step promised to secure far into the future a seemingly endless supply of land for territorial expansion.

The Louisiana Purchase raised two important constitutional questions: Did the United States have the power to acquire foreign territory, and, if so, could territory such as Louisiana be governed and admitted to the Union as a state on the basis of equality with the original states? Republicans were proponents of the theory of strict construction, which limited federal authority to specifically enumerated powers. Yet the Constitution said nothing of a right to acquire territory. If so sweeping a power were considered to be implied, it would discredit the doctrine of strict construction and go far toward legitimizing the Hamilton theory of implied powers.

Jefferson at first proposed to resolve the dilemma by amending the Constitution to grant the federal government the requisite authority to purchase territory. His advisers argued, however, that it might be dangerous to allow the purchase treaty to be delayed while waiting for a constitutional amendment to be ratified. Napoleon might change his mind and the opportunity be lost. The president's advisers also argued that the power to acquire territory was inherent in the very existence of the United States as a sovereign nation—a proposition that challenged the Republican theory of the Union as a compact among states. Jefferson reluctantly but prudently accepted this view.

Concerning the government and disposition of the Louisiana lands, sharp controversy arose when the president asked Congress to approve and implement the purchase treaty. The focal point of dispute was a provision in the treaty stating that "The inhabitants of the ceded territory shall be incorporated in the Union of the United States, and admitted as soon as possible, according to the principles of the Federal Constitution, to the enjoyment of all the rights, advantages, and immunities of citizens of the United States; and in the mean time they shall be maintained and protected in the free enjoyment of their liberty, property, and the Religion which they profess." This provision was essentially a promise of eventual statehood for the people of Louisiana, and Federalists strongly objected to it on the ground that under the Constitution the admission of new states was left to the discretion of Congress. Fearful that the creation of new southern and western states would further weaken their already declining political position, Federalists held that territory could be acquired by conquest or purchase, but must be governed as a colony. Republicans answered that the treaty did not positively guarantee statehood, inasmuch as territorial status would satisfy the requirements set forth therein. Whether states should be admitted from the Louisiana Territory would be left to the future discretion of Congress.

The Senate ratified the treaty in October 1803, 26 to 5, and both houses then appropriated the money and made temporary provisions for the govern-

[Left margin handwritten notes:]
JEFFERSON PROP. / REPUBLICAN DILEMMA FOR JEFF. IF "STRICT INTERPRETATION" APPLIES AN AMMENDMENT TO ENABLE HIM / JEFFERSON HAS NO RIGHT TO BUY TERRITORY TO BUY LAND

FEDERALISTS WANTED NEW LANDS GOVERNED AS COLONIES. REPUBLICANS WANTED NEW STATES.

ment of the new territory. Since a majority of Congress did not believe that the people of the acquired territory were yet ready for a large amount of self-government, the first governing act provided that all military, civil, and judicial authority in Louisiana should be vested in appointees of the president. Since the Constitution explicitly gave Congress the power to "make all needful Rules and Regulations" respecting the territory of the United States, there was inherent in this measure no serious question of congressional authority. However, objection was raised to the autocratic nature of the territorial government, and soon the administration sponsored another measure providing for a gradual preparation of the French and Spanish inhabitants of Louisiana for self-government. This second law provided for government by a powerful governor and a weak council to be appointed by the president from the property-holding residents of the territory.

American immigrants were soon settling in Louisiana and demanding greater participation in the government. Consequently, in 1805 a third act gave the Territory of Orleans, as the lower part of the Louisiana purchase was termed, a territorial government very similar to that outlined in the Northwest Ordinance of 1787. The vast area north of the present state of Louisiana contained few white people and was temporarily attached to Indiana Territory for purposes of administration. Thus did the territory acquired from France rapidly come to have a constitutional status practically identical with that of the original territory of the United States.

It is customary to say that the significance of the Louisiana episode was to weaken the strict-construction–states'-rights mode of constitutionalism. Certainly the Republicans departed from their avowed principles of '98, in part because exigencies demanded it. In a deeper sense, however, the reversal of roles between Republicans and Federalists on strict versus broad construction and the compact theory of the Union was testimony to the strength and appeal of these constitutional principles. In order for constitutional rhetoric to have effect it need not be applied with consistency. Indeed, when groups or parties shift constitutional positions, as Federalists and Republicans started to do in these years, they do so because they believe the new theories and principles they espouse embody values in the political culture on the basis of which they can appeal to public opinion in the altered circumstances in which they find themselves. The significance of the Louisiana controversy, therefore, lies not in some supposed cynicism about constitutional principles that political expediency inspires, or even in the cautionary reminder that practice must temper theory. Rather it lies in the insight it offers into the development of a distinctively American form of constitutional politics, based on rhetoric and principles that have the power to influence public opinion because they express fundamental values.

The Embargo

If the annexation of Louisiana created a new and expanded Union which in Republican eyes was merely an expansion of the republican empire of liberty, the major event in Jefferson's second term—the embargo—transformed Republican constitutionalism in a more questionable way by interjecting federal executive authority deeply into the commercial life of the society. Professing the enlightened purpose of avoiding war, Jefferson imposed on the country an apparatus of coercion that seriously threatened republican liberty.

Caught between warring France and England, Jefferson hoped to be able to force the depradating European powers to respect American neutrality and maritime rights by denying them the benefits of American trade. Accordingly, in December 1807 he proposed to Congress an embargo on all foreign commerce. After only four days of debate Congress adopted the measure by large majorities. The act placed a ban on all U.S. ships bound to any foreign port and required ships in the coastal trade to post bond double the value of the cargo as a guarantee that the goods would be relanded in the United States. The embargo did not close American ports to European imported goods carried in the ships of other nations. In 1808 three supplementary measures were passed tightening the shutdown of American shipping. Their principal effect was to prohibit exports by land as well as by sea and to strengthen executive enforcement of the embargo. Conceived as a defensive measure intended to buy time and preserve American maritime resources against the eventuality of a war with Great Britain, the embargo by the end of 1808 became in Jefferson's view an offensive weapon of economic coercion by which to purify the republic by ridding it of corrupt commercial interests.

The first of several constitutional issues raised by the embargo concerned the nature and scope of the commerce power, the main constitutional basis of the law. According to Republicans, the commerce power was complete and could be extended to include outright prohibitions upon all commercial activity. Some administration supporters drew a distinction between federal power over interstate commerce and federal power over foreign commerce. They admitted that Congress could not constitutionally lay any outright prohibitions upon commerce between the states, but they insisted that federal power over commerce with foreign nations was of a more complete character, since the commerce clause was reinforced in that field by the government's control over foreign affairs. The Federalist opposition, on the other hand, insisted upon an extremely narrow definition of the commerce power. The right to regulate, they said, implied only the right to protect in order to extend benefits thereto. The power was not restrictive, and certainly was not prohibitive. They also said the commerce power could not be used for any ulterior purpose—that is, any purpose other than the protection of commerce itself.

Under the circumstances, the action of Congress in passing the embargo went far toward settling the question of its constitutionality. Confirmation of the congressional judgment came from the federal judiciary and, ironically, from a Federalist judge. In October 1808, in the federal district court for Massachusetts, Judge John Davis upheld the embargo in very broad terms in the case of *U.S.* v. *The William.* "The degree or extent of the prohibition" imposed on foreign commerce, Davis said, must properly be left to "the discretion of the national government, to whom the subject appears to be committed." Davis rejected the contention that the commerce power could be used only for the protection of commerce itself: "the power to regulate commerce is not confined to the adoption of measures exclusively beneficial to commerce itself, or tending to its advancement; but in our national system, as in all modern sovereignties, it is also to be considered as an instrument for other purposes of general policy and interest." He also sustained the embargo under the war power as a preparation for war, and under the necessary-and-proper clause as appropriate for the protection of the nation's inherent sovereignty.

The scope of executive authority was a second constitutional issue raised by the embargo. The several acts of Congress gave the president sweeping authority to enforce the ban on trade as he saw fit through military and revenue officers, and even required his special permission before any ship could depart for an American port adjacent to foreign territory. Subordinate enforcement officers operated without benefit of search warrants or court process, giving rise to questions of unreasonable search and seizure in possible violation of the Fourth Amendment. No search-and-seizure issue was ever presented in litigation, but the scope of executive authority was nevertheless questioned in an important lower federal court decision handed down by a Republican Supreme Court Justice, William Johnson.

The collector of the port of Charleston, South Carolina, acting under discretionary authority given by Congress in the fourth Embargo Act, gave clearance to a ship bound for Baltimore, but then detained it on subsequent orders from Jefferson implementing the statute. The owner of the ship petitioned the federal circuit court for a writ of mandamus directing the collector to clear the vessel; Justice Johnson, sitting on circuit, decided for the shipowner. Johnson held that the collector had discretionary authority from Congress that the president could not override. More broadly and provocatively, Johnson declared: "The officers of our government, from the highest to the lowest, are equally subjected to legal restraint; and it is confidently believed that all of them feel themselves equally incapable, as well from law as from inclination, to attempt an unsanctioned encroachment on individual liberty." Through the attorney general, Jefferson denied the court's authority to issue a writ of mandamus, and his lieutenants in Congress introduced a bill making customs collectors expressly subject to executive direction. To combat the growing public disregard of the embargo, the bill authorized the president to use military force—without the requirement of a proclamation—to compel obedience to the policy. In January 1809 Congress passed this extraordinary enforcement act.

It would have been difficult to enforce the embargo even in a centralized unitary state. In the decentralized federal republic the task was extremely difficult. Jefferson devoted nearly all his energies to supervising enforcement of the embargo, becoming, in the words of a recent biographer, "commissar of the nation's economy." Normally a skilled and persuasive political tactician, Jefferson in this instance failed to prepare the public for the sacrifices demanded of it, and strangely refrained from presenting a justification of the policy when dissatisfaction with it spread. Enforcement of the embargo was carried out for the most part under federal admiralty jurisdiction, under *in rem* proceedings which did not require juries. It was possible, however, for defendants charged with violating the embargo laws to seek trial by jury at common law. In New England especially, jury trials provided a forum for protesting the administration policy and usually ended in acquittal.

Enforcement of the embargo has been estimated as being 95 percent effective—astonishing evidence of the extent to which federal authority had been accepted as legitimate in the space of a generation. Yet incidents of illegal trade and militant opposition to the series of laws became increasingly conspicuous—and politically costly. In New York, for example, along the Canadian border where resistance was particularly intense, Jefferson proclaimed an insurrection and ordered several persons prosecuted for treason. The suit was unsuccessful. Republican Supreme Court Justice Brockholst Livingston held on circuit, in the case of *U.S.* v. *Hoxie,* that no matter how violent, refusal to obey a law in time of peace could not be construed as levying war against the United States.[2]

Laudable as Jefferson's intentions were, the embargo proved to be destructive of republican liberty. The economic distress it caused, added to the political and constitutional costs it exacted, marked it an egregious failure. In March 1809, as Jefferson left office, Congress repealed the embargo.

The War of 1812 and National Republican Mercantilism

If in his first term Jefferson was on the whole successful in governing according to his party's original tents, his doctrinaire adherence to peaceful coercion in his second term served to discredit both executive authority and agrarian republicanism. During the successor administrations of James Madison and James Monroe the party's identification with the principles of the Virginia and Kentucky Resolutions became increasingly tenuous as the need to generate and exercise power—required by the War of 1812 and then by the

2. Article III, Section 3, of the Constitution defines treason as levying war against the United States or adhering to their enemies, giving them aid and comfort.

task of internal economic development—became more compelling. In the postwar period Republicans combined centralizing elements of Hamiltonian political economy with the expansionist and populistic republicanism of their original outlook. The result was a policy of national mercantilism. Meanwhile, the Federalist party, where it continued to exist, had recourse to the opposition philosophy of strict construction and states' rights set forth by the Republicans in 1798.

Bitterly opposed to the War of 1812, Federalists seized on the issue of federal control of the state militia to challenge the authority of the general government. The Constitution dealt with the problem in a seemingly clear way by giving Congress the power "To provide for calling forth the Militia to execute the Laws of the Union, suppress Insurrections, and repel Invasions." Congress was also authorized "To provide for organizing, arming, and disciplining the Militia, and for governing such Part of them as may be employed in the Service of the United States."[3] Against the manifest intention of these provisions, several New England states under Federalist control refused to permit their militia to be commanded by federal officers or to become an integral part of the army of the United States. Furthermore, all of the New England states attempted to ban service of their militia outside their borders and in effect built up separate state armies for their own defense against British attack.

Federalist discontent came to a head in the Hartford Convention, called by Massachusetts in December 1814. Although the idea of secession had been urged by extremist Federalists, moderates who controlled the convention proposed state interposition and amendment of the Constitution as milder alternatives to disunion. The states were urged to protect their citizens against unconstitutional federal militia and conscription legislation, and to request the federal government to permit the separate states to defend themselves and receive federal tax credits for such action. The Hartford Convention also proposed seven amendments to the federal constitution. One proposal would eliminate the three-fifths clause in the Constitution and base representation in the House of Representatives solely upon free population. Embargoes were to be limited to sixty days. A two-thirds vote of both houses of Congress would be required to admit a new state, to interdict commerce with foreign nations, or to declare war except in case of actual invasion. Naturalized citizens were to be disqualified from federal elective or appointive office. No president was to serve two terms, and no two successive presidents were to come from the same state. The final resolution proposed the calling of another convention if the war continued and the federal government failed to respond favorably to the recommendations of the convention.

Federalist sponsors of states'-rights–based constitutional reform fared no better than the Republicans had in 1798–99. Only Connecticut and Massachu-

---

3. Article I, Section 8.

setts approved the Hartford proposals, while nine states disapproved or dissented. From a practical standpoint the chief consequence of the proceedings was further to discredit the Federalist party in the arena of national politics. Constitutionally, the convention was significant because it endorsed—and thus nationalized—the state's-rights–strict-construction idea as a basic axiom of American politics. Useful especially for opposing the policies of the federal government, this constitutional method had first been asserted by southern agrarians in the Sedition Act crisis. Now it was taken up by New England merchants and shown to have national appeal, even though, as before, the interest it served was narrowly sectional. In adopting the stance they did, the Federalists were on the opposite side of the constitutional fence. This shift signified the emergence of a structure of politics based on constitutional principles and rhetoric—such as states' rights and strict construction—which embodied basic American political values. Carried to the extreme of state sovereignty, as it eventually would be in the antebellum period, the states'-rights idea had disunionist consequences. But used as it was in the Hartford Convention to repudiate secession and support the moderate alternatives of state interposition and constitutional amendment, the states'-rights idea helped to strengthen the emerging system of constitutional politics within the federal framework.

After 1815, with the threat to national independence removed in foreign affairs and the Federalist challenge eliminated at home, the Republican party turned its attention to the country's internal economic development. In dealing with this issue Republicans employed centralizing constitutional instruments in a context of mercantilism that carried the party further from the principles of '98.

Despite the emphasis in the American constitutional tradition on governmental limitations and guarantees of individual liberty, the mercantilist conception of positive government actively promoting and regulating economic affairs continued to have appeal during the revolutionary and early national periods. In this pre–laissez-faire era the question was not whether government would intervene, but how it would do so and to what extent. In the 1790s Hamilton's policies intruded federal authority into the commercial life of the nation, and Republican administrations, notwithstanding Jefferson's frequent paeans to frugal and minimal government, early showed themselves willing to use power for what they regarded as suitably republican purposes, as in the Louisiana Purchase. From 1815 to 1825 Republicans employed broad construction to fashion a democratized, westward-looking mercantilism—the famous American System of Clay, Calhoun, and Webster.

Republican mercantilism resembled Federalist policy in certain respects, but was notably different in others. It comprehended a national bank, but not a national debt intended to connect the most powerful commercial groups with the government, as in Federalist political economy. The Republican outlook was also distinguished from Hamiltonianism by its commitment to territorial and political expansion and by its concern for both agrarian and commercial development. Furthermore, although Republican mercantilists exercised federal power vigorously, they took a more favorable view of states' rights than the Federalists. Centralizing though it was in comparison to the localist tendency of the party's opposition phase, Republican mercantilism nevertheless looked to a balance between the states and the federal government. Republicans expressed this balanced conception of Union in legislative programs in which, to a limited extent, federal and state governments shared power and responsibility in banking, internal improvements, and land distribution.

As with the Federalists twenty years earlier, the first step in creating a Republican system of mercantilism was to establish a national bank. In 1811 Congress, dominated by Republicans, had refused to grant a new charter to the Bank of the United States. Since that time, however, many strict-constructionist Republicans had changed their mind about the wisdom and constitutionality of a national bank. The demise of the first bank in 1811 had caused the states to charter a number of state banking institutions, many of which failed to observe the elementary rules of sound banking practice. They had issued large quantities of paper money, much of it of little or no value, which circulated as part of the nation's monetary system and often caused great confusion in commercial and industrial circles. The Constitution specifically forbade the states to coin money and emit bills of credit, but as John C. Calhoun pointed out, the chartering of state banks had enabled the states to elude this restriction and usurp control of the monetary system. The absence of a national bank also proved a serious handicap to federal fiscal policy and financial activities during the War of 1812, for the government not only lacked any adequate agency of deposit, but it also missed the financial assistance such a bank might have been able to extend.

The Republican nationalists accordingly brought about the passage of a national bank bill in January 1815. Madison vetoed the measure as inadequate, but at the same time indicated his belief that the bank was constitutional, and in his annual message of December 1815 he again recommended passage of a national bank law. In January 1816, accordingly, Calhoun, as chairman of the special committee on uniform national currency, introduced a bill to incorporate a new Bank of the United States for twenty years with a capital of $35,000,000, one-fifth of which was to be subscribed by the federal government.

Calhoun defended this measure's constitutionality by holding that it was a necessary and proper means to the establishment of a uniform national currency. The main object of the framers of the Constitution in giving Congress the power to coin money and regulate its value, he thought, must have been to give steadiness and fixed value to the currency of the United States. The various states, through their banking activities, had recently worked the defeat of this end and had actually taken over control of the nation's monetary system. Consequently, he concluded, it was the duty of Congress to recover control over the monetary system, and this could best be done through the medium of a national bank.

Congress passed the bill creating the second Bank of the United States (BUS) in 1816. The measure was centralizing to the extent that it created a federal agency, but it also recognized the rights and powers of the states by giving state banks a role in the national fiscal system. In contrast to 1791, when the first Bank of the United States was chartered, numerous state banks were now in existence (most of them created by Republicans under state law after 1800), and these banks constituted an interest powerful enough to prevent establishment of a federal bank had they been so disposed. Most state banks recognized the need for national coordination, however, and supported the act of 1816. In 1817 the BUS and the state banks agreed to resume redemption of their notes in specie and thereafter created forms of cooperation in the management of the banking business that resulted in a national fiscal system.

Internal improvements was a more contentious constitutional problem, the resolution of which passed through a series of stages. Expansionist in outlook, Republicans early supported the construction or improvement of roads, canals, waterways, and harbors in order to promote commerce and internal communications. The act admitting Ohio to the Union in 1802, for example, provided that 5 percent of the revenue from public land sales be directed toward the building of roads. In 1806 Jefferson recommended to Congress the application of surplus federal revenue to public education and internal improvements, to be undertaken after the adoption of a constitutional amendment authorizing legislation for this purpose. Congress ignored the suggestion of a constitutional amendment and authorized construction of the National Road, from Cumberland, Maryland, to the Mississippi River. Only a few miles of the road were constructed before foreign policy problems caused the temporary abandonment of internal improvement projects, including a ten-year plan prepared by Secretary of the Treasury Albert Gallatin in 1808.

The War of 1812 having demonstrated the need for more effective internal transportation and communication, Madison in 1815 and 1816 advocated a federal program. Like Jefferson, he regarded a constitutional amendment as necessary to give Congress the power to carry out such a program. Republicans in Congress thought otherwise, however, and, employing broad construction, passed the so-called Bonus Bill, setting aside the $1,500,000 bonus paid by the national bank for its charter and the United States government's bank dividends as a permanent fund for internal improvements. John C. Calhoun of South Carolina cited the general-welfare clause as a constitutional basis for the bill, arguing on the example of the Louisiana Purchase and the National Road that federal appropriations need not be confined to enumerated powers. Others cited the commerce power as constitutional justification, insisting that Congress could authorize projects crossing state lines or confined to single states.

Having accepted broad construction on the bank question, Madison rejected it with respect to internal improvements. He vetoed the Bonus Bill on the ground that, no power for this purpose having been enumerated in the Constitution, approval would have the effect of acknowledging or creating a general legislative power in the federal government. In particular the general-welfare clause should not be interpreted or employed as Congress proposed, Madison reasoned, lest the whole scheme of enumeration and limitation of powers be abandoned. Nor in Madison's view did the general-welfare clause authorize appropriations of money beyond the enumerated powers of Congress.

A kind of constitutional dialogue now ensued between Republican president and Congress that resulted in a compromise on the internal-improvements question. President James Monroe in 1817 advocated a constitutional amendment authorizing federal legislation in this sphere, and an amendment was brought in giving Congress power to appropriate money accordingly. The House believed it already possessed this power, however, and passed a resolution in 1818 stating that Congress could appropriate money for post roads, military highways, and canals. On the other hand, it rejected a resolution stating that the federal government had the power to construct internal improvements. In 1819 Secretary of War John C. Calhoun submitted plans for a comprehensive system of internal improvements that called for both direct federal construction on a military basis and federal-state cooperation in the form of federal appropriations and state construction.

Monroe accepted federal-state cooperation in his Cumberland Road veto of 1822, and it subsequently became the basis for a federally sponsored program of internal improvements. The bill that Monroe vetoed provided for federal toll gates and maintenance, and gave the federal government certain jurisdictional rights over the road within the various states. Monroe rejected it on the ground that collecting tolls was an exercise of local sovereignty and thus an invasion of the state police power. But he said Congress could appropriate money for internal improvements with the consent of the states affected. It was this approach that was adopted in the General Survey Act of 1824.

The act of 1824 authorized comprehensive surveys by army engineers of routes for roads and canals judged by the president to be in the national interest. It took the view that actual construction and operation of internal improvements lay within state jurisdiction. In the next several years Congress appropriated money to several interstate canal projects that were constructed by private corporations incorporated under state law, or by the states themselves. By the mid-1830s, too, Congress ceded the Cumberland National Road to the states through which it passed. This resolution of the question and the consistent rejection of exclusively federal projects may be said to have vindicated the states'-rights–strict-construction point of view. But the more important point is that a national policy took shape under federal sponsorship in a way that respected the sensibilities of states'-rights advocates.

Republican Constitutional Interpretation

Republican national mercantilism encouraged a dynamic approach to constitutional interpretation that regarded the Constitution more as an instrument of power than as a source of limitations. Republican constitutionalism also looked to the legislature and ultimately the people as authoritative expositors of the Constitution. Madison subscribed to this view when he said, in his bank bill veto message of 1815, that all question of the bank's constitutionality had been precluded by "repeated recognition under varied circumstances of the validity of such an institution in acts of the legislative, executive, and judicial branches of the Government, accompanied by indications, in different modes, of a concurrence of the general will of the nation." Calhoun said the same thing in defending the Bonus Bill in 1816. He admitted that the Constitution was founded on positive and written principles rather than precedents, but he insisted that continuous popular approval of internal improvements was "better evidence of the true interpretation of the constitution, than the most refined and subtle arguments."

Henry Clay went further in holding that changes in circumstances created or led to the discovery of new constitutional powers. Clay reasoned that whereas in 1811 the Bank of the United States recharter bill was unconstitutional, in 1816 it was constitutional because conditions had changed and a national bank was now necessary to give effect to the enumerated powers of the Constitution. Carried to its logical extreme this method of interpretation would eliminate all fixed limitations on the federal government and create an utterly elastic fundamental law that could be changed by the legislature itself. The result would negate the very premise of American constitutionalism that governmental and especially legislative power must be kept subordinate to the organic law of the Constitution. A few states'-rights critics attacked the idea that federal legislation could settle constitutional questions on the ground that it would make the Constitution a dead letter, but these fears were exaggerated. Nevertheless, Republicans showed the potential for expansion of government power inherent in a pragmatic, instrumental conception of the Constitution in a way that was prophetic of government in the twentieth century.

The mercantilist phase of Republican constitutionalism came to a culmination—and produced a strong strict-construction–states'-rights reaction—in the administration of John Quincy Adams (1825–29). Stating that the purpose of civil government was to improve the condition of its constituents, Adams in his annual message to Congress in 1825 asserted that the exercise of delegated powers under the Constitution was "a duty as sacred and indispensable as the usurpation of powers not granted is criminal and odious." Adams acknowledged that the Constitution was a charter of limited powers, but, citing the enumerated powers of Congress and also the general-welfare and necessary-and-proper clauses, he said that to refrain from exercising these powers "would be treachery to the most sacred of trusts." The limiting Constitution thus became an authorizing and empowering instrument. Arguing that "liberty is power," Adams urged upon Congress a multitude of governmental projects, from the founding of a national university to the construction of roads and canals on a vast scale. Pointing to recent state accomplishments in the internal-improvements field that he offered as motivation for more extensive federal efforts, he admonished Congress not "to slumber in indolence" or be "palsied by the will of our constituents."

Adams's appeal to positive government and broad construction aroused vigorous opposition. For nearly two decades, since Jefferson's departure from the principles of '98, an old Republican faction centering on the agrarians John Randolph and John Taylor of Virginia had steadily criticized the centralizing trend in Republican constitutionalism. By the mid-1820s this link with the opposition Jeffersonian tradition had, through the political enterprise of Martin Van Buren of New York, developed into a coalition of southern planters, northern farmers, and small entrepreneurs that appealed to the principles of states' rights and strict construction. President Adams, meanwhile, lacking a broad political base to begin with since he owed his election to the House of Representatives, lost what little political capital he had through his high-toned appeal to public improvement under federal auspices. Committed to a kind of commonwealth vision of the national interest, Adams nevertheless appeared as a defender of a narrow northeastern commercial and industrial interest. Thus the stage was set for yet another "revolution"—the triumph of Jacksonian democracy—which its supporters hoped would arrest the trend toward centralization and restore states' rights to a more prominent position.

TEN

The Place of the Judiciary in the Constitutional System and the Origins of Judicial Review

THE DECISIVE ROLE acquired by the judiciary in interpreting and applying the written Constitution has caused American constitutionalism to be highly legalistic and juridical compared to the constitutional systems of England and European nations. The primary basis of judicial power has been judicial review, the practice by which courts determine the legitimacy of legislative acts by considering them against the requirements of a written constitution. Moreover, judicial review has given rise to the judicial monopoly theory of constitutional interpretation—the belief that final authority to state the meaning of the Constitution and to settle constitutional controversies belongs exclusively to the courts. This outlook differs greatly from that which prevailed in the early years of the new government. The "least dangerous branch," as Hamilton described it, the judiciary occupied an uncertain position in relation to the other branches of government. Courts struggled to defend their independence against legislatures and executives, and to vindicate their authority to settle constitutional disputes over individual rights. Problematic also was the structure of the American judicial system. The organization of federal courts, their relationship to the state courts, and the place, if any, of the English common law in national law were all highly controversial matters.

The Judiciary Act of 1789

During the American Revolution legislatures dominated constitutional change, expanding their power and frequently interfering in disputes over private rights. Although the judiciary was recognized as a coordinate branch of government under the separation-of-powers theory, its power was tenuous and uncertain. Controversy at the state level centered on whether judges would be appointed or elected, and whether they should enjoy tenure during good behavior or serve a limited term. The underlying issue was the responsibility or political accountability of the judiciary to the community, and until it was settled the administration of justice was uneven, if not capricious, in many states. Dissatisfaction with this situation became widespread in the 1780s and contributed to the demand for constitutional reform at the continental level. A major concern of the Constitutional Convention, therefore, was to create a national judicial system that would provide a more uniform administration of justice than the courts of the states were able to provide.

In accordance with the separation-of-powers doctrine, the Constitutional Convention created a judicial department and vested in it "the judicial Power of the United States." The judicial power extended "to all cases, in law and equity, arising under this constitution, the laws of the United States, and treaties made . . . under their authority," and to cases involving ambassadors, public ministers, admiralty jurisdiction, controversies between states and between citizens of different states. Desiring a uniform judicial system for the nation, the framers differed over how best to establish it. All agreed that a single tribunal—the Supreme Court—ought to stand at the apex of the system. But it was not at all clear whether the national judicial system below the Supreme Court ought to consist of state courts, acting in a dual state and federal capacity, or lower federal courts. Unable to decide the question, the convention chose neither alternative, but rather authorized Congress to create inferior federal courts at its discretion. It also stipulated tenure during good behavior, placed appointment in the hands of the executive, and endorsed a limited form of judicial review as part of the system of checks and balances.

The first Congress promptly enacted legislation creating a system of inferior federal courts. The work principally of centralist-minded Federalists, especially Oliver Ellsworth of Connecticut, the Judiciary Act of September 24, 1789, incorporated the principle of federal supremacy into the national judicial system. It provided for a Supreme Court consisting of a chief justice and five associate justices; thirteen federal district courts of one judge each—one district for each of the eleven existing states and two additional districts, in Virginia and Massachusetts, for Kentucky and Maine; and three circuit courts, each composed of two justices of the Supreme Court sitting in conjunction with one district court judge. The jurisdiction of the various courts was stated in great detail, and, to a lesser degree, their organization and procedure.

Although the Judiciary Act upheld the principle of federal supremacy, it was in essence a compromise between states' rights and centralization. The centralizers' chief accomplishment was Section 25 of the act, which brought the state courts directly under federal appellate jurisdiction by providing for appeals from state courts to the federal judiciary. Under this section, appeals could be taken to the United States Supreme Court whenever the highest state court having jurisdiction of a case (1) ruled against the constitutionality of a federal treaty or law; (2) ruled in favor of the validity of a state act which had been challenged as contrary to the Constitution, treaties, or laws of the United States; or (3) ruled against a right or privilege claimed under the Constitution or federal law. In effect, this meant that appeals would be taken in all instances where the state judiciary assertedly failed to give full recognition to the supremacy of the Constitution or to the treaties and laws of the United States, as provided by Article VI of the Constitution.

This provision, which solved the problem of conflicts between state and national spheres of authority, was to become the very crux of American federalism. If the Constitution and federal laws and treaties were to be "the supreme Law of the Land," it was vital that they be interpreted with reasonable uniformity. Unless the Supreme Court were given authority to review the decisions of state courts in disputes between the states and the federal government over their respective powers, it would be possible for state courts practically to nullify federal authority, just as state legislatures had virtually nullified the authority of Congress under the Confederation. Therefore, the nationalists insisted that the Supreme Court must be the final interpreter of the Constitution and as such must have the right to receive appeals from state courts.

The Constitutional Convention had not specifically provided for appeals from state to federal courts, but Ellsworth and the other centralizers in Congress assumed the right to be implied in the Constitution. In 1789 and for many years afterward, the critics of Section 25 of the Judiciary Act claimed that the Constitution specifically placed the responsibility for upholding federal supremacy upon the state courts and that Congress had no authority to subject their decisions to review by the Supreme Court of the United States. This opposition was motivated by the fear that the state judiciaries and state powers would be gradually absorbed by federal authority, a fear that made it almost impossible for this group to see the necessity for the uniform upholding of federal supremacy throughout the Union.

Although the creation of inferior federal courts was a centralist victory, it was balanced by the granting of a significant amount of jurisdiction to the state courts. Some Federalists thought that the inferior federal courts should have all the judicial authority that the Constitution made available—that is, in "all cases in law and equity" arising under the Constitution, laws, and treaties. In the opinion of these lawmakers Congress had no discretion in the matter, but must vest in the lower courts the entire judicial power allowed by the Constitution. This centralizing effort failed, however, with the result that the federal courts had limited exclusive original jurisdiction and much concurrent original jurisdiction with the state courts.

Federal district courts received exclusive original jurisdiction in admiralty and maritime cases and in cases involving crimes and offenses cognizable under the authority of the United States. At the least, this meant crimes specified by act of Congress; whether it also refered to crimes at common law was a disputed issue. Unlike the situation today, federal circuit courts were to be the main courts of general original jurisdiction in the federal system and could hear suits of a civil nature at common law or in equity where the matter in dispute exceeded the sum of $500. But the state courts were given concurrent original jurisdiction in civil suits at common law or equity; and because they were more numerous, they could be expected to be the principal courts of first instance in the national judicial system. The influence of the states was further apparent in the decision to have the federal courts adopt the methods and procedures of the state courts. Section 34 of the Judiciary Act stated that "The laws of the several States, except where the Constitution, treaties, or statutes of the United States shall otherwise require or provide, shall be regarded as rules of decision in trials at common law in the courts of the United States in cases where they apply."

The Federal Judiciary in the 1790s

The federal judiciary was slow to acquire a position of prestige and importance. During the first three years of its existence the Supreme Court had no cases to decide. Most legal matters were handled through the state courts, and many people were jealous of the potential power of the new federal judicial system. Only gradually did the Supreme Court's work grow in volume and importance; it was the federal circuit courts, where Supreme Court justices presided, that first brought federal judicial authority home to the people. Through the charges to grand juries by judges of these courts, the public was informed regarding the basic principles of the new government and the provisions of important federal statutes. And although the state courts predominated, the volume of business in the federal courts was more considerable than historians have usually assumed.

The basic question concerning the judiciary in the 1790s was its relationship to the political branches of government. The courts were subjected to much political pressure. At both the state and federal level judges tried to deal with this situation by drawing a distinction between law and politics that would reserve the former sphere—especially matters of individual right—to courts, while allowing legislatures and executives to prevail in the latter. Federal courts sought to establish this distinction by restricting their decisions and opinions to the adjudication of specific cases duly brought before them. Thus in 1792, in the so-called *Hayburn's* case, certain circuit court judges

Hayburn's Case 1792

expressed their disagreement with a recent act of Congress which provided that the circuit courts should pass upon certain claims of disabled veterans of the Revolutionary War. "Neither the Legislative nor the Executive branches," said the judges, "can constitutionally assign to the judicial any duties but such as are properly judicial and to be performed in a judicial manner."

The following year President Washington, desiring legal advice on the questions of neutrality, had his secretary of state address a letter to Chief Justice John Jay asking the justices of the Supreme Court whether the chief executive might seek their advice on questions of law. The judges were also presented with a list of specific questions on international law and neutrality. After due consideration the judges declined to give their opinion on the questions of law on the grounds that the constitutional separation of the three departments prevented them from deciding extrajudicial questions.

The function of the federal judiciary that was of the greatest public concern was its determination of the compatibility of state constitutions, statutes, and court decisions with "the supreme Law of the Land." This function was of the utmost importance in the operation of the federal system of government, for it not only tended to establish the Court as the final interpreter of the Constitution, but it also emphasized the supremacy of the national government. The guardianship of the distribution of powers between the states and the central government was not explicitly assigned by the Constitution to the federal courts, but the Judiciary Act of 1789 had taken a long step in that direction by providing for appeals from state to federal courts on constitutional questions.

Considerable popular dissatisfaction was aroused in 1796 by the Supreme Court decision in the case of *Ware v. Hylton,* concerning conflict between a Virginia statute and the Treaty of Peace with England ending the Revolutionary War. The issue was whether the treaty, which stipulated that neither side should meet with any lawful impediment to the recovery of full value of all debts contracted before the treaty, overrode statutes passed by the Virginia legislature that made other provisions for payment of pre-war debts. Declaring that a treaty "cannot be the supreme law of the land . . . if any act of a State Legislature can stand in its way," the Supreme Court stated that the plaintiff was entitled to recover his debt. In holding against the state the Court provoked criticism of the judges as pro-British Federalists.

Even more serious opposition to federal judicial authority had been excited by the decision in *Chisholm v. Georgia* (1793), a case involving the right of the federal judiciary to summon a state as defendant and to adjudicate its rights and liabilities. The Constitution expressly gave the federal courts jurisdiction over "controversies between a state and citizens of another state." In the campaign for the ratification of the Constitution in the various states prominent Federalists had assured their apprehensive opponents that this provision would not encompass suits against states without their consent. Almost from the establishment of the federal judiciary, however, suits were instituted against states by citizens of other states. In *Chisholm* v. *Georgia*, two citizens of South Carolina, executors of a British creditor, brought suit in the Supreme Court against the state of Georgia for recovery of confiscated property. The state refused to appear and presented a written protest denying the jurisdiction of the Court. Meanwhile the Georgia legislature considered a resolution declaring that the exercise of such authority by the federal judiciary "would effectually destroy the retained sovereignty of the States."

The Supreme Court rendered its decision in favor of Chisholm, and the individual justices presented elaborate opinions explaining the nature of the federal union and the extent of federal judicial authority. The majority of justices, especially John Jay and James Wilson, discussed at length the nature of sovereignty and maintained that under the Constitution sovereignty was vested in the people of the United States for "purposes of Union" and in the people of the several states for "more domestic concerns." In ordaining and establishing the Constitution the people acted "as sovereigns of the whole country." They established, said Chief Justice Jay, "a constitution by which it was their will, that the state governments should be bound, and to which the state constitutions should be made to conform." Consequently, the state of Georgia, "by being a party to the national compact," in order "to establish justice," consented to be suable by individual citizens of another state. In dissenting from the decision Justice James Iredell, while admitting that sovereignty under the Constitution was divided between the United States and the individual states, denied that the English common law, under which a sovereign could not be sued without its consent, had been superseded either by constitutional provision or by statute law.

Opposition to the decision promptly appeared, especially in those states where suits similar to Chisholm's were pending or were instituted against the state. Georgia refused to permit the *Chisholm* verdict to be executed. The day following the decision there was initiated congressional action, which a year later resulted in the submission of the Eleventh Amendment to the states for ratification. It provided: "The Judicial power of the United States shall not be construed to extend to any suit in law or equity, commenced or prosecuted against one of the United States by Citizens of another State, or by Citizens or Subjects of any Foreign State." Because of indifference or Federalist opposition the amendment was not ratified by the requisite number of states until January 1798. Thus for the only time in its history the federal judiciary had its jurisdiction directly curtailed by constitutional amendment.

Judicial Reform: The Judiciary Act of 1801

The controversy in which the federal judiciary found itself as a result of *Chisholm* v. *Georgia* was exceptional, for more often than not the federal courts labored in obscurity. Technical or professional problems afflicted the

[handwritten margin notes: "Political background to Marbury vs Madison"]

national court system from the outset, however, and when political and economic circumstances in the late 1790s caused the federal judiciary to become strategically important, reforms affecting the organization and jurisdiction of the national courts gained support in Congress. The result of this heightened interest in judicial power was the Judiciary Act of 1801.

From the beginning of the national court system in 1789 dissatisfaction arose with the organization of the circuit courts. Supreme Court justices did not like riding circuit nine months out of the year, as they were required to do. More important, they did not like acting in an appellate capacity in the Supreme Court on matters that they had already decided as circuit court judges. As early as 1790, therefore, proposals were introduced into Congress for removing Supreme Court justices from circuit duty and creating a separate circuit court judiciary. Nothing came of these measures, however, because the federal judiciary lacked the political significance needed to achieve such a reform.

This situation began to change in the late 1790s as a result of economic controversies involving Federalist land speculators and Republican-controlled state courts. In several states large land companies became embroiled in disputes arising out of the interpretation and application of state land laws. Under the Judiciary Act of 1789 these matters lay within the jurisdiction of state courts; accordingly, in Georgia, Kentucky, Pennsylvania, and Virginia, where major disputes existed and Republicans were in control, Federalist speculators faced the prospect of litigation in unfriendly courts that tended to favor settlers. Under these circumstances land companies took an interest in judicial reorganization since it offered the possibility, through a change in the jurisdiction of federal courts, of gaining access to a more sympathetic forum than the states would provide.

The Sedition Act crisis further stimulated political interest in the federal judiciary. Even before the act was passed, suits were brought in federal courts under the common law of seditious libel. More suits were initiated after adoption of the measure, and as tension mounted in 1799, Federalists who heretofore had ignored the judiciary began to see expansion of federal court jurisdiction as a means of containing the Republican insurgency. Suddenly, the technical problems of judicial organization and jurisdiction acquired large importance. Regarded in 1799 as a defense against potential Republican subversion, judicial reform after the election of 1800 seemed necessary to combat the decline of public order that Federalists feared would result from Jefferson's triumph. In this situation they adopted the Judiciary Act of 1801.

The act established six new circuit courts with their own judiciary, thereby requiring the appointment of sixteen circuit judges. It also provided for several new district courts. This increase in judicial personnel—the appointment of the famous "midnight judges" by outgoing president John Adams—was the most obvious and politically conspicuous result of the act. The Federalists' partisan purpose was plain enough. Losing power and fearing

[handwritten left margin notes: "There was precedent for the 11th Amendment in 1798", "land law dispute between Federalist speculators and Republican State legislatures", "Important to Marbury"]

[handwritten bottom notes: "Midnight judges", "Jud. Act 1801"]

revolution, they wanted reliable conservatives on the federal bench to maintain the status quo. An additional provision of the act, reducing the size of the Supreme Court from six justices to five effective with the next vacancy, eliminated tie votes, but also deprived the incoming president of his first appointment. It further emphasized the law's partisan aim.

But more important constitutionally than the appointment of Federalist judges was the expansion of federal jurisdiction authorized by the act of 1801. Here the major change concerned the circuit courts. Previously, their role as courts of first instance in private law matters was circumscribed by the requirement that the amount of money involved in a controversy had to be more than $500, and by the extension of concurrent jurisdiction to state courts. By contrast, under the act of 1801 circuit courts were given trial jurisdiction in all cases in law and equity arising under the Constitution and under laws and treaties passed in pursuance of it. In other words, the act gave circuit courts the full measure of judicial power authorized by the Constitution, thus going far toward creating the uniform judicial system envisioned by the framers of the Judiciary Act of 1789. The act of 1801 also removed the $500 requirement in civil litigation, and expressly gave circuit court jurisdiction over cases involving disputed land titles without regard to the amount involved. Finally, the act made it easier to remove from state to federal courts without regard to jurisdictional amount, and enlarged the jurisdiction of federal courts in diversity cases (that is, between citizens of different states). Previously, diversity jurisdiction arose only between a citizen of the state in which a suit was brought and a citizen of another state. Now any suit between citizens of different states was triable in any federal circuit court.

The immediate purpose of these provisions was to protect Federalist political and economic interests threatened by the Republican party's rise to power. But this political motivation should not obscure the corollary aim of reforming the circuit court system, or the effect the law had in promoting a more uniform administration of justice and bringing the federal judiciary closer to the people. If the state judiciary served as the people's courts in the first decade of the government, it was by no means certain that they alone were capable of fulfilling this function. Had the act of 1801 remained in effect, it might have popularized federal authority and detracted from the influence of the state courts. Indeed, it was this fear that caused Republicans to repeal the judicial legislation of 1801.

Federal Common Law

An additional reason why the Judiciary Act of 1801 was controversial concerned the question of a federal common law of crimes. The English common law, modified for local circumstances, was adopted or received by the American colonies throughout the eighteenth century as the basis of separate systems of private law. After the Revolution the states continued to adapt English rules and decisions, and around 1800 began to keep records of their own courts' proceedings. They thus created an indigenous body of common law on the English basis. The question necessarily arose, however, as to whether the English common law had also entered into national as well as state law. Federalists argued in the affirmative. Their theory was that the common law had been law for the empire as a whole and at the time of the Revolution was received into a general body of national law. Republicans held in contrast that the state courts alone had common law jurisdiction. For federal courts to entertain suits at common law, they contended, was a usurpation of states' rights.

There is evidence to suggest that the framers of the Constitution and the members of the first Congress regarded the common law as part of federal law. In drafting the judiciary article of the Constitution, the convention rejected language that would have confined the jurisdiction of the Supreme Court to all cases arising under the laws of the national legislature. Similarly, Congress in the Judiciary Act of 1789 rejected a limitation of lower federal court jurisdiction to crimes defined by United States statute. In each instance the purpose appears to have been to allow federal courts to assume common law jurisdiction as well as jurisdiction in pursuance of acts of Congress. Furthermore, there are references in the Constitution to elements of the common law, such as the writ of habeas corpus, which seem to rest on the assumption that the common law was an available source of national law.

At any rate, it is clear that many federal judges and other officers in the first few years of the government acted on the theory that the criminal common law was part of United States law. This was reflected in the government's decision to prosecute in the lower federal courts offenses that were not declared to be crimes under any act of Congress, and also in the instructions which judges gave to juries. Moreover, several cases at common law were successfully prosecuted in jury trials, which suggests that public opinion did not oppose the idea that the criminal common law had been received into federal jurisdiction. Yet the question of a federal common law had by no means been resolved, nor was it perceived as having any special political significance.

Toward the end of the 1790s, however, as the ideological differences between Federalists and Republicans crystallized, the issue of federal common law became politically controversial. *United States* v. *Worrall*, a circuit court case of 1798, illustrates this transition. Worrall was indicted at common law for attempting to bribe the United States commissioner of revenue, despite the fact that no congressional statute designated this act a federal crime. The jury found Worrall guilty, and he was convicted. Attention in the case focused, however, on the argument of defense counsel Alexander James Dallas, a Republican, who attacked the notion of a federal common law jurisdiction. The very idea of federal common law, he argued, was contrary to the nature of the Union. Citing the Tenth Amendment, Dallas said the powers of the federal government were delegated and strictly limited. The federal judiciary, accordingly, derived its authority solely from the Constitution and acts of Congress; the common law was not available as a source of jurisdiction. Dallas insisted that to allow the national courts to assume a common law jurisdiction would undermine state judicial authority and consolidate power in the federal government.

During the foreign policy crisis of 1798, Federalists relied on the criminal common law to deal with the threat to national security which they perceived in Republican criticism of the government. Hence they initiated prosecution of Republican editors in the lower federal courts under the common law of seditious libel. The passage of the Sedition Act provided a statutory basis for prosecuting for seditious libel in place of or in addition to the common law. Yet Republicans remained keenly aware of the threat to state power implicit in the assumption of federal common law jurisdiction. They were justifiably alarmed when Congress, in the Judiciary Act of 1801, extended the jurisdiction of the federal circuit courts to all cases in law or equity arising under the Constitution and laws of the United States. For under this sweeping authorization it was likely that the doctrine of a national common law, already supported by a majority of the Supreme Court, would gain acceptance throughout the federal judiciary.

Republicans not only feared that federal courts would supersede state courts in the administration of justice, but they also saw in the idea of federal common law the danger of centralized legislative power. This apprehension was based on the fact that the common law dealt with virtually every aspect of social life and that it was subject to legislative revision. If the United States had a common law, Republicans reasoned, Congress would be able to legislate on anything the common law touched, which meant in effect a general legislative power. In 1800 Thomas Jefferson stated: "If the principle were to prevail of a common law being in force in the U.S.," it would "possess the general government at once of all the powers of the state governments and reduce [the country] to a single consolidated government." In the opinion of the Republican *Virginia Argus,* the doctrine of a national common law "gives the Federal Government and its Courts jurisdiction over every subject that has hitherto been supposed to belong to the States; instead of the General Government being instituted for particular purposes, it embraces every subject to which government can apply."

After 1800 Republicans were in a position to resolve the question of federal common law on their own terms. Eventually, they did so in the Supreme Court case of *U.S.* v. *Hudson and Goodwin* in 1812. Ironically, the case began with Republican efforts to bring federal common law indictments against Federalist editors for libeling President Thomas Jefferson. Jefferson ordered the indictments dropped when he learned of them, but one case made its way to the Supreme Court. In *U.S.* v. *Hudson and Goodwin,* Republican Justice William Johnson held the indictment invalid on the ground that federal courts had no common law criminal jurisdiction. In orthodox Jeffersonian fashion, Johnson argued that the powers of the federal government were strictly enumerated, including the powers of the judiciary. Federal courts, other than the Supreme Court, were created by Congress and possessed only the jurisdiction that Congress gave them. Accordingly, criminal indictments could not be based on the common law, but must depend on statutes of Congress defining particular acts as federal crimes.

The Revolution of 1800 and the Judiciary

Rejection of a federal common law formed part of a more general strategy toward the judiciary that the Republican party pursued during the first Jefferson administration. Upon assuming power the party was hostile to Federalist interpretations of the Constitution, but owing to the internal division between radicals and moderates it lacked a clearly defined policy toward the judiciary. The radicals expressed a democratic tendency in republican thought dating from the Revolution which sought to make the judiciary directly responsive to the political will of the community. This view argued that federal and state judges should be popularly elected, should hold limited tenure, and should be accountable to the political branches. Furthermore, radicals insisted that justice be dispensed at the most local level, and not necessarily by persons trained in the law. Moderates, on the other hand, preferred a strong and independent judiciary, appointed during good behavior and recruited from professionally trained lawyers. Instead of demanding judicial deference to legislatures, moderates desired the separation of law and politics.

From their criticism of the "midnight judges," the Republicans could be expected to repeal the Judiciary Act of 1801. In actuality their decision to do so did not take shape until the Federalists provoked it by trying to force the administration to deliver the commission of one William Marbury as justice of the peace for the District of Columbia. Initially, pursuing his conciliatory strategy toward the Federalists, Jefferson had been content simply to call attention to the recently enacted judicial law and to submit a summary of the business of the federal courts intended to show that the new circuit courts were not needed. In January 1802, however, after the Supreme Court agreed to receive Marbury's request for a preliminary writ that would lead to his getting his commission, Jefferson agreed to seek repeal.

In the congressional debate over repeal of the 1801 statute, a controversy developed concerning the constitutional authority of Congress to deprive the judges appointed under the act of their offices by abolishing the positions they held. Federalist spokesmen answered the question emphatically in the negative by maintaining that repeal would violate the provision of the Constitution which guaranteed tenure during good behavior to federal judges. Republicans replied that the creation and abolition of inferior courts were left by the

Constitution to the discretion of Congress, and that the offices did not become the vested property of the judges. Senators and congressmen from Kentucky and Virginia in particular were well aware of the widespread sentiment among their constituents for the complete abolition of the inferior federal courts lest the decisions of those courts jeopardize existing land titles in those states. To the Federalist charge that the repeal bill was a partisan attempt to control what the Constitution had placed above partisanship, the Republicans retorted that the Judiciary Act of 1801 was the original sin in that respect.

The Republicans had their way, and on March 31, 1802, the repeal bill became law. The immediate effect was to revive the judicial system based on the Judiciary Act of 1789. Promptly, the Republicans enacted another law providing for annual instead of semiannual sessions of the Supreme Court, the effect being to postpone the Court's next session until February 1803. The law's sponsors evidently hoped thereby to discourage any of the displaced circuit judges from attacking the validity of the Repeal Act before the Court.

In April 1802 the Republican-dominated Congress passed a new Circuit Court Act by which the country was divided into six instead of three circuits, to each of which was assigned a separate justice of the Supreme Court, who, together with a district judge, should compose the circuit court. As new states were later admitted into the Union, this federal judicial system was extended, with no basic change being made until after the Civil War.

Impeachment of Federal Judges

If the repeal of the Judiciary Act was more a vindication of congressional power over inferior federal courts than an attack on the judiciary, the impeachment of federal judges in 1804–1805 reflected the desire of the radical faction of the Republican party to subordinate the judiciary to the political branches of the government.

Under the Constitution impeachment is the only legal method of removing federal executive and judicial officers. The House of Representatives is authorized to impeach "all civil Officers of the United States" for "Treason, Bribery, or other high Crimes and Misdemeanors," whereupon they are to be tried before the Senate. Jefferson's supporters were inclined to take an extremely broad view of the impeachment power. By the more partisan Republicans it was considered a proper instrument for removing from office judges who had fallen too far out of step with public opinion. This conception made impeachment largely a political proceeding in which any judge could be removed from office should both the House and the Senate think it expedient to do so.

To the Federalist argument that the judiciary should be above political considerations, Jefferson's supporters replied that the federal judiciary had already entered the political arena and that it must abide by the consequences.

More moderate Republicans were not willing to go this far, but they held that "high crimes and misdemeanors" might be construed broadly, so that bad judicial ethics or misconduct on the bench would become impeachable offenses. Some judges had taken advantage of their responsibility in charging grand juries to make political speeches from the bench; others had left their work to participate in political campaigns; still others had interpreted and applied the Sedition Law with gross partisanship. Many moderate Republicans thought these offenses properly impeachable.

The Republicans first tested the impeachment process against Judge John Pickering of the District Court of New Hampshire. In February 1803, while the *Marbury* case was pending (discussed below), Jefferson sent to the House of Representatives a message accompanied by documentary evidence showing that Pickering was guilty of intoxication and profanity on the bench. The House later impeached the judge on charges of malfeasance and general unfitness for office because of his loose morals and intemperate habits. In March 1804 Pickering was tried before the Senate, where it became obvious that he was insane.

This raised the question of the extent of the impeachment power in a most embarrassing form. It could hardly be argued plausibly that an insane man's conduct constituted either high crime or misdemeanor, since such offenses implied "a vicious will" on the part of the person involved. Yet unless the impeachment power was to be construed broadly enough to remove Pickering, the precedent would be established that there was actually no method of removing an incompetent or incapacitated judge from office.

A majority even of the Republican senators were apparently persuaded that Pickering, being insane, could not properly be convicted on any of the specific counts in the House impeachment. Nonetheless, they believed Pickering unfit for office and either abstained from voting or joined their colleagues in voting that the accused was "guilty as charged." He was convicted by a 19-to-7 vote and removed from office. The Pickering impeachment was so confused and contradictory, however, that it was not thereafter treated as having established the general power of impeachment for mere incompetence or incapacity in office.

Following Pickering's conviction, the Republicans moved to impeach Justice Samuel Chase of the Supreme Court. Republican leaders were generally agreed that Chase's conduct on the bench in the sedition cases had been inexcusable; moreover, they felt that he had forfeited any claim to judicial impartiality by actively campaigning for Adams in 1800. In 1803 he provided additional grounds for impeachment, when in a long charge to a Baltimore grand jury he severely criticized Congress for abolishing the circuit judges and jeopardizing the "independence" of the judiciary. He also attacked the Jefferson administration and its doctrine "that all men, in a state of society, are entitled to enjoy equal liberty and equal rights." Universal suffrage, he contended, would cause "our republican Constitution" to "sink into a mobocracy."

Led by John Randolph of Virginia, a radical Republican strongly committed to the twin doctrines of states' rights and agrarianism, the House of Representatives in January 1804 appointed a committee to inquire into Chase's conduct. This resulted in the House's impeachment of Chase on March 12 by a strictly partisan vote of 73 to 32. To prosecute the case against Chase the House appointed a committee of managers, headed by Randolph, who presented eight articles of impeachment. No infraction of law was alleged. The first seven articles concerned Chase's "oppressive conduct" as a presiding judge in several criminal trials of 1800 which had arisen under the Sedition Act. The final article related to the Baltimore address, which was characterized as "an intemperate and inflammatory political harangue," designed "to excite the fears and resentment . . . of the good people of Maryland against their State government . . . [and] against the Government of the United States."

In February 1805 the trial got under way before the Senate. The vital issue concerned the proper scope of impeachment under the Constitution. The counsel for the defense did not claim that Chase was above reproach, but they consistently maintained that an offense, to be impeachable, must be indictable in law. On the other hand, certain members of the impeachment committee, notably Randolph, took the extreme view that impeachment was not necessarily a criminal proceeding at all, but rather that on occasion it could be resorted to as a constitutional means of keeping the courts in reasonable harmony with the will of the nation, as expressed through politically responsible departments. The other House managers did not adhere to such a broad interpretation of impeachment. They argued logically that, since impeachment was the only constitutionally recognized method of removing federal judges, the terms "high Crimes and Misdemeanors" must necessarily include all cases of willful misconduct in office, whether indictable in law or not.

The Senate was composed of thirty-four members, twenty-five Republicans and nine Federalists. With twenty-three votes necessary for conviction, the Republicans clearly had the requisite two-thirds majority, provided balloting on the articles of impeachment followed strict party lines. But several moderate Republicans remained unconvinced of Chase's guilt, being persuaded neither by the evidence nor by the prosecution's arguments. Several Republican senators also had been antagonized either by Randolph's extreme position or by his opposition to certain legislative measures sponsored by party moderates. Moreover, the president himself maintained a hands-off policy. As a consequence, the Republican leadership failed to obtain the necessary two-thirds majority for conviction on each article of impeachment. On three articles there was a simple majority to convict, but even on the last article, where the prosecution had its strongest case, the vote fell four short of the necessary twenty-three.

The failure to impeach Chase ended the Republicans' antijudiciary campaign at the national level and left the federal court system pretty much as it was in 1800. In the next several years moderate and radical Republicans further contested issues of judicial reform in the states, and there, too, the moderates generally succeeded in establishing a systematic and uniform administration of justice free from political control. Although the removal of Chase would not necessarily have led to action against other Supreme Court justices or to the destruction of judicial independence, his successful defense signified the abandonment of impeachment as a political device. This outcome, in the opinion of most students of constitutional history, has been salutary because it has furnished protection against a potential instrument of legislative hegemony.

Meanwhile, on another front the Supreme Court had taken steps to achieve an accommodation with the political branches of the government that was also intended to guard judicial independence. This additional means of defense was the doctrine of judicial review, announced in the famous case of *Marbury* v. *Madison* in 1803.

Judicial Review

In a general sense the practice by which courts pass on the constitutionality of acts of the legislature was an outgrowth of the English idea of fundamental law. Given the history of English courts' involvement in political matters, it appears to have been almost inevitable that the American judiciary, after the adoption of written constitutions, should assume to preserve the fundamental law through judicial review. Whether or not judicial review was the logical culmination of Anglo-American constitutional development, however, the fact is that it began to emerge in recognizable form in the 1780s as a means of restraining state legislatures. The founding fathers accepted judicial review, and in the first decade after ratification the federal judiciary acted on the assumption that it could declare acts of Congress unconstitutional. Pathbreaking as it was in the development of modern judicial power, therefore, John Marshall's assertion of judicial review in *Marbury* v. *Madison* rested on intellectual and institutional tendencies that began at least during the Revolution.

Judicial review involves more than a simple declaration that an act of a legislature is invalid. A crucial question concerns the scope and effect of the judicial ruling. Does it, of its own force, eliminate the unconstitutional law from the statute book and fix the meaning of the Constitution for the executive and legislative branches? Or does it simply resolve the instant case? Furthermore, can the judiciary, under the power of judicial review, consider and decide any conceivable question that might arise in the constitutional system? Different answers have been given to these questions.

The basic task that Marshall was to describe as the essence of judicial review—the assessment of the compatibility of a questioned statute with a written constitutional requirement—continues to characterize orthodox judicial review theory. This similarity notwithstanding, it is the differences between judicial review in the early national period and in the modern era that stand out as more important. In the twentieth century the judiciary has monopolized constitutional interpretation, and judicial review has become a powerful instrument of policy-making. By contrast, in the early years of the republic it was principally a means of holding the legislature in check and protecting courts against legislative encroachment. Similarly, where we now take it for granted that Supreme Court decision-making is political, in the early nineteenth century defenders of judicial review drew a distinction between law and politics, reserving the former sphere to the judiciary and the latter to the political branches. However political early instances of judicial review may appear in retrospect, jurists in Marshall's era *thought* that their office obligated them to eschew politics and confine themselves to legal considerations. It was in this intellectual context, and in the hostile climate produced by Republican efforts to make the judiciary more politically accountable, that judicial review emerged.

Although the Constitution did not in express terms give courts the power to pass on the constitutionality of legislative acts, most members of the Constitutional Convention regarded this power—narrowly conceived—as legitimate. Its textual basis was the supremacy clause and Article III, Section 2, of the Constitution, which states that the judicial power shall extend to all cases in law and equity arising under the Constitution. The purpose of judicial review was to keep the legislature within proper limits. The framers, therefore, believed the judiciary was under no obligation to enforce an act of Congress that plainly contradicted a specific provision of the Constitution. The courts could take cognizance of the Constitution; it was not a rule simply for the legislature, but for the entire government. The power not to enforce a concededly unconstitutional act did not entail a power to interpret the fundamental law. Indeed, if there was any doubt as to whether legislation violated the fundamental law, judges must enforce it. Realizing that much of the Constitution was concerned with political matters beyond the competence of the courts, the framers did not intend the judiciary to have a general power to interpret or decide every conceivable constitutional issue that might arise. In addition to limiting the legislature, judicial review furnished the courts with a means of self-protection against legislative encroachment. Most members of the convention believed the courts would have a special warrant to review acts that raised questions about the exercise of judicial power.

Occasionally in the 1790s the Supreme Court acted on the assumption that it could refuse to enforce an unconstitutional act. In *Hylton* v. *United States* (1796), for example, legislation levying a tax on carriages came before the Court. The specific issue was whether the levy in question was a direct tax or an excise. If the former, it would conflict with the constitutional provision requiring all direct taxes to be apportioned among the states according to population. The Court held that only land taxes and capitations or head taxes were direct taxes, and that the carriage tax was an indirect tax, and therefore constitutional. But the opinion assumed that the Court had no obligation to enforce an act of Congress that was void or in conflict with the Constitution. By 1800 this view of judicial power was widely accepted.

The narrow conception of judicial review that found favor among the judiciary was compatible with the departmental theory of constitutional interpretation endorsed by most lawmakers and executives at the time. According to the departmental theory, the Constitution was the fundamental political law of the nation which combined matters of strictly legal import, such as habeas corpus and trial by jury, with matters of broad political import, such as the distribution of power among the parts of government. The Constitution was both ordinary law, enforceable in the courts, and a set of political rules for the conduct of government by the executive and legislative branches. Distinguishing between law and politics, the departmental theory held that politico-constitutional questions were for the political branches to decide, and legal-juridical questions for the judiciary. The theory thus avoided the dangers of legislative control of constitutional interpretation, as in England.

The departmental theory of interpretation first appeared in the debate over the removal power, in the first Congress, where many members asserted their right and duty to settle the meaning of the Constitution. Formulated initially by Federalists, the theory was endorsed also by the Republicans. Thus Jefferson wrote in 1801 that each of the three equal and independent branches of government "must have a right in cases which arise within the line of its proper functions, where, equally with the others, it acts in the last resort and without appeal, to decide on the validity of an act according to its own judgment, and uncontrolled by the opinions of any other department." Madison similarly acknowledged the responsibility of the judiciary to expound the meaning of the Constitution and the laws "in the ordinary course of government," especially with regard to property and other individual rights and the administration of justice. He denied, however, that any one department had greater power than any other to mark out the limits of the powers of the other departments.

Marbury v. Madison

The theory of judicial review advanced by John Marshall in *Marbury* v. *Madison* was congruent with this approach to constitutional interpretation. The case arose out of Marbury's attempt, already noted, to assume his position as justice of the peace for the District of Columbia. His commission had been signed and sealed but not delivered when Jefferson took office. Believing the appointment had not been consummated, Jefferson ordered James Madison, his secretary of state, to withhold the commission. Thereupon Marbury, acting under Section 13 of the Judiciary Act of 1789, applied to the Supreme Court for a rule or preliminary writ to Madison to show cause why a mandamus should not be issued directing the secretary of state to deliver the commission.

When the preliminary writ was issued, Madison ignored it as a judicial interference with the executive department.

At the Supreme Court's next session in February 1803, Marshall handed down an opinion on Marbury's application for a mandamus. Addressing the logically necessary first phase of the jurisdiction question—whether the issue raised by Marbury was justiciable—Marshall asked: "Has the applicant a right to the commission he demands?" His answer was in the affirmative. When a commission has been signed and sealed, Marshall said, the appointment is legally complete. "To withhold his commission," he added, "is an act deemed by the court not warranted by law, but violative of a vested legal right." The chief justice next asked if the applicant's rights have been violated, "do the laws of his country afford him a remedy?" Again Marshall answered yes: "Having this legal title to the office, he [the applicant] has a consequent right to the commission; a refusal to deliver which is a plain violation of that right, for which the laws of his country afford him a remedy."

Having found the issue justiciable, Marshall at this point properly considered whether the Supreme Court had jurisdiction over it. Was the proper remedy for the applicant "a mandamus issuing from this Court"? Under the Judiciary Act of 1789, Section 13, the Supreme Court had been authorized "to issue . . . writs of *mandamus* . . . to . . . persons holding office under the authority of the United States." Since the secretary of state definitely came within that description, "if this court is not authorized to issue a writ of mandamus to such an officer, it must be because the law is unconstitutional." Marshall then argued that the Constitution prescribed specifically the Supreme Court's original jurisdiction, that this jurisdiction did not include the power to issue writs of mandamus to federal officials, and that Congress had no power to alter this jurisdiction. Therefore, the attempt of Congress in the Judiciary Act of 1789 to give the Supreme Court authority to issue writs of mandamus to public officers "appears not to be warranted by the constitution." Consequently, Marbury's application for a mandamus was denied.

Having declared void a section of the Judiciary Act of 1789, Marshall then passed to his now famous argument defending the Court's power to hold acts of Congress unconstitutional. His argument rested more upon certain general principles of constitutional government than upon specific provisions of the Constitution itself. First he observed that the Constitution was "the fundamental and paramount law of the nation," which the courts had a duty to regard. He then said it was "emphatically, the province and duty of the judicial department, to say what the law is." He reasoned that if a law was in opposition to the Constitution, and both the law and the Constitution applied to a particular case, it was "the essence of judicial duty" to determine which of the conflicting rules governed the case. If then courts are to regard the Constitution, and the Constitution is superior to any ordinary act of the legislature, the Constitution must govern the case. Quoting the supremacy clause for additional support, Marshall concluded that "the particular phraseology of the constitution of the United States confirms and strengthens the principle, supposed to be essential to all written constitutions, that a law repugnant to the constitution is void, and that the courts, as well as other departments, are bound by that instrument." Judicial review expresses the Court's duty to refuse to enforce a void or unconstitutional law.

Taken out of context, Marshall's syllogism—the courts declare the law, the Constitution is law, therefore the courts declare the meaning of the Constitution—can be read as an assertion of the modern judicial monopoly theory of judicial review, which holds that the Supreme Court can apply and interpret the Constitution as though it were ordinary law. In fact this was not what Marshall meant. Early in the opinion Marshall acknowledged a sphere of political questions arising under the Constitution exclusively reserved for executive determination. "By the constitution," Marshall observed, "the President is invested with certain important political powers, in the exercise of which he is to use his own discretion, and is accountable only to his country in his political character and to his own conscience." Matters entrusted to the president under his constitutional powers were political because they concerned "the nation, not individual rights," Marshall said. The decision of the executive was conclusive concerning the propriety of actions taken in this sphere.

The scope of Marshall's theory of judicial review was further qualified by the fact that the law declared unconstitutional in *Marbury* v. *Madison* specifically dealt with the judiciary. Marshall made no general assertion that a judicial decision regarding the constitutionality of an act of Congress was binding on the political branches. Nor did he contend that the interpretation of the judiciary was superior to or entitled to precedence over that of Congress or the executive. He claimed no more than that each department should have final authority to pass on constitutional questions affecting its own duties and responsibilities. This was the essence of the departmental theory of constitutional interpretation. Marshall's version of the theory gave the judiciary an advantage over the political branches, since most legislation potentially involved questions of individual legal right that could be construed as appropriate for judicial determination. But the judicial interpretation of the Constitution would have only such force as its logic and persuasiveness might give it.

In the political context created by the Republican assault on the judiciary, Marshall's opinion necessarily carried political overtones. The chief justice had pointedly yet shrewdly lectured Jefferson on the legal rights of persons appointed to office and claimed for the judiciary authority to settle constitutional controversies involving individual rights. In a larger and more important sense, however, Marshall's opinion signified prudent retreat in the face of a threat to judicial independence. Though critical of the executive, Marshall refused to issue the mandamus, thus letting the administration win the battle. He recognized, moreover, a sphere of discretionary political action in which the judiciary lacked competence to judge of constitutionality or determine the meaning of the Constitution. Acquiescing to this extent in the political power that Jefferson represented, Marshall nevertheless established a limit beyond which the political branches could not go. This was the sphere of law, or individual legal right, which belonged to the judiciary and upon which the political departments could not encroach. In this sphere lay protection against undue political influence. Bold as Marshall's strategy was in *Marbury* v. *Madison,* his assertion of judicial review was thus basically defensive in nature.

The Supreme Court's accommodationist outlook was evident a few days later in the case of *Stuart* v. *Laird* (1803) where the constitutionality of the Judicial Repeal Act of 1802 was at issue. As noted, Federalists regarded the repeal of the 1801 law as unconstitutional because it deprived judges of good-behavior tenure as guaranteed by the Constitution. They also argued—and it is known that Marshall agreed—that the Constitution did not authorize Congress to require Supreme Court justices to sit on circuit courts because that entailed the exercise of original jurisdiction, which only the Constitution could confer. Yet in *Stuart* v. *Laird* Marshall accepted the Circuit Court Act of 1802 as constitutional on the ground that "practice and acquiescence" in the assignment of circuit-court duty to Supreme Court justices dating from the Judiciary Act of 1789 had fixed the meaning of the Constitution on this point. Significantly, the question of depriving judges of good-behavior lifetime tenure did not arise, because Stuart was merely a litigant protesting the transfer of his case from a court constituted under the act of 1801 to one organized under the act of 1802. The power of Congress to organize the lower federal courts was thus the issue, and Marshall upheld it.

The political drama surrounding *Marbury* v. *Madison* notwithstanding, Marshall's decision signaled a desire to stay out of partisan controversy and defer to the political branches, provided the latter respected the independence of the judiciary and its authority to settle constitutional disputes involving individual rights. This position was agreeable to moderate Republicans, who desired an independent and strong judiciary and did not deny the right of the judiciary to decide questions of constitutionality in matters that specifically concerned it. The Federalists' decision to bring the *Marbury* case forward had in part provoked Republicans into repealing the Judiciary Act of 1801, but Marshall's accommodation of political majoritarianism in his *Marbury* opinion strengthened the Republican moderates in their ensuing struggle with the radicals over impeachment. The radicals' failure at impeachment left the moderates in control of the party and the independence of the judiciary assured.

The Burr Trial and Judicial Independence

Political controversies threatening to the courts would recur, but the foundation of judicial independence had been laid. Chief Justice Marshall's handling of the celebrated trial of Aaron Burr for treason in 1807, in the face of tremendous political pressure from the Jefferson administration, demonstrated the point.

In 1806, his political career in ruins after the tragic duel with Alexander Hamilton, Burr formed a scheme either to seize Mexico for the United States or, as many Republicans believed, to detach the southwestern states and territory from the rest of the Union. Whatever his ultimate objective, Burr procured—although he did not attend—the assemblage of a small armed force on Blennerhassett's Island in the Ohio River and conducted it down the river toward New Orleans. Subsequently, the conspiracy collapsed, and Burr was captured and brought for trial in Richmond. Jefferson, who even before Burr's arrest publicly pronounced him guilty of treason, personally directed the prosecution and worked fervently to secure his conviction. Marshall, however, presiding over the United States Circuit Court for Virginia, successfully resisted the administration's attempt to use prosecution for treason as a political instrument.

The main issue in the trial was whether Burr's actions constituted treason as defined in the Constitution. Article III, Section 3, states: "Treason against the United States, shall consist only in levying War against them, or in adhering to their Enemies, giving them Aid and Comfort. No Person shall be convicted of Treason unless on the Testimony of two Witnesses to the same overt Act, or on Confession in open Court." The defense contended that Burr could have had no part in any overt act of levying war against the United States since he was not present during the assemblage on Blennerhassett's Island. The defense thus drew a distinction between the real act of levying war, which was treason, and the act of advising such action, which was only "constructive treason." The prosecution argued the English common law doctrine that "in treason all are principals," and that Burr as procurer of the unlawful gathering was as guilty as any of the men who attended it.

The framers of the Constitution had deliberately defined treason narrowly, in reaction against the practice in Britain and in many European countries, where the offense had been loosely defined to include a variety of political acts against the state. In the Burr trial Marshall adhered to the framers' narrow conception of treason. He first declared that the element of force was essential to any attempt to prove that the act of levying war had occurred. Yet the government had not proved this fact in relation to the motley assemblage in question. Marshall further distinguished between the act of levying war, which was treason, and the act of advising such action, which was not. More difficult was the question of whether the abettor or procurer of a treasonable assemblage, as the Republicans regarded Burr, could be charged with treason.

Six months earlier in another case arising out of Burr's military adventure, *Ex parte Bollman and Swartwout,* the Jefferson administration had tried to indict two of Burr's assistants for treason. The Supreme Court ordered the two prisoners released on a writ of habeas corpus because of insufficient evidence. But Chief Justice Marshall, making a bow toward the Jeffersonian point of view, had stated that if an assemblage was gathered to effect a treasonable purpose by force, all who performed a part in it, however minute or remote, were also traitors. In the Burr trial Marshall in a similar vein raised the question of whether one who procured a treason could be said to have taken part in levying war. He refused to answer it, however, on the ground that it was not essential to a decision in the case. It was sufficient to point out merely that the government's indictment of Burr was faulty.

Burr was indicted on a general charge of levying war on Blennerhassett's Island. Yet he had not been present on the island, and Marshall rejected the government's argument that he had been "constructively present." Even if the government had indicted Burr for procuring treason, Marshall reasoned, which it had not, the specific overt act must be attested by two witnesses, in accordance with the Constitution. On this statement of the law the Republican jury found Burr not guilty. Marshall has been accused of allowing his dislike of Jefferson to politicize his decision, but in fact he courageously resisted Jefferson's attempt to write constructive treason into constitutional law. Marshall thus vindicated the integrity of the judiciary on behalf of individual rights and fair criminal procedure.

Between 1804 and 1807 three Republican justices—William Johnson, H. Brockholst Livingston, and Thomas Todd—were appointed to the Supreme Court. But they were moderates sympathetic to a strong and independent judiciary and thus acceptable to Federalists like Marshall. The subsequent appointment of Joseph Story and Gabriel Duval placed on the Court two additional Republicans who differed little from Marshall on the role of the judiciary and the importance of upholding national power. Federalists and Republicans thus reached a consensus on the place of the federal judiciary in the constitutional system which prepared the way for a series of major Supreme Court decisions in the next two decades. These decisions established the basic principles of American constitutional law.

Marshall gives instructions to the jury that the jury could only convict Burr of treason only if they found he had committed "overt acts" against the U.S. As Burr had not acted yet and was gone when Fed troops tried to take Blennerhassetts Isl. (he was down river 40 miles from Natchez) he ditched his supplies and took to the hills. They couldn't prove he took arms himself.

ELEVEN

John Marshall and
Constitutional Nationalism

AS CHIEF JUSTICE OF THE SUPREME COURT from 1801 until his death in 1835, John Marshall was a staunch nationalist and upholder of property rights. He was not, however, as the folklore of American politics would have it, the lonely and embattled Federalist defending these values against the hostile forces of Jeffersonian democracy. On the contrary, Marshall's opinions dealing with federalism, property rights, and national economic development were consistent with the policies of the Republican party in its mercantilist phase from 1815 to 1828. Never an extreme Federalist, Marshall opposed his party's reactionary wing in the crisis of 1798–1800. Like almost all Americans of his day, Marshall was a Lockean republican who valued property not as an economic end in itself, but rather as the foundation of civil liberty and a free society. Property was the source both of individual happiness and of social stability and progress.

Marshall evinced strong centralizing tendencies in his theory of federalism and rejected the compact theory of the Union expressed in the Virginia and Kentucky Resolutions. Yet his outlook was compatible with the Unionism that formed the basis of the post-1815 American System of the Republican party. Not that Marshall shared the democratic sensibilities of the Republicans; like his fellow Federalists, he tended to distrust the common people and saw in legislative majoritarianism a force that was potentially hostile to constitutionalism and the rule of law. But aversion to democracy was not the hallmark of Marshall's constitutional jurisprudence. Its central features rather were a commitment to federal authority versus states' rights and a socially productive and economically dynamic conception of property rights. Marshall's support of these principles placed him near the mainstream of American politics in the years between the War of 1812 and the triumph of Jacksonian democracy.

Judicial Nationalism

In the long run, the most important decisions of the Marshall Court were those upholding the authority of the federal government against the states. *Marbury* v. *Madison* provided a jurisprudential basis for this undertaking, but the practical significance of judicial review in the Marshall era concerned the state legislatures rather than Congress. The most serious challenge to national authority resulted from state attempts to administer their judicial systems independent of the Supreme Court's appellate supervision as directed by the Judiciary Act of 1789. In successfully resisting this challenge, the Marshall Court not only averted a practical disruption of the federal system, but it also evolved doctrines of national supremacy which helped preserve the Union during the Civil War.

Marshall's first major defense of federal judicial authority came in *U.S.* v. *Peters* in 1809. The case arose out of litigation in which one Gideon Olmstead sought to recover from the state of Pennsylvania certain proceeds from the sale of a prize ship captured and sold during the Revolution. In 1803, after several years, Olmstead's title was affirmed by Judge Richard Peters in the U.S. District Court for Pennsylvania. The state legislature thereupon passed a law defying the federal court decree and authorizing the governor to use the state militia to protect the rights of the state against any process that might issue from federal authority. This action, plus Republican threats to impeach him, so intimidated Judge Peters that he refused to sign his own court order disposing of the case. Olmstead then appealed to the United States Supreme Court and obtained a writ of mandamus directing Judge Peters to issue the writ of execution.

Chief Justice Marshall's opinion in *U.S.* v. *Peters* was a strong defense of federal authority. "If the legislatures of the several states," he said, "may, at will, annul the judgments of the courts of the United States, and destroy the rights acquired under those judgments, the constitution itself becomes a solemn mockery, and the nation is deprived of the means of enforcing its laws by the instrumentality of its own tribunals." Marshall also denied that the suit was either commenced or prosecuted against the state in violation of the Eleventh Amendment. The Pennsylvania legislature ultimately yielded, but not before it protested the Supreme Court action and recommended a constitutional amendment creating an impartial tribunal to settle constitutional disputes.

A second assertion of federal judicial authority against state power came in *Fletcher* v. *Peck* in 1810. This case arose out of the famous Yazoo land fraud, in which the Georgia legislature rescinded earlier land-grant legislation passed by lawmakers who had been bribed. For reasons to be discussed below in connection with the contract clause, the Supreme Court held the rescinding measure to be unconstitutional. This was the first time the high court invalidated a state law as contrary to the Constitution, previous state laws having been negated because of conflict with federal laws and treaties.

The most important vindication of federal judicial authority against state power occurred in the controversy over the appellate jurisdiction of the Supreme Court. It will be recalled that Section 25 of the Judiciary Act of 1789 provided that whenever the highest state court rendered a decision against a person who claimed rights under the federal Constitution, laws, or treaties, the judgment could be reviewed, and possibly reversed, by the Supreme Court. At the time some of the states'-rights advocates approved this arrangement because it gave the state courts a share in a jurisdiction which might otherwise have been assigned exclusively to federal courts. Others saw only the danger to the sovereignty of the states if their highest courts could be overruled by the federal judiciary.

The first important controversy over the question of the Supreme Court's appellate jurisdiction from state courts grew out of an old case involving the vast lands of Lord Fairfax, a Virginia loyalist. During the Revolution, Virginia confiscated his estate and also enacted a law denying the right of an alien to inherit real property. After the Revolution, Virginia according to this law refused to allow Fairfax's English heir to inherit the estate, despite his rights under treaties with Great Britain. The Virginia Court of Appeals eventually upheld the state laws, but the case was taken on writ of error to the United States Supreme Court, where the Virginia decision was reversed. Since Marshall had earlier participated in the litigation, he absented himself, and the Court's decision was rendered by Justice Story. The decision practically emasculated the state's alien-inheritance and confiscation laws, which had been enforced by the state judiciary for a generation. The Virginia judges, headed by Spencer Roane, responded by declaring Section 25 of the Judiciary Act unconstitutional, and by refusing to carry into effect the Supreme Court's mandate.

This refusal caused the case to be taken again to the Supreme Court as *Martin* v. *Hunter's Lessee* (1816). Story again rendered the opinion and presented a powerful argument in support of the Court's right to review decisions of state courts. He maintained that, since Congress constitutionally could have vested all federal jurisdiction in the federal courts, the voluntary granting of concurrent jurisdiction in certain cases to the state courts did not divest the Supreme Court of its appellate jurisdiction. In other words, the concurrent jurisdiction clauses of the Judiciary Act had incorporated the state courts, for certain cases, into the federal judicial system. Story declared, moreover, that the Constitution, laws, and treaties of the United States could be maintained uniformly as the supreme law of the land only if the Supreme Court had the right to review and to harmonize the decisions of all inferior courts applying that supreme law. Story thus appealed to the structure of the federal system and the logic of federal supremacy and national uniformity as the basis of his decision, rather than to a specific constitutional text.

The Court's stand was repeatedly attacked by the states'-rights Virginians. Judge Spencer Roane presented their ablest argument. He maintained not only that the Constitution established a federal rather than a consolidated union, but also that it contained no provision that authorized the central government to be the final judge of the extent of its own power, legislative or judicial. Nor, he argued, was there any clause in the Constitution that expressly denied the power of state courts to pass with finality upon the validity of their own legislation. To be sure, he said, the judges in every state were bound by the Constitution to uphold "the supreme law of the land," even when it was in conflict with the constitution and laws of any state; but they were bound as state judges only, and, therefore, their decisions were not subject to review or correction by the courts of another jurisdiction. Hence, he contended, Section 25 of the Judiciary Act was unconstitutional. In fact, Roane concluded, the state's sovereignty could not be protected against federal encroachment if the final decision on the constitutionality of both federal and state acts rested with the Supreme Court.

The Court's opportunity to answer Roane came in *Cohens* v. *Virginia* (1821). The Cohens were convicted by a Virginia court of selling lottery ticket in violation of a state statute, although they claimed the protection of an act of Congress authorizing a lottery for the District of Columbia. When the Cohens appealed to the Supreme Court under Section 25 of the Judiciary Act, counsel for Virginia denied the Court's right of review and insisted that a state could never be subjected to any private individual's suit before any judicial tribunal without the state's own consent. This immunity resulted, the state claimed, in part from the sovereign nature of the states, "as properly sovereign now as they were under the confederacy," and in part from the Eleventh Amendment, which prohibited the federal judiciary from taking jurisdiction of a suit prosecuted against a state.

Marshall began his opinion by defining the extent of federal judicial power. The jurisdiction of the federal courts under the Constitution, he observed, extended to two general classes of cases. In the first class, jurisdiction depended upon the "character of the cause," and included "all cases in law and equity arising under this constitution, the laws of the United States, and treaties made, or which shall be made, under their authority." In the second class, jurisdiction depended on the character of the parties, and included controversies between two or more states, between a state and citizens of another state, and between a state and foreign states' citizens or subjects. Any case falling within either of these classes, Marshall said, came within the jurisdiction of the federal courts, even though one of the parties might be a state of the Union.

Marshall then examined Virginia's contention that because of the sovereign, independent character of the states they could not be sued without their consent. The chief justice replied that for some purposes the states were no longer sovereign—they had surrendered some of their sovereignty into the keeping of a national government. Maintenance of national supremacy, he continued, made it necessary for the states to submit to federal jurisdiction; the contrary situation would prostrate the government "at the feet of every state in the Union."

Nor did the Eleventh Amendment, which protected the states against suits by a private individual of another state, exempt the state of Virginia from federal jurisdiction in the present instance. The present action, Marshall said, was not commenced or prosecuted by an individual against a state; rather the appeal was merely part of an action begun by the state against the Cohens, and thus the state could not claim immunity from the appeal by virtue of the Eleventh Amendment.

Finally, Marshall turned to Virginia's argument that in any event there existed no right of appeal from the state courts to the United States Supreme Court, because the state and federal judicial systems were entirely distinct and the Constitution did not provide for such appeals. Marshall's reply again was to cite the doctrine of national supremacy and to argue that the maintenance of that supremacy made such appeals necessary. "America has chosen to be, in many respects, and to many purposes, a nation; and for all these purposes, her government is complete; to all these objects, it is competent. The people have declared, that in the exercise of all powers given for these objects it is supreme. It can, then, in effecting these objects, legitimately control all individuals or governments within the American territory." In a government so constituted, Marshall continued, the national judiciary must be able to decide whether or not the constitution and laws of any state are conformable to the federal Constitution and laws, and for this purpose the Supreme Court's right to hear appeals from the state courts was a necessity.

The Court then decided the specific question at issue in favor of Virginia, holding that the congressional lottery ordinance was limited to the city of Washington and that the Cohens, therefore, had no legal right to sell tickets in Virginia.

Virginia's nominal victory brought the state little satisfaction. It was overshadowed by the Court's sweeping and definitive interpretation of its right of appellate jurisdiction over decisions of the highest state courts in all questions involving national powers. Accordingly, Virginia states' rightists, led by Judge Roane, attacked the Court's assertion of authority over the states. Roane tried to persuade ex-president Madison to join the attack, but the latter refused. Thomas Jefferson, however, ever hostile toward Marshall and doctrinaire in his states'-rights agrarianism, denounced the decision as another step in the scheme of the Supreme Court to consolidate power in the federal government.

Marshall's Theory of Federalism

Scarcely less important than the Supreme Court's defense of federal judicial authority was its refutation of the Jeffersonian strict-construction–compact theory of the Union. Although Marshall expounded his alternative theory of national supremacy in many opinions, in none did he give it more forceful expression than in *McCulloch* v. *Maryland* (1819).

The famous bank case arose out of state efforts to tax the second Bank of the United States. The bank had been created with little controversy in 1816, but within a few years it became the object of widespread hostility because of its speculative operations and occasionally fraudulent financial practices. Several southern and western states took action to prevent the bank from operating within their borders, prohibiting it either directly in the state constitution or indirectly by heavy taxation. The state of Maryland chose the latter course, levying a tax in 1818 on the bank's Baltimore branch. The validity of the law was upheld in the state courts, whereupon the bank appealed the case to the federal Supreme Court.

The case was elaborately argued by six of the greatest lawyers in the country, including Daniel Webster and William Pinckney for the bank, and Luther Martin and Joseph Hopkinson for Maryland. Three days after the close of the argument, on March 6, 1819, the chief justice handed down the unanimous judgment of the Court. Upholding the constitutional power of Congress to charter the bank and to have exclusive control over it, he denied the right of Maryland to interfere with the federal government by taxing its agencies, and declared the state law unconstitutional.

The first important question involved in the case was whether Congress had power to incorporate a bank. In answering this question Marshall analyzed the nature of the American union. His argument was directed to upholding the doctrines of national sovereignty and broad construction. He rested national sovereignty on a popular base, asserting that the federal government derived its authority from the constituent act of the people of the United States, rather than from the states as sovereign entities. Marshall's formulation of the nature of this union did not avoid the ambiguity inherent in the historical facts concerning ratification of the Constitution. He observed that the Constitution was "submitted to the people" for ratification, and they acted on it "by assembling in convention." Acknowledging that the people acted separately in the several state ratification conventions—the point focused on by advocates of states' rights—Marshall said: "It is true they assembled in their several States." He discounted the significance of this fact, however, denying it meant that the people acted as separate political communities: ". . . and where else should they have assembled?" he asked. "No political dreamer was ever wild enough to think of breaking down the lines which separate the States, and of compounding the American people into one common mass. Of consequence, when they act, they act in their States." But they do not act *as* states, or as a plural nation, but rather as people of the United States, a single nation.

Marshall's theory of federalism acknowledged that sovereignty was divided between the states and the national government. But the national government, he said, "though limited in its powers, is supreme within its sphere of action." Marshall meant that the Constitution created limited government in the sense of giving the federal government responsibility and power for dealing with certain ends and objects of government, not all the conceivable or possible objects of government. This was only reasonable, he explained. Yet this question was "not left to mere reason," he observed further. The people in express terms decided it by writing the supremacy clause into the Constitution.

Marshall then set forth what was essentially the same doctrine of broad construction and implied powers that Hamilton had advanced in his bank message of 1791. He admitted that the right to establish a bank was not among the enumerated powers of Congress, but he held that the national government also possessed implied powers as well as those enumerated in the Constitution. Implied powers, he said, could be drawn from two sources. First, every legislature must by its very nature have the right to select appropriate means to carry out its powers. Second, he pointed to the necessary-and-proper clause, which he construed as broadly as Hamilton had previously done. "Necessary and proper," he said, did not mean "absolutely indispensable," for there were various degrees of necessity. Then followed the test for determining the constitutionality of an implied power, stated almost in the words of Hamilton's original formula: "Let the end be legitimate, let it be within the scope of the constitution, and all means which are appropriate, which are plainly adapted to that end, which are not prohibited, but consist with the letter and spirit of the constitution, are constitutional."

The second question involved in the case was whether the state of Maryland could constitutionally tax a branch of the national bank. In defending Maryland's right to tax the bank, counsel for the state had resorted to the states'-rights argument of dual federalism. The states and the federal government, according to this view, constituted two mutually exclusive fields of power, the sphere of authority of each being an absolute barrier to the encroachment of the other. The right to charter corporations was a state power, and the state, therefore, had a right to regulate or exclude from its limits corporations not chartered by itself.

In refuting this argument Marshall again invoked the principle of national supremacy. He cited the supremacy clause of the Constitution and observed that when state law conflicted with national law, the latter must prevail. Since the bank was a lawful instrument of federal authority, the congressional statute establishing it overcame any state attempt to limit or control the bank's functions. The very structure and logic of the constitutional system demanded this result. In no state, Marshall reasoned, would the people trust the legislature of another state to exercise power over them since they would have no control over it. By the same token it was impermissible for a state to tax the operations of the federal government, because it would be acting "on institutions created, not by their own constituents, but by people over whom they claim no control." Thus a state legislature might tax banks and other institutions of its consituents who had leverage over the lawmakers at the polls. The federal government might tax state-chartered institutions, since the people of the states were represented in Congress. But the state of Maryland could not tax an agency of the federal government because the people of the United States had no means of controlling or removing the legislators of Maryland.

Marshall recognized the divided sovereignty of American federalism and acknowledgd a sphere in which the states were supreme. At no time did he hold the United States to be a unitary nation or espouse an unqualified centralization. Nevertheless, Marshall's theory of Unionism unequivocally insisted on federal supremacy in cases where an apparently legitimate state power conflicted with a properly exercised federal power. Marshall rejected the view that some state powers when properly exercised were exclusive—that is, capable of excluding a constitutional exercise of federal power. He declared in *McCulloch* v. *Maryland:* "Such is the paramount character of the constitution, that its capacity to withdraw any subject from the action of even this power [that is, the state taxing power], is admitted." The practical consequence, as Marshall stated in *Cohens* v. *Virginia,* was that in exercising its powers over the objects assigned it by the Constitution, the federal government "can . . . legitimately control all individuals or governments within the American territory."

Marshall's opinion in *McCulloch* v. *Maryland* aroused immediate interest because of its impact on the bank question. Provoked by the simultaneously occurring Missouri Compromise debate on slavery, however, a few perceptive states'-rights critics grasped its long-range theoretical significance. In a series of essays the ever-vigilant Judge Spencer Roane and his colleague Judge William Brockenbrough of Virginia attacked Marshall's opinion as a prescription for consolidation. In their view Marshall's profession of federal constitutional limitations was negated by the doctrine of implied powers and broad construction. Marshall replied in a series of anonymous essays in which he denied the charge of consolidation and insisted that the McCulloch opinion dealt strictly with the problem of the means to be used in executing the specified powers of Congress. He did not, however, retract his argument that state powers, though otherwise legitimate, could not displace federal authority. In effect, Marshall held that conflicts between state and federal exercises of power must be resolved in favor of the federal government because the Constitution intended and required that result.

The Supreme Court withstood a second states'-rights challenge to federal authority in *Osborn* v. *The Bank of the United States* (1824). The case arose when Ohio disregarded the *McCulloch* decision and persisted in its attempt to levy a $50,000 tax on the bank. To prevent collection of the tax, the bank obtained an injunction against Osborn, the state auditor, and subsequently instituted a suit for damages against him. The Supreme Court dismissed the state's contention that the tax was constitutional. The crucial question, therefore, was whether the bank's suit was a suit against a state in violation of the Eleventh Amendment. On the flimsy ground that the state was not the actual party on record, the Court held that it was not. When acting under authority of an unconstitutional statute, the Court declared, an agent of a state is personally responsible for any injury inflicted in his attempt to execute an act. This involved a transfer to constitutional law of the principle of private law that every man is responsible for the wrongs he inflicts—an important means of protecting personal liberty in view of the fact that governments could not be sued for torts. Nevertheless, the decision further negated the purpose of the Eleventh Amendment by reducing the scope of state immunity to litigation.

Vested Rights and the Contract Clause

In defending the Bank of the United States against state attack the Supreme Court protected a key feature of the Republican party's policy of national mercantilism. In a series of other cases dealing with the contract and commerce clauses of the Constitution, the Marshall Court similarly encouraged mercantilist policy.

Marshall's decisions in this sphere have usually been described as conservative because they upheld private property rights. The description is misleading if it is taken to imply that Marshall's critics and opponents in the states did not also wish to uphold private property as a basic social value. On the contrary, as constitutional historian Edward S. Corwin has written, capitalist expansion, private property, and vested rights were the prepossession of the entire nation. There was, however, conflict between groups seeking economic benefits and advantages at the state level and those seeking benefits at the national level. It is important to note also that Marshall's defense of vested rights and contracts, instead of protecting established, passive wealth, encouraged economic growth that altered the status quo. Only if one assumes that state policies are by definition democratic and serve the interest of the people can one regard Marshall's anti–states'-rights economic decisions as a conservative defense of the status quo.

The contract clause of the Constitution (Article I, Section 10) was intended to safeguard property rights against state paper-money laws, debtor relief measures, and acts setting aside court decisions. It forbade the states to emit bills of credit, make anything but gold and silver legal tender in payment of debts, or enact any law impairing the obligation of contracts. These provisions gave expression to one of the basic principles of American constitutionalism—the doctrine of vested rights. Moreover, there is nothing in the language of the contract clause to suggest it is limited to private contracts.

A direct outgrowth of the natural rights philosophy of the Revolutionary period, the doctrine of vested rights held that certain rights were so fundamental to an individual as to be beyond governmental control. Constitutional government existed for the protection of these natural rights, which were derived from the very nature of justice. Some rights were specified in the bills of rights to state constitutions, but these lists were not to be considered exclusive. Among the most important rights was the individual's right to be secure in his possession of private property. Therefore, the legislature of a state did not have an unlimited right to interfere in an arbitrary manner with private property. According to the doctrine of vested rights, it was the duty of the courts to declare invalid statutes considered violative of existing property rights, not necessarily by virtue of any specific provision in the federal or state constitution but rather on the grounds that such statutes violated the fundamental nature of all constitutional government.

In 1795, Justice William Paterson in the Circuit Court for Pennsylvania stated this doctrine of vested rights in guarded terms in the case of *Vanhorne's Lessee* v. *Dorrance.* The decision turned upon the invalidity of an act of the Pennsylvania legislature which attempted to vest the ownership of some disputed land in one party after the land had been originally granted to another party. Paterson asserted that "the right of acquiring and possessing property and having it protected, is one of the natural inherent and unalienable rights of man. . . . The legislature, therefore, had no authority to make an act divesting one citizen of his freehold, and vesting it in another, without a just compensation. It is inconsistent with the principles of reason, justice, and moral rectitude; it is incompatible with the comfort, peace, and happiness of mankind; it is contrary to the principles of social alliance in every free government." Paterson also declared the Pennsylvania act unconstitutional because it impaired the obligation of a contract and thus was prohibited by Article I, Section 10, of the Constitution.

The doctrine of vested rights was refined and restricted somewhat by the Supreme Court in *Calder* v. *Bull* (1798). The decision in this case hinged upon whether the provision in Article I, Section 10, of the federal Constitution forbidding states to enact ex post facto laws encompassed a prohibition upon state laws which interfered with the decisions of the state courts affecting property and contractual rights. The justices hesitated to interfere with a legislative practice that had been employed extensively in certain states and decided that "ex post facto laws extend to criminal, and not to civil cases." As Justice Iredell expressed it, "Some of the most necessary and important acts of legislation are . . . founded upon the principle, that private rights must yield to public exigencies."

In another opinion Justice Samuel Chase nonetheless found occasion to recognize the doctrine of vested rights. "There are certain vital principles in our free Republican governments," he said, "which will determine and overrule an apparent and flagrant abuse of legislative powers; as to authorize manifest injustice by positive law; or to take away that security for personal liberty, or private property, for the protection whereof the government was established. An act of the Legislature (for I cannot call it a law) contrary to the great first principles of the social compact, cannot be considered a rightful exercise of legislative authority."

In the next three decades the doctrine of vested rights was frequently invoked by state courts as a means of restricting state legislative power. These decisions did not establish an absolute guarantee against state interference with property holdings, but they did require convincing justification in public policy before a state could legislate in this sphere. In a series of obscure and generally nonpolitical cases state courts applied vested-rights ideas to impose limitations on states' powers of taxation, eminent domain, and local sovereignty. In the process they pioneered the exercise of judicial review.

Instinctive as the doctrine of vested rights was in America, it proved less effective as a means of negating legislative acts than specific constitutional provisions. Its chief political drawback was that it could mean anything the judiciary wanted it to mean—a possibility that was bound to arouse opposition among supporters of popular sovereignty and legislative ascendancy. Increasingly, therefore, courts substituted documentary guarantees of property rights for the vested-rights doctrine. During the Marshall era the contract clause of the Constitution, infused with vested-rights meaning, served as the main instrument for protecting private property against legislative interference.

The first case involving the contract clause was *Fletcher* v. *Peck* (1810), the Yazoo land fraud case. In 1795 the Georgia legislature, influenced in part by bribery of many of its members, had granted millions of acres of land along the Yazoo River to certain land companies. At its next session the legislature rescinded the grant, but not before some of the land had been sold to innocent third parties. The status of the Yazoo lands was debated repeatedly in Congress and dragged through the courts until it finally reached the Supreme Court in 1810.

Chief Justice Marshall, speaking for the Court, upheld the original grant made by the Georgia legislature on the ground that the courts could not inquire into the motives of legislators no matter how corrupt those motives might be. Marshall's intent was not to uphold fraudulent transactions, which could be corrected by courts at common law, but rather to establish as a matter of general jurisprudence that courts could not lightly second-guess legislatures. More important, legislatures could not simply invalidate contracts. Thus Marshall challenged the validity of the rescinding act on the ground that it was a fundamental interference with private rights and hence beyond the constitutional authority of any legislative body—an allusion to the doctrine of vested rights.

Marshall was not willing to rest the decision entirely on such general principles, however, and he next held that the Georgia rescinding act came within the constitutional provision forbidding any state to impair the obligation of contracts. He defined a contract as "a compact between two or more parties," and as "either executory or executed." Either kind of contract contained obligations binding on the parties. A grant made by a state and accepted by the grantee, he added, is in substance an executed contract, the obligation of which still continues. The constitutional provision, he observed, made no distinction between public and private contracts. The rescinding act was therefore invalid.

Two years later, in *New Jersey* v. *Wilson* (1812), the Court extended the contract clause to protect and perpetuate a state grant of exemption from taxation. Some years before the Revolution, New Jersey had granted the Delaware Indians exemption from taxation on certain lands held by them. After the Revolution the lands in question were sold to white men, and when New Jersey attempted to tax them, the owners appealed to the courts, claiming that the original grant of tax exemption had passed to the new owners. When the case reached the Supreme Court, Marshall wrote an opinion holding that New Jersey's attempt to tax the lands involved constituted an impairment of New Jersey's obligation of contract. The decision had the effect of impairing New Jersey's indispensable power of taxation. Marshall's opinion was accepted by the entire Court and has never been repudiated by that body. As a consequence many later state constitutions either prohibited or sharply limited legislative grants of tax immunity.

Green v. *Biddle* (1823), a case involving the relationship between the contract clause and political agreements between states, provided yet another example of the Supreme Court's willingness to promote land speculation in the face of state regulation. At the time of Kentucky's separation from Virginia, the two states had entered into an agreement by which Kentucky recognized the validity of land titles issued under Virginia law. Land titles in Kentucky were nonetheless extremely confused because of the large number of overlapping and conflicting claims, and for many years after 1792 they gave rise to a constant procession of lawsuits in the state's courts. In order to remedy this situation, the Kentucky legislature enacted a series of laws providing that no claimant should be awarded possession of land to which he proved title without compensating the occupant for the latter's improvement; in default thereof, the disputed title was to rest in the occupant upon payment of the value of the land without improvements.

The Supreme Court, speaking through Justice Bushrod Washington, held that the contract clause in the Constitution applied to contracts between two states as well as those between private persons or between a state and a private individual. The Court also denied Kentucky's claim that the agreement in question was invalid because Congress had not given its assent to the agreement as required by the Constitution. The Constitution, Justice Washington observed, required no particular mode of consent by Congress, and he held that Congress had implicitly assented to the compact when it admitted Kentucky to the Union.

The opinion provoked widespread criticism, for the prevailing opinion was that the Convention of 1787 had never intended to include interstate political agreements within the contract clause. In Congress there arose a renewed demand for reform and restriction of the federal judiciary. Kentucky, embittered because the Court's decision benefited numerous absentee landowners, continued for the most part to enforce its own laws, thereby virtually ignoring the Court's ruling. Moreover, later cases involving interstate issues were usually decided under the interstate compact clause.

The Corporation in Constitutional Law

In expanding the contract clause to protect vested rights the Supreme Court encouraged an expansive, dynamic agrarian capitalism that supplied venture capital for more general economic development. The growth of the corporation, which the Supreme Court also promoted through its interpretation of the contract clause, was the chief manifestation of this wider economic purpose.

In the colonial period, as we have seen, the corporation was principally a method of political organization, although occasionally it served as the means by which government accomplished broad social purposes such as providing transportation facilities for the public. In the early nineteenth century the corporation became an instrument of general economic development. Legally, a corporation was a voluntary association of individuals who upon application to the legislature received specific and exclusive powers and privileges for carrying on a particular enterprise or activity. Though consisting of private persons, the legal character of the corporation was that of a public institution created by legislative authority and subject to governmental regulation and control. Nevertheless, the fact that private individuals actually managed them made corporations also in some sense private as well as public institutions.

In the period 1800 to 1820, as corporations came to serve a wider variety of productive purposes going well beyond their traditional use in building transportation facilities, hospitals, and the like, the *de facto* private character of the corporation was elevated into constitutional principle. In the case of *Terrett* v. *Taylor* in 1815, the Supreme Court took this step by announcing a distinction between public and private corporations and the degree of government control to which they were subject. Justice Joseph Story explained for the Court that public corporations, by which he meant counties, townships, and cities, could be modified by the legislature. Private corporations, however, which presumably meant all other kinds of incorporated bodies, enjoyed more substantial protection against legislative interference under "the principles of natural justice" and "the fundamental laws of every free government." Story did not say how much protection private corporations were entitled to, and he probably did not intend businesses incorporated under state law to be completely beyond the scope of subsequent legislative regulation. But by recognizing what had previously been thought a contradiction in terms—that is, a private corporation—Story enabled an increasingly large segment of business enterprise to receive the protection that the vested-rights doctrine and its documentary constitutional equivalent, the contract clause, gave to individual citizens.

Building on Story's distinction between public and private corporations but eschewing his natural law orientation, the Supreme Court in *Dartmouth College* v. *Woodward* (1819) brought private corporations under the protection of the contract clause. In doing so Chief Justice Marshall further expanded the contract clause by ruling that a charter of incorporation was a private contract protected against legislative infringement by the Constitution.

The case grew out of the efforts of the New Hampshire legislature to alter the charter granted by George III in 1769 to the trustees of Dartmouth College, conveying to them "forever" the right to govern the institution and to fill vacancies in their own body. The charter continued unchanged throughout the Revolutionary period, but in 1816 the Republican governor and legislature, believing that the old charter was based upon principles more congenial to monarchy than to "a free government," attempted to bring the college under public control. Accordingly, they passed laws that virtually took the control of the institution from the hands of the Federalist-dominated trustees and placed it under a board of overseers appointed by the governor. The trustees thereupon turned for relief to the state judiciary, but the New Hampshire Superior Court upheld the legislature's acts, chiefly on the ground that the college was essentially a public corporation whose powers and franchises were exercised for public purposes and were, therefore, subject to public control. The trustees of the college then appealed the case upon writ of error to the Supreme Court.

By a vote of 5 to 1, the Court decided that the New Hampshire laws in question were unconstitutional as impairment of the obligation of contract. The chief justice, in giving the opinion of the Court, admitted an important constitutional argument of the state: that "the framers of the constitution did not intend to restrain the states in the regulation of their civil institutions, adopted for internal government." He went to great length, however, to demonstrate that Dartmouth College was not a public institution subject to state control but instead was a "private eleemosynary institution." Although he cited no authorities, Marshall declared that the charter granted by the British crown to the trustees was a contract within the meaning of the Constitution. By virtue of the Revolution, he said, the powers and duties of government had devolved upon the people of New Hampshire. At any time prior to the adoption of the Constitution the power of the state to repeal or alter the charter was restricted only by the state constitution, but after 1789 that power was further restrained by the obligation-of-contract clause.

The *Dartmouth College* decision aided business interests at a time when privately funded internal-improvement companies, including some in Virginia in which Marshall had an interest, were vulnerable to legislative attack. Marshall's purpose, however, was not to place private corporations beyond public control, but rather to assure capitalists the expectation of a reasonable return on their investment in return for providing public improvements and services useful to the community at large. The legislative charter was an instrument both of promotion and of regulation, for the mutual benefit of both private entrepreneur and the society. Accordingly, Marshall's *Dartmouth College* opinion made it clear that state legislatures might reserve the right to repeal or to modify the charters that they granted, and in the future most legislatures took advantage of this right. In the coming decades the number and importance of private corporations in the fields of transportation, finance, and industry rapidly expanded, but this expansion was due less to their legally protected position than to the economic advantages they offered.

The Contract Clause and Bankruptcy Laws

In the context of the panic of 1819, state bankruptcy laws raised further constitutional questions about the scope of the contract clause as a limitation on state legislative power. The Supreme Court insisted on the applicability of the clause in bankruptcy matters, but, responding to changing political circumstances in the 1820s, it eventually permitted the states a degree of latitude in this field.

Sturges v. *Crowninshield* (1819) involved the constitutionality of a New York law for the relief of insolvent debtors from debts contracted before the law was enacted. Two related issues were involved: first, whether the state had the right to enact any bankruptcy legislation in the light of the provision in the Constitution specifically delegating to Congress the power to make uniform laws on bankruptcy; and second, whether the New York act violated the contract clause. Marshall held that state bankruptcy legislation was permissible in the absence of any federal statute, provided the act in question did not violate other constitutional requirements. However, he also held that the New York law impaired the obligation of contracts. Any law, said Marshall, that released a man in whole or in part from his agreement to pay another man a sum of money at a certain time impaired the obligation of contracts and could not be reconciled with the Constitution.

Sturges v. *Crowninshield* resulted in a general limitation of state authority over bankruptcy matters. The economic depression caused by the panic of 1819, however, led several states to seek a loophole in the decision by enacting bankruptcy laws applying solely to debts contracted after the statute's passage. Reflecting a shift toward the states'-rights point of view, the Supreme Court approved this type of legislation.

In *Ogden* v. *Saunders* (1827) the Court decided, 4 to 3, that a state bankruptcy law discharging both the person of the debtor and his future acquisition of property did not impair the obligation of contracts entered into after the passage of the law. Six justices offered opinions, which revealed that the Court was not only badly divided on the present question but had also been divided in *Sturges* v. *Crowninshield.* Justice Johnson now admitted that the earlier decision had been arrived at as a compromise among the justices rather than as an act of "legal adjudication." Johnson and other states'-rights–minded justices, it appeared, had acquiesced in the invalidation of state laws regulating anterior contracts only with the proviso that the opinion be so guarded as to secure the states' power over posterior contracts. It was this latter point that the present majority now insisted upon.

Among the majority justices Johnson offered a neo-Jeffersonian defense of state authority to regulate contractual dealings and relationships. In his view, "all the contracts of men receive a relative, and not a positive interpretation: for the rights of all must be held and enjoyed in subserviency to the good of the whole. The state construes them, the state applies them, and the state decides how far the social exercise of the rights they give us over each other can be justly asserted." This was substantially an anticipation of the later doctrine of the state's police power.

Marshall vigorously dissented, the first and only time he did so on an important question of constitutional law. Arguing that the Constitution protected all contracts, past or future, from state legislation that in any manner impaired their obligation, he maintained that the position of the majority would virtually destroy the contract clause. He admitted, however, that the constitutional prohibition of the impairment of the obligation of contracts did not prohibit a state legislature from changing the remedies for the enforcement of contracts.

On another issue raised in *Ogden* v. *Saunders* Johnson joined Marshall in a majority opinion. They both declared that a state's insolvency law could not discharge a contract owed to a citizen of another state, since such action would produce "a conflict of sovereign power, and a collision with the judicial powers granted to the United States." In sum, the Court's position was that state bankruptcy and insolvency laws were unconstitutional when they operated on contracts entered into before their passage, but were constitutional with respect to contracts entered into after their passage. Second, they were unconstitutional if they invalidated a contract owed to a citizen of another state. Thus the Court took the first important step in restricting the scope of the contract clause as it had been interpreted between 1810 and 1819.

The Commerce Clause

If the contract clause protected corporate development against undue state interference, the commerce clause provided a means of creating a national free-trade area as an encouragement to economic expansion. In a series of commerce power cases the Supreme Court in the 1820s pursued this nationalistic economic purpose, although here, too, it made concessions to the states'-rights point of view.

One of the chief objectives of the framers of the Constitution had been to replace the confused condition of foreign and interstate commercial relations prevailing in 1787 with an orderly and uniform system. Consequently, the Constitution empowered Congress "to regulate Commerce with foreign Nations, and among the several States, and with the Indian Tribes." After the adoption of the Constitution the volume of both foreign and interstate commerce increased rapidly. Congress early made legal provision for the regulation of ships and cargoes from foreign countries and passed a law providing for the licensing of vessels engaged in the important coastal trade. On the other hand, Congress took virtually no positive action for the control of interstate commerce, but such commerce flourished without much federal aid or regulation, since the states abandoned their former discriminations against vessels and products from other states.

The constitutional definition of commerce and the power of Congress over it meanwhile were subjects of intermittent controversy. By 1820 two theories existed. The first, deriving from the view that seems generally to have prevailed in the eighteenth century and that Alexander Hamilton supported, interpreted commerce "among the states" to mean all commercial activity in the United States, irrespective of state lines. The power of Congress in this view was a plenary legislative power, the same as it would be if the United States were a unitary government. The second theory, advanced originally by Jefferson in his bank opinion of 1791, held that the language of Article I, Section 8, referred to commerce *between* two or more states—that is, interstate commerce. In this territorially rather than functionally defined conception, either commerce was confined to a single state, in which case it was beyond the scope of federal legislative power, or it crossed from one state into another, in which case Congress could legislate concerning it. In 1824, when the Supreme Court first addressed the question, neither of these theories had gained acceptance in constitutional law, although the evidence of congressional debate on internal-improvements legislation suggests that the interstate view was gaining favor.

The Marshall Court's first venture into commerce clause interpretation dealt with the strategically important steamboat business. During the first quarter of the nineteenth century the steamboat was developed into an important means of transportation in the coastal trade and especially on the rivers and lakes of the interior of the country. By the 1820s the free development of interstate trade by this new means of transportation was being threatened by attempts of various states to grant exclusive privileges to various interests over the steam navigation of "state waters." This policy led to retaliation of state against state. Thus monopoly and localism were joining hands in a movement of state restriction upon interstate commerce that was reminiscent of the days of the Confederation.

In 1808 Robert Fulton and Robert Livingston, pioneers in the development of a practical steamboat, secured from the New York legislature a grant of the exclusive right to operate steamboats on the state's waters. From this monopoly Aaron Ogden secured the exclusive right to engage in steam navigation across the Hudson River between New York and New Jersey. Thomas Gibbons, however, proceeded to engage in competition with Ogden, claiming the right under a license granted under the federal coasting act. Ogden's suit to restrain Gibbons from engaging in this interstate navigation was sustained by the New York courts in 1819 and 1820, with Chancellor James Kent, perhaps the most learned jurist in America, upholding Ogden and the steamboat monopoly act. Gibbons appealed to the United States Supreme Court, where the case of *Gibbons* v. *Ogden* was finally heard in 1824.

Chief Justice Marshall, in handing down the unanimous decision of the Court, devoted himself to four main points or questions. First, what does commerce comprehend? Second, to what extent may Congress exercise its commercial regulatory power within the separate states? Third, is congressional power to regulate interstate commerce exclusive, or does a state have concurrent power in this field? Fourth, should the commerce power of Congress (and inferentially other powers, too) be construed broadly for the national welfare or be construed strictly in order to protect the reserved powers of the states?

In discussing the first question, Marshall rejected the argument of Ogden's counsel that commerce should be narrowly defined as "traffic" or the mere buying or selling of goods, including only such transportation as was purely auxiliary thereto. "Commerce, undoubtedly, is traffic," he said, "but it is something more; it is intercourse." It encompasses navigation and general commercial relations. The meaning of the word, he added, is just as comprehensive when applied to "commerce among the several states" as when applied to foreign commerce, where it admittedly comprehends "every species of commercial intercourse."

Turning to the second and vital question of the power to regulate commerce, Marshall accepted the more confining interstate view, although, perhaps significantly, he did not use that term. "Comprehensive as the word 'among' is," he wrote in explication of the language of the commerce clause, "it may very properly be restricted to that commerce which concerns more states than one." The corollary was that congressional power did not extend to "that commerce, which is completely internal, which is carried on between man and man in a state, or between different parts of the same state, and which does not extend to or affect other states." Although this language can be interpreted as permitting federal regulation of intrastate commerce if it can be shown to have an effect on business in another state, its clearer import was to endorse the states'-rights or *interstate* restriction on the commerce power of the federal government.

As Marshall adopted the more limited view of congressional power, so he in effect conceded a concurrent state power to regulate commerce in the absence of federal legislation. Counsel for Gibbons had argued that the constitutional grant of power to Congress was exclusive, meaning that whether or not Congress legislated, the states had no concurrent power over interstate commerce. Justice Johnson endorsed this more centralizing view, but Chief Justice Marshall did not. Instead, he struck down the New York monopoly grant on the ground that it conflicted with the federal Coasting Act of 1793. He went on to explain that the states could pass inspection laws and other health and safety measures which might have a remote effect on commerce. Formally, Marshall held such laws to be an exercise of the states' reserved powers—what would later be called the police power—rather than the commerce power. Nevertheless, in a practical sense Marshall recognized a concurrent state commerce power and thus acknowledged the heightened concern for states' rights in the mid-1820s.

Although conceding more scope to the states'-rights point of view than he ordinarily did, Marshall's opinion was strongly centralizing in answering the fourth question of whether the enumerated powers of Congress should be construed narrowly or broadly. At the outset, in the most emphatic terms, he rejected strict construction, arguing that it "would cripple the government, and render it unequal to the objects for which it is declared to be instituted." In closing he reiterated his criticism of those who, by narrowly contracting federal power, would "explain away the constitution of our country, and leave it a magnificent structure indeed, to look at, but totally unfit for use." And in asserting congressional power over commerce he described it as plenary, limited only by the "wisdom and discretion of congress, their identity with the people, and the influence which their constituents possess at elections." Regarding the matter thus as a political question, Marshall in effect denied the judiciary any role in restraining congressional exercise of the commerce power.

Because monopolies were unpopular, the Gibbons decision, unlike most of Marshall's centralizing opinions, received wide popular approval. It had the useful effect, moreover, of keeping steamboat navigation and subsequently railroad transportation free of the impediment of state monopolies and competitive on a national scale. At the same time, however, the decision failed to prevent the states from regulating interstate commerce in other respects. In subsequent years states legislated on pilotage, turnpikes, ferries, canal boats, railroads, and the immigrant passenger trade in ways that clearly had interstate effect. Thus *Gibbons* v. *Ogden* did not thwart the powerful current of state mercantilism and economic policy-making that characterized Jacksonian democracy.

Before these results became clear, however, the Marshall Court handed down two further opinions drawing a line between state powers and constitutionally protected commerce. In the first of these cases, *Brown* v. *Maryland* (1827), Marshall formulated the "original-package" doctrine. The question at issue was whether a Maryland statute requiring wholesalers of imported goods to take out a special license came within the state's taxing power or infringed upon the federal commerce power. The chief justice declared that whenever imported goods became "mixed up with the mass of property in the country," they became subject to the state's taxing power, but that as long as the goods remained the property of the importer and in the original form or package, any state tax upon them constituted an unconstitutional interference with the regulation of commerce. The principle was stated so broadly that it would apply to interstate as well as foreign commerce and to any degree of state taxation.

Two years later, however, in *Willson* v. *Black Bird Creek Marsh Company* (1829), Marshall upheld a Delaware law authorizing the damming of a creek to exclude water from a marsh, even though the stream was navigable and had occasionally been used in the coasting trade. Wilson's vessel was licensed under the same coasting act as that cited in *Gibbons* v. *Ogden,* and Marshall, therefore, might have held that the state statute infringed upon the federal commerce power. Instead he held that the federal government had not yet acted, and that the state's regulation was valid in the absence of any federal statute. Thus Marshall and the Court anticipated an important doctrinal trend that would become the central theme in commerce clause interpretation under Marshall's successor, Roger B. Taney.

Marshall's Contribution to American Constitutionalism

John Marshall's signal achievement was to vindicate federal authority against state attempts to deny the supervisory power of the federal government, which would have made the federal union in effect a confederation of sovereign states. Marshall accomplished this purpose by writing into constitutional law the theory of national-supremacy federalism. Its central principle was that the federal government, founded by the constituent act of the people of the United States, possessed sovereign power in relation to the objects or purposes assigned to it by the Constitution. In the proper exercise of its constitutional powers, this government could control any person or other government within the territorial United States.

Under Marshall's leadership the Supreme Court blocked state efforts to repudiate the appellate power of the federal judiciary and declared unconstitutional acts of more than half of the state legislatures. By invalidating state laws the Court prevented the states from becoming the final arbiter in disputes between themselves and the federal government. Opponents of the Supreme Court tried to curb its power through congressional action, especially between

1819 and 1827, when state laws were being set aside at almost every session of the Court. The most drastic attempt to restrict the Court was initiated by Senator Richard Johnson of Kentucky, who proposed to constitute the Senate a court of last resort in all cases involving the constitutionality of state laws or to which a state should be a party. Bills were also introduced to increase the size of the Supreme Court and to require more than a bare majority decision to invalidate a state law. None of these measures was adopted. In 1831 the House Judiciary Committee reported a bill repealing Section 25 of the Judiciary Act of 1789, under which the Supreme Court heard cases on appeal from the state courts, but this proposal was also defeated.

Reflecting the growing reaction against Republican national mercantilism, the Supreme Court in the last decade of the Marshall era gave broader scope to state powers and less consistent protection to property rights. The state of Georgia defied judgments of the Supreme Court in cases concerning the rights of Indian tribes, and in 1833 the Court handed down an exceedingly important states'-rights decision in holding, in Barron v. Baltimore, that the Fifth Amendment and the Bill of Rights limited only the federal government and not the states. Nevertheless, when John Marshall died in 1835 constitutional law firmly and unequivocally recognized the sovereignty of the federal government and its supremacy over the states. Moreover, the Court had acquired sufficient influence and institutional autonomy to enable it effectively to settle constitutional disputes. Despite its expansion of judicial authority and prestige, however, the Marshall Court rarely challenged the political branches of the government. For the most part, its policies complemented those of the national legislature.

The use of Marshall's nationalist doctrines to support federal regulatory legislation in the twentieth century has led many scholars to regard his constitutional outlook as anticipating modern judicial liberalism, with its emphasis on the creation of new governmental powers to meet new social conditions and needs. To be sure, Marshall's doctrine of implied powers emphasized the exercise of federal power rather than its limitation. Moreover, in McCulloch v. Maryland, in language that has often been taken as foreshadowing modern judicial activism, Marshall declared: "We must never forget that it is a constitution we are expounding . . . intended to endure for ages to come, and consequently, to be adapted to the various crises of human affairs." Yet Marshall did not mean that new powers could be fashioned out of whole cloth by judicial or legislative interpretation for purposes or objects not encompassed by the Constitution.

Answering the confining literalism of the Virginia strict constructionists, who attacked the theory of implied powers as a prescription for centralization, Marshall denied any intention of augmenting the powers of Congress or engaging in "latitudinous" or "liberal" construction of the Constitution in this regard. Defending his opinion in McCulloch v. Maryland in a series of anonymous newspaper essays in 1819, Marshall stated that the Court's chief concern in that case was with the means by which delegated powers were employed and the purposes of federal authority carried out. He reiterated what he had written in the *McCulloch* opinion: that if Congress, "under the pretext of executing its powers," should "pass laws for the accomplishment of objects not intrusted to the government," the judiciary would declare them unconstitutional. Marshall, of course, recognized the fact of social change, but he denied that social change, except as it was translated into proposals for constitutional amendments, changed the Constitution. In the fundamental purposes it defined and in the powers it assigned to the federal government, the Constitution was in Marshall's view a fixed, objective structure, not a growing, living organism as later generations—seeking to escape the restrictions of the written Constitution—would conceive of it. Finally, though emphasizing implied powers, Marshall never disavowed the jurisprudential theory of *Marbury* v. *Madison.* This theory enjoined courts impartially to declare the law, rather than in legislative fashion to make law and apply it on grounds of expediency as an instrument of policy.

Although Marshall was not a judicial activist in the significant sense of rejecting the constitutional decisions and positions advanced by the other branches of the government, a subtle change entered into the exercise of judicial review during his chief justiceship that permitted or facilitated later judicial activism. The Court, and Marshall especially, gradually adopted the practice of citing the text of the Constitution in applying the fundamental law, rather than relying on arguments from structure and relationship in the organization of the government, general principles of reason and justice (such as the doctrine of vested rights), or the spirit of the Constitution. This development occurred in relation to contract clause and federalism cases in particular. The decisions showed a tendency to treat the Constitution as ordinary supreme law, rather than as fundamental political principles that are authoritative not because they are written in a text but because they are universally accepted as fundamental. The long-range significance was to encourage judicial exposition of the text of the Constitution in a legalistic and literalistic way, and to assimilate interpretation of the Constitution into the methods used to apply and interpret ordinary law. This development may have been the inevitable result of the attempt to establish limited government on the basis of a written constitution. It showed the difficulty, as the act of foundation faded into history, of maintaining the constitutional outlook and fundamental principles of the framers.

TWELVE

Jacksonian Democracy and Dual Federalism

THE ELECTION OF ANDREW JACKSON as a states'-rights candidate in 1828 effected a political realignment which established the basic direction of constitutional change for the next generation. Intended to restore the decentralized constitutionalism of Jeffersonian republicanism, the movement over which Jackson presided was the catalyst in creating the American two-party system essentially in its modern form. As a direct corollary of that development, Jackson as chief executive strengthened and democratized presidential power beyond anything Jefferson had contemplated. Consciously identifying himself with the people, Jackson stimulated reforms through methods of direct political action which often disregarded established institutions and constitutional procedures.

In an age of intense nationalism and increasing nationalization of social and cultural life, Jacksonian democracy paradoxically resulted in a shift of power from the federal government to the states. This shift was a response to the localism of American politics and to the need of an increasingly apprehensive class of southern slaveholders to protect their peculiar institution against political attack. Based in a constitutional sense on the evolution of strict construction and states' rights into the theory of dual federalism, Jacksonian democracy was committed to the restoration of republicanism, the defense of slavery, and the preservation of the Union. When changes in public attitudes toward slavery subsequently caused these purposes to become contradictory, Democratic dual federalism was transformed into the militantly pro-slavery doctrine of state sovereignty under which the South moved resolutely toward secession and civil war.

Jacksonian Constitutionalism

Joined loosely under the Jacksonian banner were three distinct sectional groups: plain republicans of the North; western farmers, frontiersmen, and entrepreneurs; and southern planters. Old Republicans in New York and Virginia, led by Martin Van Buren and Thomas Ritchie, respectively, in the early 1820s began to organize a party to oppose the centralizing policies of the Adams administration. Critical of the speculative tendencies encouraged by the American System, as manifested in the panic of 1819, Van Buren spoke for northern farmers, artisans, and working men in arguing for a return to the laissez-faire, strict-construction, and states'-rights outlook of agrarian republican theory. Van Buren found a ready ally in the Virginia states'-rights critics of federal supremacy, who saw an ominous threat to the South in the recently concluded Missouri crisis.

In 1819 a united front of Federalist and northern Republican anti-slavery representatives denied Missouri, a slave territory, admission to the Union. A compromise was eventually reached that permitted Missouri to enter the Union as a slave state, but that prohibited slavery in Louisiana Purchase territory north of 36°30' latitude. Perceiving a threat to the southern social order, Virginia Republicans looked for protection to a national political organization based on states' rights and strict construction which could prevent federal power from being used against slavery. Accordingly, they agreed to cooperate with Van Buren, who subsequently brought into the emerging coalition a western element. Though more for entrepreneurial than ideological reasons, the original Jackson men from Tennessee, Kentucky, and Ohio shared the antibanking, laissez-faire views of the old Republicans. They contributed to the party furthermore an anti-eastern bias and democratic resentment against the special privilege on which the American System depended. Finally, for political as well as pro-slavery reasons, a contingent of South Carolina politicians led by John C. Calhoun joined the Jackson movement in protest against the national mercantilism of the Adams administration.

Placed in office under a popular mandate that rejected centralization and promised to restore government to the people, but was vague on specific questions of policy, the Jackson administration defined its old Republican and dual-federalist character in dismantling the American System. In pursuing this goal Jackson made vigorous use of federal executive power. He was also aided by a highly disciplined national party organization that introduced into political life an aggressively egalitarian outlook. Yet the essence of the old Republican spirit was local and individual liberty. And while this liberty was threatened by mercantilist centralization, it was also threatened by the opposite doctrine of state sovereignty and nullification. From the Jacksonian standpoint, union was essential for republican liberty not so much as a source of power for the attainment of social purposes, but rather as a territorially expanding framework within which the states and the people could pursue their interests and govern themselves. The theory of dual federalism expressed this balanced conception of the Union and the heightened importance of the states in Democratic constitutionalism.

Taking as its point of departure the orthodox notion of federalism as divided sovereignty, dual federalism posited the existence of mutually exclusive and reciprocally limiting spheres of state and federal power, neither of which was superior to the other in a categorical sense. Dual-federalist theory attached as much importance to the Tenth Amendment, reserving to the states or the people powers not delegated to the general government, as John Marshall did to the supremacy clause. But Jacksonians by no means abandoned the idea of federal sovereignty. The nullification crisis of 1832–33, which saw Jackson repudiate South Carolina's assertion of state sovereignty, demonstrated the dual-federalist commitment to Union and federal sovereignty. As an alternative to centralizing mercantilism, however, the historical and political logic of dual federalism was to enlarge the power of the states. Accordingly, its chief practical significance consisted in self-denying actions by the federal government which allowed national economic policy-making to be determined by the states.

The Jackson administration first clarified its old Republican–dual-federalist identity in relation to the internal-improvements question. By 1828 a substantial program of federally supported internal improvements existed, which many western Democrats, despite their dissatisfaction with the American System in general, favored. In 1830, however, in order to reassure northern and southern old Republicans of the party's commitment to strict construction, Jackson vetoed four internal-improvement bills, including one for twenty miles of turnpike in Kentucky called the Maysville Road.

Jackson rejected the narrowest states'-rights view of the internal-improvements question—namely, Madison's argument that the federal government could take no action in this field without a constitutional amendment. He accepted as constitutional the practice of appropriating federal money for state or privately constructed improvements. But he held that a genuine national purpose must justify such expenditures, and he concluded that no such purpose was present in the Maysville appropriation, a purely local project lying entirely within the state of Kentucky. To disregard this requirement, reasoned Jackson, "would of necessity lead to the subversion of the federal system." Because western demands persisted, the Maysville veto did not lead to the discontinuation of federal support for internal improvements. In fact, the Jackson administration approved other measures scarcely more national or less local than the Kentucky road. In doing so, however, the administration did not formulate a coherent national policy but rather acquiesced in state demands. And as the Democratic party became more ideologically consistent in the late 1830s, the national government withdrew entirely from the internal-improvements field and left it to the states. The culmination of this approach was President James K. Polk's veto in 1846 of a bill appropriating federal money for river and harbor improvements on the narrow states'-rights ground that Congress possessed no power whatsoever in this sphere.

On other issues the Jackson administration deferred to the states, in accordance with old Republican–dual-federalist principles. A problem that arose in the mid-1830s was how to dispose of a surplus in the federal Treasury caused by the imminent extinguishment of the national debt and continued high revenues from government land sales. The Whig party, successor to the Adams-Clay National Republicans of 1832, in orthodox mercantilist fashion proposed to distribute the proceeds of land sales to the states, with the proviso that the money be applied to education, internal improvements, or the reduction of state taxes. In support of the proposal Henry Clay argued that the public domain was a great national heritage which should be used by the federal government for the benefit of all the people. Democrats, on the other hand, proposed to reduce the price of public lands and ultimately dispose of the federal surplus by ceding all public lands to the states in which they lay. They thus sought to appeal both to western land hunger and to the old Republican fear of federal power and prestige, which they believed derived in part from the national government's control of the public domain. Jackson vetoed a distribution bill in 1833, but in 1836 Democrats passed a measure that satisfied the states'-rights point of view by depositing the federal surplus (about $30 million) on account with the states. Constitutionally, Democrats distinguished between depositing money, which was acceptable, and making an outright gift, which was not. It was understood, however, that the deposits would never be recalled, so in effect the act of 1836 gave money to the states with no strings attached.

Georgia and Federal Indian Policy

In Indian affairs the Jackson administration also acquiesced to the states, allowing them to determine national policy for all practical purposes. Denied citizenship, exempted from taxation, and not counted in the apportionment of representation and direct taxes, Indians within the territorial limits of the United States occupied an indefinite status under the Constitution. From the start of the government, however, following the British example, federal officials employed the constitutionally prescribed power to regulate commerce with the Indian tribes, and the treaty-making and war powers to license and regulate trade with the Indians and to sign treaties with them for the acquisition of Indian lands. The government's purpose was to remove the Indians so white settlement could proceed, while protecting them in unceded lands. Unable to carry out this purpose, the government in the 1820s urged the removal of the Indian tribes to the West. Several southern states within whose limits the tribes resided expedited the process by taking independent action against the Indians, and the Jackson administration supported these efforts by securing the adoption of the Indian Removal Act of 1830. The measure appropriated $500,000 for treaties that would remove the southeastern tribes west of the Mississippi.

In the early 1830s matters came to a head in a conflict between the state of Georgia, backed by the Jackson administration, and the Cherokee Indians. In 1802 Georgia ceded her western lands to the United States in return for a promise to secure for the state at federal expense all Indian lands lying within the state "as early as the same can possibly be obtained on reasonable terms." The Indians in Georgia were the Creeks and Cherokees, tribes that had adopted an agricultural way of life and were determined not to give up their lands. Federal evacuation proceeded very slowly, therefore, and the Georgia government, dissatisfied with federal inaction, in 1826 ordered state surveys of lands that the Creeks had been "persuaded" to cede. President Adams threatened to use the army to restrain Georgia's surveyors, and an open conflict between federal and state authority was averted only by the capitulation of the Creeks and their removal west. The conflict continued, however, when the Cherokees in 1827 adopted a written constitution and proclaimed themselves an independent state. In response to this action the Georgia legislature extended state law over Indian territory, annulled all Indian law, and directed the seizure of all Indian lands.

In accordance with the newly asserted jurisdiction, the state presently tried and convicted a Cherokee Indian, one Corn Tassel, for murder. The United States Supreme Court shortly granted Corn Tassel a writ of error, but the state refused to honor it. The governor, with the support of the legislature, declared that he would resist all interference from whatever quarter with the state's courts. Suiting actions to words, the state promptly executed the Indian.

Consistent with his states'-rights outlook, President Jackson denied that Indians could become an independent nation within sovereign states, and said it was absurd to make treaties with Indian tribes as though they were sovereign nations. He therefore refused to take any action in defense of Indians' rights secured by earlier treaties. Friends of the Cherokees, however, sought an injunction in the Supreme Court to restrain Georgia from seizing the Indian lands. In *Cherokee Nation* v. *Georgia* (1831) the Court held in an opinion of Chief Justice Marshall that an Indian tribe was neither a state in the Union nor a foreign nation within the meaning of the Constitution and, therefore, could not maintain an action in the federal courts. But Marshall added that the Indians were "domestic dependent nations" under the sovereignty and dominion of the United States, who had an unquestionable right to the lands they occupied until title should be extinguished by voluntary cession to the United States. This equivocal decision left Georgia defiant and the Cherokees unprotected.

In *Worcester* v. *Georgia* (1832), a case involving the conviction by the state of two Protestant missionaries for residence on Indian lands without a license from the state, Marshall went further and held that the Cherokee nation was a distinct political community. It had territorial boundaries, he said, within which "the laws of Georgia can have no force, and which the citizens of Georgia have no right to enter but with the assent of the Cherokees themselves or in conformity with treaties and with the acts of Congress." Georgia openly flouted this decision, however, refusing either to appear at the bar of the Court or to order the release of the missionaries.

President Jackson took no steps to implement the Supreme Court's decision, but he was under no legal obligation to do so. The Supreme Court remanded the case to the Superior Court of Georgia, and under the Judiciary Act of 1789 the Court could issue a final order disposing of the case only after it had been remanded once without effect. Plainly, the Georgia court would ignore the decision, but it was up to Samuel Worcester and his fellow missionary to continue the litigation by appealing again to the federal judiciary, at which time the Supreme Court might have issued a final order possibly placing the executive under an obligation to act. This next step was never taken, however, because the concurrently unfolding South Carolina nullification crisis in December 1832 gave the administration, the state, and the missionaries reason to compose the conflict.

Seeking to isolate South Carolina politically by avoiding any provocation of Georgia that might drive her into the arms of the nullifiers, the Jackson administration applied pressure on Governor Lumpkin of Georgia to pardon the missionaries without conceding the correctness of the Supreme Court decision. This would eliminate any possibility of federal authority being arrayed against the state as a final outcome of the case. For their part the missionaries and their sponsors were now convinced that Cherokee removal was inevitable, the Supreme Court notwithstanding. They were also fearful that continued legal resistance, possibly requiring the federal executive to oppose the state, would drive Georgia into alliance with South Carolina. They therefore dropped the case, whereupon the governor of Georgia pardoned them. Jackson went on to face down the South Carolina nullifiers, and federal Indian removal policy proceeded in accordance with the southern states' demands.

The Bank War

The principal event that established the old Republican–dual-federalist identity of the Democratic party was the bank war of 1832. The pivotal institution in Republican national mercantilism, the second Bank of the United States came under attack in the 1820s as an agency of corrupt financial speculation and aristocratic privilege that undermined republican virtue, liberty, and states' rights. In 1832, long before its charter was to expire, the bank's supporters pushed a recharter bill through Congress. Jackson vetoed the measure as a violation of the republican equal-rights idea and the principle of dual federalism.

Although the constitutionality of the bank seemed to have been long since settled so that even its opponents did not object to it as unconstitutional in the congressional debate of 1832, Jackson reopened the question by noting the numerous opinions that had been expressed over the years against the bank's constitutionality, especially in the states. Acknowledging the Supreme Court's affirmation of the bank in *McCulloch* v. *Maryland,* he discounted the significance of this decision by arguing that the political branches were not bound by the judiciary's reading of the Constitution, but rather were obliged to interpret the fundamental law for themselves. Jackson pointed out, moreover, that in the McCulloch case the Court said the degree of necessity of a legislative act, under the necessary-and-proper clause, was a matter of political discretion. Permitted thus to examine the bill on its merits, Jackson described the bank as a potentially "self-elected directory" possessing monopolistic power that was capable of influencing elections and controlling the affairs of the nation. Especially insofar as it was connected with foreign capital, reasoned Jackson, the bank was a "danger to our liberty and independence."

Examining the matter in a more technical and specific constitutional sense, Jackson condemned the bank as a violation of dual-federalist principles. The recharter bill restricted Congress in various particulars concerning the capital of existing or future banks in the District of Columbia, and Jackson seized on this provision as an unconstitutional attempt by Congress to limit its own sovereign power. The argument was strained, as though Jackson included it out of a theoretical requirement to acknowledge federal sovereignty. More convincingly, and to the point of the dual-federalist enlargement of state powers, Jackson then argued that by exempting the private business of the bank from state taxation, the recharter bill, "as a means of executing the powers delegated to the General Government," attacked "the substantive and most essential powers reserved by the States." The framers of the Constitution, Jackson declared, never imagined "that any portion of the taxing power of the States not prohibited to them nor delegated to Congress was to be swept away and annihilated as a means of executing certain powers delegated to Congress." The contrast with John Marshall's doctrine of national-supremacy federalism was profound: Whereas Marshall held that federal power properly exercised could stop the state taxing power, Democratic dual federalism permitted the states to exclude the exercise of a constitutional federal power.

The bank veto was the first in a series of steps that ultimately committed the federal government to a radical hard-money policy and drove many entrepreneurial-minded Democrats into the National Republican and later the Whig party. In 1833 Jackson withdrew federal deposits from the Bank of the United States and placed them in twenty-three state banks, thereby encouraging speculative tendencies. After the charter of the BUS expired, Congress in 1840 enacted a subtreasury system for receiving, transferring, and paying out federal funds. The constitutional theory behind this scheme, according to President Martin Van Buren, was that the federal government had no authority to associate itself in any way with private banking activities or business pursuits and was, therefore, obliged to manage its money without the assistance of private institutions. The Whigs in 1841 repealed the subtreasury legislation, but were twice prevented from creating another national bank by President John Tyler, successor to William Henry Harrison. Tyler, a states'-rights, strict constructionist from Virginia, held that Congress had no constitutional power "to create a national bank to operate *per se* over the Union." He would accept a national bank only if the establishment of the bank's branches was made dependent on the positive consent of the states in which the bank would operate. Finally, when the Democrats returned to power under President James K. Polk, they reestablished the independent treasury system in 1846, leaving control of the nation's banking system to the states.

Nullification: Calhoun's Theory

If the bank war revealed the states'-rights side of Democratic dual federalism, Jackson's response to the nullification crisis in South Carolina showed his commitment to the federal-supremacy side. The crisis that came to a head in South Carolina in the winter of 1832–33 had its origins in economic difficulties caused by the spread of cotton cultivation to the Southwest and by a decline in the agricultural export trade. The latter was attributable to the contraction of credit in the international market, but South Carolinians blamed it on the protective tariff. They despised the tariff not only for economic reasons, but also because it represented an external authority that was capable of disrupting, if not destroying, the state's distinctive slave-based social order. Provoked by the "Tariff of Abominations," the most highly protective impost law ever adopted by Congress, as well as by recent slave uprisings and abolitionist attacks, the South Carolina legislature in 1830 issued the South Carolina Exposition. Secretly written by Vice-President John C. Calhoun, the Exposition condemned the tariff as unconstitutional and asserted the power of the state to nullify federal legislation. Suddenly, nullification became the central issue in South Carolina politics, as a States Rights party formed in its defense and a Unionist party in opposition. Matters assumed an even more serious aspect in 1831 when Vice-President Calhoun publicly endorsed nullification and advanced a constitutional argument to defend it.

Although its association with secession and hence its disunionist connotation have cast the doctrine as a constitutional perversity, nullification dealt with and depended on familiar features in the constitutional order. This fact gave it a degree of plausibility. The general problem Calhoun faced was that of protecting minorities against the tyranny of the majority. Madison had proposed to deal with this fundamental issue by expanding the size of the republic, and from time to time the institutions of the Senate, the executive veto, and judicial review offered constitutional means of safeguarding minority interests. These instruments not being politically available to South Carolina in the late 1820s, however, Calhoun feared that the power of the numerical majority acting in the national legislature would overwhelm the interests of his state and region. To guard against this eventuality, he proposed that the states judge the constitutionality of federal legislation and nullify federal acts that contradicted their interests or encroached on their reserved rights.

Calhoun derived the power of nullification in the first place from his general theory of sovereignty. Since the time of the Revolution, Americans had posited divided sovereignty as the basis of American federalism. Calhoun rejected this approach, however, and returned to the older European and English idea of sovereignty as unitary and indivisible. He was consistent with the American constitutional tradition in speaking of the people as the ultimate sovereign, but he identified the people exclusively with the states in declaring that sovereignty was "an entire thing" and that "to divide is to destroy it." Drawing on Madison and Jefferson's old Republican principles of '98, Calhoun invoked the familiar compact theory of the Union as the immediate source of the power of nullification. Independent sovereign communities after the separation from Great Britain, the states in this view created the Articles of Confederation and were the constituent power in forming the federal union in 1787. The Constitution was a compact, in the nature of a treaty, between equal sovereign states. Delegating certain powers to the general government as their agent, the states did not surrender their sovereignty, something by nature indivisible. Accordingly, the federal government possessed no sovereignty, but merely such limited powers as the states chose to give it in order to carry out their purposes.

In positing nullification on these foundations, Calhoun employed another well-established feature of American constitutionalism—the popularly elected convention. Should the people of a state object to a law or action of the federal government, they could, acting outside their legislature in a state convention, judge it unconstitutional and declare it null and void within the limits of the state. This negation would be but a suspensory veto, however; to settle the controversy finally Calhoun invoked yet another familiar constitutional device, the amending power. A convention of all the states would consider the nullified federal act, and if three-fourths of them approved, nullification would be confirmed. Finally, if the nullifying state was overruled and it persisted in regarding the terms of the compact violated, it could secede from the Union.

It is easy to point out historical weaknesses in Calhoun's theory, ignoring as it did the seemingly clear intention of the framers to divide sovereignty and make the federal government supreme over the states. Every theory of the Union in the nineteenth century can be criticized on historical grounds, however, and Calhoun's doctrine, for all its flaws, was supported by the fact that during the Revolution state sovereignty was more apparent than Confederation sovereignty. Because secession eventually occurred, moreover, Calhoun's theory appears inherently disunionist. Yet in conception and intention it was not a disunionist doctrine. Eschewing a national-party organization to protect the South and prevent sectional division, such as the Jacksonian Democrats employed, Calhoun used the doctrinaire and seemingly impractical legal instrument of nullification. His purpose, however, was not simply to protect South Carolina, but to protect South Carolina *in the Union.* Nullification was a way of maintaining the Union. Calhoun did not abandon the national sentiment that had earlier led him to support a centralizing conception of federalism. In the altered circumstances of the 1830s, he expressed his love of the Union in the theory of state sovereignty and nullification. Far from being the purpose or end of nullification, secession was a desperate final alternative that signified its failure as an instrument of constitutional politics.

Nevertheless, Calhoun's argument for nullification marked a significant turning point in nineteenth-century constitutionalism. Up to this time debate over federalism had tended to focus on the division and allocation of powers between the federal government and the states. People could argue about the locus of specific powers without having to challenge the Union. Calhoun's insistence on a unitary conception of sovereignty, however, had the effect of forcing a more precise definition of the federal-state relationship. The result was the introduction of an element of doctrinal rigidity which caused people to differ over the principle of union itself.

The Nullification Crisis: Federal Sovereignty Vindicated

In the winter of 1832–33 South Carolina employed the doctrine of nullification to challenge the authority of the federal government. In November 1832 a state convention, called by State Rights party legislators who had been elected on an antitariff, pronullification platform, adopted an ordinance declaring the federal Tariff Acts of 1828 and 1832 null and void and instructing the state legislature to pass all legislation necessary to give it full effect. The convention decreed that the ordinance could not be questioned in any case in law or equity in the state courts; prohibited an appeal of any case in which it might be involved to the Supreme Court; required state officers and jurors in cases involving the ordinance to swear an oath to obey and enforce it; and stated that any federal effort to enforce the tariff acts or coerce the state would cause South Carolina to secede from the Union. The nullifying convention also announced that the people of South Carolina owed allegiance to the state alone, not to the federal government, and it issued an appeal for a general convention of the states to consider the tariff problem. Meeting a few days later, the state legislature adopted a test oath act for judges and jurors and a replevin act authorizing the owner of imported goods seized for nonpayment of duties to recover them or twice their value from customs officials. The legislature also authorized the governor to call out the militia to enforce the laws of the state.

President Jackson had long-standing personal reasons for disliking Calhoun. These, combined with his love of the Union and belief in federal sovereignty, led him to condemn the nullification ordinance in a proclamation to the people of South Carolina in December 1832. Jackson started with the Jeffersonian compact theory of the Union, noting that the states gave up certain powers in the process of constituting the general government. He relied on Federalist theory, however, in stating that the Union formed by the Constitution was not a league, but a government in which all the people of the nation were represented and which operated directly upon them. Moreover the Constitution as a compact created a "binding obligation" and was backed by an explicit sanction that made an attempt to destroy the government by force an offense punishable under the public law of self-defense. The states had no power to annul a law of the United States; the very idea, said Jackson, was incompatible with the existence of the Union. And the states had no right to secede. "To say that any State may at pleasure secede from the Union," Jackson explained, "is to say that the United States are not a nation." Asserting that disunion by armed force was treason, he urged the citizens of South Carolina to uphold the Constitution and laws and announced his intention to enforce the tariff laws.

On January 16, 1833, after potential conflict with the state of Georgia had been averted by the settlement of the controversy over Indian removal, Jackson requested that Congress take steps that would "solemnly proclaim that the Constitution and the laws are supreme and the Union indissoluble." He asked Congress not for new authority to use against the nullifiers—legislation of 1795 and 1807 authorized the executive to use force to uphold federal laws—but rather for means that would facilitate the exercise of power already possessed and enable the government to thwart the nullifiers without actually using military power. Congress complied by adopting the act of March 2, 1833, for enforcing the tariff—known as the Force Act. The legislation authorized the president to employ his authority in support of federal law against any obstruction, civil or military, even if the obstruction be made by authority of a state. The statute provided judicial protection for federal officers enforcing national law, including for the first time a provision permitting federal courts to issue a writ of habeas corpus against a state officer.[1] And it authorized the president to close ports of entry or alter collection districts, were such steps necessary to collect customs duties. The bill thus asserted the sovereignty of the federal

---

1. The writ of habeas corpus, in Anglo-American law the traditional means of maintaining personal liberty against wrongful detention, was mainly important in state law. Under the Judiciary Act of 1789, federal courts could issue a writ of habeas corpus against officers of the national government. Persons wrongfully detained by state officers thus had no means of securing release by turning to federal authority.

government and its authority to enforce its statutes directly upon individuals by force if necessary.

Although Jackson unhesitatingly defended federal authority, he regarded the protective tariff as an instrument of anti-republican privilege. Even before the nullification ordinance, therefore, he favored its downward revision. Jackson's outlook made possible a compromise which enabled South Carolina partially to secure its objective. While the Force Act defended federal sovereignty, a tariff law announced a gradual reduction in duties to a 20 percent maximum in 1842. Meanwhile strong displays of Unionist sentiment in other southern states left South Carolina politically isolated and helped weaken the nullifiers' resolve. In January a States Rights party convention recommended virtual suspension of nullification until Congress acted on the compromise tariff bill, a step that effectively ended the crisis. After Congress lowered the tariff the South Carolina convention reassembled and rescinded the ordinance of nullification against the tariff, though in a final and futile attempt to save face it adopted another ordinance nullifying the Force Act.

If South Carolina primarily sought a change in federal tariff policy, its resort to nullification was partially successful. Clearly, however, the nullifiers were trying to fashion a new constitutional instrument for defending southern interests, and on this score they suffered a crushing defeat.

While based on the states'-rights–compact theory of the Virginia and Kentucky Resolutions, Calhoun's doctrine of nullification went beyond the principles asserted by Jefferson and Madison. Indeed, Calhoun transformed states' rights into a doctrine of state sovereignty with profound implications for the federal system. Believing that the South would ultimately fight to defend slavery against abolitionist attack, he concluded that the only way to preserve the Union was to give the southern minority a constitutional means of protecting itself. Calhoun continued to support nullification even after it failed to gain acceptance as a legitimate constitutional instrument, but most South Carolinians abandoned it. With most Southerners, they became convinced that if a "sovereign" state's remonstrances against objectionable federal policy proved unavailing, the only alternatives were to submit or secede.

If the nullification crisis was a crucial turning point in the transformation of states' rights into state sovereignty, it was equally significant in the development of Unionism. Prior to this time union was a rationally and deliberately chosen instrument for the promotion of republican values. It was an artifice, utilitarian device, and experiment. And implicit in its experimental nature was the possibility—which was occasionally made explicit—that rational, pragmatic reasons might require the abandonment of union. On more than a few occasions states'-rights men talked of secession, while defenders of the Union spoke of the practical value of federalism as a framework of liberty. Unionists did not insist on the permanence or indissolubility of the Union. But they did when Calhoun broached his doctrine of nullification. Now for the first time defenders of federal authority asserted that the Union was permanent. Andrew

Jackson offered the most famous statement of the theory of perpetual union, but Daniel Webster and Henry Clay among the National Republicans (later Whigs) were equally firm in their support of the idea. After fifty years, union was becoming an end in itself, a political absolute rooted in history, geography, and sentiment. Not that it ceased to function as a means of securing republican liberty, but the traditional utilitarian basis of Unionism gradually evolved into a transcendent, organic rationale.

Jackson expressed both the older instrumental conception of union and the new organic, absolute approach. His famous Jefferson Day exclamation of 1830—"our Federal Union—It must be preserved"—as well as his proclamation of 1833 asserting the indissolubility of the Union rested ultimately on the idea that the United States had a right, as a living organism, to defend its existence. However, Jackson also saw Calhoun and the nullifiers as ambitious men bent on undermining republican government. Therefore, he also defended the Union as a means of maintaining republican liberty. Jacksonian adviser Amos Kendall expressed this in 1832 when he said: "With us the Union is *sacred.* Its preservation is the only *means* of preserving our civil liberty." In his proclamation to South Carolina, Jackson similarly reasoned that the crisis of the Union involved the future of "all free governments" and concluded that its successful defense would "inspire new confidence in republican institutions."

Dual federalism thus blended the potentially contradictory elements of states' rights and federal sovereignty. It struck a compromise between Calhoun's doctrine of state sovereignty and the National Republican or Whig preference for centralization. Whigs held that the Constitution was a completed or executed contract, made by the people of the United States, which created a permanent sovereign government. In this view the Union was older than the states. Calhoun's theory was precisely the opposite: Sovereign states, antedating the Union, entered into a contractual agreement or constitutional compact which required their continuing consent to make it effective and from which they could withdraw if the terms of the contract were violated. Democratic dual federalism regarded the Union as a continuing contract, but also as a binding agreement that imposed a perpetual obligation on the states. In the Jacksonian view, Whig centralization threatened liberty, while Calhoun's state sovereignty and nullification threatened union. Dual federalism was intended to promote republican liberty in a permanent, indissoluble, and expanding Union.

The Modern Two-Party System

The bank war and the nullification crisis served further to catalyze the Jacksonian political realignment in ways that permanently altered the constitutional system. Banking- and business-minded Democrats on the one hand,

and Calhoun's South Carolina followers on the other, left the party and joined the National Republicans in the aftermath of these events. By 1834 this anti-Jackson coalition called itself the Whig party. The constitutional significance of these changes lay in the fact that by 1840 they produced the second American party system.

The first party system, lasting from 1794 to about 1815, performed a representative, constitutional function by providing mechanisms for choosing officials, shaping public opinion, and mediating generally between the people and the government. Despite the more democratic style of the Republicans in contrast to the Federalists, however, the system was closer to the deferential, leader-oriented factional conflict of colonial politics than to the modern, mass-based party struggles of the nineteenth century. The parties of the early national period lacked comprehensive, articulated organization reaching to the local level and mobilizing voter participation. Moreover, party leaders persisted in seeing organized partisan opposition as dangerous to the government; the idea of a legitimate opposition, and hence of parties themselves, was not yet accepted. Federalists and Republicans were elite-led groups who assumed that the people would recognize their virtue and entrust them with the management of public affairs. Once the people made the correct choice, the defeated party would disappear.

The political realignment that occurred from 1828 to 1840 changed all of this. Disciplined, mass-based, permanent organizations emerged as characteristic of American politics as partisan activity was democratized and institutionalized. The process of political democratization had begun in the colonial period and had received a tremendous impetus with the forming of republican governments and the expansion of the suffrage during the Revolution. It continued in the early nineteenth century as both Federalists and Republicans competed in efforts to broaden the suffrage. Property and taxpayer qualifications for voting and officeholding were removed in most states, with liberalizing changes in Connecticut, Massachusetts, and New York from 1818 to 1821 forming a decisive turning point in the movement for democracy. Only in Rhode Island, Virginia, and Louisiana did serious suffrage restrictions remain. Meanwhile several new states—Indiana, Illinois, Alabama, Mississippi, and Missouri—entered the Union between 1816 and 1821 with constitutions providing for universal white manhood suffrage. Voter participation was high, moreover, especially in state and local elections where a genuine party conflict existed.

The Jackson men built on these institutional changes in the late 1820s as they formed a national party organization with a self-consciously democratic ethos and a high degree of discipline and structure. By the mid-1830s the elements of a modern party were present: leaders, cadre, constituents; a party press; effective use of patronage to hold the party together; a set of principles or an ideology to identify the party and maintain voters' loyalty and commitment; reliance on popular conventions from the local to the national level to choose party candidates (replacing the elite-dominated legislative caucus); and a uniform outlook on specific policy questions that required subordination of sectional views to a national-party perspective. Attacking the older deferential politics, the Jacksonian party also argued for rotation in office on the democratic principle that the intelligence and virtue of the common man qualified him for the duty of public services.

The Democrats as the first modern party did not serve simply a constituent or constitutional function; they had a programmatic purpose as well, expressed in their old Republican political philosophy. Nevertheless, in a very real sense the party organization existed to gain power as an end in itself. This is not to say that partisan activity could be reduced merely to the cynical pursuit of office, although there was a good deal of that involved. But parties existed for their own sake in the sense that they were now looked on as permanent organizations. And almost irrespective of the motivation of party leaders, the party system had a democratizing effect on political life.

Although Jacksonians appealed to the common man in 1828, the Democratic party was a coalition of diverse interests until the events of 1832 led it to seek a mass-voter orientation based on old Republican principles. The Whig party, in contrast, at first rejected the populistic approach to politics. Calling Jackson a tyrant for his use of presidential power, Whigs assumed the banner of resistance to executive usurpation and persisted in the older leader-oriented, local-based, deferential style of politics. They attacked Jackson as a demagogue and objected to his reliance on a "kitchen cabinet" outside the established leadership structure. In 1836 the Whigs ran four regional or favorite-son presidential candidates, a strategy aimed at preventing Van Buren from getting a majority of votes in the electoral college and throwing the election into the House of Representatives. But the strategy also reflected their "local notable" outlook and their lack of a broadly based constituency. Soundly defeated, the Whigs took a lesson in the new democratic style of politics and won the election of 1840 with their famous "log cabin" campaign that put William Henry Harrison in the White House. Thereafter, accepting each other as a legitimate opposition and organized party conflict as healthy for republican government, Whigs and Democrats competed as mass-based national organizations until the issue of slavery caused a sectional political realignment in the 1850s.

Jackson and Executive Power

In his inaugural address in 1840 President William Henry Harrison, promising to arrest what he called a trend toward monarchy, warned against the danger of excessive concentration of power in the federal government. Exaggerated as this view of recent presidential history was, it suggests something of the impact that Jackson's actions had on the development of the executive branch. Mainly concerned with expanding the power of the states where questions of federalism arose, Jackson nevertheless used executive power vigorously in his dealings with Congress in a conscious effort to democratize the presidential office.

Perceiving himself the champion of the people, Jackson was determined to play an independent role in the formation of national policy. To this end he willingly defied both Congress and the Supreme Court when it became necessary for him to do so. Nor were instruments of presidential power wanting, even though they had long lain dormant. Jackson ultimately made use of three of these instruments of power—the veto power, his power over appointments and removals, and his position as a party leader.

It was Jackson's bank veto that first led him to assert comprehensively his ideas on executive independence. His veto message set forth two fairly distinct constitutional concepts, both of which infuriated the Whigs—that the Supreme Court was not the final arbiter of all constitutional questions, and that the president could exercise a judgment independent of Congress upon matters of policy, presumably even where constitutional issues were not involved.

Constitutional questions, Jackson said, could not be regarded as settled merely because the Supreme Court had passed upon them. "The Congress, the Executive, and the Court," he asserted, "must each of itself be guided by its own opinion of the Constitution. Each public officer who takes an oath to support the Constitution swears that he will support it as he understands it, and not as it is understood by others. It is as much the duty of the House of Representatives, of the Senate, and of the President to decide upon the constitutionality of any bill or resolution which may be presented to them for passage of approval as it is of the supreme judges when it may be brought before them for judicial decision. The opinion of the judges has no more authority over Congress than the opinion of Congress has over the judges, and on that point the President is independent of both."

Although Jackson's position contradicted a developing tendency to regard the judiciary as the final authority on constitutional questions, it possessed a reliable basis in the departmental theory of review established in the Jeffersonian era. More important was Jackson's objection to the bank not only on the basis of constitutionality strictly considered, but also for reasons of policy. Ten previous exercises of the executive veto power had rested mainly on constitutional grounds, although occasionally expediency was the justification. Jackson's bank veto and his six internal-improvement vetoes changed this pattern. In addition to the dual-federalist objections already discussed, Jackson opposed the bank as an unwise and inexpedient interference with republican liberty. The Whigs argued from a strict separation-of-powers theory that the executive was not part of the legislature and hence could not use the veto out of policy considerations such as lawmakers might entertain; the veto could be employed only when Congress had clearly overstepped its constitutional authority. There was no compelling reason, however, to regard the president as other than a genuine participant in the legislative process and thus entitled to consider the substantive policy as well as the constitutional form of legislation. Presidents after Jackson accepted his broad conception of the executive veto, which anticipated later nineteenth-century checks on legislative power in the form of constitutional revision by popularly elected conventions and judicial review.

Having decided to remove government deposits from the Bank of the United States, Jackson continued the struggle with Congress over currency policy in yet another constitutional controversy concerning the removal power. In accordance with the bank's charter, the president ordered the secretary of the Treasury, Louis McLane, to remove the deposits. McLane refused to do so, however, whereupon Jackson replaced him with William Duane, who also refused on the ground that as secretary of the Treasury he had discretionary authority from Congress to decide the matter. Jackson then read to the cabinet a paper, written by Attorney General Roger B. Taney, asserting the president's power to impose his will on his subordinates. When Duane continued recalcitrant, Jackson replaced him with Taney, who promptly removed the deposits. The Senate proceeded to request a copy of Jackson's cabinet paper, and when Jackson denied the request, the Senate censured him for assuming unconstitutional powers. Jackson replied with a "Protest" in which he argued, on the theory of a unitary executive, that the entire executive power was vested in the president; that the power to remove officers charged with assisting in executing the law belonged to the president as well; and that the secretary of the Treasury was a subordinate officer who in managing the public money was subject to the supervision and control of the president.

The basic issue was whether the president, through his constitutionally implied power of dismissal, could dictate to the secretary of the Treasury how he should exercise the discretionary power vested exclusively in him by Congress. The Whigs argued that the Constitution specifically granted Congress control over public funds, and that Congress in 1789 had purposely placed the Treasury Department under congressional rather than executive control. Therefore, the president had no constitutional right either to dismiss the secretary or to force removal of the public deposits under presidential authority. There was something to this argument, but Jackson was on solid ground in insisting on executive unity and responsibility. This had been the accepted theory and practice of the government from its inception, although Congress in creating the Treasury Department departed from it by making the secretary accountable to itself as well as to the president. Jackson based his actions on the well-established belief that the power of removal, like that of appointment, was inherent in executive power and subject only to specific constitutional limitations.

Jackson had the last word in his struggle to remove the deposits, but an extreme assertion of executive power by the Jackson administration was rebuffed by the Supreme Court in the case of *Kendall* v. *U.S. ex rel. Stokes* in

1838. Amos Kendall, postmaster general, refused to enforce government contracts with a fraud-tainted mail transport firm, Stockton and Stokes. Stokes got Congress to pass a law giving the solicitor in the Treasury Department power to settle the dispute; the solicitor decided for Stokes; Stokes then filed suit for a writ of mandamus compelling Kendall to pay the firm. Kendall refused, arguing that he was subject only to the direction of the president and that even in applying an act of Congress the judiciary could not control his actions. The Supreme Court viewed this argument as a denial of congressional power to impose duties it thought proper on an executive officer and rejected it. The position of the administration, said the Court, would give the president power to control the legislation of Congress. Describing the action of the postmaster general as merely ministerial, the Court held that Kendall must pay Stokes, in accordance with the act of Congress. The decision placed a modest restraint on the executive without interfering with his determination of discretionary political matters.

State Constitutional Change

Numerous changes in state government, usually the result of state constitutional conventions, had a democratizing effect on the constitutional order. One manifestation of this trend, as noted previously, was the extension of the franchise and the increased electoral participation that resulted from the formation of disciplined, mass political parties. Democratization also occurred in the reapportionment of state legislatures, demanded in the name of political equality by western or up-country groups who were underrepresented in relation to eastern mercantile interests and tidewater planters. In Virginia a notable struggle over reapportionment took place in 1829–30, in which entrenched eastern interests retained political control in a new constitution. About 1850, however, most of the southeastern states granted representation to western regions.

In the interest of establishing more direct popular control of government, the new constitutions drafted between 1820 and 1850 increased restrictions on the power and discretion of state legislatures. Earlier constitutions embodied the assumption that the legislature was the sovereign voice of the free people, and they had placed but few constitutional checks upon legislature authority. The extravagant state banking laws and internal-improvements schemes of the generation after 1815 led to a growing popular distrust of the integrity and capacity of state legislators, a distrust that greatly increased after the financial collapse of many of the states following the panic of 1837.

As a result, the constitutions drafted in the 1840s imposed substantial limitations upon legislative discretion. Generally, they placed limitations upon the time, frequency, and expense of legislative sessions; abolished the legislature's right to enact special legislation benefiting individuals or corporations;

required a two-thirds vote or popular approval for the creation of state banks or public-works projects; and limited the amount of the state debt and the objects for which it could be contracted. Many of the constitutions contained lengthy provisions which were legislative in character rather than organic, an additional indication of unwillingness to trust legislative discretion completely.

While legislative authority declined, the power of the governor was increased. The earlier constitutions had in general given the governor no veto or had permitted the legislature to override a veto by a majority vote, while the new documents usually granted the executive a more effective veto power. The new constitutions also granted the governor much of the appointive power hitherto lodged in the legislature. These provisions reflected growing recognition of the governor as an influential political and executive leader and a valuable constitutional check upon the legislature rather than as a mere ceremonial head of the state.

The new constitutions also generally provided for the popular election of nearly all state and county administrative officers, including even minor officials. The responsibilities of the electorate were thus multiplied in a sometimes bewildering fashion that increased the need of party functionaries to oversee the electoral process. At some point the theoretically democratic character of mass political parties might be contradicted by their perhaps necessarily manipulative tactics, but for the time being the belief prevailed that the party was the embodiment of the people. What disturbed many conservatives was the fear that popular power, organized in mass parties and exercised through executive and legislative institutions, would weaken traditional constitutional restraints on governmental power.

Highly controversial were the provisions in several state constitutions for popular election of the judiciary. A few of the constitutions adopted in the 1820s provided for the popular election of judges of inferior courts, and the Mississippi constitution of 1832 carried a far more radical provision that called for the choice of supreme court judges by the electorate. For a time no other state followed Mississippi in this procedure, but in 1846 New York wrote a similar provision into its new constitution. Conservatives and even many moderates fought hard against such radicalism, but they were unable to stem the tide. Within a few years nearly all the western states framed constitutions incorporating the principle of an elective judiciary, and many of the eastern states did likewise. To guarantee popular control of the judiciary still further, many of the new constitutions empowered the legislature to remove any judge simply by a majority vote.

Popular Sovereignty

After the establishment of republican governments during the Revolution Americans generally assumed that popular sovereignty was properly manifested in prescribed constitutional forms and procedures. Nevertheless, the revolutionary tradition of direct political action in the name of the sovereign people, carried on "out of doors" or outside established institutions and procedures, continued to have influence and was vigorously asserted by many reform-minded groups in the 1830s and 1840s.

The settlement of the western territories provided a continuing opportunity for the implementation of a more immediate and spontaneous conception of republican self-government and popular sovereignty. Congress had formal power to create territories and supervise their transformation into states, but settlers often impatiently took matters into their own hands by creating governments without congressional authorization and seeking admission to the Union. Considering the undeveloped nature and scope of federal administrative authority and the fact that the Constitution nowhere refers to a *congressional* power to make or create states, there was warrant in this popular response. Manifest from the beginning of the government, it was illustrated in 1836 when settlers in Michigan Territory grew tired of waiting for Congress to grant permission to form a state government. Without federal approval they drafted a constitution, elected state officers, and sent representatives to Washington to demand recognition as a state. Congress acceded to the popular demand by agreeing to a compromise that acknowledged both the right of the people in the territory to create a state and of Congress to control the process.

The tendency to take direct political action in the name of the people was not confined to the territories. In Maryland in 1836, for example, Democratic state senators seeking reapportionment of the legislature threatened to boycott the deliberations of that body in an attempt to force the Whig majority to reform the state constitution. They were prepared by this action to destroy the government and, in the words of a contemporary, to throw the state government into a state of nature in which the people could write a new constitution. To that end, acting without formal authority, they elected delegates to a constitutional convention. The Whigs yielded, agreeing to accept constitutional reforms providing for greater popular participation in government. At about the same time in Pennsylvania the "Buckshot War" also evinced the power of aroused citizens acting in defiance of established authority. After a bitterly contested election, crowds of Democratic partisans fell on the capital at Harrisburg to force Whig officials in the state Senate to acknowledge their party's apparent victory at the polls. The popular protest, carried directly to the state house, prevented Whigs from organizing the house of representatives, whereupon the governor called out the state militia to secure order. In the face of this popular demonstration, Whig officials acknowledged Democratic control of the state assembly.

The largest and most significant expression of direct-action popular sovereignty in the Jacksonian era was the Dorr Rebellion in Rhode Island in 1842. Rhode Island was still governed under the colonial charter granted in 1662, and although changes had occurred, an exclusive oligarchy, protected by a stiff property requirement for voting and officeholding, controlled the state government. After reformers unsuccessfully sought in the 1830s to broaden the suffrage through established constitutional methods, they held a convention without the authorization of the charter government. Professing popular sovereignty and allegiance to the true principles of republican government, they wrote a constitution and formed a parallel state government. In the face of this challenge, the charter government passed a treason law directed at the irregular action, invoked martial law, and appealed to the president of the United States to assist in putting down the insurrection. The Dorr Rebellion, so named for its leader, Democrat Thomas Wilson Dorr, failed when the majority of the people in the state continued to support the charter government. They did so in large part because state officials, provoked into action by the Dorrites, drafted a new constitution embodying the reformers' demands. Dorr and his fellow defenders of popular sovereignty refused to acquiesce in this result, however, and persisted in their attempt to vindicate what they termed "peaceable revolution": the right of the people to alter their government whenever they pleased without regard to existing authority.

Long after the desired democratic reforms had been introduced into the state government, the Dorrites' defense of popular sovereignty eventuated in the Supreme Court decision in *Luther* v. *Borden* (1849). Not surprisingly, the Court rejected the popular-sovereignty argument. Asked to decide which of the competing governments in Rhode Island in 1842 had been the legitimate republican state government, the Court formally disavowed an answer on the ground that it was a political question beyond the competence of the judiciary to decide. In effect, however, the Supreme Court acknowledged the charter government as legitimate and repudiated the Dorrites by holding, in an interpretation of the guarantee-of-republican-government clause, that the action of Congress in seating representatives stamped the seal of republican legitimacy on the government that sent them. In the case of Rhode Island in 1842, of course, this meant the charter government. The Supreme Court thus defended stability and order, and gave broad latitude to states to regulate civil and political liberty within their boundaries. In the context of increasing sectional hostility and southern fear of abolitionist-inspired attacks on slavery as a state institution, this defense of existing state authority was politically significant.

Related to these specifically governmental applications of direct-action popular sovereignty was an outburst of rioting throughout the country in the 1830s aimed at a variety of social problems and grievances. Mobs formed with alarming frequency—there were fifty-three in 1834–35—to protest any number of things from banking policy to blacks' civil rights. Riots were not directed against the existing order, however, but rather, in the eyes of participants, were exercises of the people's right to correct abuses that could not be rectified through established legal channels. They were a form of popular sovereignty, collective expressions of the power of individuals to govern themselves. To some degree local officials seem to have accepted this view of rioting, for they usually refrained from vigorous and heavy applications of force to control the mobs. In some sense officials regarded popular riots as compatible with the existing political order, as had been the case in the colonies in the eighteenth century, when rioting was often accepted as an instrument of political protest.

Nevertheless, despite the rioters' acceptance of the existing order, their actions challenged the rule of law and inspired apprehension over the future of republican constitutionalism. It is significant that Abraham Lincoln's first important political act—his Springfield Lyceum address of 1838—condemned the recent wave of riots as a threat to American institutions. Warning that rioting would destroy the people's attachment to the government, Lincoln insisted on respect for law as a safeguard for republican liberty. He urged that reverence for the Constitution and the law become "the *political religion* of the nation."

Confidence in the virtue, wisdom, and ability of the people thus had important consequences for American constitutionalism, not all of them unambiguously beneficial or positive. Carried to an extreme, popular sovereignty contained tendencies inimical to limited government and the rule of law. Similarly ambiguous was Andrew Jackson's constitutional role and legacy. As the tribune of the people, his bold exercise of presidential power changed the contours of the executive office but perhaps weakened the spirit of constitutional restraint that existed in the early national period. In any event, the states eagerly grasped the power that developed upon them as a result of dual-federalist theory and practice, frequently facilitated by Jackson's executive actions. They were aided, moreover, by Supreme Court decisions, under Jacksonian Chief Justice Roger B. Taney, which wrote dual federalism into constitutional law.

THIRTEEN

Jacksonian Jurisprudence: The Taney Court and Constitutional Law

SEVERAL YEARS ELAPSED before the Democratic party, having gained control of the presidency, acquired dominant influence on the Supreme Court. At the start of his administration President Jackson appointed John McLean of Ohio to the Court; in 1835 he named three more justices, James Wayne of Georgia, Philip Barbour of Virginia, and, as chief justice, Roger B. Taney of Maryland. Then, after Congress increased the size of the Supreme Court to nine members in 1837, President Martin Van Buren appointed two more Democrats, John McKinley of Alabama and John Catron of Tennessee. These changes in the membership of the high bench were, of course, intended to shape the development of public law in accordance with the principles of the Democratic party. The Taney Court, therefore, lost little time confirming and extending the acquisition of power by the states under the theory of dual federalism.

The shift in the Court's political complexion raised in a particularly acute from the problem of accommodating social and political change while maintaining continuity in the law. Political folklore long attributed to the Taney Court a revolutionary impact, positing a fundamental conflict between its constitutional outlook and that of the Marshall Court. Modern scholarship has corrected this overdrawn judgment. It is clear, for example, that in the last years of Marshall's tenure the Supreme Court to some extent reflected the rising states'-right sentiment. In effect it permitted states to exercise a concurrent power to regulate interstate commerce (*Willson* v. *Black Bird Creek Marsh Co.,* 1829); upheld the state taxing power against a corporation's claim of implied immunity under a charter grant (*Providence Bank* v. *Billings,* 1830); and refused to apply the Fifth Amendment as a restriction on the states (*Barron* v. *Baltimore,* 1833). By the same token, the new Democratic justices by no means abandoned or overturned the leading constitutional doctrines laid down in the Marshall era. In economic matters especially, they followed the example of the Marshall Court in protecting property rights and facilitating capitalist expansion, although they tended to favor the states rather than the national government for this purpose. Sanctity of contract, interpreted to include legislative charter grants, remained a basic premise of constitutional law. The Taney Court also demonstrated continuity of outlook with its predecessor in enlarging the jurisdiction of the federal judiciary. Nevertheless, the Marshall and Taney Courts differed in significant respects.

The most important change in constitutional law that occurred in the Jacksonian era concerned the nature of the Union and federal-state relations. Rejecting the Marshall Court's bias toward national supremacy, the Taney justices acknowledged the exclusive power of the states in relation to the federal government. The theory of dual federalism, as Jackson's policies showed, did not formally deny federal sovereignty. Nevertheless, its historic purpose was to expand the power of the states relative to the federal government, and after it was transformed into the doctrine of state sovereignty it denied federal sovereignty entirely. The relative decline in national power resulting from dual federalism was not necessarily fatal to the Union. Yet, subordinated as it was to the ambitions of the slave power in the 1850s, dual federalism failed to restrain—if it did not positively encourage—southern disunionism. To be sure, Roger B. Taney was never so inflexible in his conception of state sovereignty as John C. Calhoun or even some of his southern colleagues on the Court. His interest in capitalist expansion, inherently centralizing in its effect, kept him from agrarian localist extremes. In the final analysis, however, Taney's commitment to slavery, like that of the party whose views he represented, caused him to reject the idea of authentic federal legislative sovereignty, thus facilitating the disintegration of the Union.

The New Era in Constitutional Law

The 1837 term of the Supreme Court revealed the new emphases and interests of the Democratic majority. The Court decided three cases carried over from earlier years dealing with paper money and state banking, state regulation of interstate commerce, and state encouragement of economic development through corporation charters. These were all key issues in Jacksonian politics, and in each instance the Supreme Court, ignoring or reinterpreting precedents from the Marshall era, endorsed the exercise of state power. The results delighted Democrats and appalled Whigs, who read them as evidence of a dangerous expansion in governmental power, politicization of the rule of law, and general decline in constitutional morality. *Briscoe* v. *The Bank of Kentucky* (1837), the paper-money–state banking case, illustrates the conflicting attitudes and aspirations provoked by the emergence of a distinctive Jacksonian jurisprudence.

The *Briscoe* case involved the constitutional status of state bills of credit. In *Craig* v. *Missouri* (1830) the Marshall Court had held that interest-bearing notes issued by the state of Missouri were bills of credit and thus prohibited by the Constitution. The Bank of the Commonwealth of Kentucky was created and owned by the state, which authorized it to issue notes for public circulation as legal tender, chose its officers, and was heavily involved in its management. Although there were differences between the situations in Missouri and Kentucky, chiefly in the fact that acts of the Kentucky bank were taken in its own name rather than the state's, for all practical purposes they were the same. The Supreme Court, however, sensitive to states' rights and the need for a circulating medium to fill the void left by the demise of the Bank of the United States, professed to see a difference. John McLean for the Court held that the bank notes in question were not constitutionally prohibited bills of credit because they were not issued by a state and were not designated to circulate as money on the faith and credit of the state. Justice Story dissented, arguing that the state and the bank were in effect the same and that the notes were state bills of credit. As a Whig, Story appreciated the need for a circulating medium, but believed private banks chartered by states could supply this want. In his view the Constitution plainly prohibited states from issuing paper money, and he thought the Court was engaging in a subterfuge by regarding the Kentucky bank as private. Exaggerated as Story's lamentation on the passing of the old order may have been, his dissent underscored the expedient nature of the decision.

The Charles River Bridge *Case*

The most important case in the early years of the Taney era, from the standpoint of constitutional philosophy, was the famous controversy in Massachusetts over the Charles River Bridge. In the *Dartmouth College* case the Marshall Court had held that state-issued charters of incorporation were contracts in the sense of the Constitution and could not be abrogated or impaired. Under that ruling states could reserve the right to modify corporation charters. But many states failed to do so, and disputes arose over the precise nature of privileges bestowed on corporations by legislative charters. Treating the charter as a contract was a useful means of guaranteeing entrepreneurs the security they deserved for making public improvements. It was also true, however, that corporations could act in ways injurious to the public, and this fact stimulated anticorporation sentiment among both old Republican and entrepreneurial-minded Jacksonians. Not the fundamentally contractual nature of state-granted charters, therefore, but rather the scope of corporate privilege under them was the issue in the Massachusetts bridge case.

As well as the increased economic importance of the corporation, developments in the field of transportation formed the context for the bridge controversy. A transportation revolution was occurring. Turnpike travel in the early nineteenth century was superseded by canal and river transport, which in turn were challenged by the railroad. At each stage the existing mode of commerce and transportation, protected by legal franchises awarded by the state, fought the superior competitive advantage possessed by the newer mode. Sound public policy suggested the wisdom of encouraging new forms of transportation and enterprise in general. Yet it seemed equally important, in order to assure technological progress in the future, to protect those willing to venture their capital in risky public improvement projects. Although new modes of transportation were not involved in the bridge case, the legal principles that resolved it had application in this dynamic sector of the nineteenth-century economy.

In 1785 the Massachusetts legislature had incorporated the Charles River Bridge Company for a period of forty years, and had empowered it to erect a bridge over the Charles River and to collect tolls for passage over the bridge. In 1792 the life of the original charter was extended to seventy years. Before the expiration of the charter, however, the legislature authorized another corporation, the Warren Bridge Company, to erect another bridge over the Charles River at a point less than three hundred yards from the earlier bridge. By the terms of its charter, the new corporation was to turn its bridge over to the state as soon as its expenses of construction were paid; it was, therefore, potentially toll-free and threatened to destroy almost entirely the value of the earlier bridge. Accordingly, in 1829 the Charles River Bridge Company sought an injunction against the construction of the new bridge, on the grounds that the older charter by implication gave it sole and exclusive right to operate a bridge at the point in question during the life of its charter, and that the second charter, therefore, constituted an impairment of the obligation of contracts.

In *Charles River Bridge* v. *Warren Bridge* (1837), the Supreme Court denied that the state had violated the contractual rights of the Charles River Bridge Company in chartering the new bridge. Chief Justice Taney in his majority opinion disarmed his critics by citing at the outset an opinion of John Marshall, in *Providence Bank* v. *Billings* (1830), rejecting the idea that a state bank charter by implication gave exemption from state taxation. Marshall had said the taxing power was too important to be relinquished by presumption; Taney extended the idea to all the powers of state government as he described the central tenet of Jacksonian dual federalism—the doctrine of the police power. "The object and end of all government," Taney declared, "is to promote the happiness and prosperity of the community by which it is established; and it can never be assumed, that the government intended to diminish its power of accomplishing the end for which it was created." Rejecting the argument for an implied corporate privilege, he added: "We cannot deal thus with the rights reserved to the States, and by legal intendments and mere technical reasoning, take away from them any portion of that power over their own internal police and improvement, which is so necessary to their well being and prosperity."

Taney argued further that to allow the old bridge to block the construction of the new one would jeopardize progress in internal improvements. The old turnpike companies, he warned, would claim in their charters "unknown and undefined property in a line of travelling" and would ask courts to keep canals and railroads from being built. Millions of dollars of investments would be threatened, and the country would stand still until the claims of obsolete enterprises were satisfied. Only then, said Taney, would these companies permit the states "to avail themselves of the lights of modern science, and to partake of the benefit of those improvements which are now adding to the wealth and prosperity, and the convenience and comfort of every other part of the civilized world." In other words, creative destruction of existing property rights was occasionally necessary to achieve economic progress.

To be sure, Taney did not disavow the rule of the *Darmouth College* case that a state charter of incorporation was a contract. He held that charter grants must be interpreted strictly, that corporation privileges could not be created by implication, and that ambiguities must be resolved in favor of the state. Modern commentators have concluded, therefore, that he merely refrained from extending the principle of the *Dartmouth College* decision. Yet in reality the difference between Marshall and Taney was much greater than this formal analysis suggests, for Taney abandoned the entire conceptual approach employed in the *Dartmouth College* case. This becomes apparent when one considers Justice Story's dissenting opinion.

As Story saw it, the state wanted a bridge built and the proprietors sought a profit; the two parties, therefore, reached an understanding and entered into a contract in the form of the charter of incorporation. The Charles River Bridge Company got the right to collect tolls and in return built and operated a bridge which it promised to give to the state after a period of years. According to Story, the bridge company never would have agreed to the contract if the investors had thought the legislature was reserving the right to destroy the enterprise by chartering a free bridge right next to it. This elementary perception was common sense and common law, said Story, and it must control the disposition of the matter. The charter must be interpreted, in other words, as a contract in private law.

It was this private-law contractual character of the transaction that Taney denied. Instead he argued that the charter was like a royal grant. Plausible as this analogy may appear, it contained revealing—and for Story disturbing— implications about Jacksonian constitutional philosophy. For it amounted to the substitution of a ruler-subject relationship for the relationship between equals that was implicit in the private-law contract theory. If the charter was like a royal grant, then the state legislature was like a king. Possessing sovereign power, it had the right to determine the public good and override the rights of individuals in order to obtain it. Story contended on the contrary that legislatures were not like kings; they were not sovereign. Rather, the people were sovereign, and legislative power was limited.

Story desired to encourage venture capital and economic progress, as did the majority of the Court. He did not defend static, unproductive vested rights. In his view, however, economic development required predictability and certainty of legal outcomes that would guarantee investors a return on their investment. Moreover, he believed the means chosen by Taney to promote economic progress threatened basic principles of republican constitutionalism. Taney would lodge sovereign power in the state government, backed by the will of the majority. The result would be the triumph of political expediency over the rule of law. In reaching this conclusion Story, whose emotional involvement in the case was considerable, perhaps exaggerated. Yet historians generally agree that Taney's opinion, for all its legalistic cleverness and plausibility, was heavily instrumental and pragmatic, a response to the social and economic demands of the Jacksonian majority. Story's dissent reflected an older conception of republican constitutional morality, Taney's a newer approach that emphasized the creation and exercise of power in the name of state legislative sovereignty, guided by political expediency rather than fixed constitutional principle. Whether the active government posited in Taney's politicized constitutional vision would be limited and responsible government, and thus consistent with the American constitutional tradition, remained to be seen. In any event, more was at stake in the bridge case than simply the question of interpreting corporation charters.

The Taney Court consistently adhered to the rule of strict construction of charter grants, and in an important related development held that state exercises of the power of eminent domain that abrogated charters were not violations of the contract clause. The power of eminent domain refers to the government's power to expropriate private property for public purposes. In *West River Bridge Company* v. *Dix* (1848), the Supreme Court for the first time ruled on the constitutionality of this power. The state of Vermont had granted a franchise to a bridge company to collect tolls, but subsequently took it away with a view toward constructing a free public highway. Although the bridge company got compensation, it argued that the taking impaired the obligation of the contract. It also condemned the theory of an eminent-domain power as a new and despotic doctrine that would enable states to take property unrestrainedly. The Supreme Court upheld the taking as constitutional. For the Court, Justice Peter V. Daniel asserted that every sovereign political community had the right and duty, under the power of eminent domain, to protect its interests and welfare, both in external relations and in its interior polity and social life. Paramount to all private rights vested under the government, said Daniel, the eminent-domain power was retained by the states when they entered the Union and could be used to promote the public good.

The Sanctity of Contract

Despite the anticorporation overtones emanating from decisions based on the rule of strict interpretation of charter grants, the Taney Court more than adequately protected property rights and encouraged corporation growth. It scrupulously guarded corporate privileges that were specifically identified in charters. In the notable case of *Gelpcke* v. *Dubuque* (1864), it went so far as to hold that a state supreme court decision interpreting the state constitution to permit rupudiation of a bond issue violated the contract clause.

The *Gelpcke* case involved a provision in the Iowa state constitution limiting state indebtedness to $100,000. The legislature circumvented the restriction by authorizing municipalities to issue bonds, and the city of Dubuque did so in order to get a railroad. The railroad was never built, however, and taxpayers filed suit against payment of the bonds. They were upheld by the state supreme court, which declared the bond issue in violation of the state constitution. The United States Supreme Court, for the first time overruling a state court decision interpreting the state's own constitution, reversed the decision. It held the bond issue valid as a contract which at the time it was made was sanctioned by state law. At stake were millions of dollars' worth of bond issues all over the country, and even though there seemed to be justice in the complaint of communities that had to pay for railroads that were never built, the Court insisted on the sanctity of contractual obligations.

In cases involving state debtor-relief laws and private contractual rights between individuals, the Court also enforced the contract clause. In part this was because much current legislation of this kind, especially the debtor-relief legislation arising out of the long depression following the panic of 1837, concerned property rights in land and mortgages, toward which most of the justices were more sympathetic than they were toward corporate property. In the outstanding case of this kind, *Bronson* v. *Kinzie* (1843), the Court declared invalid as an impairment of the obligation of contracts two Illinois laws restricting foreclosure sales and giving debtors certain broad rights to repurchase foreclosed property. Most state bankruptcy statutes of the day were not as radical as these, however; they seldom attempted to reduce or modify the debt, but instead contented themselves with softening the methods of execution by permitting installment payments, extending redemption dates, and the like. The Court customarily upheld this type of law under the doctrine advanced by Marshall in *Sturges* v. *Crowninshield* that the state could rightfully modify the legal "remedy" or method of enforcing a contract as long as it did not impair the terms of the contract itself.

The Supreme Court's application of the contract clause reflected the social approval of contract at this time as an instrument of economic growth. Under the supervision of the state courts, contract law was one of the most dynamic areas of private law. Used to extend market operations and introduce

greater stability and predictability into economic exchange, it had major consequences for public policy. Philosophically, contract law interpretation shifted
from a precommercial point of view which had allowed courts to judge the
essential fairness of business dealings. The new basis of contract law adjudication was the laissez-fair belief that individuals should be free to bargain as they
saw fit in order to promote their own interests. The corollary was that courts
would enforce contracts without regard to their moral content. In any event,
as American political practice had drawn heavily on contract theory, so the
burgeoning commercial capitalism of the antebellum era utilized the legal
instrument of contract.

The Legal Status of Corporations

Closely related to the use of contract was reliance on the corporation as
a means of economic expansion. Corporations were increasingly popular for
their economic usefulness. Yet they were also objects of hostility because of
the exclusive legal privileges they enjoyed, such as the power of eminent
domain and freedom from competition. These privileges were obtained by
special acts of the state legislatures. One response to the problem of the
corporation, therefore, was to adopt general incorporation laws permitting
anyone to secure the benefits that corporate status provided. The alternative
was to prohibit corporations or strictly to regulate them through legislation.
States that pursued the latter course frequently attempted to restrict corporations created in other states. Accordingly, cases came before the Supreme
Court questioning the status of corporations under the rules of interstate
relations, or comity, and also under the diversity-of-citizenship clause of the
Constitution. In both situations the Taney Court acted favorably toward corporations, and extended legal protection to them.

Bank of Augusta v. Earle was the most important of three cases in 1839
dealing with the power of a state to exclude foreign (that is, out of state)
corporations. An Alabama citizen refused to pay the bills of exchange of a
Georgia bank on the ground that a foreign corporation had no legal right to
make a contract within a sovereign state. Counsel for the bank argued that a
corporation, like a citizen, could enter another state and engage in business
under the protection of the privileges-and-immunities clause of the federal
Constitution.

The Court's decision, rendered by Chief Justice Taney, recognized the
general right of a corporation to do business under interstate comity within
other states. But it also recognized the right of the states to exclude foreign
corporations by positive action if they so desired. Taney also refused to recognize corporations as possessing all the legal rights guaranteed to natural persons under the Constitution. Accordingly, he held that a corporation could
have legal existence only in the state creating it, and that it could not migrate

to another state by virtue of any right bestowed in the privileges-and-immunities clause, though it might do business in other states if they consented. The immediate question was whether this consent must be expressed or merely implied. Taney maintained that "the silence of the state authorities" in face of extensive activities by outside corporations gave presumption of the state's acquiescence. Alabama law prohibited out-of-state banking but was ambiguous as to whether selling bills of exchange was included in banking. Disavowing any intention of determining state policy, Taney nevertheless did precisely that by adopting the rule of comity and interpreting Alabama law so as to allow the bills in question. His carefully constructed opinion plainly upheld the power of states to prohibit or regulate foreign corporations, and states subsequently enacted much legislation of this sort. On balance, however, the decision was more favorable to corporations than to their critics.

Although the Court continued to deny corporations citizenship status under the privileges-and-immunities clause (a question of great complexity and uncertainty because of the problem of defining the status of free Negroes), it recognized corporations as citizens under the clause giving federal courts jurisdiction in controversies between citizens of different states. The Marshall Court had held that only if all members of a corporation were residents of another state could a citizen bring suit against it in federal court under the diversity clause. As corporations grew more numerous there was dissatisfaction with this rule, which made it practically impossible for them to go into the national courts. In *Louisville, Cincinnati and Charleston Railroad Company* v. *Letson* (1844) the Taney Court opened the federal courts to the new business associations by holding that a corporation was a citizen of the state in which it was chartered, irrespective of where its members resided. States'-rights judges, such as Peter V. Daniel and John A. Campbell, objected to this change, but the Court affirmed it in *Marshall* v. *Baltimore and Ohio Railroad Company* (1854). Although corporations did not at this time uniformly seek access to the federal courts, and continued to be denied the more comprehensive citizenship that potentially lay in the privileges-and-immunities clause, the Letson rule proved beneficial to them because it led to the creation by the federal courts of a more uniform body of commercial law beyond the reach of state power. Thus in a field where slavery was not involved, the Taney Court tended toward centralization, albeit of a judicial rather than a legislative kind.

The Commerce Power and Dual Federalism

In questions of economic policy the Court tried to balance the need for nationally protected commercial development against promotional and occasional regulatory tendencies in the states. But in a variety of controversial internal social matters that came to it through commerce clause litigation it conspicuously deferred to the states under the theory of dual federalism. From the 1820s, when John Marshall broadly expounded the federal commerce power, Southerners were keenly aware of the potential harm that could come to slavery from this source. By 1837 an abolition movement existed in the northern states; Southerners were defending slavery as a positive good; and Democratic politicians had difficulty keeping the slavery question out of national politics. Under the circumstances the Supreme Court, with five Southerners forming a majority, was acutely sensitive to the danger to slavery inherent in a broad definition of commerce that would regard slaves as articles of commerce and in an expansive conception of congressional power to regulate interstate commerce. Accordingly, in contrast to the Marshall Court, the Taney Court defined commerce narrowly and allowed the states to exercise the police power in ways that affected interstate commerce. Eventually, the Court recognized a concurrent state power to regulate interstate commerce in the absence of congressional legislation.

New York v. Miln, one of the three major cases of the 1837 term carried over from the Marshall era, revealed the dual-federalist approach the Court would take in commerce-power controversies. The case involved the validity of a New York law requiring masters of ships arriving in New York to report certain data on all passengers brought into port. The law had been attacked as an interference with congressional authority over foreign commerce, but Justice Barbour, speaking for five of the seven justices, held the law valid as a legitimate exercise of the state's police power, since the state's internal welfare was the obvious purpose of the statute. Unlike the act in Gibbons v. Ogden, he said, the New York law did not conflict with any act of Congress so as to raise a question about the scope of the state police power in relation to the federal commerce power. Barbour said further that the act was legitimate even if considered as a commercial regulation because Congress had not acted. He thus suggested that the states possessed a concurrent commerce power. In good dual-federalist fashion, however, Barbour based his decision on what he called the "impregnable" doctrine of the police power: that a state has the same unlimited jurisdiction over persons and things within its territorial limits as a foreign nation, except as restrained by the Constitution. The authority of a state in exercising the police power to promote the well-being of the community, said Barbour, "is complete, unqualified, and exclusive." Nevertheless, Barbour took the opportunity to state that goods were articles of commerce, but persons were not. This dictum was immediately relevant to the slavery issue, and it provoked objections from northern justices.

The relation between slavery and the commerce power came under discussion in Groves v. Slaughter (1841). The case involved a provision of the Mississippi constitution intended to prohibit the introduction of slaves into the state for the purpose of selling them. The specific question was whether the constitutional provision operated of its own force, in which case the sale of slaves after its adoption would be illegal, or whether it needed to be implemented by legislation, in which case the sale of slaves would not be illegal. The

Court approved the sale in question, reasoning that the constitution was not effective until implemented by legislation.

The relationship between the Mississippi prohibition of slaves and the federal commerce power was not at issue in *Groves* v. *Slaughter* and did not need to be resolved. Nevertheless, Justice McLean of Ohio addressed it in a separate opinion. Rejecting the conclusion of the *Miln* case, he asserted that slaves *were* articles of commerce, and indeed were persons under the Constitution. He also said that Congress had exclusive power over interstate commerce. Nevertheless, he retreated from this bold position in saying, contradictorily, that the states had exclusive power over slavery. Thinking no doubt of his own state, Ohio, McLean declared that each state had a right to protect itself against "the inconveniences and danger of a slave population." This right, he added, was "higher and deeper than the Constitution." In one of the many ironies that characterized the sectional struggle over slavery, Chief Justice Taney accepted this conclusion, but for entirely different reasons. State regulation of the introduction or control of slaves within their territorial limits, said Taney, could not be controlled by Congress under the commerce power or any other power.

In the *License Cases* (1847) the Court upheld state power, although the justices were unable to agree on a single rationale for the decision. The cases concerned the validity of three statutes of Massachusetts, Rhode Island, and New Hampshire regulating and taxing the sale of alcoholic liquors. The laws were attacked on the ground that in taxing liquor imported from outside the state they in effect imposed unconstitutional regulations upon interstate commerce and so were void. The New Hampshire case was of particular interest, for here the tax had been levied upon liquor still in the "original package," in apparent violation of the dictum in *Brown* v. *Maryland*. There was considerable difference among the justices about certain legal details, evident in nine different opinions written by six justices. But certain propositions stood out clearly amid the welter of legal reasoning. The justices were in general agreement that the fact that a state tax law levied for internal police purposes has an incidental effect upon interstate commerce did not thereby make it invalid.

Four justices—Taney, John Catron, Samuel Nelson, and Levi Woodbury—also thought the states had a concurrent right to regulate interstate commerce in the absence of federal action; and it was on this basis that the first three sustained the New Hampshire law. The federal commerce power, Taney maintained, was not exclusive. "It appears to me to be very clear," he said, "that the mere grant of power to the general government cannot, upon any just principles of construction, be construed to be an absolute prohibition to the exercise of any power over the same subject by the States. . . . In my judgment, the State may nevertheless, for the safety or convenience of trade, or for the protection of the health of its citizens, make regulations of commerce for its own ports and harbors, and for its own territory; and such regulations are valid unless they come in conflict with a law of Congress." The basis of this power in Taney's view, however, was not a concurrent commerce power, but rather "the powers of government inherent in every sovereignty . . . the power to govern men and things within the limits of its dominion." Leaving Northerners like McLean to use the language of the police power, Taney took the high road of state sovereignty.

In the *Passenger Cases* (1849) it became clear, however, that the various justices were still far from agreement upon the precise line between the states' internal police power and the commerce power and upon the question of whether the commerce power was exclusive or concurrent. The cases involved the validity of New York and Massachusetts statutes imposing head taxes upon alien passengers arriving in the states' ports. Five justices thought the acts a direct regulation of interstate commerce and so void, McLean flatly declaring that the federal commerce power was lodged exclusively in the federal government and could not be exercised by the states even in the absence of congressional action. Amid the confusion of eight separate opinions, the Court at least seemed to have decided that persons were articles of commerce. This perception and the vindication of federal authority in the absence of congressional legislation caused many Southerners to fear that state inspection laws aimed at preventing the abduction of slaves and laws barring entry of free Negro seamen in southern ports would be held unconstitutional. Justice Wayne of Georgia made it clear, however, that in his view states could separate slaves and free Negroes from commerce and protect their institutions against federal encroachment by means of the commerce power. For the minority, Chief Justice Taney argued that the state laws in question were specifically aimed at the prevention of disease and pauperism and hence were valid exercises of state sovereignty. States could not, Taney insisted, be forced to admit persons whom the federal government might choose to admit. They could remove or prohibit any one they chose, employing their reserved power of "self-preservation" as independent sovereignties. This was not a concurrent power, said Taney, and any act of the federal government in conflict with it was void.

Disagreement among the justices over the nature of the commerce power was largely reconciled in *Cooley* v. *Pennsylvania Board of Wardens* (1851), a case in which the Court upheld a Pennsylvania statute regulating pilotage in the port of Philadelphia. Justice Benjamin Curtis, a Boston Whig lawyer recently appointed to the Court, speaking for six justices, said that the power to regulate commerce involved a vast field, some phases of which were national in character and so demanded congressional action. Here federal power was properly exclusive. Other aspects of commerce were local in character and demanded a diversity of local regulations. Here the states properly had a concurrent power to legislate in the absence of federal action. There was thus a limited concurrent state power over interstate commerce, exercisable only where Congress had not yet acted. Pennsylvania's regulation of pilotage came within this power.

This doctrine of "selective exclusiveness" took a more restrained view of state authority over commerce than Taney previously had. The important point for the advocates of dual federalism, however, was the concurrent power of the states or the nonexclusiveness of federal power, and since Curtis's opinion embodied this idea, Taney silently agreed with it. Justice Daniel alone protested that state power over local commerce was original and inherent in the states and not subject to federal control. McLean and Wayne dissented outright from the majority decision, insisting on the exclusive character of the federal commerce power. The Cooley rule expressed in a formal way the pragmatic approach that had characterized the Court's disposition of commerce-power cases. Although it focused attention on the nature of commerce rather than on the nature of congressional power, it provided no guidelines for distinguishing between national and local commerce. The rule was an eloquent statement of indefiniteness. Yet, as Professor Swisher has observed, with the statement, the indefiniteness seemed more manageable.[1]

At the same session at which the *Cooley* case was decided, the Court in *Pennsylvania* v. *Wheeling Bridge Company* (1851) showed its willingness to respect federal authority over commerce when the exercise of that power came into conflict with that of the states. The state of Pennsylvania had attacked the bridge company's right to construct a bridge over the Ohio River under the supposed authority of Virginia statutes, claiming that the prospective bridge would interrupt interstate river navigation. The case attracted great popular interest because it involved a conflict between rival transportation systems— rivers and railroads—which was an important economic issue at the time. The Court held, with Justice McLean delivering the opinion, that the bridge was an interference with the federal commerce power as exercised by Congress in the coasting license acts. Its construction was, therefore, unlawful. Subsequently, however, Congress declared the bridge not to be an obstruction to navigation, and in a second case in 1856 the Supreme Court acquiesced in this view.

The Taney Court's commerce decisions expressed its dual-federalist conception of the Union. Without disavowing federal supremacy, the Court treated the existence of the states with their reserved powers as a limitation on federal authority. The state police power, or as Taney preferred to call it, state sovereignty, marked out certain subjects as exclusively within the jurisdiction of the states and beyond the reach of the national government. This feature of dual federalism subsequently enabled it to serve the South's need for an instrument of constitutional power with which to protect slavery against federal intervention.

---

1. Carl B. Swisher, *History of the Supreme Court of the United States,* Vol. V: *The Taney Period 1836–64* (1974), p. 407.

The Taney Court and Judicial Nationalism

Although unsympathetic to a broad construction of national legislative power, the Taney Court significantly expanded federal judicial power. One aspect of this expansion, in response especially to the growth of the market economy, was the enlargement of federal court jurisdiction. Another aspect, the practical upshot of many of the rules of interpretation evolved in contract and commerce clause cases, was an expansion of the federal courts' discretionary policy-making authority. Occasionally, the Taney justices made deferential gestures toward legislative authority, but these were more apparent than real. Eventually, the *Dred Scott* decision, in which the Court tried to settle the most explosive political issue of the day, gave the lie to the idea that the Taney justices were guided by a philosophy of judicial restraint. In fact, under pressure to defend slavery the Court regarded itself as uniquely qualified to umpire conflicts within the federal system. This attitude can be seen as continuous with the judicial nationalism of the Marshall era, but its subordination to pro-slavery state sovereignty caused it to be a distorted expression of the Marshall legacy.

Ironically, the Taney Court's concern for economic expansion led it to acquire a common law jurisdiction denied to the Marshall Court. In 1812, it will be recalled, the Supreme Court held in *United States* v. *Hudson and Goodwin* that the federal courts possessed no common law criminal jurisdiction. In another case, *Wheaton* v. *Peters* (1834), it reiterated that there was no federal common law. In exercising jurisdiction in diversity-of-citizenship cases, moreover, the federal courts were required, under Section 34 of the Judiciary Act of 1789, to use the laws of the several states as rules of decision in trials at common law where the federal Constitution, statutes, or treaties were not controlling. Although in 1789 Congress seemingly intended to include state court decisions in the state law which the federal judiciary was instructed to apply, several judges in the Jacksonian era sought to escape this restriction. One means of doing so was to employ equity jurisprudence—a body of rules distinct from the common law—in diversity cases, in disregard of state court equity rulings. Justice Joseph Story, fearful of growing state power and the decline of federal authority, pursued this objective in his circuit court opinions. In *United States* v. *King* (1849), the Supreme Court, after Story's death, accepted the argument for federal equity jurisprudence.

More important was the attempt to fashion a federal common law jurisdiction. Despite repeated denials by the Supreme Court that a federal common law existed, compelling economic reasons urged federal judges in the 1830s to expand their power in this direction. Left to their own devices, states discriminated against out-of-state businesses and generally created conditions of legal uncertainty and instability that discouraged national economic development. Occasionally, in diversity litigation, the Supreme Court under John

Marshall had refused to be guided by state laws that were flagrantly hostile to interstate commercial interests. But the accepted interpretation of Section 34 of the Judiciary Act, which made state court decisions the rule of decision in interstate controversies, apparently blocked any serious attempt to counteract the particularity of state legislation by establishing a uniform commercial law.

Economic pressures following the panic of 1837, however, led the Supreme Court to attempt to rectify this situation. In *Swift* v. *Tyson* (1842), it held that federal courts need not be bound by state court decisions in settling conflicts between citizens of different states that did not involve the federal Constitution, laws, or treaties. The case arose when one Tyson purchased land with a bill of exchange which through a separate transaction ended up in the possession of Swift. The original transaction turned out to be fraudulent, and Tyson argued that under New York law, including state court decisions that the federal courts were required to follow according to Section 34, the bill of exchange was invalid because it was corrupted by the original fraud. For a unanimous Court, Justice Story held that the bill must be paid. In matters of a general nature not conditioned by local circumstances or governed by local statute, he reasoned, as in the construction of contracts and questions of general commercial law, the federal courts in diversity cases were not bound by state statutes or court rulings. Interpreting Section 34, Story said that state court decisions were not part of the "laws of the states" which federal courts were obliged to follow in diversity suits. Court decisions, he explained, were not laws; at most they were evidence of what the law was. Section 34, according to Story, thus referred to state statute law only. Moreover, it applied only to strictly local matters, not to questions of general commercial law. Story concluded by saying that the federal courts were free to resolve these broader questions according to their own interpretation of "the general principles and doctrines of commercial jurisprudence."

The Supreme Court subsequently affirmed *Swift* v. *Tyson* with a view toward creating a uniform body of national commercial law. This law would be functionally the same as the common law in its nonstatutory origins and judicial means of development, although historically it derived from the international law merchant rather than from the common law of England. At any rate the decision promised to expand the sphere of federal judicial authority significantly. Nationalists like Story assumed that the state courts would seek to apply the same principles of general commercial law in matters of general or extraterritorial import, and hence would be guided by federal court decisions explicating and developing this law. In practice, however, the state courts paid small regard to the federal judiciary's attempts to shape a national commercial common law. The consequence, by the late nineteenth century, was the existence of separate bodies of state and federal commercial common law which were the source of much confusion.

The Taney Court achieved greater success in extending the admiralty jurisdiction of the federal courts. In England admiralty jurisdiction applied only in tidal waters, and in 1825, in *The Thomas Jefferson,* the Supreme Court adopted this rule as a limitation on the admiralty and maritime jurisdiction of the federal judiciary. Subsequently the expansion of river and lake navigation and commerce led business interests to seek the extension of admiralty law to inland lakes, rivers, and waterways. Accordingly in 1845, for the benefit of businessmen in the interior of the country, Congress passed a law providing for the use of the forms and remedies of admiralty law in matters of tort and contract involving navigation and commerce on lakes and navigable waters between states and territories. In *Propeller Genesee Chief* v. *Fitzhugh* (1851) the Supreme Court upheld the broadened federal jurisdiction. Chief Justice Taney overruled the earlier Marshall decision, pointing out the inappropriateness of the tidal-waters limitation in light of the development of navigation in the interior of the nation. Resolving a matter that Congress had left ambiguous, Taney based the expanded federal jurisdiction on the admiralty power rather than on the commerce clause. To make the commerce power the basis of the new jurisdiction, he said, would unduly extend federal legislative power into land commerce.

Expansion of judicial discretion in decision-making, in contrast to formal jurisdiction, also occurred under Taney. An example was the invitation issued in the *Letson* case for corporations to enter the forum of the federal courts. The Court's pragmatic, case-by-case interpretation of the contract and commerce clauses further reflected the willingness of Jacksonian judges to assume a larger policy-making role. And when rules for deciding future conflicts were announced, as in the *Cooley* case, their practical import often was to enlarge the scope of judicial discretion. The *Cooley* rule of selective exclusiveness, for example, really meant that the Court would decide what was national commerce and what local.

These facts offer a corrective to the view sometimes advanced that the Taney Court rejected the political activism of the Marshall Court in favor of judicial restraint. Taney's defenders point to his dissent in the *Wheeling Bridge* case, for example. There he announced that as the Supreme Court had never exercised jurisdiction over the construction of bridges over navigable streams, and as Congress had power over the entire subject, it would be "too near the confines of legislation" for the Court to determine the question. The outstanding illustration of Taney's judicial restraint, however, is usually considered to be his opinion in *Luther* v. *Borden* (1849), announcing the doctrine of political questions.

As noted previously, the Court in this case formally refused to decide which of two competing governments in Rhode Island during the Dorr Rebellion was the legitimate state government. The question was political, declared Taney, and thus beyond the proper scope of judicial power. Yet Taney in effect did decide the question, in his interpretation of the guarantee-of-republican-government clause. He gratuitously defined the duties of the political branches under the guarantee clause and for all practical purposes acknowledged the existing charter government of Rhode Island as the legitimate state government. In actuality, *Luther* v. *Borden* expressed more of judicial assertiveness than restraint.

Unlike John Marshall, whose exercise of judicial power basically complemented the political branches of the national government, Taney conceived of the Supreme Court as a supranational and suprapolitical guardian of the Constitution. He saw the Court as the umpire of the federal system, charged with the responsibility of preventing the competing sovereignties—the states and the federal government—from invading each other's sphere of authority. Discussing the difficulty of drawing a line between federal and state power over commerce, Taney in the *License Cases* reasoned that as the Constitution did not attempt to fix the line of demarcation, and as neither Congress nor the states could enlarge their powers by legislation, "the question is necessarily one for judicial discretion."

Taney's strongest assertion of the role of the Supreme Court appeared in *Ableman* v. *Booth,* the famous fugitive slave case on the eve of the Civil War. Using ostensibly centralizing rhetoric, Taney spoke of the need to uphold national law, in this instance the Fugitive Slave Act of 1850. It was equally necessary, however, to protect the states against federal encroachment. The Supreme Court, said Taney, was created in order to provide this reciprocal protection, although it was not created by the federal government, "but by the people of the States." The judicial power was intended to maintain the supremacy of United States laws, and to guard the states against any invasion of their reserved rights by the federal government. "So long, therefore, as this Constitution shall endure," Taney declared, "this tribunal must exist with it, deciding the angry and irritating controversies between sovereignties, which in other countries have been determined by the arbitrament of force."

Evenhanded as this dual-federalist, judicial supremacist doctrine appears to be, its application was guided by a commitment to the defense of slavery that invariably led the Taney Court to uphold state power. When the sectional struggle over slavery reached a climax in the late 1850s, Taney's dual federalism was ultimately subordinated to or became indistinguishable from a theory of state sovereignty that categorically denied national legislative sovereignty. In practical effect dual federalism was a doctrine of state power that encouraged the disunionist tendencies of the slave power. To give Taney his due it must be said that, like Calhoun, he was motivated also by a genuine desire to preserve the Union. Yet in Taney's view the fundamental purpose of the Union was to protect state interests and institutions, and preeminently the institution of slavery. This became the ultimate test of constitutional and political legitimacy under the doctrine of dual federalism.

State Mercantilism

In matters distinct from slavery the chief significance of dual federalism was to release state power for economic and social purposes. It remains briefly to consider the use that the states made of the power that devolved upon them during the era of dual federalism.

The formal division of sovereignty in American federalism notwithstanding, the states exercised most of the real power of government in the period before the Civil War. The distribution of economic resources was the major public policy issue, and although prior to Jackson's administration the federal government adopted policies on the tariff, land, money and banking, immigration, and patents for inventions, after 1832 it withdrew from much of this activity. The states meanwhile formulated mercantilist policies under the police power, the concurrent power over interstate commerce, and the power of eminent domain. They chartered corporations, including banks; built or funded internal improvements; allocated land and other natural resources; and distributed legal privileges and immunities that enabled entrepreneurial activity to flourish. Frequently, states expropriated property to promote economic development. State legislatures could take property under the law of eminent domain on condition that there be a legitimate public purpose and that the owner be given just compensation. Moreover, states sometimes delegated the power of eminent domain to turnpike, canal, bridge, railroad, and manufacturing companies.

State courts played an especially key role in state mercantilism by reshaping the common law into an instrument of economic progress. Perhaps the most fundamental change effected by the state judiciary was to redefine the legal conception of property in a manner appropriate to an expanding capitalist economy. In the eighteenth century the basic tenet of property law was the absolute right of a landowner to undisturbed enjoyment of his property. This was a static conception consistent with the outlook of an agrarian society. In the nineteenth century, by contrast, state common law courts sanctioned uses of property that were injurious to adjacent landowners. Damage to another's property was considered justified if it was economically and socially beneficial, as in the construction of dams and mills.

State courts in effect subsidized the development of the economy by fashioning legal doctrines and rules that shifted the cost of economic and technological change from the entrepreneur to the community. In tort law, for example, courts rejected the eighteenth-century standard of strict liability under which damages could be recovered for an injury regardless of its cause or the intention of the injuring party. Instead they formulated the negligence doctrine. This doctrine stated that damages for injuries occurring as a result of industrial or commercial activity (such as the operation of a railroad) could be recovered only on a showing of carelessness by the operating company or corporation. Furthermore, by redefining the legal meaning of injury, state courts were able to limit the effect of the just-compensation doctrine in situations where the power of eminent domain was exercised by transportation companies. Similarly, the law of nuisance, which in the eighteenth century protected landowners against interference with their property, was narrowly interpreted to prevent the award of damages for encroachment on property rights resulting from productive economic activity. Courts thus expressed the judgment of society that a certain amount of injury to person and property was a reasonable price to pay for economic progress.

State mercantilist policies in effect determined national economic policy, with results that were often haphazard, prodigal, and corrupt. Competition among groups for distributionist advantages from government was keen and figured largely in party battles between Whigs and Democrats. Nevertheless, a strong social consensus supported economic growth, and, because of the nature of distributionist policy, it was possible for government to satisfy competing interest-group demands by giving something to each. By the 1850s, moreover, the old Republican animus against commercial development had disappeared from Democratic rhetoric, and Jacksonians as well as Whigs promoted internal improvements.

Central as it was, however, economic development was not the only concern of the states in the era of dual federalism. Suffrage, representation, and other political and constitutional problems, as we have seen, were important and contentious issues. Much as Americans might agree on the necessity of private property, government by consent, constitutional limitations, and national union, the application of these fundamental principles stirred deep controversy. The organization and distribution of power were at issue, and while economic policy sometimes provided the occasion for conflict in this sphere, by the 1850s a more difficult problem—one that was not amenable to solution in the piecemeal, decentralist way that characterized distribution policy—had emerged to dominate American politics. That problem, which concerned not only the distribution of power but the very nature of the Union and the future of the republic, was the problem of slavery.

FOURTEEN

Slavery and the Constitution

The existence of Negro slavery in the American republic created an internal contradiction that eventually threatened not only the existence of the Union, but also constitutionalism and the rule of law. Slavery violated the principles of equality and consent announced in the Declaration of Independence on which the nation was founded. This contradiction, which was confirmed by the economic unprofitability of the institution, made slavery the object of abolitionist legislation in the northern states during and after the Revolution. Yet because it was a basic feature of the social and economic system in states whose support was essential to the creation of a stronger Union in 1787, slavery was recognized as a local institution in the Constitution, although not expressly identified because of the moral opprobrium attaching to it. Throughout the early national period slavery remained a quiescent issue, until diverging sectional attitudes and interests, briefly though with alarming intensity, made it a divisive national problem in the Missouri crisis of 1819–20. Controversy lessened and tensions eased with the formation of the Jacksonian Democratic coalition in the 1820s. By combining northern republicanism with the southern defense of slavery, the Democratic party generally succeeded in keeping the slavery question out of national politics in the 1830s.

The rise of an organized abolition movement made this task more difficult, and by the 1840s the nation's drive toward territorial expansion caused the abandonment of the agreements and understandings which for a generation had assigned slavery a subordinate place in American politics. Territorial expansion and the westward movement preeminently involved the founding of new communities and social institutions which could decisively influence the future development of the nation. In this context the possibility of slavery expansion into the interior of the continent was fraught with enormous consequences. It forced Americans to resolve fundamental ambiguities about the nature of the Union and the meaning of American nationality.

In the first half of the nineteenth century changes in culture, society, and

economy produced an increasing degree of national uniformity and integration. At the same time geographical and territorial expansion enlarged the size
of the nation. This process of nationalization, whether considered from a
social-cultural or a geographical perspective, required coming to grips with the
question of slavery. Would slavery, which by the end of the Revolutionary era
had been placed outside the mainstream of American values as the South's
"peculiar" institution, assume a dominant influence on American politics and
society? In constitutional terms the question was whether the law of slavery,
a creature of the state police power or state sovereignty, would become nationalized and made ascendant over the institutions of republican liberty—prescribed by the Declaration of Independence and incompletely and imperfectly
established in the Constitution—that existed in the northern states.

Slavery and Republican Government

If slavery became the overriding issue in American politics only in the
mid-nineteenth century, it had a long legal and constitutional history that
placed limits on the way in which it could be dealt with politically. Although
slavery had existed throughout human history, in Western societies it was
never regarded as part of the natural order, but was seen as requiring the
support and justification of positive law. In the American colonies in the
seventeenth century local labor needs, economic exigency, racial prejudice,
and the impulse toward European commercial expansion combined to transform the indentured servitude of black Africans into lifetime bondage. In the
formative stages of this transformation positive law as adopted by colonial
legislatures performed an important legitimizing function. By the time of the
American Revolution slavery was legally recognized in all of the American
colonies. Starting during the Revolution, however, the marginal economic
value of slavery in the northern states permitted its gradual abolition, in
accordance with the ideal of republican liberty. Although given prospective
rather than immediate effect, gradual emancipation rendered slavery a local
rather than a national institution.

The Constitutional Convention confirmed the character of slavery as a
local institution. Although it might be argued that recognition of slavery in the
Constitution made it in some sense a national institution, the framers' chief
purpose in this regard was to affirm state rather than federal power over the
institution. Indeed, one of the fundamental ideas on which the Union may be
said to have rested was that only the states could abolish or regulate slavery
in the states where it existed. The corollary was that the federal government
should remain divorced from the institution. Nevertheless, this separation was
not absolute. Congress was authorized to abolish the international slave trade
after twenty years; fugitive slaves (referred to in the language of the Constitution as persons "held to service or labor") could arguably become the subject

of congressional legislation; and the federal promise to protect the states against insurrection, expressed in the guarantee-of-republican-government clause, could require the federal government to suppress slave rebellions.

In addition to the provisions already noted, the framers permitted the states to count three-fifths of their slave population (described as "other than free" persons) in the basis for apportionment of representatives. Yet while recognizing slavery in the short run, they also took steps that pointed to the possible abolition of slavery. The provision for ending the slave trade after twenty years, despite the discretionary nature of the grant of power to Congress, was one such indication. Another was the exclusion of slavery from the Northwest Territory, an action of the Confederation Congress that was confirmed by the new federal legislature. To be sure, Southerners approved the Northwest Ordinance, evidence that it was not uniformly perceived as auguring the eventual abolition of slavery. But the Ordinance expressed a resolve to stop the spread of slavery, and in practical effect it proved an essential barrier to the expansion of slavery into the states formed in the Northwest Territory in the next fifty years. If the Revolutionary generation for reasons of political necessity acknowledged slavery as an existing institution, its actions also marked the beginning of an anti-slavery political tradition. The refusal to mention the word "slavery" in the Constitution was a mark not merely of humanitarian sensibility, but of moral disapproval. It meant that the Constitution did not in principle support the institution. As James Madison said at the Constitutional Convention, it would be "wrong to admit in the Constitution the idea that there could be property in man."

Allowed to remain more or less implicit at the Constitutional Convention, an attitude of neutrality toward slavery on the part of the federal government was expressly declared in the first Congress. At the urging of Quaker abolitionists, the House of Representatives created a special committee to consider the powers of Congress in relation to slavery. Although stopping well short of any finding of a general power of emancipation in the federal government, the committee took the position that Congress could indirectly regulate conditions in which slaves were held. But this was objectionable to the South. At the instance of James Madison, a substitute resolution was approved stating that Congress had no authority to interfere in slave emancipation or in the treatment of slaves. Madison's resolution concluded that the states alone possessed authority to regulate slavery. This change was acquiesced in by many northern representatives who were previously inclined toward an anti-slavery position, but who in order to win southern support for the assumption of state debts now refrained from backing any measures hostile to slavery.

The existence of slavery in some of the states of the Union caused the rule of federal neutrality gradually to acquire a degree of pro-slavery coloration. For example, when the District of Columbia was incorporated in 1802, the slave laws of Maryland and Virginia were adopted as local law in the federal city. Members of Congress and government officials who were slaveowners could thereafter bring their slaves with them as they accomplished the public business. In later years, pressure to abolish the slave trade in the District of Columbia was a persistent issue that signified the emergence of slavery as an issue in national politics. The federal government became involved with slavery in other respects as well. Slavery was permitted to exist by local action in the Southwest Territory after 1790, and the federal government made diplomatic efforts to gain compensation from England for slaves captured and emancipated during the Revolution and the War of 1812. Federal officials also assisted slaveowners in the extradition of fugitive slaves from Canada.

Limited federal involvement did not gainsay the fact that slavery in a legal and constitutional sense was a local or municipal institution. South of the Mason-Dixon line it became the object of elaborate systems of state constitutional, statutory, and common law that were intended to protect it and to resolve the massive contradictions that it posed to liberal and republican political principles. In the northern states, on the other hand, legislative and judicial action was taken to exclude slavery through guarantees of personal liberty. Constitutional problems concerning slavery usually took the form of conflicts between states over the law to be applied in resolving disputes over personal liberty. One of the most important sources of anti-slavery jurisprudence relied on in these conflicts was the famous English case of *Somerset* v. *Stewart* (1772).

James Somerset was a slave brought to England from Jamaica in 1769, who was captured after escaping and held in detention for subsequent sale. Through the intervention of British abolitionists, Somerset obtained a writ of habeas corpus from Lord Mansfield, chief justice of King's Bench, who ruled that he was free by virtue of having lived in England, where slavery was not recognized. In words that had a profound influence on the American anti-slavery movement in the nineteenth century, Mansfield said that seizing a slave was "so high an act of dominion" that it "must be recognized by the law of the country where it is used." Mansfield stated further: "The state of slavery is of such a nature, that it is incapable of being introduced on any reasons, moral or political; but only [by] positive law. . . . It's so odious, that nothing can be suffered to support it but positive law." Narrowly construed, the decision meant that an escaped slave could not be captured and sold in England, or, by analogy, in any free state. Interpreted more broadly it meant that the law of slavery under which a slave was held did not by implication or presumption extend into a free polity. For slavery to exist, it must be recognized in positive law. Most broadly, Mansfield's opinion could be transformed into the doctrine that slavery was illegal because it violated natural law.

Slavery may have been a violation of natural law, but as long as only the tiniest part of the population accepted that proposition the institution retained its legitimacy in the constitutional order. The *Somerset* case initially, therefore, had little influence outside abolitionist circles. Nevertheless, it was potentially of great importance because the conflict-of-laws situation that it presented offered a parallel to the way slavery questions might be raised in the United States. Given the legal status of slavery as a municipal institution and the presumption against federal involvement, constitutional problems concerning slavery arose most frequently in the context of interstate relations.

In essence the slavery controversy in the United States involved a fundamental conflict between opposing legal systems. Law in the southern states gave positive recognition to slavery, and generally assumed further that persons of color were slaves until they could prove themselves free. Because *Negro* slavery existed in the South, to assume otherwise would create serious difficulties in maintaining the basic principle of southern law—the right of the master to his property. An essential buttress to this principle was the right of recaption, a common law right that permitted the owner of property—in this instance slave property—to recapture it without judicial or other legal process, provided only that he do so in a manner consistent with public peace and order.

In the free states, on the other hand, the law presumed the freedom of all persons and provided legal means for guaranteeing personal liberty irrespective of color. The privilege of the writ of habeas corpus, by which courts could inquire into the causes of a person's detention and secure his release, and the right of personal replevin, a common law process for dealing with property that could also be used to win freedom for slaves, were the principal legal instruments employed to uphold the presumption of freedom. Trial by jury, a requirement under the process of personal replevin and occasionally in habeas corpus proceedings, was a third instrument for the protection of liberty. Under the constitutional dispensation that gave states virtually complete power to regulate personal liberty and civil rights, the presumption was strong that states could maintain the freedom of all persons within their jurisdiction.

The fundamental question in interstate controversies over slavery was whether the law of slavery of a southern state was valid and effective outside the state. For example, did a slave who entered a free state acquire personal liberty, or did his or her slave status continue in the free state? Five situations presented this conflict of laws: slaves brought for permanent residence in a free state; sojourning slaves brought for a limited period into a free state; *in transitu* slaves being taken from one slave jurisdiction to another; and fugitive slaves entering a free state. A fifth situation occurred when a slave who was emancipated in a free state returned to the slave state of origin, and the question arose whether his or her slave status resumed.

From 1790 to about 1830 free and slave states accommodated each other on questions concerning the extraterritorial or extrajurisdictional effect of their laws. Employing the rules of comity, by which sovereign states as a matter of discretion and convenience choose to recognize the laws of another jurisdiction, northern states permitted sojourning and *in transitu* slaves to reside temporarily on free soil and cooperated in the return of fugitive slaves. On the other hand, southern states acknowledged that indefinite or permanent residence in a free state resulted in emancipation, and southern courts recognized this condition of freedom in controversies caused by the return of former slaves to the South.

In the 1830s, however, after Nat Turner's Rebellion and with the emergence of abolitionism in the North and pro-slavery apologetics in the South, the period of accommodation ended. Now the *Somerset* doctrine, asserting the incompatibility of slavery and natural law and insisting on positive law as the only basis for slavery, became directly relevant. In 1836, for example, the Massachusetts Supreme Court incorporated *Somerset* doctrine in *Commonwealth* v. *Aves,* a case involving the personal liberty of a sojourner slave from Louisiana. Chief Justice Lemuel Shaw held the slave free on the ground that Louisiana slave law had no application in Massachusetts. Slavery was contrary to the constitution and laws of Massachusetts, said Shaw, and any attempt to bring a slave into the state automatically resulted in emancipation. Furthermore, slavery was so repugnant to natural law that it had to be established by positive law. Similar rulings against sojourner slave status were forthcoming in other northern states. Southern states for their part reciprocated by refusing to recognize the personal liberty acquired by blacks from residence in free states or territories.

The Problem of Fugitive Slaves

The most contentious issue in relations between free and slave states concerned the return of fugitive slaves. Yet since the rendition of fugitives was dealt with in the federal Constitution, it was arguably a subject over which the national government had power to act. Indeed, it was pressure for national action on the fugitive slave question that first significantly weakened the rule of federal nonintervention with regard to slavery.

Article IV, Section 2, of the Constitution provided that persons "held to Service or Labour" in one state who escaped into another state were not thereby to be "discharged from Service" but were to be "delivered up on Claim of the Party to whom such Service or Labour shall be due." The precise meaning of this section was vague in that it did not make clear what agency, state or federal, was charged with its execution. Article IV of the Constitution dealt with various matters of interstate comity, and from this it might have been assumed that the mutual return of fugitive slaves was an obligation imposed upon the states rather than the federal government. This supposition was strengthened by the fact that power to enact a fugitive slave law was not among the enumerated powers of Congress.

In spite of this ambiguity, Congress in 1793 enacted a fugitive slave law. This statute provided that fugitives escaping from one state into another might be seized by the master or his agent, brought before any federal or state court within the state, and returned under warrant upon proof of identity. The act thus put the responsibility for the return of fugitives upon both federal and state courts, and so made state officials agents for the enforcement of a federal constitutional provision. Various states, North and South, also enacted fugitive slave laws which provided legal processes for the seizure, detention, and return of fugitives through state police officers and courts. This system of joint federal-state responsibility worked well enough for a long time, and no one thought to challenge its constitutionality.

The fugitive slave law of 1793 gave a significant advantage to the southern states, for it meant that the law of slavery would, or at least ought to, prevail over the law of freedom in the event of conflict over runaway slaves. It gave extraterritorial effect to the municipal law of slavery. The corollary was that the free states were constitutionally prevented from exercising plenary power over the personal liberty and civil rights of all persons within their territorial limits.

As anti-slavery sentiment spread, dissatisfaction with this constitutional limitation increased and led to the adoption of personal liberty laws. The object of these laws was to throw legal safeguards around alleged fugitives and protect free Negroes from kidnapping. The Pennsylvania personal liberty law of 1826, for example, ostensibly intended to enforce the federal Fugitive Slave Act, imposed stringent requirements on persons claiming alleged fugitives, provided for jury trial and Negro testimony, and prohibited lower state magistrates from taking cognizance of fugitive slave cases under the federal law. Connecticut also imposed the latter restriction and, together with Illinois, New York, and Vermont, guaranteed fugitives a jury trial.

The constitutionality of the Pennsylvania personal liberty law and the federal Fugitive Slave Act of 1793 came before the Supreme Court in the case of *Prigg* v. *Pennsylvania* (1842). Edward Prigg, a slaveholders' agent from Maryland, had seized a runaway in Pennsylvania. Upon being denied a warrant in the state courts he had forcibly carried the slave back to Maryland without benefit of further legal proceedings. Returning to Pennsylvania, he was indicted and convicted of violating the kidnapping clause in the act of 1826. This verdict was sustained by the Pennsylvania Supreme Court, and an appeal was thereupon taken to the United States Supreme Court.

Justice Story, giving the opinion of the Court, held the Pennsylvania law to be in conflict with the federal law and thus unconstitutional. Story began by positing the right to recapture fugitive slaves as a self-executing, fundamental constitutional right, available to the master without the aid of federal legislation or judicial process in any state. But, he reasoned, since the right of recaption was confined to no territorial limits, and since the subject demanded uniform national treatment to prevent states from adopting conflicting measures upholding the right, the power over fugitive slaves belonged exclusively to Congress. Rejecting the anti-slavery argument that Congress lacked power to enact fugitive slave legislation and that the entire subject lay within state jurisdiction, Story pronounced the 1793 act constitutional. Because the Pennsylvania law conflicted with it by denying the right to recapture fugitive slaves, it must be struck down.

The *Prigg* decision constituted a major victory for the slave interest. In the most unequivocal terms Story wrote into constitutional law the southern states' right of recaption. He described this as "an absolute and positive right . . . pervading the whole Union with an equal and supreme force, uncontrolled and uncontrollable by State sovereignty or State legislation." On the surface the decision was highly centralizing in its effect. Yet in reality it endorsed state sovereignty by upholding the slave states' right of recaption, which was now imposed on the free states in derogation of their desire to protect personal liberty. With reason abolitionists promptly condemned the result. Yet Story's opinion also contained a dissonant note that proved to have anti-slavery potential.

The discordant note appeared in Story's interpretation of the exclusive nature of federal power over fugitive slaves. His opinion was unclear as to whether states could, if they wished, assist in enforcing the federal fugitive slave law and, if they did not so wish, whether they could be compelled to do so. Story said yes on the first count and no on the second. The act of 1793 plainly conferred authority on the states, and as Story regarded this measure as constitutional, he obviously was prepared to accept reliance on state officers as constitutionally permissible. Undoubtedly, state magistrates "may, if they choose," Story noted, exercise the authority over fugitive slaves conferred on them by the federal statute. States could also use the police power to arrest, restrain, and remove fugitive slaves from their borders. What they could not do was adopt additional regulations inhibiting the exercise of the right to recapture runaway slaves. Nevertheless, Story refrained from saying that states had a duty or obligation to assist in the rendition of fugitives. On the contrary, he declared that states could not be compelled to enforce provisions of the Constitution entrusting duties to the federal government. Thus if state officers might choose to cooperate in returning fugitives, the states could also prohibit such cooperation.

These utterances offered a degree of solace to anti-slavery men and women and provided northern states with an instrument with which to protect personal liberty in controversies over alleged fugitives. In a concurring opinion Chief Justice Taney attacked Story's emphasis on federal exclusivity on the ground that it would encourage state noncooperation; the states had a duty to assist in enforcing the fugitive slave law, Taney argued. And in fact a majority of the justices believed that states could legislate in support of the federal rendition process, as they held in *Moore* v. *Illinois* in 1852. However, anti-slavery lawyers, judges, and legislators put Story's dictum to precisely the opposite use. They cited it as authority for denying jurisdiction over fugitive cases, thus freeing alleged runaways. They also used it to justify legislation prohibiting state officials from enforcing the federal fugitive slave law and denying the use of state facilities for that purpose.

The Supreme Court was thus widely if inaccurately perceived as having prohibited state action to assist in the return of fugitives. One direct consequence was the enactment in several northern states of personal liberty laws aiming at noncooperation. A second consequence was a determined effort by Southerners, in part provoked by the new personal liberty laws, to adopt a more stringent fugitive slave law based exclusively on federal power. A few years later, as part of the Compromise of 1850, Congress adopted such a measure.

The Fugitive Slave Act of 1850 provided for the appointment, by federal circuit courts, of federal commissioners who were given concurrent jurisdiction with federal district courts over fugitive slave questions. Upon presentation of satisfactory proof of ownership, the federal commissioner was authorized to permit the claimant to remove the fugitive slave or, if circumstances warranted, to entrust the rendition to a federal marshal. The act provided no jury trial, nor did it permit the alleged fugitive slave to testify. Moreover, the decision of the federal commissioner was declared conclusive as against the issuance of a state writ of habeas corpus.

Anti-slavery men and women regarded these provisions as a gross violation of rights guaranteed in the Fifth and Sixth Amendments. They contended that Congress had no power over fugitive slaves, and that since the decision-making process envisioned in the law was essentially judicial, reliance on federal commissioners violated the requirements of the Constitution concerning the exercise of judicial power. Defenders of the Fugitive Slave Act cited Story's *Prigg* opinion as authority. They held further that the rendition of fugitives was a ministerial rather than a judicial process, and hence not subject to the procedural guarantees appropriate to a court of law.

The Nationalization of the Slavery Question

If the fugitive slave problem involved both state and federal governments, other aspects of the slavery question mainly concerned the federal government. A consensus on the wisdom and desirability of federal neutrality toward slavery had long served to keep the issue subordinated and out of the mainstream of political controversy. As the fugitive slave question showed, however, public opinion in the 1840s increasingly demanded that slavery be dealt with as a national issue. The Compromise of 1850, followed by the formation of the Republican party as an exclusively sectional anti-slavery organization in 1854, signified the abandonment of the idea of federal neutrality and the nationalization of the slavery problem. When that happened the Union itself was placed in jeopardy.

The Constitutional Convention made an exception to the rule of federal neutrality by confining the subject of the slave trade to Congress. Article I, Section 9, of the Constitution stated: "The migration or importation of such persons as any of the States now existing shall think proper to admit, shall not be prohibited by the congress prior to the year one thousand eight hundred and eight." This language undoubtedly empowered Congress to ban the international slave trade, and possibly also the domestic or interstate traffic in slaves. Whether it did depended on the meaning of "such persons." Obviously, the term referred to slaves, whom the founding fathers once again refused to name out of deference to moral sensibility. But if it referred only to slaves, as everyone assumed when the Constitution was written and ratified, then the clause could be construed as giving Congress the power, after 1808, to prohibit the migration of slaves, as opposed to their importation; in other words, as prohibiting the interstate slave trade. By the early nineteenth century, however, this interpretation was obviously unacceptable to Southerners because of its anti-slavery potential. They insisted that the clause, and the words "such persons," referred to white aliens as well as Negroes. The term "importation," they reasoned, described Negro slaves, and "migration" white foreigners. Southerners thus tried to restrict the emigration-and-importation clause—and hence congressional power over commerce—to matters pertaining to entry into the United States from abroad. Under this interpretation Congress in 1808 legislated against the international slave trade.

The southern view of the importation-and-migration clause and also of the commerce power, earnestly supported by Madison and Jefferson, eventually prevailed. In the wake of the Missouri crisis Southerners feared in the 1820s that the federal commerce power would be employed against the domestic slave trade, even as it had been used against the international slave trade. From a constitutional standpoint the fear was not unfounded, for in 1804 Congress had legislated against the internal slave trade. The Orleans (Louisiana) territorial act of that year forbade the importation of slaves from abroad, and also "from any port or place within the limits of the United States." Although the act was not enforced, and a year later the domestic slave trade ban dropped from further territorial legislation in Louisiana, it showed the possibility of an anti-slavery interpretation of the commerce power.

Controversies over southern states' black seamen's laws in the 1820s raised further questions about the federal commerce power and slavery. In 1822 South Carolina, reacting to an alleged slave uprising, passed a law providing that all free Negroes who came as sailors into the ports of the state should be arrested by the local sheriff and held in jail until their ship was ready to sail. In the case of *Elkison* v. *Deliesseline* (1823) in federal circuit court, Justice William Johnson held the South Carolina law unconstitutional as an encroachment on the exclusive power of Congress over foreign and interstate commerce. South Carolina ceased to enforce the statute against British Negroes after the English government protested that it violated a commercial treaty with the United States. But, disregarding the federal court ruling, South Carolina applied the law against Negroes from northern states.

In the 1830s, as we have seen, the scope of the commerce power and its relation to slavery came before the Supreme Court. Despite some vacillation, the Taney Court held generally that persons—and most importantly slaves— were not articles of commerce. Rather, the entire subject of slavery was subject to the police power under the doctrine of state sovereignty. Even an anti-slavery–tending justice such as McLean of Ohio, who regarded the federal commerce power as exclusive, agreed that slaves were beyond the scope of the federal commercial authority. The Court thus gave no encouragement to the possible use of the commerce power to prohibit or regulate the interstate slave trade.

Other questions concerning slavery obtruded on national politics in the 1830s, despite Jacksonian efforts to keep the issue muted. One controversy concerned federal and state powers in relation to the delivery of mail. The abolitionists early adopted the device of flooding the mails with quantities of pamphlets, newspapers, and circulars addressed to Southerners and in some instances to slaves themselves. Southerners, not unnaturally, hotly resented this practice as an attempt to stir up servile insurrection, and postmasters in the South often took it upon themselves, without formal legal sanction, to destroy such material. President Jackson sympathized with the southern attitude in this matter, and in December 1835 he recommended the passage of a federal censorship law.

Calhoun and other Southerners, however, fearing the centralizing effects of federal postal censorship, opposed Jackson's suggestion. Instead, in February 1836, a Senate committee under Calhoun's chairmanship reported a bill providing that it should be unlawful for any deputy postmaster knowingly to receive and mail any matter "touching the subject of slavery, directed to any person or post-office in any state where by the laws thereof their circulation is prohibited." Calhoun recognized congressional power to regulate the mail, but saw this as a mere delegated power subordinate to the states' power and right to enforce laws necessary for their peace and security. The southern states' laws recognizing and protecting slavery, an expression of state sovereignty, had primacy, and the federal government as agent of the states was obligated to uphold them.

The Senate rejected Calhoun's bill, whereupon Congress passed a law prohibiting federal postmasters from refusing to deliver mail to its proper address. Apparently a blow for liberty and anti-slavery, the law was never enforced in the South. Nonenforcement was premised on the theory that federal power over the mail ceased upon reception in the state, at which point state power became exclusive and state laws governing the circulation of incendiary material took effect. Consistent with its policy of subordinating slavery while accommodating southern interests, the Jackson administration acquiesced in this solution to the problem.

Controversy also developed over abolitionist petitions and memorials asking Congress to abolish slavery in the District of Columbia. Since the federal government presumably had full police power in the District, the petitions had a plausible constitutional foundation, but they infuriated southern congressmen, who not without reason regarded them as attempts to drive a wedge into the institution of slavery. In any event, they said, Congress had no lawful authority to interfere with slavery in the District, for the institution was protected by a federal contract with the states of Virginia and Maryland. This contract had been incorporated in the act of 1802, which organized government in the District and by which Congress had promised not to interfere with the domestic institutions and property rights of residents in the ceded areas.

The debate over slavery in the District was notable for the reliance of both pro- and anti-slavery men on the due-process clause of the Fifth Amendment. Drawing on traditional vested-rights doctrine, defenders of slavery held that the Fifth Amendment guarantee against deprivation of life, liberty, and property without due process of law prevented any federal interference with slave property in the District of Columbia. Anti-slavery reformers used the amendment to condemn the deprivation of slaves' liberty without due process of law (as well as without jury trial and judicial process). Moreover, both groups advanced a substantive interpretation of the Fifth Amendment due-process clause. Regardless of the procedure or forms employed, they reasoned, no act of Congress was legitimate or constitutional which, depending on one's point of view, in substance or effect destroyed property in slaves or deprived black persons of their liberty.

The right to petition Congress was seemingly protected by the First Amendment, but the steady flow of abolitionist petitions in Congress nevertheless inspired southern congressmen to find some means of banning them. Southerners contended that the First Amendment guaranteed the right of petition only upon subjects within the constitutional competence of Congress, and that Congress was under no obligation to receive petitions upon matters beyond its lawful concern. Slavery, they pointed out, was a domestic institution of the states over which Congress had no authority; hence petitions on slavery could be lawfully rejected. Many northern delegates in Congress, anxious to suppress anti-slavery agitation, were sympathetic with this attitude, although others thought that any house rule barring petitions would violate the Constitution.

After some months of intermittent debate, the House of Representatives in May 1836 adopted a "gag rule" intended to bar abolitionist petitions entirely. The rule, drawn by Representative Henry Pinckney of South Carolina, stated that "all petitions, memorials, resolutions, propositions, or papers relating in any way, or to any extent whatsoever, to the subject of slavery, or the abolition of slavery, shall, without being either printed or referred, be laid upon the table, and no further action whatever shall be had thereon." The resolution passed, 117 to 68, over the bitter protests of John Quincy Adams of Massachusetts, who denounced the proposal as "a direct violation of the constitution of the United States, the rules of this House, and the rights of my constituents." In spite of Adams's continued opposition, the House strengthened the rule in 1840 to ban outright any attempt to introduce petitions on slavery. This was a more extreme prohibition than that of 1836, which had merely established a uniform rule for disposing of memorials.

Adams made the repeal of the House gag rule a *cause célèbre,* which he carried on for years, much to the displeasure of his colleagues. He was finally successful in obtaining repeal in 1844, largely because the growth of northern anti-slavery sentiment had convinced most northern congressmen that it would be politically unwise to support the rule any longer.

Protective of slavery as the gag rule was, it failed to satisfy Calhoun and the South Carolinians, who wanted Congress categorically to reject anti-slavery petitions without even receiving them. In order to bind congressional opinion more firmly to the southern point of view, Calhoun in December 1837 introduced state-sovereignty resolutions into the Senate. The resolutions held that the several states had voluntarily entered the Union as independent and sovereign states, retaining "sole and exclusive" control of their domestic institutions, and that the federal government was a common agent of the several states and, therefore, "bound so to exercise its powers as to give . . . increased stability and security to the domestic institutions of the states that compose the union." It was, therefore, "the solemn duty of the government to resist all attempts by one portion of the Union to use it as an instrument to attack the domestic institutions of the other states." The resolutions added that "domestic slavery, as it exists in the Southern and Western states of this Union composes an important part of their domestic institutions," and warned that all attacks against it on the part of other states of the Union, including even attempts to abolish slavery in the District of Columbia or the territories, were "a violation of the mutual and solemn pledge given to protect and defend each other" when the states adopted the Constitution. The resolutions ended with an implied threat of secession were southern rights denied and the equality of the Union thereby destroyed. All but the last of these resolutions passed the Senate by large majorities, partly because they involved no specific political interest of the moment and partly because certain senators found it expedient to conciliate Calhoun. However, Calhoun's main argument on the nature of the Union went unchallenged in debate, so far had the conception of national sovereignty evidently disintegrated since 1789.

Calhoun's resolutions marked the firm union of the pro-slavery and state-sovereignty arguments. As Calhoun put it in debate, the resolutions were aimed directly at the proposition that the United States was "one great Republic." Such a doctrine, he said, would strengthen the abolitionists and prepare the ground for an attack on slavery in the southern states through the medium of the national government. From this time onward, Calhoun invariably called forth the logic of his resolutions in support of southern interests in the slavery debate, and other southern statesmen were quick to see the advantage and do the same. The resolutions thus became the basis of the main southern argument concerning slavery in the territories as developed in the debate preceding the Compromise of 1850.

Slavery in the Territories

The issue that forced final abandonment of federal neutrality toward slavery concerned the expansion of slavery into the territories. The movement for continental expansion in the 1840s carried American settlement to the Pacific coast, demanded the annexation of Texas, and provoked the Mexican War. In this new political situation the Democratic party could no longer subordinate the slavery question. Bitter political controversy ensued which called into question the long-settled congressional policy dealing with slavery in the territories. This issue lay at the heart of the conflict between North and South that brought the nation to the brink of war in 1850.

At the beginning of the government, congressional power to legislate on slavery in the territories was unquestioned, despite the somewhat anomalous position territories occupied in the constitutional system. The Union consisted of organized states in which federal and state authority coexisted. States possessed the power of local self-government, but in unorganized national territory they had no such authority. Indeed, in the Confederation period the creation of a national territory was contingent on the denial of state claims to the area. Congress could, therefore, govern unorganized national territory, regulating property, personal liberty, civil rights, and social and political organization, even as the states did within their borders. Congressional authority was described in Article IV, Section 3, of the Constitution, which declared: "The Congress shall have power to dispose of and make all needful Rules and Regulations respecting the Territory or other Property belonging to the United States."   *N.W ORDINANCE CONNECTION*

Whatever qualifications on congressional power this language later seemed to imply, for more than fifty years it provided ample authority for federal legislation against slavery in the national domain. The first and perhaps most important exercise of the power occurred in 1789, when Congress confirmed by legislation the prohibition of slavery adopted by the Confederation Congress in the Northwest Ordinance of 1787. Other anti-slavery measures followed: In 1798 Congress prohibited slave importation from abroad in the Mississippi territorial act; in 1804 it excluded both the domestic and foreign slave trade from Louisiana Territory; in 1805 it created Michigan Territory and in 1809 Illinois Territory with slavery excluded. Meanwhile, in legislation creating territories south of the Ohio River Congress refrained from prohibiting slavery, permitting local settlers to introduce, establish, or recognize it if they chose. This dual approach—prohibition of slavery north and toleration of it south of a sectional dividing line—was challenged but eventually reaffirmed in the Missouri crisis of 1819–20.

Constitutionally, the Missouri crisis involved the questions of whether Congress could prohibit slavery in the territories, and whether in admitting new states it could impose conditions affecting their internal organization. The

[margin handwritten notes, left side:] NORTHWEST ORDINANCE & LOUISIANA PURCHASE & SLAVERY ISSUE

controversy began when Missouri, a slave territory, applied for admission to the Union. Led by anti-slavery Federalists, the House passed an enabling bill that admitted Missouri, but required it gradually to abolish slavery. The Senate rejected this proposal, recommending instead a compromise by which Missouri would be brought into the Union as a slave state balanced by the admission of Maine as a free state. Slavery would also be prohibited in Louisiana Purchase territory north of 36°30′, a line extending Missouri's southern border.

In debate, anti-slavery men argued that Congress could govern the territories as it saw fit and impose restrictions on them in the nature of a contract enforceable after the territory became a state. They also held that Congress could set conditions on statehood, as it had done in relation to several states, including the prohibition of slavery in the constitutions of Ohio, Indiana, and Illinois. Southerners contended that Congress could not impose terms on statehood lest it impair the equal sovereignty to which the states were entitled. Significantly, Southerners acknowledged that Congress could legislate against slavery in the territories, although they said such restrictions would cease to apply after the attainment of statehood. The first stage of the crisis ended when Congress admitted Missouri as a slave state and prohibited slavery in the Louisiana Purchase Territory north of 36°30′.[1]

As noted previously, the Missouri Compromise provoked southern apprehension about possible anti-slavery uses of federal legislative power and led northern republicans and southern planters to form an alliance aimed at protecting slavery through a national political party. When in the 1840s territorial expansion again dominated national politics, this apprehension grew into open repudiation of the constitutional theory and practice concerning slavery in the territories that had prevailed for several decades.

The annexation of Texas in 1845, which many Northerners saw as a form of pro-slavery aggression, severely tested the long-standing Democratic policy of keeping slavery out of national politics. Texas declared its independence from Mexico in 1836, at which time discussion of annexation to the United States began. Fearful of British anti-slavery influence in the independent republic, the Tyler administration in 1844 concluded a treaty of annexation that would have brought Texas into the Union as a territory. The treaty was rejected in the Senate, however, whereupon President Tyler stated his desire to have Texas annexed by any means compatible with the Constitution. Since Texas was a sovereign independent state, annexation by treaty approved by the Senate appeared the proper course of action, as the administration's diplomatic efforts showed. Equal representation of the states in the Senate made that body the appropriate institution to decide whether a foreign state should be admitted to the Union of states. Yet political expediency drove Tyler and the Democratic party in Congress to argue that Texas could be admitted directly and

---

1. The second phase of the Missouri crisis concerned the attempt by Missouri to exclude free Negroes from the state and the question of Negro citizenship. See below, pp. 271–272.

immediately as a state, under the provision of the Constitution declaring that "New States may be admitted by the Congress into this Union. . . ." Under authority of this provision, Congress in December 1844 by a joint resolution voted to admit Texas as a state into the Union. Many Northerners denounced the action as constitutional sophistry designed to strengthen the slavery interest. The admittance of Texas as a state effectively changed the rules concerning slavery and national politics.

Northern resentment increased when the expansionist Polk administration declared war against Mexico in 1846. A large minority in the North regarded the war as one of conquest waged for the purpose of gaining more slave territory. Accordingly, northern Democrats, in order to allay northern apprehensions, maintain party unity in support of the war, and relegate slavery to the subordinate place it had occupied for over two decades, introduced the Wilmot Proviso into Congress in August 1846. The strategy backfired, however. Within a few months the proviso became a symbol of northern resolve to keep the slave power from dominating the government, and a practical instrument for protecting new national territory—and, by implication, the nation—against the blight of slavery.

Introduced by Representative David Wilmot of Pennsylvania, an anti-abolitionist, anti-Negro Democrat in the Van Buren wing of the party, the proviso stated that as an express and fundamental condition to the acquisition of any territory from Mexico, "neither slavery nor involuntary servitude shall ever exist in any part of said territory." Constitutionally, the measure was thoroughly orthodox, since Congress on numerous occasions had legislated to prohibit slavery in territories. In a sense it was politically orthodox, too, in its intention to bank the fires of pro- and anti-slavery agitation in national politics. Yet in a more profound sense the proviso was politically radical, for it proposed to abrogate the dividing-line approach to territorial policy that had existed implicitly since 1789 and explicitly since the Missouri crisis. Indeed, in the southern view the policy of dividing national territory and new states evenly between slavery and freedom was so solidly established that it was to be regarded as having the force of constitutional law. From this perspective the proviso was unconstitutional.

The Wilmot Proviso initiated a fourteen-year controversy over the power of Congress over slavery in the territories. Four distinct positions on the question emerged. The proviso itself from 1846 to 1850 represented the views of dissident Democrats, anti-slavery–minded Whigs, and moderate political abolitionists in the Liberty party—the diverse groups that converged in the Free-Soil party of 1848. Constitutionally, this position held that Congress had full sovereignty over the territories by virtue of the territorial clause and the federal treaty and war powers. Existing constitutional law as seen in congressional legislation affirmed plenary federal legislative power, and the Supreme Court in *American Insurance Co.* v. *Canter* (1828) had declared that Congress in legislating for the territories exercised the powers both of the general government and of the states. A more radical version of the free-soil position held that the Fifth Amendment guarantee against federal deprivation of liberty without due process of law prohibited slavery in the territories and prevented Congress from recognizing the institution there. Still another variation applied the Somerset doctrine, insisting that the natural condition of all territory was freedom and that slavery could exist only by virtue of positive municipal legislation. The lands acquired from Mexico had been free under Mexican law; therefore, their normal condition was freedom, which Congress was powerless to change by introducing slavery.

A second position recognized congressional power over slavery in the territories, but advocated discretionary use of the power in extending the Missouri line to the Pacific coast. Because this position acknowledged federal authority over slavery, most Southerners rejected it. Yet a surprising number did not, even though extending the dividing line would not positively, but only by implication, establish slavery south of 36°30'. Actually, extension of the Missouri line would have guaranteed a larger area for free soil than was secured by the territorial legislation that eventually was adopted in the Compromise of 1850. However, when the idea of extending the dividing line was broached in 1846, northern free-soilers categorically rejected it, probably because it implied equal moral and political standing for slavery and freedom.

A third position on the territorial question, supported by many if not yet a majority of Southerners in the period 1846 to 1850, denied congressional power to interfere with slavery and insisted on the right of slaveowners to take their property into the territories under the doctrine of state sovereignty and the protection of the Fifth Amendment. This position, identified most clearly with Calhoun, was subsequently expressed by Chief Justice Taney in the *Dred Scott* decision. It held that Congress could not exercise local police power such as was required to legislate concerning municipal institutions. It also denied that the people of a territory, not yet having attained statehood, possessed sovereignty. The conclusion that followed was that only the states were sovereign and capable of legislating on slavery as a municipal institution. Accordingly, the states were the source of police-power legislation for the territories.

Calhoun's theory of federal agency provided the means by which the states could exercise this power. The agent or trustee of the sovereign states, the federal government in this view was charged with protecting their interests, but was denied sovereign legislative authority for dealing with slavery. Federal power rather was limited, ministerial, nondiscretionary. Moreover, the recognition of slavery in the Constitution—as in the fugitive slave clause—was taken as a recognition of slave-state law and as indicating a commitment to give the law of slavery priority over the law of freedom in the event of conflict, such as might occur in the territories. In other words, under the theory of state sovereignty and federal agency the slave states were regarded as the only authoritative source of law and policy for dealing with questions of slavery outside the states that had abolished it. In relation to slavery in the territories, as in the matter of fugitive slaves, the laws of the southern states would have extrajurisdictional effect and determine policy for the nation.

The common-property doctrine was a corollary of the state-sovereignty theory of congressional nonintervention. The doctrine asserted that the territories were the common property of the states, held in trust for them by their agent, the federal government. The agent had no right to act against the property interests of any of the sovereign principals and hence could not ban slavery in the territories, an act construed as against slave-state rights in the common property.

From still another angle—that of individual property rights—Southerners argued against congressional interference with slavery in the territories. The idea here was that slave property was entitled to no less protection against legislative interference than any other property under the doctrine of vested rights and the guarantees of the Constitution. Slaveholders were citizens who had a right under the Fifth Amendment to take their property into national territory. This did not mean, argued defenders of southern rights such as Calhoun and Jefferson Davis, that Congress should establish slavery in the territories by legislative act; on the contrary, all that was sought was protection of the same rights of national citizenship that non-slaveholders enjoyed in entering the national domain.

The property-rights strategy contained a further implication about the enforcement of constitutional rights that encouraged reliance on judicial power to resolve the controversy over slavery in the territories. Disavowing protection of slavery by act of Congress, Southerners also rejected the idea of territorial sovereignty and the notion of vigilante-style, self-help protection by private individuals. The alternative, consistent with time-honored tenets of American constitutionalism, was to seek protection in a court of law. Accordingly, as part of their strategy for dealing with the territorial question, Southerners after 1846 included recourse to the federal judiciary for the protection of slave property rights.

The fourth position on slavery in the territories that emerged in the period 1846 to 1850 was popular sovereignty. Advanced as a compromise solution by the party of pro-slavery accommodation and national unity, Democratic popular sovereignty located the all-important police power not in Congress or in the states, but in the people of the territory. Theorists of this doctrine seized on the language of the territorial clause, which authorized Congress "to dispose of and make all needful Rules and Regulations respecting the Territory or other Property of the United States." They concluded that it did not give Congress plenary, discretionary, sovereign power to govern. At most Congress could draw territorial boundaries and provide forms of government; the substance of sovereignty lay in the people of the territory.

The historic role that local self-government or "squatter sovereignty" played in the development of American territorial policy, far more than this labored interpretation of the Constitution, provided the basis for the widespread appeal of popular sovereignty in the 1840s. Congress had passed territorial acts establishing forms of government and enabling legislation that permitted or recognized the attainment of statehood. But for all practical purposes the people of the territories had governed themselves, adopting local laws and police regulations, founding municipal institutions, and creating new states for admission into the Union. Popular sovereignty was thus not an instrument of recent invention when Lewis Cass, Stephen A. Douglas, and other Democrats proposed it as a solution to the question of slavery in the territories in 1847. Instead of the dividing line that had served since 1820 as the organizing principle of territorial policy on slavery, and in preference to the alternatives of free-soil restriction or categorical support of slavery under the state-sovereignty doctrine, Democrats insisted that people at the local level should decide whether slavery should enter the newly acquired western territories.

The Compromise of 1850

The territorial question was one of several North-South issues that produced a crisis of the Union in 1850. California, seized from Mexico and settled rapidly, had skipped the territorial stage of organization and sought admission to the Union as a free state. The border between Texas and New Mexico, a source of bitter contention, needed to be drawn, and the lands of the Mexican cession outside of California had to be organized into territories and the status of slavery therein resolved. Finally, the abolitionist demand for the abolishment of the slave trade in the District of Columbia and the southern demand for a stronger fugitive slave law were highly charged issues on which action seemed long past due.

The Wilmot Proviso forms the proximate starting point for a narrative of the events culminating in the Compromise of 1850. Twice the proviso was passed by the House of Representatives but defeated in the Senate. In 1848 two attempts were made to resolve the dispute over slavery in the new territories. A Senate committee headed by John Clayton of Delaware proposed to organize California and New Mexico as separate territories with the status of slavery therein to be determined by the territorial court, with a right of appeal to the Supreme Court. As a concession to the North, Oregon, which because of southern opposition had for years gone without a territorial government, would be organized as a free territory. The Clayton compromise passed the Senate, but failed in the House. A second compromise was offered by Stephen A. Douglas, who proposed to extend the Missouri Compromise line through the new territories to the Pacific Ocean. Douglas's proposal also passed the Senate, but died in the House as northern members stood by the Wilmot Proviso.

In 1848 Oregon was organized as a free territory. In approving the Oregon bill President Polk observed that as the territory lay north of the 36°30'

Missouri line, it could be regarded as a continuation of the traditional dividing-line approach to slavery in the territories. This view had little appeal for most Northerners, however, who insisted on admitting California as a free state without regard to the Missouri line. As pressure to admit California mounted in 1849, Southerners, facing the prospect of free-state superiority in the Senate, dug in their heels and demanded satisfaction of some sort in the organization of the former Mexican lands. Their demand made Utah and New Mexico territorial legislation the central focus of compromise strategy in Congress in 1850.

In February 1850, after months of bitter debate and amid serious talk of secession in South Carolina, Georgia, and Mississippi, Henry Clay offered an elaborate eight-point plan for the Senate's consideration. By the first resolution, California was to be admitted to the Union at once without any restrictions upon its right to exclude or include slaves. In effect this meant California's admission as a free state. Second, the New Mexico Territory was to be organized without any restrictions or limitations upon the status of slavery. Clay's third and fourth resolutions fixed the western Texan boundary so as to deprive the state of the disputed region between the Del Norte and the Rio Grande rivers but proposed to compensate Texas by the assumption by the federal government of the state's preannexation public debt. The fifth resolution submitted that it was "inexpedient" to abolish slavery in the District of Columbia, but the sixth proposed that the trade in imported and exported slaves be banned in the District. The seventh resolution asked for a more effective fugitive slave law, while the eighth stated merely that Congress had no authority over the interstate slave trade.

When it proved impossible to get even a scaled-down version of this compromise plan through the Senate (that is, the so-called Omnibus bill linking California, New Mexico, and Utah), Douglas broke Clay's original proposal into separate pieces of legislation. Aided by the death of anticompromise-minded President Zachary Taylor, in September 1850 he guided the separate bills through the Senate principally with the support of northern Democratic votes. A few days later Douglas Democrats secured passage of the several measures in the House of Representatives. The first and decisive bill dealt with New Mexico Territory and also included the Texas boundary and debt. Most important for purposes of sectional compromise, it embodied the doctrine of popular sovereignty.

In its original formulation the New Mexico bill prohibited the territorial legislature from legislating on slavery. Although some Northerners, on the theory that Mexican anti-slavery law had made the territory free, could support this provision, Southerners who believed that Mexican law had lapsed and that slaveholders could take their property there under constitutional protection provided most of the backing for this restriction on the territorial legislature. But to deny the territorial legislature power to act on slavery contradicted too bluntly Douglas's conception of popular sovereignty and seemed to threaten passage of the bill. Accordingly, the ban on legislation concerning slavery was dropped, and the power of the territorial legislature was described as "extending to all rightful subjects of legislation consistent with the Constitution of the United States." Another section stated that the territory, when admitted as a state, was to be received with or without slavery as its constitution provided. Still another provision, in the manner of the Clayton compromise, permitted judicial determination of questions concerning title to slaves or personal liberty, with appeal to the Supreme Court.

Popular sovereignty as incorporated in the New Mexico and Utah territorial bills served principally as a means of uniting the Democratic party; only indirectly, through the instrumentality of the party, was it the basis of North-South compromise. The special appeal of popular sovereignty was its ambiguity about *when* the people in a territory could take action for or against slavery. Douglas and the northern Democrats interpreted the removal of the ban on legislation dealing with slavery as authorizing the territorial legislature to act on slavery from the moment it was created. Southerners, however, believed that only when the people of a territory wrote a state constitution and applied for admission to the Union could they take action on slavery. They reasoned that until statehood was attained, slaveholders as United States citizens had a constitutional right to take their property into the territory—a right that could presumably be upheld in the territorial court and the Supreme Court. The New Mexico and Utah territorial bills did not expressly endorse either of these points of view. Accordingly, interpreting the legislation in their different ways, enough southern and northern Democrats were able to support the measures to assure their passage.

The abandonment of the Wilmot Proviso in favor of popular sovereignty was the critical step in achieving the Compromise of 1850. Democrats acted mainly to preserve party unity. Equally decisive, however, was the willingness of northern representatives, some of free-soil inclination, to accept popular sovereignty after standing firmly behind the Wilmot Proviso. Their reasons for doing so remain unclear, but the most important factors seem to have been their belief that climate and geography would keep slavery out of the Southwest, their lack of legislative organization, and their responsiveness to public fear of disunion and desire for compromise. The result was a significant concession to the South—regardless of whether the northern or southern view of popular sovereignty would prevail.

After passage of the New Mexico bill, the other Compromise measures were rapidly adopted. Utah Territory was organized on the same basis as New Mexico; California was admitted as a free state; a new fugitive slave law was enacted; and the slave trade in the District of Columbia was abolished. Although Douglas's legislative strategy made it possible for members of Congress to vote only for the particular measures they favored, avoiding compromise in the more important sense of voting for measures that conflicted with their sectional interest, the country welcomed the acts of 1850 as a deliverance from

a genuine crisis that threatened to disrupt the Union. Surely, this perception
was justified. Yet a decade later it was less clear that northern willingness to
treat the combination of issues as a true crisis, requiring accommodation to
southern threats of secession and demands for concessions on the slavery
question, had been the wisest course.

It is, of course, impossible to say whether the South would have seceded
in 1850 if northern support for the Wilmot Proviso had persisted or President
Taylor had lived to insist solely on the admission of California as a free state.
What is clear is that the South, gaining confidence in its ability to use the threat
of secession as an effective political instrument, secured a stronger fugitive
slave law and legislation denying congressional power to legislate on slavery
in the territory acquired from Mexico. Moreover, the new territorial policy of
popular sovereignty, unlike the Wilmot Proviso and in contrast even to the
dividing-line approach of the Missouri Compromise, contained no hint of
moral condemnation of slavery.

It was not exactly clear what the term meant, but both North and South
agreed that popular sovereignty opened the possibility of "nationalizing" slavery. Federal law had never recognized or established slavery in a positive sense;
at most, south of 36°30', it had remained silent on the matter. Slavery was
properly viewed, therefore, as a local institution, and freedom as national.
Although popular sovereignty in a technical sense continued the posture of
congressional silence toward slavery, in effect it would allow slavery to enter
lands from which it had been previously excluded by law (that is, Mexican
law). Theoretically neutral, popular sovereignty in the territorial legislation of
1850 signified a subtle shift toward a pro-slavery territorial policy, no matter
how much Douglas might protest that it would also permit the prohibition of
slavery. Conceivably, the adoption of popular sovereignty in 1850 might even
imply the substitution of a policy of toleration toward slavery in other national
territories, as yet unorganized, where the dividing line of the Missouri Compromise had been projected but not actually applied. As the movement for
territorial expansion proceeded in the 1850s, this question became the focal
point of sectional conflict over the place of slavery in the American republic.

FIFTEEN

Slavery and the Crisis of the American Republic

IN A POLITICAL SYSTEM that had accommodated the fact of Negro slavery for seventy-five years, there was ample reason to think that the Compromise of 1850, intended to end sectional agitation of the slavery question, would accomplish its purpose. The two major parties agreed on the wisdom of the Compromise measures, which settled the constitutional status of slavery in the former Mexican territory while permitting the Missouri Compromise Act to remain in effect in the lands of the Louisiana Purchase. Slavery in the territories was thus a closed issue, should the status quo be accepted as permanent. The parties could persist in their rivalry as national organizations, moreover, and the Union, threatened by sectional polarization in the recent crisis, would endure. Nor would it be necessary to resolve the fundamental ambiguity that had existed from the beginning of the government about the nature of the Union. The federal republic could be at once a confederation of equal sovereign states, expressing the diversity and particularity of American politics, and also a unitary sovereign government expressing the sense of nationality that Americans shared.

It proved impossible, however, to subordinate the slavery issue politically, to prolong the existence of the national party system on which the existence of the Union depended, or to persist in the flexible and politically useful ambiguity about the nature of the Union that had helped sustain the parties as legitimate representative institutions. Ironically, the decision of both Whigs and Democrats to support the Compromise of 1850 had the indirect consequence of weakening the party system, and permitting slavery once again to dominate politics. It was not the moral and political force of the slavery question that directly undermined the parties. These factors could, of course, add momentum to any attack on the party system, but problems arising out of the social and economic issues of the age were more immediate, concrete, and threatening to political stability. This was true even though these issues had provided the rationale for party conflict since the 1830s.

The Political Realignment of the 1850s

By 1854, when the slavery question again challenged the integrity of national parties by attracting people to sectional loyalties, party bonds were weakened by changing attitudes toward socioeconomic issues. Whigs had stood for a national bank, the protective tariff, internal improvements, a restrictive public land policy, and, in general, federal government promotion of economic development. Democrats were antibank and pro–hard money, favored a liberal land distribution policy, opposed the protective tariff and internal improvements, and generally demanded federal nonintervention in the economy. By 1850, however, many western Democrats had shifted to support of banks, internal improvements, and homestead legislation requiring positive government action, thus blurring the lines between the parties. Moreover, conflicts between Democrats who supported and Whigs who opposed democratizing state constitutional reform had largely been resolved by 1852, so this issue, too, was removed from the field of electoral competition. The effect of these changes was to diminish the legitimacy of the parties in the eyes of voters, who saw fewer real differences between them. Increasingly, the parties seemed concerned solely with privilege and power, rather than with the genuine interests of their constituents.

As these older issues were composed, new ones took shape as a result of commercial expansion, the growth of cities, and the great influx of immigrants that came to the United States principally from Ireland and Germany between 1846 and 1854. The existing parties were not able to deal with the social dislocation and resentment caused by these developments within the traditional framework of electoral conflict. The Whigs, for example, were responsive in the 1840s to nativist criticism of immigrant groups. In the early 1850s, trying to compete with the Democrats, they sought to attract the immigrant vote. Unsuccessful against the Democrats, the traditional party of the immigrant, they managed only to eliminate another difference between the parties. Nativist and temperance groups, fearful of the effect of immigration on American society, therefore pursued their reform purposes in new parties, which began to appear at the state level in 1851. These developments weakened the major parties by causing them to appear useless and hence illegitimate in the eyes of voters. And when both parties agreed to submerge differences over slavery and accept the Compromise of 1850, the effect was similar.

To large numbers of people, therefore, the national parties in the early 1850s seemed corrupt and irrelevant, if not dangerous to republican values. The moribund state of the parties, however, which allowed voters to embrace exclusively sectional alignments, only became apparent after slavery was reintroduced into national politics. This fateful step was taken by Stephen A. Douglas, the chief architect of the Compromise of 1850, acting in response to pressures within the Democratic party arising out of the ambiguous meaning of popular sovereignty.

The Kansas-Nebraska Bill

In the Kansas-Nebraska bill Douglas pushed through Congress a popular-sovereignty proposal that almost immediately caused the formation of an exclusively sectional free-soil party. Besides being ideologically committed to popular sovereignty, Douglas was under tremendous pressure from southern Democrats who, fearful that slavery would be "de-nationalized," insisted on concessions that decisively affected the legislative history of the measure. These concessions were to be used to impose discipline on a party that, though officially committed to the Compromise of 1850, remained seriously divided internally.

Many northern Democrats of free-soil proclivity who had left the party in 1850 returned to it during the election of 1852, in which Franklin Pierce of New Hampshire defeated the Whig candidate, General Winfield Scott. Typified by the Barnburners of New York, these apostates were welcomed back by moderate supporters of the administration, but were strongly opposed by hard-line, pro-slavery administration men. In the South similar conflict existed between those who had called for a southern-rights party in 1850 and those who had stood by the Union irrespective of party lines. In this confused situation President Franklin Pierce tried to alleviate internal strife by distributing the patronage to all factions. His policy was notably unsuccessful, however, and when Congress met at the end of 1853, it was left for the ambitious Douglas of Illinois to try to unify the party through a vigorous program of western expansion.

Since 1845 Douglas had been trying to organize Nebraska Territory, the remaining unorganized portion of the Louisiana Purchase lands lying north of the Indian territory. A major reason for wanting to do so was to facilitate the construction of a transcontinental railroad from Illinois to the Pacific coast. Douglas believed an aggressive western policy based on Nebraska would provide the Democratic party with an important national issue, enhance his stature as a national figure, and even make him a logical choice for the presidency. Yet a major obstacle stood in Douglas's way: a group of southern senators who were prepared to oppose the organization of Nebraska Territory unless the legislation benefited the South. This meant, in particular, concessions on the slavery question that could be forced on free-soil northern Democrats.

In December 1853, Senator Augustus C. Dodge of Iowa introduced a bill to organize the Nebraska Territory. The bill was referred to the Senate committee on territories, of which Douglas was chairman. Douglas added provisions borrowed from the New Mexico and Utah territorial acts of 1850 stipulating that Nebraska Territory, when admitted into the Union as a state or states, "shall be received . . . with or without slavery as their constitution may prescribe at the time of their admission." Another section provided that all questions involving title to slaves in the territory should be tried in the territorial courts, with appeal to the Supreme Court.

This bill technically did not repeal the Missouri Compromise restriction on slavery, for Douglas realized that to do so would excite free-soil opinion. Nevertheless, because of southern demands for concessions on slavery, and because he was genuinely committed to the approach, Douglas argued that popular sovereignty should be made the basis of settlement in Nebraska. He would accomplish this, however, not by repealing the Missouri Compromise restriction on slavery, but by ignoring it. He believed popular sovereignty was sufficiently expressed in the provisions already mentioned and in an accompanying committee report which asserted that the bill embodied the principles of the Compromise of 1850. These principles, the report explained, were intended to apply to all national territories, not simply the former Mexican lands, and were meant to avoid future agitation of the slavery issue by reserving to local settlers the right to decide questions concerning slavery. Douglas drew a parallel between the situation in 1850 and the present one. As the status of slavery in the Mexican cession lands was uncertain because of doubts about the effect of the Mexican law abolishing slavery, he explained, so there were doubts, based on the theory of congressional nonintervention in the territories, about the constitutionality of the Missouri Compromise restriction on slavery. As in 1850, Douglas said the sound course was to rely on the right of local self-determination.

The committee report notwithstanding, Southerners rejected Douglas's proposal because it permitted the Missouri restriction on slavery to remain in effect in the decisive period of settlement before the territory might form a constitution and seek statehood. A right to choose slavery at that point was no right at all. Acknowledging the fact, and the impossibility of reconciling popular sovereignty with the Missouri restriction, Douglas now began the process of accommodation to the slave interest that reopened the sectional struggle at a new level of intensity. The reluctance with which he proceeded in his unpleasant yet politically necessary task, as though aware of the momentous consequences his actions would produce, can be seen in the successive formulations of the Nebraska bill that he offered in the hope of avoiding outright repeal of the thirty-four-year-old Missouri law.

First, to the original bill Douglas added a section, which he later said had been omitted through a "clerical error," stating that to avoid any misunderstanding about the purpose of the legislation, its true intent was to apply the principles of the Compromise of 1850 and to leave all questions pertaining to slavery in the territories to the decision of the people therein, through their appropriate representatives. This was characteristically ambiguous in its re- fusal to say which territorial representatives were to act on slavery and when they should do so, but it implied that the Missouri restriction would cease to have effect. Not satisfied with this formulation, James Dixon of Maryland, a southern Whig trying to restore his party's credentials as a defender of south- ern rights, proposed outright repeal of the Missouri Compromise. Alarmed by this proposal, which swiftly found favor among Southerners of *both* parties, Douglas tried to keep control of the situation by bringing in a second Nebraska bill that moved closer toward repeal. It stated that the Missouri Compromise restriction on slavery was "superseded by the principles of the legislation of 1850" and accordingly was "inoperative." The bill also divided the area into two territories: Kansas, directly west of a slave state (Missouri), and Nebraska, directly west of a free state (Iowa). Sensing the gravity of the situation, Doug- las took the extraordinary step of getting President Pierce's personal written endorsement of the bill as an administration measure.

Still it was not enough. Coincidental with the introduction of Douglas's second bill, free-soil members of Congress published the "Appeal of Indepen- dent Democrats," a vigorous denunciation of the *original* Nebraska bill as tantamount to a repeal of the Missouri Compromise. If that was to be the northern reaction, Southerners were determined to have outright repeal, and Douglas was in no position to deny them. Accordingly, in February 1854 he brought in yet a third Nebraska bill. This one stated that the Missouri Com- promise, "being inconsistent with the principles of non-intervention by Con- gress with slavery in the States and territories, as recognized by the legislation of 1850, is hereby declared inoperative and void." The word "repeal" was not used, but it was a distinction without a difference. The bill also stated that its true intent was not to legislate slavery into or exclude it from any territory or state, but "to leave the people thereof free to form and regulate their own domestic institutions in their own way, subject only to the Constitution of the United States."

Having condemned Douglas's first attempt to shift the basis of Nebraska territorial organization from slavery restriction to popular sovereignty, anti- slavery men were relentless in attacking subsequent versions of the bill. In their view Douglas had violated a national commitment, expressed in the Missouri Compromise, to keep lands north of 36°30′ free, when it was too late to reclaim the territory lying south of the dividing line from the rule of slavery. Free- soilers also denied that anyone in 1850 thought popular sovereignty as applied to Utah and New Mexico extended as well to all unorganized national terri- tory.

For their part, Democrats adhered to the principle of popular sovereignty, which through artful ambiguity was still able to provide a common ground on which the northern and southern wings of the party could stand. Both groups agreed on congressional nonintervention. Beyond that they disagreed over

when popular sovereignty became effective in relation to slavery: at the outset
of the territorial period, as Douglas believed, or only upon admission to the
Union, with the right of slave property constitutionally protected up to that
time, as Southerners contended. Each side could read into the Kansas-Nebraska bill its own conception of popular sovereignty. But in the final analysis
the "true" meaning of popular sovereignty would depend on the interpretation
given the provision in the Nebraska bill stating that the people of the territories
and the states could shape and regulate their own local institutions, "subject
to the Constitution of the United States." And to explain what these words
meant it was likely that the Supreme Court, already invited by another section
of the Kansas-Nebraska bill to settle disputes over slavery in the territory,
would be consulted.

The Kansas-Nebraska Act, approved by Congress in March 1854, immediately provoked a political upheaval. Anti-Nebraska and anti-administration
coalitions quickly formed, and within a few months there existed an exclusively sectional anti-slavery organization—the Republican party. Alongside it
appeared another new political grouping, the Native American or Know-
Nothing party, which expressed the social and cultural pressures that eroded
traditional party loyalties in the early 1850s. For a while the two new parties
competed on equal terms, but by 1856 the Republicans achieved major party
status while the Native American party was virtually extinct. Meanwhile the
Democratic party experienced internal realignment as former southern Whigs
joined its ranks. From 1856 to 1860 the Democrats continued to be a national
party, but their outlook and policies became increasingly pro-slavery.

The Dred Scott *Case*

Revived with a vengeance in the debate over the Kansas-Nebraska Act,
agitation of the slavery question grew more fierce in the attempt to implement
popular sovereignty in Kansas between 1855 and 1858. Pro-slavery and anti-
slavery groups erected territorial governments, and in June 1856 hostilities
broke out between them. Although the Pierce administration recognized the
pro-slavery government, Congress became deadlocked on the issue when the
House of Representatives approved, but the Senate rejected, a bill to make
Kansas a free state. In these highly charged circumstances, amounting virtually to civil war in the territory, the Supreme Court attempted to settle the
question of the status of slavery in the territories.

Dred Scott was a Negro slave, formerly the property of one Dr. Emerson,
a surgeon in the United States Army. In 1834, Emerson took Scott to the free
state of Illinois, and thence in 1836 to Fort Snelling, in what was then the
Wisconsin Territory, free soil under the Missouri Compromise and the act of
1836 organizing Wisconsin's territorial government. Eventually, Emerson returned to Missouri, taking Scott with him. The surgeon died shortly thereafter,

and title to Scott eventually passed to John F. A. Sanford, a citizen of New York.

In 1846 Scott brought suit in the Missouri state courts for his freedom. At the time this action apparently had no political import. Though Scott won a favorable decision in the lower courts, the Missouri Supreme Court eventually rejected his plea, on the grounds that the laws of Illinois and of free territory did not have extraterritorial status in Missouri and could not affect his status as a slave after his return. Scott's attorney then began, in 1854, a new suit against Sanford in the United States Circuit Court for Missouri. The case was now frankly political in character, and both sides pressed it through to a conclusion in order to obtain a judicial opinion upon slavery in the territories.

Scott's right to sue Sanford in a federal court rested upon his contention that he was a citizen of the state of Missouri, and that the case involved a suit between citizens of different states. Sanford replied to Scott's suit with a plea in abatement—that is, a demand that the court dismiss the case for want of jurisdiction, on the ground that since Scott was a Negro he was not a citizen of Missouri. To this plea, Scott demurred. The circuit court sustained the demurrer (thereby implying that Scott might be a citizen), but it then returned a verdict in favor of Sanford. Scott now appealed to the Supreme Court of the United States on a writ of error.

The Court first heard argument on the case in February 1856, at the height of the Kansas furor. Opinion was divided on the question of jurisdiction, however, and this division, combined with a reluctance to take up politically controversial issues in an election year, led the justices to order the case reargued at its next term, in December 1857. In contrast to its first appearance on the docket, the case now aroused enormous interest, and the arguments of counsel, which went heavily into the question of congressional power over slavery in the territories, were closely attended. Nevertheless, the Court's initial response was to dismiss the case for want of jurisdiction. A clear and recent precedent for such a decision was available. In 1850, in *Strader* v. *Graham,* the Court without dissent had refused to consider the argument that a slave automatically became free through residence in a free state, and had held instead that the decision of the state courts was final in determining the slave status of a Negro. A majority of seven justices apparently now believed this precedent to be a decisive one, and in accordance with their wishes Justice Samuel Nelson actually prepared an opinion for the Court based on *Strader* v. *Graham,* a course avoiding all discussion of slavery in the territories.

It proved impossible, however, because of the tremendous interest the case had generated and because of the strength of the pro-slavery point of view on the Court, to maintain this attitude of restraint. In fact the decision to use the *Strader* precedent and avoid the explosive territorial question was not as settled as it appeared; at least two and perhaps four justices—all Southerners—were preparing concurring opinions in which they would deal with it. Accordingly, a few days after agreeing to an opinion from Justice Nelson, the Court, at the urging of Justice Wayne of Georgia, voted to take up all of the controversial issues raised in the reargument and entrust the writing of a new opinion to Chief Justice Taney. Undoubtedly, the by now habitual tendency of politicians to refer to the territorial issue as a "judicial question," a tendency expressed in the provision for judicial determination of all questions concerning slavery in the territories in legislation of 1848, 1850, and 1854, had its effect as the Court now changed its mind. It seems equally clear, however, that the desire of pro-slavery justices to settle the territorial question and remove it from politics influenced the decision to take up the disputed matters.

One further step was necessary. That was to enlist at least one northern justice on the majority side to avoid the appearance of a strictly sectional decision. To this end Justice Catron of Tennessee asked the help of President-elect James Buchanan in persuading Justice Grier of Pennsylvania to join the majority. Buchanan did so, and in turn was permitted to learn that the Court's imminent decision in the *Dred Scott* case would dispose of the territorial question. Buchanan, who had hoped for judicial assistance in quieting the struggle in Kansas, now made bold to say in his inaugural address on March 4, 1857, that the point of time when the people of a territory could decide the question of slavery was "a judicial question, which legitimately belongs to the Supreme Court of the United States, before whom it is now pending, and will, it is understood, be speedily and finally settled." "In common with all good citizens," Buchanan added, he would "cheerfully submit" to the Court's decision, "whatever this may be."[1]

On March 6, 1857, by a 7 to 2 vote, the Supreme Court decided that Scott could not sue, and that he was still a slave. In his opinion for the Court, Chief Justice Taney explained that Scott could not sue because he was not a citizen of the United States. And he was not a citizen because he was a Negro and a slave.

At the time the Constitution was written, Taney said, Negroes were not citizens of any states; therefore, none became a citizen of the United States. After the start of the government Negroes might become state citizens, for the states could make anyone they pleased a citizen. But this was state citizenship for strictly local purposes and it did not make a person a citizen of the United States. In contradiction to accepted doctrines of constitutional law, Taney thus asserted that state citizenship and national citizenship were absolutely separate. More precisely, he held that two kinds of state citizenship existed: one for national purposes, as expressed in the diversity-of-citizenship and privi-

---

1. Buchanan evidently thought the Court would deal with the problem of resolving the ambiguity in popular sovereignty; hence his reference to the power of the people in a territory over slavery. The Court, however, was interested in settling the larger and more fundamental issue of congressional power over slavery in the territories.

leges-and-immunities clauses of the Constitution, and one for exclusively state purposes. Because they were excluded from state citizenship in 1789—the only time, in Taney's view, when state-created citizenship conferred national citizenship—Negroes could never thereafter, except presumably by constitutional amendment, become state citizens in the sense of the Constitution and entitled to sue in federal courts as citizens of the United States.

Taney's opinion on citizenship resolved a long-standing controversy over the status of free Negroes in the United States. American law since the Revolution recognized no gradations of citizenship: Persons were either citizens or aliens. Public law also adhered to the traditional doctrine that place of birth determined citizenship. By these standards blacks born free in the United States were citizens, and some states, though discriminating against them in respect of political rights, so recognized them and protected them in the rights of personal liberty, property, access to courts, domestic relations, and the like—the rights that legally appertained to citizenship. Southerners, however, guided by the widespread discrimination against blacks that everywhere existed in the United States, denied that Negroes were citizens. In the southern view, at least as far as Negroes were concerned, citizenship did not confer the minimal rights of civil liberty, but rather was a condition to be deduced from the possession of all the civil rights of every other person in the community under like circumstances. Although as late as the 1830s some southern courts held to traditional birthright citizenship and recognized free Negroes as citizens, by the time of the *Dred Scott* case the weight of southern legal opinion was against Negro citizenship.

Taney's opinion resolved the question by denying that blacks were U.S. citizens or state citizens under the Constitution. Yet they were not aliens. Indeed, Taney said, born in the United States, whether slave or free, blacks owed allegiance to the government. In effect, Taney placed Negroes in a third category between citizenship and alienage, as subject-nationals or quasi-citizens. This determination was nowhere recognized in the American law of citizenship, but it was not greatly at variance with the actual conditions of Negro life in the antebellum period.

An important feature of Taney's opinion was his discussion of national citizenship based on the privileges-and-immunities clause of the Constitution. This was another question in antebellum constitutional law that was rendered problematic by the presence of large numbers of free Negroes in the United States. Whether Negroes as state citizens enjoyed national protection under the privileges-and-immunities clause had been an issue since the Missouri crisis of 1820. At that time Missouri sought admission to the Union under a constitution that excluded free Negroes from the state. Northerners argued that this restriction violated the privileges-and-immunities clause by denying rights to Negroes who were state citizens under the Constitution, and thus entitled to national protection. Congress failed to resolve the issue, and in succeeding years anti-slavery constitutionalists fashioned a doctrine of national citizenship under the privileges-and-immunities clause for the protection of blacks.[2]

In the *Dred Scott* case Chief Justice Taney accepted a broad, nationalistic view of the privileges-and-immunities clause. He was at pains, however, precisely because of the apparent protective force of this constitutional provision, to refute the idea of Negro citizenship and exclude blacks from the political community of the nation. If Negroes were regarded as state citizens under the Constitution, he observed, other states would have to receive them and acknowledge their right to paramount federal protection of the privileges and immunities of citizens. Negroes would be exempt from the operation of special laws and police regulations essential to public safety in the slave states, and would be entitled to freedom of speech, the right to keep and bear arms, the right of assembly, and so on. The effect, Taney predicted, would be to produce discontent and insubordination in slave society.

Taney had given as a second reason why Scott was not a citizen the fact that he was a slave. The chief justice might have made this point simply by citing the opinion of the lower Missouri courts, with a reference to *Strader* v. *Graham* as precedent. Instead he proceeded to consider the effect of Scott's residence on free soil, a matter enabling him to discuss the constitutional status of slavery in the territories. Republican critics at once pronounced Taney's subsequent denial of congressional power over slavery in the territories obiter dictum. In a legal sense the charge was mistaken, for the case was before the Court on a writ of error, and contemporary practice permitted the Court to consider all phases of an opinion taken from the lower courts on a writ of error, even though a decision on any one point might be sufficient to dispose of the case. Nevertheless, though Taney's course was not inconsistent with accepted procedure, he acted as he did not strictly out of legal obligation. He also wished to demolish the idea of congressional power to restrict slavery in the territories—the central tenet of anti-slavery constitutionalism since the introduction of the Wilmot Proviso.

Taney began his argument on the effects of Scott's residence on free soil with the novel contention that federal authority over the territories was derived from the power to acquire territory by treaty and to create new states, not from the clause empowering Congress to make necessary rules and regulations for governing the territories. The latter clause, he said, was a mere emergency provision applying only to lands ceded by the original states to the Confederation; it did not validate federal authority in territories acquired after 1789. That authority, Taney went on to explain, was not a general, discretionary, sovereign legislative power, but rather a limited, protective power appro-

---

2. Congress admitted Missouri on condition that its constitution not be interpreted as authorizing the passage of any law excluding the citizens of any state from enjoying the privileges and immunities guaranteed by the Constitution of the United States. The requirement was a dead letter from the outset.

priate to the trusteeship or agency function that properly belonged to the federal government. Whatever the government acquired, Taney said, it acquired "for the benefit of the people of the several States who created it. It is their trustee acting for them, and charged with protecting the interests of the whole people of the Union." Moreover, congressional power over the person and property of a citizen "can never be a mere discretionary power." Citizens of the United States who migrate to the territories, Taney admonished, "cannot be ruled as mere colonists, dependent on the will of the General Government, to be governed by any laws it may think proper." The federal government could thus exercise no power of internal police, nor infringe any property right enjoyed by a citizen under the laws of his own state.

Additional strictures on congressional power derived from the Fifth Amendment. Federal authority in the territories, Taney observed, was limited by the various provisions in the federal Bill of Rights, including the Fifth Amendment guarantee of due process of law. "And an act of Congress," said the chief justice, "which deprives a citizen of the United States of his liberty or property, merely because he came himself or brought his property into a particular Territory of the United States, and who had committed no offence against the laws, could hardly be dignified with the name of due process of law." Taney thus invoked the doctrine of vested interests, tied it to the due-process clause in the Fifth Amendment, and applied it to property in slaves.

Taney then concluded that the Missouri Compromise Act prohibiting slavery north of the 36°30' line was "not warranted by the Constitution" and was, therefore, void. Dred Scott's residence on free soil had not made him a free man, since slavery had not lawfully been excluded from the Wisconsin Territory. The federal government, in short, could not lawfully exclude slavery from any of the territories. And for good measure, although it was not an issue in the case, Taney announced that a territorial legislature lacked power to prohibit slavery under the doctrine of popular sovereignty. If Congress could not interfere with property rights, he said, it could not authorize a territorial government to do so. Congress "could confer no power on any local government established by its authority, to violate the provisions of the Constitution."

Thus, on the one hand, Taney discovered in the Constitution restrictions on federal and territorial legislative power and, on the other hand, positive protection of slave property going far beyond the right of recaption in fugitive slave cases that marked the most aggressive grasp of pro-slavery constitutionalism to this time. In describing limits on legislative power and the sanctity of property rights, Taney invoked fundamental principles of American constitutionalism. But in employing them for the defense of slavery he transmuted them in ways that, in the eyes of an ever larger segment of the public, contradicted the very purpose of republican constitutionalism. The febrile state of Taney's mind as he attempted, more openly than ever before, to destroy anti-slavery constitutionalism was evident in his assertion that "the right of property in a slave is distinctly and expressly affirmed in the Constitution."

This was manifestly untrue. With equal license and imagination he concluded: "No word can be found in the Constitution which gives Congress a greater power over slave property, or which entitles property of that kind to less protection than property of any other description. The only power conferred is the power coupled with the duty of guarding and protecting the owner in his rights."

Justices Nelson, Daniel, Campbell, Catron, Wayne, and Grier all concurred in Taney's conclusion that Scott was a slave, although they arrived at this finding by varying routes. Nelson entered the opinion originally prepared for the seven majority justices, deciding the case on the authority of *Strader v. Graham*. Daniel merely restated Calhoun's doctrine of federal agency as prohibiting any interference with slavery. Campbell admitted the efficacy of the territories clause, but thought strict construction properly limited federal authority to mere administrative and conservatory acts, and to the enumerated powers of Congress. Catron thought the Louisiana Purchase treaty, which had guaranteed existing property rights in the territory, had made illegal any restriction on property rights in slaves within the confines of the original purchase. Wayne and Grier indicated more or less complete assent to Taney's opinion.

Justices Curtis and McLean dissented on Scott's status and on the validity of the Missouri Compromise. Denying the contention that because Scott was a Negro he was not a citizen, Curtis argued that free Negroes were citizens and had been accepted as such in 1787. Moreover, state citizenship was primary and automatically conferred national citizenship. As for Scott's personal status, it had been determined by his residence on free soil. And as for congressional power in the territories, it was supreme and plenary, and included power over slavery which had been exercised on numerous occasions. The minority concluded that the Missouri Compromise was valid and that Scott was a free man.

The legal effect of the *Dred Scott* decision was profound. Although the federal government had never claimed power over slavery in the states where it existed, Congress had prohibited slavery in national territory. By the same token, it had never established or recognized slavery by positive legislation. Although sanctioned by the Constitution, slavery had, therefore, always been considered a local institution, existing only by force of positive municipal law. Freedom was thought of as national. The *Dred Scott* decision altered this situation by asserting a positive constitutional right to take slave property into national territory, a right that Congress could not restrict. In a very real sense, therefore, it made slavery national and freedom local. Moreover, although restricted to the territories in the instant case, Taney's assertion of an expressly affirmed constitutional right to own slave property could conceivably be given national scope and effect, like the right of recaption in fugitive slave cases.

The *Dred Scott* case had important political as well as legal consequences. For several years the controversy over slavery in the territories had been conducted in two distinct forums. In the first, free-soilers upholding congressional power to restrict slavery had opposed Democrats insisting on congressional nonintervention. In the second arena of controversy, Democrats disagreed among themselves over the stage of territorial organization at which anti-slavery legislation might be adopted. The *Dred Scott* decision principally affected the former controversy. It struck at the Republican party's constitutional rationale, forcing anti-slavery men to denounce the opinion as obiter dictum or to question the authority of the Supreme Court as final arbiter of constitutional disputes. But the decision also exacerbated the conflict within the Democratic party over the meaning of popular sovereignty. It upheld the property right of slaveowners against the power of a territorial legislature to restrict slavery. In effect it endorsed the pro-slavery conception of popular sovereignty and repudiated the Douglas version.

The Lincoln-Douglas Debates

The legal and political effects of the *Dred Scott* decision were dramatically interjected into national politics in the Lincoln-Douglas debates of 1858, a brilliant episode in constitutional politics that explored the problem of slavery in the American republic. Abraham Lincoln and Stephen A. Douglas were competing for a senatorial seat from Illinois. They were also in effect vying for leadership of free-soil opinion in the North. The outcome of the struggle to implement popular sovereignty in Kansas invested their contest with this broad significance.

After prolonged and violent conflict, anti-slavery forces prevailed in Kansas, and by the fall of 1858 the territory was a free-soil area. The Buchanan administration had brought forward and had approved in the Senate the fraudulent pro-slavery Lecompton constitution—fraudulent because it had been ratified in an election which allowed no genuine choice between slavery and freedom. The Lecompton constitution, however, was rejected by the House of Representatives. Congress then provided for another territorial election on the Lecompton constitution, and it was defeated by an overwhelming margin. As the dust settled, it became clear that destabilization of the party system had progressed ominously. For Douglas and the northern Democrats had strenuously opposed the Lecompton charter, in the process breaking with the Buchanan administration. Popular sovereignty, so long an effective means of intraparty compromise, turned out in this instance to be a free-soil instrument. And it was this perception, however turbulent and costly the implementation of popular sovereignty had been, that made the contest between Lincoln and Douglas so critically important. Douglas's rejection of the Lecompton fraud brought him free-soil favor, and if victorious in 1858 he stood a chance of leading a free-soil popular front across the North. If, on the other hand, Lincoln won or made a strong showing, northern opinion would continue to be divided, yet also alienated against the South. The result would be a highly volatile, even dangerous situation.

Republicans and Democrats had together opposed the Lecompton constitution, but Lincoln, conceding nothing to Douglas, emphasized the differences of principle between the parties. In the debates he reaffirmed Republican opposition to slavery on both moral and political grounds. If slavery was not wrong, he said, nothing was wrong. At bottom the issue was "the right or wrong of slavery in this Union." Moreover, slavery contradicted the fundamental principle of equality, expressed in the Declaration of Independence. Lincoln did not insist on civil rights equality between Negroes and whites; he was in fact generally pessimistic about race relations in the United States. Yet he believed that all persons were equal in at least this respect: that they had the right not to be governed without their consent—the right, in other words, of personal liberty. The Republican party expressed this principle in opposing the expansion of slavery into the territories.

Stop the spread of slavery, Lincoln argued in 1858, and the people would believe once again—as at the founding of the nation—that slavery was in the course of ultimate extinction. Restore the country to its commitment to republican freedom, he reasoned, and slavery actually would be placed on a course toward ultimate extinction. The Union would then endure. It could not continue to exist, however, half slave and half free: Either the one condition or the other must be nationalized. Lincoln refused to say when or how slavery might be ended, but by focusing on the morality of slavery and speaking of its eventual elimination he took a radical position. At the same time, however, he presented a moderate aspect by arguing simply for a policy of slavery restriction, which he identified with the founding fathers, and by acknowledging the lack of federal power to interfere with slavery in the states where it existed.

Douglas defended popular sovereignty, unrestricted by any higher moral principle, as the touchstone of republican government and as the only basis of national unity. In his view majority rule was not a means to an end, but a self-justifying end in itself. In practical effect it meant that each political community, whether state or territorial, had the right to shape its domestic institutions, subject only to the requirements of the Constitution. And if slave labor was the choice of some communities, that choice was not inconsistent with republican government. Answering Lincoln's prediction that either slavery or freedom must be nationalized, Douglas said the government had been founded on such a division and could continue only on that basis. For this reason Douglas professed indifference to the moral aspect of slavery, saying he did not care whether it was voted up or down. To agitate the moral issue and try to settle it uniformly for the entire republic, he warned, would provoke conflict and disrupt the Union. In the final analysis, he declared on several occasions, the integrity of the Union was more important than the liberty of Negro slaves.

Douglas had always said that popular sovereignty was subject only to the Constitution, and it was in this context that Lincoln raised the issue of the legal effect of the *Dred Scott* decision. In Lincoln's view the case provided dramatic evidence of the legal tendency toward slavery expansion. The first step, he said, had been the Kansas-Nebraska Act removing the Missouri Compromise barrier against slavery extension. Moreover, although that act dealt with a territory, it stated that Congress had no intention of legislating slavery into any *state;* the purpose of the act was said to be to leave the people free to form local institutions subject only to the federal Constitution. Did this perhaps imply, asked Lincoln, that there were constitutional exceptions to the power of states to prohibit slavery? And did the disavowal of congressional intent to legislate on slavery in the states perhaps imply a power so to legislate?

Lincoln next pointed to Justice Nelson's statement, in his concurring opinion in the *Dred Scott* case, that "except in cases where the power is restrained by the Constitution of the United States, the law of the State is supreme over the subject of slavery within its jurisdiction." The fugitive slave clause, of course, constituted an exception to the states' absolute power over slavery, but did the *Dred Scott* decision create an additional and more threatening exception? What did it mean to say, as Chief Justice Taney had, that "the right of property in a slave is distinctly and expressly affirmed in the Constitution"? Perhaps, Lincoln suggested, it meant that the free states would be forced to recognize slave property generally. In his famous "house-divided" speech in August 1858, he expressed this fear: "We shall all lie down pleasantly dreaming that the people of Missouri are on the verge of making their State free, and we shall awake to the reality instead that the Supreme Court has made Illinois a slave State."

In addition to posing this issue, Lincoln pointedly asked Douglas how he could reconcile popular sovereignty with the *Dred Scott* decision. Did not the right of constitutionally protected slave property supersede the right of a territorial community to exclude slavery? Douglas's answer, the famous Freeport doctrine, defended popular sovereignty as effective and legitimate, the *Dred Scott* decision notwithstanding. It did not matter what the Supreme Court said about the abstract question of property in slaves, Douglas explained, for slavery could not exist without the protection of local legislation. And if the people did not like slavery, they could pass "unfriendly legislation" preventing the adoption of the legal supports that slavery required.

Douglas had expressed the substance of the Freeport doctrine before; indeed, Southerners themselves, before the split over the Lecompton constitution, in similar terms had reassured northern audiences with this argument. Now, however, Douglas's reiteration of the local-sovereignty principle attracted national attention because of his break with the Buchanan administration. From Lincoln's standpoint there was little to be gained by placing Douglas at odds with the South and hence closer to free-soil opinion. But intellectually and morally Lincoln put Douglas in an untenable position.

Douglas had said local sovereignty was subject to the Constitution; like most politicians he took Supreme Court decisions as authoritative expositions of the Constitution, and stated that he accepted the *Dred Scott* decision. Yet he was now saying, in effect, that he would negate it. Lincoln captured the contradiction—and Douglas's flawed sense of constitutional morality—in charging that the Freeport doctrine amounted to saying that "a thing may be lawfully driven away from where it had a lawful right to be."

In the opinion of some historians, Lincoln was irresponsible in speaking of a "second *Dred Scott* decision" that would further nationalize slavery in the free states. Yet if Southerners could be apprehensive about the effect of slavery restriction in "denationalizing" slavery and causing its eventual destruction, Republicans were warranted in pointing to the possibility of further slave advances, directed by the national judiciary, under the logic of the *Dred Scott* opinion. There were cases in northern state courts dealing with slaves in transit that the Supreme Court could have used to provide limited recognition of the right to hold slave property in the free states under the Fifth Amendment. In *Lemmon* v. *The People* (1860), for example, the New York courts upheld, over a challenge made by a slaveowner, a state law prohibiting transit of slaves and freeing by a writ of habeas corpus any person held as a slave within the borders of the state. The Supreme Court could have entertained such a suit and overturned the state law as a violation of the Fifth Amendment. Such a ruling, applying the Fifth Amendment to the states, would appear to run counter to *Barron* v. *Baltimore* (1833), where the Court held that the first eight amendments were restrictions only on the federal government. The *Barron* case, however, was not unequivocally accepted as binding precedent in the antebellum period. In fact, arguments were frequently advanced in federal and state courts asserting the applicability of the Fifth Amendment and the Bill of Rights to the states. Thus if the Taney Court were to persist in its drive to destroy anti-slavery constitutionalism, another "Dred Scott" decision was by no means an impossibility. And that the Taney Court would so persist seemed apparent from its attack on northern personal liberty laws in the famous fugitive slave case of 1859, *Ableman* v. *Booth*.

State Sovereignty Vindicated: Ableman *v.* Booth

Despite a few highly publicized fugitive slave escapes, the Pierce and Buchanan administrations vigorously enforced the Fugitive Slave Act of 1850. Still, some slaves managed to escape, and of those who did only a small number were actually subjected to the rendition process. Southerners were dissatisfied with this circumstance, and their resentment was compounded by the adoption of new personal liberty laws in the northern states in the 1850s. Laws in Connecticut, Rhode Island, Massachusetts, Michigan, Maine, Ohio, and Wisconsin provided counsel for alleged fugitives, guaranteed them the writ of habeas corpus and trial by jury, denied the use of state jails for arrested fugitives, prohibited state officers from assisting in the return of fugitives, and punished kidnapping of free Negroes. *Ableman* v. *Booth* arose in this context.

The case began in 1854 when an abolitionist editor in Wisconsin, Sherman Booth, forcibly assisted in the escape of a fugitive slave. He was convicted in federal district court of violating the fugitive slave law and was fined $1,000. The Wisconsin Supreme Court then issued a writ of habeas corpus, and on hearing, freed Booth, holding his conviction illegal and the fugitive slave law void. The Wisconsin court insisted on its right to free its citizens from illegal confinement, even though examination into the constitutionality of federal law was involved. United States District Marshal Ableman then sought and obtained a writ of error in the federal Supreme Court, to review the Wisconsin court's finding. The Wisconsin Supreme Court refused to receive notice of the United States Supreme Court's writ, and in fact ignored the subsequent review completely.

In March 1859 Chief Justice Taney gave the opinion of the Supreme Court upholding Booth's conviction and denying the power of a state court to interpose its authority to prevent possibly illegal detention in federal hands. Using dual-federalist analysis, Taney said the federal and state governments were sovereign in their respective spheres, and the federal judiciary had an obligation to guard each in the exercise of the powers assigned it. In the instant case, said Taney, the state judiciary was interfering in the execution of federal law and asserting its supremacy over the courts of the United States. Denying the right of the state judiciary to interfere in federal cases, the chief justice upheld the supremacy of the federal Constitution and defended the role of the federal judiciary as the final tribunal to decide constitutional issues. He condemned the action of the Wisconsin court as unconstitutional, destructive of national sovereignty, and tantamount to "lawless violence."

Conventional wisdom has regarded *Ableman* v. *Booth* as a landmark decision in the development of constitutional nationalism, and the position of the Wisconsin Supreme Court as dangerously nullificationist in tendency. It is pertinent to note, however, that in the 1850s habeas corpus law concerning the powers of state courts in relation to federal authority was unsettled. According to one view, states could discharge persons illegally detained by the federal government, even when the constitutionality of federal actions was involved. It is significant, too, that Taney defended national judicial rather than legislative authority. He said nothing about congressional power, except to assert the constitutionality of the Fugitive Slave Act of 1850. His main concern was to exercise judicial power as the agent of the slave states. Despite the appearance of national centralization, therefore, *Ableman* v. *Booth* gave extrajurisdictional effect to the law of slavery, in accordance with the doctrine of state sovereignty and federal trusteeship. And by holding that the states could not inquire into confinement under federal authority, Taney effectively demolished the personal liberty laws of the free states.

Secession

The culmination of pro-slavery constitutionalism was the demand for enactment of a federal slave code in the territories. This was the ultimate expression of extrajurisdictional application of slave-state law through the agency of the federal government. A secondary demand was for repeal of the personal liberty laws. Douglas's Freeport doctrine spurred the former proposal, while free-state attempts at interposition in fugitive slave cases, as in Wisconsin, provoked the latter. In the increasingly tense atmosphere that surrounded these demands, John Brown's raid on the federal arsenal at Harpers Ferry, Virginia, in November 1859 heightened southern fear of a free-soil victory in the election of 1860.

In the campaign of 1860 four parties competed for control of the national government. The Democratic party, in reality split since the fight over the Lecompton constitution, now formally divided into two parties. Douglas ran for the northern Democrats on the basis of popular sovereignty and a promise to abide by Supreme Court decisions. Southern Democrats nominated John C. Breckinridge of Kentucky and insisted on federal protection of the rights of persons and property in the territories. The Republican nominee was Abraham Lincoln, who ran on a platform proclaiming that due process of law under the Fifth Amendment guaranteed freedom in the territories. The Republican platform also denounced popular sovereignty as a fraud and condemned the view that the Constitution of its own force carried slavery into the territories. Finally, a small body of Whigs from the upper South organized as the Constitutional Union party and ran John Bell of Tennessee for president. Fearful of what might happen if either Lincoln or Breckinridge were elected, the Constitutional Unionists deplored agitation of the slavery question. Advocating no policy, they simply appealed to patriotism, respect for the Constitution and the Union, and enforcement of the laws.

Lincoln carried every northern state but New Jersey, winning 180 electoral votes. Douglas won only Missouri and New Jersey, securing 12 votes. Breckinridge carried eleven southern states for 72 votes, while Bell won 39 votes in Kentucky, Tennessee, and Virginia. The vote thus resolved itself into a direct conflict between northern free-soilers and southern proponents of slavery expansion for control of the electoral college. Although winning only a minority of the popular vote, Lincoln's electoral college majority won him the presidency.

Secession, justified on the basis of state sovereignty, was the direct result of the election of 1860. It is important to recall, however, that before this event changed the political situation, state sovereignty was intended to serve the southern constitutional purpose of preserving the Union on the basis of pro-slavery principles. Because slavery violated the principles of equality and consent set forth in the Declaration of Independence, however, the southern attempt to interpret the Constitution and direct the course of national political development for the protection of slavery was bound to fail. Although the implications of this fact could not be fully understood in 1860, Southerners understood that Lincoln's election fundamentally altered the situation. As events soon revealed, Lincoln was determined to stop the spread of slavery. From the southern point of view, to contemplate this prospect was to contemplate disaster. However much Republicans might deny federal authority over slavery in the states where it existed, agree to enforce the fugitive slave law, and support the repeal of personal liberty laws, Southerners perceived a mortal threat to their way of life. They saw no distinction between direct and indirect attacks on slavery, between proposals to keep slavery out of the territories and demands for outright abolition. At some point the objective realities of slavery restriction symbolized the South's deepening sense of social and economic alienation from the North. By the same token, free-soil opposition to slavery extension and to secession symbolized northern social fears and aspirations.

In retrospect it is easy to conclude that had southern members of Congress stayed where they were and remained calm, they could still have exercised considerable influence over national policy. Secession has, therefore, often seemed a great blunder—ill conceived, overreactive, irrational. Yet the triumph of a party committed to the ultimate extinction of slavery would probably have proven decisive in shaping national policy even without secession and war. Majority opinion, becoming increasingly anti-slavery and anti-southern, in time would have supported restrictions on the institution. In the short run the practical results of the election would have been evident in the appointment of Republican postmasters, customs collectors, and sundry government officials—a process that would have interfered with and possibly ended pro-slavery control of thought and behavior in the South. The South was, therefore, justified in fearing the accession to national power of an exclusively sectional anti-slavery party.

State sovereignty as the basis of secession was now used to destroy the Union and the constitutional system. Yet years of theorizing about secession caused it to appear—or enabled Southerners to regard it—as a legitimate constitutional instrument. Like Calhoun before them, the secession theorists of 1860 held that the several states retained complete sovereignty, and that the Union was a mere league, from which member states might withdraw at their pleasure. The Constitution was a compact between the states. Sovereignty was indivisible and could be neither divided nor delegated; therefore, the federal government had no sovereignty. The Constitution was thus a mere treaty, and the Union a mere league. From this it followed that secession was a self-evident right, since it could hardly be denied that a sovereign state could withdraw from a league at any time it chose to do so.

Jefferson Davis, perhaps the most brilliant secession theorist of the times, frequently adduced two additional historical arguments in support of secession. First, he pointed to the fact that the Constitutional Convention had rejected state coercion. If a state could not be coerced, Davis contended, then it was manifestly impossible to prevent it from withdrawing from the Union at will. Davis also pointed to the resolutions adopted by the various state conventions when ratifying the Constitution. The Virginia convention, in particular, had resolved that "rights granted by the people may be resumed by the people at their pleasure," while New York and Massachusetts had enacted similar resolutions. Davis interpreted these resolutions as specifically reserving to the various states the right to withdraw from the compact should they desire to do so.

The South justified secession on the ground that actions of the northern states, as parties to the original constitutional compact, violated the commitment to protect slavery that was incorporated in the Constitution as the very basis of Union. According to the Mississippi legislature, "slavery existed prior to the formation of the Federal Constitution, and is recognized by its letter, and all efforts to impair its value or lessen its duration by Congress, or any of the free States, is a violation of the compact of Union." Specifically, the northern states had violated and obstructed the fugitive slave law by passing personal liberty laws; made attacks on slavery in the South by permitting abolition societies to exist; tried to exclude slavery from the territories, thus denying the rights of the southern states there; opposed the *Dred Scott* decision and its guarantee of southern citizens' property rights; and launched a direct assault on the slave system of the South in the Harpers Ferry raid.

These arguments were by no means frivolous or patently inaccurate, for in some sense slavery *was* recognized in the constitutional settlement on which the republic was founded. The recognition, however, was nowhere so clear and explicit, nor did it approve slavery in principle, as Southerners claimed. Opinion about slavery in 1787 was far more ambivalent, even among Southerners themselves, than the secessionists could possibly have acknowledged. Furthermore, the text of the Constitution implied moral disapprobation of slavery, and the constitutional settlement in 1787 more broadly considered included antislavery actions that Northerners could point to as evidence of the framers' desire to see slavery ultimately abolished. Indeed, a stronger argument could be made against secession on constitutional grounds. The components of the argument included the silence of the Constitution on the subject; the existence of federal powers not subject to state interference; the supremacy clause; the rejection of the Articles of Confederation by the popularly elected state conventions that ratified the Constitution; and the legitimacy and primacy of majority rule in a republican system of government. Ultimately slavery's denial of equality and consent was reflected by the repudiation, in the secession movement, of the principles of equality and consent on which free government rests. Because the Constitution must be interpreted in light of the Declaration of Independence, and because Southerners failed to understand or rejected the principles of the Declaration, their application of state sovereignty to secede from the Union lacked constitutional legitimacy.

South Carolina seceded first. As soon as the result of the election became known, the state legislature called a constitutional convention which met at Charleston on December 17, 1861. Three days later, the convention by unanimous vote adopted an ordinance of secession. The ordinance purported to repeal the ordinance of 1787, whereby the state had ratified the Constitution. The convention also adopted a declaration of the causes of secession, which presented the southern theory of the Union and the various southern grievances of the hour. Alabama, Georgia, Florida, Mississippi, Louisiana, and Texas had also called conventions, all of which met in January and voted for secession by large majorities. Thus all seven states of the lower South had seceded by the end of January.

Attempts at Compromise

Meanwhile Buchanan's administration in Washington was involved in a paralyzing dilemma: If it did nothing to check the secessionist movement, the Union would most assuredly be dissolved; on the other hand, if the government used force against the seceding states, a terrible civil war might result. There was no assurance that the North was ready to support such a drastic policy. Moreover, the employment of force would probably precipitate secession in several of the remaining slave states of the upper South, then on the verge of leaving the Union.

Confronted by this quandary, President Buchanan stalled for time and awaited developments. In his annual message in December, he laid the responsibility for the current crisis at the door of the northern people's "intemperate interference" with slavery. He added, however, that Lincoln's election was not just cause for secession, and he also warned the South that no constitutional right of secession existed, since the Union had been intended to be permanent. He then nullified whatever force these last observations had with the statement that if a state chose to secede, there existed no constitutional remedy against its action, however illegal it might be. Buchanan's constitutionalism was thus the quintessence of futility. Senator William H. Seward ironically commented that "the message shows conclusively that it is the duty of the President to execute the law—unless someone opposes it; and that no state has the right to go out of the Union—unless it wants to." In justice to Buchanan, however, it must be observed that the political dilemma in which he found himself was a very real one, and that his policy of watchful waiting was basically the course that Lincoln adopted after his inauguration.

In reality, Buchanan hoped that Congress would again effect some sort of last-minute compromise. Moderate Democrats, both North and South, were working desperately to that end. The House on December 4, 1860, appointed a committee of thirty-three, one member from each state, to consider compromise proposals, and two days later the Senate created a committee of thirteen for the same purpose. The Republicans dominated the House committee, but the Senate group represented all factions, and included Seward of New York and Ben Wade of Ohio for the Republicans, Stephen A. Douglas of Illinois and John J. Crittenden of Kentucky for the moderate Democrats, and Robert Toombs of Georgia and Jefferson Davis of Mississippi for the secessionists.

The most significant proposals presented were the Crittenden Resolutions, introduced to the Senate and the compromise committees by Senator Crittenden on December 18. These were recommendations for amendments to the Constitution that would extend the Missouri Compromise line to the Pacific, prohibiting slavery north and guaranteeing it south of 36°30'. This proposal, it should be noted, went beyond the 1820 Compromise by positively legislating slavery in national territory, something Congress had never before done. It was intended to apply, moreover, to existing territories and those "hereafter acquired." Other proposed amendments denied Congress power to abolish slavery in the District of Columbia or in places subject to federal jurisdiction where slavery existed in the surrounding state; denied Congress power to interfere with the domestic slave trade; and guaranteed federal compensation to slaveholders who were prevented from recovering fugitive slaves. Additional resolutions called for enforcement of the fugitive slave law, repeal of the personal liberty laws, and, on the North's behalf, reinforcement of the laws against the African slave trade.

The compromise attempt failed mainly because the Republican party opposed it, although a large share of responsibility belongs to southern members of Congress who if they had stayed in Washington might have altered the outcome. Republicans believed Lincoln's election did not menace the South and that concessions to the southern states were, therefore, unnecessary. The party could not accept a solution that established slavery in the territories, for that would have contradicted its constitutional rationale, its election promises, and its very reason for being. It was especially important to reject any plan to legislate slavery into territories south of 36°30' that might be acquired in the future, for the expansionist pressures that had affected American politics for two decades appeared likely to continue. Southerners had encouraged filibustering ventures into Nicaragua and Cuba in the 1850s, and anticipated Caribbean expansion as a means of maintaining their political power. Republicans were, therefore, categorically opposed to the dividing-line approach to the slavery question incorporated in the Crittenden Compromise. And if they needed any further reason for rejecting compromise, it could be found in the widespread belief that the Compromise of 1850 had been a grievous mistake because it only encouraged southern aggressiveness.

In February 1861 Congress did belatedly adopt a constitutional amendment guaranteeing slavery within the states in perpetuity against federal interference. "No amendment shall be made to the Constitution," the proposal stated, "which will authorize or give to Congress the power to abolish or interfere, within any state, with the domestic institutions thereof, including that of persons held to labor or service by the laws of said state." Eventually, three states, Ohio, Maryland, and Illinois, ratified the amendment, but it came too late and conceded too little to influence the course of events.

The Unionist-dominated Virginia legislature also sponsored an unsuccessful peace conference. In response to Virginia's call, delegates from twenty-one states assembled at Washington on February 4, under the chairmanship of ex-president Tyler. The conference got nowhere. The seven seceded states refused to send delegates, while the northern delegations were for the most part controlled by Republicans determined to make no substantial concessions. Eventually, the conference adopted the substance of the Crittenden amendments, with some modifications, as well as a proposed amendment that the United States acquire no new territory except by a four-fifths vote of the Senate, with a majority of both free- and slave-state senators concurring. When presented in Congress, these proposals were overwhelmingly defeated. Almost all hope of compromise was now gone.

Formation of the Confederacy

On February 4, 1861, the very day when the futile peace conference met in Washington, delegates from the seven seceded states gathered in Montgomery, Alabama, for the purpose of forming a central government. They shortly adopted a temporary constitution converting themselves into a provisional congress and instructing the congress to elect a provisional president and vice-president. On March 11, the congress adopted a permanent constitution and submitted it to the seceded states for ratification.

The Confederate constitution closely resembled that of the United States, although it contained a number of important differences. Certain provisions underscored state sovereignty. The preamble read, "We the people of the Confederate States, each state acting in its sovereign capacity . . . do ordain and establish this Constitution . . ." This implied that the resultant government arose out of a compact between sovereign states, and not between the people thereof. The right of secession might thereby be inferred. However, the constitution mentioned no such right, and in fact three different proposals guaranteeing the right were killed in convention without reaching the floor.

Other provisions grew directly out of the slavery controversy. Congress was forbidden to pass any law impairing the right of property in slaves. Citizens with their slaves were granted the right of transit and sojourn in other states, and such sojourn did not thereby impair ownership in such slaves. Negro slavery was specifically recognized in any territories the Confederacy might acquire. The foreign slave trade, however, except with slaveholding states of the United States, was forbidden. The South's long-standing grievance against the protective tariff was reflected in a clause forbidding import duties for the benefit of industry, while congressional appropriations for internal improvements, except those in navigational facilities, were also prohibited.

Substantial changes were made in the executive department. The president and vice-president were given six-year terms and made ineligible for reelection. The president was specifically granted a separate unconditional removal power over principal officers, and over minor officials for reasons of misconduct or incapacity. This provision evidently reflected the long quarrel over the removal power under the United States Constitution.

The president also had more effective control over money matters than did the president of the United States under the Constitution. He could veto separate items in appropriations bills, while the congress could appropriate money only by two-thirds vote of both houses unless the funds were requested by the executive. Another clause enabled the congress to grant cabinet officers a seat on the floor of either house to discuss matters pertaining to their departments. Such a provision might conceivably have led to the emergence of a parliamentary system of government, although no such tendency appeared during the Confederacy's brief history.

The new government also prepared to treat with the United States to effect a settlement with respect to "common property," the territories, debts, and the like. For this purpose the Confederate congress accredited two commissioners to Washington. The new government also proceeded to take over certain forts, arsenals, and other United States property lying within the Confederacy. Apparently, it expected the government at Washington to offer little resistance to the establishment of a new nation.

Lincoln and the Secession Crisis

On March 4, 1861, the Buchanan administration ended and the responsibilities of the presidential office devolved upon Abraham Lincoln. In his inaugural address of March 4, perhaps the most important state paper in American history, President Lincoln explained the principles on which the United States would resist secession and the policy it would employ in an attempt peacefully to maintain the integrity of the Union.

Repudiating the southern compact theory of the Union, Lincoln stated that the Union was older than the Constitution. Formed by the Articles of Association in 1774, it was matured and continued by the Declaration and the Articles of Confederation, and made into a more perfect Union in the Constitution. Observing that perpetuity is implied in the fundamental law of all national governments, Lincoln declared that in contemplation of the Constitution and "universal law," "the Union of these States is perpetual." In discussing the origin of the Union, he said the United States was "a government proper," not an association of states in the nature of a contract. The implication was that it was made by "the American people," whom in his discussion of his duties as chief executive Lincoln referred to as "my rightful masters." From this analysis it followed that no state, merely upon its own volition, "can lawfully get out of the Union." Lincoln asserted: ". . . *resolves* and *ordinances* to that effect are legally void; and . . . acts of violence, within any State or States, against the authority of the United States, are insurrectionary or revolutionary, according to circumstances." He concluded that "in view of the Constitution and the laws, the Union is unbroken."

President Lincoln next considered the South's grievances and the problem of how to resolve constitutional controversies in a constitutional republic. He granted that if a majority should deprive a minority of any clearly written constitutional right, it would morally justify revolution. He asserted that Southerners had never been denied any right "plainly written in the Constitution." The problems of practical administration that produced the crisis in which the country now found itself concerned questions such as whether Congress could prohibit slavery in the territories, to which the Constitution gave no express answer. These questions in Lincoln's view were to be settled by the people according to the principles and institutions of democratic politics. Indirectly referring to the *Dred Scott* case, he observed that while the decisions of the Supreme Court were entitled to high respect and consideration by the other departments of the government, "the policy of the government, upon vital questions, affecting the whole people," could not properly "be irrevocably fixed by the decisions of the Supreme Court." Were that to occur, "the people will have ceased to be their own rulers, having, to that extent, practically resigned their government into the hands of that eminent tribunal."

Many constitutional controversies therefore had to be dealt with in the forum of democratic politics, in presidential and congressional elections that would identify key constitutional principles and interpretations and translate those constitutional views into public policy through legislation. Returning to fundamentals, Lincoln said that where there were democratic elections, there were majorities and minorities. As was always the case in a democracy, so in the present crisis: "If the minority will not acquiesce, the majority must, or the government must cease. There is no other alternative; for continuing the government, is acquiescence on one side or the other." Lincoln believed majority rule was the superior principle. If the minority, refusing to acquiesce, carried its protest to the point of secession, it established a precedent and a practice the central idea of which is "the essence of anarchy." Minority rule, in other words, inherently promoted division and ruin. In contrast, Lincoln asserted the republican principle. He declared: "A majority, held in restraint by constitutional checks and limitations, and always changing easily, with deliberate changes of popular opinions and sentiments, is the only true sovereign of a free people."

The plain implication of Lincoln's analysis was that the new administration would uphold not only the promise contained in the Republican platform to maintain the right of each state "to order and control its own domestic institutions," to which he expressly referred, but also the promise to oppose the spread of slavery into the territories. As for the immediate conflict between the seven deep South states and the Union, Lincoln said he would fulfill his constitutional duty to take care that the laws be executed in all the states. This did not necessarily entail "bloodshed and violence," and he said "there shall be none, unless it be forced upon the national authority." The president would use force to collect duties and imposts, and to hold, occupy, and possess the property and places belonging to the government. Beyond this, Lincoln said there would be no invasion or use of force "against, or among the people anywhere." Striking a conciliatory note, he announced moreover that he would not do all that strict legal right entitled him to do in the way of upholding federal authority. Where hostility to the United States was so great as to prevent local citizens from holding office, for example, Lincoln stated that he would not appoint "obnoxious strangers." That would be "irritating" and impracticable, and he would rather "forego for the time being the uses of such offices." Similarly Lincoln said that the mails would be delivered, "unless repelled."

The new president thus took a position that was at once firm and conciliatory. Above all he saw clearly what Buchanan had not seen—that coercion of a seceding state was technically unnecessary and irrelevant, and that the proper answer to secession was the coercion of individuals resisting federal authority. Lincoln went on to warn the South to consider well the possible disadvantages involved in resorting to the undoubted right of revolution. Successful secession would solve none of the South's existing problems relating to the North and the Union; the same problems would exist after secession as before. He ended with an attempt to stir southern sentiment and loyalty for the Union. "The mystic chords of memory stretching from every battlefield and patriot grave to every living heart and hearthstone all over this broad land, will yet swell the chorus of the Union when again touched, as surely they will be, by the better angels of our nature."

Lincoln never wavered in the policy toward secession announced in his inaugural address. He did, however, proceed with great caution in its application. He desired above all else to avoid the charge of deliberately waging war upon the South. Moreover, he believed that a policy of caution might hold the states of the upper South in the Union, while the rash application of force would make their secession certain. The Virginia Unionists, in particular, were pleading with him to make no move, lest it precipitate their state's secession.

The issue of federal authority in the South very shortly focused upon Fort Sumter, in Charleston Harbor. Although the Confederates had taken over nearly all other federal properties, Buchanan had refused to surrender Sumter, and Lincoln continued this policy. When Lincoln notified the governor of South Carolina of his intention to replenish the fort's supplies, Confederate military officials replied, on April 12, 1861, with an attack on the fort. The bombardment ended the agonizing interim between secession and war. Four more states, Virginia, Tennessee, Arkansas, and North Carolina, shortly seceded. Lincoln called for troops to suppress the "rebellion," and the Civil War had begun.

Lincoln's policy before and after his inaugural has been severely criticized by certain historians, who charge him with partial responsibility for the coming of secession and war. First, they assert, Lincoln's coldness toward the Crittenden Compromise and his general unwillingness to extend to the South any assurances on the territorial question inspired the remaining six states in the lower South to follow South Carolina out of the Union. Second, Lincoln's critics contend that the policy set forth in his inaugural address made war and further secession inevitable.

It is highly probable that the attitude of Lincoln and other Republican leaders toward the South after November 1860 strengthened the hand of the secessionists and thereby contributed to disunion. When the Republicans confined their assurances to a promise not to interfere with slavery in the southern states, the secessionists were enabled to argue that the forthcoming administration would ignore southern constitutional rights in the territories as enunciated in the *Dred Scott* case. Since the Republicans were willing to treat one set of constitutional rights in so cavalier a manner, the secessionists said, what assurance was there that a Republican administration might not ultimately attack slavery within the states themselves?

Behind the concern with Lincoln's responsibility for the war lies the more complex question of the North's reasons for resisting secession. Implicit in the criticism of Lincoln is the view that war is not justified, especially not a war for mere nationalism. But while Northerners opposed secession out of a drive for national self-preservation, it was a particular kind of nationalism, possessing a distinct political character, that sustained them. From the founding of the nation, American nationality was defined with reference to republican self-government and citizenship. Moreover, the Union government was not a unitary, centralized state, but a federal republic that permitted substantial local autonomy. In resisting secession, therefore, Northerners defended republican self-government, identifying it with the Union as the basis of American nationality. Criticism of Lincoln's role rests on the further assumption that slavery would eventually have been abolished by peaceful means, or been transformed into a form of free labor. This is a purely speculative assumption that rests on none of the historical evidence concerning the nature of American Negro slavery in the context of the constitutional system.

Northerners also resisted secession as a threat to constitutionalism. Here continuity is evident between antebellum struggles and the wartime crisis. For among the reasons for opposing slavery was its contradiction not only of the principles of equality and consent, but also of constitutionalism and the rule of law. Congressional gag rules, the mobbing of abolitionist speakers, interference with the mails and the denial of free speech in the South, fugitive slave recaptures that abrogated free states' due process of law—all were taken as illustrating in northern eyes the lawless, coercive, and anticonstitutional tendencies encouraged by the imperious rule of the slave power. Secession escalated this lawlessness into open repudiation of the rule of law. It was, as Lincoln said in his inaugural address, "the essence of anarchy" and an unjustified revolution against constitutional government. In opposing secession, therefore, Republicans were defending the peaceful methods of constitutional politics.

After secession and the assault on Fort Sumter, the preeminent issue in American politics shifted from the future of slavery in the American republic to the preservation of the Union and the Constitution. Ambiguous by design, combining elements both of a confederation expressing the size and diversity of the American people and of a unitary government expressing their shared values, the federal republic would receive clearer constitutional definition in the trial of civil war.

SIXTEEN

The Civil War

THE CIVIL WAR WAS A CONSTITUTIONAL CRISIS of the most profound sort, for it called into question not only the existence of the Union, but also constitutionalism and the rule of law. Northern protest against the illegality of secession notwithstanding, the withdrawal of the southern states followed by the attack on Fort Sumter raised anew, after three-quarters of a century, the problem of continental political organization. The decentralized Union, part confederation and part unitary government, might be restored to its antebellum condition; a centralized, consolidated Union might emerge from the war; should the South prevail, two or more independent confederations of states might be the result. Equally uncertain was the continuation of constitutional politics. Although war was anticipated by the Constitution, fratricidal, civil war was not. Born of deep-seated cultural and social differences, the conflict that began in 1861 generated enormous pressure to set aside the methods of constitutionalism in favor of arbitrary rule.

The first constitutional issue presented by the outbreak of hostilities was the adequacy of the Constitution in time of war. Many Unionists thought the war abrogated the Constitution in all matters related to the suppression of the rebellion, and made available the rules of warfare under international law. Most Northerners believed, however, that although wartime adjustments would be necessary, constitutional law must continue to provide the institutional and legal setting in which the struggle should be carried on. No categorical shift to an all-war footing, requiring the suspension of constitutional procedures and rules, took place.

Believing the Constitution adequate, Americans throughout the Civil War and Reconstruction frequently clung to settled political and governmental habits. Yet one of the sources of strength in the constitutional system, and a principal reason why it was perceived as adequate, was the flexibility and responsiveness of existing constitutional institutions. Of these none was more important than the executive power, now wielded by a Republican president

committed to the preservation of the Union and willing to employ the resources of his office to defend the Constitution. The first clear evidence of the
adequacy of the Constitution—startling for the contrast it offered to the Buchanan administration—was Lincoln's decisive direction of the government
after the attack on Fort Sumter.

Lincoln and the Constitution

The period between November 1860 and April 1861 witnessed the rapid
disintegration of national authority, the spectacular spread of secession, and
the founding of the Confederate States of America. Never before or since has
the United States government under the Constitution been so near total collapse. Despite this grave situation Congress adjourned on March 4 and most
members went home. Under such foreboding circumstances the awesome
responsibility for saving the nation fell upon the new and inexperienced president, fresh from the prairies of Illinois. Lincoln surprised his enemies and
detractors, and pleased his friends, by responding to the attack on Fort Sumter
with imagination and vigor. Unlike many of his contemporaries, Lincoln
believed that the Constitution was adequate to the supreme test of self-preservation, and he acted accordingly.

Neither the nature nor the location of the war power was established
beyond debate by the Constitution. Although Unionists firmly believed that
the national government possessed full powers to wage war successfully, they
differed sharply among themselves over the relative authority of Congress and
the president in the exercise of these powers. The Constitution specifically
empowers Congress to declare war, to raise and support armies, to maintain
a navy, and to provide for the government and the regulation of the land and
naval forces, including militia employed in the United States service. The
president is constituted the commander in chief of the national military forces
and is vested with the full executive power of the government. Clashes between
Congress and president during the War of 1812 and the Mexican War over the
exercise of war powers had been neither serious nor conclusive in results. In
this respect the Civil War was to be vastly different.

On April 15, immediately after the attack on Fort Sumter, Lincoln took
action that extended the powers of the executive beyond their traditional
limits. His first action was to call for 75,000 volunteers to suppress the insurrection. He also summoned Congress into extraordinary session but set the
convening date far ahead to July 4. His failure to convene Congress immediately to provide additional legislation to cope with the grave national crisis
defies conclusive explanation. His wish that members of Congress should
acquaint themselves with the public temper before convening certainly did not
justify the delay of eighty days. Undoubtedly Lincoln, like most Northerners,
failed to realize how effectively the secessionists had overpowered the Union-

ists in the lower South, and hence he seriously underestimated the task of restoring national authority. Perhaps he also thought the current states'-rights doctrines had so undermined Congress's power to cope with the emergency that the Union would have to be saved by some as yet largely untested source of national authority. This he found in the presidential oath and in the office of commander in chief.

Accordingly, Lincoln proceeded rapidly to prepare the nation for war without either aid or new authority from Congress. He not only determined the existence of rebellion and called forth the militia to suppress it, but he also proclaimed a blockade of the ports of the rebel states, an act equivalent legally to a declaration of war. Realizing soon that such steps were inadequate for the emergency, on May 3 he called for 42,034 United States volunteers to serve for three years, and he actually received a much larger number. He also directed that large additions be made to the regular army and to the navy. He had $2 million paid out of the federal Treasury, and he pledged the government's credit for the unprecedented sum of a quarter of a billion dollars, all without statutory authority. He had the privilege of the writ of habeas corpus suspended in certain places and ordered the arrest and military detention of citizens who were represented to him as being engaged in or contemplating "treasonable practices."

When Congress met in special session in July 1861, Lincoln justified his actions in a penetrating analysis of the constitutional questions involved and the purpose of the war. The fundamental issue, embracing not simply the fate of the United States but also "the whole family of man," was "whether a constitutional republic, or a democracy," could maintain its territorial integrity against domestic foes. More broadly, Lincoln said the question was whether a discontented minority could "break up their Government, and thus practically put an end to free government upon the earth." "Is there, in all republics," he asked, "this inherent, and fatal weakness?" "Must a government, of necessity, be too *strong* for the liberties of its own people, or too *weak* to maintain its own existence?" This analysis left no choice, Lincoln stated, "but to call out the war power of the Government; and so to resist force, employed for its destruction, by force, for its preservation."

Lincoln explained that the measures adopted after the attack on Fort Sumter, "whether strictly legal or not, were ventured upon, under what appeared to be a popular demand, and a public necessity." Extraordinary though the actions were, the president believed that "nothing has been done beyond the constitutional competency of Congress," and he trusted that Congress would ratify the steps taken. Lincoln discussed in greater detail the suspension of the writ of habeas corpus. Noting criticism of this action as illegal, Lincoln defended it as consistent with his constitutional duty to enforce the laws. Pointing to the general resistance to all law enforcement in the southern states, he asked: ". . . are all the laws, *but one,* to go unexecuted, and the government itself go to pieces, lest that one be violated?" To allow that to happen would ·

break the official oath, and for the sake of a law that was "made in such tenderness of the citizen's liberty, that practically, it relieves more of the guilty, than of the innocent."

The argument has been made that Lincoln conceded the illegality of his emergency actions, believing them justified outside the Constitution by the necessity of preserving the government. The argument is erroneous because Lincoln in fact denied that any law was violated. He pointed out that the Constitution authorizes the suspension of the privilege of the writ of habeas corpus when the public safety requires it, but is silent as to which branch of the government can suspend the writ. Lincoln reasoned that since the provision was made for an emergency, the framers of the Constitution could not have intended that only Congress can suspend it. In a message to Congress in 1862 Lincoln commented further on his actions at the start of the war. "It became necessary for me to choose," he wrote, "whether, using only the existing means, agencies, and processes which Congress had provided, I should let the government fall at once into ruin, or whether, availing myself of the broader powers conferred by the Constitution in cases of insurrection, I would make an effort to save it with all its blessings for the present age and for posterity." Choosing the latter course, he said he took measures "some of which were without any authority of law." But "the government was saved from overthrow," in accordance with constitutional design and intention, and on the basis of constitutional powers. The action thus was constitutionally lawful.

Lincoln was neither a constitutional dictator, as some sympathetic scholars have depicted him, nor an unconstitutional dictator, as his detractors from the Civil War to the present have charged. The assertion is baseless in either case because the Constitution provides necessary emergency power, which Lincoln exercised under procedures and institutions for enforcing accountability to the people and to other branches of government that functioned throughout the Civil War. Lincoln was fully aware of the political and constitutional dimensions of the problem. Referring to the necessity of action by the executive to defend the public safety, he said: "If he uses the power justly, the people will probably justify him; if he abuses it, he is in their hands, to be dealt with by all the modes they have reserved to themselves in the constitution." Lincoln understood that the Constitution provides emergency power, and that the statesmanship of presidents who exercise this power will always be controversial. His reference to the people's reserved powers under the Constitution explains why "dictatorship" is an inapt description of American government in times of crisis. The text and forms of the Constitution—most especially the separation of powers—make it possible and indeed virtually assured that political criticism will be brought to bear by coordinate institutions as a restraint on emergency power. The American Constitution does not provide for the kind of unlimited, absolute power implied in the concept of dictatorship, whether constitutional or otherwise.

The great majority of the members of Congress—those from the Confederate states having withdrawn or having been expelled—approved the president's course, but they divided sharply over the constitutional justification of his actions. Intermittently throughout the special session of 1861 the Senate debated a proposed joint resolution which enumerated, approved, and validated the president's extraordinary acts, proclamations, and orders. The resolution had the support of the vast majority of Republicans, including some who assumed that certain of the president's acts were illegal when performed. Other Republicans, while approving the president's course, questioned the proposed method of validating his suspension of the writ of habeas corpus and his proclamation of a blockade. Owing to this disagreement the resolution never came to a vote. Instead a less specific and less comprehensive validating clause was attached as a rider to an act to increase the pay of privates and on the last two days of the session was rushed through both houses, with only five Democratic senators from border slave states recorded in opposition. By this law all of the president's acts, proclamations, and orders respecting the army, navy, militia, and volunteers were approved and "in all respects legalized and made valid, to the same intent and with the same effect as if they had been issued and done under the previous express authority and direction of the Congress." This congressional ratification of part of the president's extraordinary acts left the blockade and the suspension of the privilege of habeas corpus resting entirely upon presidential authority.

The measured congressional endorsement of Lincoln's crisis management reflected institutional jealousy more than political differences. By the winter of 1861 political disagreement over policy toward slavery was noticeable, but constitutional rivalry continued to provide the principal basis for congressional actions in relation to the conduct of the war. On numerous issues debate occurred over the relative authority of the president and Congress in the exercise of war powers under the Constitution. Conservative Republicans contended that the rights of war were executive, not legislative, and that questions of military necessity, by their very nature, must be decided by military commanders acting under the authority of the president as commander in chief. The majority of Republicans held in contrast that Congress's power to declare war encompassed full belligerent rights against an enemy, and hence that Congress possessed complete powers of sovereignty in the conduct of war. To buttress this position they invoked the principles of civilian control of the military and legislative regulation of executive power. And they rested these principles in turn on a theory of the separation of powers that gave Congress a decisive role in the constitutional system.

Constitutional orthodoxy since the founding of the government stipulated an admixture of separation of powers and checks and balances. The founding fathers believed that by separating the functions of government into three distinct branches, and by giving each branch a share of the power belonging to the others, consolidationist tendencies could be restrained. Civil War

Republicans, however, returned to an earlier theory of the separation of powers that, by ignoring or deemphasizing checks and balances, made the lawmaking power the center of the government. In effect it denied a legislative role
to the executive. Republican congressmen argued that the objects and duration
of the war were proper subjects of legislation. Congress did not have tactical,
battlefield authority, but it could, under the lawmaking authority that the
Constitution entrusted to it, control the conduct of the war through military
legislation as well as through confiscation and emancipation measures. "Only
in the manner and in the mode we may prescribe by law," said Senator John
Sherman of Ohio, could the president conduct the war. Senator Jacob Howard
of Michigan declared: "It is idle to talk of a war-making power independent
of the law-making power." In a pre-bureaucratic age when legislatures were
ascendant, and when their authority was enhanced by close identification with
the people, Congress presented a formidable challenge to executive power.

In December 1861 Congress created its own version of crisis government
in the Joint Committee on the Conduct of the War. By no means the result
of a radical cabal, the creation of the committee expressed a general legislative
intention to restrain executive power and affirm civilian control of the military.
Military defeat, resentment against the West Point officer class, and a desire
to promote anti-slavery purposes spurred the formation of the committee. In
conducting numerous investigations and publishing voluminous reports of its
findings, the committee was severely critical of Democrats and conservative
generals. Plainly, it tried to steer military policy in an anti-slavery direction,
and occasionally its criticism was excessive and unwarranted. Yet considering
that the subject of war powers lacked precise definition and that no model
existed on which to pattern congressional-executive relations in an emergency
of this sort, the committee was justified in following the well-established practice of legislative investigation of military campaigns. The Joint Committee
played a less important role in military affairs after Lincoln reorganized the
Union command in 1864. On the whole it facilitated executive-legislative
cooperation and strengthened the Union's crisis government.

The Supreme Court, like Congress, was divided over the constitutionality
of Lincoln's assumption of broad war powers, but a majority of the justices
upheld his position. In the *Prize Cases* (1863) Justice Robert Grier declared
for the majority that, although the president did not have power to initiate war,
when it was begun by insurrection he was "bound to accept the challenge
without waiting for any special legislative authority." Grier concluded:

Whether the President in fulfilling his duties, as Commander-in-Chief, in suppressing
an insurrection, has met with such armed hostile resistance, and a civil war of such
alarming proportions as will compel him to accord to them the character of belligerents,
is a question to be decided by him, and this court must be governed by the decisions
and acts of the Political Department of the government to which this power was

intrusted. "He must determine what degree of force the crisis dem. tion of blockade is, itself, official and conclusive evidence to the c war existed which demanded and authorized a recourse to such a m circumstances peculiar to the case.

A minority of four justices insisted that the basic war power be Congress and not to the president. Justice Samuel Nelson summar.   .e minority position when he declared:

The President does not possess the power under Constitution to declare war or recognize its existence within the meaning of the law of nations, which carries with it
belligerent rights, and thus change the country and all its citizens from a state of peace
to a state of war; that this power belongs exclusively to the Congress of the United
States and, consequently, that the President had no power to set on foot a blockade
under the law of nations.

Under these circumstances President Lincoln continued to formulate as well as to execute most of the essential war policies. In 1862 the War Department commissioned Professor Francis Lieber, a German immigrant and an authority on international law, to codify for the first time in America the rules and regulations for the conduct of armies in the field. The result, General Orders No. 100, was promulgated in April 1863 as the laws of war for the Union armies. All this was done without congressional authorization, despite the fact that the Constitution specifically grants this power and responsibility to Congress. On the other hand, Congress on July 17, 1862, did make a thorough revision of the Articles for the Government of the Navy. Both sets of regulations, extensively revised, continued to be used through World War II.

In such other important fields as emancipation, reconstruction, and the impairment of civil rights, the president largely determined governmental policy, either in the absence of congressional action or in virtual disregard of it. In September 1862 he disregarded the emancipation section of the Second Confiscation Act and based his preliminary Emancipation Proclamation upon his power as commander in chief. In December 1863 he merely announced to the new Congress his own reconstruction program, and when Congress formulated a sterner plan in the Wade-Davis bill, he killed it with a pocket veto.[1]

For almost two years after the outbreak of hostilities Lincoln continued to suspend the habeas corpus privilege on his own authority. Both Republicans and Democrats repeatedly challenged his constitutional authority on the ground that the clause of the Constitution authorizing suspension was in Article I, Section 9, which deals with the powers of Congress and not those of the president. Nevertheless, in September 1862 he issued a proclamation

---

1. See below, p. 322.

subjecting broad categories of "disloyal" persons to martial law and suspending the privilege of habeas corpus in all cases involving such persons.

At its next session Congress, on March 3, 1863, finally passed the Habeas Corpus Act, by which the president, during the rebellion, was "authorized to suspend" the privilege of the writ in all cases in which he thought the public safety might require it. The phraseology was intentionally ambiguous, designed to win the support of those who believed that Congress was recognizing an existing presidential power as well as of those who believed that Congress was thereby conferring the power upon the president. Lincoln did not issue a fresh proclamation invoking this new authority until six months later, nor did the administration later materially alter its policy in making arbitrary arrests.

Although the Supreme Court never rendered a decision directly involving the location of the suspending powers, in the *Prize Cases* it did give indirect approval to the president's action in suspending the habeas corpus privilege. The suspension of the writ was not directly involved, but the Court held that when war was forced upon the United States, the president was obligated to take all appropriate steps to meet it "without waiting for any special legislative authority."

In nonmilitary matters Lincoln assumed an attitude of deference toward Congress that contributed to the postwar weakening of the presidency. Yet virtually single-handedly at the beginning of the war he discovered within the confines of the Constitution the power of emergency rule that permanently altered the presidential office. In an unprecedented situation he used the war power in unprecedented ways to affect not merely military but also civil and political affairs. Although the republican civic tradition recognized the need for emergency dictatorship, the founding fathers made no express provision for emergency government other than to anticipate the suspension of the writ of habeas corpus. One of Lincoln's accomplishments was to constitutionalize the doctrine of emergency prerogative that had arisen since the start of the government.

The Legal Nature of the War

Although it was hardly an issue in the decision to meet the attack on Fort Sumter, once hostilities began it was necessary to deal with the constitutional question of the legal nature of the war. Was the conflict basically an insurrection, a rebellion, or an international war? This was an important question, since a variety of legal rights and responsibilities hinged upon the answer. An insurrection is legally construed to be an organized and armed uprising for public political purposes; it may seek to overthrow the government, or it may seek merely to suppress certain laws or to alter administrative practice. A rebellion in general is considered to have a much more highly developed political and military organization than an insurrection; in international law it conveys belligerent status. Generally, such belligerent status implies that the belligerent government is attempting by war to free itself from the jurisdiction of the parent state, that it has an organized *de facto* government, that it is in control of at least some territory, and that it has sufficient proportions to render the issue of the conflict in doubt. An international war, on the other hand, is one between two or more independent states who are recognized members of the family of nations.

In international law the rights of parties to an armed conflict vary greatly with their status. Insurgents have a very limited status; they are not mere pirates or bandits, but their activities do not constitute "war" in the *de jure* sense, and they cannot claim against neutrals the privileges of the laws of war. A full rebellion, on the other hand, is a "war" so far as international law is concerned and the rebel government possesses all the belligerent rights of a fully recognized international state, toward both neutrals and the parent state. Needless to say, a parent state may attempt by force to suppress either an insurrection or a rebellion. In domestic law rebels may be criminals in the eyes of the parent state, and answerable to its courts if their movement fails. Thus under the United States Constitution insurrection and rebellion constitute treason, for which the laws provide severe penalties.

The southern secessionists took the position that the armed conflict was an international war between the United States and the Confederate States of America. The Confederates believed that secession had been constitutional and that they had not only a *de facto* government entitled to full belligerent rights but also a *de jure* government whose independence and sovereignty should be recognized by foreign powers. In their hope of winning the war the Southerners counted heavily upon the aid and the intervention of foreign nations and they were bitterly disappointed when little aid was forthcoming. Even after the collapse of the Confederacy all true Southerners held that the struggle had been a "War between the States."

The official position of the Union government was that secession was a constitutional impossibility and nullity, and hence that the so-called Confederates were engaged in an insurrection against their lawful government. When the Confederates fired upon Fort Sumter, President Lincoln proclaimed on April 15, 1861, that the execution of federal laws was being obstructed "by combinations too powerful to be suppressed by the ordinary course of judicial proceedings." Therefore, he called for militia to suppress the insurrection, in much the same way that Washington had done in the Whisky Rebellion of 1794. Both Congress and the Supreme Court later supported Lincoln's theory of the war, even though the war attained enormous proportions.

In harmony with this insurrection theory the Union government throughout the war was meticulously careful to avoid any act that even suggested official recognition of the Confederacy as a *de jure* independent state. At first the United States attempted to deny that the Confederacy possessed even belligerent status. Thus in 1861 the State Department objected strongly to foreign powers granting belligerent rights to the Confederacy. Throughout the war the Lincoln administration maintained that no peace terms could be considered unless they were premised upon the legal nonexistence of the Confederacy and the complete submission of the "rebels" to Union authority. In theory Union spokesmen commonly insisted that they were dealing only with the "pretended government" of the "so-called Confederate States of America."

In practice, however, the Union government was very soon impelled to concede belligerent rights to the Confederates. The impotency of Buchanan's administration had permitted southern resistance to federal authority to become too extensive and powerful to be treated as mere insurrection. At the outbreak of hostilities Lincoln proclaimed a blockade of southern ports, an act that according to international law virtually recognized the belligerency of the Confederacy. Soon afterward the Lincoln administration abandoned its declared purpose of treating Confederate seamen as pirates. Threats of reprisal upon captured Unionists as well as humanitarian considerations induced the government to treat all captives as prisoners of war.

After initial protests the United States acquiesced in the recognition by foreign nations of the belligerent status of the Confederate government. In short, practical considerations led the Union government to treat the Confederates as belligerents, even though it still refused to recognize their belligerency in any direct, formal manner.

Congress agreed fully with the president that the United States could claim against the Confederates both sovereign rights and those rights arising out of the international law of war. This double status greatly influenced federal laws and policies. For example, Congress enacted a new treason law providing severe punishment for all those found guilty of supporting the rebellion, while other congressional acts held such persons to be public enemies.

The Supreme Court also sustained this dual status for the Confederates. In this connection the most important decision was in the *Prize Cases,* decided in March 1863, involving the legality of the capture of neutral ships and cargoes. These seizures occurred soon after Lincoln had issued his proclamations of blockade of Confederate ports on April 19 and 27, 1861, and before Congress had formally recognized the existence of war. In upholding the legality of the captures, Justice Robert Grier declared for the Court that it would and must accept the president's decision that the armed insurgents had become so formidable by April 19, 1861, that they must be accorded belligerent status. "A civil war," he asserted, "is never solemnly declared; it becomes such by its accidents—the number, power, and organization of the persons who originate and carry it on. . . . It is not the less a civil war, with belligerent parties in hostile array, because it may be called an 'insurrection' by one side, and the insurgents be considered as rebels and traitors." Therefore, the Court held that as far as foreign nationals were concerned the conflict was a civil war, fought according to the laws of nations, with both sides possessed of belligerent rights and responsibilities. In subsequent decisions the Court maintained the same position.

While the war from a military standpoint was between the belligerents, in constitutional theory the insurrection doctrine remained of great importance during both the war and the reconstruction period. Many war acts and words of the Unionists were based upon the assumption that they were fighting to suppress a gigantic insurrection, even though Union officials often spoke of the war as a rebellion. At the conclusion of the war no peace treaty was drawn up. Instead the subjugated Confederates threw themselves upon the mercy of the Union government, which thus was free to develop a reconstruction program premised upon the insurrection theory.

The Problem of Internal Security

The government's difficulty in determining the status of the Confederate foe had its parallel in the adoption of internal security measures to deal with opponents of the war. The constitutional issue raised here concerned the government's authority to impair civil liberties in wartime. This authority was problematic because of the prevailing Anglo-American concept of the rule of law—that the officers of government are always subject to the law and prohibited from exercising arbitrary authority over citizens. The peaceful conditions that had prevailed except for a few brief periods since the adoption of the Constitution had accustomed the American people to a policy of noninterference with civil rights by the federal government. There had been very few occasions for suspension of the habeas corpus privilege, censorship of the press, or the establishment of martial law. There was in America no tradition or important precedent for military rule or summary procedure even for a war emergency.

At one level the internal security problem was simple and clear-cut: The Constitution defined and limited treason to levying war against the United States or adhering to its enemies and giving them aid and comfort. Thus any participation in insurrection or rebellion against the federal government constituted treason. Congress was authorized to declare the punishment of treason, but no attainder of treason should work corruption of blood or forfeiture except during the life of the person attainted. Therefore, the only constitutional method of procedure against traitors was by judicial conviction under treason statutes passed by Congress. Accordingly, in 1790 Congress had passed a law against treason, providing the death penalty for anyone convicted. Though no one had ever been executed for treason against the United States, this law was still operative in 1861.

The nature and scope of the Civil War soon demonstrated the practical impossibility of enforcing the existing treason law against Confederates. Sev-

eral million southern people were adhering to the "rebellion," while hundreds
of thousands of them were actually bearing arms against the United States. As
explained above, for practical and humanitarian reasons the captured soldiers
and sailors had to be treated as prisoners of war. Few civilian Confederates
were captured during the early phases of the war, and with sympathetic
witnesses and juries the possibilities of conviction for treason seemed remote
even where the federal courts were open. Moreover, many persons in the
border states and in the North were engaging in disloyal activities that did not
amount to full treason. These activities were designed to bring about Union
defeat and included spying, sabotage, recruiting for the enemy, stealing military supplies for potential Confederate invasions of the North, carrying on
treasonable correspondence, plotting to split the remaining Union states, and
otherwise aiding the enemy. Other persons professed loyalty to the Union but
openly opposed the government's policy of suppressing the rebellion by complete subjugation of the Confederacy. Their activities were confined to discouraging enlistments, aiding desertion, circulating disloyal literature, and
denouncing the Lincoln administration.

Recognizing the complex nature of the internal security problem, Congress enacted special legislation to adapt the punishment of treason to the
emergency and to define as crimes disloyal acts that were less than treasonous.
The Seditious Conspiracy Act of July 31, 1861, the first such law to be adopted
since the Sedition Act of 1798, provided a heavy fine and imprisonment for
anyone convicted of conspiring to overthrow the United States government,
or to levy war against the United States, or to oppose by force the authority
of the government, or to interfere forcibly with the execution of federal laws,
or to seize property of the United States. Technically, this act dealt with
conspiracy and not with treason. Critics of the measure were partly right in
contending that it nullified existing constitutional law prohibiting "constructive treason." However, they overlooked the fact that new emergencies often
call for new statutes or new interpretations of laws.

In July 1862 Congress passed a more comprehensive war measure, the
Second Confiscation Act. For reasons of political compromise the act brought
together three distinct subjects—treason, confiscation, and emancipation—
and proposed to deal with them in discrete ways. The treason sections were
the work of conservative Republicans who, insisting on strict legal orthodoxy,
proposed to punish leading rebels only after trial and conviction under criminal law procedures. This part of the 1862 law declared the penalty for treason
to be either death or heavy fine and imprisonment at the discretion of a court.
It also declared engaging in or aiding rebellion against the United States to be
distinct from the crime of treason, with a separate penalty of fine and imprisonment. Finally, the act provided for freeing the slaves of anyone convicted of
either treason or rebellion.

As federal judicial authority existed nowhere in the South, the act of July
1862 as a punishment for treason and rebellion was intended to serve a postwar

rather than a wartime purpose. Accordingly, in its treason and rebellion sections it employed the ordinary legislative power of the government over individual citizens, rather than the war power under international law. The administration, therefore, did not contradict congressional purpose in pursuing, as it did, a cautious and lenient policy of enforcement. Grand juries brought numerous indictments for treason, especially in the border states, but few cases were prosecuted to completion. Instead, the district attorney usually continued the indictment from one term of court to another until eventually the case was dismissed. It is significant that despite the vast extent of rebellion, the government did not execute a single person for treason or even carry out completely a sentence of fine or imprisonment. This policy of leniency continued after the war, under a different president and in very different political circumstances. Even Jefferson Davis, former president of the Confederacy, escaped official punishment, although his treason case dragged through the federal courts for more than three years.

Unable to enforce treason and rebellion statutes in the South, the administration chose not to apply them rigorously in the North. Instead it adopted an internal security policy of dealing with suspected persons through military arrests and the suspension of the privilege of habeas corpus. In the early part of the war this policy was restricted to definite localities specified in presidential proclamations. Its operation was entrusted to the State Department, which directed arrests through an elaborate secret service as well as through federal marshals and military authorities. The national situation was very critical at the time, and hundreds of arrests were made. Prisoners were not told why they were arrested, and often the authorities acted without sufficient investigation or evidence to provide a reasonable basis for definite charges. With the habeas corpus privilege suspended, prisoners were held without legal action until the emergency which had led to their arrest had passed. Judges often sought to secure the release of such prisoners, but provost marshals and other military officers were usually under orders to disregard judicial mandates and to resist the execution of writs. This procedure resulted in numerous conflicts between civil and military authorities, with the latter necessarily prevailing.

In 1862 the administration both modified and extended its policy. In February the control of arbitrary arrests was transferred to the War Department, and the policy was mitigated by establishing a commission to provide for the examination and release of political prisoners. On September 24, however, the president issued a sweeping proclamation declaring that all persons discouraging enlistments, resisting the draft, or "guilty of any disloyal practice affording aid and comfort to rebels . . . shall be subject to martial law, and liable to trial and punishment by courts-martial or military commissions." Further, the habeas corpus privilege was suspended for all persons arrested or already imprisoned on such charges. Thereafter thousands of citizens suspected of disloyalty were summarily arrested and imprisoned in all parts of the country.

In the actual use of such extraordinary powers the Lincoln administration generally manifested considerable circumspection and leniency. The broad prerogatives assumed and announced in proclamations were not always exercised. Since arrests were often precautionary, designed to prevent violence or interference with military or other governmental activities, many prisoners were released within a short time. Those detained were usually treated without undue harshness.

Nevertheless, Lincoln's policy of suspending the privilege of the writ of habeas corpus encountered bitter opposition among Democrats. Leading the attack was Chief Justice Taney, who in *Ex parte Merryman* (1861), a case involving a Maryland secessionist arrested for destroying railroad bridges, tried unsuccessfully to prevent the president from withholding the writ in military emergencies. After Union officers ignored Taney's writ of habeas corpus ordering the release of Merryman, the chief justice, in the federal circuit court at Baltimore, delivered an opinion stating that Lincoln acted without warrant in suspending the writ, since only Congress could do so. Taney argued for exclusive congressional control from the fact that the habeas corpus clause occurs in Article I, Section 9, which deals with the legislative power. The president's only power where the rights of citizens are involved, said Taney, is to take care that the laws "be faithfully carried into execution as they are expounded and adjudged by the co-ordinate branch of the government, to which that duty is assigned by the Constitution." Instead of performing his constitutional duty of assisting the judiciary in enforcing its judgments, Taney asserted, the chief executive in this case had actually thrust aside the judicial authorities and substituted military government.

Lincoln's reply to Taney came in his July 4, 1861, special message to Congress. He justified the arrest and detention of individuals "dangerous to the public safety" on the ground that courts were incapable of dealing adequately with organized rebellion. As noted, he argued that since the Constitution permits suspension of the writ of habeas corpus during a rebellion and does not specify which branch of the government is to exercise the suspending power, the president in an emergency must be allowed to use his discretion in the matter. Later Lincoln emphasized the precautionary or preventive purpose of the arbitrary arrests, which were made "not so much for what has been done, as for what probably would be done."

In a more elaborate opinion Attorney General Edward Bates refuted Taney's contention that the president had violated his constitutional duty of executing the laws. The executive, he insisted, was not subordinate to the judiciary, but was one of three coordinate departments of government. Moreover, the president's oath to "preserve, protect, and defend the Constitution" makes it particularly his duty to put down a rebellion since the courts are too weak to do so. Bates cited *Martin* v. *Mott* (1827) to support the president's discretionary power in the manner of discharging his duty.[2] Therefore, if the

2. In this case, which arose out of the War of 1812, the Supreme Court upheld the president's right, under authority of Congress, to be the sole judge of the existence of those contingencies

president in case of rebellion or insurrection considers the suspension of the habeas corpus privilege necessary for the public safety, he may order it on his own authority.

The Habeas Corpus Act of 1863

Unwilling categorically to defer to executive authority on this important war-related issue, Congress in the Habeas Corpus Act of March 3, 1863, attempted to regularize and modify the president's control of political prisoners so that the authority of the courts would be respected without restricting too seriously the executive and military authorities. The Habeas Corpus Act served the additional purpose, insofar as doubt persisted, of legitimizing the government's internal security program. Under the statute the president was "authorized to suspend" the habeas corpus privilege, and military officers were relieved from the obligation to answer the writ. On the other hand, the secretaries of state and war were required to furnish lists of political prisoners to the federal courts, and if grand juries found no indictments against them, they were to be released upon taking the oath of allegiance. Thus to some extent congressional authority and regulations were substituted for executive authority, and judicial procedure rather than executive discretion was made the basis for the detention of prisoners.

The Habeas Corpus Act also contained indemnity sections which granted broad immunity to federal enforcement officers and extended the jurisdiction of federal courts at the expense of state judiciaries. These provisions were necessary because federal officers carrying out conscription, internal security, revenue, and emancipation policies had in numerous instances been the object of suits in northern state courts charging them with violation of state laws and infringement of the civil rights of private individuals. This litigation, which specified unlawful seizure, false arrest, assault and battery, and the like, could seriously impede Union war policies. A bridge was needed within the federal system by which federal officers detained or charged by states could be protected, in accordance with well-established common law principles. Accordingly, the act of March 1863 provided that any order made by or under the authority of the president should be a defense in all courts to any action or prosecution for any search, seizure, arrest, or imprisonment. Provision was also made for the removal of suits of this type from state to federal courts and for imposing a two-year limitation upon the initiation of such suits.

The Habeas Corpus Act in practice did not greatly alter internal procedures already in operation. For some time commissions appointed by the

specified in the Constitution upon which the militia might be called out. The Court held further that the president's decision was binding upon state authorities and that the state militia in federal service was subject to the authority of officers appointed by the president.

secretary of war had been reviewing cases of civilians detained on suspicion of disloyal actions and releasing those against whom there was insufficient evidence for civil or military prosecution. For this reason executive authorities were slow in furnishing the courts with lists of prisoners. Furthermore, in implementing the Habeas Corpus Act Judge Advocate General Joseph Holt ruled controversially that it did not apply to prisoners triable by military commissions. This ruling left the executive department without restraint in cases where martial law was instituted. But this was consistent with congressional policy as expressed in the Articles of War, which denied ordinary judicial process for civilians held for military offenses such as spying and sabotage. Thus, although release of political prisoners continued to be at the discretion of the War Department, the policy was in substantial accord with what members of Congress and the northern public regarded as procedurally fair and militarily effective.

The institution of martial law and the limited use of military tribunals for the trial of civilians in the loyal states represented the most serious departure from normal constitutional procedure in the government's internal security program. Since portions of all the border states were at various times during the war occupied by Confederate troops or hostile guerrillas, martial law was employed there as an essential means of military security. Moreover, disloyalty to the Union in these areas was so widespread and so violent that the president considered martial law necessary for the preservation of peace and order. Usually, martial law was applied in specified limited districts where the situation seemed most serious, but in July 1864 Lincoln put the whole state of Kentucky under martial law. At the time of Lee's invasion of Pennsylvania in 1863, the president, in response to the petitions of many citizens, proceeded to put that area under martial law.

In all these instances, however, actual interference with the civil authorities was generally held to a minimum, and the power over citizens entrusted to the military authorities was sparingly used. Political and judicial officers continued to function except as interruption was necessary for the military authorities to preserve order and punish military crimes. In short, the federal government made no effort to carry martial law beyond certain specified objectives considered necessary for the successful prosecution of the war.

More important to constitutional law was the actual trial and conviction of citizens before military tribunals. In regions under martial law military commissions could properly be used for the trial of civilians who had committed offenses of a military character, such as sniping or spying. The vast majority of cases brought before military commissions in the border states were of this general type, and many individuals were convicted and punished, sometimes severely, for such offenses. Little adverse criticism was made at that time, and little has been made since.

A great legal controversy arose, however, when citizens were subjected to military tribunals in regions remote from military operations and where the civil courts were unimpeded by the course of the war. This situation developed during 1863 and 1864, especially in Ohio, Indiana, and Illinois, where many Democrats were so opposed to the administration's new war policies that they were demanding a negotiated peace and obstructing the prosecution of the war.

The most famous wartime military tribunal case involved Clement L. Vallandigham, a former Democratic congressman from Ohio who in 1863 was placed under military arrest and tried by a military commission for a public speech bitterly denouncing the Lincoln administration. The commission found Vallandigham guilty of disloyal sentiments with the object of weakening the government. Subsequently, the case was carried to the Supreme Court, on the argument that the jurisdiction of a military commission did not extend to a citizen who was not a member of the military forces. In *Ex parte Vallandigham* (1864) the Supreme Court refused to review the case, declaring that its authority, derived from the Constitution and the Judiciary Act of 1789, did not extend to the proceedings of a military commission because the latter was not a court. The Supreme Court, said Justice James Wayne in the official opinion, "cannot without disregarding its frequent decisions and interpretation of the Constitution in respect to its judicial power, originate a writ of certiorari to review or pronounce any opinion upon the proceedings of a military commission." Neither in this case nor in any other during the war did the Court deny or even question officially the president's authority to establish military commissions for the trial of civilians in nonmilitary areas.

In every different political circumstances after the war the Supreme Court held in *Ex parte Milligan* (1866) that the military commission by which an Indiana citizen was tried and convicted for actual subversive activity was unlawful. The Court stated not only that the executive had violated the Habeas Corpus Act of 1863 by ignoring the requirement of indictment by a grand jury, but also that Congress lacked authority to institute military commissions to try civilians in areas remote from the theater of war where the courts were open. Politically, this case was important for reconstruction policy and will be discussed in that context.[3] Concerning its importance in the history of constitutional law, the judgment of the victors has prevailed. The Court's opinion in the *Milligan* case was not a realistic approach either in relation to the Civil War experience or in providing for a future contingency of a similar kind. There was ample ground for believing, as Lincoln did, that disloyalty in the North might become so violent, unless held in check by military authority, that it would materially bolster Confederate morale and thus jeopardize the Union cause, or at least prolong the war and bring about additional loss of life. Therefore, his policy of arbitrary arrests and military trials for suspected citizens was essentially precautionary and in case of civil war justifiable.

3. See below, pp. 337, 352.

Federal Centralization of Authority

Between 1801 and 1861 an irregular but considerable decentralization of constitutional and political authority had taken place in the United States. During these years population had increased rapidly and had spread over a vast area. The states had more than doubled in number, and their governments, rather than the federal government, had assumed most of the new governmental functions that had evolved. In general during this period all three branches of the federal government had interpreted federal powers somewhat narrowly, with the result that the people looked to the state governments rather than to Washington for the performance of many positive governmental services. Relatively little federal administrative machinery had been developed. States'-rights tendencies were strong in the free as well as the slave states. Consequently, in 1861 the loyal state governments assumed that they would play important roles in the prosecution of the war.

In 1861 and 1862 the governors and other state officials to a large degree took the lead in mobilizing the nation for war. They not only raised the militia called for initially by the president, but they also directed the recruiting of most of the regiments of federal volunteers. In addition the states often provided the troops with equipment, subsistence, and transportation. Such state governors as John A. Andrew of Massachusetts, Oliver P. Morton of Indiana, and Richard Yates of Illinois were more energetic and more efficient than Secretary of War Simon Cameron in mobilizing troops. Before Congress met in July 1861, more than a quarter of a million men had been mobilized, largely by state initiative.

Inevitably, friction and confusion arose between federal and state authorities in these military matters. Federal recruiting officers sometimes clashed with governors over the raising of troops and the appointing of officers. Early in the war some states actually competed with the War Department in the purchase of arms and equipment. The president had the unpleasant task of trying to placate conflicting parties and to coordinate their activities. This task was made somewhat easier by the fact that at the time practically all free-state governors were Republicans, but it was also made more difficult by the fact that the governors under the federal system are not constitutional subordinates of the president, even in the raising and control of troops. It was conflicting authority of this kind as well as the decline of volunteering which caused Congress and the administration eventually to turn to a national conscription policy.

A different type of controversy arose in April 1861 between the federal government and the border slave states, especially Kentucky and Maryland. Many people, perhaps a majority, in those states accepted the doctrine of state sovereignty, yet they wanted neither secession nor war. In Kentucky the governor emphatically refused to supply troops to the federal government and the state senate formally declared that the state would maintain an armed neutrality, neither severing connection with the Union nor taking up arms for either side. This attempt to take a middle position was not only impractical but also contrary to both the letter and the spirit of the Constitution. The power of neutrality is an integral part of the war-making power, which is specifically and necessarily assigned to the federal government.

At about the same time the state authorities of Maryland sought to prevent the passage of federal troops through the state on the way to the national capital. This action was flagrantly unconstitutional; for, as Marshall had pointed out in *McCulloch* v. *Maryland,* in matters which belong to the United States federal authority must be supreme and unimpeded by state interference. Within a brief time the Lincoln administration, by employing a waiting policy in Kentucky and a firm policy in Maryland, was able to maintain federal authority in both states and to secure a considerable degree of cooperation from state authorities.

Another case where national authority definitely won out over states' rights was in the partition of Virginia. The western portion of the state was geographically a part of the Ohio Valley, and for many years before 1861 the people there had disagreed politically and economically with the eastern Virginians. When the Virginia convention adopted an ordinance of secession, the westerners refused to be bound thereby, and in June 1861 organized a new Unionist or restored government for Virginia, which was recognized for most purposes by the federal government. This Unionist state government, meeting at Wheeling, authorized the western counties to frame a constitution for a new state of West Virginia; this, in turn, was ratified by the voters. Thus in an irregular manner the "state" of Virginia complied with the constitutional requirement of giving consent to the erection of a new state within its borders.

On December 31, 1862, Congress passed an act providing for the admission of West Virginia as a state as soon as it had provided for the gradual abolition of slavery. During the congressional debate on the subject the Republican majority took the position that the admission would aid in suppressing the rebellion, while conservative opponents contended that the real state of Virginia had not given its consent to partition. Although the cabinet also was divided over the constitutionality of the act, Lincoln reluctantly signed it, believing then, as he did throughout the war, that the determining consideration should be whether the measure aided or hampered the restoration of the Union. On June 20, 1863, West Virginia officially became a separate state.

The Supreme Court in *Virginia* v. *West Virginia* (1870) indirectly declared the process of separation to be constitutional by affirming the existence of "a valid agreement between the two States consented to by Congress." Thus did the federal government's policy of broad constitutional construction, in conjunction with what was virtually a revolution within a state, effect the partitioning of one of the oldest and largest states in the Union.

During 1862 Congress and the administration came to realize that more

vigorous assertion of federal authority was necessary for the effective prosecution of the war. Two years of unwarranted decentralization and reliance upon
state performance of certain war functions had proved unsatisfactory and may
have prolonged the war. Gradually and reluctantly, therefore, the federal
government adopted centralizing measures and policies. By 1863 it was exercising authority commensurate with that intended by the framers of the Constitution, having regained much that had been dissipated during two generations dominated by states'-rights doctrines and practices.

In order to finance the war the federal government had to resume definite
control of the important fields of currency and banking, which had been left
largely to the states since the 1830s. Between February 1862 and March 1863
Congress authorized the issuance of $450,000,000 in fiat money or greenbacks,
which were made legal tender for both public and private debts. Even more
significant was the enactment of the National Banking Act of February 25,
1863, with important modifications made by new laws in 1864 and 1865.
Although these measures did not create a centralized national bank like those
of 1791 and 1817, they did provide for an extensive system of national banking
institutions, which under federal supervision could issue bank notes based
largely upon United States bonds and guaranteed by the federal government.
The 1865 law, which levied a 10 percent tax on all state bank notes, soon had
the intended effect of driving these notes out of existence and leaving a uniform
national currency based fundamentally upon the credit of the United States.

After a lapse of some thirty years the federal government once more
assumed a prominent role in the field of internal improvements and transportation. In pursuance of an act of Congress, the president in May 1862 took
official possession of all railroads and directed that all railroad companies and
their employees hold themselves in readiness for the transportation of troops
and munitions at the order of military authorities. Only in a very few instances
did the government take more than nominal control of northern railroads, but
through this act it did obtain effective cooperation from the railroads. In the
South the federal government, through the military authorities, actually re-
paired and operated many miles of railroads.

Congress took steps also to sponsor the construction of new railroad lines.
In March 1863 a select committee of the House, in order to provide more
adequately for the transportation of military forces and supplies, recommended that the federal government charter a special railroad line between
Washington and New York to which the government would give its patronage
and over which it would enjoy priorities and have extensive powers of regulation. Constitutional and political opposition to the federal government taking
such a direct part in the railroad business, plus some effective lobbying by
competing railroad lines, prevented the enactment of the measure. However,
the Pacific Railroad Act of 1862, supplemented by another act in 1864, enabled
the federal government to charter two corporations to build a railroad from
Omaha to the Pacific and to grant them large tracts of land and extensive loans.

This action proved to be only the beginning of the active part that the government was to play in rail transportation after the Civil War.

In general, however, the federal government attempted little or no regulation of private enterprise. Congress encouraged great industrial and agricultural expansion by the enactment of increasingly high protective tariff rates and by paying high prices for food, clothing, munitions, and other military supplies. But there were no price ceilings, no rationing, and practically no governmental controls over agriculture, commerce, industry, or labor.

Compulsory Military Service

The gigantic military task of conquering the Confederacy forced the federal government to reexamine the place of military forces under the Constitution. Practically no one seriously questioned the traditional American principle that the military authority is always subject to ultimate civilian control. The Constitution, in Article I, Section 8, gave Congress blanket power "to raise and support armies" and to provide for calling forth, organizing, arming, disciplining, and governing the militia when employed in federal service. By law and precedent three forms of military organization were available in 1861: the regular army, United States volunteers called into service during emergencies for limited periods, and the militia, which was in a degree both a state and a federal organization. In the War of 1812 and the Mexican War all troops had been raised by voluntary recruiting, although in the earlier struggle conscription had been seriously considered by Congress.

In April 1861 Lincoln called for 75,000 militia under the law of 1795, but the great bulk of the army raised in 1861, and in fact throughout the war, consisted of federal volunteers. When the supply of volunteers seemed inadequate, Congress, in July 1862, enacted a new Militia Act, which provided that the militia should include all male citizens between the ages of eighteen and forty-five and authorized the president to issue regulations to cover any defects in state laws for employment of the militia. With no more specific basis than this provision, the president in August 1862 assigned quotas to the states and ordered a draft through the state governors to fill any unfilled quotas. Under this curious mixture of federal and state authority the first men were conscripted in 1862. The chief constitutional significance of this entire procedure lies in the small amount of statutory law considered necessary to transform the old obligation for militia duty into compulsory federal military service.

The president and Congress soon realized that the militia could not be made into an effective national army and on March 3, 1863, enacted a comprehensive conscription law. All able-bodied male citizens between twenty and forty-five, and foreigners who had declared their intention to become citizens, were "to constitute the national forces" and were declared liable for military service upon call by the president. No reference was made to the militia, and a complete federal system of enrollment and administration was established. Any person failing to report after due service of notice was to be considered a deserter, and any person convicted of resisting the draft or of aiding or encouraging the same was subject to fine and imprisonment.

Such a drastic departure from previous American experience was bound to encounter serious opposition on constitutional as well as political grounds. In regions where pro-southern sentiment was strong, resistance to the draft took place in various forms, and federal troops were sometimes needed for enforcement. The Conscription Act was repeatedly denounced as un-American and unconstitutional in Congress, in the courts, in the press, in the public forums, and on the streets. From New York, where violent antidraft riots raged for four days in July 1863, Governor Horatio Seymour wrote to the president, declaring bluntly that conscription was unconstitutional and requesting its suspension. Except for minor interruptions, however, the draft was applied when necessary to meet quotas.

The constitutionality of the Conscription Act never came before the Supreme Court, but it was challenged in some of the lower courts without decisive results. Of all the constitutional arguments in support of conscription perhaps the most forceful was made by the president himself. In legal logic that was reminiscent of John Marshall at his best, Lincoln declared:

It is the first instance, I believe, in which the power of Congress to do a thing has ever been questioned in a case when the power is given by the Constitution in express terms. . . .

The case simply is, the Constitution provides that the Congress shall have power to raise and support armies; and by this act the Congress has exercised the power to raise and support armies. This is the whole of it. It is a law made in literal pursuance of this part of the United States Constitution. . . . The Constitution gives Congress the power, but it does not prescribe the mode, or expressly declare who shall prescribe it. In such case Congress must prescribe the mode, or relinquish the power. There is no alternative. . . . If the Constitution had prescribed a mode, Congress could and must follow that mode; but, as it is, the mode necessarily goes to Congress, with the power expressly given. The power is given fully, completely, unconditionally. It is not a power to raise armies if State authorities consent; nor if the men to compose the armies are entirely willing; but it is a power to raise and support armies given to Congress by the Constitution without an if.

Opponents of conscription usually resorted to states'-rights and strict-construction arguments and emphasized the distinction between the militia and the army. Many believed with Chief Justice Taney that although both federal and state governments exercised sovereign powers over the same territory and the same people at the same time, each was altogether independent of the other within its own sphere of action. They argued that the militia was primarily a state institution, and, therefore, the extent to which the Conscription Act interfered with this state institution by bringing state militiamen and state civil officials within the draft constituted a violation of the Constitution.

The preponderance of logic as well as legal public opinion supported the constitutionality of conscription. The power to raise armies as well as the power to declare war are expressly given to Congress without qualification as to means, and conscription may reasonably be considered a "necessary and proper" means to "carry into effect" these powers. To restrict federal powers within the narrow limits proposed by draft opponents would in effect have denied the United States the assured power to suppress the rebellion.

Union War Aims

Ultimately, the task of readying the machinery of war yielded in importance to the question of the uses to which it was put. At the outset the purpose of the war from the northern point of view was obvious: to restore the Union and preserve the Constitution. Thus Lincoln in his special message to Congress of July 4, 1861, said the issue was whether the republic could maintain its territorial integrity. Dwelling at length on the illegality of secession, he argued the perpetuity of the Union and the indestructibility of the states. And after some hesitation caused by Democratic demands for a concise and extremely restrictive expression of war aims, Congress agreed with him. In July 1861 it adopted the Crittenden-Johnson Resolutions declaring that the war was waged not for any purpose of conquest or subjugation, but to preserve the Union and the states with their rights and institutions unimpaired.

The means chosen to fight the war, however, as congressmen who passed the Crittenden-Johnson Resolutions well knew, might also affect its purpose and results. This was evident from the start in discussions of confiscation and emancipation. Each of these actions could be proposed as an expedient war measure, yet, if thoroughly and rigorously applied, each could also produce not merely a restored but a constitutionally changed Union.

Confiscation of enemy property was an ancient war usage, and most legal authorities had maintained that international law sanctioned a nation's right to confiscate. Yet by 1861 Western nations had largely abandoned the practice. Moreover, the United States Constitution provided safeguards for citizens' property by prohibiting such devices as bills of attainder and deprivation of property without due process of law. Nevertheless, under the dual-status theory of the nature of the war confiscation became a major issue in northern politics.

One view of confiscation intended it to weaken the Confederacy by seizing rebel property through military means. It would shorten the war and make the rebels pay much of the cost. A second view held that the property of leading Confederates should be confiscated as a punishment for rebellion and a guarantee of security for the future, but that this result could only ensue after trial and conviction of individual Southerners for treason under the ordinary criminal law. As is apparent, this approach treated treason and confiscation together, as parts of the same legal process. A third view of confiscation, in the nature of a compromise between the first two, proposed to take enemy property under the war power, but to do so through the agency of federal courts. It was this approach that was embodied in the Confiscation Act of July 1862.

The act, as noted above, contained treason sections intended to punish individuals through *in personam* proceedings in national courts under federal criminal jurisdiction. The confiscation sections, based on international law and the "enemy" aspect of the dual-status doctrine, provided for *in rem* proceedings in federal courts against the property of Southerners as enemies. In other words, property would not be taken as a punishment against individuals guilty of treason, but, in a borrowing from admiralty and revenue law, as a condemnation of things in themselves, independent of the guilt of the owner. The act directed the president to seize the property of officials of the Confederate government and, after sixty days' warning, the property of all other persons supporting the rebellion. The government could obtain title to the property only by instituting proceedings against the forfeited property of persons engaging in rebellion, in federal district courts where the property was located.

Conservatives had reason to complain about the method employed in the Confiscation Act, for in effect it punished rebels by taking away their property without the criminal trial that proper constitutional procedure required in matters of treason. It contrasted with the First Confiscation Act of August 1861, a measure important mainly for its emancipation content, which, ignoring treason, declared the forfeiture of all property used for insurrectionary purposes. The act of 1862 also had the effect of confiscating the property of persons guilty of treason beyond their lifetime, or permanently, in violation of the constitutional stipulation that limited forfeiture of property as a punishment for treason to the life of the guilty party. Lincoln objected to the Confiscation Act for both of these reasons. He prepared a veto message, whereupon Congress, in an unusual maneuver, passed an explanatory joint resolution removing part of the president's objections. The resolution stated that the law was not to be construed as working "a forfeiture of the real estate of the offender beyond his natural life." Satisfied by this restriction, Lincoln signed the bill.

Although the Confiscation Act expressed a radical desire for more forceful prosecution of the war, it also showed the persistence of constitutional restraint. Most important in this respect was the requirement of judicial procedure for the seizure of property. Despite congressional rhetoric that presented the act as a war measure, reliance on courts and judicial process marked it principally as a postwar instrument. What would come of it then, of course, could not be foretold. But despite the restriction on permanent forfeiture of property, it provided a framework for dealing with leading rebels and effecting potentially decisive changes in southern politics and society that would assure

the future security of the Union. Meanwhile, because of the judicial requirement, wartime enforcement was limited to the northern and border states,
where a small amount of rebel-owned property was located.

Emancipation

The Confiscation Act contained emancipation provisions that in an even
more pointed way raised the question of war aims. If anything was clear in the
pre-war Republican platform, it was the constitutional inability of the federal
government to interfere with slavery in the states. Moreover, most authorities
on international law held that even during time of war a belligerent did not
possess a legal right to emancipate the enemy's slaves except as they were used
for military purposes. This was a major qualification, however, which figured
in Republican thinking from the start of the war. In approving the Crittenden-
Johnson Resolutions, for example, some Republican lawmakers said that while
it was not the government's intention to abolish slavery, abolition might be a
necessary result of the war. It did not take long for events to show the accuracy
of this prediction. In August 1861 Congress passed a confiscation act that
declared forfeit all claims to the labor of slaves employed in military efforts
in support of the rebellion. Emancipation could thus be a means of conducting
the war.

Nevertheless, although he signed the First Confiscation Act, Lincoln
scrupulously placed preservation of the Union uppermost. Believing emancipation likely to alienate needed border-state and southern Unionist allies, he
repudiated an emancipation order issued by General John C. Frémont in
September 1861. In December, however, Lincoln urged voluntary emancipation on the states, and in March 1862 proposed a formal plan of gradual,
compensated emancipation. In his view this program recognized the constitutional rights of the states and the property rights of slaveholders. Congress
accepted Lincoln's plan to the extent of passing a resolution offering cooperation and financial support to any state adopting gradual abolition. But when
no positive results were forthcoming from the border area, both president and
Congress turned to more straightforward emancipation measures.

Congress moved the more rapidly. In the first half of 1862 it forbade
military officers to return fugitive slaves, prohibited slavery in the territories,
and abolished slavery in the District of Columbia, with compensation for loyal
owners. More important was the emancipation part of the Confiscation Act
of 1862. This provided that all slaves of persons engaged in rebellion or in any
way giving aid thereto, who should be captured or escape to Union lines, "shall
be deemed captives of war, and shall be forever free of their servitude, and not
again held as slaves." The legislation, however, provided no means of implementing the decree of emancipation, or any guarantee of freed slaves' personal
liberty.

The absence of legal machinery for effecting emancipation is evidence that members of Congress were primarily concerned with depriving the South of its labor supply and gathering resources for the Union war effort. (The act also authorized the use of Negroes for military labor.) Emancipation was more a military expedient than an expression of a consciously humanitarian liberation policy. The omission of legal devices for achieving freedom was also partly attributable to unwillingness to use *in rem* proceedings, appropriate to property, for the emancipation of slaves, whom Republicans viewed as *persons*. Moreover, legal uncertainties about national court jurisdiction in relation to slavery may help explain congressional reticence in regard to emancipation instruments. The main result of the Confiscation Act in any case was to confirm and legitimize the *de facto* emancipation that was occurring with the advance of Union armies.

Lincoln made no serious attempt to enforce the emancipation section of the act of July 1862 largely because he was himself shaping a more aggressive policy against slavery. In July 1862 he drafted for cabinet consideration an emancipation proclamation. Then, after the battle of Antietam in September, he issued a preliminary order stating that the war would continue to be prosecuted for the restoration of the Union, but that in all areas where the people were still in rebellion on January 1, 1863, all persons held as slaves would be free. On January 1, Lincoln announced the definitive proclamation. "As a fit and necessary war measure for suppressing the rebellion," he declared that in all the seceded states except Tennessee and parts of Louisiana and Virginia, all persons held as slaves "are, and henceforth shall be, free; and that the Executive Government of the United States, including the military and naval authorities thereof, will recognize and maintain the freedom of said persons."

The constitutional basis of the Emancipation Proclamation was the war power. It was the extraordinary military emergency alone that could justify departure from the constitutional rule against federal interference with slavery in the states. Opponents of the administration emphatically condemned Lincoln's proclamation as entirely unconstitutional and as a gross usurpation of power on the part of the executive. They argued that the federal government had no authority over slavery in the states under any circumstances, and that the laws of war did not warrant such a blanket destruction of private property.

More practically relevant was the question of the legal effect of the Emancipation Proclamation. Extreme conservatives argued that its utter unconstitutionality deprived it of any legal consequences. At the opposite pole, radicals held that the proclamation conferred a right of personal liberty on slaves regardless of their circumstances. Moderate Unionists, accepting the validity of the proclamation as a war measure, said that any legal effect it had would depend on its actual implementation by the advance of Union arms, and this was closest to the truth. There was agreement, moreover, that the Emancipation Proclamation did not abolish slavery as an institution recognized in the laws and constitutions of the southern states. Accordingly, constitutional amendments for the abolition of slavery were introduced into Congress in 1864. The Thirteenth Amendment, proposed by Congress in January 1865 and ratified by the states in December, completed the legal process begun by the Emancipation Proclamation.

Although in a constitutional and legal sense emancipation was an expedient military measure, its substantive moral and political content made it impossible to employ without at the same time altering the general understanding of the purpose of the war. Henceforth, the aim of the war was to preserve the Union and destroy slavery. Yet the military basis of emancipation ought not to obscure the historic anti-slavery purpose of the Republican party, or the identity of constitutional and political principle between emancipation and defense of the Union. Both slavery and secession denied the republican principle of equality and government by consent, and both defense of the Union and wartime emancipation were intended to uphold this principle. In adopting military emancipation, therefore, the administration did not place the war effort on a higher moral and ideological plane than that on which defense of the Union rested. Rather it provided a solution to the problem of slavery in the American republic that was consistent with the principles on which resistance to secession was based.

Constitutional Significance of the Civil War

Amid change and upheaval, one of the most significant facts of wartime constitutional history was the continuous operation of political parties in the North. Elections were held and constitutional politics persisted. This fact testifies to the adequacy of the Constitution and the American people's commitment to constitutionalism. It also throws light on the Union's ultimate success. Party organization was a means by which federal authorities mobilized and sustained popular energies in support of the war. Moreover, party loyalties restrained states'-rights tendencies and brought federal and state governments into closer harmony, in contrast to the partyless South where states' rights impeded the Confederate war effort. Risky though elections were, especially with opponents of the war involved, they were important in focusing and reinforcing northern popular attitudes toward the war. A reciprocal effect was also evident. With the Union and the Constitution in the balance, wartime elections restored in the public mind an appreciation of the importance of party competition for republican government.

The most important constitutional result of the war was the repudiation of state sovereignty and the compact theory of the Union, with its corollary right of secession. For years ambiguity over the nature of the Union was not only tolerable, but useful as an ingredient in party competition. The federal Union was part confederation, part unitary government. Under the pressure of events concerning slavery this ambiguity eventually became intolerable, and

on the eve of the war Southerners denied categorically that the federal government possessed sovereignty. Sovereignty resided entirely in the states; citizens
owed allegiance to them rather than to the federal government. Ambiguity
over the nature of the Union was unacceptable for the additional reason that
it was incompatible with the process of nationalization that occurred in the
nineteenth century. Americans were becoming more unified and integrated in
society, culture, and economy. Yet their government was weak and ineffectual.
By 1860 there was doubt as to whether it was in any genuine sense a sovereign
government.

The war settled this question unequivocally: The United States was indeed
a sovereign nation, not a league of sovereign states. As a consequence of this
sovereignty, much centralization took place during the war. Yet states' rights,
as distinct from state sovereignty, were not extinguished. Increased centralization produced not a unitary state, but a new and vigorous federalism in which
both states and federal government gained power. Of course, by comparison
with antebellum and wartime Democrats, Republicans were centralizers. But
they retained a strong respect for states' rights. They were in fact states'-rights
nationalists. The political theorist Francis Lieber expressed the party's point
of view when he defended nationalism, yet warned against consolidation:
"Centralism is the convergence of all the rays of power into one central point
. . . nationalization is the diffusion of the same life-blood through a system of
arteries, throughout a body politic." The Supreme Court captured the twin
concerns of Civil War Republicans in declaring, in *Texas* v. *White* (1869):
"The Constitution, in all its provisions, looks to an indestructible Union,
composed of indestructible States."

The second major constitutional result of the war was emancipation. The
South's peculiar institution was irreparably shattered, yet in a constitutional
sense the resolution of this issue had only begun in 1865. Emancipation raised
a series of questions about the rights of the states and the federal government
in relation to personal liberty and civil rights that would go far toward defining
the balance of power in the reconstructed Union.

SEVENTEEN

Reconstruction: The Nationalization
of Civil Rights

RESTORING THE SECEDED STATES TO THE UNION was the central issue in American politics from 1865 to 1869. This was preeminently a constitutional question involving the distribution of power between the states and the federal government. Considered from a strictly legal standpoint, reunification presented perplexing difficulties. Social and economic turmoil resulting from the destruction of slavery vastly complicated the problem, if it did not make a peaceful solution virtually impossible. In addition to states' rights and federal supremacy, reconstruction concerned the status and rights of the former Confederates, on the one hand, and the status and rights of the emancipated slaves, on the other. The first group, if secession was the legal nullity it was proclaimed to be in official Union war policy, could ironically claim a right to participate in the reorganization of state governments in the South. The second group, if the promise of emancipation were to be made good by effective guarantees of civil rights, also had a legitimate claim to participate in reconstruction politics. The task of postwar Union policy was to reconcile the demands of these conflicting groups while restoring the federal system according to northern republican principles.

Wartime Reconstruction

Reconstruction as a problem in constitutional politics began with the disruption of the Union in the months before Sumter and continued throughout the war. The first ideas on the subject to be given practical expression were those advanced by President Lincoln at the beginning of the war. In his message to Congress in July 1861 and in a series of executive actions in subsequent months, Lincoln held that secession was null and void, and that the so-called seceded states were, therefore, still in the Union. He admitted that the southern states were out of their normal relationship to the other states and the federal government since they had no loyal governments and were controlled by persons in rebellion against federal authority. But the states, as political entities distinguished from their governments, still were in the Union. Hence all that was necessary for reconstruction was the suppression of actual military rebellion, the creation of loyal state governments by loyal citizens, and the resumption of normal relations with the federal government.

Lincoln assumed that it was the duty of the federal government to assist the states in reconstruction. The justification for this assumption he found in Article IV, Section 4, of the Constitution, by which the United States guarantees every state in the Union a republican form of government. All subsequent reconstruction schemes drew upon this constitutional provision as justification for federal controls. Lincoln further assumed that the president had authority to carry through a competent reconstruction program with little congressional assistance. A principal step in the plan was the suppression of rebellion, already being accomplished under the president's war powers. Lincoln admitted that in practice Congress would have final authority to pass upon presidential reconstruction, since it could seat delegates from southern states at its discretion. President Andrew Johnson was later to claim that Congress could not lawfully refuse to seat delegates from reconstructed states, but Lincoln did not advance this argument.

As long as the war was fought to restore "the Union as it was and the Constitution as it is," as conservatives described the government's aims, reconstruction was relatively unproblematic. Early in the war Congress began to consider a legislative solution to the essentially civil rather than military problem of governmental organization which lay at the heart of reconstruction. As in the conduct of the war, the separation of powers as a basic constitutional principle introduced into reconstruction politics an element of institutional rivalry between president and Congress. This rivalry was accentuated by military emancipation, which in an important sense altered the shape of reconstruction as a constitutional problem. If carried to its logical conclusion, emancipation would require changes in the laws and constitutions of the southern states when they reentered the Union. No longer could personal liberty be the exclusive concern of state power. By the same token, the silence and disability of the federal government in matters of personal liberty and civil rights, so conspicuous a part of the pre-war Constitution, would also end. If emancipation were to be made secure, the Constitution must in some form recognize the extension of federal power into an area of law and policy previously reserved to the states.

In the first two years of the war Lincoln tried with only limited success to stimulate Unionist sentiment in the occupied South by holding elections for members of Congress. In December 1863 he assumed more direct—though by no means exclusive—control of state restoration by issuing a Proclamation of Amnesty and Reconstruction. The proclamation committed the government to a reconstruction policy that confirmed emancipation and invited a small number of loyal white Southerners to organize state governments with a minimum of federal supervision. With the exception of certain Confederate officials, it offered a pardon to anyone engaged in rebellion who agreed to take an oath of loyalty to the United States. It further declared that whenever the number of loyal persons qualified to vote within a state equaled 10 percent of the total qualified voters in 1860, they would be permitted to form a state government. Reconstructed governments were promised protection under the constitutional provision guaranteeing each state a republican form of government. Lincoln's amnesty proclamation also required participants in state reorganization to swear an oath supporting the Emancipation Proclamation and all acts of Congress dealing with slavery. To abandon emancipation, said Lincoln, would give up a vital lever of power and would be "a cruel and astounding breach of faith" toward Negroes. The president promised not to retract or modify the Emancipation Proclamation, or to return any freed blacks to slavery.

Under this proclamation loyal state governments were organized before the end of the war in Tennessee, Arkansas, and Louisiana. The loyal voters in Union-occupied areas in these states first elected delegates to constitutional conventions. These conventions repudiated secession, abolished slavery, drafted new state constitutions, and provided for new state governments, which were set up in 1864. A loyal government in Virginia had been created under a similar arrangement in 1862. Thus four loyal state governments existed in the South before the war ended.

Congress endorsed Lincoln's policy of December 1863 because it satisfied the demand of virtually all Republicans that emancipation be made the basis of reconstruction. Yet Congress did not regard executive action alone as sufficient for effecting national reunification. Nor did Congress approve of the administration's policy on freedmen's rights which was adopted in occupied Louisiana, the centerpiece of presidential reconstruction. Lincoln's amnesty and reconstruction proclamation in effect allowed white southern Unionists to determine questions concerning the status, rights, labor conditions, and other circumstances of the freed people. Republicans in Congress, however, looking beyond emancipation to the general problem of civil liberty that blacks would face, proposed to establish under federal auspices legal guarantees of personal liberty and civil rights for the former slaves. Republican lawmakers articulated these concerns in the Wade-Davis reconstruction bill of July 1864.

Based on the guarantee-of-republican-government clause of the Constitution, the Wade-Davis bill required conventions in the seceded states, supported by a majority of the adult white male population, to draft new constitutions that would disenfranchise Confederate civil and military officers, repudiate the Confederate debt, and abolish slavery and guarantee the freedom of all persons. Furthermore, the bill prohibited the recognition or enforcement of state slavery laws, authorized federal courts to issue writs of habeas corpus for the release of freed slaves illegally detained on claims of labor, made kidnapping of former slaves a federal crime, and required that state laws for the trial and punishment of white persons should extend to all persons.

Lincoln pocket-vetoed the bill because it proposed to abolish slavery in the states, and would have negated the steps taken to organize a loyal government in Louisiana and effectively postponed restoration of other states until after the war. Emphasizing their political value as governments-in-exile, Lincoln wanted to maintain the restored governments, however flimsy they seemed. In an attempt at compromise, congressional leaders in the winter of 1864–65 revived the Wade-Davis plan, with Louisiana exempted and limited Negro suffrage included.[1] The compromise failed, however, as the majority of Republicans were willing to entrust reconstruction policy—for the time being at least—to the president. In retaliation, congressional radicals blocked the readmission of the reconstructed government of Louisiana. Although other aspects of reconstruction were dealt with in the Thirteenth Amendment and the Freedmen's Bureau Act of March 3, 1865, at the end of the war no comprehensive policy existed for readmitting the seceded states to the Union.

Theories of Reconstruction

The Confederate surrender focused attention on constitutional issues of reconstruction which had long been discussed, but which now possessed an immediacy and importance previously denied them. Of these none was more perplexing than the status of the seceded states. This was the kind of legalistic question that was at once dismissed as theoretical, yet subjected to endless and highly emotional debate. Clearly, there was something real at stake, and although the issue was in a sense abstract—like all constitutional issues when they become the subject of political debate and action—its resolution had practical consequences. For the powers legally available to the government depended on the status that the states and their people occupied. The status of the states had symbolic value, moreover, as an issue through which lawmakers could identify themselves politically and appeal to public opinion.

With understandable inconsistency, Southerners at the end of the war took up the official Union theory and argued that if secession was unconstitutional and without legal effect, then the states were still in the Union and qualified to resume their place in Congress with no strings attached. All that was necessary in this view was for state officers to take an oath to support the Constitution. A second view, endorsed by President Andrew Johnson, held that although the former Confederate states were still in the Union, they were

1. The bill authorized blacks in Union military service to vote.

temporarily disqualified from resuming their place in the federal system because of the treason in which their officers had engaged. Placed by events in a kind of constitutional limbo, the states could be revived and prepared for readmission through the exercise of the president's power of pardon and the war power.

At the opposite end of the political spectrum, radical theories of reconstruction aimed at establishing direct federal rule over the South for the purpose of achieving political and social revolution. One theory held that although secession was illegal, it was nevertheless an accomplished fact which placed the Confederate states in the status of enemies. Defeated as a belligerent, the states were conquered provinces with no internal political or constitutional rights whatever. Another radical theory, much discussed in the early stages of the war, was derived from constitutional rather than international law. It argued that although secession was unconstitutional, it had the legal effect of causing the states to revert to a territorial condition. This theory was careful to state that the former Confederate states were not out of the Union. But it insisted that lawful state governments, through the destructive actions of Southerners themselves, had ceased to exist in the states. As a consequence the states became, in law and in fact, unorganized territory subject to the legislative power of Congress.

Identified with Thaddeus Stevens and Charles Sumner, these theories were more provocative than influential. They conceded too much to secession as the cause of constitutional change in the southern states and departed too drastically from traditional federalism. What was needed from the northern point of view was a theory of reconstruction that would regard the states as still in the Union and allow loyal citizens voluntarily to reorganize their government, but that would at the same time provide sufficient national power to assure that the reorganized states adhered to acceptable standards of republicanism for the future security of the Union.

The disorganized-states theory of reconstruction (also called the forfeited-rights theory) fulfilled these conflicting political and constitutional requirements. Taking as its point of departure the guarantee clause of the Constitution, the theory held that the seceded states were still in the Union. Nevertheless, secession and war had deprived them of republican governments and left them in a disorganized condition. "The fact, as well as the constitutional view of the condition of affairs in the States enveloped by the rebellion," asserted Representative Henry Winter Davis of Maryland, "is that a force has overthrown, or the people, in a moment of madness, have abrogated the governments which existed in those States, under the Constitution." The seceded states, said Davis, were "by law . . . people forming a State without a political organization, called State government." In this disorganized condition the states were subject to federal jurisdiction, and, in particular, to legislative authority to guarantee them a republican form of government. The states were not, however, subject to absolute national control; their existence as states constituted a limitation on the federal government. As a reconstruction instrument under the disorganized-states theory, therefore, the guarantee clause provided temporary federal control that would be civil rather than military in nature, thus fulfilling a fundamental requirement of republicanism. It would also permit the people of the seceded states voluntarily to exercise a degree of local self-government, another requirement of republicanism. This moderate approach to the constitutional problem of reconstruction appealed to the majority of Republicans. It formed the basis for the Wade-Davis bill of 1864, and, with one additional theoretical component, the Military Reconstruction Act of 1867.

The additional element sustaining the act of 1867 was the grasp-of-war theory. This was a way of describing not the status of the states, but the legitimacy of federal power over them for purposes of reconstruction. Derived from the idea that the Confederacy was a belligerent under international law, it asserted that the federal government held the seceded states temporarily under the war power and could demand changes in their constitution and laws necessary to guarantee the results of the war and the future security of the Union. Like Lincoln's wartime crisis government, this theory justified departure from normal constitutional requirements in the name of ultimate restoration of the Constitution. In a situation where perfect consistency with the theory of rebellion on which the war was officially fought presented intolerable political risks, the grasp-of-war theory set aside the normal states'-rights limitations on the federal government in order to reestablish federalism, with appropriate modifications.

Johnson's Policy of Reconstruction

Political circumstances favored Andrew Johnson on his accession to the executive office in April 1865. Though a Democrat and a Southerner, Johnson enjoyed a strong position in relation to the Republican party, whose vice-presidential candidate he had been in 1864. Most Republicans were moderates who wanted to secure the results of the war by guaranteeing genuine freedom to emancipated slaves and by excluding leading Confederates from reconstruction politics. Convinced of the soundness and virtue of their party's free-labor, free-speech, and equality-before-the-law principles, they wanted to extend these principles to the South. Their purposes were to republicanize the region, unite the nation, and secure political control of federal and state governments for their party. But the main body of Republicans was averse to political, social, and economic revolution in the South, and was prepared to accept the leadership of the new president in the initial stages of reconstruction.

After a period of uncertainty in which he gave the appearance of having radical inclinations, Johnson formally initiated a reconstruction policy that in broad outline was similar to Lincoln's. In a proclamation of May 29, Johnson pardoned all persons lately engaged in rebellion, except for high Confederate officials and Confederate supporters who possessed more than $20,000 in property. Persons accepting amnesty were required to take an oath of loyalty to the national government, which included a promise to abide by and support all federal laws and proclamations adopted during the war concerning the emancipation of slaves.

At the same time, Johnson issued a proclamation appointing W. W. Holden provisional governor of North Carolina and outlining a plan of presidential reconstruction for that state. The governor was to call a constitutional convention of delegates chosen by and from loyal voters accepting the presidential amnesty. The convention was to "alter and amend" the state constitution and to take the necessary steps to restore the state to its normal constitutional status. Significantly, the proclamation said nothing of Negro suffrage, although in subsequent statements the president advocated extension of the franchise to Negro taxpayers and to literate Negroes. In the course of the next six weeks Johnson issued similar proclamations for the remaining southern states where Lincoln-sponsored governments had not been erected. Meanwhile, he had extended full recognition to the four Lincoln governments.

Between August 1865 and March 1866, conventions met in all of the seven unreconstructed states. These bodies, except in South Carolina, passed resolutions declaring the various ordinances of secession to have been null and void. South Carolina, clinging to discredited constitutional theory, merely repealed the ordinance. All of the conventions formally abolished slavery within their respective states. With the exception of South Carolina and Mississippi, all repudiated the state debt incurred in rebellion. The conventions also provided for elections of state legislative, executive, and judicial officers.

The newly elected legislatures met shortly and, except in Mississippi, ratified the Thirteenth Amendment. Johnson virtually insisted upon ratification, and it was by this device that the requisite three-fourths majority of the states was secured for the adoption of the amendment. This requirement of ratification was altogether inconsistent with the theoretical sovereignty of the new governments; however, this technical consideration attracted little notice. The new legislatures also chose United States senators, and provided for the election of House members. Thus by the time Congress met in December 1865, the Johnson reconstruction program was approaching completion in every southern state. All that remained was for Congress to seat the southern delegates, and presidential reconstruction would be complete.

Although willing to accept the legitimacy of Johnson's policy, Republicans in Congress thought it far from conclusive. As under Lincoln, they believed that executive action was constitutionally insufficient and that national legislation was needed to reconstruct the Union. Politically, too, they had objections to Johnson's course of action. It was unsettling, to say the least, that many former Confederates were among the newly elected southern representatives and senators applying for seats in Congress. Republicans also had doubts about the wisdom of presidential policy as they observed the initial efforts of the reconstructed states to fix the status and rights of the freedmen in the so-called black codes. For these reasons, they blocked the admission of southern representatives and senators, by means of a Republican party caucus order instructing the clerks in each house to ignore the seceded states in the roll call. Congressional leaders then secured the appointment of a Joint Committee on Reconstruction, composed of nine representatives and six senators, carefully balanced between radical and moderate viewpoints, who were instructed to make a thorough study of the entire reconstruction problem and to report upon whether any of the southern states ought to be represented in Congress. Another resolution was passed pledging that neither house would seat representatives from the seceded states until the Joint Committee made its report.

Placed on the defensive by the swift restoration of state governments in the South, Congress undertook to review not only executive policy, but also measures dealing with emancipation and the freedmen that in effect formed a partial reconstruction policy. These measures were the Thirteenth Amendment and the Freedmen's Bureau Act.

Federal Freedmen's Policy in 1865

Approved for submission to the states in January 1865 and ratified in December with the support of eight southern states, the Thirteenth Amendment declared that neither slavery nor involuntary servitude, except as a punishment for crime, shall exist in the United States or its territories. The amendment further gave Congress power to enforce the prohibition by appropriate legislation.

The Thirteenth Amendment profoundly altered the federal system by curtailing previously exclusive state power over personal liberty. For the first time it gave the federal government authority in this sphere. Moreover the amendment authorized the federal government to enforce the prohibition of slavery against violation from whatever source, whether state government or private individual. For purposes of the amendment, in other words, the existence of the states was not to constitute a limitation on federal power.

Seemingly simple and straightforward, the Thirteenth Amendment nevertheless gave rise to vexing problems of interpretation that remained unresolved in December 1865. If it was obvious that the amendment placed 4 million black persons in a new condition of freedom, it was by no means clear precisely what additional civil rights it conferred upon them beyond personal liberty. For a moment's reflection suggested that the right of personal liberty needed to be amplified and supported with other rights in order to fulfill the promise of emancipation. Accordingly, Republican congressmen who framed the amendment asserted that it would confer fundamental civil rights on the freed slaves:

the right to labor and enjoy the fruits thereof; to own property, make contracts, and exercise related economic rights; to bring suit and testify in courts of law; to enter into marriage and receive the protection of the private household; to speak and write freely and to be educated.

If it was hard to say what civil rights the prohibition of slavery bestowed by implication, it was harder to say how—that is, under the jurisdiction of which government, state or federal—these rights would be enforced. It was plain that Congress could legislate to prevent the illegal detention or reenslavement of freed persons or anyone else. But could it regulate and protect civil rights in general, as a corollary of its power to protect personal liberty? If so, it would replace the states in this sphere of public policy. In adopting the Thirteenth Amendment, however, Republicans made no claim for such a sweeping federal power. In fact, they rejected a proposed anti-slavery amendment introduced by Senator Charles Sumner declaring all persons equal before the law and authorizing Congress to enforce legal equality in a comprehensive way. Nor did Democratic opponents of the Thirteenth Amendment argue that under the enforcement section Congress would have power to legislate directly on civil rights, in derogation of the state police power. The main argument against the amendment was that it represented an unconstitutional exercise of the amending power.[2] As restored southern governments in late 1865 began to pass demeaning and discriminatory laws regulating the black population, however, and as the freedmen were victimized by violence, Republicans adopted a broader view of federal legislative power—or felt free to express ideas previously held but for political reasons not publicly revealed. By December 1865 this reconsideration or discovery of national legislative power under the Thirteenth Amendment was in the process of formation.

A second aspect of federal freedmen's policy in December 1865 provided legal protection for emancipated slaves in the southern states. The origins of this policy lay in wartime efforts by the War and Treasury Departments to manage post-emancipation problems among the large black refugee population of the South. Ending the long period of incapacity concerning slavery and personal liberty, the federal government, under the pressure of war, reached deep into local affairs. It recruited freedmen for the Union army, gathered them in refugee camps, and organized them under a free labor system on plantations in the occupied South. Early in the war it even undertook a few abortive overseas colonization ventures. Political controversy surrounded these various programs as many anti-slavery militants charged the Lincoln administration with failing adequately to protect the rights and well-being of

---

2. Democrats argued that by interfering with the domestic institutions of the states, the Thirteenth Amendment revolutionized the federal system and was tantamount to the creation of a new constitution. If the amending power could be used to destroy slavery, Democrats contended, it could also be used to deprive states of power over other local institutions such as schools, property arrangements, and the like.

the emancipated slaves. Often War and Treasury Department officials worked at cross-purposes in trying to gain control of freedmen's policy. In March 1865 Congress resolved this intragovernmental squabbling by passing the Freedmen's Bureau Act. The law created an agency in the War Department, to continue during the war and for one year thereafter, that was charged with extending welfare relief and protection to freedmen and white refugees and with establishing them in temporary occupancy of abandoned lands.

The Freedmen's Bureau began operations in May 1865. At once it became heavily involved in providing legal protection for freedmen through special military courts appointed by bureau head General Oliver Otis Howard. Responsible to the executive through the secretary of war, the Freedmen's Bureau found itself at odds with the civil governments restored by the president. It also clashed with the president himself, who encouraged the bureau to turn questions involving freedmen's rights over to state courts in return for the modification of state laws restricting and discriminating against blacks. To some extent General Howard complied with this request, but the agreement did not hold. Irrespective of state laws, local law enforcement officials continued to discriminate against blacks. By the time Congress assembled in December 1865, bureau officials were seeking stronger legislative authorization for protecting the liberty and rights of the freedmen.

Protection was mainly necessary against the black codes and the actions of state officials. Adopted by the reorganized state governments in 1865 and 1866, the black codes from the white southern point of view conferred new rights and a higher status on the mass of blacks. From a northern perspective, however, the laws bore a disturbing resemblance to the antebellum slave codes. They contained harsh vagrancy and apprenticeship provisions whose apparent purpose was to bind the ex-slaves to the soil and strip them of all the practical attributes of freedom. The penal sections provided for more severe and arbitrary punishment for Negroes than for whites, while several codes also called for racial segregation in schools and other public facilities. The black codes, in short, imposed an inferior citizenship upon the freedmen, along with a potential system of partial bondage. Many northern congressmen believed they violated the Thirteenth Amendment, unless the amendment's provisions against "involuntary servitude" were to be construed in the narrowest possible sense.

The Moderate Republican Policy of 1866

Responding to these varied influences and pressures, Congress in 1866 adopted a reconstruction policy aimed at protecting the liberty and rights of the freed blacks. This issue was the outstanding point of contention in the struggle between parties and sections that dominated postwar politics. Shaped by Republican moderates, the policy of 1866 proposed to accept the restored

Johnson governments if they would agree to protect Negro civil rights. As states'-rights nationalists, the moderates desired the states to remain the principal centers of republicanism, protecting and regulating civil liberty under new national guarantees of equality before the law for American citizens.

The first step in this policy was the enactment of the second Freedmen's Bureau bill in February 1866. Introduced by Senator Lyman Trumbull of Illinois, the bill extended the life of the bureau indefinitely. More important, it placed Negro civil rights in the seceded states under federal military protection. Any person in any of the formerly seceded states charged with depriving a freedman of his civil rights was to be tried by a military tribunal or a Freedmen's Bureau agent in accordance with martial law. No presentment or indictment was required.

These provisions precipitated a serious constitutional debate in both houses of Congress. Democrats and more conservative Republicans, led by Senators Garrett Davis of Kentucky and Reverdy Johnson of Maryland, attacked the Trumbull bill as hopelessly unconstitutional, arguing that control of civil rights was not one of the enumerated or implied powers of Congress and, therefore, was exclusively reserved to the states. They argued also that the provisions for the military trial of civilians violated the procedural guarantees of the Fifth Amendment, which specifically enjoined presentment and indictment in federal criminal trials except in the armed forces and in the militia in time of war and which thus clearly implied a general immunity for civilians from peacetime military trial.

Republicans expressed the more capacious understanding of Thirteenth Amendment liberty and national power that events were forcing upon them. Lyman Trumbull argued that the constitutional amendment gave Congress a new power to legislate to protect civil rights, or at least those essential to the blacks' new status of freedom as opposed to slavery. But the clearer and more certain basis of the Freedmen's Bureau bill was the grasp-of-war theory. Accordingly, Trumbull defended the military-trial provisions on the ground that disturbed conditions persisted in the South and civil authority had not yet been completely restored. The bill's provisions were seen as temporary, however, for federal military power could not indefinitely govern local affairs in the manner now required. The task of providing permanent civil guarantees of Negro citizenship and rights remained.

Johnson vetoed the Freedmen's Bureau bill, calling the provisions for military trials a violation of the Fifth Amendment and questioning the capacity of the present Congress to function at all. A Congress that barred eleven states outright, the president said, was not legally capable of enacting any legislation, especially for the states it excluded. Congress sustained the veto by a narrow margin, but this was to be Johnson's last reconstruction victory of any consequence. In July, Congress was to pass another Freedmen's Bureau bill, very like the earlier measure, over Johnson's veto.

The second component in the moderate Republican policy was the Civil

Rights Act of 1866. The purpose of this law was to provide a permanent guarantee of rights equality. The first question to be resolved concerned the citizenship of the freed people. To this end the bill declared that "all persons born or naturalized in the United States and not subject to any foreign power, except Indians not taxed," were citizens of the United States. The bill then stated that citizens of the United States, irrespective of race, color, or previous condition of servitude, should have the same right in every state "to make and enforce contracts, to sue, be parties, and give evidence, to inherit, purchase, lease, sell, hold, and convey real and personal property," and to enjoy the "full and equal benefit of all laws and proceedings for the security of person and property, as is enjoyed by white citizens." The rights thus enumerated were given sanction in Section 2, which declared that any person who under color of any law, statute, ordinance, regulation, or custom deprived any inhabitant of rights secured by the act was guilty of a misdemeanor and upon conviction was subject to fine and imprisonment. The bill gave United States district courts exclusive jurisdiction over crimes committed against the act and concurrent jurisdiction to district and circuit courts over civil and criminal cases involving persons unable to enforce in state courts rights secured by the act.

In debate Republicans had little difficulty defending the attribution of citizenship to blacks. Chief Justice Taney himself in the *Dred Scott* opinion had insisted that control over citizenship was vested exclusively in Congress under the naturalization power. Executive and legislative actions during the Civil War had repudiated the Supreme Court's denial of Negro citizenship in the *Dred Scott* case. But as these actions were arguably not legally conclusive, and in view of the degraded status the black codes imposed on the freedmen, it was expedient formally to overrule Taney's exclusion of blacks from citizenship. This the Civil Rights Act did.

The Republican Congress accepted the idea of dual citizenship. But the citizenship which the Civil Rights Act conferred was dual and mutually reinforcing, in contrast to the strictly separate spheres of state and federal citizenship described by Taney in the *Dred Scott* case. Republicans viewed American citizenship as a single entity, in the nature of concentric circles of state and federal power. National citizenship encompassed state citizenship and consisted of general rights such as those the Civil Rights Act enumerated. State citizenship was concerned with the specific entitlement of individuals to these categorical rights under state law. For example, every citizen had a right to make contracts, but the precise manner of exercising the right was determined and regulated by the states. National citizenship thus consisted of fundamental civil rights that were implemented in the sphere of state law, with the federal government acting as ultimate guarantor. In effect, the content of national citizenship was equality before states' laws as state citizens.

More problematic than the attribution of citizenship in the congressional debate was the delineation of civil rights. Especially alarming to conservatives was a clause in Trumbull's original bill which stated that "there shall be no discrimination in civil rights and immunities." This guarantee seemingly transferred the protection of all such rights from their historic lodgment with the states to the federal government. Democrats and several conservative Republicans objected that it would prevent the states from making any legal distinction whatever between Negroes and whites. Trumbull argued that the Thirteenth Amendment gave Congress power to legislate on civil rights in this plenary fashion, but most Republicans disagreed. Accordingly, they struck out the sweeping "no-discrimination" clause.

More controversial still were the nature and scope of federal power employed in the Civil Rights Act. As the black codes indicated, the chief threat to freedmen's rights at this time came from the restored state governments, although private injury and discrimination were also widespread. Could Congress, and did the act, prohibit both official and private denial of civil rights, or only the former? Contemporary opinion was divided. Some Republicans held that the Thirteenth Amendment gave Congress plenary power to legislate against denials of rights from whatever source, as a necessary corollary of its power to prohibit slavery. Others held that Congress could not assume the power of local police and criminal law jurisdiction which this comprehensive and sweeping conception of rights protection implied. In this view Congress under the Thirteenth Amendment could legislate only in case of a denial of civil rights by state governments. There was, in other words, a state action limitation on congressional power, a stipulation that state action denying rights had to occur before Congress could legislate. Most Republicans appear to have supported this moderate view, believing—naively—that if state officers could be got to respect Negroes' rights and enforce state laws for the protection of person and property, private injury would cease. In a typical expression of this outlook, Representative James Wilson of Iowa said that the Civil Rights Act applied to state officers alone, rather than to all persons, because Congress was not legislating a general criminal code for the states.

Indeed, if the Civil Rights Act worked as its framers intended, it would itself prove to be a temporary measure. The expansion of federal jurisdiction contemplated by the act was potentially very considerable, as persons who were discriminated against in state courts through the application of unequal state laws could transfer their cases to the federal courts. Republican moderates believed that, facing this prospect, the states would drop their discriminatory laws in order to retain jurisdiction over the range of ordinary civil and criminal matters that had traditionally lain within their exclusive authority. The point was to get the states to treat their citizens equally. The act "will have no operation in any State where the laws are equal," said Trumbull, "where all persons have the same civil rights without regard to color or race."

Johnson vetoed the civil rights bill, advancing the same conservative state's-rights objections he had offered to the Freedmen's Bureau bill. However, on April 9 Congress passed the bill over his veto. Although the Democratic minority and a scattering of Republicans continued to support his

administration, the Republican majority henceforth promptly passed all reconstruction measures of any consequence over his veto.

The Fourteenth Amendment

Plainly the Civil Rights Act of 1866 rested on the Thirteenth Amendment. Among several Republicans, however, doubt persisted about the suffi-
ciency of this constitutional basis. This doubt critically influenced the drafting
of another constitutional amendment authorizing national civil rights legislation in clear and unmistakable terms. This new measure was the work of the
Joint Committee on Reconstruction, which for several months had been considering all aspects of the reconstruction question necessary for a comprehensive peace settlement.

In January 1866 the Joint Committee introduced a proposed constitutional amendment to exclude outright from the basis of congressional representation any person whose political rights were denied or abridged by the state
on account of race or color. By implication this measure enjoined Negro
suffrage under penalty of a reduction in the representation of any state not
granting it. The amendment passed the House late in January, but the less
radical Senate rejected it. After some further delay, the Joint Committee on
April 30 reported out a far more comprehensive constitutional amendment,
destined to emerge with some modifications as the Fourteenth Amendment.

The opening sentence of Section 1 of the proposed amendment provided
that:

All persons born or naturalized in the United States, and subject to the jurisdiction
thereof, are citizens of the United States and of the State wherein they reside.

Thus the lack of a citizenship clause in the original Constitution was formally
remedied. National citizenship now became primary and state citizenship
secondary; thereby the issue of the locus of citizenship, discussed in the Missouri Compromise and later debates and left in a confused condition by the
Dred Scott decision, was finally put to rest. The clause also obviously conferred
outright national and state citizenship upon Negroes, as was its intent.

Sections 2 and 3 dealt with the problem of southern representation.
Section 2 as reported by the committee was a compromise. It based state
representation in the House upon the whole number of people in each state
and so abrogated the three-fifths clause, but it excluded from the basis of
representation those persons denied the franchise for any reason other than
"participation in rebellion, or other crime." This section in effect ensured that
the conservative white population should not be able to take advantage of
increased state representation together with Negro disfranchisement to place
the southern states and Democrats in control in Washington once more. At

the same time, the section did not categorically bestow the vote upon Negroes.

As originally drafted by the Joint Committee, Section 3 unconditionally disfranchised all participants in the late rebellion until March 4, 1870. Many moderate Republicans thought this at once too severe and too temporary. It passed the House, but was then unanimously stricken out in both houses and a substitute provision by Senator Jacob Howard of Michigan put in its place. Howard's provision merely barred from state and federal offices all participants in rebellion who had formerly held political office and in that capacity taken an oath to support the Constitution. It further empowered Congress to remove this disability by a two-thirds vote.

Section 4 recited the obvious—it guaranteed the United States public debt and outlawed debts incurred in rebellion against the United States. Section 5 empowered Congress to enforce the amendment by appropriate legislation.

By far the most important part of the Fourteenth Amendment was the guarantee of civil rights contained in Section 1. Originally, the Joint Committee, using a formulation of Representative John Bingham of Ohio, proposed to give Congress power "to make all laws necessary and proper to secure to the citizens of each State all privileges and immunities of citizens in the several States, and to all persons in the several States equal protection in the rights of life, liberty, and property." Although Bingham later said this meant only that Congress could correct state laws that denied equal rights, the language seemed unequivocally to transfer legislative power over civil rights from the states to the federal government. It appeared to have the same revolutionary impact on the federal system as the "no-discrimination" clause of the original civil rights bill. Sensitive to moderate and conservative objections, the Joint Committee, therefore, substituted an alternative civil rights section, also drawn by Bingham, which remained in the amendment as adopted: "No state shall make or enforce any law which shall abridge the privileges and immunities of citizens of the United States; nor shall any State deprive any person of life, liberty, or property, without due process of law; nor deny to any person within its jurisdiction equal protection of the laws."

These provisions expressed the state-action theory of federal legislative power over civil rights. For a few radicals with abolitionist backgrounds, the language of Section 1 had a clear and sweeping liberal humanitarian content that banned all forms of discrimination against blacks in law, politics, and society. Most Republican lawmakers, however, saw Section 1 as a restatement in broader terms of the Civil Rights Act, expressed in a form that prevented subsequent national legislative repeal. Most also saw it as removing all doubt about the constitutionality of the Civil Rights Act.

The Fourteenth Amendment nationalized civil rights, but it did so in a way that respected traditional federal values. The states had been the principal regulators of personal liberty and civil rights, and they would continue to perform that function. Now, however, they would do so under federal supervisory authority and national guarantees of rights protection, as expressed in the

Thirteenth and Fourteenth Amendments and the Civil Rights Act. National-ization of civil rights, in other words, was not to be accomplished by direct centralization and consolidation of legislative power in Congress. To be sure, by comparison with the pre-war Constitution, the reconstruction amendments pointed in that direction, and there were Republicans who endorsed a central-ist or unitary solution. They argued, for example, that if under the rule of slavery the right of recapturing fugitive slaves could be enforced as a national constitutional right against any interference whatever, whether from state government or private individuals, then surely under the rule of freedom the basic rights of citizenship could be protected by the federal government in the same direct and exclusive manner. Yet this view did not achieve majority support. The moderate center, when they considered the implications and ramifications of this more radical approach, rejected it. The revolution in federalism that began under wartime exigencies thus stopped at a halfway point.

The Fourteenth Amendment, passed by both houses of Congress on June 13, 1866, was part of a comprehensive reconstruction settlement submitted by the Joint Committee on Reconstruction. Eschewing the conquered provinces and territorialization theories, the committee adhered to the disorganized-governments–guarantee-clause conception of reconstruction. It declared that the states lacked legitimate civil governments and said the people must form and ratify new constitutions establishing republican government. The commit-tee also took the position that while the federal government would determine the fundamental conditions, the people in the states should voluntarily accept the elements of a new republican order. Thus the guarantee clause offered a middle ground between exclusive federal control of reconstruction and virtu-ally complete local autonomy or self-reconstruction, as under President John-son's policy.

The Republican moderates in control of Congress were prepared to recog-nize the Johnson governments provided they agreed to protect the civil rights of all citizens, secure a "just equality of representation," and protect against rebel debt claims. These terms referred to the Fourteenth Amendment and to a bill introduced in April providing that any seceded state that ratified the amendment would be readmitted to Congress. Unwilling to make any formal commitment to receive the states, radicals blocked this bill. But the promise of readmission was clear. It was borne out when Tennessee was granted representation in Congress in July 1866 after ratifying the Fourteenth Amend-ment.

However, the other ten seceded states rejected the Fourteenth Amend-ment. Believing that time was on their side and that the northern public would not endorse the moderate program, let alone more radical proposals, southern political leaders denounced the amendment. They looked to the congressional elections of 1866 as a means of strengthening President Johnson's position. Should Johnson's supporters win control of Congress, the president could secure admission of the southern states on his own terms. Dubbed "masterly inactivity," this strategy in fact proved to be a grave mistake, for moderate and radical Republicans made heavy gains at Johnson's expense in the fall elections.

Meanwhile, as the northern public grew increasingly impatient with the failure of Congress to adopt a reconstruction plan, events were driving moderate and radical Republicans closer together. Johnson's unwillingness to accept any degree of federal civil rights protection, on the ground that it violated the rights of the states, strengthened Republican unity and resolve. The upshot of this political process was the adoption of a more radical congressional policy in the Military Reconstruction Act of 1867.

EIGHTEEN

Congressional Reconstruction

WHEN CONGRESS CONVENED IN DECEMBER 1866, the need for a reconstruction policy had grown more imperative. Radicals might be willing to keep the former Confederate states waiting for a generation, but most Northerners were disturbed by the constitutional anomaly of ten reconstructed state governments remaining unrepresented in the national legislature. Complicating the situation was the problem of protecting the liberty of the freed slaves, which most Northerners regarded as necessary on both political and humanitarian grounds. The object of official state discrimination in the black codes, Negroes were increasingly the victims of private injury and denial of rights. Southern abuse of the freedmen was a major reason why the states were not yet readmitted to Congress. Yet, paradoxically, the condition of the freedmen was also a source of pressure to restore the states to the Union, on the theory that they would then be subject to the constraints of national civil rights guarantees. Still another issue demanding congressional attention was the challenge to national authority presented by civil and criminal suits in southern state courts against Union military personnel. These suits alleged violation of local citizens' civil rights through actions taken in the performance of military duties during and after the war. In short, a law-and-order problem existed in the South to add urgency to the task of adopting a reconstruction policy.

Long since alienated from the Republican party, President Johnson rejected the northern majority's perception of events. Intent on restoring the states with virtually all their antebellum rights intact, Johnson used his authority to frustrate federal protection of freedmen and Unionists. In April 1866, for example, he issued a proclamation declaring the insurrection ended and pronouncing the former rebellious states restored to the Union. In time of peace, Johnson observed, military tribunals and suspension of the writ of habeas corpus were a threat to civil liberty and individual rights. The president's message encouraged white Southerners and alarmed the Union military command, which in July 1866 authorized the use of military tribunals to try persons charged with crimes against federal officers and freedmen whom state officials failed to prosecute. In August Johnson issued another proclamation criticizing reliance on military government in place of civil authority, and in December 1866 the Supreme Court issued a similar warning. In its opinion in the *Milligan* case the Court held that in places remote from the theater of war, where the civil courts were open, military trial of civilians was unconstitutional. This dictum seemed to threaten existing operations of the army carried out under the provisions of the Freedmen's Bureau Act. It increased the uncertainty facing Congress as it turned once again to the problem of formulating a reconstruction policy.

The Military Reconstruction Acts of 1867

Although Republicans were united in opposition to Johnson's policy, moderate and radical factions continued to disagree in their approach to reconstruction. Radicals wanted to remove the Johnson governments, exclude all former rebels from citizenship, and force the states to write new constitutions and form new governments based on Negro suffrage. Seeking to revolutionize the South through confiscation, land redistribution, and public education programs, they would deny Southerners representation indefinitely until they were genuinely penitent and republicanized. Moderates clung to the Fourteenth Amendment as a basic reconstruction policy. Averse to political and social revolution, they wanted to recognize the Johnson governments on condition that they accept the obligation to protect the civil rights of all citizens equally.

Anxious both to restore federalism and to guarantee citizenship equality, moderates laid heavy stress on securing legislation that would expressly promise to readmit the states when they ratified the Fourteenth Amendment. As the southern states had already rejected this approach when they repudiated the Fourteenth Amendment, however, moderates could hardly regard it as a sufficient plan of reconstruction. Accordingly, they now accepted Negro suffrage as an essential additional step. Initially opposed to black voting out of a belief that the freedmen were unprepared for it and in deference to the constitutional rule that gave the states exclusive power to regulate voting, moderates now saw enfranchisement of Negroes as a way of solving both the civil rights and reconstruction questions. Armed with the vote, blacks would be able to protect themselves and demand recognition of their rights as citizens. Negro suffrage would also supply the political support needed in the southern states to get the Fourteenth Amendment adopted and the states readmitted. Perhaps most important, it would make continuing federal intervention in local affairs unnecessary.

Radical and moderate agendas aside, the most pressing need was to deal with the law-and-order problem. To this end the Joint Committee on Reconstruction in January 1867 introduced a military government bill authorizing the use of military tribunals for civil purposes. It was this bill, amended to accommodate the radical and moderate points of view on reconstruction, that became the Military Reconstruction Act of March 2, 1867.

The original bill divided the unrestored seceded states into five districts, under the command of military officers who were authorized to employ military tribunals to protect the person and property of all citizens and bring to trial disturbers of the peace and criminals. Any interference by state governments with the exercise of military power under the act was declared null and void. Based on the disorganized-states–republican-government theory of reconstruction, the act declared the existing civil governments in the South to be provisional only and subject to the paramount authority of the United States to abolish, modify, control, or supersede them. Thus Congress rejected the radical demand that the Johnson governments be removed, though it placed them on notice in that regard. Yet the radical point of view was satisfied in the requirement that the states form new constitutions guaranteeing Negro suffrage. On the other hand, while former rebels were excluded from the constitution-making process, the standard of exclusion was to be the Fourteenth Amendment, the moderates' lodestar. And the act further satisfied the moderates by providing that when the states ratified the Fourteenth Amendment, they would be readmitted to Congress.

The Military Reconstruction Act embodied more of the radical point of view than did the congressional policy of 1866. It was perceived in the South—and by most historians ever since—as a supremely radical measure that subjugated the states outright and imposed on them a political and social revolution. There is much truth in this assessment. It is equally important, however, to point out that within the range of reconstruction policies being contemplated, the act was a compromise that denied the radicals much of what they wanted—especially abolition of the Johnson governments, confiscation, and land redistribution. Moreover, it contained key moderate elements, including the all-important promise to readmit the states once they accepted the Fourteenth Amendment. This fact serves to remind us that the fundamental problem was how to restore the seceded states to the Union rather than how to govern them. Furthermore, in a reflection of the persistent faith in—or constitutional necessity of—local self-government, the act left the initiative in devising ways of proceeding to the Johnson governments themselves. It made no stipulation as to the steps to be taken in drafting new constitutions.

Johnson vetoed the military reconstruction bill, whereupon Congress overrode his veto. The states, however, refused to implement the act. Congress therefore adopted the Reconstruction Act of March 23, 1867. This measure gave the military commanders instructions for starting the constitution-making process and specified in detail the procedure to follow in holding elections for a constitutional convention. After a second veto and override by Congress, Johnson enforced the reconstruction acts as narrowly as possible in order to maintain the existing governments and minimize change. Attorney General Henry Stanbery, for example, sought to disfranchise as few white Southerners as possible. He ruled that military-appointed registration boards, entrusted with the power to determine ineligibility for voting because of participation in the rebellion, could not exclude persons who wished to take the required oath denying disqualification, whether they were lying or not. Vigorous opposition promptly appeared in Congress and in the army against what Republicans regarded as the administration's obstructionist course. When additional conflicts arose over attempts of military commanders to remove state officers, Congress passed a third Reconstruction Act in July 1867. This law set aside the attorney general's rulings on disqualification for rebellion and confirmed the authority of military commanders to remove state officers. From this point Johnson pursued his conservative objectives through use of the removal power, replacing the more radical military commanders and trying to drive Secretary of War Stanton out of the cabinet. Within a year his actions provoked the House of Representatives to impeach him.

From the conservative point of view, the congressional policy of 1867 was hopelessly unconstitutional. It centralized power in the federal government and invaded states' rights. Furthermore, it imposed military government on states in disregard of the guarantee-of-republican-government clause, denied representation to states lawfully entitled to it, and imposed illegal conditions on those states before readmitting them to representation. From the Republican perspective, however, the policy was constitutional under the guarantee clause and the grasp-of-war theory, as the Supreme Court acknowledged in *Texas* v. *White* (1869). Yet even this radical plan of 1867, while stipulating conditions the states must meet in order to resume their place in the Union, left much to be carried out by the states themselves. Essentially, it was a policy of internal reconstruction by Southerners. Congress intended no permanent centralization of power. On the contrary, the Reconstruction Act was a temporary expedient for restoring the states and making permanent federal control unnecessary.

Nevertheless, the congressional policy of 1867 portended a political revolution in the South. Reconstruction would in large part be accomplished by a new class of Southerners created by congressional enfranchisement of the freedmen and formally organized as the Republican party. In the enrollment of eligible voters the proportion of Negroes was very large. In Alabama, for example, 104,000 out of 165,000 registered voters were Negroes. In only five states, however, were black voters a majority. Moreover, the white majority in the other states and in the South as a whole was not, as legend would have it, composed principally of carpetbagger immigrants from the North.

The new electorate was purified by the exclusion of former rebels, but the extent of this proscription was limited. The test employed—which applied only to election to and service in the state constitutional conventions—was the moderate Fourteenth Amendment one barring persons who had sworn an oath to uphold the Constitution as state or federal officers and then joined the rebellion. The number of Southerners excluded under this test has been estimated at approximately 100,000, a number that may seem large or small depending on one's perspective. Plainly the policy did not proscribe a majority of white Southerners, although quantitative evaluation is beside the point since the purpose was to exclude the key political leaders of the existing southern establishment. Nevertheless, the number proscribed was far fewer than the categorical elimination of former rebels that radicals had hoped for. Furthermore, although permanent disfranchisement of persons excluded by the Fourteenth Amendment became an issue in state reconstruction politics, in only three states was it adopted. By and large, new state governments were formed in the South without a wholesale purge of the old political class or the removal of existing state governments.

In the fall of 1867, then, all ten unreconstructed southern states voted by large majorities to call constitutional conventions. Their principal purpose was to establish a new political order based on universal male suffrage and civil rights equality. But other significant changes also occurred. In general the new state charters strengthened state government against local autonomy, reorganized local government, made many offices elective that had been appointive, reapportioned legislative representation more equitably, and effected legal and penal reforms. Taxation and finance systems were modified, and in what was probably the most important single reform, free public education was introduced into the South. Drawn up by the new class of smaller farmers, business and industrial groups, and blacks, the reconstruction constitutions reflected typical mid-nineteenth-century progressive social and economic ideas.

Because the Reconstruction Act of March 23, 1867, required that a constitution must be ratified in an election in which a majority of all registered voters in the state participated, many enfranchised whites stayed away from the polls in an effort to prevent adoption of the new constitutions. In Alabama this device temporarily succeeded. In March 1868, however, Congress passed the fourth Reconstruction Act providing that the new constitutions could be ratified by a simple majority of those voting. In all the remaining states except Mississippi the constitutions were ratified by large majorities. Accordingly, in June 1868 Congress voted to readmit Alabama, Arkansas, North Carolina, South Carolina, Georgia, Florida, and Louisiana. Texas, Mississippi, and Virginia were readmitted in 1870, after being required to ratify a new constitutional amendment protecting Negro suffrage.

The Impeachment of Johnson

As the Reconstruction Acts went into effect in 1867–68, a constitutional crisis unique in the history of the republic gripped the government at Washington. After months of backing and filling and two false starts, a frustrated, embittered, yet withal reluctant Congress impeached President Johnson out of a conviction that he had improperly obstructed the carrying out of congressional reconstruction policy.

Beginning in March 1867, Congress adopted a series of acts intended to restrict the president's authority as much as possible. The Army Appropriation Act of March 2, 1867, required that all army orders be issued through the general of the army, and that the general in command of the army should not be removed without the Senate's consent. The third Reconstruction Act of July 19, 1867, vested the entire power to appoint and remove officials under the act in the general of the army, a direct transfer of the president's appointive power to a subordinate official. Of even greater significance was the Tenure of Office Act, also enacted on March 2, 1867. This law was intended to destroy the president's power to remove subordinate officials without the Senate's consent. It provided that all executive officials appointed with the Senate's consent should hold office until a successor was appointed and qualified in the same manner. Thus no presidential removal would be valid under the act until the Senate consented by ratifying the nomination of a successor. A partial exception was made for cabinet officers, who were to hold office only during the term of the president appointing them, and for one month thereafter.

Another section of the act provided for ad interim appointments. When the Senate was not in session, the president could remove an official for crime, misconduct, or incapacity and fill the vacancy so created with an ad interim appointment. But the president was obliged to report the removal to the Senate within twenty days after that chamber next convened. If the Senate then refused its consent to the removal, the office reverted to the former incumbent. Accepting or holding an office in violation of the statute was made a misdemeanor punishable by fine and imprisonment.

This statute reopened the old dispute over the president's removal power. As the reader is aware, the First Congress had decided that the president possessed a separate right of removal without the Senate's consent. Also, Jackson had successfully reaffirmed that right in 1833, and it had since been commonly exercised. Johnson's veto recalled these facts and denounced the bill as an unconstitutional usurpation of executive authority; however, Congress promptly passed the measure over his veto.

Meanwhile the radical leaders had been searching for plausible grounds upon which to impeach the president. In the spring of 1867 a House investigating committee had covered every possible charge thoroughly and had been forced to report in July that no adequate grounds for impeachment existed. The investigation continued, however, and in December the committee, under the direction of Representative George S. Boutwell of Massachusetts, recommended impeachment, although no specific grounds for such a step were presented.

In the debate that followed, the radical leaders contended that the phrase "high crimes and misdemeanors" was not to be construed narrowly, but that it embraced essentially political acts tending to undermine the government and the Constitution. This broad view was in part supported by the history of impeachment proceedings in Congress. Five times the House of Representatives had voted to impeach federal judges, but only once did it limit its charge to an indictable crime. On pne occasion—the impeachment of demented Judge John Pickering in 1804—a nonindictable offense was the ground for conviction. Moreover, constitutional commentators throughout the nineteenth century agreed that impeachment was at bottom political rather than narrowly legalistic in character. It was intended to deal not with single offenses otherwise indictable under federal statute or common law, but with abuse of power and public trust. On the other hand, it was true that judgments by the Senate in impeachment trials supported the view that the power could be used only against defined, indictable offenses. For in all but one instance—that of Judge Pickering—nonindictable offenses had not led to conviction.

Boutwell drew the issue when, conceding that it might not be possible "by specific charge" to arraign Johnson for his "great crime," he nonetheless urged the president's impeachment on the ground that he had promoted the restoration of rebels to power. Representative James F. Wilson of Iowa, a Republican, answered that though Johnson was "the worst of the Presidents, . . . [i]f we cannot arraign the President for a specific crime for what are we to proceed against him? . . . If we cannot state upon paper a specific crime how are we to carry this cause to the Senate for trial?" The House then rejected the committee report, 100 to 57.

At this point Johnson gave the Republican majority what they demanded: a flagrant violation of a federal statute, the Tenure of Office Act. The president had long been at odds with Secretary of War Edwin M. Stanton, who had openly aligned himself with the congressional radicals and had refused to resign. In August 1867 Johnson removed Stanton from office and appointed General Grant in his place. The removal and appointment were made ad interim (that is, while the Senate was not in session), and so did not constitute a violation of the Tenure of Office Act. In accordance with the act, Johnson gave the Senate reasons for removing Stanton, thereby implying that Stanton was covered by the statute. In December 1867 the Senate refused to confirm the appointment, whereupon Grant resigned and Stanton resumed office.

In February 1868 Johnson forced the issue by summarily removing Stanton as secretary of war and appointing Major General Lorenzo Thomas as his successor. Since the Senate was then in session, the president's act appeared to be a specific violation of the Tenure of Office Act. This was precisely what the radical leaders had been waiting for, since the president had now presumably committed the specific statutory offense that many hesitant Republicans considered necessary for impeachment. Two days later, on February 24, the House voted, 128 to 47, to impeach the president.

On March 2 and 3 the House voted eleven articles of impeachment against Johnson. The first three articles charged the president with deliberately violating the Tenure of Office Act in removing Stanton and appointing Thomas. Articles 4 to 8 charged the president with entering into a conspiracy with Thomas to violate the same law. Conspiracy to violate a federal statute was a punishable offense by a statute of July 31, 1861. Article 9 charged Johnson with having attempted to subvert the provision in the Army Appropriation Act of 1867, which made all orders issuable through the general of the army. Article 10, inserted at the insistence of the radicals, shifted the indictment to the broad political basis by charging Johnson with attempting to "bring into disgrace, ridicule, hatred, contempt, and reproach the Congress of the United States." Article 11 summarized the previous counts and also charged Johnson with obstructing the enforcement of the Reconstruction Act of March 2, 1867.

On March 30 the impeachment trial began before the Senate, with Chief Justice Salmon P. Chase presiding. The first important matter of contention was the Senate's judicial status. Was the Senate sitting as a court or as a political body? The issue was extremely important. If the Senate was a regular court, then it was bound by legal rules of evidence. Presumably, also, it could convict the president only if it found him guilty of a specific offense either at common law or as defined in a federal statute. It could not rightfully convict the president merely as a political enemy of Congress. On the other hand, if the Senate sat as a political body, not only could it hear evidence usually inadmissible in a regular court of justice, but also it might conceivably convict the president of a political offense.

Johnson's attorneys argued that the trial was strictly a judicial proceeding. The Constitution, they pointed out, adhered strictly to a common law terminology in describing impeachment. The Senate was empowered to "try" impeachments, make a conviction, and enter a judgment. With equal force they contended that if impeachment was a mere political proceeding, then the whole long-established constitutional relationship between executive and Congress would be threatened. Were the president removable merely because he was politically unacceptable to Congress, executive independence would be destroyed and parliamentary ascendancy would replace the American presidential system.

The prosecution, on the other hand, argued that the nature of impeachment made the Senate something more than a court. Offenses other than those known to the common law were impeachable. Impeachment, they said, could be pressed for improper motive, or even "action against the public interest." If not, what other method was there for getting rid of an incompetent officeholder? Here they cited the Pickering precedent.

The issue was technically settled in favor of the defense. Early in the trial the Senate voted 31 to 19 to permit the chief justice to settle all questions of law, evidence, and the like, unless the Senate overruled him. The implication was that the chief justice was the presiding officer in a regular court, the senators sitting as associate justices. In reality, however, this ruling hardly destroyed the political character of the proceedings—on the part of both the opponents of the president and his supporters. On each side senators were prepared to vote according to their political convictions regardless of the evidence. Nor should this be taken as a total constitutional irregularity or failing. Whether one employs the broadly political or narrowly legalistic definition of "high crimes and misdemeanors," impeachment could hardly be expected to occur except in highly charged political circumstances. Under such conditions political convictions and principles rightly exert influence. The paradox of impeachment was that it required the use of judicial standards and rules to resolve what was essentially a political-constitutional crisis.

The principal argument in the trial centered on Johnson's supposed violation of the Tenure of Office Act. The prosecution argued that Johnson had committed a deliberate violation of a constitutional statute, clearly an impeachable offense. Johnson's attorneys in reply argued that the Tenure of Office Act did not apply to Johnson's removal of Stanton at all. The act specified that cabinet officers were to hold office during the term of the president appointing them, and for one month thereafter. Stanton had been appointed by Lincoln, not Johnson, and Johnson had never reappointed him but had merely tacitly assented to Stanton's continuance in office. The prosecution replied that Johnson was merely an "acting President" serving Lincoln's unexpired second term—a weak argument, for since Tyler's time vice-presidents succeeding to office had been considered as presidents-in-full.

The cornerstone of Johnson's defense, however, was the contention that the Tenure of Office Act was unconstitutional. Counsel for the president cited the debates in the First Congress on the removal power, Jackson's successful removal of Duane, and the established practice of eighty years, all of which supported the contention that the removal power was an executive prerogative separate and distinct from the power of appointment. Against the weight of these precedents the House managers retorted that the Tenure of Office Act was a formal declaration of the meaning of the Constitution, and, therefore, finally settled a long-mooted constitutional issue. This was tantamount to the assertion that Congress possessed a final right of constitutional interpretation even with regard to issues apparently settled by long-established practice.

Finally, the defense contended that Johnson's deliberate violation of law had not been subversive, but that the president had merely wished to test the act's constitutionality by bringing it before the courts. The president's action was, therefore, not a misdemeanor but an attempt to institute judicial proceedings. This argument the prosecution dealt with effectively. The president, they said, must like everyone else bear responsibility for his acts. If he violated a law on the grounds that it was unconstitutional, he must face the consequences if the proper tribunal, in this case the Senate, decided that the law was valid. If the Senate decided that the Tenure of Office Act was constitutional, then Johnson had committed a misdemeanor and must be punished regardless of intent.

On May 16 the Senate began balloting upon the impeachment articles.

The Republican majority in the Senate, intent on securing a conviction, instructed the chief justice to poll the Senate first on Article 11, which included all possible charges and supposedly offered the greatest chance of conviction.

The final vote on Article 11 was 35 "guilty" and 19 "not guilty," one vote short of the two-thirds majority required by the Constitution for impeachment. After an adjournment to May 26, the Senate voted on Articles 2 and 3. On both articles the vote was again 35 to 19, after which the Senate voted to adjourn as a tribunal *sine die*. Decisive votes were cast by seven Republican senators—Fessenden, Fowler, Grimes, Henderson, Ross, Trumbull, and Van Winkle—who joined with the Democratic minority in favor of acquittal. Historians have lauded these Republicans for selflessly rising above politics for the sake of constitutional principle, but in fact they had ample political reason to favor Johnson's acquittal. As conservative Republicans and hard-money men, they opposed the political and economic views of radical senator Ben Wade of Ohio, president pro tempore of the Senate, who would become president if Johnson were removed. Furthermore, by mid-May Johnson's actions on reconstruction had allayed much of the apprehension that led to the vote for impeachment in February. At the urging of conservative Republicans, Johnson appointed General John M. Schofield, a conservative who had enforced the reconstruction acts in Virginia, as secretary of war. He also agreed to submit the constitutions of Arkansas and South Carolina to Congress instead of withholding them. These developments suggested an end of executive obstructionism toward congressional reconstruction policy and enabled conservative Republicans to follow their constitutional inclination and vote for acquittal.

Historians have usually condemned Congress for using the impeachment power improperly to punish Johnson for mere political disagreements, on the assumption that political convictions ought to have played no part in the process. It is hard to agree with this premise, however. The purpose of impeachment is to deal with fundamental political controversies. It was intended by the founding fathers as a means by which Congress, ordinarily prevented from interfering with the discretionary powers of the president, might restrain the chief executive when his actions threatened the safety of the republic or the integrity of the constitutional order. Necessarily, impeachment is employed in situations which require political evaluation and judgment, so that it misses the point to criticize Congress for letting politics enter into impeachment decisions. Of course, it can always be objected that if the legislature can impeach for other than a clearly defined crime, there is a danger that it will use the power irresponsibly to pursue petty political objectives and punish the executive for mere disagreements of policy. If constitutionalism has any reality, however, this is an unlikely danger.

The pertinent question about impeachment is whether the political considerations involved are transient and trivial, or whether they obliterate all other considerations and influences. In Johnson's case it seems clear that while political passions ran deep—on both sides of the question—they did not banish a concern for fair procedure. It seems clear, furthermore, that Republicans had genuine reason to object to Johnson's legally correct but nonetheless obstructionist enforcement of the Reconstruction Acts. It is well to remember also that no model existed to guide lawmakers in exercising the impeachment power; Congress necessarily had to interpret the Constitution as it went along. No one could say what was constitutionally correct in the impeachment of a president because it had never been done.

The decisive constitutional interpretation that Congress made in 1868 was to require evidence of an indictable offense, a clear violation of positive law, as warrant for impeaching a president. Once Congress committed itself to this position, the strength of its case depended on the nature and purpose of the law that Johnson violated. And the Tenure of Office Act proved to be a weak foundation for the undertaking. Not that the removal power belonged so unequivocally to the president that Congress had absolutely no business trying to regulate it in any way. The weight of constitutional history favored the president's position on removals, but it did not render all other approaches to the problem of removals patently unconstitutional.

What weakened the congressional position was that the Tenure of Office Act was passed with a view toward catching Johnson. His violation of the law was a pretext by which to reach his more substantively objectionable actions; it was symbolic of his overall obstructionist course. But once seized on and made the basis of impeachment proceedings, as the constitutional conservatism of the Republican majority required, violation of the Tenure of Office Act could not be dealt with merely as a symbol or legitimate pretext for Johnson's grave political offenses. It had to be considered on its merits, in isolation from the pattern of events that gave rise to it. Or at least the defense succeeded in presenting the lonely violation of law in this way. And from this perspective Johnson's disregard of the act assumed far less serious, not to say trivial, proportions, especially in light of the history of the removal power. When presidential impeachment next became an issue a century later, the lesson of the Johnson trial seemed to be that the impeachment power could be used only for indictable crimes, not political offenses no matter how serious they might be.

National Enforcement of Civil Rights

Johnson's acquittal was followed by the readmission of all but three ex-Confederate states in the summer of 1868. In November General Ulysses S. Grant was elected president on a platform that announced the restoration of peace. Reconstruction was not over yet, however, for though the new southern state constitutions provided for Negro suffrage, there was nothing to prevent revocation of the guarantee should conservatives regain control of state governments. In the northern states, moreover, attempts to enfranchise

Negroes in several states and territories had met with defeat between 1865 and 1867, so that in all but a few states blacks were denied the suffrage. Republicans naturally wanted these votes, too, and, therefore, had political as well as ideological reasons for amending the Constitution to make Negroes voters throughout the nation.

Like civil rights, regulation of the suffrage before the war belonged exclusively to the states. The Constitution provided that members of the House of Representatives should be elected by those who were qualified to vote for the most numerous branch of the state legislature. This meant that while the right of suffrage in federal elections was lodged in the national Constitution, it did not actually arise until the franchise was conferred by the states. During the Civil War the disorganization of loyal state governments created a situation in which it was plausible, under the grasp-of-war and republican-government theories, to assert federal control over the suffrage. At the end of the war Negro suffrage was a leading radical reconstruction demand, but it was soon eclipsed by the more immediate problem of guaranteeing civil rights. Nevertheless, Negro suffrage was indirectly, though ineffectually, stipulated in the Fourteenth Amendment provision reducing the representation of states which denied blacks the right to vote. In January 1867 Congress enfranchised Negroes in the District of Columbia and the territories, and in March, as noted previously, the Military Reconstruction Act instituted black suffrage in the ten unreconstructed former rebel states.

The Fifteenth Amendment, framed in early 1869 and ratified in March 1870, authorized the federal government to regulate voting in limited respects without denying basic state control of the subject. It stated that "the right of citizens of the United States to vote shall not be denied or abridged by the United States or by any State on account of race, color, or previous condition of servitude." Section 2 gave Congress power to enforce the amendment by appropriate legislation. A moderate formulation, the Fifteenth Amendment not only embodied the state-action idea as a limitation on congressional power, but it also eschewed the radical demand for universal male suffrage. In other words, rather than confer the right to vote, it conferred the right not to be discriminated against in voting on racial grounds. Nor did the amendment, as radicals had proposed, protect blacks against exclusion from officeholding or prohibit states from employing literacy and property tests in regulating voting rights. As in other civil rights measures, Republican congressmen sought to achieve a balance between placing rights under national guarantees and maintaining traditional federalism.

Negro suffrage was the leading and by far the most bitter point of contention in the campaign waged by conservative white, ex-Confederate Southerners to wrest control of the reconstructed state governments from southern Republicans. Whereas official state action was the chief threat to Negro rights in the early postwar period, the main danger after 1868 came from the private violence of individuals and terrorist groups attempting to keep blacks from the polls. In part aided by tactics of intimidation, conservatives regained control of Georgia, Tennessee, Virginia, and North Carolina in 1870, and threatened to drive Republicans from power elsewhere in the South. To meet the political crisis presented by this movement, Congress passed additional civil rights laws known as the Enforcement Acts.

The purpose of the new laws was to enforce the Fourteenth and Fifteenth Amendments. The first measure, adopted in May 1870, prohibited state election officials from discriminating among voters on the basis of color in the application of local election laws. It also made bribery and intimidation of voters by individuals a federal crime and, in a section directed at terrorist groups, outlawed conspiracies to prevent citizens from exercising federal constitutional rights. The second Enforcement Act of February 1871 placed congressional elections in cities of over 20,000 population under direct federal supervision. The most important of the new civil rights laws, however, was the Ku Klux Act of April 1871.

Adopted in response to President Grant's request for action to stem southern violence directed against blacks, the Ku Klux Act represented the most far-reaching assertion of federal legislative power to enforce civil rights in the Reconstruction era. In an attempt to stop private violence, Congress stretched the state-action theory to its outer limit. As initially drafted, the bill proposed to punish violations of civil rights resulting from specific crimes of murder, assault, arson, etc., as carried out by individuals. Moderate and conservative Republicans thought the bill extended federal power too far into local affairs, however. Accordingly, they modified it to punish only the general crime of denying equal protection of the law and privileges and immunities of citizens. Reference to specific crimes was thus dropped. The act was directed at individuals on the theory that the failure of the states to punish private violence against blacks was a form of state action justifying congressional legislation. Where conspiracies and violence deprived persons of constitutional rights, the measure declared, "such facts will be deemed a denial by such State of the equal protection of the laws." The act also prohibited acts of individuals that prevented state officers from giving citizens equal protection of the law. Finally, it authorized the president to suspend the writ of habeas corpus and employ military power to deal with conspiracies against civil rights.

Enormous obstacles impeded federal civil rights enforcement, the largest of which was the overwhelming opposition of the vast majority of whites in the South. In the context of the country's deep-seated commitment to federalism, this fact in the long run was sufficient to cause the failure of the national enforcement effort. Nevertheless, in the crisis atmosphere of 1870–71 federal officials applied the civil rights law with vigor. In October 1871 Grant suspended the writ of habeas corpus and imposed martial law in South Carolina. Elsewhere federal officers initiated prosecutions, and by 1872 the Ku Klux Klan had been disbanded. The gain was merely temporary, however, for southern conservatives, who were opposed to the Klan now that it had outlived its usefulness, resorted to more sophisticated legal or quasi-legal forms of intimidation and coercion to deny black civil rights. At the same time, President Grant and the main body of Republicans, expressing northern opinion, desired reconciliation. In short, the next few years revealed that the task of enforcing Negro civil and political rights in the South was beyond the constitutional capacity of the federal government and the moral and ideological commitment of the Republican party.

Party moderates known as Liberal Republicans led the movement for reconciliation and an end to federal interference in southern affairs. In 1872 Congress took action under Section 3 of the Fourteenth Amendment, passing a broad amnesty act restoring the right of officeholding to nearly all ex-Confederates. This measure was adopted shortly after Liberal Republicans and Democrats met in Cincinnati and nominated Horace Greeley for president on a platform that called for "the immediate and absolute removal of all disabilities on account of the rebellion." Grant and the regular Republicans, benefiting from the sense of outrage that accounts of southern terrorism produced in the North, easily defeated the Liberal Republican–Democratic ticket in the election of 1872. But they failed to persist in civil rights enforcement. Costs were high, appropriations from Congress for civil rights enforcement were low, federal district judges in the South were unsympathetic, and federal officers often lacked competence. And always, of course, there was the profound and enduring white hostility. By 1873 government attorneys dropped most of the charges against former Klansmen. Altogether between 1870 and 1877 the government had a 34 percent success rate in prosecuting violations of the enforcement acts in the South.

As the northern desire to secure justice for the freedmen waned, the expedient political purpose that had also motivated the policy of civil rights enforcement remained. It was true that if justice were to be done, the Republican party must do it and must, therefore, be maintained in power. Yet after it became clear that justice could not be done, the quest for power naturally persisted and contributed to a further discrediting of the entire rights-enforcement enterprise. Recognizing the impossibility of sustaining Republican regimes in the South without permanent federal intervention, Republicans concentrated on keeping their hold on the North. Accordingly, more than half the money appropriated for federal supervision of elections under the Enforcement Act of 1871 was spent in northern and border states (where were located 63 of 68 cities of over 20,000 population affected by the act).

Under these circumstances Republicans refused to pass legislation interfering in the internal affairs of the southern states. Southern conservatives now had virtually a free hand. By 1875, operating mainly through the Democratic party, they had recovered control in eight of the eleven former Confederate states. Only in South Carolina, Florida, and Louisiana did Republican regimes still exist.

Meanwhile, in the election of 1874 the Republicans lost control of the

House of Representatives. The effect on them, perhaps paradoxically, was to spur one final civil rights effort. Partly in an attempt to retain the loyalty of southern blacks and partly as a sentimental tribute to exhausted idealism and the recently deceased Senator Charles Sumner, the lame-duck Congress passed the Civil Rights Act of 1875. Originally introduced by Sumner in 1870, the bill declared that all persons were entitled to the full and equal enjoyment of public accommodations in inns, transportation facilities, and places of public amusement. It punished any person who denied others equal access in these places. While its focus on social as opposed to political and legal discrimination gave the bill a radical appearance, significantly it had been stripped of its school desegregation features. It was generally thought to be practically unenforceable. Constitutionally, the act expressed a moderate interpretation of congressional power under the Fourteenth Amendment. Although it dealt with private denials of rights, Republicans upheld the act on the theory that the prohibited discrimination was in effect carried on under state authority—by businesses or institutions created or regulated by state law or in which the state had a substantial interest. Thus it did not depart from, though it went to the verge of, the state-action theory of the Fourteenth Amendment.

The Election of 1876

The presidential election of 1876, which resulted in a bitter political and constitutional controversy, greatly hastened the disintegration of congressional reconstruction.

The election at first appeared to have resulted in a victory for Samuel J. Tilden, the Democratic candidate. An early tabulation gave him 184 undisputed electoral votes, with but 185 votes necessary for election. Rutherford B. Hayes, the Republican candidate, had 165 undisputed votes. However, it soon appeared that Hayes had a chance to win. South Carolina, Florida, and Louisiana, with nineteen electoral votes, emerged as disputed states. Conflict also developed in Oregon, where one Republican elector was ineligible because he was a federal officeholder. Eventually all four states submitted dual electoral returns to Congress. If the disputed electoral votes of all four were added to the Republican column, Hayes would win.

Unfortunately, there was no constitutional provision governing such a situation, nor was there any clear precedent for solving the problem. The Constitution stipulated merely that electoral returns were to be opened by the president of the Senate in the presence of both houses, and should then be counted. After some initial confusion, a joint Senate-House committee on January 18 reported a bill creating an Electoral Commission of Fifteen to decide all disputed returns. The commission was to be composed of five representatives (three Democrats and two Republicans), five senators (three Republicans and two Democrats), and four justices of the Supreme Court, who were to name a fifth justice. The four justices designated were those assigned to the First, Third, Eighth, and Ninth Circuits, which in reality meant Nathan Clifford, Stephen J. Field, William Strong, and Samuel Miller—two Democrats and two Republicans. It was generally understood that the fifth justice would probably be David Davis of Illinois, who was nominally a Republican but very moderate in his viewpoint. The bill provided that the commission's decision on all disputed returns should be final unless an objection were sustained by the separate vote of both houses.

Nearly all Democrats and most Republicans supported this proposal. The Democrats believed that the commission would settle at least one disputed return in their favor and so elect Tilden. This expectation was badly shaken when the Illinois legislature elected Davis to the Senate. As a result the fifth justice named was Joseph Bradley, who was a staunch Republican, and thus the Republicans controlled the commission by a count of eight votes to seven.

When the electoral votes were counted in joint session, the returns from the four states were all disputed and were, therefore, referred to the commission. The commission settled the dispute by refusing "to go behind the election returns." It held that it had power merely to decide what electors had been certified in the proper manner by the correct returning board, in accordance with the state law; and that it could not investigate the actual popular vote to determine whether the returning board had correctly counted that vote. The commission based this conclusion on the argument that each state under the Constitution was entitled to choose its electors as it saw fit. The federal government, the commission held, had no constitutional power to control this process, for to do so would be an intrusion upon the sovereign sphere of state authority. In accordance with this rule, the commission decided, by a vote of eight to seven in each instance, that the Republican electors in South Carolina, Florida, and Louisiana had been properly certified and that their vote was valid.

The Oregon case was more difficult, but the commission resolved it by deciding that under Oregon law the secretary of state alone was the properly constituted returning board and that he had originally certified the election of the three Republican electors. Thus the commission by a partisan vote of eight to seven decided every disputed return in favor of the Republicans. The House dissented from the commission's report in every instance, but the Senate concurred, and, therefore, the commission's decisions stood. Hayes was accordingly declared elected, 185 votes to 184, the final decision being formally reached on March 3, the day before the scheduled inauguration.

With some merit Democrats contended that the Republicans stole the election. Hayes electors were evidently "counted in" in Florida and Louisiana under heavy Republican pressure. The commission also made all its decisions by a straight partisan majority; plainly, the eight Republican members were concerned mainly with placing Hayes in the White House. But the charges of fraud were so difficult to sort out that there really was not time for a thorough investigation. Furthermore the commission's decision had a certain consistency in constitutional theory. The contention that federal authority over state choice was limited to fixing the identity of the electors lawfully certified by the legal state agency for this purpose had a great deal of force. Electors are technically state officials, and the Constitution does indeed give each state the right to choose its electors as it wishes. To "go behind the returns" and subject a state election to scrutiny and analysis might well be considered an act of doubtful constitutionality.

Hayes's election marked the practical end of congressional reconstruction and federal control of the South. The Republicans had already lost control of the House, and the new president was a moderate who did not approve of continued federal interference in state affairs. Hayes at once withdrew federal troops from the three Republican-controlled southern states. The Democrats shortly assumed control in all of them, thereby bringing the Republican era in the South to a close.

Reconstruction and the Judiciary

If from the congressional and executive perspectives reconstruction policy effectively ended with the election of 1876, it persisted in constitutional law. Congress first shaped the public law of civil rights through constitutional amendment and legislation, but the Supreme Court had the last word as it confirmed and clarified changes emanating from the legislature.

The judicial history of reconstruction involves two separate considerations: the decisions of the Supreme Court in reconstruction-related cases, and the jurisdiction of the national courts as a critical feature in federalism. Doctrinally, the Court recognized reconstruction as an essentially political question in which judicial intervention would be inappropriate. Maintaining a neutrality that was sympathetic to the congressional reconstruction program, the Court in its interpretation of the reconstruction amendments on the whole confirmed the moderate states'-rights nationalist outlook evinced in Congress. Jurisdictionally a similar nationalist pattern of change emerged. Although Congress was careful to guard its reconstruction policies against possible judicial obstruction, it relied heavily on judicial power in its southern program and significantly enlarged federal court jurisdiction.

The announcement of the Court's decision in *Ex parte Milligan* in April 1866 had given pause to congressional Republicans, and the publication of the opinion in the case in December provoked further apprehension. By ruling against military trial of civilians where civil courts were open, the Court appeared to jeopardize the protection of freedmen's rights by existing Freedmen's Bureau courts, and by military tribunals that Congress might create in the future. In January 1867, in *Cummings* v. *Missouri,* the Court again acted adversely to Republican interests. It struck down, as a bill of attainder and ex post facto law, a provision in the Missouri constitution of 1865 requiring voters, ministers, attorneys, and candidates for public office to swear that they had never engaged in rebellion against the United States, or given aid to rebels, or even expressed any sympathy for their cause. The same day, by an identical 5–4 margin, the Court in *Ex parte Garland* held the Federal Test Act of 1865, imposing a similar oath upon federal attorneys, unconstitutional on the same grounds. These decisions prompted sharp criticism of the Supreme Court, and in January 1868 the House passed a bill requiring a two-thirds vote of the Court in order to declare an act of Congress unconstitutional. The Senate, however, allowed the bill to die.

Meanwhile the Court, in *Mississippi* v. *Johnson* (1867), refrained from seizing upon a dubious opportunity to rule upon the constitutionality of the congressional Reconstruction Acts of March 1867. In April attorneys for the Johnson government in Mississippi, then about to be replaced by a federal military administration, asked the Court to issue an injunction restraining the president from enforcing the two acts in question, on the ground that they were unconstitutional. This request was, to say the least, extraordinary, for although the Court, beginning with *Marbury* v. *Madison,* had several times held the executive to be amenable to judicial writ, the present petition was utterly unprecedented in that it asked the justices to interpose their authority directly against that of the president in his execution of an act of Congress. Attorney General Stanbery, appearing before the Court in response to the petition, called the request "scandalous" and in derogation of the president's properly constituted authority.

In a unanimous decision, the Court rejected Mississippi's plea. In an opinion that followed Stanbery's argument almost precisely, Chief Justice Chase drew a distinction between mere ministerial acts involving no discretion and large executive acts such as those carrying into effect a statute of Congress. The former, he said, could be enjoined; the latter involved political discretion and could not be. Such an injunction would amount to interference with the political acts of the legislative and executive branches of the government; defiance of it, Chase pointed out, would create an absurd situation.

In February 1868, in *Georgia* v. *Stanton,* the Court dismissed a similar suit in which the states of Georgia and Mississippi asked injunctions restraining the secretary of war and General Grant from enforcing the Reconstruction Acts. The suits, said the Court, involved proposed adjudication of political questions over which the Court had no jurisdiction. In February 1868, however, the Court consented to hear argument in *Ex parte McCardle,* a case arising in a Mississippi military tribunal, and carried on appeal under the authority of the Habeas Corpus Act of 1867. The case by implication involved the constitutionality of the Reconstruction Acts, since the appellant McCardle contended that the military tribunal which existed by virtue of the acts had no lawful authority.

When it thus became apparent that the Court might dare to declare the

Reconstruction Acts invalid, the Republican majority immediately moved to end the possibility. In March, Congress passed a bill dealing with appeals in customs and revenue cases. Attached was a rider repealing the Supreme Court's jurisdiction in all cases arising under the Habeas Corpus Act of 1867. The rider was admittedly designed to kill the *McCardle* case. Johnson gave the bill a blistering veto, but Congress immediately overrode the veto. In April 1869, accordingly, the Court dismissed McCardle's plea on the ground that the new act had destroyed its jurisdiction in the case. Whether or not the justices had acted in part out of a sense of caution is uncertain; however, their constitutional position was entirely sound. As Chief Justice Chase pointed out in his opinion, the Court holds its appellate jurisdiction entirely at the discretion of Congress, so that it was no longer empowered to act.

That the Court had not in any undue sense capitulated to Congress became clear in October 1869 when it accepted jurisdiction in a similar case. Edward M. Yerger, arrested and tried by a military commission for killing an army officer, sought release from an army prison in Mississippi on a writ of habeas corpus. In light of congressional repeal of part of the Habeas Corpus Act of 1867, the question was whether the Court had jurisdiction. Chief Justice Chase held in the affirmative, on the ground that the repeal of the sections of the 1867 law under which McCardle's suit was brought left intact the still very substantial habeas corpus jurisdiction of the Supreme Court under the Judiciary Act of 1789. Although in the *Yerger* case the Court did not examine the validity of the detention, its response to the jurisdictional question showed a distinct sense of judicial independence.

Not because it was cowed, but because reconstruction was fundamentally a political question, the Supreme Court steered clear of pronouncements concerning the constitutionality of the Reconstruction Acts of 1867. In *Texas* v. *White* (1869), it expressed this point of view while endorsing the congressional theory of reconstruction. The case involved an action by the Johnson government of Texas to recover title to certain United States bonds formerly the property of the state but sold by the Confederate state government during the war. It offered an opportunity to pass on the status of both the Confederate and Johnson state governments, and hence to analyze theories of secession and reconstruction.

Chief Justice Chase first presented the orthodox Lincoln theory of secession. The United States, said Chase, was an indissoluble Union of indissoluble states. Hence secession did not destroy the state of Texas, or the obligations of Texans as citizens of the United States. The pretended Confederate state government, though for some purposes a *de facto* government, was in its relations to the United States a mere illegal combination. Nevertheless, Chase reasoned, the war altered the relationship of the state to the Union. Its government refused to recognize its constitutional obligations, assumed the character of an enemy, and after the war ceased to exist. In consequence, Chase declared, "the rights of the State as a member, and of her people as citizens of the Union, were suspended." It had no government. Under the circumstances the national government—and Congress in particular—had to assume the responsibility for reestablishing the state's relationship with the Union. As congressional reconstruction theorists had done, Chase cited the opinion of the Supreme Court in *Luther* v. *Borden* that Congress had power under Article IV, Section 4, to guarantee republican governments in the states and to recognize the correct government in any state. Chase specifically refrained from expressing any opinion on the constitutionality of the Reconstruction Acts.

If it was proper for the judiciary to avoid preeminently political questions, it was necessary to settle conflicts concerning individual rights that involved the nature and scope of federal power under the new civil rights laws and constitutional amendments. In resolving questions of this sort, the Supreme Court played a major role in determining the long-range impact of reconstruction on the Constitution, as well as the lasting legal benefits of congressional reconstruction policy.

The earliest judicial interpretation of reconstruction civil rights legislation supported a broad view of national power. In 1867, for example, Chief Justice Chase, in the circuit court case *In re Turner* (1867), upheld the Civil Rights Act of 1866 under the Thirteenth Amendment in the course of striking down a Maryland apprenticeship law for blacks. In another circuit decision, *U.S.* v. *Rhodes* (1866), Justice Noah Swayne held the Civil Rights Act constitutional and interpreted the Thirteenth Amendment in sweeping fashion as a guarantee of free institutions, not merely a prohibition of chattel slavery. In litigation arising a few years later under the Enforcement Acts, federal judges exhibited a similarly extensive view of federal power. Thus in circuit court decisions Supreme Court Justices William B. Woods and William Strong upheld congressional power to legislate directly against private civil rights offenders when states, through inaction, denied Negro citizens equal protection of the laws.

By 1873 civil rights enforcement zeal was flagging, however, and judicial decisions reflected the changing northern outlook. The *Slaughterhouse Cases,* the occasion for the Supreme Court's first interpretation of the Fourteenth Amendment, revealed the moderate nationalist position that would characterize the Court's reconstruction decisions for the next decade. Asserting that the Fourteenth Amendment was intended to protect Negro rights, Justice Samuel F. Miller, for a 5–4 majority, dismissed the contention of a group of white butchers from New Orleans that a Louisiana law creating a monopoly in the slaughtering trade deprived them of rights of United States citizenship under the Fourteenth Amendment. Blacks were thus not directly involved in the case, but they would be affected by the Court's definition of Fourteenth Amendment rights.

Employing states'-rights nationalist theory, Justice Miller described federal and state citizenship as separate yet partially overlapping systems of rights. According to Miller, national citizenship comprehended the relatively few rights arising from an individual's direct relationship with the federal government, such as the right to receive protection abroad, the right of access to the federal government, and the right to enjoy benefits secured by American treaties with foreign countries. He noted further that national citizenship included rights defined by the Constitution, such as the rights of assembly and petition enumerated in the First Amendment and the privilege of the writ of habeas corpus identified in Article I, Section 9. State citizenship in contrast was broader, and included the wide array of rights of person and property that characterized republican civil liberty generally. In Miller's view, the effect of the Fourteenth Amendment was to place the rights of national citizenship under the protection of Congress, and prohibit the states from violating them. The privileges-and-immunities clause accomplished this purpose.

Justice Miller did not espouse the view, attributed to him by the minority opinion of Justice Field in *Slaughterhouse,* that the Fourteenth Amendment effected no alteration in federal-state relations in respect of the rights of citizens. The amendment protected, against state encroachment, constitutional rights that were previously protected only against the federal government, under *Barron* v. *Baltimore* (1833). The amendment thus changed federal and state jurisdiction. It did not, however, create new federal rights, nor did it shift to federal citizenship protection the great mass of ordinary rights that pertained to state citizenship, including the freedom from unreasonable monopolies. The Fourteenth Amendment signified a completion of federal jurisdiction, not a revolution in federalism that placed all the fundamental rights of a free person or citizen under national guarantee, as the dissenting justices proposed. Acceptance of the argument against the Louisiana law, Miller asserted, would make the Supreme Court "a perpetual censor upon all legislation of the States, on the civil rights of their own citizens." Moreover, if the Court could regulate the states in this sweeping manner, so too could Congress, producing a revolution in federalism. Yet it was manifestly not the intent of Congress and the states in adopting the Fourteenth Amendment, Miller observed, "to transfer the security and protection of all the civil rights . . . from the States to the federal government." Miller's interpretation recognized the expansion of federal power intended by Congress in the Fourteenth Amendment, and the purpose of preserving the states as the centers of republican government in respect of ordinary civil rights.

In the next several years a series of decisions interpreted the reconstruction amendments and civil rights laws from the moderate states'-rights nationalist perspective. The Supreme Court's central purpose in these decisions was to vindicate federal power to protect civil rights, while maintaining the states' primary jurisdiction in regulating civil rights. In *United States* v. *Cruikshank* (1874), for example, a circuit court case in which scores of Louisiana whites were indicted under the Enforcement Act of 1870 for conspiracy to deprive Negroes of their rights as United States citizens, Justice Joseph P. Bradley held that the Fourteenth Amendment authorized federal legislation only against state action denying rights. Under the Thirteenth and Fifteenth Amendments

Congress could prohibit private denial of rights, Bradley reasoned, but only where the denial was motivated by racial hostility rather than ordinary criminal intent. Because the government's indictment of the Colfax, Louisiana, rioters failed to specify their intention to deprive blacks of civil rights on account of race, Bradley found it invalid.

The Supreme Court affirmed this decision in 1876. Reiterating the state-action theory of the Fourteenth Amendment, Chief Justice Morrison R. Waite held that the amendment "adds nothing to the rights of one citizen as against another. It simply furnishes a federal guaranty against any encroachment by the States upon the fundamental rights which belong to every citizen as a member of society." Waite did not deny that Congress could punish private discrimination under the Thirteenth and Fifteenth Amendments. But he ruled the indictment invalid under the Thirteenth Amendment (and also the Civil Rights Act of 1866) because it did not expressly aver racial hostility as the basis for the denial of rights. In *United States* v. *Harris* (1883) the Supreme Court invalidated an indictment of whites for denial of Negro rights on the ground that the Ku Klux Act of 1871, the basis of the indictment, failed to respect the state-action limitation of the Fourteenth Amendment. The act was not framed, explained Justice William B. Woods, so as to take effect only after it was established that states had denied civil rights. Rather, it punished private wrongs irrespective of state efforts in enforcing civil rights.

Similarly, in the *Civil Rights Cases* of 1883 the Supreme Court struck down the Civil Rights Act of 1875 because it was directed against private discrimination, not state action. Yet, though it was small consolation to blacks, the Court again recognized the possibility of federal legislation punishing private individuals under the Fourteenth Amendment on a showing of state failure to protect citizens against private wrongs. Justice Bradley also held in the *Civil Rights Cases* that under the Thirteenth Amendment Congress could legislate to protect the fundamental rights inherent in freedom, to abolish the "badges and incidents" of slavery. Yet regard for federalism required placing a limit even on this power to abolish slavery, in the sense of drawing a distinction between essential civil rights and social rights. Like his moderate Republican colleagues, Bradley rejected the contention that denial of equal access to public accommodations was a "badge" of slavery that Congress could prohibit.

In voting rights cases the Supreme Court also accommodated the retreat from reconstruction without surrendering to the conservative demand for a complete denial of federal power and restoration of antebellum federalism. Indeed, in this sphere the Court upheld extensions of national power more firmly than in the civil rights field generally. In *United States* v. *Reese* (1876), the leading case, the Court pointed out the obvious but important fact, clearly understood by its framers, that the Fifteenth Amendment did not confer the right of suffrage on anyone. It merely prohibited the states or the United States from excluding a person from the franchise because of race, color, or previous condition of servitude. The primary control of suffrage remained with the states. Accordingly, the Court threw out an indictment of a Kentucky voting official for refusing to count a Negro's vote, on the ground that the law on which the indictment was based, the Enforcement Act of 1870, did not in express terms restrict itself to racially motivated offenses. It unconstitutionally provided penalties for obstructing or hindering any person from voting in any election. With respect to state elections, Congress could only legislate against discrimination based on race, but it could direct its sanction against both state and private individual action.

The Waite Court affirmed more extensive federal power to protect voting rights in national elections. Initially in the early 1870s lower federal courts held that the right to vote in federal elections derived from state constitutions and laws. In *Ex parte Yarbrough* (1884), however, the Supreme Court declared that voters in national elections owed their right of suffrage to the federal Constitution, although it was necessary to consult state constitutions and laws to find out the qualifications for voting. The *Yarbrough* case was significant also for establishing federal power to protect the right to vote in national elections against private discrimination, whether racially motivated or not. In *Ex parte Siebold* (1880), *Ex parte Clark* (1880), and *United States* v. *Gale* (1883), the Court upheld convictions of state officers for fraudulent interference with national elections. Thus the Court in general affirmed federal power to guard the right to vote in state elections against racially inspired denial by either state officers or private individuals, and in federal elections against denial from any source and for any reason whatever.

Formal state discrimination against blacks, the reason for adopting civil rights laws and amendments in the first place, also came under the Court's ban. Thus in *Strauder* v. *West Virginia* (1880) the Court found a law limiting jury duty to whites to be in violation of the equal protection clause of the Fourteenth Amendment. In *Ex parte Virginia* (1880) it declared the action of a state judge in excluding blacks from jury service a violation of the Civil Rights Act of 1875. And in *Neal* v. *Delaware* (1880) it held that although a state's constitution and laws did not exclude blacks, the exclusion of Negroes from jury service in actual practice denied equal protection. Yet the Court undercut the force of these decisions when it ruled in *Virginia* v. *Rives* (1880) that the absence of Negroes from a jury did not necessarily mean a denial of right. By the cautious exercise of discretionary authority local officials could practically exclude Negroes.

The Court in the 1870s and early 1880s was hardly inclined to stop the retreat from reconstruction undertaken by the political branches and the northern public. Nevertheless, the Court generally confirmed the moderate nationalist view of the changes in federalism intended by the framers of the reconstruction amendments. And though most of the short-run consequences of the Court's decisions were practically debilitating for civil rights enforcement, the confirmation of national power, even if in doctrines and dicta that would not be employed for decades, prevented the adoption of the extreme conservative view that denied virtually any change in federal–state relations. The Court, like Congress, tried to fashion instruments for national protection of civil rights while, in deference to federalism, allowing the states to retain primary responsibility for the administration of justice in ordinary civil and criminal matters. As between these conflicting purposes, compromise was necessary.

The ultimate abandonment of the reconstruction equal-rights purpose came in the 1890s with the acceptance of the "separate-but-equal" doctrine by a very different Supreme Court. In *Plessy* v. *Ferguson* (1896) the Court found no constitutional objection to a Louisiana law requiring separate railway coaches for whites and blacks, provided that Negroes were furnished accommodations equal to whites. Formal racial classification, which the Court had earlier condemned, was thus legitimized, and was rapidly extended to schools and most other social institutions. In respect of political rights, too, the Court at this time acquiesced in southern disfranchisement devices. In *Williams* v. *Mississippi* (1898) it approved a law authorizing literacy tests by which blacks could effectively be excluded from elections. In the same case the Court endorsed the poll tax as a valid prerequisite for the franchise. Yet even in the militantly racist atmosphere of the early twentieth century, reconstruction did not quite end. In 1915 the Supreme Court, in *Guinn* v. *United States,* struck down "grandfather laws" which disfranchised Negroes by extending the franchise only to those whose ancestors had had the right to vote in 1866. And in 1917, in *Buchanan* v. *Warley,* the Court ruled unconstitutional municipal ordinances prohibiting blacks from moving into white neighborhoods. With this rejection of an official apartheid policy the equal-rights story pointed ahead to the "Second Reconstruction" of the mid-twentieth century.

If Supreme Court opinions during reconstruction frequently revealed an assertive independence, the legislation by which Congress marked out the scope of judicial power also expressed confidence in the national judiciary. In this technical and often pedestrian sphere of policy Republican lawmakers enlarged national power to overcome pre-war incapacities born of excessive concern with states' rights.

Removal of cases from state to federal courts was a major source of expanded national judicial power. As noted previously, this process began in the Habeas Corpus Act of 1863, which permitted removal from states to federal courts of civil and criminal cases involving all acts performed under orders by national officials. This bridge in the federal system was widened in the Civil Rights Act of 1866, the Internal Revenue Act of 1866, and the voting rights Enforcement Act of 1871. In these statutes removal was intended to facilitate the carrying out of substantive policies; in others expansion of federal court jurisdiction was the chief object. The most important of these measures was the Jurisdiction and Removal Act of 1875, which permitted removal in all suits arising under the Constitution, laws, and treaties of the United States; suits in which the United States was a plaintiff; suits between citizens of different states; and suits between citizens and aliens. The act also gave the lower federal courts original jurisdiction in all cases arising under the Constitution, laws, and treaties. Thus the old Federalist party objective of giving the national courts jurisdiction as broad as the Constitution permitted, expressed in the short-lived Judiciary Act of 1801, was finally achieved.

Another extremely important change in federalism was accomplished by legislation enlarging the habeas corpus jurisdiction of federal courts. The decisive statute for this purpose was the Habeas Corpus Act of February 5, 1867. Under the Judiciary Act of 1789 the writ of habeas corpus had application only to persons held under federal authority, in executive confinement. It could not, in other words, be used to secure release from state detention. The Habeas Corpus Act of 1867, however, broke down this barrier of state power. It made the writ available "in all cases where any person may be restricted of his or her liberty in violation of the Constitution, or of any treaty or law of the United States." Although in 1867 Congress repealed the part of the law that allowed the Supreme Court to review a lower federal court's disposition of a habeas corpus petition, federal courts retained the power under the act to review even the highest state court decisions.

Both for political and technical-professional reasons Congress altered the organization of the federal court system in the 1860s. Before the war five of nine judicial circuits comprised slave states exclusively. In order to reduce southern influence in the judicial system Congress in 1862 redrew the lines to put the slave states into three circuits. It also added a tenth circuit for the West Coast and increased the number of Supreme Court judges to ten. In 1866, principally on the advice of the Court itself, Congress reduced the size of the Court from ten to seven, effective with the next two vacancies (Justice Catron had died in 1865). It further changed circuit lines so that only one circuit, the Fifth, would consist exclusively of former slave states, and it reduced the number of circuits to nine. Additional reform occurred in 1869 when, with the Court numbering eight justices, Congress increased its size to nine and added nine circuit court judges to relieve Supreme Court justices of some of the burden of riding circuit. Shortly after passage of this act a Supreme Court vacancy occurred, and President Grant had two appointments to make. He named Republicans Bradley and Strong, and the augmented Court, reversing the decision in *Hepburn* v. *Griswold* (1870), upheld the Legal Tender Act of 1862 as constitutional in the *Second Legal Tender Cases* (1871). Democrats cried "court packing," but the charge was groundless, for Congress enlarged the Court mainly to give it an odd number of justices and eliminate tie votes.

The Constitutional Significance of Reconstruction

The enormous expansion of federal power since the New Deal, as well as the acceptance of the idea of racial equality in the mid-twentieth century, have made it difficult to appreciate the constitutional significance of Reconstruction as it appeared to the Civil War generation. From their perspective reconstruction restored the states to a properly balanced federal Union, under rules and principles of equal rights that brought republican government to the former slave states and secured the liberty and basic civil rights of the freed blacks. From a late-twentieth-century perspective, the restoration of federalism occurred at the expense of genuine black freedom and equal rights. If this difference in perception is inevitable and perhaps irreconcilable, it is nevertheless remarkable that in a society so strongly committed to the idea of Negro inferiority the doctrine of equal rights found expression as fully as it did in the constitutional amendments and laws of the day.

The most significant constitutional change occurring between 1860 and 1880 was the extension of national power over personal liberty and civil rights through the Thirteenth, Fourteenth, and Fifteenth Amendments, the Civil Rights Act of 1866, and the Enforcement Acts of the 1870s. The corollary of this expansion of federal power was the destruction of state sovereignty and the curtailment of states' rights. No longer were the states autonomous in matters of individual rights. Civil rights were thus nationalized. But only in limited ways did this nationalization employ the constitutional technique of centralization. States retained their primary responsibility and power to regulate civil rights. They did so, however, under national equal-rights guarantees that gave the federal government a qualified but potentially effective power to protect the rights of American citizens. The twentieth-century liberal correlation of centralized national power and individual liberty owes much of its appeal to the accomplishments of the Union government in abolishing slavery and introducing equal-rights principles into American constitutional law.

Nevertheless, by 1880 nationalizing civil rights energies were all but exhausted as Northerners acquiesced in the restoration of conservative white rule and the end of federal intervention in the South. Changes in economy and society had, of course, continued to take place throughout the Reconstruction period. These changes now became central issues in constitutional politics as Americans tried to adjust their still largely decentralized governmental system to the new social environment created by the industrial revolution of the late nineteenth century.

APPENDIX
ONE

Declaration of Independence in Congress, July 4, 1776

THE UNANIMOUS DECLARATION OF THE THIRTEEN UNITED STATES OF AMERICA

When in the Course of human events, it becomes necessary for one people to dissolve the political bands which have connected them with another, and to assume among the Powers of the earth, the separate and equal station to which the Laws of Nature and of Nature's God entitle them, a decent respect to the opinions of mankind requires that they should declare the causes which impel them to the separation.

We hold these truths to be self-evident, that all men are created equal, that they are endowed by their Creator with certain unalienable Rights, that among these are Life, Liberty and the pursuit of Happiness. That to secure these rights, Governments are instituted among Men, deriving their just powers from the consent of the governed, That whenever any Form of Government becomes destructive of these ends, it is the Right of the People to alter or to abolish it, and to institute new Government, laying its foundation on such principles and organizing its powers in such form, as to them shall seem most likely to effect their Safety and Happiness. Prudence, indeed, will dictate that Governments long established should not be changed for light and transient causes; and accordingly all experience hath shown, that mankind are more disposed to suffer, while evils are sufferable, than to right themselves by abolishing the forms to which they are accustomed. But when a long train of abuses and usurpations, pursuing invariably the same Object evinces a design to reduce them under absolute Despotism, it is their right, it is their duty, to throw off such Government, and to provide new Guards for their future security.—Such has been the patient sufferance of these Colonies; and such is now the necessity which constrains them to alter their former Systems of Government. The history of the present King of Great Britain is a history of repeated injuries and usurpations, all having in direct object the establishment of an absolute Tyranny over these States. To prove this, let Facts be submitted to a candid world.

He refused his Assent to Laws, the most wholesome and necessary for the public good.

He has forbidden his Governors to pass Laws of immediate and pressing importance, unless suspended in their operation till his Assent should be obtained; and when so suspended, he has utterly neglected to attend to them.

He has refused to pass other Laws for the accommodation of large districts of people, unless those people would relinquish the right of Representation in the Legislature, a right inestimable to them and formidable to tyrants only.

He has called together legislative bodies at places unusual, uncomfortable, and distant from the depository of their Public Records, for the sole purpose of fatiguing them into compliance with his measures.

He has dissolved Representative Houses repeatedly, for opposing with manly firmness his invasions on the rights of the people.

He has refused for a long time, after such dissolutions, to cause others to be elected; whereby the Legislative Powers, incapable of Annihilation, have returned to the People at large for their exercise; the State remaining in the mean time exposed to all the dangers of invasion from without, and convulsions within.

He has endeavoured to prevent the population of these States; for that purpose obstructing the Laws for Naturalization of Foreigners; refusing to pass others to encourage their migrations hither, and raising the conditions of new Appropriations of Lands.

He has obstructed the Administration of Justice, by refusing his Assent to Laws for establishing Judiciary Powers.

He has made Judges dependent on his Will alone, for the tenure of their offices, and the amount and payment of their salaries.

He has erected a multitude of New Offices, and sent hither swarms of Officers to harass our people, and eat out their substance.

He has kept among us, in times of peace, Standing Armies without the Consent of our legislatures.

He has affected to render the Military independent of and superior to the Civil Power.

He has combined with others to subject us to a jurisdiction foreign to our constitution, and unacknowledged by our laws; giving his Assent to their acts of pretended Legislation:

For quartering large bodies of armed troops among us:

For protecting them, by a mock Trial, from Punishment for any Murders which they should commit on the Inhabitants of these States:

For cutting off our Trade with all parts of the world:

For imposing taxes on us without our consent:

For depriving us in many cases, of the benefits of Trial by Jury:

For transporting us beyond Seas to be tried for pretended offences:

For abolishing the free System of English Laws in a neighbouring Province, establishing therein an Arbitrary government, and enlarging its Boundaries so as to render it at once an example and fit instrument for introducing the same absolute rule into these Colonies:

For taking away our Charters, abolishing our most valuable Laws, and altering fundamentally the Forms of our Governments:

For suspending our own Legislatures, and declaring themselves invested with Power to legislate for us in all cases whatsoever.

He has abdicated Government here, by declaring us out of his Protection and waging War against us.

He has plundered our seas, ravaged our Coasts, burnt our towns, and destroyed the lives of our people.

He is at this time transporting large armies of foreign mercenaries to compleat the works of death, desolation and tyranny, already begun with circumstances of Cruelty & Perfidy scarcely paralleled in the most barbarous ages, and totally unworthy the Head of a civilized nation.

He has constrained our fellow Citizens taken Captive on the high Seas to bear Arms against their country, to become the executioners of their friends and Brethren, or to fall themselves by their Hands.

He has excited domestic insurrections amongst us, and has endeavoured to bring on the inhabitants of our frontiers, the merciless Indian Savages, whose known rule of warfare, is an undistinguished destruction of all ages, sexes and conditions.

In every stage of these Oppressions We have Petitioned for Redress in the most humble terms: Our repeated Petitions have been answered only by repeated injury. A Prince, whose character is thus marked by every act which may define a Tyrant, is unfit to be the ruler of a free people.

Nor have We been wanting in attentions to our British brethren. We have warned them from time to time of attempts by their legislature to extend an unwarrantable jurisdiction over us. We have reminded them of the circumstances of our emigration and settlement here. We have appealed to their native justice and magnanimity, and we have conjured them by the ties of our common kindred to disavow these usurpations which, would inevitably interrupt our connections and correspondence. They too have been deaf to the voice of justice and of consanguinity. We must, therefore, acquiesce in the necessity, which denounces our Separation, and hold them, as we hold the rest of mankind, Enemies in War, in Peace Friends.

We, therefore, the Representatives of the united States of America in

General Congress, Assembled, appealing to the Supreme Judge of the world for the rectitude of our intentions, do in the Name, and by authority of the good People of these Colonies, solemnly publish and declare, That these United Colonies are, and of Right ought to be Free and Independent States; that they are Absolved from all Allegiance to the British Crown, and that all political connection between them and the State of Great Britain, is and ought to be totally dissolved; and that as Free and Independent States, they have full power to levy War, conclude Peace, contract Alliances, establish Commerce, and to do all other Acts and Things which Independent States may of right do. And for the support of this Declaration, with a firm reliance on the Protection of Divine Providence, we mutually pledge to each other our Lives, our Fortunes and our sacred Honor.

JOHN HANCOCK.

BUTTON GWINNETT.	JOSEPH HEWES.
LYMAN HALL.	JOHN PENN.
GEO. WALTON.	EDWARD RUTLEDGE.
WM. HOOPER.	THOS. HEYWARD, JR.

APPENDIX
TWO

Articles of Confederation

TO ALL to whom these Presents shall come, we the undersigned Delegates of the States affixed to our Names send greeting.

Whereas the Delegates of the United States of America in Congress assembled did on the fifteenth day of November in the Year of our Lord One Thousand Seven Hundred and Seventy-seven, and in the Second Year of the Independence of America agree to certain articles of Confederation and perpetual Union between the States of Newhampshire, Massachusetts-bay, Rhodeisland and Providence Plantations, Connecticut, New York, New Jersey, Pennsylvania, Delaware, Maryland, Virginia, North-Carolina, South-Carolina and Georgia in the Words following, viz.

"Articles of Confederation and perpetual Union between the States of Newhampshire, Massachusetts-bay, Rhodeisland and Providence Plantations, Connecticut, New-York, New-Jersey, Pennsylvania, Delaware, Maryland, Virginia, North-Carolina, South-Carolina and Georgia.

ARTICLE I. The stile of this confederacy shall be "The United States of America."

ARTICLE II. Each State retains its sovereignty, freedom and independence, and every power, jurisdiction and right, which is not by this confederation expressly delegated to the United States, in Congress assembled.

ARTICLE III. The said States hereby severally enter into a firm league of friendship with each other, for their common defence, the security of their liberties, and their mutual and general welfare, binding themselves to assist each other, against all force offered to, or attacks made upon them, or any of them, on account of religion, sovereignty, trade or any other pretence whatever.

ARTICLE IV. The better to secure and perpetuate mutual friendship and intercourse among the people of the different States in this Union, the free inhabitants of each of these States, paupers, vagabonds and fugitives from justice excepted, shall be entitled to all privileges and immunities of free citizens in the several States; and the people of each State shall have free ingress and regress to and from any other State, and shall enjoy therein all the privileges of trade and commerce, subject to the same duties, impositions and restrictions as the inhabitants thereof respectively, provided that such restrictions shall not extend so far as to prevent the removal of property imported into any State, to any other State of which the owner is an inhabitant; provided also that no imposition, duties or restriction shall be laid by any State, on the property of the United States, or either of them.

If any person guilty of, or charged with treason, felony, or other high misdemeanor in any State, shall flee from justice, and be found in any of the United States, he shall upon demand of the Governor or Executive power, of the State from which he fled, be delivered up and removed to the State having jurisdiction of his offence.

Full faith and credit shall be given in each of these States to the records, acts and judicial proceedings of the courts and magistrates of every other State.

ARTICLE V. For the more convenient management of the general interests of the United States, delegates shall be annually appointed in such manner as the legislature of each State shall direct, to meet in Congress on the first Monday in November, in every year, with a power reserved to each State, to recall its delegates or any of them, at any time within the year, and to send others in their stead, for the remainder of the year.

No State shall be represented in Congress by less than two, nor by more than seven members; and no person shall be capable of being a delegate for more than three years in any term of six years; nor shall any person, being a delegate, be capable of holding any office under the United States, for which he, or another for his benefit receives any salary, fees or emolument of any kind.

Each State shall maintain its own delegates in a meeting of the States, and while they act as members of the committee of the States.

In determining questions in the United States, in Congress assembled, each State shall have one vote.

Freedom of speech and debate in Congress shall not be impeached or questioned in any court, or place out of Congress, and the members of Congress shall be protected in their persons from arrests and imprisonments, during the time of their going to and from, and attendance on Congress, except for treason, felony, or breach of the peace.

ARTICLE VI. No State without the consent of the United States in Congress assembled, shall send any embassy to, or receive any embassy from, or enter into any conference, agreement, alliance or treaty with any king, prince or state; nor shall any person holding any office of profit or trust under the United States, or any of them, accept of any present, emolument, office or title of any kind whatever from any king, prince or foreign state; nor shall the United States in Congress assembled, or any of them, grant any title of nobility.

No two or more States shall enter into any treaty, confederation or alliance whatever between them, without the consent of the United States in Congress assembled, specifying accurately the purposes for which the same is to be entered into, and how long it shall continue.

No State shall lay any imposts or duties, which may interfere with any stipulations in treaties, entered into by the United States in Congress assembled, with any king, prince or state, in pursuance of any treaties already proposed by Congress, to the courts of France and Spain.

No vessels of war shall be kept up in time of peace by any State, except such number only, as shall be deemed necessary by the United States in Congress assembled, for the defence of such State, or its trade; nor shall any body of forces be kept up by any State, in time of peace, except such number only, as in the judgment of the United States, in Congress assembled, shall be deemed requisite to garrison the forts necessary for the defence of such State; but every State shall always keep up a well regulated and disciplined militia, sufficiently armed and accoutred, and shall provide and constantly have ready for use, in public stores, a due number of field pieces and tents, and a proper quantity of arms, ammunition and camp equipage.

No State shall engage in any war without the consent of the United States in Congress assembled, unless such State be actually invaded by enemies, or shall have received certain advice of a resolution being formed by some nation of Indians to invade such State, and the danger is so imminent as not to admit of a delay, till the United States in Congress assembled can be consulted: nor shall any State grant commissions to any ships or vessels of war, nor letters of marque or reprisal, except it be after a declaration of war by the United States in Congress assembled, and then only against the kingdom or state and the subjects thereof, against which war has been so declared, and under such regulations as shall be established by the United States in Congress assembled, unless such State be infested by pirates, in which case vessels of war may be fitted out for that occasion, and kept so long as the danger shall continue, or until the United States in Congress assembled shall determine otherwise.

ARTICLE VII. When land-forces are raised by any State for the common defence, all officers of or under the rank of colonel, shall be appointed by the Legislature of each State respectively by whom such forces shall be raised, or in such manner as such State shall direct, and all vacancies shall be filled up by the State which first made the appointment.

ARTICLE VIII. All charges of war, and all other expenses that shall be incurred for the common defence or general welfare, and allowed by the United States in Congress assembled, shall be defrayed out of a common treasury, which shall be supplied by the several States, in proportion to the value of all land within each State, granted to or surveyed for any person, as such land and the buildings and improvements thereon shall be estimated according to such mode as the United States in Congress assembled, shall from time to time direct and appoint.

The taxes for paying that proportion shall be laid and levied by the authority and direction of the Legislature of the several States within the time agreed upon by the United States in Congress assembled.

ARTICLE IX. The United States in Congress assembled, shall have the sole and exclusive right and power of determining on peace and war, except in the cases mentioned in the sixth article—of sending and receiving ambassadors—entering into treaties and alliances, provided that no treaty of commerce shall be made whereby the legislative power of the respective States shall be restrained from imposing such imposts and duties on foreigners, as their own people are subjected to, or from prohibiting the exportation or importation of and species of goods or commodities whatsoever—of establishing rules for deciding in all cases, what captures on land or water shall be legal, and in what manner prizes taken by land or naval forces in the service of the United States shall be divided or appropriated—of granting letters of marque and reprisal in times of peace—appointing courts for the trial of piracies and felonies committed on the high seas and establishing courts for receiving and determining finally appeals in all cases of captures, provided that no member of Congress shall be appointed a judge of any of the said courts.

The United States in Congress assembled shall also be the last resort on appeal in all disputes and differences now subsisting or that hereafter may arise between two or more States concerning boundary, jurisdiction or any other cause whatever; which authority shall always be exercised in the manner following. Whenever the legislative or executive authority or lawful agent of any State in controversy with another shall present a petition to Congress, stating the matter in question and praying for a hearing, notice thereof shall be given by order of Congress to the legislative or executive authority of the other State in controversy, and a day assigned for the appearance of the parties by their lawful agents, who shall then be directed to appoint by joint consent, commissioners or judges to constitute a court for hearing and determining the matter in question: but if they cannot agree, Congress shall name three persons out of each of the United States, and from the list of such persons each party shall alternately strike out one, the petitioners beginning, until the number shall be reduced to thirteen; and from that number not less than seven, nor more than nine names as Congress shall direct, shall in the presence of Congress be drawn out by lot, and the persons whose names shall be so drawn or any five of them, shall be commissioners or judges, to hear and finally determine the controversy, so always as a major part of the judges who shall hear the cause shall agree in the determination: and if either party shall neglect to attend at the day appointed, without reasons, which Congress shall judge sufficient, or being present shall refuse to strike, the Congress shall proceed to nominate three persons out of each State, and the Secretary of Congress shall strike in behalf of such party absent or refusing; and the judgment and sentence of the court to be appointed, in the manner before prescribed, shall be final and conclusive; and if any of the parties shall refuse to submit to the authority of such court, or to appear or defend their claim or cause, the court shall nevertheless proceed to pronounce sentence, or judgment, which shall in like manner be final and decisive, the judgment or sentence and other procedings being in either case transmitted to Congress, and lodged among the acts of Congress for the security of the parties concerned: provided that every commissioner, before he sits in judgment, shall take an oath to be administered by one of the judges of the supreme or superior court of the State where the cause shall be tried, "well and truly to hear and determine the matter in question, according to the best of his judgment, without favour, affection or hope of reward:" provided also that no State shall be deprived of territory for the benefit of the United States.

All controversies concerning the private right of soil claimed under different grants of two or more States, whose jurisdiction as they may respect such lands, and the states which passed such grants are adjusted, the said grants or either of them being at the same time claimed to have originated antecedent to such settlement of jurisdiction, shall on the petition of either party to the Congress of the United States, be finally determined as near as may be in the same manner as is before prescribed for deciding disputes respecting territorial jurisdiction between different States.

The United States in Congress assembled shall also have the sole and exclusive right and power of regulating the alloy and value of coin struck by their own authority, or by that of the respective States—fixing the standard of weights and measures throughout the United States—regulating the trade and managing all affairs with the Indians, not members of any of the States, provided that the legislative right of any State within its own limits be not infringed or violated—establishing and regulating post-offices from one State to another, throughout all the United States, and exacting such postage on the papers passing thro' the same as may be requisite to defray the expenses of the said office—appointing all officers of the land forces, in the service of the United States, excepting regimental officers—appointing all the officers of the naval forces, and commissioning all officers whatever in the service of the United States—making rules for the government and regulation of the said land and naval forces, and directing their operations.

The United States in Congress assembled shall have authority to appoint a committee, to sit in the recess of Congress, to be denominated "a Committee of the States," and to consist of one delegate from each State; and to appoint such other committees and civil officers as may be necessary for managing the general affairs of the United States under their direction—to appoint one of their number to preside, provided that no person be allowed to serve in the office of president more than one year in any term of three years; to ascertain the necessary sums of money to be raised for the service of the United States, and to appropriate and apply the same for defraying the public expenses—to borrow money, or emit bills on the credit of the United States, transmitting every half year to the respective States an account of the sums of money so borrowed or emitted,—to build and equip a navy—to agree upon the number of land forces, and to make requisitions from each State for its quota, in proportion to the number of white inhabitants in such State; which requisition shall be binding, and thereupon the Legislature of each State shall appoint the regimental officers, raise the men and cloath, arm and equip them in a soldier like manner, at the expense of the United States; and the officers and men so cloathed, armed and equipped shall march to the place appointed, and within the time agreed on by the United States in Congress assembled: but if the United States in Congress assembled shall, on consideration of circumstances judge proper that any State should not raise men, or should raise a smaller number of men than the quota thereof, such extra number shall be raised , officered, cloathed, armed and equipped in the same manner as the quota of such State, unless the legislature of such State shall judge that such extra number cannot be safely spared out of the same, in which case they shall raise officer, cloath, arm and equip as many of such extra number as they judge can be safely spared. And the officers and men so cloathed, armed and equipped, shall march to the place appointed, and within the time agreed on by the United States in Congress assembled.

The United States in Congress assembled shall never engage in a war, nor grant letters of marque and reprisal in time of peace, nor enter into any treaties or alliances, nor coin money, nor regulate the value thereof, nor ascertain the sums and expenses necessary for the defence and welfare of the United States, or any of them, nor emit bills, nor borrow money on the credit of the United States, nor appropriate money, nor agree upon the number of vessels of war, to be built or purchased, or the number of land or sea forces to be raised, nor appoint a commander in chief of the army or navy, unless nine States assent to the same: nor shall a question on any other point, except for adjourning from day to day be determined, unless by the votes of a majority of the United States in Congress assembled.

The Congress of the United States shall have power to adjourn to any time within the year, and to any place within the United States, so that no period of adjournment be for a longer duration than the space of six months, and shall publish the journal of their proceedings monthly, except such parts thereof relating to treaties, alliances or military operations, as in their judgment require secrecy; and the yeas and nays of the delegates of each State on any question shall be entered on the Journal, when it is desired by any delegate; and the delegates of a State, or any of them, at his or their request shall be furnished with a transcript of the said journal, except such parts as are above excepted, to lay before the Legislatures of the several States.

ARTICLE X. The committee of the States, or any nine of them, shall be authorized to execute, in the recess of Congress, such of the powers of Congress as the United States in Congress assembled, by the consent of nine States, shall from time to time think expedient to vest them with; provided that no power be delegated to the said committee, for the exercise of which, by the articles of confederation, the voice of nine States in the Congress of the United States assembled is requisite.

ARTICLE XI. Canada acceding to this confederation, and joining in the measures of the United States, shall be admitted into, and entitled to all the advantages of this Union: but no other colony shall be admitted into the same, unless such admission be agreed to by nine States.

ARTICLE XII. All bills of credit emitted, monies borrowed and debts contracted by, or under the authority of Congress, before the assembling of the United States, in pursuance of the present confederation, shall be deemed and considered as a charge against the United States, for payment and satisfaction whereof the said United States, and the public faith are hereby solemnly pledged.

ARTICLE XIII. Every State shall abide by the determinations of the United States in Congress assembled, on all questions which by this confederation are submitted to them. And the articles of this confederation shall be inviolably observed by every State, and the Union shall be perpetual; nor shall any alteration at any time hereafter be made in any of them; unless such alteration be agreed to in a Congress of the United States, and be afterwards confirmed by the Legislatures of every State.

And whereas it has pleased the Great Governor of the world to incline the hearts of the Legislatures we respectively represent in Congress, to approve of, and to authorize us to ratify the said articles of confederation and perpetual union. Know ye that we the undersigned delegates, by virtue of the power and authority to us given for that purpose, do by these presents, in the name and in behalf of our respective constituents, fully and entirely ratify and confirm each and every of the said articles of confederation and perpetual union, and all and singular the matters and things therein contained: and we do further solemnly plight and engage the faith of our respective constituents, that they shall abide by the determinations of the United States in Congress assembled, on all questions, which by the said confederation are submitted to them. And

that the articles thereof shall be inviolably observed by the States we respectively represent, and that the Union shall be perpetual.

In witness whereof we have hereunto set our hands in Congress. Done at
Philadelphia in the State of Pennsylvania the ninth day of July in the year of
our Lord one thousand seven hundred and seventy-eight, and in the third year
of the independence of America.

APPENDIX THREE

The Constitution of the United States

WE THE PEOPLE OF THE UNITED STATES, in order to form a more perfect Union, establish Justice, insure domestic Tranquility, provide for the common defence, promote the general Welfare, and secure the Blessings of Liberty to ourselves and our Posterity, do ordain and establish this Constitution for the United States of America.

ARTICLE. I

Section 1. All legislative Powers herein granted shall be vested in a Congress of the United States, which shall consist of a Senate and House of Representatives.

Section 2. The House of Representatives shall be composed of Members chosen every second Year by the People of the several States, and the Electors in each State shall have the Qualifications requisite for Electors of the most numerous Branch of the State Legislature.

No Person shall be a Representative who shall not have attained to the Age of twenty five Years, and been seven Years a Citizen of the United States, and who shall not, when elected, be an Inhabitant of that State in which he shall be chosen.

Representatives and direct Taxes shall be apportioned among the several States which may be included within this Union, according to their respective Numbers, which shall be determined by adding to the whole Number of free Persons, including those bound to Service for a Term of Years, and excluding Indians not taxed, three fifths of all other Persons. The actual Enumeration shall be made within three Years after the first Meeting of the Congress of the

United States, and within every subsequent Term of ten Years, in such Manner as they shall by Law direct. The Number of Representatives shall not exceed one for every thirty Thousand, but each State shall have at Least one Representative; and until such enumeration shall be made, the State of New Hampshire shall be entitled to chuse three, Massachusetts eight, Rhode-Island and Providence Plantations one, Connecticut five, New-York six, New Jersey four, Pennsylvania eight, Delaware one, Maryland six, Virginia ten, North Carolina five, South Carolina five, and Georgia three.

When vacancies happen in the Representation from any State, the Executive Authority thereof shall issue Writs of Election to fill such Vacancies.

The House of Representatives shall chuse their Speaker and other Officers; and shall have the sole Power of Impeachment.

Section 3. The Senate of the United States shall be composed of two Senators from each State, chosen by the Legislature thereof, for six Years; and each Senator shall have one Vote.

Immediately after they shall be assembled in Consequence of the first Election, they shall be divided as equally as may be into three Classes. The Seats of the Senators of the first Class shall be vacated at the Expiration of the second Year, of the second Class at the Expiration of the fourth Year, and of the third Class at the Expiration of the sixth Year, so that one third may be chosen every second Year; and if Vacancies happen by Resignation, or otherwise, during the Recess of the Legislature of any State, the Executive thereof may make temporary Appointments until the next Meeting of the Legislature, which shall then fill such Vacancies.

No Person shall be a Senator who shall not have attained to the Age of thirty Years, and been nine Years a Citizen of the United States, and who shall not, when elected, be an Inhabitant of that State for which he shall be chosen.

The Vice President of the United States shall be President of the Senate, but shall have no Vote, unless they be equally divided.

The Senate shall chuse their other Officers, and also a President pro tempore, in the Absence of the Vice President, or when he shall exercise the Office of President of the United States.

The Senate shall have the sole Power to try all Impeachments. When sitting for that Purpose, they shall be on Oath or Affirmation. When the President of the United States is tried, the Chief Justice shall preside: And no Person shall be convicted without the Concurrence of two thirds of the Members present.

Judgment in Cases of Impeachment shall not extend further than to removal from Office, and disqualification to hold and enjoy any Office of honor, Trust or Profit under the United States: but the Party convicted shall nevertheless be liable and subject to Indictment, Trial, Judgment and Punishment, according to Law.

Section 4. The Times, Places and Manner of holding Elections for Senators and Representatives, shall be prescribed in each State by the Legislature thereof, but the Congress may at any time by Law make or alter such Regulations, except as to the Places of chusing Senators.

The Congress shall assemble at least once in every Year, and such Meeting shall be on the first Monday in December, unless they shall by Law appoint a different Day.

Section 5. Each House shall be the Judge of the Elections, Returns and Qualifications of its own Members, and a Majority of each shall constitute a Quorum to do Business; but a smaller Number may adjourn from day to day, and may be authorized to compel the Attendance of absent Members, in such Manner, and under such Penalties as each House may provide.

Each House may determine the Rules of its Proceedings, punish its Members for disorderly Behaviour, and, with the Concurrence of two thirds, expel a Member.

Each House shall keep a Journal of its Proceedings, and from time to time publish the same, excepting such Parts as may in their Judgment require Secrecy; and the Yeas and Nays of the Members of either House on any question shall, at the Desire of one fifth of those Present, be entered on the Journal.

Neither House, during the Session of Congress, shall, without the Consent of the other, adjourn for more than three days, nor to any other Place than that in which the two Houses shall be sitting.

Section 6. The Senators and Representatives shall receive a Compensation for their Services, to be ascertained by Law, and paid out of the Treasury of the United States. They shall in all Cases, except Treason, Felony and Breach of the Peace, be privileged from Arrest during their Attendance at the Session of their respective Houses, and in going to and returning from the same; and for any Speech or Debate in either House, they shall not be questioned in any other Place.

No Senator or Representative shall, during the Time for which he was elected, be appointed to any civil Office under the Authority of the United States, which shall have been created, or the Emoluments whereof shall have been encreased during such time; and no Person holding any Office under the United States, shall be a Member of either House during his Continuance in Office.

Section 7. All Bills for raising Revenue shall originate in the House of Representatives; but the Senate may propose or concur with Amendments as on other Bills.

Every Bill which shall have passed the House of Representatives and the

Senate shall, before it become a Law, be presented to the President of the United States; if he approve he shall sign it, but if not he shall return it, with his Objections to that House in which it shall have originated, who shall enter the Objections at large on their Journal, and proceed to reconsider it. If after such Reconsideration two thirds of that House shall agree to pass the Bill, it shall be sent, together with the Objections, to the other House, by which it shall likewise be reconsidered, and if approved by two thirds of that House, it shall become a Law. But in all such Cases the Votes of both Houses shall be determined by yeas and Nays, and the Names of the Persons voting for and against the Bill shall be entered on the Journal of each House respectively. If any Bill shall not be returned by the President within ten Days (Sundays excepted) after it shall have been presented to him, the Same shall be a Law, in like Manner as if he had signed it, unless the Congress by their Adjournment prevent its Return, in which Case it shall not be a Law.

Every Order, Resolution, or Vote to which the Concurrence of the Senate and House of Representatives may be necessary (except on a question of Adjournment) shall be presented to the President of the United States; and before the Same shall take Effect, shall be approved by him, or being disapproved by him, shall be repassed by two thirds of the Senate and House or Representatives, according to the Rules and Limitations prescribed in the Case of a Bill.

Section 8. The Congress shall have Power To lay and collect Taxes, Duties, Imposts and Excises, to pay the Debts and provide for the common Defence and general Welfare of the United States; but all Duties, Imposts and Excises shall be uniform throughout the United States.

To borrow Money on the credit of the United States;

To regulate Commerce with foreign Nations, and among the several States, and with the Indian Tribes;

To establish an uniform Rule of Naturalization, and uniform Laws on the subject of Bankruptcies throughout the United States;

To coin Money, regulate the Value thereof, and of foreign Coin, and fix the Standard of Weights and Measures;

To provide for the Punishment of counterfeiting the Securities and current Coin of the United States;

To establish Post Offices and Post Roads;

To promote the Progress of Science and useful Arts, by securing for limited Times to Authors and Inventors the exclusive Right to their respective Writings and Discoveries;

To constitute Tribunals inferior to the supreme Court;

To define and punish Piracies and Felonies committed on the high Seas, and Offences against the Law of Nations;

To declare War, grant Letters of Marque and Reprisal, and make Rules concerning Captures on Land and Water;

To raise and support Armies, but no Appropriation of Money to that Use shall be for a longer Term than two Years;

To provide and maintain a Navy;

To make Rules for the Government and Regulation of the land and naval Forces;

To provide for calling forth the Militia to execute the Laws of the Union, suppress Insurrections and repel Invasions;

To provide for organizing, arming, and disciplining, the Militia, and for governing such Part of them as may be employed in the Service of the United States, reserving to the States respectively, the Appointment of the Officers, and the Authority of training the Militia according to the discipline prescribed by Congress;

To exercise exclusive Legislation in all Cases whatsoever, over such District (not exceeding ten Miles square) as may, by Cession of particular States, and the Acceptance of Congress, become the Seat of the Government of the United States, and to exercise like Authority over all Places purchased by the Consent of the Legislature of the State in which the Same shall be, for the Erection of Forts, Magazines, Arsenals, dock-Yards, and other needful Buildings;—And

To make all Laws which shall be necessary and proper for carrying into Execution the foregoing Powers, and all other Powers vested by this Constitution in the Government of the United States, or in any Department or Officer thereof.

Section 9. The Migration or Importation of such Persons as any of the States now existing shall think proper to admit, shall not be prohibited by the Congress prior to the Year one thousand eight hundred and eight, but a Tax or duty may be imposed on such Importation, not exceeding ten dollars for each Person.

The Privilege of the Writ of Habeas Corpus shall not be suspended, unless when in Cases of Rebellion or Invasion the public Safety may require it.

No Bill of Attainder or ex post facto Law shall be passed.

No Capitation, or other direct, Tax shall be laid, unless in Proportion to the Census or Enumeration herein before directed to be taken.

No Tax or Duty shall be laid on Articles exported from any State.

No Preference shall be given by any Regulation of Commerce or Revenue to the Ports of one State over those of another: nor shall Vessels bound to, or from, one State, be obliged to enter, clear, or pay Duties in another.

No Money shall be drawn from the Treasury, but in Consequence of Appropriations made by Law, and a regular Statement and Account of the Receipts and Expenditures of all public Money shall be published from time to time.

No Title of Nobility shall be granted by the United States: And no Person holding any Office of Profit or trust under them, shall, without the Consent of the Congress, accept of any present, Emolument, Office, or Title, of any kind whatever, from any King, Prince, or foreign State.

Section. 10. No State shall enter into any Treaty, Alliance, or Confederation; grant Letters of Marque and Reprisal; coin Money; emit Bills of Credit; make any Thing but gold and silver Coin a Tender in Payment of Debts; pass any Bill of Attainder, ex post facto Law, or Law impairing the Obligation of Contracts, or grant any Title of Nobility.

No State shall, without the Consent of the Congress, lay any Imposts or Duties on Imports or Exports, except what may be absolutely necessary for executing it's inspection Laws: and the net Produce of all Duties and Imposts, laid by any State on Imports or Exports, shall be for the Use of the Treasury of the United States; and all such Laws shall be subject to the Revision and Controul of the Congress.

No State shall, without the Consent of Congress, lay any Duty of Tonnage, keep Troops, or Ships of War in time of Peace, enter into any Agreement or Compact with another State, or with a foreign Power, or engage in War, unless actually invaded, or in such imminent Danger as will not admit of delay.

ARTICLE. II.

Section. 1. The executive Power shall be vested in a President of the United States of America. He shall hold his Office during the term of four Years, and, together with the Vice President, chosen for the same Term, be elected, as follows

Each State shall appoint, in such Manner as the Legislature thereof may direct, a Number of Electors, equal to the whole Number of Senators and Representatives to which the State may be entitled in the Congress: but no Senator or Representative, or Person holding an Office of Trust or Profit under the United States, shall be appointed an Elector.

The Electors shall meet in their respective States, and vote by Ballot for two Persons, of whom one at least shall not be an Inhabitant of the same State with themselves. And they shall make a List of all the Persons voted for, and of the Number of Votes for each; which List they shall sign and certify, and transmit sealed to the Seat of the Government of the United States, directed to the President of the Senate. The President of the Senate shall, in the Presence of the Senate and House of Representatives, open all the Certificates, and the Votes shall then be counted. The Person having the greatest Number of Votes shall be the President, if such Number be a Majority of the whole Number of Electors appointed; and if there be more than one who have such Majority, and have an equal Number of Votes, then the House of Representatives shall immediately chuse by Ballot one of them for President; and if no Person have a Majority, then from the five highest on the List the said House shall in like Manner chuse the President. But in chusing the President, the Votes shall be taken by States, the Representation from each State having one Vote; A quorum for this Purpose shall consist of a Member or Members from two thirds of the States, and a Majority all the States shall be necessary to a Choice. In every Case, after the Choice of the President, the Person having the greatest Number of Votes of the Electors shall be the Vice President. But if there should remain two or more who have equal Votes, the Senate shall chuse from them by Ballot the Vice President.

The Congress may determine the Time of chusing the Electors, and the Day on which they shall give their Votes; which Day shall be the same throughout the United States.

No Person except a natural born Citizen, or a Citizen of the United States, at the time of the Adoption of this Constitution, shall be eligible to the Office of President, neither shall any Person be eligible to that Office who shall not have attained to the Age of thirty-five Years, and been fourteen Years a Resident within the United States.

In Case of the Removal of the President from Office, or of his Death, Resignation, or Inability to discharge the Powers and Duties of the said Office, the Same shall devolve on the Vice President, and the Congress may by Law provide for the Case of Removal, Death, Resignation or Inability, both of the President and Vice President, declaring what Officer shall then act as President, and such Officer shall act accordingly, until the Disability be removed, or a President shall be elected.

The President shall, at stated Times, receive for his Services, a Compensation, which shall neither be encreased or diminished during the Period for which he shall have been elected, and he shall not receive within that Period any other Emolument from the United States, or any of them.

Before he enters on the Execution of his Office, he shall take the following Oath or Affirmation:—"I do solemnly swear (or affirm) that I will faithfully execute the Office of President of the United States, and will to the best of my Ability, preserve, protect and defend the Constitution of the United States."

Section. 2. The President shall be Commander in Chief of the Army and Navy of the United States, and of the Militia of the several States, when called into the actual Service of the United States; he may require the Opinion, in writing, of the principal Officer in each of the executive Departments, upon any Subject relating to the Duties of their respective Offices, and he shall have Power to grant Reprieves and Pardons for Offences against the United States, except in Cases of Impeachment.

He shall have Power, by and with the Advice and Consent of the Senate, to make Treaties, provided two thirds of the Senators present concur; and he shall nominate, and by and with the Advice and Consent of the Senate, shall appoint Ambassadors, other public Ministers and Consuls, Judges of the supreme Court, and all other Officers of the United States, whose Appointments are not herein otherwise provided for, and which shall be established by Law; but the Congress may by Law vest the Appointment of such inferior Officers, as they think proper, in the President alone, in the Courts of Law, or in the Heads of Departments.

The President shall have Power to fill up all Vacancies that may happen during the Recess of the Senate, by granting Commissions which shall expire at the End of their next Session.

Section. 3. He shall from time to time give to the Congress Information of the State of the Union, and recommend to their Consideration such Measures as he shall judge necessary and expedient; he may, on extraordinary Occasions, convene both Houses, or either of them, and in Case of Disagreement between them, with Respect to the Time of Adjournment, he may adjourn them to such Time as he shall think proper; he shall receive Ambassadors and other public Ministers; he shall take Care that the Laws be faithfully executed, and shall Commission all the Officers of the United States.

Section. 4. The President, Vice President and all civil Officers of the United States, shall be removed from Office on Impeachment for, and Conviction of, Treason, Bribery, or other high Crimes and Misdemeanors.

ARTICLE. III.

Section. 1. The judicial Power of the United States, shall be vested in one supreme Court, and in such inferior Courts as the Congress may from time to time ordain and establish. The Judges, both of the supreme and inferior Courts, shall hold their Offices during good Behaviour, and shall, at stated Times, receive for their Services, a Compensation, which shall not be diminished during their Continuance in Office.

Section. 2. The judicial Power shall extend to all Cases, in Law and Equity, arising under this Constitution, the Laws of the United States, and Treaties made, or which shall be made, under their Authority;—to all Cases affecting Ambassadors, other public Ministers and Consuls;—to all Cases of admiralty and maritime Jurisdiction;—to Controversies to which the United States shall be a Party;—to Controversies between two or more States;—between a State and Citizens of another State;—between Citizens of different States,—between Citizens of the same State claiming Lands under Grants of different States, and between a State, or the Citizens thereof, and foreign States, Citizens or Subjects.

In all cases affecting Ambassadors, other public Ministers and Consuls, and those in which a State shall be Party, the supreme Court shall have original Jurisdiction. In all the other Cases before mentioned, the supreme Court shall have appellate Jurisdiction, both as to Law and Fact, with such Exceptions, and under such Regulations as the Congress shall make.

The Trial of all Crimes, except in Cases of Impeachment, shall be by Jury; and such Trial shall be held in the State where the said Crimes shall have been committed; but when not committed within any State, the Trial shall be at such Place or Places as the Congress may by Law have directed.

Section. 3. Treason against the United States, shall consist only in levying War against them, or in adhering to their Enemies, giving them Aid and Comfort. No Person shall be convicted of Treason unless on the Testimony of two Witnesses to the same overt Act, or on Confession in open Court.

The Congress shall have Power to declare the Punishment of Treason, but no Attainder of Treason shall work Corruption of Blood, or Forfeiture except during the Life of the Person attainted.

ARTICLE. IV.

Section. 1. Full Faith and Credit shall be given in each State to the public Acts, Records, and judicial Proceedings of every other State. And the Congress may by general Laws prescribe the Manner in which such Acts, Records and Proceedings shall be proved, and the Effect thereof.

Section. 2. The Citizens of each State shall be entitled to all Privileges and Immunities of Citizens in the several States.

A person charged in any State with Treason, Felony, or other Crime, who shall flee from Justice, and be found in another State, shall on Demand of the executive Authority of the State from which he fled, be delivered up, to be removed to the State having Jurisdiction of the Crime.

No Person held to Service or Labour in one State, under the Laws thereof, escaping into another, shall, in Consequence of any Law or Regulation therein, be discharged from such Service or Labour, but shall be delivered up on Claim of the Party to whom such Service or Labour may be due.

Section. 3. New States may be admitted by the Congress into this Union; but no new State shall be formed or erected within the Jurisdiction of any other State; nor any State be formed by the Junction of two or more States, or Parts of States, without the consent of the Legislatures of the States concerned as well as of the Congress.

The Congress shall have Power to dispose of and make all needful Rules and Regulations respecting the Territory or other Property belonging to the United States; and nothing in this Constitution shall be so construed as to Prejudice any Claims of the United States, or of any particular States.

Section. 4. The United States shall guarantee to every State in this Union a Republican Form of Government, and shall protect each of them against Invasion; and on Application of the Legislature, or of the Executive (when the Legislature cannot be convened) against domestic Violence.

ARTICLE. V.

The Congress, whenever two thirds of both Houses shall deem it necessary, shall propose Amendments to this Constitution, or, on the Application of the Legislatures of two thirds of the several States shall call a Convention for proposing Amendments, which, in either Case, shall be valid to all Intents and Purposes, as Part of this Constitution, when ratified by the Legislatures of three fourths of the several States, or by Conventions in three fourths thereof, as the one or the other Mode of Ratification may be proposed by the Congress; Provided that no Amendment which may be made prior to the Year One thousand eight hundred and eight shall in any Manner affect the first and fourth Clauses in the Ninth Section of the first Article; and that no State, without its Consent, shall be deprived of it's equal Suffrage in the Senate.

ARTICLE. VI.

All Debts contracted and Engagements entered into, before the Adoption of this Constitution, shall be as valid against the United States under this Constitution, as under the Confederation.

This Constitution, and the Laws of the United States which shall be made in Pursuance thereof; and all Treaties made, or which shall be made, under the Authority of the United States, shall be the supreme Law of the Land; and the Judges in every State shall be bound thereby, any Thing in the Constitution or Laws of any State to the Contrary notwithstanding.

The Senators and Representatives before mentioned, and the Members of the several State Legislatures, and all executive and judicial Officers, both of the United States and of the several States, shall be bound by Oath or Affirmation, to support this Constitution; but no religious Test shall ever be required as a Qualification to any Office or public Trust under the United States.

ARTICLE. VII.

The Ratification of the Conventions of nine States, shall be sufficient for the Establishment of this Constitution between the States so ratifying the Same.

Done in Convention by the Unanimous Consent of the States present the Seventeenth Day of September in the Year of our Lord one thousand seven hundred and Eighty seven and of the Independence of the United States of America the Twelfth. In witness thereof We have hereunto subscribed our Names,

G°: WASHINGTON–Presidᵗ
and deputy from Virginia

New Hampshire	John Langdon Nicholas Gilman		Geo: Read Gunning Bedford jun
Massachusetts	Nathaniel Gorham Rufus King	Delaware	John Dickinson Richard Bassett Jaco: Broom
Connecticut	Wᵐ Samˡ Johnson Roger Sherman		
New York	Alexander Hamilton	Maryland	James McHenry Dan of Sᵗ Thoˢ Jenifer Danˡ Carroll
New Jersey	Wil: Livingston David A. Brearley. Wᵐ Paterson. Jona: Dayton	Virginia	John Blair– James Madison Jr.
Pennsylvania	B. Franklin Thomas Mifflin Robᵗ Morris Geo. Clymer Thoˢ. FitzSimons Jared Ingersoll James Wilson Gouv Morris	North Carolina	Wᵐ. Blount Richᵈ Dobbs Spaight. Hu Williamson
		South Carolina	J. Rutledge Charles Cotesworth Pinckney Charles Pinckney Pierce Butler.
		Georgia	William Few Abr Baldwin

Amendments to the Constitution

ARTICLES IN ADDITION TO, and Amendment of the Constitution of the United States of America, proposed by Congress, and ratified by the Legislatures of the several States, pursuant to the fifth Article of the original Constitution.

ARTICLE I.

Congress shall make no law respecting an establishment of religion, or prohibiting the free exercise thereof; or abriding the freedom of speech, or of the press; or the right of the people peaceably to assemble, and to petition the Government for a redress of grievances.

ARTICLE II.

A well regulated Militia, being necessary to the security of a free State, the right of the people to keep and bear Arms, shall not be infringed.

ARTICLE III.

No Soldier shall, in time of peace be quartered in any house, without the consent of the Owner, nor in time of war, but in a manner to be prescribed by law.

ARTICLE IV.

The right of the people to be secure in their persons, houses, papers, and effects, against unreasonable searches and seizures, shall not be violated, and no Warrants shall issue, but upon probable cause, supported by Oath or affirmation, and particularly describing the place to be searched, and the persons or things to be seized.

ARTICLE V.

No person shall be held to answer for a capital, or otherwise infamous crime, unless on a presentment or indictment of a Grand Jury, except in cases arising in the land or naval forces, or in the Militia, when in actual service in time of War or public danger; nor shall any person be subject for the same offence to be twice put in jeopardy of life or limb; nor shall be compelled in any criminal case to be a witness against himself, nor be deprived of life, liberty, or property, without due process of law; nor shall private property be taken for public use, without just compensation.

ARTICLE VI.

In all criminal prosecutions, the accused shall enjoy the right to a speedy and public trial, by an impartial jury of the State and district wherein the crime shall have been committed, which district shall have been previously ascertained by law, and to be informed of the nature and cause of the accusation; to be confronted with the witnesses against him; to have compulsory process for obtaining witnesses in his favor, and to have the Assistance of Counsel for his defence.

ARTICLE VII.

In Suits at common law, where the value in controversy shall exceed twenty dollars, the right of trial by jury shall be preserved, and no fact tried by a jury, shall be otherwise re-examined in any Court of the United States, than accoridng to the rules of the common law.

ARTICLE VIII.

Excessive bail shall not be required, nor excessive fines imposed, nor cruel and unusual punishments inflicted.

ARTICLE IX.

The enumeration in the Constitution, of certain rights, shall not be construed to deny or disparage others retained by the people.

ARTICLE X.

The powers not delegated to the United States by the Constitution, nor prohibited by it to the States, are reserved to the States respectively, or to the people. [The first ten amendments went into effect December 15, 1791.]

ARTICLE XI.

The Judicial power of the United States shall not be construed to extend to any suit in law or equity, commenced or prosecuted against one of the United States by Citizens of another State, or by Citizens or Subjects of any Foreign State. [January 8, 1798.]

ARTICLE XII.

The Electors shall meet in their respective states, and vote by ballot for President and Vice-President, one of whom, at least, shall not be an inhabitant of the same state with themselves; they shall name in their ballots the person voted for as President, and in distinct ballots the person voted for as Vice-President, and they shall make distinct lists of all persons voted for as President, and of all persons voted for as Vice-President, and of the number of votes for each, which lists they shall sign and certify, and transmit sealed to the seat of the government of the United States, directed to the President of the Senate;—The President of the Senate shall, in the presence of the Senate and House of Representatives, open all the certificates and the votes shall then be counted;—The person having the greatest number of votes for President, shall be the President, if such number be a majority of the whole number of Electors appointed; and if no person have such majority, then from the persons having the highest numbers not exceeding three on the list of those voted for as President, the House of Representatives shall choose immediately, by ballot, the President. But in choosing the President, the votes shall be taken by states, the representation from each state having one vote; a quorum for this purpose shall consist of a member or members from two-thirds of the states, and a majority of all the states shall be necessary to a choice. And if the House of Representatives shall not choose a President whenever the right of choice shall devolve upon them, before the fourth day of March next following, then the Vice-President shall act as President, as in the case of the death or other constitutional disability of the President.—The person having the greatest number of votes as Vice-President, shall be the Vice-President, if such number be a majority of the whole number of Electors appointed, and if no person have a majority, then from the two highest numbers on the list, the Senate shall choose the Vice-President; a quorum for the purpose shall consist of two-thirds of the whole number of Senators, and a majority of the whole number shall be necessary to a choice. But no person constitutionally ineligible to the office of President shall be eligible to that of Vice-President of the United States. [September 25, 1804.]

ARTICLE XIII.

Section 1. Neither slavery nor involuntary servitude, except as a punishment for crime whereof the party shall have been duly convicted, shall exist within the United States, or any place subject to their jurisdiction.

Section 2. Congress shall have power to enforce this article by appropriate legislation. [December 18, 1865.]

ARTICLE XIV.

Section 1. All persons born or naturalized in the United States, and subject to the jurisdiction thereof, are citizens of the United States and of the State wherein they reside. No State shall make or enforce any law which shall abridge the privileges or immunities of citizens of the United States; nor shall any State deprive any person of life, liberty, or property, without due process of law; nor deny to any person within its jurisdiction the equal protection of the laws.

Section 2. Representatives shall be apportioned among the several States according to their respective numbers, counting the whole number of persons in each State, excluding Indians not taxed. But when the right to vote at any election for the choice of electors for President and Vice President of the United States, Representatives in Congress, the Executive and Judicial officers of a State, or the members of the Legislature thereof, is denied to any of the male inhabitants of such State, being twenty-one years of age, and citizens of the United States, or in any way abridged, except for participation in rebellion, or other crime, the basis of representation therein shall be reduced in the proportion which the number of such male citizens shall bear to the whole number of male citizens twenty-one years of age in such State.

Section 3. No person shall be a Senator or Representative in Congress, or elector of President and Vice President, or hold any office, civil or military, under the United States, or under any State, who, having previously taken an oath, as a member of Congress, or as an officer of the United States, or as a member of any State legislature, or as an executive or judicial officer of any State, to support the Constitution of the United States, shall have engaged in insurrection or rebellion against the same, or given aid or comfort to the enemies thereof. But Congress may by a vote of two-thirds of each House, remove such disability.

Section 4. The validity of the public debt of the United States, authorized by law, including debts incurred for payment of pensions and bounties for services in suppressing insurrection or rebellion, shall not be questioned. But neither the United States nor any State shall assume or pay any debt or obligation incurred in aid of insurrection or rebellion against the United States, or any claim for the loss or emancipation of any slave; but all such debts, obligations and claims shall be held illegal and void.

Section 5. The Congress shall have power to enforce, by appropriate legislation, the provisions of this article. [July 28, 1868.]

ARTICLE XV.

Section 1. The right of citizens of the United States to vote shall not be denied or abridged by the United States or by any State on account of race, color, or previous condition of servitude—

Section 2. The Congress shall have power to enforce this article by appropriate legislation.—[March 30, 1870.]

ARTICLE XVI.

The Congress shall have power to lay and collect taxes on incomes, from whatever source derived, without apportionment among the several States, and without regard to any census or enumeration. [February 25, 1913.]

ARTICLE XVII.

The Senate of the United States shall be composed of two senators from each State, elected by the people thereof, for six years; and each Senator shall have one vote. The electors in each State shall have the qualifications requisite for electors of the most numerous branch of the State legislature.

When vacancies happen in the representation of any State in the Senate, the executive authority of such State shall issue writs of election to fill such vacancies: *Provided,* That the legislature of any State may empower the executive thereof to make temporary appointments until the people fill the vacancies by election as the legislature may direct.

This amendment shall not be so construed as to affect the election or term of any senator chosen before it becomes valid as part of the Constitution. [May 31, 1913.]

ARTICLE XVIII.

After one year from the ratification of this article, the manufacture, sale, or transportation of intoxicating liquors within, the importation thereof into, or the exportation thereof from the United States and all territory subject to the jurisdiction thereof for beverage purposes is hereby prohibited.

The Congress and the several States shall have concurrent power to enforce this article by appropriate legislation.

This article shall be inoperative unless it shall have been ratified as an amendment to the Constitution by the legislatures of the several States, as provided in the Constitution, within seven years from the date of the submission thereof to the States by Congress. [January 29, 1919.]

ARTICLE XIX.

The right of citizens of the United States to vote shall not be denied or abridged by the United States or by any State on account of sex.

The Congress shall have power by appropriate legislation to enforce the provisions of this article. [August 26, 1920.]

ARTICLE XX.

Section 1. The terms of the President and Vice-President shall end at noon on the twentieth day of January, and the terms of Senators and Representatives at noon on the third day of January, of the years in which such terms would have ended if this article had not been ratified; and the terms of their successors shall then begin.

Section 2. The Congress shall assemble at least once in every year, and such meeting shall begin at noon on the third day of January, unless they shall by law appoint a different day.

Section 3. If, at the time fixed for the beginning of the term of the President, the President-elect shall have died, the Vice-President-elect shall become President. If a President shall not have been chosen before the time fixed for the beginning of his term, or if the President-elect shall have failed to qualify, then the Vice-President-elect shall act as President until a President shall have qualified; and the Congress may by law provide for the case wherein neither a President-elect nor a Vice-President-elect shall have qualified, declaring who shall then act as President, or the manner in which one who is to act shall be selected, and such person shall act accordingly until a President or Vice-President shall have qualified.

Section 4. The Congress may by law provide for the case of the death of any of the persons from whom the House of Representatives may choose a President whenever the right of choice shall have devolved upon them, and for the case of the death of any of the persons from whom the Senate may choose a Vice-President whenever the right of choice shall have devolved upon them.

Section 5. Sections 1 and 2 shall take effect on the 15th day of October following the ratification of this article.

Section 6. This article shall be inoperative unless it shall have been ratified as an amendment to the Constitution by the legislatures of three-fourths of the several States within seven years from the date of its submission. [February 6, 1933.]

ARTICLE XXI.

Section 1. The eighteenth article of amendment to the Constitution of the United States is hereby repealed.

Section 2. The transportation or importation into any State, Territory or possession of the United States for delivery or use therein of intoxicating liquors, in violation of the laws thereof, is hereby prohibited.

Section 3. This article shall be inoperative unless it shall have been ratified as an amendment to the Constitution by convention in the several States, as provided in the Constitution, within seven years from the date of the submission thereof to the States by the Congress. [December 5, 1933.]

ARTICLE XXII.

Section 1. No person shall be elected to the office of the President more than twice, and no person who has held the office of President, or acted as President, for more than two years of a term to which some other person was elected President shall be elected to the office of the President more than once. But this Article shall not apply to any person holding the office of President when this Article was proposed by the Congress, and shall not prevent any person who may be holding the office of President, or acting as President, during the term within which this Article becomes operative from holding the office of President or acting as President during the remainder of such term.

Section 2. This article shall be inoperative unless it shall have been ratified as an amendment to the Constitution by the legislatures of three-fourths of the several States within seven years from the date of its submission to the States by the Congress. [February 27, 1951.]

ARTICLE XXIII.

Section 1. The District constituting the seat of government of the United States shall appoint in such manner as the Congress may direct:

A number of electors of President and Vice-President equal to the whole number of Senators and Representatives in Congress to which the District would be entitled if it were a State, but in no event more than the least populous State; they shall be in addition to those appointed by the States, but they shall be considered, for the purposes of the election of President and Vice-President, to be electors appointed by a State; and they shall meet in the District and perform such duties as provided by the twelfth article of amendment.

Section 2. The Congress shall have the power to enforce this article by appropriate legislation. [March 29, 1961.]

ARTICLE XXIV.

Section 1. The right of citizens of the United States to vote in any primary or other election for President or Vice President, for electors for President or Vice President, or for Senator or Representative in Congress, shall not be denied or abridged by the United States or any State by reason of failure to pay any poll tax or other tax.

Section 2. The Congress shall have power to enforce this article by appropriate legislation. [January 23, 1964.]

ARTICLE XXV.

Section 1. In case of the removal of the President from office or of his death or resignation, the Vice President shall become President.

Section 2. Whenever there is a vacancy in the office of Vice President, the President shall nominate a Vice President who shall take office upon confirmation by a majority vote of both Houses of Congress.

Section 3. Whenever the President transmits to the President pro tempore of the Senate and the Speaker of the House of Representatives his written declaration that he is unable to discharge the powers and duties of his office, and until he transmits to them a written declaration to the contrary, such powers and duties shall be discharged by the Vice President as Acting President.

Section 4. Whenever the Vice President and a majority of either the principal officers of the executive departments or of such other body as Congress may by law provide, transmit to the President pro tempore of the Senate and the Speaker of the House of Representatives their written declaration that the President is unable to discharge the powers and duties of his office, the Vice President shall immediately assume the powers and duties of the office as Acting President.

Thereafter, when the President transmits to the President pro tempore of the Senate and the Speaker of the House of Representatives his written declaration that no inability exists, he shall resume the powers and duties of his office unless the Vice President and a majority of either the principal officers of the executive departments or of such other body as Congress may by law provide, transmit within four days to the President pro tempore of the Senate and the

Speaker of the House of Representatives their written declaration that the President is unable to discharge the powers and duties of his office. Thereupon Congress shall decide the issue, assembling within forty-eight hours for that purpose if not in session. If the Congress, within twenty-one days after receipt of the latter written declaration, or, if Congress is not in session, within twenty-one days after Congress is required to assemble, determines by two-thirds vote of both Houses that the President is unable to discharge the powers and duties of his office, the Vice President shall continue to discharge the same as Acting President; otherwise, the President shall resume the powers and duties of his office. [February 10, 1967.]

ARTICLE XXVI.

Section 1. The right of citizens of the United States, who are eighteen years of age or older, to vote shall not be denied or abridged by the United States or by any State on account of age.

Section 2. The Congress shall have power to enforce this article by appropriate legislation [June 30, 1971.]

Bibliography

Abbreviations used: *AHR (American Historical Review); AJLH (American Journal of Legal History); Annals (Annals of the American Academy of Political and Social Science); APSR (American Political Science Review); CWH (Civil War History); JAH (Journal of American History); JP (Journal of Politics); JSH (Journal of Southern History); MVHR (Mississippi Valley Historical Review); Pres. Studies Q. (Presidential Studies Quarterly); PSQ (Political Science Quarterly); WMQ (William and Mary Quarterly); Western Pol. Q. (Western Political Quarterly).*

I. *American Constitutional History and Constitutionalism: Primary Sources and General Works*

The indispensable starting point for modern study of the Constitution is Leonard W. Levy, Kenneth W. Karst, and Dennis J. Mahoney, eds., *The Encyclopedia of the American Constitution,* 4 vols. (1986). Edward S. Corwin *et al.,* eds., *The Constitution of the United States: Analysis and Interpretation* (1952, 1964, 1973 eds., 1976 and 1978 suppl.), is an annotation of the constitutional text on the basis of Supreme Court decisions. Corwin, *The Constitution and What It Means Today,* 14th ed., rev. Harold W. Chase and Craig R. Ducat (1978), is a similar work of briefer scope. Francis Newton Thorpe, ed., *The Federal and State Constitutions, Colonial Charters and Other Organic Laws,* 7 vols. (1909), and William F. Swindler, comp., *Sources and Documents of United States Constitutions,* 10 vols. (1973–79), are basic documentary collections. Primary sources for constitutional development as seen through the national legislature are *Statutes at Large of the United States of America 1789–1873,* 17 vols. (1850–73; *United States Statutes at Large* (1874–   ); United States Code, 16 vols. (1977; 4 vols., 1979 suppl.); *Annals of Congress, 1789–1824; Register of Debates in Congress, 1825–1837; Congressional Globe,*

1833–73; *Congressional Record, 1873–   ; American State Papers; Documents, Legislative and Executive,* 38 vols. (1832–61), covering the First through the Fourteenth Congress. Reports, Executive Documents, and Miscellaneous Papers of the House of Representatives and the Senate, referred to as the Congressional Serials Set, start with the Fifteenth Congress. Executive documents are presented in *Compilation of the Messages and Papers of the Presidents,* 20 vols. to 1929; *Public Papers of the Presidents of the United States* (1958–   ), beginning with the Truman administration; *Code of Federal Regulations* (1938–   ), an annual codification of administrative rules; *Federal Register* (1936–   ), a daily listing of administrative rules and agency decisions; *Official Opinions of the Attorneys-General.* Decisions of the Supreme Court are found in *United States Reports* (1970–   ). Before 1875 reports of decisions were published under the names of the official court reporters: Dallas, Cranch, Wheaton, Peters, Howard, Black, Wallace. The decisions of the Supreme Court are also published in *United States Supreme Court Reports: Lawyers' Edition,* and *The Supreme Court Reporter.* Lower federal court decisions are found in *Federal Cases, 1789–1879; Federal Reporter, 1880–1924; Federal Reporter, 1924–   2d ser.; Federal Supplement, 1932–   ; American Law Reports—Federal, 1969–   .*

Documentary collections of materials in constitutional history include Philip S. Kurland and Ralph Lerner, eds., *The Founders' Constitution,* 5 vols. (1987); Melvin I. Urofsky, ed., *Documents of American Constitutional and Legal History,* 2 vols. (1989); Henry Steele Commager, ed., *Documents of American History,* 9th ed. (1973); Donald O. Dewey, ed., *Union and Liberty: A Documentary History of American Constitutionalism* (1969); James M. Smith and Paul L. Murphy, eds., *Liberty and Justice, Forging the Federal Union: American Constitutional Development to 1869* (1965); Smith and Murphy, eds., *Liberty and Justice—The Modern Constitution: American Constitutional Development since 1865* (1968); Allen Johnson, ed., *Readings in American Constitutional History, 1776–1876* (1912); Allen Johnson and William T. Robinson, eds., *Readings in Recent American Constitutional History, 1876–1926* (1927). Among the better constitutional law casebooks and treatises are Gerald Gunther, *Cases and Materials on Constitutional Law* (1975); Paul A. Freund *et al., Constitutional Law: Cases and Other Problems,* 4th ed. (1977); Paul Brest, *Processes of Constitutional Decision Making: Cases and Materials* (1975); Lawrence H. Tribe, *American Constitutional Law* (1988); Walter F. Murphy *et al., American Constitutional Interpretation* (1986). Stanley I. Kutler, ed., *The Supreme Court and the Constitution: Readings in American Constitutional History,* 2d ed. (1977), is a collection of Supreme Court opinions.

The intellectual roots of constitutional government in the United States may be explored in a variety of works dealing with European and English constitutionalism. Especially relevant are Charles H. McIlwain, *Constitutionalism, Ancient and Modern* (1940; 1947); Edward S. Corwin, *The "Higher Law" Background of American Constitutional Law* (1955); J. W. Gough,

Fundamental Law in English Constitutional History (1955); Francis D. Wormuth, *The Origins of Modern Constitutionalism* (1949); M. J. C. Vile, *Constitutionalism and the Separation of Powers* (1967); J. G. A. Pocock, *The Ancient Constitution and Feudal Law: A Study of English Historical Thought in the Seventeenth Century* (1957). Pocock, *The Machiavellian Moment: Florentine Political Thought and the Atlantic Republican Tradition* (1975), emphasizes positive liberty defined as participation in the political life of the community, rather than negative liberty or restraints upon government. On this distinction see Isaiah Berlin, "Two Concepts of Liberty," in *Four Essays on Liberty* (1969).

Carl J. Friedrich, *Constitutional Government and Democracy: Theory and Practice in Europe and America,* 4th ed. (1968), is magisterial in scope and enlightening in its insights into the nature of constitutionism. An excellent recent analysis of the roots of American constitutionalism is Harvey Wheeler, "Constitutionalism," in Fred I. Greenstein and Nelson W. Polsby, eds., *Handbook of Political Science, vol. 5: Governmental Institutions and Processes* (1975). Pertinent also is J. Roland Pennock and John W. Chapman, eds., *Constitutionalism: Nomos,* vol. 20 (1979), a collection of essays dealing with philosophical and historical aspects of the subject in Europe and America. Other important works on constitutionalism are Robert Eden, "Tocqueville on Political Realignment and Constitutional Forms," *Review of Politics,* 48 (1986); Gerald Stourzh, "Constitution: Changing Meanings of the Term from the Early Seventeenth to the Eighteenth Century," in Terence Ball and J.G.A. Pocock, eds., *Conceptual Change and the Constitution* (1988); Harvey C. Mansfield, Jr., "Constitutional Government: The Soul of Modern Democracy," *The Public Interest,* No. 86 (1987); Louis Fisher, *Constitutional Dialogues: Interpretation as Political Process* (1988); Giovanni Sartori, "Constitutionalism: A Preliminary Discussion," *APSR* 56 (1962); W. H. Morris-Jones, "On Constitutionalism," *APSR* 59 (1965); K. C. Wheare, *Modern Constitutions* (1958); William Yandell Elliott, *The Pragmatic Revolt in Politics: Syndicalism, Fascism and the Constitutional State* (1928); Harro Höpfl and Martyn P. Thompson, "The History of Contract as a Motif in Political Thought," *AHR* 84 (1979); Kirk Thompson, "Constitutional Theory and Political Action," *JP* 31 (1969).

Martin E. Spencer, "Politics and Rhetorics," *Social Research,* 37 (1970), is a perceptive analysis of the way in which constitutional rules and principles shape the conduct of American government and politics. A similar point is made in Arthur E. Bestor, "The American Civil War as a Constitutional Crisis," *AHR* 69 (1964). The nature of constitutional politics in the United States is illuminated in Edward S. Corwin, "The Constitution as Instrument and as Symbol," *APSR* 30 (1936); Corwin, "Constitution v. Constitutional Theory," *APSR* 19 (1925); Karl Llewellyn, "The Constitution as an Institution," *Columbia Law Review* 34 (1934); Gerald Garvey, *Constitutional Bricolage* (1971); Glendon Schubert, "The Rhetoric of Constitutional Change,"

Journal of Public Law 16 (1967); Daniel J. Boorstin, "The Perils of Indwelling Law," in *The Decline of American Radicalism: Reflections on America Today* (1970); John Brigham, *Constitutional Language: An Interpretation of Judicial Decision* (1978); Charles L. Black, Jr., *Structure and Relationship in Constitutional Law* (1969); William F. Harris II, "Bonding Word and Polity: The Logic of American Constitutionalism," *APSR* 76 (1982).

Commentaries on the Constitution have always to some extent provided a record of constitutional development. The most important works in this genre for the early national period and nineteenth century are James Madison, Alexander Hamilton, John Jay, *The Federalist;* James Wilson and Thomas McKean, *Commentaries on the Constitution of the United States of America* (1792); St. George Tucker, *Blackstone's Commentaries, with Notes of Reference to the Constitution and Laws of the Federal Government of the United States, and of the Commonwealth of Virginia* (1797); John Taylor, *An Inquiry into the Principles and Policy of the Government of the United States* (1814); Taylor, *New Views of the Constitution of the United States* (1823); William Rawle, *A View of the Constitution of the United States of America* (1825); Nathaniel Chipman, *Principles of Government, a Treatise on Free Government, Including the Constitution of the United States* (1833); Joseph Story, *Commentaries on the Constitution of the United States,* 3 vols. (1833); James Kent, *Commentaries on American Law,* 4 vols. (1826–30); John Alexander Jameson, *A Treatise on Constitutional Conventions, Their History, Power, and Modes of Proceeding* (1867); Thomas M. Cooley, *A Treatise on Constitutional Limitations Which Rest upon the Legislative Power of the States of the American Union* (1868); Christopher G. Tiedeman, *A Treatise on the Limitations of the Police Power in the United States* (1886). Notable commentaries in the twentieth century are Westel Woodbury Willoughby, *The Constitutional Law of the United States,* 3 vols. (1924), and, most recently, Bernard Schwartz, *A Commentary on the Constitution of the United States,* 5 vols. (1963–68).

Early constitutional histories that retain scholarly value are Herman Eduard von Holst, *The Constitutional and Political History of the United States,* 7 vols. (1877–92); George Ticknor Curtis, *Constitutional History of the United States,* 2 vols. (1889); James Shouler, *Constitutional Studies, State and Federal* (1897); James Bryce, *The American Commonwealth,* 2 vols. (1888); Henry Jones Ford, *The Rise and Growth of American Politics: A Sketch of Constitutional Development* (1898); Francis Newton Thorpe, *The Constitutional History of the United States,* 3 vols. (1901). There is much solid constitutional history in Andrew C. McLaughlin and Albert Bushnell Hart, eds., *Cyclopedia of American Government,* 3 vols. (1914). Twentieth-century works include William Seal Carpenter, *The Development of American Political Thought* (1930); Andrew C. McLaughlin, *The Foundations of American Constitutionalism* (1932); McLaughlin, *A Constitutional History of the United States* (1935); Erik M. Eriksson and David N. Rowe, *American Constitutional History* (1933); Homer C. Hockett, *The Constitutional History of the United States, 1776–1876,* 2 vols. (1939); Carl B. Swisher, *American Constitutional*

Development (1943, 1954); Arthur E. Sutherland, *Constitutionalism in America: Origins and Evolution of Its Fundamental Ideas* (1965). The contribution of Edward S. Corwin, perhaps the pre-eminent constitutional historian of the twentieth century, is well represented in Alpheus T. Mason and Gerald Garvey, eds., *American Constitutional History: Essays by Edward S. Corwin* (1964); Richard Loss, ed., *Presidential Power and the Constitution: Essays by Edward S. Corwin* (1976); and Corwin's "Introduction" to *The Constitution of the United States: Analysis and Interpretation* (1952).

Recent general accounts of constitutional and legal history are Kermit L. Hall, *The Magic Mirror: Law in American History* (1989); Daniel A. Farber and Suzanna Sherry, *A History of the American Constitution* (1990); Melvin I. Urofsky, *A March of Liberty: A Constitutional History of the United States* (1988); Kermit L. Hall and James W. Ely, Jr., eds., *An Uncertain Tradition: Constitutionalism and the History of the South* (1989); David J. Bodenhamer and James W. Ely, Jr., eds., *Ambivalent Legacy: A Legal History of the South* (1984); Symposium: "The Constitution and American Life," *JAH* 74 (1987). More specialized works that cover a broad sweep of constitutional history include Charles Warren, *The Supreme Court in United States History*, 2 vols. (1922); Charles Grove Haines, *The American Doctrine of Judicial Supremacy* (1911, 1932); Louis B. Boudin, *Government by Judiciary*, 2 vols. (1932); Conyers Read, ed., *The Constitution Reconsidered* (1938); Benjamin F. Wright, *The Growth of American Constitutional Law* (1942); G. Edward White, *The American Judicial Tradition: Profiles of Leading American Judges* (1976); Robert J. Steamer, *The Supreme Court in Crisis: A History of Conflict* (1971); Leon Friedman and Fred L. Israel, eds., *The Justices of the United States Supreme Court 1789–1969*, 4 vols. (1969); John R. Schmidhauser, *The Supreme Court as Final Arbiter in Federal-State Relations, 1789–1957* (1958). William M. Wiecek, *The Guarantee Clause of the U.S. Constitution* (1972), is concerned with controversy over the nature of republican constitutionalism. Notable recent studies of judicial history include John V. Orth, *The Judicial Power of the United States: The Eleventh Amendment in United States History* (1987); Christopher Wolfe, *The Rise of Modern Judicial Review: From Constitutional Interpretation to Judge-Made Law* (1986); David P. Currie, *The Constitution in the Supreme Court: The First Hundred Years, 1789–1888* (1985); William M. Wiecek, *Liberty under Law: The Supreme Court in American Life* (1988).

The formal amendment process, usually considered less worthy of study than methods of informal constitutional change, receives illuminating treatment in Alan P. Grimes, *Democracy and the Amendments to the Constitution* (1978), and Clement E. Vose, *Constitutional Change: Amendment Politics and Supreme Court Litigation since 1900* (1972). Herbert W. Horwill, *The Usages of the American Constitution* (1925), employs an English mode of analysis to describe what Americans sometimes refer to as extraconstitutional practices and institutions. M. Judd Harmon, ed., *Essays on the Constitution of the United States* (1978), provides broad analysis of constitutional development based on current scholarship, while recent constitutional tendencies are described in American Academy of Political and Social Science, *The Revolution, the Constitution, and America's Third Century: The Bicentennial Conference on the United States Constitution,* 2 vols. (1980), and Charles L. Black, Jr., and Bob Eckhardt, *The Tides of Power: Conversations on the American Constitution* (1976).

On the writing of constitutional history, see Paul L. Murphy, "Time to Reclaim: The Current Challenge of American Constitutional History" *AHR* 69 (1963); Herman Belz, "The Realist Critique of Constitutionalism in the Era of Reform," *AJLH* 15 (1971); Glendon A. Schubert, "The Future of Public Law," *George Washington Law Review* 34 (1966); James G. Randall, "The Interrelation of Social and Constitutional History," *AHR* 35 (1929). Harry N. Scheiber, "American Constitutional History and the New Legal History: Complementary Themes in Two Modes," *JAH* 68 (1981), discusses the relationship between public law and private law. This relationship is illustrated in Lawrence M. Friedman, *A History of American Law* (1973); James W. Hurst, *Law and Social Process in United States History* (1960); Hurst, "Legal Elements in United States History," *Perspectives in American History,* vol. 5 (1971); Harry N. Scheiber and Lawrence M. Friedman, eds., *American Law and the Constitutional Order: Historical Perspectives* (1988); Wythe Holt, ed., *Essays in Nineteenth-Century American Legal History* (1976); Stephen B. Presser and Jamil S. Zainaldin, eds., *Law and American History: Cases and Materials* (1980). The use of history in constitutional adjudication is examined in Charles A. Miller, *The Supreme Court and the Uses of History* (1969); Alfred H. Kelly, "Clio and the Court: An Illicit Love Affair," *Supreme Court Review 1965* (1966); Julius Goebel, Jr., "Constitutional History and Constitutional Law," *Columbia Law Review* 38 (1938). Michael Kammen, *A Machine That Would Go of Itself: The Constitution in American Culture* (1986), contains a wealth of information concerning attitudes toward the Constitution among the educated public.

Four good bibliographical aids are Alpheus T. Mason and D. Grier Stephenson, Jr., comps., *American Constitutional Development* (1977); Earlean M. McCarrick, *U.S. Constitution: A Guide to Information Sources* (1980); Stephen M. Millett, comp., *A Selected Bibliography of American Constitutional History* (1975); Kermit L. Hall, comp., *A Comprehensive Bibliography of American Constitutional and Legal History, 1896–1979* (5 vols., 1982).

II. *The Founding of the Colonies and Constitutional Development in the Seventeenth Century*

Two valuable general studies of early American constitutional development are Donald S. Lutz, *The Origins of American Constitutionalism* (1988), and Jack P. Greene, *Peripheries and Center: Constitutional Development in the*

Extended Politics of the British Empire and the United States, 1607–1788 (1986). The best general works dealing with constitutional aspects of colonization are John E. Pomfret, *Founding the American Colonies, 1583–1660* (1970); Wesley Frank Craven, *The Southern Colonies in the Seventeenth Century* (1949); Craven, *The Colonies in Transition 1660–1713* (1968). Of lasting importance for the study of early American constitutional development are Herbert L. Osgood, *The American Colonies in the Seventeenth Century,* 3 vols. (1904–7), and Charles M. Andrews, *The Colonial Period of American History,* 4 vols. (1935–39). Andrew C. McLaughlin, *The Foundations of American Constitutionalism* (1932) is a classic statement of the significance of the corporation and covenant in the formation of American government. William Robert Scott, *The Constitution and Finance of English, Scottish and Irish Joint-Stock Companies to 1720,* 3 vols. (1912), provides detailed information about the colonizing activities of English merchant-adventurers. John P. Davis, *Corporations: A Study of the Origin and Development of Great Business Combinations and Their Relation to the Authority of the State,* 2 vols. (1905), is a superior analysis of the influence of the corporation on the colonial constitution. Still worthwhile are a series of seminal articles by Herbert L. Osgood: "The Corporation as a Form of Colonial Government," *PSQ* 11 (1896); "The Proprietary Province as a Form of Colonial Government," *AHR* 2 (1897); "The Political Ideas of the Puritans," *PSQ* 6 (1891).

On the development of government in Virginia, see Sigmund Diamond, "From Organization to Society: Virginia in the Seventeenth Century," *American Journal of Sociology* 63 (1958); Wesley Frank Craven, "And So the Form of Government Became Perfect," *Virginia Magazine of History and Biography* 77 (1969); Warren Billings, "The Growth of Political Institutions in Virginia, 1634 to 1676," *WMQ* 31 (1974).

Valuable works on Massachusetts include Samuel Eliot Morison, *Builders of the Bay Colony* (1930); Frances Rose-Troup, *The Massachusetts Bay Company and Its Predecessors* (1930); Perry Miller, *Orthodoxy in Massachusetts, 1630–1650* (1933); Charles H. McIlwain, "The Transfer of the Charter to New England and Its Significance in American Constitutional History," *Massachusetts Historical Society Proceedings* 63 (1929), reprinted in McIlwain *Constitutionalism and the Changing World* (1939); T. H. Breen, *The Character of the Good Ruler: A Study of Puritan Political Ideas in New England, 1630–1730* (1970); Robert E. Wall, Jr., *Massachusetts Bay: The Crucial Decade, 1640–1650* (1972); Richard P. Gildrie, *Salem, Massachusetts, 1626–1683: A Covenant Community* (1972); Richard S. Dunn, *Puritans and Yankees: The Winthrop Dynasty of New England, 1630–1717* (1962). George Langdon, Jr., *Pilgrim Colony: A History of New Plymouth, 1620–1691* (1966), is a standard account, while Mary Jeane Anderson Jones, *Congregational Commonwealth: Connecticut 1636–1662* (1968), relates developments in that New England colony.

The early constitutional history of Maryland is described in Newton D. Mereness, *Maryland as a Proprietary Province* (1901), and Matthew P. Andrews, *The Founding of Maryland: Province and State* (1933). Studies of the later proprietary colonies include John E. Pomfret, *The Province of East New Jersey, 1609–1702: The Rebellious Proprietary* (1962); Pomfret, *The Province of West New Jersey 1609–1702: A History of Organization of an American Colony* (1956); Wesley Frank Craven, *New Jersey and the English Colonization of North America* (1964); J. S. Bassett, *The Constitutional Beginnings of North Carolina* (1894); Hugh T. Lefler and Albert R. Newsome, *The History of a Southern State: North Carolina* (1954); Edwin R. Bronner, *William Penn's 'Holy Experiment': The Founding of Pennsylvania 1681–1701* (1962); Mary Maples Dunn, *William Penn: Politics and Conscience* (1967); Gary B. Nash, "The Framing of Government in Pennsylvania: Ideas in Contact with Reality," *WMQ* 23 (1966); Robert C. Ritchie, *The Duke's Province: A Study of New York Politics and Society, 1664–1691* (1977).

On the political and constitutional changes of the later seventeenth century, see David S. Lovejoy, *The Glorious Revolution in America* (1972); Lois G. Carr and David W. Jordan, *Maryland's Revolution in Government 1689–1692* (1974); Wilcomb E. Washburn, *The Government and the Rebel: A History of Bacon's Rebellion in Virginia* (1957); Bernard Bailyn, "Politics and Social Structure in Seventeenth Century Virginia," in James M. Smith, ed., *Seventeenth Century America: Essays in Colonial History* (1959); Michael G. Hall, *Edward Randolph and the American Colonies, 1676–1703* (1960); Philip S. Haffenden, *New England in the English Nation, 1689–1713* (1974); Lawrence H. Leder, *Robert Livingston, 1654–1728, and the Politics of Colonial New York* (1961); Jerome R. Reich, *Leisler's Rebellion: A Study of Democracy in New York, 1664–1720* (1953). Wesley Frank Craven, *The Colonies in Transition* (1968), and Clarence L. VerSteeg, *The Formative Years, 1607–1763* (1964), are good on this period. Michael Kammen, *Deputyes and Libertyes: the Origins of Representative Government in Colonial America* (1969), sees decisive acquisitions of power by the colonial assemblies in the seventeenth century. Stephen Saunders Webb, *The Governors-General: The English Army and the Definition of the Empire, 1569–1681* (1979), contends that centralized military rule characterized the British empire form the outset. This interpretation is disputed in J. M. Sosin, *English America and the Restoration Monarchy of Charles II: Transatlantic Politics, Commerce, and Kinship* (1980). Viola F. Barnes, *The Dominion of New England: A Study in British Colonial Policy* (1923), and Louise P. Kellogg, "The American Colonial Charter," American Historical Association *Annual Report, 1903,* vol. I, are worthwhile accounts of the early British imperial system.

III. *The Colonial Constitution in the Eighteenth Century*

The growth of assembly power as the basis of effective local autonomy forms the central theme in accounts of eighteenth-century constitutional development. Influential have been Bernard Bailyn, *The Origin of American Politics* (1968) and *The Ideological Origins of the American Revolution* (1967), both of which identify English republican writers as the chief source of American constitutional thought. Other valuable studies include Jack P. Greene, *The Quest for Power: The Lower Houses of Assembly in the Southern Royal Colonies, 1689–1776* (1963); Greene, "Political Mimesis: A Consideration of the Historical and Cultural Roots of Legislative Behavior in the British Colonies in the Eighteenth Century," *AHR* 75 (1969); Lawrence Leder, *Liberty and Authority: Early American Political Ideology, 1689–1763* (1968); J. R. Pole, *Political Representation in England and the Origins of the American Republic* (1966); Stanley N. Katz, "The Origins of American Constitutional Thought," *Perspectives in American History,* III (1969); Alfred de Grazia, *Public and Republic: Political Representation in America* (1951); George N. Dargo, *Roots of the Republic: A New Perspective on Early American Constitutionalism* (1974); Patricia Bonomi, *Politics and Society in Colonial New York* (1971); George Edward Frakes, *Laboratory for Liberty: The South Carolina Legislative Committee System, 1719–1776* (1970); Lucille Griffith, *The Virginia House of Burgesses, 1750–1774* (1963); Raymond C. Bailey, *Popular Influence upon Public Policy: Petitioning in Eighteenth Century Virginia* (1979); James Henretta, "Salutary Neglect": Colonial Administration under the Duke of Newcastle (1972); Stanley N. Katz, *Newcastle's New York: Anglo-American Politics, 1732–1753* (1968); M. Eugene Sirmans, *Colonial South Carolina: A Political History 1663–1763* (1967). Important older accounts are Mary P. Clarke, *Parliamentary Privilege in the American Colonies* (1943); Evarts B. Green, *The Provincial Governor in the English Colonies of North America* (1898); Leonard W. Labaree, *Royal Government in America: A Study of the British Colonial System before 1783* (1930); Labaree, *Conservatism in Early American History* (1948); Beverly W. Bond, Jr., *The Quit-Rent System in the American Colonies* (1919).

The Lockean, liberal individualist view of colonial constitutional thought is found in William Seal Carpenter, *The Development of American Political Thought* (1930); Benjamin F. Wright, Jr., *American Interpretations of Natural Law* (1931); Max Savelle, *Seeds of Liberty: The Genesis of the Amreican Mind* (1948); Clinton L. Rossiter, *Seedtime of the Republic* (1953). The problem of democracy in early America has received intensive study, especially the question of suffrage requirements. Key works examining this issue are B. Katherine Brown, "Freemanship in Puritan Massachusetts," *AHR* 50 (1954); Brown, "Puritan Democracy: A Case Study," *MVHR* 50 (1963); Robert F. and Katherine Brown, *Virginia: 1705–1788: Democracy or Aristocracy?* (1964); Robert F. Brown, *Middle Class Democracy and the Revolution in Massachusetts, 1691–1780* (1955), all of which argue that democracy existed in colonial America. This view is disputed in Timothy H. Breen, "Who Governs: The Town Franchise in Seventeenth Century Massachusetts," *WMQ* 27 (1970), and Robert E. Wall, Jr., "The Decline of the Massachusetts Franchise, 1647–

1666," *JAH* 69 (1972). A rewarding treatment of the subject is J. R. Pole, "Historians and the Problem of Early American Democracy," *AHR* 67 (1962). See also John C. Rainbolt, "The Alteration in the Relationship between Leadership and Constituents in Virginia, 1660 to 1720," *WMQ* 27 (1970); Richard V. Buel, "Democracy and the American Revolution: A Frame of Reference," *WMQ* 22 (1965); Roy N. Lokken, "The Concept of Democracy in Colonial Political Thought," *WMQ* 16 (1959); John B. Kirby, "Early American Politics—the Search for Ideology: An Historiographical Analysis and Critique of the Concept of Deference," *JP* 32 (1970). Albert E. McKinley, *The Suffrage Franchise in the Thirteen English Colonies in America* (1905), and Chilton Williamson, *American Suffrage from Property to Democracy, 1760–1860* (1960), provide essential data concerning suffrage laws and practices.

The reception of the common law and the development of colonial legal and judicial institutions are discussed in William E. Nelson and Robert C. Palmer, *Liberty and Community: Constitution and Rights in the Early American Republic* (1987); Lawrence M. Friedman, *A History of American Law* (1973); George L. Haskins, *Law and Authority in Early Massachusetts: A Study in Tradition and Design* (1960); Herbert A. Johnson, "American Colonial Legal History: A Historiographical Interpretation," in *Perspectives in Early American History,* ed. Alden T. Vaughn and George A. Billias (1973); David H. Flaherty, ed., *Essays in the History of Early American Law* (1969); Stanley N. Katz, "The Politics of Law in Colonial America: Controversies over Chancery Courts and Equity Law in the Eighteenth Century," *Perspectives in American History,* vol. 5 (1971); Julius Goebel, Jr., *History of the Supreme Court of the United States,* vol. 1: Antecedents and Beginnings (1971); Erwin C. Surrency, "The Courts in the American Colonies," *AJLH* 11 (1967); George A. Billias, ed., *Law and Authority in Colonial America* (1965); Stanley N. Katz, "Looking Backward: The Early History of American Law," *University of Chicago Law Review* 33 (1966); Herbert A. Johnson, "The Prerogative Court of New York, 1686–1776," *AJLH* 18 (1973); Milton M. Klein, *The Politics of Diversity: Essays in the History of Colonial New York* (1974); Richard B. Morris, *Studies in the History of American Law, with Special Reference to the Seventeenth and Eighteenth Century* (1930); Paul S. Reinsch, *English Common Law in Early American Colonies* (1899); Francis R. Aumann, *The Changing American Legal System: Some Selected Phases* (1940).

There are numerous recent studies examining oligarchical control of local government and the relationship between town government and provincial authority. See, in particular, Michael Zuckerman, *Peaceable Kingdoms: New England Towns in the Eighteenth Century* (1970); David G. Allen, "The Zuckerman Thesis and the Process of Legal Rationalization in Provincial Massachusetts," *WMQ* 29 (1972); L. Kinvin Wroth, "Peaceable Kingdoms: The New England Town from the Perspective of Legal History," *AJLH* 15 (1971); Bruce C. Daniels, *The Connecticut Town: Growth and Development, 1635–1790* (1979); Bruce C. Daniels, ed., *Town and County: Essays on the*

Structure of Local Government in the American Colonies (1978); Kenneth A. Lockridge and Alan Kreider, "The Evolution of Massachusetts Town Government, 1640 to 1740," *WMQ* 23 (1966); Hendrik Hartog, "The Public Law of a County Court: Judicial Government in Eighteenth Century Massachusetts," *AJLH* 20 (1976). Roy H. Akagi, *The Town Proprietors of the New England Colonies: A Study of their Development, Organization, Activities, and Controversies, 1620–1770* (1924) is a superior older work.

IV. *The American Revolution, the State Constitutions and the Articles of Confederation*

Works describing the nature and development of the British imperial system include Lawrence Henry Gipson, *The British Empire before the Revolution*, 14 vols. (1936–68); Dora Mae Clarke, *The Rise of the British Treasury: Colonial Administration in the Eighteenth Century* (1960); Michael Kammen, *A Rope of Sand: The Colonial Agents, British Politics, and the American Revolution* (1968); Alison G. Olson, "Parliament, Empire, and Parliamentary Law, 1776," in *Three British Revolutions: 1641, 1688, 1776,* ed. J. G. A. Pocock (1980); Thomas C. Barrow, *Trade and Empire: The British Customs Service in America, 1660–1775* (1967); Lawrence Harper, *The English Navigation Laws: A Seventeenth Century Experiment in Social Engineering* (1939); O. M. Dickerson, *The Navigation Acts and the American Revolution* (1951); F. P. Wickwire, *British Subministers and Colonial America, 1766–1783* (1966); George Louis Beer, *Origins of the British Colonial System* (1908) and *The Old Colonial System* (1912).

The debate about parliamentary power and the status of the colonies in the empire has produced some of the classic works in constitutional history. These include Charles H. McIlwain, *The American Revolution: A Constitutional Interpretation* (1923); Randolph G. Adams, *The Political Ideas of the American Revolution* (1922); Robert L. Schuyler, *Parliament and the British Empire* (1929); Carl L. Becker, *The Declaration of Independence* (1922); Herbert L. Osgood, "England and the Colonies," *PSQ* 2 (1887); Claude H. Van Tyne, *The Causes of the War of Independence* (1922); Andrew C. McLaughlin, "The Background of American Federalism," *APSR* 12 (1918); Charles F. Mullett, *Fundamental Law and the American Revolution, 1760–1776* (1933); Julian P. Boyd, *Anglo-American Union: Joseph Galloway's Plans to Preserve the British Empire* (1941). More recent works that should be consulted are James H. Kettner, *The Development of American Citizenship, 1608–1870* (1978); Edmund S. Morgan, "Colonial Ideas of Parliamentary Power, 1764–1776," *WMQ* 5 (1948); Harvey Wheeler, "Calvin's Case and the McIlwain-Schuyler Debate," *AHR* 61 (1955–56); Walter F. Bennett, *American Theories of Federalism* (1964); Barbara A. Black, "The Constitution of the

Empire: The Case for the Colonists," *University of Pennsylvania Law Review*
124 (1976); David Ammerman, "The British Constitution and the American
Revolution: A Failure of Precedent," *William and Mary Law Review* 17
(1976). Two major works challenging the recent republican ideological interpretation of the Revolution are John Phillip Reid, *Constitutional History of the
American Revolution: The Authority of Rights* (1986), and John Phillip Reid,
Constitutional History of the American Revolution: The Authority to Tax
(1987).

Charles M. Andrews, "The American Revolution: An Interpretation,"
AHR 31 (1926), is a classic statement of the thesis that the movement for
independence was essentially constitutional in nature. See also R. A. Hum-
phreys, "The Rule of Law and the American Revolution," *Law Quarterly
Review* 53 (1937). More recent studies that advance this view are Daniel J.
Boorstin, *The Genius of American Politics* (1953); Edmund S. Morgan and
Helen M. Morgan, *The Stamp Act Crisis: Prologue to Revolution* (1953);
Edmund S. Morgan, *The Birth of the Republic, 1763–1789* (1956); David S.
Lovejoy, "Rights Imply Equality: The Case against Admiralty Jurisdiction in
America, 1764–1776," *WMQ* 16 (1959). A more sophisticated version of this
thesis is developed by Bernard Bailyn, *The Ideological Origins of the American
Revolution* (1967), and Bailyn, "Political Experience and Enlightenment Ideas
in Eighteenth Century America," *AHR* 67 (1962). Works which emphasize
the importance of English republican and eighteenth-century Enlightenment
ideas in the American Revolution include Edmund S. Morgan, "The American
Revolution Considered as an Intellectual Movement," in Morton White and
Arthur Schlesinger, Jr., eds., *Paths of American Thought* (1973); Gordon
Wood, *The Creation of the American Republic, 1776–1787* (1969); Hannah
Arendt, *On Revolution* (1963); J. G. A. Pocock, "1776: The Revolution against
Parliament," in Pocock, ed., *Three British Revolutions: 1641, 1688, 1776*
(1980); William H. Nelson, "The Revolutionary Character of the American
Revolution," *AHR* 70 (1965); William D. Liddle, " 'A Patriot King, or None':
Lord Bolingbroke and the American Renunciation of George III," *JAH* 65
(1979); Garry Wills, *Inventing America: Jefferson's Declaration of Independence* (1978); Morton White, *The Philosophy of the American Revolution*
(1978); Pauline Maier, *From Resistance to Revolution: Colonial Radicals and
the Development of American Opposition to Britain, 1765–1776* (1972); Alan
Rogers, Empire and Liberty: American Resistance to British Authority, 1755–
1763 (1974); Stanley N. Katz, "Republicanism and the Law of Inheritance in
the American Revolutionary Era," *Michigan Law Review* 76 (1977); Library
of Congress Symposia on the American Revolution: *The Development of a
Revolutionary Mentality* (1972); Willi Paul Adams, "Republicanism in Political Rhetoric before 1776," *PSQ* 85 (1970). An interesting older work on this
subject is George M. Dutcher, "The Rise of Republican Government in the
United States," *PSQ* 55 (1940).

The problem of fundamental law and the new American conception of constitutionalism that emerged during the Revolution are analyzed in Edward S. Corwin, "The 'Higher Law' Background of American Constitutional Law," *Harvard Law Review* 42 (1928–29), reprinted under the same title in book form in 1955; Charles H. McIlwain, "The Fundamental Law behind the Constitution of the United States," in *Constitutionalism in a Changing World* (1939); Charles F. Mullett, "Coke and the American Revolution," *Economica* 12 (1932); Bailyn, *The Ideological Origins of the American Revolution;* Thomas C. Grey, "Origins of the Unwritten Constitution: Fundamental Law in American Revolutionary Thought," *Stanford Law Review* 30 (1978). Donald S. Lutz, "From Covenant to Constitution in American Political Thought," *Publius* 10 (1980), surpasses previous studies in the thoroughness and precision with which it traces the development of American thinking on constitutions. See also Donald S. Lutz, *The Origins of American Constitutionalism* (1988).

For detailed description of the first state constitutions the following works are worth consulting: Donald S. Lutz, *Popular Consent and Popular Control: Whig Political Theory in the Early State Constitutions* (1980); Willi Paul Adams, *The First American Constitutions: Republican Ideology and the Making of the State Constitutions in the Revolutionary Era* (1980); Allan Nevins, *The American States during and after the Revolution, 1775–1789* (1924); Benjamin F. Wright, "The Early History of Written Constitutions in America," in *Essays in History and Political Theory in Honor of Charles Howard McIlwain,* ed. Carl Wittke (1936); Wright, *Consensus and Continuity, 1776–1787* (1958); W. F. Dodd, "The First State Constitutional Conventions, 1776–1783," *APSR* 2 (1908); W. C. Morey, "The First State Constitutions," *Annals* 4 (1893); W. C. Webster, "A Comparative Study of the State Constitutions of the American Revolution," *Annals* 9 (1897); Thad W. Tate, "The Social Contract in America, 1774–1787: Revolutionary Theory as a Conservative Instrument," *WMQ* 22 (1965); Fletcher Green, *Constitutional Development of the South Atlantic States, 1776–1860* (1930); John N. Shaeffer, "Public Consideration of the 1776 Pennsylvania Constitution," *Pennsylvania Magazine of History and Biography* 98 (1974); Ronald M. Peters, *The Massachusetts Constitution of 1780: A Social Compact* (1974); Jere N. Daniell, *Experiment in Republicanism: New Hampshire Politics and the American Revolution 1741–1794* (1970); Peter S. Onuf, "State-Making in Revolutionary America: Independent Vermont as a Case Study," *JAH* 67 (1981).

The relationship between the separation-of-powers doctrine and the theory of mixed government has been one of the more perplexing questions in colonial and revolutionary constitutional history. The best analysis of the problem is M. J. C. Vile, *Constitutionalism and the Separation of Powers* (1967). Other pertinent works are W. B. Gwyn, *The Meaning of the Separation of Powers* (1965); Murray Dry, "The Separation of Powers and Republican Government," *Political Science Reviewer* 3 (1973); Martin Diamond, "The Separation of Powers and the Mixed Regime," *Publius* 8 (1978); William Seal Carpenter, "The Separation of Powers in the Eighteenth Century," *APSR* 22

(1928); Francis G. Wilson, "The Mixed Constitution and the Separation of Powers," *Southwestern Social Science Quarterly* 15 (1934); Benjamin F. Wright, "The Origin of the Separation of Powers in America," *Economica* 13 (1933); Malcom P. Sharpe, "The Classical American Doctrine of the Separation of Powers," *University of Chicago Law Review* 2 (1935).

The progressive interpretation of Revolutionary constitution making, concerned more with social and economic interests than constitutional principles and ideas, is well illustrated in Merrill Jensen, *The Founding of a Nation* (1968); Jensen, *The American Revolution within America* (1974); Jensen, "Democracy and the American Revolution," *Huntington Library Quarterly* 20 (1957); Elisha P. Douglass, *Rebels and Democrats: The Struggle for Equal Political Rights and Majority Rule during the American Revolution* (1955); Jackson Turner Main, *The Upper House in Revolutionary America, 1763–1788* (1967); Main, *The Sovereign States 1775–1783* (1973).

The development of a distinctive national outlook and loyalty in the colonial and Revolutionary period is discussed in Harry M. Ward, *"Unite or Die": Intercolony Relations, 1690–1763* (1971); J. M. Bumsted, " 'Things in the Womb of Time': Ideas of American Independence, 1633 to 1763," *WMQ* 31 (1974); Edwin G. Burrows and Michael Wallace, "The American Revolution: The Ideology and Psychology of National Liberation," *Perspectives in American History* 6 (1972); Max Savelle, "Nationalism and Other Loyalties in the American Revolution," *AHR* 67 (1962); John Blassingame, "American Nationalism and Other Loyalties in the Southern Colonies, 1763–1775," *JSH* 34 (1968); Thomas C. Barrow, "The American Revolution as a Colonial War for Independence," *WMQ* 25 (1968). The central importance of political and constitutional ideas in defining American nationality is perceptively analyzed in Yehoshua Arieli, *Individualism and Nationalism in American Ideology* (1964).

The Articles of Confederation are interpreted as expressing the democratic spirit of the Revolution in various works of Merrill Jensen. See his *The Articles of Confederation: An Interpretation of the Social-Constitutional History of the American Revolution, 1774–1781* (1940), and *The New Nation: A History of the United States during the Confederation 1781–1789* (1950). Andrew C. McLaughlin, *The Confederation and the Constitution, 1781–1789* (1905) is the classic nationalist interpretation of the Confederation era. It is complemented by the more recent accounts of Morgan, *The Birth of the Republic;* Wright, *Consensus and Continuity;* Forrest Mcdonald, *E Pluribus Unum: The Formation of the American Republic 1776–1790* (1965). There is an excellent analysis of the problem of sovereignty in the Confederation period in Claude H. Van Tyne, "Sovereignty in the American Revolution: An Historical Study," *AHR* 12 (1907).

Recent general accounts of the Confederation are Jerrilyn Greene Marston, *King and Congress: The Transfer of Political Legitimacy, 1774–1776* (1987); H. James Henderson, *Party Politics in the Continental Congress* (1974);

Joseph L. Davis, *Sectionalism in American Politics, 1774–1787* (1977); Jack N. Rakove, *The Beginnings of National Politics: An Interpretive History of the Continental Congress* (1979). Studies of institutional development in the Confederation era include Herbert A. Johnson, "Toward a Reappraisal of the Federal Government: 1783–1789," *AJLH* 8 (1964); Edmund C. Burnett, *The Continental Congress* (1941); Jennings B. Sanders, *The Presidency of the Continental Congress 1774–1789: A Study in American Institutional History* (1930); Sanders, *Evolution of the Executive Departments of the Continental Congress, 1774–1789* (1935); Charles C. Thach, *The Creation of the Presidency, 1775–1789* (1922); Jay Caesar Guggenheimer, "The Development of the Executive Departments, 1775–1789," in J. Franklin Jameson, ed., *Essays in the Constitutional History of the United States in the Formative Period, 1775–1789* (1889). Peter Onuf, "Toward Federalism: Virginia, Congress, and the Western Lands," *WMQ* 34 (1977), is an illuminating discussion of the territorial character of governmental sovereignty in American federalism. Arthur Bestor, "Constitutionalism and the Settlement of the West: The Attainment of Consensus, 1754–1784," in John Porter Bloom, ed., *The American Territorial System,* and Robert F. Berkhofer, Jr., "Jefferson, the Ordinance of 1784, and the Origins of the American Territorial System," *WMQ* 29 (1972), analyze an important aspect of Confederation policy making.

V. *The Federal Constitution of 1787*

Key studies of the movement for constitutional reform that led to the federal convention are Edward S. Corwin, "The Progress of Constitutional Theory between the Declaration of Independence and the Meeting of the Philadelphia Convention," *AHR* 30 (1925); Merrill Jensen, "The Idea of a National Government during the American Revolution," *PSQ* 58 (1943); E. J. Ferguson, "The Nationalists of 1781–1783 and the Economic Interpretation of the Constitution," *JAH* 56 (1969); Wood, *The Creation of the American Republic.*

Max Farrand, ed., *The Records of the Federal Convention of 1787,* 4 vols. (1911–37), provides the basic documentary foundation for study of the convention. The most authoritative recent studies of the making of the Constitution are Forrest McDonald, *Novus Ordo Seclorum: The Intellectual Origins of the Constitution* (1985); Richard B. Morris, *The Forging of the Union, 1781–1787* (1987); Calvin C. Jillson, *Constitution Making: Conflict and Consensus in the Federal Convention of 1787* (1988). The following works offer good narrative accounts of the convention: Andrew C. McLaughlin, *A Constitutional History of the United States* (1935); McLaughlin, *The Confederation and the Constitution, 1781–1789* (1905); Max Farrand, *The Fathers of the Constitution* (1913); Charles Warren, *The Making of the Constitution* (1929); David G. Smith, *The Convention and the Constitution* (1965); Clinton L. Rossiter, *1787: The Grand*

Convention (1966). Among the more useful of numerous biographical studies are Irving Brant, *James Madison: Father of the Constitution* (1950) and Charles P. Smith, *James Wilson, Founding Father, 1742–1798* (1956).

An excellent study of the politics of the convention is Calvin C. Jillson, "Constitution-Making; Alignment and Realignment in the Federal Convention of 1787," *APSR* 75 (1981). Other valuable analyses are John P. Roche, "The Founding Fathers: A Reform Caucus in Action," *APSR* 55 (1961); Stanley Elkins and Eric McKitrick, "The Founding Fathers: Young Men of the Revolution," *PSQ* 76 (1961); Arnold A. Rogow, "The Federal Convention: Madison and Yates," *AHR* 60 (1955); Staughton Lynd, "The Compromise of 1787," *PSQ* 81 (1966); Calvin Jillson and Thornton Anderson, "Realignment in the convention of 1787: The Slave Trade Compromise," *JP* 39 (1977); Howard A. Ohline, "Republicanism and Slavery: Origins of the Three Fifths Clause in the United States Constitution," *WMQ* 28 (1971); William Cuddihy and B. Carmon Hardy, "A Man's House Was Not His Castle: Origins of the Fourth Amendment to the United States Constitution," *WMQ* 37 (1980); Robert H. Birkby, "The Politics of Accommodation: The Origin of the Supremacy Clause," *Western Pol. Q.* 19 (1966); Bernard Donahoe and Marshall Smelser, "The Congressional Power to Raise Armies: The Constitutional and Ratifying Conventions 1787–1788," *Review of Politics* 33 (1971); Frederick W. Marks III, *Independence on Trial: Foreign Affairs and the Making of the Constitution* (1973).

Numerous works analyze the achievement of the Constitutional Convention from the standpoint of political and constitutional theory. Among the more helpful in understanding the nature of the Constitution and the ideas of the framers are Rozann Rothman, *Acts and Enactments: The Constitutional Convention of 1787* (1974), written from a Kenneth Burkean symbolic perspective; Rothman, "The Impact of Covenant and Contract Theories on Conceptions of the U.S. Constitution," *Publius* 10 (1980); Martin Diamond, "Democracy and the Federalist: A Reconsideration of the Framers' Intent," *APSR* 53 (1959); Diamond, "The Declaration and the Constitution: Liberty, Democracy, and the Founders," *The Public Interest* 41 (1975); Douglass Adair, " 'That Politics May Be Reduced to a Science': David Hume, James Madison, and the Tenth *Federalist,* " *Huntington Library Quarterly* 20 (1957). Alpheus T. Mason, "The Federalist—a Split Personality," *AHR* 58 (1952); Mason, "Our Federal Union Reconsidered," *PSQ* 65 (1950).

In recent years study of the political science of the framers has focused on the question of whether the political philosophy of the Constitution is primarily that of republicanism or liberalism. Important contributions to this debate are Gordon S. Wood, *The Creation of the American Republic, 1776–1787* (1969); Gordon S. Wood, "Ideology and the Origins of Liberal America," *WMQ* 44 (1987); Thomas L. Pangle, *The Spirit of Modern Republicanism: The Moral Vision of the American Founders and the Philosophy of Locke* (1988); Ralph Lerner, *The Thinking Revolutionary: Principle and Practice in the New Republic* (1987); David F. Epstein, *The Political Theory of 'The Federalist'* (1984); John P. Diggins, *The Lost Soul of American Politics: Virtue, Self-Interest, and the Foundations of Liberalism* (1984); Michael P. Zuckert, "Federalisms and the Founding," *Review of Politics* 48 (1986); Michael P. Zuckert, "*The Federalist* at 200—What's It to Us?" *Constitutional Commentary* 7 (1990); Michael Lienesch, *New Order of the Ages: Time, the Constitution, and the Making of Modern American Political Thought* (1988); Edward J. Erler, "The Problem of the Public Good in *The Federalist,* " *Polity* 13 (1981); Jean Yarbrough, "Representation and Republicanism: Two Views," *Publius* 9 (1979); Jean Yarbrough, "Thoughts on *The Federalist*'s View of Representation," *Polity* 12 (1980). Useful historiographical commentary on the political ideas of the Constitution may be found in James H. Hutson, "The Creation of the Constitution: Scholarship at a Standstill," *Reviews in American History* 12 (1984); Peter S. Onuf, "Reflections on the Founding: Constitutional Historiography in Bicentennial Perspective," *WMQ* 44 (1987); Symposium: "*The Creation of the American Republic,* " *WMQ* 44 (1987). There are several collections of essays that explore the political ideas of the Constitution, including Terence Ball and J.G.A. Pocock, eds., *Conceptual Change and the Constitution* (1988); Leonard W. Levy and Dennis J. Mahoney, eds., *The Framing and Ratification of the Constitution* (1987); Charles R. Kesler, ed., *Saving the Republic: The Federalist Papers and the American Founding* (1987); Richard Beeman *et al.,* eds., *Beyond Confederation: Origins of the Constitution and American National Identity* (1987); Robert A. Goldwin and William A. Schambra, eds., *How Does the Constitution Secure Rights?* (1985); Robert A. Goldwin and William A. Schambra, eds., *How Democratic Is the Constitution?* (1980). Additional works that provide insight into the framers' ideas are Leonard R. Sorenson, "The Limits of Constitutional Government: Reflections toward the Conclusion of the Bicentennial Celebration of Our Constitution," *Review of Politics* 51 (1989); Richard S. Kay, "The Illegality of the Constitution," *Constitutional Commentary* 4 (1987); William E. Nelson, "Reason and Compromise in the Establishment of the Constitution: 1787–1801," *WMQ* 44 (1987); Albert Furtwangler, *The Authority of Publius: A Reading of the 'Federalist' Papers* (1984).

Federalism is analyzed philosophically in S. Rufus Davis, *The Federal Principle: A Journey through Time in Quest of Meaning* (1978), and Rozann Rothman, 'The Ambiguity of American Federal Theory," *Publius* 8 (1978). William T. Hutchinson, "Unite to Divide; Divide to Unite: The Shaping of American Federalism," *MVHR* 46 (1959), and McLaughlin, "The Background of American Federalism," *APSR* 12 (1918), approach the subject historically. A recent work that revives the perspective of earlier scholarship is Peter S. Onuf, *The Origins of the Federal Republic: Jurisdictional Controversies in the United States, 1775–1787* (1983).

Charles A. Beard's, *An Economic Interpretation of the Constitution of the United States* (1913), arguing that the framers created a strong central government to restrain democracy and protect property interests, has become a field of study unto itself that bears directly on the question of the ratification of the Constitution. Beard's views were anticipated in part by Orin G. Libby, *The Geographical Distribution of the Vote by the Thirteen States on the Federal Constitution, 1787–8* (1894), and J. Allen Smith, *The Spirit of American Government, a Study of the Constitution: Its Origin, Influence and Relation to Democracy* (1907). After a long period of intellectual hegemony, the Beard thesis was attacked by scholars who perceived an underlying consensus in American politics and who asserted the primacy of constitutional principles over class interests. See especially Morgan, *Birth of the Republic* (1956); Forrest McDonald, *We the People: The Economic Origins of the Constitution* (1958); McDonald, *E Pluribus Unum: The Formation of the American Republic, 1776–1790* (1965); Wright, *Consensus and Continuity* (1958); Robert E. Brown, *Charles Beard and the Constitution* (1956); Brown, *Reinterpretation of the formation of the American Constitution* (1963); Henry Steele Commager, "The Constitution: Was It an Economic Document?" *American Heritage* 9 (1958); Lee Benson, *Turner and Beard* (1960); Richard Hofstadter, *The Progressive Historians* (1968); Douglass Adair, "The Tenth Federalist Revisited," *WMQ* 8 (1951).

More sophisticated and empirically sound versions of the Beardian social-conflict interpretation of the Constitution appear in Jackson Turner Main, *The Antifederalists: Critics of the Constitution, 1781–1788* (1961); E. James Ferguson, *The Power of the Purse: A History of American Public Finance 1776–1790* (1961); Staughton Lynd, "Capitalism, Democracy, and the U.S. Constitution," *Science and Society* 27 (1963); Merrill Jensen, *The American Revolution within America* (1974).

Jonathan Elliot, ed., *The Debates in the Several State Conventions on the Adoption of the Federal Constitution,* 5 vols. (1936), is the basic documentary source for the study of ratification. Herbert J. Storing, ed., *The Complete Anti-Federalist,* 7 vols. (1982), supplements this record. Storing, *What the Anti-Federalists Were For,* vol. I of this collection, presents a sympathetic analysis of Antifederalist constitutional ideas. Stimulating analyses of the ratification controversy blending the insights of both the neo-Beardian and the consensus-ideological points of view on the Constitution appear in John M. Murrin, "The Great Inversion, or Court versus Country: A Comparison of the Revolutionary Settlements in England (1688–1721) and America (1776–1816)," in Pocock, ed., *Three British Revolutions: 1641, 1688, 1776* (1980), and James H. Hutson, "Country, Court, and Constitution: Antifederalism and the Historians," *WMQ* 38 (1981). Other important works are Cecelia Kenyon, "Men of Little Faith: The Anti-Federalists on the Nature of Representative Government," *WMQ* 12 (1955); Kenyon, "Republicanism and Radicalism in the American Revolution: An Old-fashioned Interpretation," *WMQ* 19 (1962); Wood, *The Creation of the American Republic;* Charles W. Roll, Jr., "We Some of the People: Apportionment in the Thirteen State Conventions

Ratifying the Constitution," *JAH* 56 (1969); Linda Grant DePauw, *The Eleventh Pillar: New York State and the Federal Constitution* (1966); Stephen R. Boyd, *The Politics of Opposition: Antifederalists and the Acceptance of the Constitution* (1979); Alpheus T. Mason, *The States Rights Debate: Antifederalism and the Constitution* (1964). The relationship between the Declaration of Independence and the Constitution is considered in Edmund S. Morgan, "The Great Political Fiction," *New York Review of Books,* March 9, 1978; Gary J. Schmitt and Robert H. Webking, "Revolutionaries, Antifederalists, and Federalists: Comments on Gordon Wood's Understanding of the American Founding," *Political Science Reviewer* 9 (1979); Martin Diamond, "The American Idea of Equality: The View from the Founding," *Review of Politics* 38 (1976).

VI. *Constitutional Development in the Early National Period*

The rapid acceptance of the Constitution as the legitimate basis for the conduct of government and politics is dealt with in Lance Banning, "Republican Ideology and the Triumph of the Constitution, 1789 to 1793," *WMQ* 31 (1974); Michael Lienesch, "The Constitutional Tradition: History, Political Action, and Progress in American Political Thought, 1787–1793," *JP* 42 (1980); Frank I. Schechter, "The Early History of the Tradition of the Constitution," *APSR* 9 (1915). Arendt, *On Revolution* (1963), contains an illuminating analysis of the nature of constitutional legitimacy as derived from the act of foundation.

On the problem of establishing the legitimacy of the new federal government, see Seymour Martin Lipset, *The First New Nation* (1963). The statecraft and policies of Alexander Hamilton in relation to the problem of legitimacy are treated in Forrest McDonald, "The Fourth Phase: The Completion of the Continental Union, 1789–1792," in E. P. Willis, ed., *Fame and the Founding Fathers* (1967); Cecelia M. Kenyon, "Alexander Hamilton: Rousseau of the Right," *PSQ* 73 (1958); Gerald Stourzh, *Alexander Hamilton and the Idea of Republican Government* (1970); Clinton L. Rossiter, *Alexander Hamilton and the Constitution* (1964); John C. Koritansky, "Alexander Hamilton's Philosophy of Government and Administration," *Publius* 9 (1979); L. K. Caldwell, "Alexander Hamilton: Advocate of Executive Leadership," *Public Administration Review* 4 (1944). Also pertinent is Louise Burnham Dunbar, *A Study of "Monarchical" Tendencies in the United States, from 1776 to 1801* (1922). An early crisis in republican law and order is dealt with in Thomas P. Slaughter, *The Whiskey Rebellion: Frontier Epilogue to the American Revolution* (1986).

Concerning the executive branch, Congress, and administration, see James Hart, *The American Presidency in Action, 1789: A Study in Constitutional History* (1948); Edward S. Corwin, *The President: Office and Powers*

(1957); Leonard D. White, *The Federalists: A Study in Administration* (1948);
Raoul Berger, *Executive Privilege: A Constitutional Myth* (1974); Forrest Mc-
Donald, *The Presidency of George Washington* (1974); Lloyd M. Short, *The
Development of National Administrative Organization in the United States*
(1923); Carl E. Prince, *The Federalists and the Origins of the U.S. Civil Service*
(1977); Ralph V. Harlow, *History of Legislative Methods before 1825* (1917);
Joseph Cooper, *The Origins of the Standing Committees and the Development
of the Modern House* (1971); George B. Galloway, *History of the House of
Representatives* (1961); Nelson Polsby, "The Institutionalization of the U.S.
House of Representatives," *APSR* 62 (1968). On the constitutional ideas and
presidency of John Adams, see John R. Howe, Jr., *The Changing Political
Thought of John Adams* (1966); Manning J. Dauer, *The Adams Federalists*
(1953); Joseph Dorfman, "The Regal Republic of John Adams," *PSQ* 59
(1944); Correa M. Walsh, *The Political Science of John Adams* (1915); Stephen
G. Kurtz, "The Political Science of John Adams, a Guide to His Statecraft,"
WMQ 25 (1968).

Jefferson's exercise of presidential power is the subject of numerous studies. Among the more useful are Dumas Malone, *Jefferson and His Time,* vols.
4 and 5 (1970–74); Merrill D. Peterson, *Thomas Jefferson and the New Nation:
A Biography* (1970); Forrest Mcdonald, *The Presidency of Thomas Jefferson*
(1976); Robert M. Johnstone, Jr., *Jefferson and the Presidency: Leadership in
the Young Republic* (1978); Noble E. Cunningham, Jr., *The Process of Government under Jefferson* (1978); Leonard D. White, *The Jeffersonians: A Study
in Administrative History* (1951); James MacGregor Burns, *The Deadlock of
Democracy: Four-Party Politics in America* (1963). Jefferson's constitutional
legacy is defined in terms of negative government and laissez-faire in Dumas
Malone, "Jefferson, Hamilton, and the Constitution," in W. H. Nelson, ed.,
Theory and Practice in American Politics (1964), and Caleb Perry Patterson,
The Constitutional Principles of Thomas Jefferson (1953). In contrast, Julian
P. Boyd, "Thomas Jefferson's Empire of Liberty," *virginia Quarterly Review*
24 (1948), and Charles M. Wiltse, *The Jeffersonian Tradition in American
Democracy* (1935), regard Jefferson as a national-minded governmental activ-
ist. Richard K. Matthews, *The Radical Politics of Thomas Jefferson: A Revi-
sionist View* (1984), presents a new left radical interpretation.

Jefferson's immediate successors in the White House are described in
Irving Brant, *James Madison: The President, 1809–1812;* Brant, *Commander
in Chief, 1812–1836* (1961); Ralph Ketcham, *James Madison: A Biography*
(1971); Edward M. Burns, *James Madison: Philosopher of the Constitution*
(1938); Abbot Smith, "Mr. Madison's War: An Unsuccessful Experiment in
the Conduct of National Policy," *PSQ* 57 (1942); Harry Ammon, *James
Monroe: The Quest for National Identity* (1971); George A. Lipsky, *John
Quincy Adams: His Theory and Ideas* (1950).

Helpful for an understanding of the conflict between Federalist and Republican constitutionalism are the following studies of political thought and

ideology: Lance Banning, "Jefferson Ideology Revisited: Liberal and Classical Ideas in the New American Republic," *WMQ* 43 (1986); Joyce Appleby, *Capitalism and a New Social Order: The Republican Vision of the 1790s* (1984); Ralph Ketcham, *Presidents Above Party: The First American Presidency, 1789–1829* (1984); Lance Banning, *The Jeffersonian Persuasion: Evolution of a Party Ideology* (1978); Richard V. Buel, *Securing the Revolution: Ideology in American Politics 1789–1815* (1972); Linda K. Kerber, *Federalists in Dissent: Imagery and Ideology in Jeffersonian America* (1970); Drew R. McCoy, *The Elusive Republic: Political Economy in Jeffersonian America* (1980). Older works worth consulting are Benjamin F. Wright, "The Philosopher of Jeffersonian Democracy," *APSR* 22 (1928); Manning J. Dauer and Hans Hammond, "John Taylor: Aristocrat or Democrat?" *JP* 6 (1944); Charles E. Merriam, "The Political Theory of Jefferson," *PSQ* 17 (1902); William Seal Carpenter, *The Development of American Political Thought* (1930).

The Sedition Act crisis is dealt with in James M. Smith, *Freedom's Fetters: The Alien and Sedition Laws and American Civil Liberties* (1956); John C. Miller, *Crisis in Freedom: The Alien and Sedition Acts* (1951); Adrienne Koch and Harry Ammon, "The Virginia and Kentucky Resolutions: An Episode in Jefferson's and Madison's Defense of Civil Liberties," *WMQ* 5 (1948); For analysis of the free-speech problem in relation to the Sedition Act, see Leonard W. Levy, "Liberty and the First Amendment," *AHR* 67 (1962); James M. Smith, "The Sedition Law, Free Speech, and the American Political Process," *WMQ* 9 (1952); Walter Berns, "Freedom of the Press and the Alien and Sedition Laws: A Reappraisal," *Supreme Court Review 1970* (1971). The nature of freedom of speech and press generally in the eighteenth century is the subject of Robert C. Palmer, "Liberties as Constitutional Provisions: 1776–1791," in William E. Nelson and Robert C. Palmer, *Liberty and Community: Constitution and Rights in the Early American Republic* (1987); Leonard W. Levy, *Legacy of Suppression: Freedom of Speech and Press in Early American History* (1960), which appears in a revised version as *Emergence of a Free Press* (1985); Lawrence H. Leder, *Liberty and Authority; Early American Political Ideology 1689–1763* (1968); George N. Dargo, *Roots of the Republic: A New Perspective on Early American Constitutionalism* (1974). Civil liberties problems during Jefferson's presidency are analyzed in Leonard W. Levy, *Jefferson and Civil Liberties: The Darker Side* (1963).

The formation of political parties has attracted the interest of many historians and political scientists. An excellent introduction to the constitutional significance of parties is Theodore J. Lowi, "Party, Policy, and Constitution in America," in William N. Chambers and Walter Dean Burnham, eds., *The American Party Systems: Stages of Political Development* (1967). For parties in the early national period see Ronald P. Formisano, "Deferential-Participant Politics: The Early Republic's Political Culture, 1789–1840," *APSR* 68 (1974); William N. Chambers, *Political Parties in a New Nation: The American Experience, 1776–1809* (1963); Paul Goodman, "The First American Party System," in Chambers and Burnham, eds., *The American Party Systems;* Richard Hofstadter, *The Idea of a Party System: The Rise of Legitimate Opposition in the United States, 1780–1840* (1969); Michael Wallace, "Changing Concepts of Party in the United States: New York, 1815–1828," *AHR* 74 (1968); John Zvesper, *Political Philosophy and Rhetoric: A Case Study of the Origins of American Party Politics* (1977); James Stirling Young, *The Washington Community, 1800–1828* (1966); Rudolph M. Bell, *Party and Faction in American Politics: The House of Representatives, 1789–1801* (1973); Joseph Charles, *The Origins of the American Party System* (1961); Noble E. Cunningham, Jr., *The Jeffersonian Republicans: The Formation of Party Organization, 1789–1801* (1957); Cunningham, *The Jeffersonian Republicans in Power: Party Operations 1801–1809* (1963); David Hackett Fischer, *The Revolution of American Conservatism: The Federalist Party in the Era of Jeffersonian Republicanism* (1965); James M. Banner, *To the Hartford Convention: The Federalists and the Origins of Party Politics in Massachusetts, 1789–1815* (1969). The relationship between ideology and political geography is treated in Rosemarie Azgarri, *The Politics of Size: Representation in the United States, 1776–1850* (1987).

The impact of party development on the formal constitutional system is perceptively shown in John J. Turner, Jr., "The Twelfth Amendment and the First American Party System," *Historian* 35 (1973). See also Lucius Wilmerding, Jr., *The Electoral College* (1958). Worthwile older works on party development are Charles A. Beard, *Economic Origins of Jeffersonian Democracy* (1915); Andrew C. McLaughlin, *The Courts, the Constitution, and Parties* (1912); Henry Jones Ford, *The Rise and Growth of American Politics: A Sketch of Constitutional Development* (1898); M. Ostrogorski, *Democracy and the Party System in the United States: A Study in Extra-Constitutional Government* (1910); Lolabel House, *A Study of the Twelfth Amendment to the Constitution of the United States* (1901).

VII. *Judicial Power and Constitutional Law in the Marshall Era*

The most thorough accounts of the establishment of the federal judicial system are Julius Goebel, *History of the Supreme Court of the United States,* vol. 1: *Antecedents and Beginnings to 1801* (1971); William W. Crosskey, *Politics and the Constitution in the History of the United States,* 2 vols. (1953); Charles Warren, "New Light on the Judiciary Act of 1789," *Harvard Law Review* 37 (1923). An illuminating analysis of the politics of judicial reform in the 1790s is Kathryn Turner, "Federalist Policy in the Judiciary Act of 1801," *WMQ* 22 (1965). The question of whether the common law was a part of federal law is considered in Robert C. Palmer, "The Federal Common Law of Crime," *Law and History Review* 4 (1986); Kathryn Preyer, "Jurisdiction to Punish: Federal Authority, Federalism and the Common Law of Crimes in the Early Republic," *Law and History Review* 4 (1986); Dwight F. Henderson, *Congress, Courts, and Criminals: The Development of Federal Criminal Law, 1801–1829* (1985); Stephen B. Presser, "A Tale of Two Judges: Richard Peters, Samuel Chase, and the Broken Promise of Federalist Jurisprudence," *Northwestern University Law Review* 73 (1978). Other valuable works are Mary K. B. Tachau, *Federal Courts in the Early Republic: Kentucky, 1789–1816* (1978); Richard E. Ellis, *The Jeffersonian Crisis: Courts and Politics in the Young Republic* (1971); William F. Swindler, "Seedtime of an American Judiciary: From Independence to the Constitution," *William and Mary Law Review* 17 (1976); Henry J. Bourguignon, *The First Federal Court: The Federal Appellate Prize Court of the American Revolution, 1775–1787* (1977); Dwight F. Henderson, *Courts for a New Nation* (1971); Kathryn Turner, "The Midnight Judges," *University of Pennsylvania Law Review* 109 (1961); Turner, "The Appointment of John Marshall," *WMQ* 17 (1960); Richard B. Morris, *John Jay: The Nation and the Court* (1967); J. Franklin Jameson, "The Predecessor of the Supreme Court," in *Essays in the Constitutional History of the United States in the Formative Period, 1775–1789* (1889).

Studies of judicial review have focused on the question of whether review was intended by the framers or was a usurpation by the courts. Pioneering works include Brinton Coxe, *Judicial Power and Unconstitutional Legislation* (1893); James Bradley Thayer, "The Origin and Scope of the American Doctrine of Constitutional Law," *Harvard Law Review* 7 (1893); Charles Grove Haines, *The American Doctrine of Judicial Supremacy* (1911, 1932); Charles A. Beard, *The Supreme Court and the Constitution* (1912); Edward S. Corwin, *The Doctrine of Judicial Review* (1914); Andrew C. McLaughlin, *The Courts, the Constitution, and Parties: Studies in Constitutional History and Politics* (1912); Horace A. Davis, *The Judicial Veto* (1914); Charles Warren, *Congress, the Constitution, and the Supreme Court* (1925); Louis Boudin, *Government by Judiciary*, 2 vols. (1932). More recent are Crosskey, *Politics and the Constitution,* denying that judicial review was part of the original constitutional system, and Raoul Berger, *Congress v. the Supreme Court* (1969), arguing that it was. Donald G. Morgan, *Congress and the Constitution: A Study in Responsibility* (1966), is an important work which examines orthodox judicial review in relation to the departmental approach to resolving constitutional controversies. William E. Nelson, "Changing Conceptions of Judicial Review: The Evolution of Constitutional Theory in the States, 1790–1860," *University of Pennsylvania Law Review* 120 (1972), relates judicial review to an emergent interest-group approach to public-policy formation. Important recent analyses of this question are Sylvia Snowiss, "From Fundamental Law to Supreme Law of the Land: A Reinterpretation of the Origin of Judicial Review," *Studies in American Political Development* 2 (1987), and Robert L. Clinton, *Marbury v. Madison and Judicial Review* (1989).

The attitude of Jefferson and the Republican party toward the judiciary is dealt with in Henry Steele Commager, "Judicial Review and Democracy,"

Virginia Quarterly Review 19 (1943); Samuel Krislov, "Jefferson and Judicial Review: Refereeing Cahn, Commager, and Mendelson," *Journal of Public Law* 9 (1960); Donald O. Dewey, *Marshall versus Jefferson: The Political Background of Marbury v. Madison* (1970); Ellis, *The Jeffersonian Crisis;* Richard B. Lillich, "The Chase Impeachment," *AJLH* 4 (1960); Kenneth Treacy, "The Olmstead Case, 1778–1809," *Western Pol. Q.* 10 (1957); Jerry W. Knudson, "The Jeffersonian Assault on the Federalist Judiciary, 1802–1805: Political Forces and Press Reaction," *AJLH* 14 (1970); Curtis Nettels, "The Mississippi Valley and the Federal Judiciary 1807–1837," *MVHR* 12 (1925).

Recent studies which refute the simplistic progressive view of John Marshall as a conservative defender of vested rights include G. Edward White, *The Marshall Court and Cultural Change 1815–1835* (1988); George L. Haskins and Herbert A. Johnson, *History of the Supreme Court of the United States,* vol. 2: *Foundations of Power: John Marshall, 1801–15* (1981); Haskins, "Law Versus Politics in the Early Years of the Marshall, 1801–15 (1981); Haskins, "Law Versus Politics in the Early Years of the Marshall Court," *University of Pennsylvania Law Review* 130 (1981); William Nelson, "The Eighteenth Century Background of John Marshall's Jurisprudence," *Michigan Law Review* 76 (1978); Robert K. Faulkner, *The Jurisprudence of John Marshall* (1968); Morton J. Frisch, "John Marshall's Philosophy of Constitutional Republicanism," *Review of Politics* 20 (1958); C. Umbamhowar, "Marshall on Judging," *AJLH* 7 (1963); Gerald Gunther, ed., *John Marshall's Defense of McCulloch v. Maryland* (1969); Bruce A. Campbell, "John Marshall, the Virginia Political Economy, and the Dartmouth College Decision," *AJLH* 19 (1975); William W. Crosskey, "John Marshall and the Constitution," *University of Chicago Law Review* 23 (1956). R. Kent Newmyer, *The Supreme Court under Marshall and Taney* (1968), is a fine work of synthesis, and Francis N. Stites, *John Marshall: Defender of the Constitution* (1981), is a capable brief biography.

The modern institutional development of the Supreme Court under Marshall is described in Donald M. Roper, "Judicial Unanimity and the Marshall Court—a Road to Reappraisal," *AJLH* 9 (1965); Donald G. Morgan, *Justice William Johnson, the First Dissenter* (1954), and Morgan, "The Origin of Supreme Court Dissent," *WMQ* 10 (1953). Specialized studies of aspects of constitutional law under Marshall include C. Peter Magrath, *Yazoo: Law and Politics in the New Republic: The Case of Fletcher v. Peck* (1966); Maurice G. Baxter, *The Steamboat Monopoly: Gibbons v. Ogden, 1824* (1972); Francis N. Stites, *Private Interest and Public Gain: The Dartmouth College Case, 1819* (1972); Albert S. Abel, "Commerce Regulation before Gibbons v. Ogden: Interstate Transportation Facilities," *North Carolina Law Review* 25 (1946). For Marshall's role in the controversy between Aaron Burr and Jefferson, see Robert K. Faulkner, "John Marshall and the Burr Trial," *JAH* 53 (1966), and Bradley Chapin, *The American Law of Treason: Revolutionary and Early National Origins* (1964). The Marshall Court's involvement in the problem of

Indian policy is examined in Joseph Burke, "The Cherokee Cases: A Study in Law, Politics, and Morality," *Stanford Law Review* 21 (1969).

Older works that interpret Marshall as a conservative nationalist are Albert J. Beveridge, *The Life of John Marshall,* 4 vols. (1916–19), still the best biography; Edward S. Corwin, *John Marshall and the Constitution* (1919); Charles Warren, *The Supreme Court in United States History,* 3 vols. (1922). For the progressive reaction to the nationalist interpretation, see Charles Grove Haines, "Histories of the Supreme Court of the United States written from the Federalist Point of View," *Southwestern Social Science Quarterly* 4 (1923); Haines, *The Role of the Supreme Court in American Government and Politics 1789–1835* (1944); Max Lerner, "John Marshall and the Campaign of History," *Columbia Law Review* 34 (1939); Wallace Mendelson, "New Light on Fletcher v. Peck and Gibbon v. Ogden," *Yale Law Journal* 58 (1949). More sympathetic assessments of Marshall, reflecting the use of his centralizing principles in New Deal liberalism, are found in W. Melville Jones, ed., *Chief Justice Marshall: A Reappraisal* (1956); George L. Haskins, "John Marshall and the Commerce Clause," *University of Pennsylvania Law Review* 104 (1955); and Edward S. Corwin, "John Marshall, Revolutionist Malgré Lui," *University of Pennsylvania Law Review* 104 (1955); Samuel J. Konefsky, *John Marshall and Alexander Hamilton: Architects of the Constitution* (1964). Standard works tracing Marshall's handling of two key problems in constitutional law are Felix Frankfurter, *The Commerce Clause under Marshall, Taney, and Waite* (1937), and Benjamin F. Wright, *The Contract Clause of the Constitution* (1938).

VIII. *Constitutional Change in the Jacksonian Era*

Basic to an understanding of the American polity is Alexis de Tocqueville, *Democracy in America,* 2 vols. (1945). Studies of executive and administrative aspects of constitutional change in the middle period include Leonard D. White, *The Jacksonians: A Study in Administrative History, 1829–1860* (1954); Richard B. Latner, *The Presidency of Andrew Jackson: White House Politics, 1829–1837* (1979); Latner, "The Kitchen Cabinet and Andrew Jackson's Advisory Cabinet," *JAH* 65 (1978); Richard P. Longaker, "Was Jackson's Kitchen Cabinet a Cabinet?" *MVHR* 44 (1957); Matthew A. Crenson, *The Federal Machine: Beginnings of Bureaucracy in Jacksonian America* (1975); Sidney H. Aronson, *Status and Kinship in the Higher Civil Service: Standards of Selection in the Administrations of John Adams, Thomas Jefferson, and Andrew Jackson* (1964); Carlton Jackson, *Presidential Vetoes, 1792–1945* (1967); Richard P. Longaker, "Andrew Jackson and the Judiciary," *PSQ* 71 (1956); Albert Somit, "Andrew Jackson as Administrator," *Public Administration Review* 8 (1948). Robert V. Remini, *Andrew Jackson and the Bank War: A Study in the Growth of Presidential Power* (1967). Executive developments after Jackson are recounted in James C. Curtis, *The Fox at Bay: Martin Van Buren and the Presidency, 1837–1841* (1970); R. J. Morgan, *A Whig Embattled: The Presidency under John Tyler* (1954); Charles G. Sellers, *James K. Polk, Continentalist, 1843–1846* (1968).

Political party development is analyzed in Richard P. McCormick, *The Second American Party System: Party Formation in the Jacksonian Era* (1966); McCormick, "Political Development and the Second Party System," in W. N. Chambers and W. D. Burnham, eds., *The American Party Systems: Stages of Political Development* (1967); Perry M. Goldman, "Political Virtue in the Age of Jackson," *PSQ* 87 (1972); Lynn L. Marshall, "The Strange Stillbirth of the Whig Party," *AHR* 72 (1967); Ronald P. Formisano, "Deferential-Participant Politics: The Early Republic's Political Culture, 1789–1840," *APSR* 68 (1974); Formisano, "Political Character, Antipartyism and the Second Party System," *American Quarterly* 21 (1969); Hofstadter, *The Idea of a Party System* (1968); Henry Jones Ford, *The Rise and Growth of American Politics* (1898); M. Ostrogorski, *Democracy and the Organization of Political Parties*, 2 vols. (1902); James S. Chase, *Emergence of the Presidential Nominating Convention, 1789–1832* (1973).

Studies of political thought and ideology that contribute to an understanding of constitutional politics in the Jacksonian era include Clinton Rossiter, *The American Quest, 1790–1860: An Emerging Nation in Search of Identity, Unity, and Modernity* (1971); Major L. Wilson, *Space, Time and Freedom: The Quest for Nationality and the Irrepressible Conflict, 1815–1861* (1974); Daniel Walker Howe, *The Political Culture of the American Whigs* (1979); Herbert Ershkowitz and William G. Shade, "Consensus or Conflict? Political Behavior in the State Legislatures during the Jacksonian Era," *JAH* 58 (1971). Richard H. Brown, "The Missouri Crisis, Slavery, and the Politics of Jacksonianism," *South Atlantic Quarterly* 65 (1966), emphasizes the proslavery outlook of the Jacksonians, while John M. McFaul, "Expediency vs. Morality: Jacksonian Politics and Slavery," *JAH* 62 (1975), criticizes this interpretation and stresses Jacksonian nationalism.

Concerned with class and group conflict in Jacksonian-Whig constitutional politics are Lee Benson, *The Concept of jacksonian Democracy: New York as a Test Case* (1961); Glyndon G. Van Deusen, *The Jacksonian Era, 1828–1848* (1959); Van Deusen, "Some Aspects of Whig Thought and Theory in the Jacksonian Period," *AHR* 63 (1958); Arthur M. Schlesinger, Jr., *The Age of Jackson* (1945).

The nullification crisis is capably analyzed in Richard E. Ellis, *The Union at Risk: Jacksonian Democracy, States' Rights, and the Nullification Crisis* (1987); James B. Stewart, " 'A Great Talking and Eating Machine': Patriarchy, Mobilization and the Dynamics of Nullification in South Carolina," *CWH* 27 (1981); Richard B. Latner, "The Nullification Crisis and Republican Subversion," *JSH* 43 (1977); Edwin A. Miles, "After John Marshall's Decision: Worcester v. Georgia and the Nullification Crisis," *JSH* 39 (1973);

William H. Freehling, *Prelude to Civil War: The Nullification Controversy in South Carolina, 1816–1836* (1966); C. S. Boucher, *The Nullification Controversy in South Carolina* (1916). Two excellent articles on political ideology in South Carolina are Kenneth S. Greenberg, "Revolutionary Ideology and the Proslavery Argument: The Abolition of Slavery in Antebellum South Carolina," *JSH* 42 (1976), and Greenberg, "Representation and the Isolation of South Carolina, 1776–1860," *JAH* 64 (1977).

Among numerous works on the constitutional thought of John C. Calhoun, see especially George Kateb, "The Majority Principle: Calhoun and His Antecedents," *PSQ* 84 (1969); Ralph Lerner, "Calhoun's New Science of Politics," *APSR* 57 (1963); William H. Freehling, "Spoilsmen and Interests in the Thought and Career of John C. Calhoun," *JAH* 52 (1965); Charles M. Wiltse, "Calhoun's Democracy," *JP* 3 (1941); Gunnar Heckscher, "Calhoun's Idea of the Concurrent Majority and the Constitutional Theory of Hegel," *APSR* 33 (1939); Darryl Baskin, "The Pluralist Vision of Calhoun," *Polity* 2 (1969); Peter J. Steinberger, "Calhoun's Concept of the Public Interest: A Clarification," *Polity* 13 (1981); August O. Spain, *The Political Theory of John C. Calhoun* (1950); Jesse Carpenter, *The South as a Conscious Minority* (1930). Andrew C. McLaughlin, "Social Compact and Constitutional Construction," *AHR* 5 (1900), is a judicious analysis of the relationship between Calhoun's theory of union and that of Jefferson and Madison in the Kentucky and Virginia Resolutions.

Valuable studies of theories of the Union in the Jacksonian period are Kenneth M. Stampp, "The Concept of a Perpetual Union," *JAH* 65 (1978); Major L. Wilson, " 'Liberty and Union': An Analysis of Three Concepts Involved in the Nullification Controversy," *JSH* 33 (1967); Charles M. Wiltse, "From Compact to National State in American Political Thought," in M. Konvitz and A. Murphy, eds., *Essays in Political Theory, Presented to George H. Sabine* (1948); Yehoshua Arieli, *Individualism and Nationalism in American Ideology* (1964); Edward S. Corwin, "National Power and State Interposition, 1787–1861," *Michigan Law Review* 10 (1912); Elizabeth C. Bauer, *Commentaries on the Constitution, 1790–1860* (1952); Paul C. Nagel, *One Nation Indivisible: The Union in American Thought* (1964).

Constitutional change at the state level is dealt with in Morton Keller, "The Politics of State Constitutional Revision, 1820–1930," in Kermit L. Hall *et al.*, eds., *The Constitutional Convention as an Amending Device* (1981). Merrill Peterson, ed., *Democracy, Liberty and Property: The State Constitutional Convention of the 1820s* (1966), a documentary collection; Bayrd Still, "An Interpretation of the Statehood Process, 1800 to 1850," *MVHR* 23 (1936); Benjamin F. Wright, "Political Institutions and the Frontier," in Dixon Ryan Fox, ed., *Sources of Culture in the Middle West* (1934); Fletcher Green, *Constitutional Development in the South Atlantic States, 1776–1860* (1930); Robert M. Ireland, *The County Courts in Antebellum Kentucky* (1972); James Q. Dealey, *Growth of American State Constitutions, 1776–1914* (1915).

The best studies of the Dorr War and its resolution in the case of *Luther v. Borden* are George M. Dennison, *The Dorr War: Republicanism on Trial, 1831–1861* (1976); Dennison, "martial Law: The Development of a Theory of Emergency Powers, 1776–1861," *AJLH* 18 (1974); William M. Wiecek, *The Guarantee Clause of the U.S. Constitution* (1972); Wiecek, " 'A Peculiar Conservatism' and the Dorr Rebellion: Constitutional Clash in Jacksonian America," *AJLH* 22 (1978); Michael Conron, "Law, Politics, and Chief Justice Taney: A Reconsideration of the *Luther v. Borden* Decision," *AJLH* 11 (1967).

IX. *Constitutional Law in the Taney Era*

Harold M. Hyman and William M. Wiecek, *Equal Justice under Law: Constitutional Development, 1835–1875* (1982), is an outstanding survey of the period based on the most recent scholarship. Carl B. Swisher, *History of the Supreme Court of the United States,* vol. 5: *The Taney Period, 1836–1864* (1974), at once magisterial and encyclopedic, provides an excellent general account of the Jacksonian judiciary. Other valuable general treatments are R. Kent Newmyer, *The Supreme Court under Marshall and Taney* (1968); Robert J. Harris, "Chief Justice Taney: Prophet of Reform and Reaction," *Vanderbilt Law Review* 10 (1957); Wallace Mendelson, "Chief Justice Taney—Jacksonian Judge," *University of Pittsburgh Law Review* 12 (1951); Mendelson, *Capitalism, Democracy and the Supreme Court* (1960); Charles Grove Haines and Foster H. Sherwood, *The Role of the Supreme Court in American Government and Politics* (1957); Charles Warren, *The Supreme Court in United States History,* 3 vols. (1922).

Two excellent interpretations of the Taney Court dealing with the problem of law and economic change are Stanley I. Kutler, *Privilege and Creative Destruction: The Charles River Bridge Case* (1971), and R. Kent Newmyer, "Justice Joseph Story, the Charles River Bridge Case and the Crisis of Republicanism," *AJLH* 17 (1973). Gerald Garvey, *Constitutional Bricolage* (1971), and Garvey, "The Constitutional Revolution of 1837 and the Myth of Marshall's Monolith," *Western Pol. Q.* 18 (1965), emphasize doctrinal continuity between the Marshall and Taney Courts. Comparison of Marshall and Taney is also the focus of Edward S. Corwin, *The Commerce Power versus States Rights* (1936); Benjamin F. Wright, *The Contract Clause of the Constitution* (1938); Felix Frankfurter, *The Commerce Clause under Marshall, Taney and Waite* (1937); Louis B. Boudin, "John Marshall and Roger B. Taney," *Georgetown Law Journal* 24 (1936).

Biographical studies which throw light on constitutional law in the Taney era include Carl B. Swisher, *Roger B. Taney* (1935); Swisher, "Mr. Chief Justice Taney," in Allison Dunham and Philip Kurland, eds., *Mr. Justice* (1964); Charles W. Smith, Jr., *Roger B. Taney: Jacksonian Jurist* (1936); R.

Kent Newmyer, *Supreme Court Justice Joseph Story: Statesman of the Old Republic* (1985); James McClellan, *Joseph Story and the American Constitution: A Study in Political and Legal Thought* (1971); Gerald T. Dunne, *Justice Joseph Story and the Rise of the Supreme Court* (1970); John P. Frank, *Justice Daniel Dissenting: A Biography of Peter V. Daniel* (1964); Alexander A. Lawrence, *James Moore Wayne: Southern Unionist* (1943); Francis P. Weisenburger, *The Life of John McLean: A Politician on the United States Supreme Court* (1937); Henry G. Connor, *John Archibald Campbell, Associate Justice of the U.S. Supreme Court, 1853–1861* (1920); Maurice G. Baxter, *Daniel Webster and the Supreme Court* (1966).

The relationship between law and economic development in the Jacksonian era forms the subject of numerous studies. Edward S. Corwin, "The Basic Doctrine of American Constitutional Law," *Michigan Law Review* 12 (1914), and Corwin, "The Doctrine of Due Process of Law before the Civil War," *Harvard Law Review* 24 (1910), are seminal articles describing judicial protection of private property against legislative interference, especially at the state level. Max Lerner, "The Supreme Court and American Capitalism," *Yale Law Journal* 42 (1933), analyzes the same phenomenon from the liberal-reform perspective. The legal history of the corporation is recounted in E. M. Dodd, *American Business Corporations until 1860* (1954), and G. C. Henderson, *The Position of Foreign Corporations in American Constitutional Law* (1918).

Accounts of state mercantilism showing how law and public policy, contrary to the myth of laissez-faire, were used to promote economic development include James Willard Hurst, *Law and the Conditions of Freedom in the Nineteenth Century United States* (1956); Lawrence M. Friedman, *A History of American Law* (1973); Harry N. Scheiber, *Ohio Canal Era: A Case Study of Government and the Economy, 1820–1861* (1969); Scheiber, "Public Economic Policy and the American Legal System: Historical Perspectives," *Wisconsin Law Review* (1980); Scheiber, "Federalism and the American Economic Order, 1789–1910," *Law and Society Review* 10 (1975); Scheiber, "The Road to Munn: Eminent Domain and the Concept of Public Purpose in the State Courts," *Perspectives in American History* 5 (1971); Charles W. McCurdy, "Stephen J. Field and Public Land Law Development in California, 1850–1866," *Law and Society Review* 10 (1976); Carter Goodrich, *Governmental Promotion of American Canals and Railroads, 1800–1890* (1960); Louis Hartz, *Economic Policy and Democratic Thought: Pennsylvania, 1776–1860* (1948); Oscar Handlin and Mary F. Handlin, *Commonwealth: A Study of the Role of Government in the American Economy: Massachusetts, 1774–1861* (1947). Theodore J. Lowi, "American Business, Public Policy, Case-Studies, and Political Theory," *World Politics* 16 (1964), presents a valuable theoretical framework for analyzing government's relationship to the economy. J. R. Pole, "Property and Law in the American Republic," in *Paths to the American Present* (1979), and Harry N. Scheiber, "At the Borderland of Law and

Economic History: The Contributions of Willard Hurst," *AHR* 75 (1970), contain perceptive historiographical commentary. Homer C. Hockett, *The Constitutional History of the United States, 1776–1876,* 2 vols. (1939), has a thorough discussion of the constitutional controversy over internal improvements. Daniel J. Elazar, *The American Partnership: Intergovernmental Cooperation in the Nineteenth Century United States* (1962), argues that federal-state sharing of power dates from the early national period.

Morton J. Horwitz, *The Transformation of American Law, 1780–1860* (1977), dealing with tort and contract law in the state courts, asserts a schematic class interpretation which contends that states in effect subsidized the process of industrialization at the expense of the public. For criticism of this thesis, see Gary T. Schwartz, "Tort Law and the Economy in Nineteenth-Century America: A Reinterpretation," *Yale Law Review* 90 (1981); A. W. B. Simpson, "The Horwitz Thesis and the History of Contracts," *University of Chicago Law Review* 46 (1979); Harry N. Scheiber, "Back to 'The Legal Mind'? Doctrinal Analysis and the History of Law," *Reviews in American History* 5 (1977); Randolph Bridwell and Ralph W. Whitten, *The Constitution and the Common Law: The Decline of the Doctrines of Separation of Powers and Federalism* (1977). The development of federal commercial common law after *Swift* v. *Tyson* is dealt with in Tony Freyer, *Harmony and Dissonance: The Swift and Erie Cases in American Federalism* (1981), and Freyer, *Forums of Order: The Federal Courts and Business in American History* (1979); Charles A. Heckman, "The Relationship of Swift v. Tyson to the Status of Commercial Law in the Nineteenth Century and the Federal System," *AJLH* 17 (1973); Heckman, "Uniform Commercial Law in the Nineteenth Century Federal Courts: The Decline and Abuse of the *Swift* Doctrine," *Emory Law Journal* 27 (1978).

Diverse aspects of federal and state constitutional change involving the judiciary in the first half of the nineteenth century are examined in Kermit L. Hall, *The Politics of Justice: Lower Federal Court Selection and the Second Party System, 1829–61* (1979); Hall, "The Children of the Cabins: The Lower Federal Judiciary, Modernization, and the Political Culture, 1789–1899," *Northwestern University Law Review* 75 (1980); Maxwell Bloomfield, *American Lawyers in a Changing Society, 1776–1876* (1976); William E. Nelson, *The Americanization of the Common Law: The Impact of Legal Change on Massachusetts Society, 1760–1830* (1975); Leonard W. Levy, *The Law of the Commonwealth and Chief Justice Shaw: The Evolution of American Law, 1830–1860* (1957); Stanley I. Kutler, "John Bannister Gibson: Judicial Restraint and the 'Positive State,' " *Journal of Public Law* 14 (1965); Jean V. Matthews, *Rufus Choate: The Law and Civic Virtue* (1980); Charles M. Cook, *The American Codification Movement: A Study of Antebellum Legal Reform* (1981); John T. Horton, *James Kent: A Study in Conservatism, 1763–1844* (1939).

Jurisprudential tendencies are traced in Perry Miller, *The Life of the Mind in America: From the Revolution to the Civil War* (1965); Roscoe Pound, *The*

Formative Era of American Law (1938); Grant Gilmore, *The Ages of American Law* (1977); William E. Nelson, "The Impact of the Antislavery Movement upon Styles of Judicial Reasoning in Nineteenth Century America," *Harvard Law Review* 87 (1974); Morton J. Horwitz, "The Rise of Legal Formalism," *AJLH* 19 (1975); Horwitz, "The Emergence of an Instrumental Conception of American Law, 1780–1820," *Perspectives in American History* 5 (1971); Karl N. Llewellyn, *The Common Law Tradition: Deciding Appeals* (1960); Harry N. Scheiber, "Instrumentalism and Property Rights: A Reconsideration of American 'Styles of Judicial Reasoning' in the 19th Century," *Wisconsin Law Review* (1975).

X. *Slavery, the Constitution and the Crisis of the Union*

The constitutional status of slavery at the beginning of the government is described in Don E. Fehrenbacher, *The Dred Scott Case: Its Significance in American Law and Politics* (1978); Robert A. Goldwin, *Why Blacks, Women, and Jews Are Not Mentioned in the Constitution, and Other Unorthodox Views* (1990); Paul Finkelman, "Slavery and the Constitution: Making a Covenant with Death," in Richard Beeman *et al.*, eds., *Beyond Confederation: Origins of the Constitution and American National Identity* (1987); Raymond T. Diamond, "No Call to Glory: Thurgood Marshall's Thesis on the Intent of a Pro-Slavery Constitution," *Vanderbilt Law Review* 42 (1989); John Alvis, "The Slavery Provisions of the Constitution," *Political Science Reviewer* 17 (1987). On the law and politics of slavery, see William M. Wiecek, *The Sources of Antislavery Constitutionalism in America, 1760–1848* (1977); Wiecek, "*Somerset:* Lord Mansfield and the Legitimacy of Slavery in the Anglo-American World," *University of Chicago Law Review* 42 (1974); David Brion Davis, *The Problem of Slavery in the Age of Revolution, 1770–1823* (1975); Donald L. Robinson, *Slavery in the Structure of American Politics, 1765–1820* (1971); William W. Freehling, "The Founding Fathers and Slavery," *AHR* 77 (1972); Arthur Zilversmit, *The First Emancipation: The Abolition of Slavery in the North* (1967); Howard A. Ohline, "Slavery, Economics, and Congressional Politics, 1790," *JSH* 46 (1980); Walter Berns, "The Constitution and the Migration of Slaves," *Yale Law Journal* 78 (1968). The colonial background for the constitutional acceptance of slavery is discussed in William M. Wiecek, "The Statutory Law of Slavery and Race in the Thirteen Mainland Colonies of British America," *WMQ* 34 (1977), and A. Leon Higginbotham, *In the Matter of Color: Race and the American Legal Process: The Colonial Period* (1978).

Two outstanding accounts of the emergence of slavery as an issue in constitutional politics are Harold M. Hyman and William M. Wiecek, *Equal Justice under Law: Constitutional Development, 1835–1875* (1982), and Fehrenbacher, *The Dred Scott Case.* Other valuable accounts are Wiecek, *The*

Sources of Antislavery Constitutionalism; Wiecek, "Slavery and Abolition before the United States Supreme Court, 1820–1860," *JAH* 65 (1978); Robert Cover, *Justice Accused: Antislavery and the Judicial Process* (1975); Donald M. Roper, "In Quest of Judicial Objectivity: The Marshall Court and the Legitimation of Slavery," *Stanford Law Review* 21 (1969); John T. Noonan, Jr., *The Antelope: The Ordeal of the Recaptured Africans in the Administration of James Monroe and John Quincy Adams* (1977); Glover Moore, *The Missouri Controversy, 1819–1821* (1953). The constitutional ideas of the abolitionists are described in the book by Wiecek cited above, and in Dwight L. Dumond, *Antislavery: The Crusade for Freedom in America* (1961); Howard Jay Graham, *Everyman's Constitution: Historical Essays on the Fourteenth Amendment, the "Conspiracy Theory," and American Constitutionalism* (1968); Jacobus ten Broek, *The Anti-Slavery Origins of the fourteenth Amendment* (1951; reprinted as *Equal under Law,* 1965). William S. Jenkins, *Pro-Slavery Thought in the Old South* (1935), and Jesse T. Carpenter, *The South as a Conscious Minority* (1930), perform a similar function for the defenders of slavery.

Among more specialized studies of constitutional controversies over slavery, Thomas D. Morris, *Free Men All: The Personal Liberty Laws of the North, 1780–1861* (1974), is an excellent account of northern attempts to protect free blacks under state law. Paul Finkelman, *An Imperfect Union: Slavery, Federalism, and Comity* (1981), treats interstate conflicts arising over the transit of slaves in free society. On the fugitive slave question, see Joseph C. Burke, "What Did the Prigg Decision Really Decide?" *Pennsylvania Magazine of History and Biography* 93 (1969); Paul Finkelman, "Prigg v. Pennsylvania and Northern State Courts: Anti-Slavery Uses of a Pro-Slavery Decision," *CWH* 25 (1979); Stanley W. Campbell, *The Slave Catchers: Enforcement of the Fugitive Slave Law, 1850–1860* (1968); William R. Leslie, "The Influence of Joseph Story's Theory of the Conflict of Laws on Constitutional Nationalism," *MVHR* 35 (1948); Larry Gara, "The Fugitive Slave Law: A Double Paradox," *CWH* 10 (1964); Allen Johnson, "The Constitutionality of the Fugitive Slave Acts," *Yale Law Journal* 31 (1920). Other slavery-related constitutional disputes are discussed in Russell B. Nye, *Fettered Freedoms: Civil Liberties and the Slavery Crisis, 1836–1860* (1949), and Clement Eaton, "Censorship of the Southern Mails," *AHR* 48 (1943).

Studies of politics and ideology in the antebellum era pertinent to an understanding of constitutional struggles over slavery include William E. Gienapp, *The Origins of the Republican Party, 1852–1856* (1987); Peter S. Onuf, *Statehood and Union: A History of the Northwest Ordinance* (1987); Eric Foner, *Free Soil, Free Labor, Free Men: The Ideology of the Republican Party before the Civil War* (1970); Richard H. Sewell, *Ballots for Freedom: Antislavery Politics in the United States, 1837–1860* (1976); Chaplain Morrison, *Democratic Politics and Sectionalism: The Wilmot Proviso Controversy* (1967); Michael F. Holt, *The Political Crisis of the 1850s* (1978); J. Mills Thornton, *Politics and Power in a Slave Society: Alabama, 1800–1860* (1978); Roy F. Nichols, *The Disruption of the American Democracy* (1948).

Allan Nevins, *The Ordeal of the Union,* 2 vols. (1947), Nevins, *The Emergence of Lincoln,* 2 vols. (1952), and David M. Potter, *The Impending Crisis, 1848–1861* (1979), are superior general accounts of the coming of the Civil War. The most perceptive analysis of the problem of slavery expansion into the territories is Arthur Bestor, "State Sovereignty and Slavery: A Reinterpretation of Proslavery Constitutional Doctrine, 1846–1861," *Journal of the Illinois State Historical Society* 54 (1961). See also Allan Nevins, "The Constitution, Slavery, and the Territories," *The Gaspar G. Bacon Lectures on the Constitution of the United States, 1940–1953* (1953).

Popular sovereignty as the solution to the territorial question is sympathetically presented in Robert Johannsen, *Stephen A. Douglas* (1972); Allen Johnson, "The Genesis of Popular Sovereignty," *Iowa Journal of History and Politics* 2 (1905); George Fort Milton, *The Eve of Conflict: Stephen A. Douglas and the Needless War* (1934). Johannsen, "Stephen A. Douglas and the Territories in the Senate," in John Porter Bloom, ed., *The American Territorial System* (1973), reviews the larger issue of territorial policy. Robert R. Russel, "What Was the Compromise of 1850?" *JSH* 22 (1956), is a cogent analysis of the legislative history of popular sovereignty in the Compromise of 1850, while Holman Hamilton, *Prelude to Conflict: The Crisis and Compromise of 1850* (1964), explains the voting alignments which supported the compromise. On the Kansas-Nebraska Act, see Roy F. Nichols, "The Kansas-Nebraska Act: A Century of Historiography," *MVHR* 43 (1956); Robert R. Russell, "The Issues in the Congressional Struggle over the Kansas-Nebraska Bill, 1854," *JSH* 29 (1963); Russell, "Constitutional Doctrines with Regard to Slavery in the Territories," *JSH* 32 (1966); Milo M. Quaife, *The Doctrine of Non-Intervention with Slavery in the Territories* (1910). Events in Kansas are analyzed in James C. Malin, *The Nebraska Question, 1852–1854* (1953), a trenchant and original work, and James H. Rawley, *Race and Politics: Bleeding Kansas and the Coming of the Civil War* (1969).

Fehrenbacher, *The Dred Scott Case,* is the most thorough and penetrating account of the Supreme Court's attempt to resolve the question of slavery in the territories. Other studies include Walter Ehrlich, *They Have No Rights: Dred Scott's Struggle for Freedom* (1979); Vincent Hopkins, *Dred Scott's Case* (1951); Wallace Mendelson, "Dred Scott's Case—Reconsidered," *Minnesota Law Review* 38 (1953); Edward S. Corwin, "The Dred Scott Decision in the Light of Contemporary Legal Doctrines," *AHR* 17 (1911). Frederick S. Allis, Jr., "The Dred Scott Labyrinth," in H. Stuart Hughes, ed., *Teachers of History: Essays in Honor of Lawrence Bradford Packard* (1954), is an able historiographical account. The question of Negro citizenship under state and federal law in the antebellum period is treated in James H. Kettner, *The Development of American Citizenship, 1608–1870* (1978). Although peripheral to the constitutional struggles that dominated national politics in the 1850s, slave law in the states has received careful study by scholars. See, in particular, A. E. Keir Nash, "Reason of Slavery: Understanding the Judicial Role in the Peculiar Institution," *Vanderbilt Law Review* 32 (1979), a book-length monograph that also surveys recent writings in the field. Also useful are Mark Tushnet, *The American Law of Slavery 1810–1860: Considerations of Humanity and Interest* (1981). Helen T. Catterall, ed., *Judicial Cases Concerning American Slavery and the Negro,* 5 vols. (1926–37), provides the basic documentary record.

The best analysis of the political and constitutional issues involved in the struggle between Lincoln and Douglas is Harry V. Jaffa, *Crisis of the House Divided: An Interpretation of the Lincoln-Douglas Debates* (1959). Of great value for understanding Lincoln's handling of the territorial question is Don E. Fehrenbacher, *Prelude to Greatness: Lincoln in the 1850s* (1962). Douglas's devotion to popular sovereignty is discussed in Robert W. Johannsen, "Stephen A. Douglas, 'Harpers Magazine,' and Popular Sovereignty," *MVHR* 45 (1959). Able accounts of the disruption of the Union after the election of Lincoln are Ralph A. Wooster, *The Secession Conventions of the South* (1962); Dwight L. Dumond, *The Secession Movement, 1860–1861* (1931); Philip S. Klein, *President James Buchanan* (1962); Charles R. Lee, *The Confederate Constitutions* (1963). Among numerous works on the secession crisis the following make significant contributions: David M. Potter, *Lincoln and His Party in the Secession Crisis* (1942); Kenneth M. Stampp, *And the War Came: The North and the Secession Crisis, 1860–1861* (1950); Richard N. Current, *Lincoln and the First Shot* (1963); Harold M. Hyman, "The Narrow Escape from a 'Compromise of 1860': Secession and the Constitution," in Hyman and Leonard W. Levy, eds., *Freedom and Reform: Essays in Honor of Henry Steele Commager* (1967); Robert W. Johannsen, "The Douglas Democracy and the Crisis of Disunion," *CWH* 9 (1963); George H. Knoles, ed., *The Crisis of the Union, 1860–1861* (1965). A. C. Cole, "Lincoln's Election an Immediate Menace to Slavery in the States," *AHR* 36 (1931), and J. G. de R. Hamilton in an article of the same title, *AHR* 37 (1932), debate the impact of the election from northern and southern points of view. Futile peace efforts are described in R. G. Gunderson, *Old Gentlemen's Convention: The Washington Peace Conference of 1861* (1961).

XI. *The Civil War and Reconstruction*

There are three excellent general accounts of Civil War constitutional history: Harold M. Hyman and William M. Wiecek, *Equal Justice under Law: Constitutional Development, 1835–1875* (1982); Harold M. Hyman, *A More Perfect Union: The Impact of the Civil War and Reconstruction on the Constitution* (1973); James G. Randall, *Constitutional Problems under Lincoln* (1926; rev. ed., 1951). Arthur Bestor, "The Civil War as a Constitutional Crisis," *AHR* 69 (1964), illuminates the configurative effect of the Constitution in shaping the crisis of the Union. An incisive analysis of northern reasons for resisting secession is Phillip S. Paludan, "The American Civil War Considered as a Crisis in Law and Order," *AHR* 77 (1972). Phillip S. Paludan, *"A People's*

Contest": The Union and Civil War 1861–1865 (1988), offers insights into wartime politics and constitutionalism.

On the constitutional issues involved in the war, see also Roy F. Nichols, "Federalism *versus* Democracy: The Significance of the Civil War in the History of United States Federalism," in *Federalism as a Democratic Process: Essays by Roscoe Pound, Charles H. McIlwain, and Roy F. Nichols* (1942); Allan Nevins, *The War for the Union,* 4 vols. (1959–71); Carl Russell Fish, *The American Civil War* (1937); William A Dunning, *Essays on the Civil War and Reconstruction* (1904); John W. Burgess, *The Civil War and the Constitution,* 2 vols. (1901); Peter J. Parish, *The American Civil War* (1975). Eric McKitrick, "Party Politics and the Union and Confederate War Efforts," in W. D. Burnham and W. N. Chambers, eds., *The American Party System: Stages of Political Development* (1967), shows the persistence of organized party activity in northern constitutional politics.

Lincoln's exercise of presidential power and constitutional outlook are analyzed in Herman Belz, "Abraham Lincoln and American Constitutionalism," *Review of Politics* 50 (1988); Herman Belz, "Lincoln and the Constitution: The Dictatorship Question Reconsidered," *Congress and the Presidency* 15 (1988); Michael Les Benedict, "Abraham Lincoln and Federalism," *Journal of the Abraham Lincoln Association* 10 (1988–89); Gary J. Jacobson, "Abraham Lincoln 'On This Question of Judicial Authority': The Theory of Constitutional Aspiration," *Western Political Quarterly* 36 (1983); Ludwell H. Johnson III, "Abraham Lincoln and the Development of Presidential War-Making Powers: Prize Cases (1863) Revisited," *CWH* 35 (1989); James G. Randall, *Lincoln the President,* 4 vols. (1945–55); Randall, "The Rule of Law under Lincoln," in *Lincoln the Liberal Statesman* (1947); Don E. Fehrenbacher, "Lincoln and the Constitution," in Cullom Davis, ed., *The Public and Private Lincoln: Contemporary Perspectives* (1979); Glen E. Thurow, *Abraham Lincoln and American Political Religion* (1976); Clinton L. Rossiter, *Constitutional Dictatorship: Crisis Government in the Modern Democracies* (1948); Dunning, *Essays on the Civil War and Reconstruction;* Andrew C. McLaughlin, "Lincoln, the Constitution, and Democracy," *International Journal of Ethics* 47 (1936); Morgan D. Dowd, "Lincoln, the Rule of Law and Crisis Government: A Study of His Constitutional Law Theories," *University of Detroit Law Journal* 39 (1962); David Donald, "Abraham Lincoln: A Whig in the White House," in *Lincoln Reconsidered: Essays on the Civil War Era* (1961). Lincoln's political thought is dealt with in Herman Belz, "The 'Philosophical Cause' of 'Our Free Government and Consequent Prosperity': The Problem of Lincoln's Political Thought," *Journal of the Abraham Lincoln Association* 10 (1988–89); John L. Thomas, ed., *Abraham Lincoln and the American Political Tradition* (1986); James A. Rawley, "The Nationalism of Abraham Lincoln," *CWH* 9 (1963); T. Harry Williams, "Abraham Lincoln— Principle and Pragmatism in Politics: A Review Article," *MVHR* 40 (1953); Thomas J. Pressly, "Bullets and Ballots: Lincoln and the 'Right of Revolution,' " *AHR* 67 (1962). William B. Hesseltine, *Lincoln and The War Governors* (1948), and Robert M. Spector, "Lincoln and Taney: A Study in Constitutional Polarization," *AJLH* 15 (1971), describe Lincoln's concentration of power in the federal executive. Gottfried Dietze, *America's Political Dilemma: From Limited to Unlimited Democracy* (1968), is severely critical of Lincoln's exercise of executive power, as are Dwight G. Anderson, *Abraham Lincoln: The Quest for Immortality* (1982); Willmoore Kendall and George W. Carey, *The Basic Symbols of the American Political Tradition* (1970); and M. E. Bradford, "The Lincoln Legacy: A Long View," *Modern Age* 24 (1980). Ludwell H. Johnson, "Jefferson Davis and Abraham Lincoln as War Presidents: Nothing Succeeds Like Success," *CWH* 27 (1981), rates Lincoln's presidential performance lower than that of the Confederate president.

Congress during the Civil War is examined in Allan G. Bogue, *The Earnest Men: Republicans of the Civil War Senate* (1981); Hyman, *A More Perfect Union;* Hyman, "Lincoln and Congress: Why Not Congress and Lincoln?" *Journal of the Illinois State Historical Society* 68 (1975); Leonard Curry, *Blueprint for Modern America: Nonmilitary Legislation of the First Civil War Congress* (1968); T. Harry Williams, "Lincoln and the Radicals: An Essay in Civil War History and Historiography," in Grady McWhiney, ed., *Grant, Lee, Lincoln and the Radicals: Essays on Civil War Leadership* (1964); Williams, *Lincoln and the Radicals* (1941); Roy F. Nichols, *Blueprints for Leviathan: American Style* (1963). Emergency government in the legislative branch is dealt with in W. W. Pierson, Jr., "The Committee on the Conduct of the War," *AHR* 22 (1918); T. Harry Williams, "The Committee on the Conduct of the War: An Experiment in Civilian Control," *Journal of the American Military Institute* 3 (1939); Hans L. Trefousse, "The Joint Committee on the Conduct of the War: A Reassessment," *CWH* 10 (1964).

Union internal security policies are dealt with in Hyman, *A More Perfect Union;* Hyman, *Era of the Oath: Northern Loyalty Tests during the Civil War and Reconstruction* (1954); Hyman and Benjamin P. Thomas, *Stanton: The Life and Times of Lincoln's Secretary of War* (1962); Charles Fairman, *The Law of Martial Rule* (1930); William F. Dukes, *A Constitutional History of Habeas Corpus* (1980). On conscription and army organization, see Eugene C. Murdock, *One Million Men: The Civil War Draft in the North* (1971); J. F. Leach, *Conscription in the United States: Historical Background* (1953); Fred A. Shannon, *The Organization and Administration of the Union Army, 1861–1865,* 2 vols. (1928); William B. Weedon, *War Government: Federal and State, 1861–1865* (1906). James F. Childress, "Francis Lieber's Interpretation of the Laws of War: General Orders No. 100 in the Context of His Life and Thought," *American Journal of Jurisprudence* 21 (1976), and Frank Freidel, "General Orders 100 and Military Government," *MVHR* 32 (1946), deal with the problem of restraining military power. Patricia L. M. Lucie, "Confiscation: Constitutional Crossroads," *CWH* 23 (1977), is particularly good on that subject, while William Whiting, *War Powers under the Constitution of the*

United States (1871), is a legal treatise dealing with most aspects of wartime constitutionalism. The constitutional results of the war are considered in Harold M. Hyman, "Law and the Impact of the Civil War," *CWH* 14 (1968), and Erwin W. Surrency, "The Legal Effects of the Civil War," *AJLH* 5 (1961).

On constitutional questions in the Confederacy, see Richard Bensel, "Southern Leviathan: The Development of Central State Authority in the Confederate States of America," *Studies in American Political Development* 2 (1987); Ludwell H. Johnson III, "The Confederacy: What Was It? The View from the Federal Courts," *CWH* 32 (1986); Charles R. Lee, Jr., *The Confederate Constitutions* (1963); Emory Thomas, *The Confederate Nation 1861–1865* (1979); Frank L. Owsley, *State Rights in the Confederacy* (1925).

Emancipation as a constitutional problem and federal policy toward freedmen are described in Randall, *Constitutional Problems under Lincoln;* Herman Belz, *A New Birth of Freedom: The Republican Party and Freedmen's Rights 1861–1866* (1976); Belz, *Emancipation and Equal Rights: Politics and Constitutionalism in the Civil War Era* (1978); Harry V. Jaffa, "The Emancipation Proclamation," in Robert A. Goldwin, ed., *100 Years of Emancipation* (1964); V. Jacque Voegeli, *Free but Not Equal: The Midwest and the Negro during the Civil War* (1967); Louis S. Gerteis, *From Contraband to Freedman: Federal Policy toward Southern Blacks, 1861–1865* (1973); Mary F. Berry, *Military Necessity and Civil Rights Policy: Black Citizenship and the Constitution, 1861–1868* (1977). Lincoln's attitude and actions on the question of freedmen's rights are explored in La Wanda Cox, *Lincoln and Black Freedom: A Study in Presidential Leadership* (1981); Don E. Fehrenbacher, "Only His Stepchildren: Lincoln and the Negro," *CWH* 22 (1974); George M. Fredrickson, "A Man but Not a Brother: Abraham Lincoln and Racial Equality," *JSH* 41 (1975).

The origins of Reconstruction as a constitutional problem during the Civil War are discussed in Herman Belz, *Reconstructing the Union: Theory and Policy during the Civil War* (1969). Works dealing with constitutional issues in Reconstruction generally are Hyman and Wiecek, *Equal Justice under Law;* Hyman, *A More Perfect Union;* Hyman, "Reconstruction and Political-Constitutional Institutions: The Popular Expression," in *New Frontiers of the American Reconstruction* (1966); Michael Les Benedict, *A Compromise of Principle: Congressional Republicans and Reconstruction, 1863–1869* (1974); Dunning, *Essays on the Civil War and Reconstruction.* A special focus on the civil rights question in Reconstruction policy is found in Patricia Lucie, "On Being a Free Person and a Citizen by Constitutional Amendment," *Journal of American Studies* 12 (1978); Belz, *Emancipation and Equal Rights;* Belz, "The New Orthodoxy in Reconstruction Historiography," *Reviews in American History* I (1973); Phillip S. Paludan, *A Covenant with Death: The Constitution, Law, and Equality in the Civil War Era* (1975); C. Vann Woodward, "Seeds of Failure in Radical Race Policy," in Hyman, ed., *New Frontiers of the American Reconstruction.* The best general accounts of Reconstruction politics are La

Wanda Cox and John H. Cox, *Politics, Principle, and Prejudice, 1865–1866: Dilemma of Reconstruction America* (1963); W. R. Brock, *An American Crisis: Congress and Reconstruction, 1865–1867* (1963); David Donald, *The Politics of Reconstruction, 1863–1867* (1965); Eric L. McKitrick, *Andrew Johnson and Reconstruction* (1960); Michael Perman, *Reunion without Compromise: The South and Reconstruction, 1865–1868* (1973); William A. Dunning, *Reconstruction, Political and Economic, 1865–1877* (1907).

The problems of maintaining order and organizing politically acceptable governments in the southern states through the use of military power are dealt with in Harold M. Hyman, "Johnson, Stanton, and Grant: A Reconsideration of the Army's Role in the Events Leading to Impeachment," *AHR* 66 (1960), and James E. Sefton, *The United States Army and Reconstruction, 1865–1877* (1967). The best analyses of the Military Reconstruction Act of 1867 are found in Benedict, *A Compromise of Principle,* and Brock, *An American Crisis.* For the constitutional theories supporting congressional Reconstruction policy, see William M. Wiecek, *The Guarantee Clause of the U.S. Constitution* (1972); Benedict, "Preserving the Constitution: The Conservative Basis of Radical Reconstruction," *JAH* 61 (1974); Belz, *Emancipation and Equal Rights;* Phillip S. Paludan, "John Norton Pomeroy: State Rights Nationalist," *AJLH* 12 (1968); Charles Larsen, "Nationalism and States' Rights in Commentaries on the Constitution after the Civil War," *AJLH* 3 (1959). James E. Sefton, *Andrew Johnson and the Uses of Constitutional Power* (1980), and Albert Castel, *The Presidency of Andrew Johnson* (1979), show greater regard for Johnson's constitutional views than most recent historians have. Jonathan T. Dorris, *Pardon and Amnesty under Lincoln and Johnson: The Restoration of the Confederates to Their Rights and Privileges* (1953), discusses that subject in exhaustive detail. The best accounts of Johnson's impeachment with emphasis on the constitutional dimension are John R. Labovitz, *Presidential Impeachment* (1978); Raoul Berger, *Impeachment: The Constitutional Problem* (1973); Michael Les Benedict, *The Impeachment and Trial of Andrew Johnson* (1973).

An extensive literature has developed on the civil rights question in Reconstruction. The efforts of the Freedmen's Bureau to deal with the problem are discussed in Donald G. Nieman, *To Set the Law in Motion: The Freedmen's Bureau and the Legal Rights of Blacks, 1865–1868* (1979); James Oakes, "Failure of Vision: The Collapse of the Freedmen's Bureau Courts," *CWH* 25 (1979); Thomas D. Morris, "Equality, 'Extraordinary Law,' and Criminal Justice: The South Carolina Experience, 1865–1866," *South Carolina Historical Magazine* 83 (1982); George R. Bentley, *A History of the Freedmen's Bureau* (1955). The southern states' legislation defining the status of the freedmen is described in Theodore B. Wilson, *The Black Codes of the South* (1965), and Gilbert T. Stephenson, *Race Distinctions in American Law* (1910).

Special attention is accorded the original intention of the framers of the Thirteenth Amendment in Ten Broek, *Equal under Law;* Belz, *A New Birth of Freedom;* G. Sidney Buchanan, *The Quest for Freedom: A Legal History of the Thirteenth Amendment,* reprinted from *Houston Law Review* 12 (1976); Howard Devon Hamilton, "The Legislative History of the Thirteenth Amendment," *National Bar Journal* 9 (1951). The relationship between the Thirteenth Amendment, the Civil Rights Act of 1866, and the Fourteenth Amendment is the focus of Mark De Wolfe Howe, "Federalism and Civil Rights," *Massachusetts Historical Society Proceedings* 77 (1965), and Hyman and Wiecek, *Equal Justice under Law.* Insight into the nature of the constitutional change effected by the prohibition of slavery is provided by Michael P. Zuckert, "Completing the Constitution: The Thirteenth Amendment," *Constitutional Commentary* 4 (1987), and Note, "The 'New' Thirteenth Amendment: A Preliminary Analysis," *Harvard Law Review* 82 (1969). The nature and purpose of the Fourteenth Amendment are discussed from differing points of view in Earl M. Maltz, *Civil Rights, the Constitution, and Congress, 1863–1869* (1990); Earl M. Maltz, "Fourteenth Amendment Concepts in the Antebellum Era," *AJLH* 32 (1988); William E. Nelson, *The Fourteenth Amendment: From Political Principle to Judicial Doctrine* (1988); Robert J. Kaczorowski, "To Begin the Nation Anew: Congress, Citizenship, and Civil Rights After the Civil War," *AHR* 92 (1987); Michael Kent Curtis, *No State Shall Abridge: The Fourteenth Amendment and the Bill of Rights* (1986); Michael P. Zuckert, "Congressional Power Under the Fourteenth Amendment—The Original Understanding of Section Five," *Constitutional Commentary* 3 (1986); Eric Schnapper, "Affirmative Action and the Legislative History of the Fourteenth Amendment," *Virginia Law Review* 71 (1985); Robert J. Kaczorowski, *The Politics of Judicial Interpretation: The Federal Courts, Department of Justice and Civil Rights 1866–1876* (1985); Daniel A. Farber and John E. Muench, "The Ideological Origins of the Fourteenth Amendment," (1977). Older works of value include Alfred H. Kelly, "The Fourteenth Amendment Reconsidered: The Segregation Question," *Michigan Law Review* 54 (1956); Alexander M. Bickel, "The Original Understanding and the Segregation Decision," *Harvard Law Review* 69 (1955); Laurent B. Frantz, "Congressional Power to Enforce the Fourteenth Amendment against Private Acts," *Yale Law Journal* 73 (1964); Charles Fairman, "Does the Fourteenth Amendment Incorporate the Bill of Rights?" *Stanford Law Review* 2 (1949); W. W. Crosskey, "Charles Fairman, 'Legislative History,' and the Constitutional Limitations on State Authority," *University of Chicago Law Review* 22 (1954); John P. Frank and Robert F. Munroe, "The Original Understanding of 'Equal Protection of the Law,' " *Columbia Law Review* 50 (1950); Joseph B. James, *The Framing of the Fourteenth Amendment* (1956); Horace E. Flack, *The Adoption of the Fourteenth Amendment* (1908). Howard J. Graham inaugurated the modern study of the Fourteenth Amendment in two pathbreaking articles: "The 'Conspiracy Theory' of the Fourteenth Amendment," *Yale Law Journal* 37–38 (1938), which demolished the argument that the framers of the amendment intended to protect corporations, and "The Early Anti-Slavery Backgrounds of the Fourteenth Amendment," *Wisconsin Law Review* 23 (1950), which identified pre-war abolitionism as the source of the civil rights prescriptions written into Section 1 of the amendment. These articles are reprinted in Graham, *Everyman's Constitution* (1968). On the economic interpretation of the Fourteenth Amendment, see also Andrew C. McLaughlin, "The Court, the Corporation, and Conkling," *AHR* 46 (1940); Louis B. Boudin, "Truth and Fiction about the Fourteenth Amendment," *New York University Law Quarterly Review* 16 (1938); James F. S. Russell, "The Railroads and the 'Conspiracy Theory' of the Fourteenth Amendment," *MVHR* 41 (1955).

The relevant modern study of the framing of the Fifteenth Amendment is William Gillette, *The Right to Vote: Politics and the Passage of the Fifteenth Amendment* (1965). Its emphasis on political expediency is challenged in La Wanda Cox and John H. Cox, "Negro Suffrage and Republican Politics: The Problem of Motivation in Reconstruction Historiography," *JSH* 33 (1967). Federal enforcement of civil and political rights in the 1870s is dealt with in Alfred Avins, "The Ku Klux Act of 1871: Some Reflected Light on State Action and the Fourteenth Amendment," *St. Louis University Law Journal* 11 (1967); William Gillette, "Anatomy of a Failure: Federal Enforcement of the Right to Vote in the Border States during Reconstruction," in Richard L. Curry, ed., *Radicalism, Racism, and Party Realignment: The Border States during Reconstruction* (1969); Everette Swinney, "Enforcing the Fifteenth Amendment, 1870–1877," *JSH* 28 (1962); Albie Burke, "Federal Regulation of Congressional Elections in Northern Cities, 1871–1894," *AJLH* 14 (1970); Richard L. Claude, *The Supreme Court and the Electoral Process* (1970); J. M. Mathew, *Legislative and Judicial History of the Fifteenth Amendment* (1909); Bertram Wyatt-Brown, "The Civil Rights Act of 1875," *Western Pol. Q.* 18 (1965); Alfred H. Kelly, "The Congressional Controversy over School Segregation, 1867–1875," *AHR* 64 (1959); Alfred Avins, "The Civil Rights Act of 1875: Some Reflected Light on the Fourteenth Amendment and Public Accommodations," *Columbia Law Review* 66 (1966); John Hope Franklin, "Enforcement of the Civil Rights Act of 1875," *Prologue* 6 (1974).

The best brief analysis of the Supreme Court and Reconstruction is Michael Les Benedict, "Preserving Federalism: Reconstruction and the Waite Court," *Supreme Court Review 1978* (1979). New insights are also provided in Robert C. Palmer, "The Parameters of Constitutional Reconstruction: *Slaughter-House, Cruikshank,* and the Fourteenth Amendment," *University of Illinois Law Review,* Vol. 1984. On the judiciary generally during the Civil War and Reconstruction, see Stanley I. Kutler, *Judicial Power and Reconstruction Politics* (1968); Charles Fairman, *History of the Supreme Court of the United States,* vol. 6: *Reconstruction and Reunion, 1864–88: Part One* (1971); David M. Silver, *Lincoln's Supreme Court* (1956); William M. Wiecek, "The Reconstruction of Federal Judicial Power: 1863–1875," *AJLH* 13 (1969); Wiecek, "The Great Writ and Reconstruction: The Habeas Corpus Act of 1867," *JSH*

36 (1970); J. David Hoeveler, Jr., "Reconstruction and the Federal Courts: The Civil Rights Act of 1875," *Historian* 31 (1969); John V. Orth, "The Eleventh Amendment and the North Carolina State Debt," *North Carolina Law Review* 59 (1981); C. Peter Magrath, *Morrison R. Waite: The Triumph of Character* (1963); Warren, *The Supreme Court in United States History;* Boudin, *Government by Judiciary.* Judicial interpretation of civil rights is the focus of Robert J. Harris, *The Quest for Equality: The Constitution, Congress and the Supreme Court* (1960); John Anthony Scott, "Justice Bradley's Evolving Concept of the Fourteenth Amendment from the Slaughterhouse Cases to the Civil Rights Cases," *Rutgers Law Review* 25 (1971).

Recent accounts of Reconstruction in the South are Eric Foner, *Reconstruction: American's Unfinished Revolution 1863–1877* (1988); Dan T. Carter, *When the War Was Over: The Failure of Self-Reconstruction in the South 1865–1867* (1985); Michael Perman, *The Road to Redemption: Southern Politics 1868–1878* (1984). Constitutional change in the former Confederate states is treated in Jack B. Scroggs, "Carpetbagger Constitutional Reform in the South Atlantic States, 1867–1868," *JSH* 27 (1961), and Richard L. Hume, "Carpetbaggers in the Reconstruction South: A Group Portrait of Outside Whites in the 'Black and Tan' Constitutional Conventions," *JAH* 64 (1977). On Reconstruction politics in the South, see also William Gillette, *Retreat from Reconstruction, 1869–1879* (1979); William R. Brock, "Reconstruction and the American Party System," and Otto H. Olsen, "Southern Reconstruction and the Question of Self-Determination," in George M. Fredrickson, ed., *A Nation Divided: Problems and Issues of the Civil War and Reconstruction* (1975). C. Vann Woodward, *Reunion and Reaction: The Compromise of 1877 and the End of Reconstruction* (1951), has long been the standard account of that subject but it is challenged in Allen Peskin, "Was There a Compromise of 1877?" *JAH* 60 (1973); Keith Polakoff, *The Politics of Inertia: The Election of 1876 and the End of Reconstruction* (1973); Michael Les Benedict, "Southern Democrats in the Crisis of 1876–1877: A Reconsideration of *Reunion and Reaction,*" *JSH* 46 (1980). The condition of Negro civil liberty in the aftermath of Reconstruction is discussed in John W. Cell, *The Highest Stage of White Supremacy: The Origins of Segregation in South Africa and the American South* (1982); Joel Williamson, *The Crucible of Race: Black-White Relations in the American South since Emancipation* (1984); Howard N. Rabinowitz, *Race Relations in the Urban South, 1865–1890* (1978); William Cohen, "Negro Involuntary Servitude in the South, 1865–1940: A Preliminary Analysis," *JSH* 42 (1976); Pete Daniel, "The Metamorphosis of Slavery, 1865–1900," *JAH* 66 (1979). Judicious assessments of reconstruction are provided in Eric McKitrick, "Reconstruction: Ultraconservative Revolution," in C. Vann Woodward, ed., *The Comparative Approach to American History* (1968); Phillip S. Paludan, "The American Civil War: Triumph through Tragedy," *CWH* 20 (1974); Cox, "Reflections on the Limits of the Possible," in *Lincoln and Black Freedom.*

XII. *The Constitutional System in the Late Nineteenth Century*

Morton Keller, *Affairs of State: Public Life in Late Nineteenth Century America* (1977), is a comprehensive account of law, politics, and administration at the federal and state levels. Its magisterial scope recalls James Bryce's classic work *The American Commonwealth,* 3 vols. (1888). An important study of the role of state government is Ballard C. Campbell, *Representative Democracy: Public Policy and Midwestern Legislatures in the Late Nineteenth Century* (1980). Worthwhile also for a general overview of the period are Loren Beth, *The Development of the American Constitution 1877–1917* (1971); Charles E. Merriam, *American Political Ideas: Studies in the Development of American Political Thought, 1865–1917* (1920); Edward R. Lewis, *A History of American Political Thought from the Civil War to the World War* (1937). Concerned especially with the emergence of a critical realistic attitude in the constitutional thought of the period are Herman Belz, "The Constitution in the Gilded Age: The Beginnings of Constitutional Realism in American Scholarship," *ALJH* 13 (1969); Martin Landau, "The Myth of Hyperfactionalism in the Study of American Politics," *PSQ* 83 (1968); Christopher Wolfe, "Woodrow Wilson: Interpreting the Constitution," *Review of Politics* 41 (1979).

The standard work on the interactions between president, Congress, and administration in this period is Leonard D. White, *The Republican Era: A Study in Administrative History, 1869–1901* (1958). Other works dealing generally with this subject include Corwin, *The President: Office and Powers;* Binkley, *President and Congress;* Stephen Horn, *The Cabinet and Congress* (1960); Paul P. Van Riper, *A History of the United States Civil Service* (1958); Woodrow Wilson, *Congressional Government* (1885); Dorothy G. Fowler, *The Cabinet Politician: The Postmasters General, 1829–1909* (1943); Henry Jones Ford, *The Rise and Growth of American Politics* (1898); Homer Cummings and Carl McFarland, *Federal Justice: Chapters in the History of Justice and the Federal Executive* (1937).

David Rothman, *Politics and Power: The U.S. Senate, 1869–1901* (1966), describes the more disciplined organizational politics that superseded the ideological conflict of the Civil War era. Additional studies of Congress are Nelson Polsby, "The Institutionalization of the House of Representatives," *APSR* 62 (1968); Neil McNeil, *Forge of Democracy: The House of Representatives* (1963); George B. Galloway, *History of the House of Representatives* (1961); George H. Haynes, *The Senate of the United States: Its History and Practice,* 2 vols. (1938).

A reassessment of political parties in the late nineteenth century has led historians to reject the older economic interpretation of American history. Outstanding examples of the revisionist view, which stresses ethnocultural as well as economic group conflict, are Paul Kleppner, *The Third Electoral*

System, 1853–1892: Parties, Voters, and Political Cultures (1979); Kleppner, *The Cross of Culture: A Social Analysis of Midwestern Politics, 1850–1900* (1970); Richard Jensen, *The Winning of the Midwest: Social and Economic Conflict, 1888–1896* (1971); Samuel T. McSeveney, *The Politics of Depression: Political Behavior in the Northeast, 1893–1896* (1972); Richard L. McCormick, "Ethno-cultural Interpretations of Nineteenth Century American Voting Behavior," *PSQ* 89 (1974). The concept of critical elections and electoral realignment has also been a dominant motif in accounts of party history. See Walter Dean Burnham, "The Changing Shape of the American Political Universe," *APSR* 59 (1965); Burnham, "Party Systems and the Political Process," in Burnham and W. N. Chambers, eds., *The American Party Systems: Stages of Political Development* (1967); James L. Sundquist, *Dynamics of the Party System: Alignment and Realignment of Political Parties in the United States* (1973); V. O. Key, "A Theory of Critical Elections," *JP* 17 (1955); Key, "Secular Realignment and the Party System," *JP* 21 (1959).

Also of value for understanding parties in the late nineteenth century are Samuel P. Hays, "Political Parties and the Community—Society Continuum," in Burnham and Chambers, eds., *The American Party Systems;* Robert D. Marcus, *Grand Old Party: Political Structure in the Gilded Age, 1880–1896* (1971); J. Morgan Kousser, *The Shaping of Southern Politics: Suffrage Restriction and the Establishment of the One-Party South, 1880–1910* (1974); Peter H. Argersinger, " 'A Place on the Ballot': Fusion Politics and Antifusion Laws," *AHR* 85 (1980); Morton Keller, "The Politicos Reconsidered," *Perspectives in American History* 1 (1967). The older progressive view of late-nineteenth century politics can be found in Matthew Josephson, *The Politicos, 1865–1896* (1938), and John D. Hicks, *The Populist Revolt* (1930). It is updated in Lawrence Goodwyn, *Democratic Promise: The Populist Moment in America* (1976).

Morton Keller, *Parties, Congress, and Public Policy* (1985), and Richard L. McCormick, "The Party Period and Public Policy: An Exploratory Hypothesis, *JAH* 66 (1979), evaluate the programmatic function of parties in relation to their constituent and cultural function. The activist role of government in economic affairs in the late nineteenth century is discussed in William M. Wiecek, *Constitutional Development in a Modernizing Society: The United States, 1803 to 1917* (1985); Jonathan Lurie, *The Constitution and Economic Change* (1988); Campbell, *Representative Democracy;* Harry N. Scheiber, "Regulation, Property Rights, and Definition of 'The Market': Law and the American Economy," *Journal of Economic History* 41 (1981); Scheiber, "Property Law, Expropriations, and Resource Allocation by Government: The United States, 1789–1910," *Journal of Economic History* 33 (1973).

The growing importance of public administration in the late nineteenth century can be seen in Woodrow Wilson's classic essay, "The Study of Administration," *PSQ* 2 (1887). Accounts of the implementation of governmental policy showing the problematic nature of public administration include Wallace D. Farnham, "The Weakened Spring of Government': A Study in Nine-teenth-Century American History," *AHR* 68 (1963); Leslie E. Decker, "The Railroads and the Land Office: Administrative Policy and the Land Patent Controversy, 1864–1896," *MVHR* 46 (1960); Decker, *Railroads, Lands, and Politics: The Taxation of the Railroad Land Grants, 1864–1897* (1964); Harold H. Dunham, *Government Handout: A Study in the Administration of the Public Lands 1875–1891* (1941). Corruption and reform in politics and administration are treated in Ari Hoogenboom, *Outlawing the Spoils: A History of the Civil Service Reform Movement 1865–1883* (1961); Hoogenboom, "Did the Gilded Age Scandals Bring Reform?" in Eisenstadt *et al.*, eds., *Before Watergate;* Eric McKitrick, "The Study of Corruption," *PSQ* 72 (1957).

Two interpretations of the movement for national regulation of the economy are Stephen Skowronek, *Building a New American State: The Expansion of National Administrative Capacities, 1877–1920* (1982), and William E. Nelson, *The Roots of American Bureaucracy, 1830–1900* (1982). Much study has been devoted to the politics, social sources, and economic rationale of railroad regulation. The best accounts dealing with these issues are Albro Martin, "The Troubled Subject of Railroad Regulation in the Gilded Age—A Reappraisal," *JAH* 61 (1974); George W. Hilton, "The Consistency of the Interstate Commerce Act," *Journal of Law and Economics* 9 (1966); Robert W. Harbeson, "Railroads and Regulation, 1877–1916: Conspiracy or Public Interest?" *Journal of Economic History* 27 (1967); George H. Miller, *Railroads and the Granger Laws* (1973); Edward A. Purcell, Jr., "Ideas and Interests: Businessmen and the Interstate Commerce Act, *JAH* 54 (1967); Gabriel Kolko, *Railroads and Regulation, 1877–1916* (1965). The difficulties faced by the ICC in its early years are analyzed in Ari Hoogenboom and Olive Hoogenboom, *A History of the Interstate Commerce Commission: From Panacea to Palliative* (1976); Robert E. Cushman, *The Independent Regulatory Commissions* (1941); I. W. Sharfman, *The Interstate Commerce Commission,* 5 vols. (1931–37); Alan Jones, "Thomas M. Cooley and the Interstate Commerce Commission: Continuity and Change in the Doctrine of Equal Rights," *PSQ* 81 (1966).

Charles L. McCurdy, "The Knight Sugar Decision of 1895 and the Modernization of American Corporation Law, 1869–1903," *Business History Review* 53 (1979), analyzes the purpose of the Sherman Antitrust Act in relation to state efforts to regulate corporations. More comprehensive treatments of this subject are James May, "Antitrust in the Formative Era: Political and Economic Theory in Constitutional and Antitrust Analysis, 1880–1918," *Ohio State Law Journal* 50 (1989); Robert H. Bork, *The Antitrust Paradox: A Policy at War with Itself* (1978); William Letwin, *Law and Economic Policy in America: The Evolution of the Sherman Anti-trust Act* (1965); Hans Thorelli, *The Federal Anti-Trust Policy: Origination of an American Tradition* (1955).

Territorial administration after the Civil War is the subject of Jack E. Eblen, *The First and Second United States Empires: Governors and Territorial Government, 1784–1912* (1968), and Earl S. Pomeroy, *The Territories and the United States, 1861–1890: Studies in Colonial Administration* (1947).

The following works provide an introduction to constitutional problems in federal Indian policy in the nineteenth century: Wilcomb E. Washburn, *Red Man's Land/White Man's Law: A Study of the Past and Present Status of the American Indian* (1971); Washburn, "The Historical Context of American Indian Legal Problems," *Law and Contemporary Problems* 40 (1976); Howard R. Berman, "The Concept of Aboriginal Rights in the Early Legal History of the United States," *Buffalo Law Review* 27 (1978); Frederick J. Martone, "American Indian Tribal Self-Government in the Federal System: Inherent Right or Congressional License?" *Notre Dame Lawyer* 51 *(1976);* Bernard W. Sheehan, *Seeds of Extinction: Jeffersonian Philanthropy and the American Indian* (1973); Ronald N. Satz, *American Indian Policy in the Jacksonian Era* (1975); Francis Paul Prucha, *American Indian Policy in the Formative Years: The Indian Trade and Intercourse Acts, 1780–1834* (1962); Robert A. Trennert, Jr., *Alternative to Extinction: Federal Indian Policy and the Beginning of the Reservation System, 1846–51* (1975); Henry E. Fritz, *The Movement for Indian Assimilation, 1860–1890* (1963). Indian policy in the twentieth century is described in William T. Hagan, *American Indians* (1961). Russell L. Barsh and James Y. Henderson, *The Road: Indian Tribes and Political Liberty* (1980), is an argument for tribal political rights within the federal system that contains useful information about the recent history of Indian policy.

Constitutional aspects of territorial annexation and colonial administration after the Spanish-American War are treated in Jose A. Cabranes, *Citizenship and the American Empire: Notes on the Legislative History of the United States Citizenship of Puerto Ricans* (1979; orig. published in *University of Pennsylvania Law Review* 127 [1978]); Whitney T. Perkins, *Denial of Empire: The United States and Its Dependencies* (1962); Julius W. Pratt, *America's Colonial Experiment: How the United States Gained, Governed, and in Part Gave Away a Colonial Empire* (1950); W. F. Willoughby, *Territories and Dependencies of the United States: Their Government and Administration* (1905); David Y. Thomas, *A History of Military Government in Newly Acquired Territory of the United States* (1904). Four excellent contemporary legal analyses of the insular problem remain pertinent: C. C. Langdell, "The Status of Our New Territories," *Harvard Law Review* 12 (1899); Simeon E. Baldwin, "The Constitutional Questions Incident to the Acquisition by the United States of Island Territory," *Harvard Law Review* 12 (1899); A Lawrence Lowell, "The Status of Our New Possessions—a Third View," *Harvard Law Review* 13 (1899); Frederick R. Coudert, "The Evolution of the Doctrine of Territorial Incorporation," *Columbia Law Review* 26 (1926).

XIII. *Constitutional Law in the Late Nineteenth Century*

A number of works refute the progressive view of the late-nineteenth-century judiciary as apologists for and defenders of laissez-faire capitalism, including Michael Les Benedict, "Laissez-Faire and Liberty: A Re-Evaluation of the Meaning and Origins of Laissez-Faire Constitutionalism," *Law and History Review* 3 (1985); Kermit L. Hall, *The Supreme Court and Judicial Review in American History* (1985); Charles W. McCurdy, "Justice Field and the Jurisprudence of Government-Business Relations: Some Parameters of Laissez-Faire Constitutionalism, 1863–1897," *JAH* 61 (1975); Mary Cornelia Porter, "That Commerce Shall Be Free: A New Look at the Old Laissez-Faire Court," *Supreme Court Review 1976* (1977); Alan Jones, "Thomas M. Cooley and Laissez Faire Constitutionalism: A Reconsideration," *JAH* 53 (1967). Other works in a revisionist vein are Robert Goedecke, "Justice Field and Inherent Rights," *Review of Politics* 27 (1965); Robert E. Garner, "Justice Brewer and Substantive Due Process: A Conservative Court Revisited," *Vanderbilt Law Review* 18 (1965); Walter F. Pratt, "Rhetorical Styles on the Fuller Court," *AJLH* 24 (1980), refuting the assumption that legal formalism adequately describes the outlook of the Supreme Court in the late nineteenth century; Charles C. Goetsch, "The Future of Legal Formalism," *AJLH* 24 (1980), an appraisal of the conservative jurist Simeon E. Baldwin; David M. Gold, "John Appleton of Maine and Commercial Law: Freedom, Responsibility, and Law in the Nineteenth Century Marketplace," *Law and History Review* 4 (1986); David M. Gold, "Redfield, Railroads, and the Roots of 'Laissez-Faire Constitutionalism,'" *AJLH* 27 (1983).

Arnold M. Paul, *Conservative Crisis and the Rule of Law: Attitudes of Bar and Bench, 1887–1895* (1960), is a fine study in the progressive tradition which explains the judicial acceptance of laissez-faire constitutionalism by reference to threats to the established order in the 1890s. Written from the same perspective are John P. Roche, "Entrepreneurial Liberty and the Commerce Power: Expansion, Contraction, and Casuistry in the Age of Enterprise," *University of Chicago Law Review* 30 (1963); Loren P. Beth, *The Development of the American Constitution, 1877–1917* (1971); William F. Swindler, *Court and Constitution in the Twentieth Century: The Old Legality, 1889–1932* (1969). Many of the standard works of progressive historiography deal with this period, including Charles Grove Haines, *The Doctrine of Judicial Supremacy* (1911; rev. ed., 1932); Edward S. Corwin, *Liberty against Government: The Rise, Flowering, and Decline of a Famous Juridical Concept* (1948); Benjamin R. Twiss, *Lawyers and the Constitution: How Laissez-Faire Came to the Supreme Court* (1942); Clyde E. Jacobs, *Law Writers and the Courts: The Influence of Thomas M. Cooley, Christopher M. Tiedeman, and John E. Dillon upon American Constitutional Law* (1954); Carl B. Swisher, *Stephen J. Field: Craftsman of the Law* (1930).

Worthwhile biographical accounts of late-nineteenth-century justices are Charles Fairman, *Mr. Justice Miller and the Supreme Court, 1862–1890* (1939); C. Peter Magrath, *Morrison R. Waite: The Triumph of Character* (1963); Willard L. King, *Melville Weston Fuller* (1950); Bruce R. Trimble, *Chief Justice Waite: Defender of the Public Interest* (1938); Fairman, "What Makes a Great Justice? Mr. Justice Bradley and the Supreme Court, 1870–

1892," *Boston University Law Review* 30 (1950); Alan F. Westin, "John Marshall Harlan and the Constitutional Rights of Negroes: The Transformation of a Southerner," *Yale Law Journal* 66 (1957); Henry J. Abraham, "John Marshall Harlan: A Justice Neglected," *Virginia Law Review* 41 (1955); D. Grier Stephenson, Jr., "The Chief Justice as Leader: The Case of Morrison R. Waite," *William and Mary Law Review* 14 (1973); Robert B. Highsaw, *Edward Douglas White: Defender of the Conservative Faith* (1981); Wallace Mendelson, "Mr. Justice Field and Laissez-faire," *Virginia Law Review* 36 (1950).

The development of substantive due process under the Fourteenth Amendment is the subject of several classic articles: Edward S. Corwin, "The Supreme Court and the Fourteenth Amendment," *Michigan Law Review* 7 (1909); Robert E. Cushman, "The Social and Economic Development of the Fourteenth Amendment," *Michigan Law Review* 20 (1922); Charles Grove Haines, "Judicial Review of Legislation in the United States and the Doctrine of Vested Rights," *Texas Law Review* 2–3 (1924); Walton H. Hamilton, "The Path of Due Process of Law," *Ethics* 48 (1938), reprinted in Conyers Read, ed., *The Constitution Reconsidered* (1938); Roscoe Pound, "Liberty of Contract," *Yale Law Journal* 18 (1909). Pertinent also are Rodney L. Mott, *Due Process of Law* (1926); Keith Jurow, "Untimely Thoughts: A Reconsideration of the Origins of Due Process of Law," *AJLH* 19 (1975); L. A. Powe, Jr., "Rehearsal for Substantive Due Process: The Municipal Bond Cases," *Texas Law Review* 58 (1975). The contrast between property rights and women's rights in the interpretation of the Fourteenth Amendment is underscored in Charles E. Corker, *"Bradwell v. State:* Some Reflections Prompted by Myra Bradwell's Hard Case That Made 'Bad Law,' " *Washington Law Review* 53 (1978).

There are rewarding discussions of judicial regulation of commerce and industry in Harry N. Scheiber, "The Road to Munn: Eminent Domain and the Concept of Public Purpose in the State Courts," *Perspectives in American History* 5 (1971); Charles Fairman, "The So-Called Granger Cases, Lord Hale, and Justice Bradley," *Stanford Law Review* 5 (1953); Breck P. McAllister, "Lord Hale and Business Affected with a Public Interest," *Harvard Law Review* 43 (1930); Charles W. McCurdy, "American Law and the Marketing Structure of the Large Corporation, 1875–1890," *Journal of Economic History* 38 (1978). On the Sherman Act and its application in the 1890s, see Charles W. McCurdy, "The Knight Sugar Decision of 1895 and the Modernization of American Corporation Law, 1869–1903," *Business History Review* 53 (1979), and Joe A. Fisher, "The Knight Case Revisited," *Historian* 35 (1973).

Important insights concerning the nature and extent of judicial power following the acceptance of substantive due process are provided in Morton Keller, *Affairs of State: Public Life in Late Nineteenth Century America* (1977); Christopher Wolfe, *The Rise of Modern Judicial Review* (1986), Wallace Mendelson, "The Politics of Judicial Supremacy," *Journal of Law and Economics* 4 (1961); Stuart S. Nagel, "Political Parties and Judicial Review in American

History," *Journal of Public Law* 11 (1962); Robert G. McCloskey, *The American Supreme Court* (1960); Alan Westin, "The Supreme Court, the Populist Movement and the Campaign of 1896," *JP* 15 (1953). Two contemporary essays of great value for understanding the new judicial review of the 1890s are James Bradley Thayer, "The Origin and Scope of the American Doctrine of Constitutional Law," *Harvard Law Review* 7 (1893), and Charles E. Shattuck, "The True Meaning of the Term 'Liberty' in Those Clauses in the Federal and State Constitutions Which Protect Life, Liberty, and Property," *Harvard Law Review* 4 (1891).

XIV. *The Constitution in an Age of Transition, 1900–1930*

Recent general analyses of progressivism expressing radical, liberal, and conservative interpretations, respectively, are Martin J. Sklar, *The Corporate Reconstruction of American Capitalism: The Market, the Law and Politics* (1988); Barry D. Karl, *The Uneasy State: The United States from 1915 to 1945* (1983); Robert Higgs, *Crisis and Leviathan: Critical Episodes in the Growth of American Government* (1987). The best introduction to progressive constitutional thought, emphasizing reformers' quest for positive government and reliance on new techniques of public administration, is M. J. C. Vile, "Progressivism and Political Science in America," in *Constitutionalism and the Separation of Powers* (1967). Richard L. McCormick, "The Discovery That 'Business Corrupts Politics': A Reappraisal of the Origins of Progressivism," *AHR* 86 (1981), effectively reasserts and links the older liberal democratic interpretation of progressive reform with the newer view which regards bureaucratic-administrative management as the essential purpose of progressivism. Good examples of the older view are Edward R. Lewis, *A History of American Political thought from the Civil War to the World War* (1937); Charles E. Merriam, *American Political Ideas: Studies in the Development of American Political Thought, 1865–1917* (1920); Charles McKinley, "The Constitution and the Tasks Ahead," *APSR* 49 (1955); J. Allen Smith, *The Spirit of American Government; A Study of the Constitution: It Origin, Influence, and Relation to Democracy* (1907; Herbert Croly, *The Promise of American Life* (1909); Frank J. Goodnow, *Social Reform and the Constitution* (1911). The bureaucratic-managerial interpretation of progressivism is best represented by Robert L. Wiebe, *The Search for Order, 1877–1920* (1967), and Louis Galambos, "The Emerging Organizational Synthesis in Modern American History," *Business History Review* 44 (1970). The managerial thesis is given a Marxian application in Gabriel Kolko, *The Triumph of Conservatism 1900–1916* (1963).

David P. Thelen, *The New Citizenship: Origins of Progressivism in Wisconsin, 1885–1900* (1972), stresses popular sovereignty and opposition to special privilege as the central themes of the reform movement. There are thoughtful interpretations also in Thomas K. McGraw, "The Progressive Legacy," in

Lewis L. Gould, ed., *The Progressive Era* (1974), and Otis A. Pease, "Urban Reformers in the Progressive Era," *Pacific Northwest Quarterly* 62 (1971). Austin Ranney, *The Doctrine of Responsible Party Government: Its Origins and Present State* (1954), analyzes the thought of leading progressives on political parties. Calvin Woodward, "Reality and Social Reform: The Transition from Laissez-Faire to the Welfare State," *Yale Law Journal* 72 (1962), is a penetrating examination of key changes in the meaning of basic political and constitutional concepts in the early twentieth century.

Students of the regulatory movement and government-business relations have debated the extent to which regulation served the needs of corporations and other economic groups or promoted the public interest. An excellent guide to this controversy is Thomas K. McCraw, "Regulation in America: A Review Article," *Business History Review* 49 (1975). The issues and evidence considered in the debate can be traced in Thomas K. McCraw, ed., *Regulation in Perspective* (1982); Robert L. Wiebe, *Businessmen and Reform: A Study of the Progressive Movement* (1962); Jonathan Lurie, "Private Associations, Internal Regulation and Progressivism: The Chicago Board of Trade as a Case Study," *AJLH* 16 (1972); Stanley P. Caine, *The Myth of Progressive Reform: Railroad Regulation in Wisconsin 1903–1910* (1970); Marver H. Bernstein, *Regulating Business by Independent Commission* (1955); Oscar E. Anderson, Jr., "The Pure-Food Issue: A Republican Dilemma 1906–1912," *AHR* 61 (1956); Bruce W. Dearstyne, "Regulation in the Progressive Era: The New York Public Service Commission," *New York History* 58 (1977); Melvin I. Urofsky, *Big Steel and the Wilson Administration: A Study in Business-Government Relations* (1969); Arthur M. Johnson, *Government-Business Relations: A Pragmatic Approach to the American Experience* (1965). On the two agencies which have received the closest study in relation to this issue, see Douglas Walter Jaenicke, "Herbert Croly, Progressive Ideology, and the FTC Act," *PSQ* 93 (1978); G. Cullom Davis, "The Transformation of the Federal Trade Commission, 1914–1929," *MVHR* 49 (1962); Gabriel Kolko, *Railroads and Regulation, 1877–1916* (1965); Richard H. K. Vietor, "Businessmen and the Political Economy: The Railroad Rate Controversy of 1905," *JAH* 64 (1977); Albro Martin, *Enterprise Denied: Origins of the Decline of American Railroads, 1897–1917* (1971). The judicial reaction to the emerging regulatory state is the subject of John Dickinson, *Administrative Justice and the Supremacy of Law in the United States* (1927).

Woodrow Wilson's contribution to the modern presidency is treated in James W. Ceaser, *Presidential Selection: Theory and Development* (1979); Earl Latham, ed., *The Philosophy and Policies of Woodrow Wilson* (1958); Arthur Link, *Woodrow Wilson: The New Freedom* (1956); Arthur W. MacMahon, "Woodrow Wilson as Legislative Leader and Administrator," *APSR* 50 (1956). Wilson's own works, *Congressional Government* (1885), and *Constitutional Government in the United States* (1908), should be consulted, as well as several contemporary accounts: Henry Jones Ford, "The Growth of Dictatorship," *Atlantic Monthly* 121 (1918); Henry Campbell Black, *The Relation of the Executive Power to Legislation* (1919); John W. Burgess, *Recent Changes in American Constitutional Theory* (1923); William Bennett Munro, "Woodrow Wilson and the Accentuation of Presidential Leadership," in *The Makers of the Unwritten Constitution* (1930). Donald F. Anderson, *William Howard Taft: A Conservative's Conception of the Presidency* (1973), emphasizes the persistence of traditional rule-of-law values in the era of reform.

Robert D. Cuff, *The War Industries Board: Business-Government Relations during World War I* (1973), shows how the war presented opportunities to realize bureaucratic-managerial reforms. Standard accounts of wartime government are Carl B. Swisher, *American Constitutional Development* (1954); Swisher, "The Control of War Preparations in the United States," *APSR* 34 (1940); William F. Willoughby, *Government Organization in War Time and After* (1919).

The bureaucratic-managerial aspect of progressivism as reflected in the career of Herbert Hoover is discussed in Ellis Hawley, *The Great War and the Search for a Modern Order: A History of the American People and Their Institutions, 1917–1933* (1979); Hawley, "Herbert Hoover, the Commerce Secretariat, and the Vision of the 'Associative State,' 1921–1928," *JAH* 61 (1974); Robert D. Cuff, "Herbert Hoover, the Ideology of Voluntarism and War Organization during the Great War," *JAH* 64 (1977); Peri E. Arnold, "The 'Great Engineer' as Administrator: Herbert Hoover and Modern Bureaucracy," *Review of Politics* 42 (1980). Concerned more broadly with the development of executive power over the bureaucracy are Peri E. Arnold, *Making the Managerial Presidency: Comprehensive Reorganization Planning 1905–1980* (1986); Barry Dean Karl, *Executive Reorganization and Reform in the New Deal: The Genesis of Administrative Management, 1900–1939* (1963); Karl, "Presidential Planning and Social Science Research: Mr. Hoover's Experts," *Perspectives in American History* 3 (1969). Larry Berman, *The Office of Management and Budget and the Presidency 1921–1979* (1979), describes the Budget Act of 1921 and its enhancement of executive power. Thomas B. Silver, *Coolidge and the Historians* (1982), is an analysis of the biases that have colored accounts of that president. The *Myers* case and the controversy over the removal power are dealt with in James Hart, *Tenure of Office under the Constitution* (1930), and Edward S. Corwin, "Tenure of Office and the Removal Power under the Constitution," *Columbia Law Review* 27 (1927).

Awareness of the growth of big government in the 1920s is documented in a number of contemporary works: Charles A. Beard and William Beard, *The American Leviathan: The Republic in the Machine Age* (1931); Carroll H. Woody, *The Growth of the Federal Government, 1915–1932* (1934); Walter Thompson, *Federal Centralization* (1923); President's Research Committee, *Recent Social Trends in the United States* (1933). Changes in federalism in this period are examined in Harry Scheiber, "The Condition of American Federalism: An Historian's View," in Frank Smallwood, ed., *The New Federalism*

(1967), and William Graebner, "Federalism in the Progressive Era: A Structural Interpretation of Reform," *JAH* 64 (1977). Charles Warren, *Congress as Santa Claus, or National Donations and the General Welfare Clause* (1932, 1978), traces the emergence of special-interest and class legislation and its effect in eroding states' rights.

Several works describe federal policy toward labor union militance, among them Jerry M. Cooper, *The Army and Civil Disorder: Federal Military Intervention in Labor Disputes* (1980); Gerald C. Eggert, *Railroad Labor Disputes: The Beginnings of Federal Strike Policy* (1967); Edwin E. Witte, *The Government in Labor Disputes* (1932); Felix Frankfurter and Nathan V. Green, *The Labor Injunction* (1930). The problem of child labor is examined in Stephen B. Wood, *Constitutional Politics in the Progressive Era: Child Labor and the Law* (1968).

The evolution of a federal police power on the one hand and the persistence of laissez-faire constitutionalism on the other form the central themes in the history of constitutional law in the progressive era. An authoritative recent study is Alexander M. Bickel and Benno C. Schmidt, Jr., *The Judiciary and Responsible Government: 1910–1921* (1984). In addition to the general works on the Supreme Court by Warren, Boudin, Wright, and McCloskey, see John E. Semonche, *Charting the Future: The Supreme Court Responds to a Changing Society, 1890–1920* (1978), and William F. Swindler, *Court and Constitution in the Twentieth Century: The Old Legality, 1889–1932* (1969). Ernst Freund, *The Police Power* (1904), is a standard treatise which illuminates the nature of the federal police power. See also John Braeman, "The Square Deal in Action: A Case Study in the Growth of the National Police Power," in Braeman *et al.,* eds., *Change and Continuity in Twentieth Century America* (1966). Conservative tendencies in the judiciary are underscored Lawrence M. Friedman, "A Search for Seizure: *Pennsylvania Coal Co. v. Mahon* in Context," *Law and History Review* 4 (1986); in John P. Roche, "Entrepreneurial Liberty and the Fourteenth Amendment," *Labor History* 4 (1963); Thomas Reed Powell, "The Supreme Court and State Police Power, 1922–1930," *Virginia Law Review* 17–18 (1931–32); Walton H. Hamilton, "Affectation with a Public Interest," *Yale Law Journal* 39 (1930); Maurice Finkelstein "From Munn v. Illinois to Tyson v. Banton: A Study in the Judicial Process," *Columbia Law Review* 26 (1927). Ray A. Brown, "Due Process of Law, Police Power, and the Supreme Court," *Harvard Law Review* 40 (1927), and Brown, "Police Power—Legislation for Health and Personal Safety," *Harvard Law Review* 42 (1929), present a favorable assessment of the Supreme Court's handling of social and economic legislation. Revisionist views of a famous conservative decision appear in Frank Strong, "The Economic Philosophy of Lochner: Emergence, Embrasure and Emasculation," *Arizona Law Review* 15 (1973); Sidney G. Tarrow, "Lochner versus New York: A Political Analysis," *Labor History* 5 (1964); Albert Mavrinac, "From Lochner to Brown v. Topeka: The Court and Conflicting Concepts of the Judicial Process," *APSR* 52 (1958). A famous liberal decision is analyzed in David Gordon, *"Swift & Co. v. United States:* The Beef Trust and the Stream of Commerce Doctrine," *AJLH* 28 (1984).

Worthwhile studies of individual judges include G. Edward White, "The Rise and Fall of Justice Holmes," *University of Chicago Law Review* 39 (1971); Samuel J. Konefsky, *The Legacy of Holmes and Brandeis: A Study in the Influence of Ideas* (1956); Mark De Wolfe Howe, *Justice Oliver Wendell Holmes,* 2 vols. (1957–63); Felix Frankfurter, *Mr. Justice Holmes and the Supreme Court* (1938); Mark Tushnet, "The Logic of Experience: Oliver Wendell Holmes on the Supreme Judicial Court," *Virginia Law Review* 63 (1977); Samuel Krislov, "Oliver Wendell Holmes: The Ebb and Flow of Judicial Legendry," *Northwestern University Law Review* 52 (1957); Symposium, "Mr. Justice Holmes: Some Modern Views," *University of Chicago Law Review* 31 (1964); Melvin I. Urofsky, *Louis D. Brandeis and the Progressive Tradition* (1981); Allon Gal, *Brandeis of Boston* (1980); Alpheus T. Mason, *Brandeis: A Free Man's Life* (1946); Mason, *William Howard Taft: Chief Justice* (1965); J. F. Paschal, *Mr. Justice Sutherland: A Man Against the State* (1951); Hoyt L. Warner, *Life of Mr. Justice Clarke: A Testament to the Power of Liberal Dissent In America* (1959); J. E. McLean, *William Rufus Day: Supreme Court Justice from Ohio* (1946); David J. Danelski, *A Supreme Court Justice Is Appointed* (1964), concerning the Pierce Butler appointment.

The progressive attack on the judiciary is discussed in Stephen Stagner, "The Recall of Judicial Decisions and the Due Process Debate," *AJLH* 24 (1980). Representative contemporary writings on this theme include W. F. Dodd, "The Growth of Judicial Power" *PSQ* 24 (1909); Louis B. Boudin, "Government by Judiciary," *PSQ* 26 (1911); Gilbert E. Roe, *Our Judicial Oligarchy* (1912). The political involvement of two renowned progressive jurists is revealed in Bruce Allen Murphy, *The Brandeis/Frankfurter Connection: The Secret Political Activities of Two Supreme Court Justices* (1982).

Progressive trends in jurisprudence are explained in David Wigdor, *Roscoe Pound: Philosopher of Law* (1973); Fred V. Cahill, *Judicial Legislation* (1952); Morton White, *Social Thought in America: The Revolt against Formalism* (1949); Benjamin N. Cardozo, *The Nature of the Judicial Process* (1921); Cardozo, *The Growth of the Law* (1924); Thomas Reed Powell, "The Logic and Rhetoric of Constitutional Law," *Journal of Philosophy* 15 (1918). Sundry problems in constitutional law are dealt with in Bruce Bringhurst, *Antitrust and the Oil Monopoly: The Standard Oil Cases, 1890–1911* (1979); M. Browning Carrott, "The Supreme Court and American Trade Associations, 1921–1925," *Business History Review* 44 (1970); Stanley I. Kutler, "Labor, the Clayton Act, and the Supreme Court," *Labor History* 3 (1962); Kutler, "Chief Justice Taft, National Regulation and the Commerce Clause," *JAH* 51 (1965); Morton Keller, "The Judicial System and the Law of Life Insurance, 1888–1910," *Business History Review* 35 (1961).

Able surveys of the constitutional problems involved in municipal government are Jon C. Teaford, *City and Suburb: The Political Fragmentation of*

Metropolitan America, 1850–1970 (1979); Teaford, *The Municipal Revolution in America: Origins of Modern Urban Government, 1650–1825* (1975); Teaford, "Special Legislation and the Cities, 1865–1900," *AJLH* 23 (1979); Anwar H. Syed, *The Political Theory of American Local Government* (1966). The argument that municipal reformers were antidemocratic elitists is made in Samuel P. Hays, "The Politics of Reform in Municipal Government in the Progressive Era," *Pacific Northwest Quarterly* 55 (1964). On local government, see also David Nord, "The Experts versus the Experts: Conflicting Philosophies of Municipal Utility Regulation in the Progressive Era," *Wisconsin Magazine of History* 58 (1975); Clifford W. Patton, *The Battle for Municipal Reform: Mobilization and Attack, 1875 to 1900* (1940); Ernest S. Griffith, *The Modern Development of City Government in the United Kingdom and the United States,* 2 vols. (1927); Howard Lee McBain, *The Law and Practice of Municipal Home Rule* (1916); Delos Wilcox, *Municipal Franchises* (1910); John F. Dillon, *Treatise on the Law of Municipal Corporations* (1872). Electoral reforms at the state level are treated in Jerrold G. Rusk, "The Effect of the Australian Ballot Reform on Split Ticket Voting: 1876–1908," *APSR* 64 (1970), and Jack L. Walker, "The Diffusion of Innovations among the American States," *APSR* 63 (1969).

Federal taxation and the politics of the Seventeenth Amendment are covered in John D. Buenker, "Urban Liberalism and the Federal Income Tax Amendment," *Pennsylvania History* 36 (1969); Buenker, "The Urban Political Machine and the Seventeenth Amendment," *JAH* 56 (1969); Sidney Ratner, *American Taxation* (1942); R. Alton Lee, *A History of Regulatory Taxation* (1973). For constitutional and legal aspects of the women's suffrage and prohibition amendments, see David Morgan, *Suffragists and Democrats: The Politics of Woman Suffrage in America* (1972), and David E. Kyvig, *Repealing National Prohibition* (1979).

XV. *The New Deal Era in American Constitutionalism*

In recent years scholars have pointed out elements of political and constitutional continuity between the efforts of the Hoover administration to combat the depression and those of the New Deal administration of Franklin D. Roosevelt. Hoover's policies and governmental attitudes are examined in Jordan A. Schwarz, *The Interregnum of Despair: Hoover, Congress, and the Depression* (1970); Alfred U. Romasco, *The Poverty of Abundance: Hoover, the Nation, the Depression* (1965); James Stuart Olson, *Herbert Hoover and the Reconstruction Finance Corporation, 1931–1933* (1977); Harris G. Warren, *Herbert Hoover and the Great Depression* (1967); Martin L. Fausold and George T. Mazuzan, eds., *The Hoover Presidencey: A Reappraisal* (1974); Craig Lloyd, *Aggressive Introvert: A Study of Herbert Hoover and Public Relations Management, 1912–1932* (1972).

New scholarship reflecting a revisionist view of the New Deal is found in

Robert Eden, ed., *The New Deal and Its Legacy: Critique and Reappraisal* (1989); Robert Higgs, *Crisis and Leviathan: Critical Episodes in the Growth of American Government* (1987); Sidney M. Milkis, "Franklin D. Roosevelt and the Transcendence of Partisan Politics," *PSQ* 100 (1985); Harvard Sitkoff, ed., *Fifty Years Later: The New Deal Evaluated* (1985); Michael E. Parrish, "The Great Depression, the New Deal, and the American Legal Order," *Washington Law Review* 59 (1984). A more traditional view of the New Deal is presented in Barry D. Karl, *The Uneasy State: The United States from 1915 to 1945* (1983), and William E. Leuchtenburg, "The New Deal and the Analogue of War," in John Braeman *et al.*, eds., *Continuity and Change in Twentieth Century America* (1965). Peter H. Irons, *The New Deal Lawyers* (1982), and Michael R. Belknap, "The New Deal and the Emergency Powers Doctrine," *Texas Law Review* 62 (1983), provide through analyses of constitutional strategy. Clinton Rossiter, *Constitutional Dictatorship: Crisis Government in the Modern Democracies* (1948), contains a good account of Roosevelt's expansion of executive power. General works on the New Deal which cast light on constitutional issues include Paul K. Conkin, *FDR and the Origins of the Welfare State* (1967); Arthur M. Schlesinger, Jr., *The Coming of the New Deal* (1958); Schlesinger, *The Politics of Upheaval* (1960); Edgar E. Robinson, *The Roosevelt Leadership, 1933–1945* (1955); James MacGregor Burns, *Roosevelt: The Lion and the Fox* (1956); Mario Einaudi, *The Roosevelt Revolution* (1959); William E. Leuchtenburg, *Franklin D. Roosevelt and the New Deal: 1932–1940* (1963).

More specialized considerations of the New Deal constitutionalism include Morton J. Frisch, "Franklin D. Roosevelt and the Problem of Democratic Liberty," *Ethics* 72 (1962); Frisch, "Roosevelt the Conservator: A Rejoinder to Hofstadter," *JP* 25 (1963); Rexford G. Tugwell, "Design for Government," *PSQ* 48 (1933); Tugwell, "The New Deal: Available Instruments of Governmental Power," *Western Pol. Q.* 2 (1949); Francis G. Wilson, "The Revival of Organic Theory," *APSR* 36 (1942); Luther Gulick, "Politics, Administration, and the 'New Deal,' " *Annals* 169 (1933); John Dickinson, "Political Aspects of the New Deal," *APSR* 28 (1934); Jane Perry Clark, "Emergencies and the Law," *PSQ* 49 (1934); Edward S. Corwin, "Some Probable Consequences of 'Nira' on Our Constitutional System," *Annals* 172 (1934); William Yandell Elliott, *The Need for Constitutional Reform: A Program for National Security* (1935); Harold Laski, "The Constitution under Strain," *Political Quarterly* 8 (1937); Norton E. Long, "Party and Constitution," *JP* 3 (1941).

The relationship between groups and regulatory agencies in constitutional politics in the New Deal era is discussed in Grant McConnell, *Private Power and American Democracy* (1966); Louis L. Jaffe, "Law Making by Private Groups," *Harvard Law Review* 51 (1937); James J. Robbins and Gunnar Heckscher, "The Constitutional Theory of Autonomous Groups," *JP* 3 (1941); Charles M. Wiltse, "The Representative Function of Bureaucracy," *APSR* 35 (1941); E. Pendleton Herring, *Group Representation before Congress*

(1929); Reinhard Bendix, "Bureaucracy and the Problem of Power," *Public Administration Review* 5 (1945); Vincent M. Barnett, Jr., "Modern Constitutional Development: A Challenge to Administration," *Public Administration Review* 4 (1944).

Roosevelt's attempt to gain greater executive control over the structure of influence created by interest groups and bureaucratic agencies is recounted in studies of executive reorganization. See especially John A. Rohr, *To Run a Constitution: The Legitimacy of the Administrative State* (1986); Peri E. Arnold, *Making the Managerial Presidency: Comprehensive Reorganization Planning 1905–1980* (1986); Barry D. Karl, *Executive Reorganization and Reform in the New Deal: The Genesis of Administrative Management 1900– 1939* (1963); Clinton L. Rossiter, "The Constitutional Significance of the Executive Office of the President," *APSR* 43 (1949); Richard Polenberg, *Reorganizing Roosevelt's Government* (1966); A. J. Wann, *The President as Chief Administrator: A Study of Franklin D. Roosevelt* (1968). Roosevelt's relations with Congress can be traced in James T. Patterson, *Congressional Conservatism and the New Deal: The Growth of the Conservative Coalition in Congress, 1933–1935* (1967); J. Joseph Huthmacher, *Robert A. Wagner and the Rise of Urban Liberalism* (1968); Lawrence H. Chamberlain, *The President, Congress and Legislation* (1946), containing the legislative history of many New Deal measures. Roosevelt's attempt to impose greater executive control on the Democratic party is analyzed in Charles M. Price and Joseph Boskin, "The Roosevelt 'Purge': A Reappraisal," *JP* 28 (1966).

The establishment of federal regulatory and social welfare structures is described in numerous works. The best accounts of industrial recovery and reform are Ellis W. Hawley, *The New Deal and the Problem of Monopoly: A Study in Economic Ambivalence* (1966), and Bernard Bellush, *The Failure of the NRA* (1975). Paul L. Murphy, "The New Deal Agricultural Program and the Constitution," *Agricultural History* 29 (1955), is a solid analysis. On the subjects indicated the following studies are reliable guides: Thomas K. McCraw, *TVA and the Power Fight, 1933–1939* (1971); C. Herman Pritchett, *The Tennessee Valley Authority: A Study in Public Administration* (1943); Irving Bernstein, *The New Deal Collective Bargaining Policy* (1950); Susan Estabrook Kennedy, *The Banking Crisis of 1933* (1973); Michael E. Parrish, *Securities Regulation and the New Deal* (1970); Sidney Fine, *The Automobile Industry under the Blue Eagle: Labor, Management, and the Automobile Manufacturing Code* (1963); Daniel Nelson, *Unemployment Insurance: The American Experience, 1915–1935* (1969); William Graebner, *A History of Retirement: The Meaning and Function of An American Institution, 1885–1978* (1980), containing an account of the Social Security Act; Roy Lubove, *The Struggle for Social Security: 1900–1935* (1968); Paul A. Kurzman, *Harry Hopkins and the New Deal* (1974), concerning administration of the federal relief program; Searle F. Charles, *Minister of Relief: Harry Hopkins and the Depression* (1963).

Samuel P. Huntington, "The Marasmus of the ICC: The Commission, the

Railroads, and the Public Interest," *Yale Law Journal* 61 (1952), covers problems in transportation regulation in the 1930s and 1940s. Otis L. Graham, *Toward a Planned Society: From Roosevelt to Nixon* (1976), is a survery of the concept of national economic planning. Donald A. Ritchie, *James M. Landis: Dean of the Regulators* (1980), provides an able survey of New Deal administrative history. Corwin D. Edwards, "Thurman Arnold and the Antitrust Laws," *PSQ* 58 (1943), argues for the effectiveness of the New Deal regulation of corporations.

Changes in federalism produced by the New Deal are considered in Harry N. Scheiber, "The Condition of American Federalism: An Historian's View," in Frank Smallwood, ed., *The New Federalism* (1967); James T. Patterson, *The New Deal and the States* (1969); Jane Perry Clark, *The Rise of a New Federalism* (1938); V. O. Key, Jr., *Administration of Federal Grants to States* (1937); H. J. Bitterman, *State and Federal Grants in Aid* (1938).

The hostility of the Supreme Court toward the New Deal before 1937 is well described in Paul L. Murphy, *The Constitution in Crisis Times, 1919–1969* (1972); William F. Swindler, *Court and Constitution in the Twentieth Century: The New Legality, 1932–1968* (1970); Robert H. Jackson, *The Struggle for Judicial Supremacy* (1941); Merlo J. Pusey, *Charles Evans Hughes,* 2 vols. (1951); Samuel Hendel, *Charles Evans Hughes and the Supreme Court* (1951); William Harbaugh, *Lawyer's Lawyer: The Life of John W. Davis* (1973). Several of Edward S. Corwin's works written in the 1930s illuminate the Court's anti-New Deal outlook. See especially *The Twilight of the Supreme Court* (1934) and *The Commerce Power versus States Rights* (1936). Gerald Garvey, "Edward S. Corwin in the Campaign of History: The Struggle for National Power in the 1930s," *George Washington Law Review* 34 (1965), is pertinent in this regard. Corwin's "Curbing the Court," *Annals* 185 (1936), is a valuable analysis of the problem of constitutional reform created by the Court's negative course.

The best accounts of the Court-packing crisis are William E. Leuchtenburg, "The Origins of Franklin D. Roosevelt's 'Court-Packing' Plan," *Supreme Court Review 1966* (1967); Leuchtenburg, "Franklin D. Roosevelt's Supreme Court 'Packing' Plan," in George Wolfskill *et al., Essays on the New Deal* (1969); Lionel V. Patenaude, "Garner, Sumners, and Connally: The Defeat of the Roosevelt Court Bill in 1937," *Southwestern Historical Quarterly* 74 (1970); Gene M. Gressley, "Joseph C. O'Mahoney, FDR and the Supreme Court," *Pacific Historical Review* 40 (1971). See also Charles A. Leonard, *A Search for a Judicial Philosophy: Mr. Justice Roberts and the Constitutional Revolution of 1937* (1971); John W. Chambers, "The Big Switch: Justice Roberts and the Minimum Wage Cases," *Labor History* 10 (1969); Barry A. Crouch, "Dennis Chavez and Roosevelt's 'Court Packing' Plan," *New Mexico Historical Review* 42 (1967); Karl A. Lamb, "The Opposition Party as Secret Agent: Republicans and the Court Fight, 1937," *Papers of the Michigan Academy of Science, Arts, and Letters* 46 (1961).

The changes in constitutional law inaugurated in 1937 are analyzed in Robert Harrison, "The Breakup of the Roosevelt Supreme Court: The Contribution of History and Biography," *Law and History Review* 2 (1984); Richard C. Cortner, *The Jones and Laughlin Case* (1970); Cortner, *The Wagner Act Cases* (1964); C. Herman Pritchett, *The Roosevelt Court: A Study in Judicial Politics and Values, 1937–1947* (1948); Alpheus T. Mason, *Harlan Fiske Stone: Pillar of the Law* (1956); Robert L. Stern, "The Commerce Clause and the National Economy, 1933–1946," *Harvard Law Review* 59 (1946); Robert G. McCloskey, "Economic Due Process and the Supreme Court: An Exhumation and Reburial," *Supreme Court Review 1962* (1963); J. Woodford Howard, Jr., *Mr. Justice Murphy: A Political Biography* (1968); Carl B. Swisher, *The Growth of Constitutional Power in the United States* (1946). The liberal commitment to maintaining pro-New Deal tendencies on the Court is vividly depicted in William E. Leuchtenburg, "A Klansman Joins the Court: The Appointment of Hugo L. Black," *University of Chicago Law Review* 41 (1973).

Broad assessments of the constitutional impact of the New Deal and the role of the Supreme Court after 1937 are found in Vincent M. Barnett, Jr., "The Political Philosophy of the New Supreme Court," *Journal of Social Philosophy and Jurisprudence* 7 (1942); Barnett, "The Supreme Court and the Capacity to Govern," *PSQ* 63 (1948); Walton H. Hamilton and George D. Braden, "The Special Competence of the Supreme Court," *Yale Law Journal* 50 (1941); Max Lerner, "The Great Constitutional War," *Virginia Quarterly Review* 18 (1942); Kenneth Culp Davis, "Revolution in the Supreme Court," *Atlantic Monthly* 166 (1940); Henry Steele Commager, *Majority Rule and Minority Rights* (1943); Edward S. Corwin, *Constitutional Revolution, Ltd.* (1941); Corwin, "The Passing of Dual Federalism" *Virginia Law Review* 37 (1950); Thomas Reed Powell, *Vagaries and Varieties in Constitutional Interpretation* (1956). Improvement in federal judicial organization as a partial response to the Court-packing crisis is described in Peter G. Fish, "Crises, Politics, and Federal Judicial Reform: The Administrative Office Act of 1939," *JP* 32 (1970). The *Erie* case is the subject of a large body of technical legal literature, the scope of which can be seen in John Hart Ely, "The Irrepressible Myth of Erie," *Harvard Law Review* 87 (1974). An interesting narrative of the case is provided in Irving Younger, "What Happened in *Erie,*" *Texas Law Review* 56 (1978).

The philosophy of legal realism that influenced the Court-packing plan and New Deal liberalism in general is well represented in Karl Llewellyn, "The Constitution as an Institution," *Columbia Law Review* 34 (1934); Charles A. Beard, "The Living Constitution," *Annals* 185 (1936); Thurman Arnold, *The Symbols of Government* (1935); Max Lerner, "Constitution and Court as Symbols," *Yale Law Journal* 46 (1937). See the analyses of these and other constitutional critics in Herman Belz, "Changing Conceptions of Constitutionalism in the Era of World War II and the Cold War," *JAH* 59 (1972); Edward A. Purcell, Jr., *The Crisis of Democratic Theory: Scientific Naturalism and the*

Problem of Values (1973); Douglas Ayer, "In Quest of Efficiency: The Ideological Journey of Thurman Arnold in the Interwar Period," *Stanford Law Review* 23 (1971).

Concerning constitutional problems during World War II, see Edward S. Corwin, *Total War and the Constitution* (1947); Bernard Schwartz, "The War Power in Britain and America," *New York University Law Quarterly Review* 20 (1945); Clinton Rossiter, *The Supreme Court and the Commander-in-Chief* (1951); Nathan Grundstein, "Presidential Subdelegation of Administrative Authority in War-time," *George Washington Law Review* 16 (1948); Louis Smith, *American Democracy and Military Power: A Study of Civil Control of the Military Power in the United States* (1951). On the internment of Japanese-Americans, see Peter Irons, *Justice at War* (1983); Peter Irons, ed., *Justice Delayed: The Record of the Japanese American Internment Cases* (1989); Charles Fairman, "The Supreme Court on Military Jurisdiction: Martial Rule in Hawaii and the Yamashita Case," *Harvard Law Review* 59 (1946); Jacobus ten Broek *et al., Prejudice, War and the Constitution: Japanese-American Evacuation and Resettlement* (1954); Roger Daniels, *Concentration Camps U.S.A.: Japanese Americans and World War II* (1971); E. V. Rostow, "The Japanese-American Cases—A Disaster," *Yale Law Journal* 54 (1945). J. Woodford Howard, Jr., "Advocacy in Constitutional Choice: The *Cramer* Treason Case, 1942–1945," *American Bar Foundation Research Journal,* vol. 1986, discusses the law of treason during the war.

XVI. *Civil Liberties and Modern Constitutionalism*

An excellent introduction to modern problems of civil liberties, distinguishing between pluralistic, community-oriented civil liberty in the nineteenth century and centralized, judicially maintained civil liberties in the twentieth century, is John P. Roche, "American Liberty: An Examination of the 'Tradition' of Freedom," in Milton R. Konvitz and Clinton Rossiter, eds., *Aspects of Liberty: Essays Presented to Robert E. Cushman* (1958). Good examples of the libertarian position are provided by Zechariah Chafee, Jr., *Free Speech in the United States* (1941); Alexander Meiklejohn, *Political Freedom: The Constitutional Powers of the People* (1965); O. K. Frankel, *The Supreme Court and Civil Liberties* (1960); Thomas I. Emerson, *Toward a General Theory of the First Amendment* (1966). Valuable recent surveys of civil liberties are Michael Les Benedict, *Civil Rights and Civil Liberties* (1987); Thomas A. Tedford, *Freedom of Speech in the United States* (1985); Lee C. Bollinger, *The Tolerant Society: Freedom of Speech and Extremist Speech in America* (1986).

Civil liberties issues are viewed from a conservative perspective in Walter F. Berns, *Freedom, Virtue and the First Amendment* (1957); Berns, *The First Amendment and the Future of American Democracy* (1976); Robert Nisbet,

The Twilight of Authority (1975). Reliable general accounts reflecting the high value placed on civil liberties protection since the New Deal are Milton R. Konvitz, *Expanding Liberties: Freedom's Gains in Post-War America* (1966); Henry J. Abraham, *Freedom and the Court: Civil Rights and Liberties in the United States* (1967); Samuel Krislov, *The Supreme Court and Political Freedom* (1968); Paul G. Kauper, *Civil Liberties and the Constitution* (1966); Martin Shapiro, *Freedom of Speech: The Supreme Court and Judicial Review* (1966).

The emergence of rights consciousness and the assertion of civil liberties claims in the late nineteenth and early twentieth centuries is described in Alexis J. Anderson, "The Formative Period of First Amendment Theory, 1870–1915," *AJLH* 24 (1980), and David M. Rabban, "The First Amendment and Its Forgotton Years," *Yale Law Journal* 90 (1981). Developments during World War I are examined in Richard Polenberg, *Fighting Faiths: The Abrams Case, the Supreme Court, and Free Speech* (1987); Paul L. Murphy, *World War I and the Origins of Civil Liberties in the United States* (1979); Stephen Vaughn, "First Amendment Liberties and the Committee on Public Information," *AJLH* 23 (1979); Fred D. Ragan, "Justice Oliver Wendell Holmes, Jr., Zechariah Chaffee, Jr., and the Clear and Present Danger Test for Free Speech: The First Year, 1919," *JAH* 58 (1971); Gerald Gunther, "Learned Hand and the Origins of Modern First Amendment Theory: Some Fragments of History," *Stanford Law Review* 27 (1975); Harry N. Scheiber, *The Wilson Administration and Civil Liberties, 1917–1921* (1960). William Preston, Jr., *Aliens and Dissenters: Federal Suppression of Radicals, 1900–1933* (1963), and H. C. Peterson and Gilbert C. Fite, *Opponents of War 1917–1918* (1957), are chronicles of wartime government restrictions.

Paul L. Murphy, *The Meaning of Freedom of Speech: First Amendment Freedoms from Wilson to FDR* (1972), is a thorough examination of civil liberties claims raised principally by radicals, labor protesters, and aliens in the 1920s. Other pertinent accounts are Donald Johnson, *The Challenge to American Freedom: World War I and the Rise of the American Civil Liberties Union* (1963); David B. Tyack, "The Perils of Pluralism: The Background of the Pierce Case," *AHR* 74 (1968); Kenneth B. O'Brien, Jr., "Education, Americanization and the Supreme Court in the 1920s," *American Quarterly* 13 (1961); David Williams, "The Bureau of Investigation and Its Critics: The Origins of Federal Political Surveillance," *JAH* 68 (1981); Robert K. Murray, *Red Scare: A Study in National Hysteria 1919–1920* (1955); Paul L. Murphy, "Communities in Conflict 1919–1930," In Alan Reitman, ed., *The Pulse of Freedom: American Liberties 1920–1970s* (1975). For developments in the 1930s, see Jerold S. Auerbach, "The Depression Decade," in Reitman, ed., *The Pulse of Freedom;* Auerbach, *Labor and Liberty: The LaFollette Committee and the New Deal* (1966); John P. Roche, *The Quest for the Dream: The Development of Civil Rights and Human Relations in Modern America* (1963); Charles H. Martin, *The Angelo Herndon Case and Southern Justice* (1976).

William A. Donohue, *The Politics of the American Civil Liberties Union* (1985), emphasizes the liberal social policy agenda of civil liberties advocates.

The incorporation of the Bill of Rights into the Fourteenth Amendment is treated in an excellent work by Richard C. Cortner, *The Supreme Court and the Second Bill of Rights* (1981). Other valuable studies of this problem are Klaus H. Heberle, "From Gitlow to Near: Judicial 'Amendment' by Absent-Minded Incrementalism," *JP* 34 (1972); Charles Warren, "The New Liberty under the Fourteenth Amendment," *Harvard Law Review* 39 (1926), unique among contemporary reactions for its understanding of the centralizing potential of the incorporation of the First Amendment into the Fourteenth; Charles Fairman, "Does the Fourteenth Amendment Incorporate the Bill of Rights? The Original Understanding," *Stanford Law Review* 2 (1949); Stanley Morrison, "The Judicial Interpretation," *Stanford Law Review* 2 (1949); W. W. Crosskey, "Legislative History and the Constitutional Limitations on State Authority," *University of Chicago Law Review* 22 (1954); Louis Henkin, "Selective Incorporation in the Fourteenth Amendment," *Yale Law Journal* 73 (1963); Robert E. Cushman, "Incorporation: Due Process and the Bill of Rights," *Cornell Law Quarterly* 51 (1966).

The preferred-freedoms doctrine as a key instrument of modern judicial liberalism and civil libertarianism is discussed in general accounts of the post-1937 judiciary and in numerous specialized studies. Alpheus T. Mason, "The Core of Free Government, 1938–40: Mr. Justice Stone and 'Preferred Freedoms,' " *Yale Law Journal* 65 (1956), is a good introduction to the problem. The author of the famous *Carolene Products* footnote, Louis Lusky, law clerk to Justice Stone, comments on its significance in "Minority Rights and the Public Interest," *Yale Law Journal* 52 (1942), and in *By What Right? A Commentary on the Supreme Court's Power to Revise the Constitution* (1975).

The development of libertarian trends in the 1940s and 1950s can be traced in the following works: Charles L. Black, Jr., "Mr. Justice Black, the Supreme Court, and the Bill of Rights," *Harper's Magazine* 222 (1961); Clyde E. Jacobs, *Justice Frankfurter and Civil Liberties* (1961); John P. Frank, "Hugo L. Black: Free Speech and the Declaration of Independence," *University of Illinois Law Forum* (1977); Philip B. Kurland, "Justice Robert H. Jackson—Impact on Civil Rights and Civil Liberties," *University of Illinois Law Forum* 1977 (1977); L. A. Powe, Jr., "Evolution to Absolutism: Justice Douglas and the First Amendment," *Columbia Law Review* 74 (1974); William J. Brennan, "The Supreme Court and the Meiklejohn Interpretation of the First Amendment," *Harvard Law Review* 79 (1965). Learned Hand, *The Bill of Rights* (1958), is a classic critique of preferred-freedoms and clear-and-present-danger libertarianism.

The controversy between liberals and conservatives over balancing in civil liberties cases is well illustrated in Laurent B. Frantz, "The First Amendment in the Balance," *Yale Law Journal* 71 (1962), attacking the balancing test, and Wallace Mendelson, "On the Meaning of the First Amendment: Absolutes in the Balance," *California Law Review* 50 (1962), criticizing the preferred-freedoms idea. Two useful accounts of this problem are C. Herman Pritchett, *Civil Liberties and the Vinson Court* (1954), and Pritchett, *The Political Offender and the Warren Court* (1958). Robert E. Cushman, *Civil Liberties in the United States: A Guide to Current Problems and Experience* (1956), and Walter Gellhorn, *American Rights: The Constitution in Action* (1960), provide a good description of civil liberties law and practice in the 1950s.

Two thoughtful studies of cold war civil liberties issues are Earl Latham, *The Communist Controversy in Washington: From the New Deal to McCarthy* (1966), and Robert A. Horn, *Groups and the Constitution* (1956). Cogent statements of the conservative position on internal security matters are Harry V. Jaffa, "On the Nature of Civil and Religious Liberty," in *Equality and Liberty: Theory and Practice in American Politics* (1965); Willmoore Kendall, *The Conservative Affirmation* (1963); Sidney Hook, *Common Sense and the Fifth Amendment* (1957). The libertarian approach receives forceful expression in Carey McWilliams, *Witch Hunt: The Revival of Heresy* (1950, 1975); Alan Barth, *The Loyalty of Free Man* (1951); Henry Steele Commager, *Freedom, Loyalty, Dissent* (1954). Worthwhile discussions of the loyalty issue also appear in Harold W. Chase, *Security and Liberty: The Problem of Native Communists, 1947–1955* (1955); Thomas I. Cook, *Democratic Rights versus Communist Activity* (1954); Harold M. Hyman, *To Try Men's Souls: Loyalty Tests in American History* (1959).

On the government's internal security regulations, see Eleanor Bontecou, *The Federal Loyalty-Security Program* (1953), containing sober criticism of the policy, and Seth W. Richardson, "The Federal Employee Loyalty Program," *Columbia Law Review* 51 (1951), a defense of the government. Anti-Communist legislation is described in Arthur E. Sutherland, "Freedom and National Security," *Harvard Law Review* 64 (1951); Carl A. Auerbach, "The Communist Control Act of 1954: A Proposed Legal-Political Theory of Free Speech," *University of Chicago Law Review* 30 (1956). Latham, *The Communist Controversy in Washington,* is excellent on congressional investigations. Also pertinent are Carl Beck, *Contempt of Congress: A Study of the Prosecutions Initiated by the Committee on Un-American Activities, 1945–1957* (1955); M. Nelson McGeary, *The Development of Congressional Investigative Power* (1940); Marshall Dimock, *Congressional Investigating Committees* (1929). State internal security efforts are covered in Walter Gellhorn, ed., *The States and Subversion* (1952), and Lawrence Chamberlain, *Loyalty and Legislative Action: A Survey of Activity by the New York Legislature 1919–1949* (1951).

The *Dennis* case provoked numerous analyses, notable among which are Edward S. Corwin, "Bowing Out 'Clear and Present Danger,' " *Notre Dame Lawyer* 27 (1952), and Wallace Mendelson, "Clear and Present Danger: From Schenck to Dennis," *Columbia Law Review* 52 (1952). Later Smith Act and McCarran Act prosecutions are reviewed in Robert Mollan, "Smith Act Prosecutions: The Effect of the Dennis and Yates Decisions," *University of*

Pittsburgh Law Review 26 (1965); Kathleen L. Barber, "The Legal Status of the Communist Party: 1965," *Journal of Public Law* 15 (1966); Frank E. Strong, "Fifty Years of Clear and Present Danger: From Schenck to Brandenburg—and Beyond," *Supreme Court Review 1969* (1970). Two broader accounts of the internal security question are Michael R. Belknap, *Cold War Political Justice: The Smith Act, the Communist Party, and American Civil Liberties* (1977), and Alan D. Harper, *The Politics of Loyalty: The White House and the Communist Issue, 1946–1952* (1969). See also Stanley I. Kutler, *The American Inquisition: Justice and Injustice in the Cold War* (1982).

The following provide good introductions to diverse aspects of civil liberties problems in the 1940s and 1950s: Edgar A. Jones, Jr., "The Right to Picket: Twilight Zone of the Constitution," *University of Pennsylvania Law Review* 102 (1954); Charles L. Black, Jr., "He Cannot But Choose to Hear: The Plight of the Captive Auditor," *Columbia Law Review* 53 (1953); Loren P. Beth, "Group Libel and Free Speech," *Minnesota Law Review* 39 (1955); Loren P. Beth, *The American Theory of Church and State* (1958); David Manwaring, *Render unto Caesar: The Flag Salute Controversy* (1962).

Constitutional questions raised by cold war collective security agreements are studied in Jacob D. Hyman, "Constitutional Aspects of the Covenant," *Law and Contemporary Problems* 14 (1949); M. G. Pausen, "Charter and Constitution: The Human Rights Provisions in American Law," *Vanderbilt Law Review* 4 (1951); Glendon Schubert, "Politics and the Constitution: The Bricker Amendment during 1953," *JP* 16 (1954); Arthur E. Sutherland, "Restricting the Treaty Power," *Harvard Law Review* 65 (1952). Samuel P. Huntington, *The Soldier and the State: The Theory and Politics of Civil-Military Relations* (1957), is pertinent for the study of cold war constitutionalism.

XVII. *The Constitution and Civil Rights*

An excellent study of the civil rights movement in the 1960s is Hugh Davis Graham, *The Civil Rights Era: Origins and Development of National Policy 1960–1972* (1990). Civil rights theory is perceptively analyzed in Aaron Wildavsky, "The 'Reverse Sequence' in Civil Liberties," *The Public Interest* No. 78 (1985). J. R. Pole, *The Pursuit of Equality in American History* (1978), and Terry Eastland and William J. Bennett, *Counting by Race: Equality from the Founding Fathers to Bakke and Weber* (1979), are good general historical accounts of civil rights problems. Other useful surveys are Charles Redenius, *The American Ideal of Equality: From Jefferson's Declaration to the Burger Court* (1981); Milton R. Konvitz, *A Century of Civil Rights* (1961); Robert J. Harris, *The Quest for Equality: The Constitution, Congress, and the Supreme Court* (1960); Jack Greenberg, *Race Relations and American Law* (1959); Derrick A. Bell, Jr., ed. *Race, Racism, and American Law* (1973).

Late-nineteenth-century civil rights issues are discussed in Charles A.

Lofgren, *The Plessy Case: A Legal-Historical Interpretation* (1988); J. Morgan Kousser, *Dead End: The Development of Nineteenth Century Litigation on Racial Discrimination in the Schools* (1986); Stephen J. Riegel, "The Persistent Career of Jim Crow: Lower Federal Courts and the 'Separate but Equal' Doctrine, 1865–1896," *AJLH* 28 (1984); Jonathan Lurie, "The Fourteenth Amendment: Use and Application in Selected State Court Civil Liberties Cases, 1870–1890—A Preliminary Assessment," *AJLH* 28 (1984); Jennifer Roback, "The Political Economy of Segregation: The Case of Segregated Streetcars," *Journal of Economic History* 46 (1986); Jennifer Roback, "Southern Labor Law in the Jim Crow Era: Exploitative or Competitive?" *University of Chicago Law Review* 51 (1984). The following works treat civil rights issues in the first half of the twentieth century: Mark V. Tushnet, *The NAACP's Legal Strategy Against Segregated Education 1925–1950* (1987); Genna Rae McNeil, *Groundwork: Charles Hamilton Houston and the Struggle for Civil Right* (1983); Catherine A. Barnes, *Journey from Jim Crow: The Desegregation of Southern Transit* (1983); Harvard Sitkoff, *A New Deal for Blacks: The Emergence of Civil Rights as a National Issue* (1978); David M. Bixby, "The Roosevelt Court, Democratic Ideology, and Minority Rights: Another Look at *United States v. Classic,*" *Yale Law Journal* 90 (1981); Roger L. Rice, "Residential Segregation by Law, 1910–1917," *JSH* 34 (1968); Daniel T. Kelleher, "The Case of Lloyd Lionel Gaines: The Demise of the 'Separate-but-Equal' Doctrine," *JNH* 56 (1971); Daniel A. Novak, *The Wheel of Servitude: Black Forced Labor after Slavery* (1978); Pete Daniel, *The Shadow of Slavery: Peonage in the South, 1901–1969* (1972); Robert L. Zangrando, *The NAACP Crusade against Lynching, 1909–1950* (1980); Clement E. Vose, *Caucasians Only: The Supreme Court, the N.A.A.C.P. and the Restrictive Covenant Cases* (1959); Donald R. McCoy and Richard T. Ruetten, *Quest and Response: Minority Rights and the Truman Administration* (1973); Richard Dalfiume, *Desegregation of the U.S. Armed Forces: Fighting on Two Fronts, 1939–1953* (1969); Randall W. Bland, *Private Pressure on Public Law: The Legal Career of Justice Thurgood Marshall* (1973); Mary F. Berry, *Black Resistance/White Law: A History of Constitutional Racism in America* (1971).

A good contemporary account of the school desegregation problem on the eve of *Brown* v. *Board of Education* is John P. Roche, "Education, Segregation and the Supreme Court—A Political Analysis," *University of Pennsylvania Law Review* 99 (1951). Richard Kluger, *Simple Justice: The History of Brown v. Board of Education and Black America's Struggle for Equality* (1975), is an exhaustive narrative of the *Brown* case. The best analysis of the actual shaping of the decision is Dennis Hutchinson, "Unanimity and Desegregation: Decision-making in the Supreme Court, 1948–1958," *Georgetown Law Journal* 68 (1979). See also Alfred H. Kelly, "The School Desegregation Case," in John Garraty, ed., *Quarrels That Have Shaped the Constitution* (1964), providing an inside view of the preparation of the argument against segregation.

A number of works have analyzed Chief Justice Warren's opinion from a jurisprudential standpoint. See in particular Charles L. Black, Jr., "The Lawfulness of the Segregation Decisions," *Yale Law Journal* 69 (1960); Ira M. Heyman, "The Chief Justice, Racial Segregation and Friendly Critics," *California Law Review* 49 (1961); Morris D. Forposch, "The Desegregation Opinion Revisited: Legal or Sociological," *Vanderbilt Law Review* 21 (1967); Morton J. Horwitz, "The Jurisprudence of *Brown* and the Dilemmas of Liberalism," *Harvard Civil Rights-Civil Liberties Law Review* 14 (1979). The southern reaction to the *Brown* decision is described in Michael R. Belknap, *Federal Law and Southern Order: Racial Violence and Constitutional Conflict in the Post-Brown South* (1987); Raymond Wolters, *The Burden of Brown: Thirty Years of School Desegregation* (1984); Tony Freyer, *The Little Rock Crisis: A Constitutional Intrepretation* (1984); James W. Ely, Jr., *The Crisis of Conservative Virginia: The Byrd Organization and the Politics of Massive Resistance* (1976); Mary L. Dudziak, "The Limits of Good Faith: Desegregation in Topeka, Kansas, 1950–1956," *Law and History Review* 5 (1987); Numan v. Bartley, *The Rise of Massive Resistance: Race and Politics in the South during the 1950s* (1969); Neil R. McMillen, *The Citizens Council: Organized Resistance to the Second Reconstruction, 1954–1964* (1971). Albert P. Blaustein and C. C. Ferguson, Jr., *Desegregation and the Law: The Meaning and Effect of the School Segregation Cases,* rev. ed. (1962), is an early study of the implications of the decision.

Surveys of the progress of school desegregation reveal the shift to integration and affirmative action as a legal remedy. Pertinent works include John Kaplan, "Segregation Litigation and the Schools," *Northwestern University Law Review* 58–59 (1963–64); Harrell R. Rodgers, Jr., "The Supreme Court and School Desegregation: Twenty Years Later," *PSQ* 89 (1975); Charles S. Bullock III and Harrell R. Rodgers, Jr., "Coercion to Compliance: Southern School Districts and School Desegregation Guidelines," *JP* 38 (1976); Symposium, "School Desegregation: Lessons of the First Twenty-five Years," *Law and Contemporary Problems* 42 (1978).

J. Harvie Wilkinson III, *From Brown to Bakke: The Supreme Court and School Integration, 1954–1978* (1979), and Lino Graglia, *Disaster by Decree: The Supreme Court Decisions on Race and the Schools* (1976), are detailed accounts which criticize the judicial shift to result-oriented integration and affirmative-action policies based on racial considerations. Also critical are Richard A. Posner, "The De Funis Case and the Constitutionality of Preferential Treatment of Racial Minorities," *Supreme Court Review 1974* (1975); Robert G. Dixon, "The Supreme Court and Equality: Legislative Classifications, Desegregation, and Reverse Discrimination," *Cornell Law Review* 62 (1977); William Van Alstyne, "Rites of Passage: Race, the Supreme Court, and the Constitution," *University of Chicago Law Review* 46 (1978); Ralph A. Rossum, "Ameliorative Racial Reference and the Fourteenth Amendment: Some Constitutional Problems," *JP* 38 (1976).

The case for result-oriented affirmative-action policies based on racial group classification is made in Owen Fiss, "The Fate of an Idea Whose Time Has Come: Anti-Discrimination Law in the Second Decade after *Brown v. Board of Education,*" *University of Chicago Law Review* 41 (1974); Fiss, "Groups and the Equal Protection Clause," *Philosophy and Public Affairs* 5 (1976); John Hart Ely, "The Constitutionality of Reverse Racial Discrimination," *University of Chicago Law Review* 41 (1974); Norman Vieira, "Racial Imbalance, Black Separatism, and Permissible Classification by Race," *Michigan Law Review* 67, (1969); William H. Hastie, "Affirmative Action in Vindicating Civil Rights," *University of Illinois Law Forum* 1975 (1975); J. Skelly Wright, "Color-Blind Theories and Color-Conscious Remedies," *University of Chicago Law Review* 47 (1980); Boris I. Bittker, *The Case for Black Reparations* (1973).

The busing problem in school desegregation is treated in Gary Orfield, *Must We Bus? Segregated Schools and National Policy* (1978). On the preferential admissions cases, see Symposium, "Regents of the University of California v. Bakke," *California Law Review* 67 (1979); Guido Calabresi, "Bakke as Pseudo-Tragedy," *Catholic University Law Review* 28 (1979); Allen P. Sindler, *Bakke, De Funis, and Minority Admissions: The Quest for Equal Opportunity* (1978); Robert M. O'Neil, *Discriminating against Discrimination: Preferential Admissions and the De Funis Case* (1975). William H. Chafe, *Civilities and Civil Rights: Greensboro, North Carolina, and the Black Struggle for Freedom* (1980), is an account of the sit-in movement. Donald B. King and Charles W. Quick, eds., *Legal Aspects of the Civil Rights Movement* (1965), is a useful survey of civil rights law in the mid-1960s.

Questions concerning voting and other political rights are examined in Abigail M. Thernstrom, *Whose Votes Count? Affirmative Action and Minority Voting Rights* (1987); Timothy G. O'Rourke, "Racial Polarization in Vote Dilution Cases Under Section 2 of the Voting Rights Act: The Impact of *Thornburg v. Gingles,*" *Journal of Law and Politics* 3 (1986); Philip L. Martin, "The Quest for Racial Representation in Legislative Apportionment," *Howard Law Journal* 21 (1978); Ward Y. Elliott, *The Rise of Guardian Democracy: The Supreme Court's Role in Voting Rights Disputes, 1845–1969* (1974); Darlene Clark Hine, *Black Victory: The Rise and Fall of the White Primary in Texas* (1979); Richard Claude, *The Supreme Court and the Electoral Process* (1970).

Employment discrimination is discussed in Herbert Hill, *Black Labor and the American Legal System,* (1977); Michael I. Sovern, *Legal Restraints on Racial Discrimination in Employment* (1966); Andrea H. Beller, "The Economics of Enforcement of an Antidiscrimination Law: Title VII of the Civil Rights Act of 1964," *Journal of Law and Economics* 21 (1978). The problem of affirmative action is analyzed in Bernard D. Meltzer, "The *Weber* Case: The Judicial Abrogation of the Antidiscrimination Standard in Employment," *University of Chicago Law Review* 47 (1980); William E. Boyd, "Affirmative Action in Employment—The *Weber* Decision," *Iowa Law Review* 66 (1980); Nathan Glazer, *Affirmative Discrimination: Ethnic Inequality and Public Pol-*

icy (1975); Thomas Sowell, *Civil Rights: Myth or Reality?* (1984); Alan H. Goldman, *Justice and Reverse Discrimination* (1979); Robert K. Fullinwider, *The Reverse Discrimination Controversy: A Moral and Legal Analysis* (1980); Ralph A. Rossum, "Plessy, Brown, and the Reverse Discrimination Cases," *American Behavioral Scientist* 28 (1985); Harvey C. Mansfield, Jr., "The Underhandedness of Affirmative Action," *National Review* 36 (1984); Michael W. Combs and John Gruhl, eds., *Affirmative Action: Theory, Analysis, and Prospects* (1986).

The state-action-private-action distinction in civil rights litigation is analyzed in Leslie F. Goldstein, "Death and Transfiguratiofn of the State Action Doctrine—*Moose Lodge v. Irvis* to *Runyon v. McCrary,*" *Hastings Constitutional Law Quarterly* 4 (1977); Erwin Chemerinsky, "Rethinking State Action," *Northwestern University Law Review* 80 (1985); Charles L. Black, Jr., "The Constitution and Public Power," *Yale Review* 52 (1962); Laurent B. Frantz, "Congressional Power to Enforce the Fourteenth Amendment against Private Acts," *Yale Law Journal* 73 (1964).

The use of Reconstruction era statutes in modern civil rights litigation is dealt with in Peter W. Low and John Calvin Jeffries, Jr., *Civil Rights Actions: Section 1983 and Related Statutes* (1988); James McClellan, "The New Liberty of Contract Under the Thirteenth Amendment: The Case Against *Runyon v. McCrary,*" *Benchmark* 3 (1987); Gerhard Casper, "Jones v. Mayer: Clio, Bemused and Confused Muse," *Supreme Court Review 1968* (1969).

There are thoughtful discussions of civil rights law in Derrick A. Bell, Jr., "Brown v. Board of Education and the Interests-Convergence Dilemma," *Harvard Law Review* 93 (1980); Earlean M. McCarrick, "Equality v. Liberty: An Unresolved Constitutional Conflict," *Polity* 10 (1978); Charles L. Black, Jr., "Civil Rights in Times of Economic Stress—Jurisprudential and Philosophic Aspects," *University of Illinois Law Forum* (1976); Walter Berns, "Racial Discrimination and the Limits of Judicial Remedy," in Robert Goldwin, ed., *100 Years of Emancipation* (1963).

XVIII. *Constitutional Law and Modern Liberalism: The Warren Era*

There has been controversy since the Court-packing fight of 1937 over the nature and function of judicial review. In the 1950s and 1960s the activist position was represented in a number of works, chief among them Eugene V. Rostow, "The Democratic Character of Judicial Review," *Harvard Law Review* 66 (1952); Alpheus T. Mason, "The Supreme Court, Temple and Forum." *Yale Law Review* 58 (1959); Charles L. Black, Jr., *The People and the Court: Judicial Review in a Democracy* (1960); Arthur S. Miller and Ronald F. Howell, "The Myth of Neutrality in Constitutional Adjudication," *University of Chicago Law Review* 27 (1960); J. Skelly Wright, "The Role of the Supreme Court in a Democratic Society—Judicial Activism or Restraint?" *Cornell Law Quarterly* 53 (1968). The judicial restraint model is described in

Felix Frankfurter, "Some Reflections on the Reading of Statutes," *Columbia Law Review* 47 (1947); Learned Hand, *The Bill of Rights* (1958); Herbert Wechsler, "Toward Neutral Principles of Constitutional Law," *Harvard Law Review* 73 (1959); Alexander M. Bickel, *The Least Dangerous Branch: The Supreme Court at the Bar of Politics* (1962); Wallace Mendelson, *Black and Frankfurter: Conflict in the Court* (1961).

The neorealist approach to judicial review is seen in Martin Shapiro, *Law and Politics in the Supreme Court: New Approaches to Political Jurisprudence* (1964); Shapiro, *Freedom of Speech: The Supreme Court and Judicial Review* (1966); Glendon A. Schubert, *Judicial Policy Making* (1965, 1974); Schubert, *The Judicial Mind: The Attitudes and Ideologies of Supreme Court Justices, 1946–1963* (1965). George Braden, "The Search for Objectivity in Constitutional Law," *Yale Law Journal* 57 (1948), anticipates this point of view in a perceptive commentary on Justices Black, Frankfurter, and Stone.

Illuminating surveys of the post–New Deal judiciary are offered by G. Edward White, *The American Judicial Tradition: Profiles of Leading American Judges* (1988); Paul L. Murphy, *The Constitution in the Twentieth Century* (1986); Martin M. Shapiro, "The Supreme Court from Warren to Burger," in Anthony King, ed., *The New American Political System* (1978); Shapiro, "The Court and Economic Rights," in M. J. Harmon, ed., *Essays on the Constitution of the United States* (1978). There are perceptive accounts in Sanford B. Gabin, *Judicial Review and the Reasonable Doubt Test* (1980); Alexander M. Bickel, *The Supreme Court and the Idea of Progress* (1970); Bickel, *Politics and the Warren Court* (1965); Philip B. Kurland, *Politics, the Constitution and The Warren Court* (1970); Robert G. McCloskey, *The Modern Supreme Court* (1972); Archibald Cox, *The Warren Court: Constitutional Decision as an Instrument of Social Reform* (1968); Richard A. Maidment, "Policy in Search of Law: The Warren Court from *Brown* to *Miranda,*" *Journal of American Studies* 9 (1975).

Justices Black and Frankfurter have been the most popular subjects of study among individual justices. The best works on Black are James J. Magee, *Mr. Justice Black: Absolutist on the Court* (1980); Gerald T. Dunne, *Hugo Black and the Judicial Revolution* (1977); Sylvia Snowiss, "The Legacy of Justice Black," *Supreme Court Review 1973* (1974); Tinsley Yarbrough, "Mr. Justice Black and Legal Positivism," *Virginia Law Review* 57 (1971); Charles A. Reich, "Mr. Justice Black and the Living Constitution," *Harvard Law Review* 76 (1963). Frankfurter's career is analyzed in Michael E. Parrish, *Felix Frankfurter and His Times: The Reform Years* (1982); H. N. Hirsch, *The Enigma of Felix Frankfurter* (1981); Gary Jacobsohn, "Felix Frankfurter and the Ambiguities of Judicial Statesmanship," *New York University Law Review* 49 (1974); Joel B. Grossman, "Role-Playing and the Analysis of Judicial Behavior: The Case of Mr. Justice Frankfurter," *Journal of Public Law* 11 (1962); Louis L. Jaffe, "The Judicial Universe of Mr. Justice Frankfurter," *Harvard Law Review* 62 (1949).

Other worthwhile accounts dealing with the post-1937 judiciary include

Bruce Allen Murphy, *Fortas: The Rise and Ruin of a Supreme Court Justice* (1988); James F. Simon, *Independent Journey: The Life of William O. Douglas* (1980); G. Edward White, *Earl Warren: A Public Life* (1982); Bernard Schwartz, *Super Chief: Earl Warren and His Supreme Court* (1983); Donald Roper, "The Jurisprudence of Arthur Goldberg: A Commentary," *Harvard Civil Rights-Civil Liberties Law Review* 8 (1973); Norman Redlich, "A Black-Harlan Dialogue on Due Process and Equal Protection: Overheard in Heaven and Dedicated to Robert M. McKay," *New York University Law Review* 50 (1975); J. Harvie Wilkinson III, "Justice John M. Harlan and the Values of Federalism," *Virginia Law Review* 57 (1971); Norman Dorsen, "The Second Mr. Justice Harlan: A Constitutional Conservative," *New York University Law Review* 44 (1969); John P. Frank, "Fred Vinson and the Chief Justiceship," *University of Chicago Law Review* 21 (1954); Glendon Schubert, *Dispassionate Justice: A Synthesis of the Judicial Opinions of Robert H. Jackson* (1969).

Two significant assessments of judicial power in the post-New Deal period are Robert A. Dahl, "Decision-Making in a Democracy: The Supreme Court as a National Policy-Maker," *Journal of Public Law* 6 (1958), and Willard Hurst, "Review and the Distribution of National Power," in Edmond Cahn, ed., *Supreme Court and Supreme Law* (1954). As the Supreme Court attempted to alter local institutions in the 1960s, a number of compliance studies were undertaken that cast light on judicial power. See, for example, Theodore L. Becker and Malcolm M. Feeley, eds., *The Impact of Supreme Court Decisions* (1973); Stephen L. Wasby, *The Impact of the United States Supreme Court: Some Perspectives* (1970); Richard M. Johnson, *The Dynamics of Compliance: Supreme Court Decision-Making from a New Perspective* (1967).

The legal literature on specific constitutional problems in the 1950s and 1960s is voluminous, but the key developments can be explored in a number of seminal studies. On reapportionment see Gordon E. Baker, *The Reapportionment Revolution* (1967); Robert G. Dixon, Jr., "The Warren Court Crusade for the Holy Grail of 'One Man-*One Vote*,' " *Supreme Court Review 1969* (1970); Dixon, *Democratic Representation: Reapportionment in Law and Politics* (1968); Richard C. Cortner, *The Apportionment Cases* (1970); Robert McKay, *Reapportionment: The Law and Politics of Equal Representation* (1964).

The school-prayer decisions are dealt with in John Herbert Laubach, *School Prayers: Congress, the Courts, and the Public* (1969); Charles E. Rice, *The Supreme Court and Public Prayer: The Need for Restraint* (1964); Paul G. Kauper, "Prayer, Public Schools and the Supreme Court," *Michigan Law Review* 61 (1963); Leo Pfeffer, "Court, Constitution, and Prayer," *Rutgers Law Review* 16 (1962). William K. Muir, Jr., *Prayer in the Public Schools: Law and Attitude Change* (1967), and Kenneth M. Dolbeare and Phillip E. Hammond, *The School Prayer Decisions: From Court Policy to Local Practice* (1971), are impact studies of Supreme Court decisions in this area.

In the field of criminal procedure, Richard C. Cortner, *The Supreme*

Court and the Second Bill of Rights (1981), is an excellent account of the application of federal constitutional requirements to the states under the due-process clause of the Fourteenth Amendment. Also valuable on this question are Adam C. Breckenridge, *Congress against the Court* (1970), a study of the legislative reaction to judicial decisions in criminal procedure; Fred P. Graham, *The Due Process Revolution: The Warren Court's Impact on Criminal Law* (1970); A. Kenneth Pye, "The Warren Court and Criminal Procedure," *Michigan Law Review* 67 (1968); Henry J. Friendly, "The Bill of Rights as a Code of Criminal Procedure," *California Law Review* 53 (1965); Jay Sigler, *Double Jeopardy: The Development of a Legal and Social Policy* (1969); Phillip Johnson, "Retroactivity in Retrospect," *California Law Review* 56 (1968).

Alfred H. Kelly, "Constitutional Liberty and the Law of Libel: A Historian's View," *AHR* 74 (1968), is a good summary of the civil libel question in its historical and contemporary aspects. Other worthwhile discussions of free-speech issues are Harry Kalven, Jr., " 'Uninhibited, Robust, and Wide-Open'—a Note on Free Speech and the Warren Court," *Michigan Law Review* 67 (1968); Donald Meiklejohn, "Public Speech and the First Amendment," *Georgetown Law Journal* 55 (1966); Arthur L. Barney, "Libel and the First Amendment—A New Constitutional Privilege," *Virginia Law Review* 51 (1965). Control of pornography is discussed in Harry M. Clor, *Obscenity and Public Morality: Censorship in a Liberal Society* (1969); Richard H. Kuh, *Foolish Figleaves? Pornography in—and out of—Court* (1969); C. Peter Magrath, "The Obscenity Cases: The Grapes of Roth," *Supreme Court Review 1966* (1967); Richard Funston, "Pornography and Politics: The Court, the Constitution, and the Commission," *Western Pol. Q.* 24 (1971).

The right to privacy receives broad examination in Alan F. Westin, *Privacy and Freedom* (1967); Adam C. Breckenridge, *The Right to Privacy* (1970); William M. Beaney, "The Constitutional Right to Privacy in the Supreme Court," *Supreme Court Review 1962* (1963). The birth-control decision is analyzed in Robert G. Dixon, "The Griswold Penumbra: Constitutional Charter for an Expanded Law of Privacy?" *Michigan Law Review* 64 (1965); William M. Beaney, "The Griswold Case and the Expanded Right to Privacy," *Wisconsin Law Review* 1966.

The expansion of equal-protection law as a basic corollary of positive government is forecast in a seminal article by Joseph Tussman and Jacobus ten Broek, "The Equal Protection of the Laws," *California Law Review* 37 (1949). For later development of the equal-protection idea, see Gerald Gunther, "Foreword: In Search of Evolving Doctrine on a Changing Court: A Model for a Newer Equal Protection," *Harvard Law Review* 86 (1972); Philip B. Kurland, "Egalitarianism and the Warren Court," *Michigan Law Review* 68 (1970); Frank I. Michelman, "Foreword: On Protecting the Poor through the Fourteenth Amendment," *Harvard Law Review* 83 (1969). Charles Reich, "The New Property," *Yale Law Journal* 73 (1964), is an important argument for a redefinition of welfare state benefits as constitutionally protected property. See also "Symposium: Law of the Poor," *California Law Review* 54 (1966). Robert M. O'Neil, *The Price of Dependency: Civil Liberties in the Welfare State* (1970), is a comprehensive study of this new area of constitutional law. The expanded rights of government employees in the 1960s are described in David H. Rosenbloom, *Federal Service and the Constitution: The Development of the Public Employment Relationship* (1971), and William W. Van Alstyne, "The Demise of the Right-Privilege Distinction in Constitutional Law," *Harvard Law Review* 81 (1968).

XIX. *The Liberal Regulatory State and the Modern Presidency: 1945–1980*

Samuel P. Huntington, *American Politics: The Promise of Disharmony* (1981), is a penetrating analysis of recent constitutional politics that emphasizes the conflict between ideals and institutions in American political culture. Theodore J. Lowi, *The End of Liberalism: Ideology, Policy, and the Crisis of Public Authority* (1969; rev. ed., 1979), describes the delegation of governmental power to private interest groups and offers a sharp critique of this liberal-pluralist method of government. James L. Sundquist, *Politics and Policy: The Eisenhower, Kennedy, and Johnson Years* (1968), and A. James Reichley, *Conservatives in an Age of Change: The Nixon and Ford Administrations* (1981), provide historical accounts of the major public policy questions that have dominated constitutional politics in the past three decades.

The relationship between private groups and regulatory agencies that forms the basis of the liberal-pluralist political economy is discussed in Earl Latham, "The Group Basis of Politics: Notes for a Theory," *APSR* 46 (1952); Peter H. Odegard, "A Group Basis of Politics: A New Name for an Ancient Myth," *Western Pol. Q.* 20 (1958); Norton E. Long, "Bureaucracy and Constitutionalism," *APSR* 46 (1952); Wolfgang G. Friedmann, "Corporate Power, Government by Private Groups, and the Law," *Columbia Law Review* 57 (1957); Grant McConnell, *Private Power and American Democracy* (1966). Andrew Shonfield, *Modern Capitalism* (1965), Michael D. Regan, *The Managed Economy* (1963), and Eugene V. Rostow, *Planning for Freedom: The Public Law of American Capitalism* (1959), focus on the problem of public and private power in the post-New Deal political economy.

In criticizing the delegation of power to private groups through the process of administrative rule making, Lowi, *The End of Liberalism,* stimulated a reconsideration of the principle of nondelegation of legislative power. See in this connection Sotirios A. Barber, *The Constitution and the Delegation of Congressional Power* (1975); James O. Freedman, "Delegation of Power and Institutional Competence," *University of Chicago Law Review* 43 (1975); Carl McGowan, "Congress, Court, and Control of Delegated Power," *Columbia*

Law Review 77 (1977). Lowi's recommendation for a return to the *Schechter* rule provides the focus for Richard F. Bensel, "Creating the Statutory State: The Implications of a Rule of Law Standard in American Politics," *APSR* 74 (1980), and Robert C. Grady, "Interest-Group Liberalism and Juridical Democracy: Two Theses in Search of Legitimacy," *American Politics Quarterly* 6 (1978).

There are perceptive observations about the modern regulatory state in John A. Rohr, *To Run A Constitution: The Legitimacy of the Administrative State* (1986); James O. Freedman, *Crisis and Legitimacy: The Administrative Process and American Government* (1978); James Q. Wilson, "The Rise of the Bureaucratic State," *Public Interest* no. 41 (1975); Hugh Heclo, "Issue Networks and the Executive Establishment," in Anthony King, ed., *The New American Political System* (1978); Richard B. Stewart, "The Reformation of American Administrative Law," *Harvard Law Review* 88 (1975); Vincent Ostrum, *The Intellectual Crisis in American Public Administration* (1974). Ernest Gellhorn and Glen O. Robinson, "Rulemaking 'Due Process': An Inconclusive Dialogue," *University of Chicago Law Review* 48 (1981), considers the ways in which administrative agencies have adapted to judicial standards and methods of operation. Kenneth W. Clarkson and Timothy J. Muris, eds., *The Federal Trade Commission since 1970* (1981), reviews the revitalization of one of the more controversial regulatory agencies in recent years. The position of trade unions in the liberal pluralist state is the subjec of Katherine Van Wezel Stone, "The Post-War Paradigm in American Labor Law," *Yale Law Journal* 90 (1981).

Historical surveys of the presidential office are Joseph M. Bessette and Jeffrey Tulis, *The Presidency in the Constitutional Order* (1981); Arthur M. Schlesinger, Jr., *The Imperial Presidency* (1973), and Fred I. Greenstein, "The Modern Presidency," in Anthony King, ed., *The New American Political System* (1978). Scholarly views toward the presidency have changed significantly in the past decade and a half. Liberal approval of a powerful presidency is seen in Harold Laski, *The American Presidency: An Interpretation* (1940); Pendleton Herring, *Presidential Leadership* (1940); Clinton Rossiter, *Constitutional Dictatorship: Crisis Government in the Modern Democracies* (1948); Rossiter, *The American Presidency* (1956); Walter Lippmann, *Essays in the Public Philosophy* (1955); Richard Neustadt, *Presidential Power: The Politics of Leadership* (1956); Louis W. Koenig, *The Chief Executive* (1964); James MacGregor Burns, *Presidential Government: The Crucible of Leadership* (1965).

There were dissenters to the liberal theory of presidential power, notably Caleb Perry Patterson, *Presidential Government in the United States: The Unwritten Constitution* (1947); Edward S. Corwin, *The President: Office and Powers* (1940, 1957); and Herman Finer, *The Presidency: Crisis and Regeneration* (1960), who argued that far too much was demanded of the chief executive. In reaction to the Vietnam War and the Watergate affair, criticism of presidential power and emphasis on the limitations of the office dominated scholarly analyses. See Aaron Wildavsky, "The Past and Future Presidency," *Public Interest* no. 41 (1975); Norton Long, "Reflections on Presidential Power," *Public Administrative Review* 29 (1969); James David Barber, *The Presidential Character* (1972); Charles M. Hardin, *Presidential Power and Accountability* (1974); Thomas E. Cronin, *The State of the Presidency* (1975); Richard M. Pious, *The American Presidency* (1979); Hugh Heclo and Lester M. Salamon, eds., *The Illusion of Presidential Government* (1981).

The president's relationship with the bureaucracy and the problem of executive management are discussed in Larry Berman, *The Office of Management and Budget and the Presidency, 1921–1979* (1979); Louis Fisher and Ronald C. Moe, "Presidential Reorganization Authority: Is It Worth the Cost?" *PSQ* 96 (1981); Harold H. Bruff, "Presidential Power and Administrative Rulemaking," *Yale Law Journal* 88 (1979); Barry Dean Karl, "Executive Reorganization and Presidential Power," *Supreme Court Review 1977* (1978); Harvey C. Mansfield, "Federal Executive Reorganization: Thirty Years Experience," *Public Administrative Review* 29 (1969). Peri E. Arnold, "The First Hoover Commission and the Managerial Presidency," *JP* 38 (1976), shows how conservative critics of FDR were reconciled to a modern conception of executive control in the Truman period. Diverse aspects of recent presidential history are covered in Richard Fenno, *The President's Cabinet* (1959); Clinton Rossiter, *The Supreme Court and the Commander-in-Chief* (1951); Glendon Schubert, *The Presidency in the Courts* (1957); Richard P. Longaker, *The Presidency and Individual Liberties* (1961).

Among works dealing with individual presidents, the following have value for constitutional history: Maeva Marcus, *Truman and the Steel Seizure Case: The Limits of Presidential Power* (1977); Francis H. Heller, ed., *The Truman White House: The Administration of the Presidency 1945–1953* (1980); Fred I. Greenstein, "Eisenhower as an Activist President: A Look at New Evidence," *PSQ* 94 (1979–80); Arthur M. Schlesinger, Jr., *A Thousand Days: John F. Kennedy in the White House* (1965); Henry Fairlie, *The Kennedy Promise: The Politics of Expectation* (1973); Doris Kearns, *Lyndon Johnson and the American Dream* (1976); Garry Wills, *Nixon Antagonistes: The Crisis of the Self-Made Man* (1970).

A number of works illustrate the disenchantment with modern liberal constitutionalism that occurred in the 1960s. See, for example, Jack L. Walker, "A Critique of the Elitist Theory of Democracy," *APSR* 60 (1966); Kirk Thompson, "Constitutional Theory and Political Action," *JP* 31 (1969); William E. Connolly, ed., *The Bias of Pluralism* (1969); Herman Belz, "New Left Reverberations in the Academy: The Anti-Pluralist Critique of Constitutionalism," *Review of Politics* 36 (1974). Still the best general analysis of radical attitudes is Ronald Berman, *America in the Sixties: An Intellectual History* (1968), while Anthony M. Platt, *The Politics of the Riot Commissions, 1917–1970* (1971), provides a good view of the public disorders of the late 1960s and the government's response to them. There are perceptive observations on the riots and protest movements in David Potter, "Changing Pattern of Social Cohesion and the Crisis of Law under a System of Government by Consent," in Eugene V. Rostow, ed., *Is Law Dead?* (1971); Walter Dean Burnham, "Crisis of American Political Legitimacy," *Society* 10 (1972); Samuel P. Huntington, "Paradigms of American Politics: Beyond the One, the Two, and the Many," *PSQ* 89 (1974); Gerald Garvey, *Constitutional Bricolage* (1971); Samuel Beer, "In Search of A New Public Philosophy," in A. King, ed., *The New American Political System* (1978).

Rostow, ed., *Is Law Dead?*, contains essays on civil disobedience and the protest movements, for which see also Wilson Carey McWilliams, "Civil Disobedience and Contemporary Constitutionalism: The American Case," *Comparative Politics* 1 (1969); Hannah Arendt, "Civil Disobedience," in *Crises of the Republic* (1972); Paul F. Power, "On Civil Disobedience in Recent American Democratic Thought," *APSR* 64 (1970). John T. Elliff, *Crime, Dissent, and the Attorney General: The Justice Department in the 1960s* (1971), is a narrative of the riots and protests.

The most pertinent background for the Watergate affair from a constitutional standpoint is the expansion of presidential power in foreign affairs and for national security purposes. On these matters, see Francis D. Wormuth and Edward B. Firmage, *To Chain the Dogs of War: The War Power of Congress in History and Law* (1989); W. Taylor Reveley III, *War Powers of the President and Congress: Who Holds the Arrows and Olive Branch?* (1981); Louis Henkin, *Foreign Affairs and the Constitution* (1972); John Norton Moore, *Law and the Indo-China War* (1972); Charles A. Lofgren, *"United States v. Curtiss-Wright Export Corporation:* An Historical Assessment," *Yale Law Journal* 83 (1973). Domestic political intelligence operations preceding President Nixon are the focus of Richard W. Steele, "Franklin D. Roosevelt and His Foreign Policy Critics," *PSQ* 94 (1979); Barton J. Bernstein, "The Road to Watergate and Beyond: The Growth and Abuse of Executive Power since 1940," *Law and Contemporary Problems* 40 (1976); Athan Theoharis, *Spying on Americans: Political Surveillance from Hoover to the Houston Plan* (1978).

Concerning the impoundment question, see Louis Fisher, *Presidential Spending Power* (1975); Abner J. Mikva and Michael Hertz, "Impoundment of Funds—the Courts, the Congress and the President: A Constitutional Triangle," *Northwestern University Law Review* 69 (1974); Warren Archer, "Presidential Impoundment of Funds," *University of Chicago Law Review* 40 (1973). John W. Dumbrell and John D. Lees, "Presidential Pocket-Veto Power: A Constitutional Anachronism?" *Political Studies* 28 (1980), is a good analysis of that issue. Valuable studies of executive privilege are Raoul Berger, *Executive Privilege: A Constitutional Myth* (1974); Archibald Cox, "Executive Privilege," *University of Pennsylvania Law Review* 122 (1974); Paul Freund, "Foreword: On Presidential Privilege," *Harvard Law Review* 88 (1974).

There are perceptive analyses of the Watergate affair and its constitutional significance in Stanley I. Kutler, *The Wars of Watergate: The Last Crisis of Richard Nixon* (1990); Nelson W. Polsby, *Political Promises: Essays and Commentary on American Politics* (1974); Alexander M. Bickel, "Watergate and the Legal Order," *Commentary* 57 (1974); Philip S. Kurland, *Watergate and the Constitution* (1978); James David Barber, "Nixon's Brush with Tyranny," *PSQ* 92 (1977–78); Paul F. Kress, "Of Action and Virtue: Notes on the Presidency, Watergate, and Liberal Society," *Polity* 10 (1978); Arthur J. Vidrich, "Political Legitimacy in Bureaucratic Society: An Analysis of Watergate," *Social Research* 42 (1975); Sanford Levinson, "The Specious Morality of the Law," *Harper's Magazine* 254 (1977). See also Ronald E. Pynn, ed., *Watergate and the American Political Process* (1975); Frederick C. Mosher *et al., Watergate: Implications for Responsible Government* (1974); Symposium, "American Political Institutions after Watergate—a Discussion," *PSQ* 89 (1974–75).

Several able works on impeachment predated the inquiry directed at President Nixon. They include Raoul Berger, *Impeachment: The Constitutional Problems* (1973); Charles L. Black, Jr., *Impeachment: A Handbook* (1974); Arthur Bestor, "Impeachment," *Washington Law Review* 49 (1973), a review of Berger's book. John R. Labovitz, *Presidential Impeachment* (1978), is an excellent recent study. Other worthwhile observations on impeachment and Watergate are found in Bernard Schwartz, "Bad Presidents Make Hard Law: Richard M. Nixon in the Supreme Court," *Rutgers Law Review* 31 (1977); David W. Dennis, "Impeachment Revisited," *Indiana Law Review* 9 (1976), the reflections of a Republican Congressman; Louis H. Pollak, "The Constitution as an Experiment," *University of Pennsylvania Law Review* 123 (1975); Leon Jaworski, *The Right and the Power: The Prosecution of Watergate* (1976).

The reaction against the imperial presidency can be seen in James L. Sundquist, *The Decline and Resurgence of Congress* (1981); Thomas E. Cronin, "A Resurgent Congress and the Imperial Presidency," *PSQ* 95 (1980); Harvey G. Zeldenstein, "The Reassertion of Congressional Power: New Curbs on the President," *PSQ* 93 (1978); Morris P. Fiorina, *Congress: Keystone of the Washington Establishment* (1977). Positive evaluations of Congress forming a basis for the reassessment of the institution in the 1970s are found in Nelson W. Polsby, "Strengthening Congress in National Policy-Making," *Yale Review* 59 (1970); Polsby, *Congress and the Presidency* (1964); Joseph Harris, *Congressional Control of Administration* (1964); Alfred deGrazia, *Republic in Crisis: Congress against the Executive Force* (1965); Roland Young, *The American Congress* (1958); James Burnham, *Congress and the American Tradition* (1959).

In the 1970s the legislative veto became the focal point of conflict between Congress and the executive and administrative departments and agencies. See John B. Henry II, "The Legislative Veto: In Search of Constitutional Limits," *Harvard Journal on Legislation* 16 (1979); Robert G. Dixon, Jr., "The Congressional Veto and Separation of Powers: The Executive on a Leash?" *North Carolina Law Review* 56 (1978); Harold H. Bruff and Ernest Gellhorn, "Congressional Control of Administrative Regulation: A Study of Legislative Vetoes," *Harvard Law Review* 90 (1977).

Significant changes in election campaign laws and political party organization as a reaction to Watergate are surveyed in Austin Ranney, "The Political Parties: Reform and Decline," in King, ed., *The New American Political System;* Michael J. Malbin, ed., *Parties, Interest Groups, and Campaign Finance Laws* (1980); Harold Leventhal, "Courts and Political Thickets," *Columbia Law Review* 77 (1977). Benjamin R. Civiletti, "Post-Watergate Legislation in Retrospect." *Southwestern Law Journal* 34 (1981), reviews the operation of a variety of reform measures in the 1970s.

XX. *Constitutional Law and the Burger-Rehnquist Court*

Vincent Blasi, ed., *The Burger Court and the Counterrevolution That Wasn't* (1983), and Richard Y. Funston, *Constitutional Counterrevolution? The Warren Court and the Burger Court: Judicial Policy Making in Modern America* (1977), are excellent general accounts which emphasize continuity in the development of constitutional law in the 1970s. Archibald Cox, *The Role of the Supreme Court in American Government* (1976), adopts a similar perspective in analyzing the policy-making activity of the Burger Court. There are good general analyses of the Burger period in Walter Berns, *The First Amendment and the Future of American Democracy* (1976); Robert J. Steamer, "Contemporary Supreme Court Directions in Civil Liberties," *PSQ* 92 (1977); Symposium, "The Burger Court: Reflections of the First Decade," *Law and Contemporary Problems* 43 (1980).

Arguing that the Burger Court departed significantly from Warren Court precedents are Edward V. Heck, "Civil Liberties Voting Patterns in the Burger Court 1975–1978," *Western Pol. Q.* 34 (1981); Robert D. Goldstein, "A *Swann* Song for Remedies: Equitable Relief in the Burger Court," *Harvard Civil Rights—Civil Liberties Law Review* 13 (1978); Alan B. Morrison, "Rights without Remedies: The Burger Court Takes the Federal Courts Out of the Business of Protecting Federal Rights" *Rutgers Law Review* 30 (1977); Tinsley E. Yarbrough, "Litigant Access Doctrine and the Burger Court," *Vanderbilt Law Review* 31 (1978).

There are able general discussion of decisions concerning federalism in A. E. Dick Howard, "The Supreme Court and Federalism," in *The Courts; The Pendulum of Federalism* (1979); Henry P. Monaghan, "The Burger Court and 'Our Federalism,'" *Law and Contemporary Problems* 43 (1980); Neil D. McFeeley, "The Supreme Court and the Federal System: Federalism from Warren to Burger," *Publius* 8 (1978). On federal-state relations under the commerce power, see Bernard Schwartz, "Commerce, the States, and the

Burger Court," *Northwestern University Law Review* 74 (1979), and Earl M. Maltz, "The Burger Court, the Commerce Clause, and the Problem of Differential Treatment," *Indiana Law Journal* 54 (1978–79).

The attitude of the Supreme Court toward state courts and local governments is considered in Richard A. Michael, "The 'New' Federalism and the Burger Court's Deference to the States in Federal Habeas Proceedings," *Iowa Law Review* 64 (1979). Worthwhile analyses of the *Usery* case are Richard E. Johnston and John T. Thompson, "The Burger Court and Federalism: A Revolution in 1976?" *Western Pol. Q.* 33 (1980), and Lawrence H. Tribe, "Unraveling National League of Cities: The New Federalism and Affirmative Rights to Essential Government Services," *Harvard Law Review* 90 (1977). The Burger Court's attitude toward litigation under Section 1983 of the U.S. Code, claiming violations of civil rights by state and local governments, is analyzed in Melvyn R. Durchslag, "Federalism and Constitutional Liberties: Varying the Remedy to Save the Right," *Michigan Law Review* 54 (1979), and Eric Schnapper, "Civil Rights Litigation after *Monell,*" *Columbia Law Review* 79 (1979). Federal-state relations as affected by the Eleventh Amendment are examined in Martha A. Field, "The Eleventh Amendment and Other Sovereign Immunity Doctrines: Congressional Imposition of Suit upon the States," *University of Pennsylvania Law Review* 126 (1978).

Concerning the Second Amendment, see Don B. Kates, Jr., "Handgun Prohibition and the Original Meaning of the Second Amendment," *Michigan Law Review* 82 (1983); Stephen P. Hallbrook, *That Every Man Be Armed: The Evolution of a Constitutional Right* (1984). Decisions concerning criminal procedure in general are discussed in Louis M. Seidman, "Factual Guilt and the Burger Court: An Examination of Continuity and Change in Criminal Procedure," *Columbia Law Review* 80 (1980); Stephen A. Saltzburg, "Foreword: The Flow and Ebb of Constitutional Criminal Procedure in the Warren and Burger Courts," *Georgetown Law Journal* 69 (1980); Robert Popper, "De-Nationalizing the Bill of Rights," in *The Courts: The Pendulum of Federalism* (1979). The fate of a key Warren Court ruling is explored in Geoffrey R. Stone, "The Miranda Doctrine in the Burger Court," *Supreme Court Review 1977* (1978).

Fourth Amendment problems are treated in William A. Schroeder, "Deterring Fourth Amendment Violations: Alternatives to the Exclusionary Rule," *Georgetown Law Review* 69 (1981); Lane Y. Sunderland, "Liberals, Conservatives, and the Exclusionary Rule," *Journal of Criminal Law and Criminology* 71 (1980); Ronald J. Bacigal, "Some Observations and Proposals on the Nature of the Fourth Amendment," *George Washington Law Review* 46 (1978). Concerning the death penalty and the Eighth Amendment, see Margaret Jane Radin, "Cruel Punishment and Respect for Persons: Super Due Process for Death," *Southern California Law Review* 53 (1980), and Kenneth M. Murchison, "Toward a Perspective on the Death Penalty Cases," *Emory Law Journal* 27 (1978).

"Symposium on the Law and Politics of Abortion," *Michigan Law Review* 77 (1979), is useful on that controversial subject. Earlier reactions to the abortion question are found in Richard E. Epstein, "Substantive Due Process by Any Other Name: The Abortion Cases," *Supreme Court Review 1973* (1974); John Hart Ely, "The Wages of Crying Wolf: A Comment on Roe v. Wade," *Yale Law Review* 82 (1973); Laurence H. Tribe, "Foreword: Toward a Model of Roles in the Due Process of Life and Law," *Harvard Law Review* 87 (1973).

Good accounts of the Burger Court's blunting of Warren Court egalitarianism are Richard Y. Funston, "The Double Standard of Constitutional Protection in the Era of the Welfare State," *PSQ* 90 (1975); Wallace Mendelson, "From Warren to Burger: The Rise and Decline of Substantive Equal Protection," *APSR* 66 (1972); Richard A. Epstein, "Foreword: Unconstitutional Conditions, State Power, and the Limits of Consent," *Harvard Law Review* 102 (1988). Subsequent equal protection developments are analyzed in Scott H. Bice, "Standards of Judicial Review under the Equal Protection and Due Process Clauses," *Southern California Law Review* 50 (1977); Richard Van Alstyne, "Cracks in 'the New Property,' " *Cornell Law Review* 62 (1977); and Tinsley E. Yarbrough, "The Burger Court and Unspecified Rights: On Protecting Fundamental and Not-So-Fundamental 'Rights' or 'Interests' through a Flexible Conception of Equal Protection," *Duke Law Journal* 1977.

The Supreme Court's renewed interest in property rights is treated in Martin Shapiro, "The Supreme Court's 'Return' to Economic Regulation," *Studies in American Political Development* 1 (1986); Frank H. Easterbrook, "Foreword: The Court and the Economic System," *Harvard Law Review* 98 (1984); William W. Van Alstyne, "The Recrudescence of Property Rights as the Foremost Principle of Civil Liberties: The First Decade of the Burger Court," *Law and Contemporary Problems* 43 (1980). For general description of free-speech decisions in the Burger era, see Archibald Cox, "Foreword: Freedom of Expression in the Burger Court," *Harvard Law Review* 94 (1980); Thomas I. Emerson, "First Amendment Doctrine and the Burger Court," *California Law Review* 68 (1980); David A. Farber, "Content Regulation and the First Amendment: A Revisionist View," *Georgetown Law Journal* 69 (1981). Commercial speech under First Amendment protection is discussed in Daniel A. Farber, "Commercial Speech and First Amendment Theory," *Northwestern University Law Review* 74 (1979), and R. H. Coase, "Advertising and Free Speech," *Journal of Legal Studies* 6 (1977). The free-speech rights of corporations are considered in David B. Keto, "The Corporation and the Constitution: Economic Due Process and Corporate Speech," *Yale Law Journal* 90 (1981).

On the law of libel, see "Symposium: Toward a Resolution of the Expanding Conflict between the Press and Privacy Interests," *Iowa Law Review* 64 (1979). Other pertinent studies of the First Amendment include Daniel A. Farber, "Civilizing Public Discourse: An Essay on Professor Bickel, Justice

Harlan, and the Enduring Significance of *Cohen v. California,"* *Duke Law Journal* (1980); Steven Shiffrin, "Government Speech," *UCLA Law Review* 27 (1980); Harry W. Wellington, "On Freedom of Expression," *Yale Law Journal* 88 (1979). The obscenity problem receives analysis in Frederick Schauer, "Speech and 'Speech'—Obscenity and 'Obscenity': An Exercise in the Interpretation of Constitutional Language," *Georgetown Law Journal* 67 (1979).

First Amendment establishment and free exercise of religion issues are examined in Leonard W. Levy, *The Establishment Clause: Religion and the First Amendment* (1986); Leo Pfeffer, "Freedom and/or Separation: The Constitutional Dilemma of the First Amendment," *Minnesota Law Review* 64 (1980); Kenneth F. Ripple, "The Entanglement Test of the Religion Clauses—a Ten Year Assessment," *UCLA Law Review* 27 (1980); Nancy H. Fink, "The Establishment Clause According to the Supreme Court: The Mysterious Eclipse of Free Exercise Values," *Catholic University Law Review* 27 (1978). Reapportionment law is reviewed in Bruce Adams, "A Model State Reapportionment Process: The Continuing Quest for 'Fair and Effective Representation,' " *Harvard Journal of Legislation* 14 (1977); Gerhard Casper, "Apportionment and the Right to Vote: Standards of Judicial Scrutiny," *Supreme Court Review 1973* (1974); Robert G. Dixon, Jr., "The Court, the People, and 'One Man, One Vote,' " in Nelson W. Polsby, ed., *Reapportionment in the 1970s* (1971).

XXI. *American Constitutionalism in the 1980s*

Thoughtful analyses of recent tendencies in American politics and constitutionalism appear in Richard A. Harris and Sidney M. Milkis, eds., *Remaking American Politics* (1988); James L. Sundquist, "Needed: A Political Theory for the New Era of Coalition Government in the United States," *PSQ* 103 (1988–89); *Mr. Madison's Constitution and the Twenty-first Century: A Project '87 Report* (1988); Theodore J. Lowi, "The Welfare State: Ethical Foundations and Constitutional Remedies," *PSQ* 101 (1986); Hugh Heclo, "General Welfare and Two American Political Traditions," *PSQ* 101 (1986); Donald L. Robinson, ed., *Reforming American Government: The Bicentennial Papers of the Committee on the Constitutional System* (1985); Harvey C. Mansfield, Jr., "Pride versus Interest in American Conservatism Today," *Government and Opposition* 22 (1987); Harvey C. Mansfield, Jr., "The American Election: Entitlements Versus Opportunity," *Government and Opposition* 20 (1985); Nelson W. Polsby, *Consequences of Party Reform* (1983); Aaron Wildavsky, *How to Limit Government Spending* (1980); James L. Sundquist, "The Crisis of Competence in Our National Government," *PSQ* 95 (1980); Samuel P. Huntington, *American Politics: The Promise of Disharmony* (1981); Theodore J. Lowi, *The End of Liberalism: Ideology, Policy, and the Crisis of Public Authority,* rev. ed. (1979); David Vogel, "The Public Interest Movement and the American Reform Tradition," *PSQ* 95 (1980–81).

Useful studies of the presidency are Theodore J. Lowi, *The Personal President: Power Invested, Promise Unfulfilled* (1985); Louis Fisher, *Constitutional Conflict between Congress and the President* (1984); John A. Rohr, *The Presidency and the Public Administration* (1989); Harold M. Hyman, *Quiet Past and Stormy Present? War Powers in American History* (1986); Donald S. Horowitz, "Is the Presidency Failing?" *The Public Interest* No. 88 (1987). Problems of divided government are explored in Gordon S. Jones and John A. Marini, eds., *The Imperial Congress: Crisis in the Separation of Powers* (1988); Richard H. Schultz, Jr., "Covert Action and Executive-Legislative Relations: The Iran-Contra Crisis and Its Aftermath," *Harvard Journal of Law and Public Policy* 12 (1989); L. Gordon Crovitz, "Crime, the Constitution and the Iran-Contra Affair," *Commentary* 84 (1987).

On the independent counsel, see Terry Eastland, *Ethics, Politics and the Independent Counsel: Executive Power, Executive Vice 1789–1989* (1989); Stephen L. Carter, "The Independent Counsel Mess," *Harvard Law Review* 102 (1988); John A. Rohr, "Public Administration, Executive Power, and Constitutional Confusion," *Public Administration Review* 49 (1989). Administrative law tendencies involving the executive branch are the subject of Martin Shapiro, "A.P.A. [Administrative Procedure Act] Past, Present, Future," *Virginia Law Review* 72 (1986); Peter L. Strauss and Cass R. Sunstein, "The Role of the President and OMB in Informal Rulemaking," *Administrative Law Review* 38 (1986); Alan B. Morrison, "OMB Interference with Agency Rulemaking: The Wrong Way to Write a Regulation," *Harvard Law Review* 99 (1986).

The role of the judiciary in American government and the nature of constitutional adjudication continue to be problematic and controversial. Two provocative interpretations of the role of the Supreme Court are Richard Funston, "The Supreme Court and Critical Elections," *APSR* 69 (1975), arguing that the Court's antimajoritarian potential is significant only during times of electoral realignment, and Jonathan D. Casper, "The Supreme Court and National Policy Making," *APSR* 70 (1976), asserting that the Court has a more consequential policy role than was recognized in Robert Dahl's influential study, "Decision-Making in a Democracy: The Supreme Court as a National Policy-Maker," *Journal of Public Law* 6 (1958). Other worthwhile general studies of the judiciary in the constitutional order are Robert F. Nagel, *Constitutional Cultures: The Mentality and Consequences of Judicial Review* (1989); William Lasser, *The Limits of Judicial Power: The Supreme Court in American Politics* (1988); Christopher Wolfe, *The Rise of Modern Judicial Review: From Constitutional Interpretation to Judge-Made Law* (1986); John Agresto, *The Supreme Court and Constitutional Democracy* (1984); Gary C. Jacobson, *The Supreme Court and the Decline of Constitutional Aspiration* (1984); Sotirios A. Barber, *On What the Constitution Means* (1984); Harry M. Clor, *"Judicial Statesmanship and Constitutional Interpretation,"* *South Texas Law Journal* 26 (1985); Sanford Byron Gabin, *Judicial Review and the Reasonable Doubt Test* (1980).

The debate between proponents of judicial restraint and of judicial activism has produced an extensive literature. The judicial restraint position is well illustrated in Gary L. McDowell, *Curbing the Courts: The Constitution and the Limits of Judicial Power* (1988); Gary L. McDowell, *The Constitution and Contemporary Constitutional Theory* (1985); Glen E. Thurow, "Judicial Review, Democracy, and the Rule of Law," in Sarah Thurow, ed., *Constitutionalism in America: The Constitution in Twentieth Century American Politics* (1988); Leslie F. Goldstein, "Judicial Review and Democratic Theory: Guardian Democracy vs. Representative Democracy," *Western Political Quarterly* 40 (1987); David P. Bryden, "Politics, the Constitution, and the New Formalism," *Constitutional Commentary* 3 (1986). Earlier contributions to this position are Raoul Berger, *Government by Judiciary: The Transformation of the Fourteenth Amendment* (1977); Louis Lusky, *By What Right? A Commentary on the Supreme Court's Power to Revise the Constitution* (1975); Nathan Glazer, "Toward an Imperial Judiciary?" *Public Interest* no. 41 (1975); William H. Rehnquist, "The Notion of a Living Constitution," *Texas Law Review* 54 (1976). Judicial activism is defended in Abram Chayes, "How the Constitution Establishes Justice," in Robert A. Goldwin and William A. Schambra, eds., *The Constitution, the Courts, and the Quest for Justice* (1989); Philip Bobbitt, *Constitutional Fate* (1984); Michael Perry, *The Constitution, the Courts, and Human Rights* (1982); Laurence Tribe, *God Save This Honorable Court: How the Choice of Supreme Court Justices Shapes Our History* (1985); Laurence Tribe, *American Constitutional Law* (1988); Frank M. Johnson, Jr., "In Defense of Judicial Activism," *Emory Law Journal* 28 (1980); Abram Chayes, "The Role of the Judge in Public Law Litigation," *Harvard Law Review* 89 (1976); Owen M. Fiss, "Foreword: The Forms of Justice," *Harvard Law Review* 93 (1979); John Hart Ely, *Democracy and Distrust: A Theory of Judicial Review* (1980); Jesse H. Choper, *The Supreme Court and the Political Branches: Judicial Review in the National Political Process: A Functional Reconsideration of the Role of the Supreme Court* (1980). See also the discussions of constitutional adjudication in Stephen R. Munzer and James W. Nickel, "Does the Constitution Mean What It Always Meant?" *Columbia Law Review* 77 (1977); Walter F. Murphy, "An Ordering of Constitutional Values," *Southern California Law Review* 53 (1980); Murphy, "The Art of Constitutional Interpretation," in M. Judd Harmon, ed., *Essays on the Constitution of the United States* (1978); Thomas C. Grey, "Do We Have an Unwritten Constitution?" *Stanford Law Review* 27 (1975). Alexander Bickel, one of the most important constitutional commentators of the post-New Deal era, is the subject of two studies which throw light on the nature and tendency of recent judicial power: Robert K. Faulkner, "Bickel's Constitution: The Problem of Moderate Liberalism," *APSR* 72 (1978); Edward A. Purcell, Jr., "Alexander M. Bickel and the Post-Realist Constitution," *Harvard Civil Rights-Civil Liberties Law Review* 11 (1976).

On the original-intent controversy, see Leonard W. Levy, *Original Intent and the Framers' Constitution* (1988); Earl M. Maltz, "The Failure of Attacks on Constitutional Originalism," *Constitutional Commentary* 4 (1987); H. Jefferson Powell, "The Original Understanding of Original Intent," *Harvard Law Review* 98 (1985); Lino A. Graglia, "How the Constitution Disappeared," *Commentary* 81 (1986); Henry P. Monoghan, "Our Perfect Constitution," *New York University Law Review* 56 (1981); Paul Brest, "The Misconceived Quest for the Original Understanding," *Boston University Law Review* 60 (1980). Karen Orren, "Standing to Sue: Interest Group Conflict in the Federal Courts," *APSR* 70 (1976), argues that excessive judicial political involvement resulting from the relaxation of rules governing access to the courts threatens the rule of law. Of related interest is Louis Henkin, "Is There a 'Political Question' Doctrine?" *Yale Law Journal* 85 (1976). Wade H. McCree, Jr., "Bureaucratic Justice: An Early Warning," *University of Pennsylvania Law Review* 129 (1981), criticizes the tendency toward bureaucratization in the judicial system, while Jethro K. Lieberman, *The Litigious Society* (1981), and Richard Neely, *How Courts Govern America* (1981), offer an explanation and justification for the recent expansion of the judicial policy-making role.

The balance between state and federal power has regained some of its former importance as criticism of centralized federal bureaucracy has increased. Good analyses of federalism are found in Leon D. Epstein, "The Old States in a New System," in Anthony King, ed., *The New American Political System* (1978); Symposium: "The State of American Federalism: 1979," *Publius* 10 (1980); Vincent Ostrum, "The Contemporary Debate over Centralization and Decentralization," *Publius* 6 (1976); Michael D. Reagan, *The New Federalism* (1972). Mary Cornelia Porter, "State Supreme Courts and the Legacy of the Warren Court: Some Old Inquiries for a New Situation," *Publius* 8 (1978), describes increased state court activism. See also Shirley S. Abrahamson, "Criminal Law and State Constitutions: The Emergence of State Constitutional Law," *Texas Law Review* 63 (1985); Ronald L. K. Collins and Peter J. Galie, "Models of Post-Incorporation Judicial Review: 1985 Survey of State Constitutional Individual Rights Decisions," *Publius* 16 (1986).

The states have also been conspicuous in proposals for an Article V convention to revise the Constitution. See the discussion of this issue in Russell L. Caplan, *Constitutional Brinksmanship: Amending the Constitution by National Convention* (1988); Grover Rees III, "The Amendment Process and Limited Constitutional Conventions," *Benchmark* 2 (1986); Wilbur Edel, *A Constitutional Convention: Threat or Challenge?* (1981); Walter E. Dellinger, "The Recurring Question of the 'Limited' Constitutional Convention," *Yale Law Journal* 88 (1979); William W. Van Alstyne, "The Limited Constitutional Convention—the Recurring Answer," *Duke Law Journal* 1979; Paul Bator et al., *A Constitutional Convention: How Well Would It Work?* (1979); Charles L. Black, Jr., "Amending the Constitution: A Letter to a Congressman," *Yale Law Journal* 82 (1972); Paul G. Kauper, ed., *The Article V Convention Process: A Symposium* (1971), reprinted from *Michigan Law Review* 66 (1968). Historical and political background is provided in Kermit L. Hall *et al.,* eds., *The Constitutional Convention as an Amending Device* (1981).

On the District of Columbia representation amendment, see Clement E. Vose, "When District of Columbia Representation Collides with the Constitutional Amendment Institution," *Publius* 9 (1979); Peter Raven-Hansen, "Congressional Representation for the District of Columbia: A Constitutional Analysis," *Harvard Journal on Legislation* 12 (1975). Constitutional problems concerning the equal-rights amendment are discussed in Jane H. Mansbridge, *Why We Lost the ERA* (1986); Ruth Bader Ginsburg, "Ratification of the Equal Rights Amendment: A Question of Time," *Texas Law Review* 57 (1979); Grover Rees III, "Throwing Away the Key: The Unconstitutionality of the Equal Rights Amendment," *Texas Law Review* 58 (1980); Samuel S. Freedman and Pamela J. Naughton, *ERA: May a State Change Its Vote?* (1978). For analysis of the equal-rights amendment and constitutional law on women's rights, see Earlean McCarrick, "The Supreme Court and the Evolution of Women's Rights," *This Constitution* No. 13 (1986); O. John Rogge, "Equal Rights for Women," *Howard Law Journal* 21 (1977); Ruth Bader Ginsburg, "Sex Equality and the Constitution," *Texas Law Review* 52 (1978); "Equal Rights for Women: A Symposium on the Proposed Constitutional Amendment," *Harvard Civil Rights-Civil Liberties Law Review* 6 (1971); Janet K. Boles, *The Politics of the Equal Rights Amendment: Conflict and the Decision Process* (1979).

The constitutional amendment dealing with presidential succession is treated in John D. Feerick, *The Twenty-fifth Amendment: Its Complete History and Earliest Application* (1976).

Table of Cases

Ableman v. Booth, 21 Howard 506 (1859): 238, 278–79
Abrams v. U.S., 250 U.S. 616 (1919): 514–15
Adair v. U.S., 208 U.S. 161 (1908): 419, 447
Adams v. Williams, 407 U.S. 144 (1972): 693
Adamson v. California, 322 U.S. 46 (1948): 521
Adderley v. Florida, 385 U.S. 39 (1966): 650
Addyston Pipe and Steel Company v. U.S., 175 U.S. 211 (1899): 420
Adkins v. Children's Hospital, 261 U.S. 525 (1923): 448, 487
Adler v. Board of Education, 342 U.S. 485 (1952): 573
Aguilar v. Felton, 105 S.Ct. 3216 (1985): 736
Alabama Power Co. v. Ickes, 302 U.S. 464 (1938): 493
Albertson v. Subversive Activities Control Board, 382 U.S. 70 (1965): 576
Alexander v. Holmes, 396 U.S. 19 (1969): 606
Almeida-Sanchez v. U.S., 413 U.S. 266 (1973): 693
Allen v. State Board of Elections, 393 U.S. 544 (1968): 608
Allgeyer v. Louisiana, 165 U.S. 578 (1897): 403
Amalgamated Food Employees Union Local 590 v. Logan Valley Plaza, 391 U.S. 308 (1968): 698
American Column and Lumber Co. v. U.S., 257 U.S. 377 (1921): 452
American Communications Association v. Douds, 339 U.S. 94 (1950): 569–71
American Federation of Labor v. Swing, 312 U.S. 321 (1941): 524
American Insurance Co. v. Canter, 1 Peters 511 (1828):256
American Power and Light Co. v. Securities and Exchange Commission, 329 U.S. 90 (1946): 492
American Steel Foundries v. Tri-City Central Trades Council, 257 U.S. 184 (1921): 450
American Textile Manufacturers Institute, Inc. v. Donovan, 452 U.S. 490 (1981): 716
Anderson v. Creighton, 107 S.Ct. 3034 (1987): 731
Apodaca v. Oregon, 406 U.S. 404 (1972): 695
Aptheker v. Secretary of State, 378 U.S. 500 (1964): 576
Argersinger v. Hamlin, 407 U.S. 25 (1972): 694

Ashwander v. Tennessee Valley Authority, 297 U.S. 288 (1936): 479
Associated Press v. National Labor Relations Board, 301 U.S. 103 (1937): 488
Associated Press v. Walker, 388 U.S. 130 (1967): 626
Avery v. Midland Co., 390 U.S. 474 (1968): 619

Baggett v. Bullitt, 377 U.S. 360 (1964): 578
Bailey v. Alabama, 219 U.S. 219 (1910): 581
Bailey v. Drexel Furniture Co., 259 U.S. 20 (1922): 448
Bailey v. Richardson, 341 U.S. 918 (1951): 572–73
Baker v. Carr, 369 U.S. 186 (1962): 615–16
Baldwin v. New York, 399 U.S. 66 (1970): 694
Ballew v. Georgia, 435 U.S. 223 (1978): 695
Baltimore v. City of Dawson, 350 U.S. 877 (1955): 592
Bank of Augusta v. Earle, 13 Peters 519 (1839): 229–30
Barenblatt v. U.S., 360 U.S. 109 (1959): 577
Barron v. Baltimore, 7 Peters 243 (1833): 198, 222, 278, 356, 511
Baumgartner v. U.S., 322 U.S. 665 (1944): 551
Bayard v. Singleton, 1 Martin 42 (1787): 86
Beauharnais v. Illinois, 343 U.S. 250 (1952): 528
Beckwith v. U.S., 425 U.S. 341 (1976): 694
Bedford Cut Stone Co. v. Journeymen Stone Cutters Association, 274 U.S. 37
    (1927): 450
Beilan v. Board of Education, 357 U.S. 399 (1958): 574
Bell v. Maryland, 378 U.S. 226 (1964): 594
Bell v. Ohio, 438 U.S. 637 (1978): 695
Benton v. Maryland, 395 U.S. 784 (1969): 623
Bethel School District No. 403 v. Fraser, 478 U.S. 675 (1986): 733
Betts v. Brady, 316 U.S. 455 (1942): 621
Bishop v. Wood, 426 U.S. 341 (1976): 682
Blum v. Stenson, 465 U.S. 886 (1984): 756
Board of Education v. Allen, 392 U.S. 236 (1968): 632
Board of Education v. Roth, 408 U.S. 564 (1972): 682
Bob-Lo Excursion Co. v. Michigan, 333 U.S. 28 (1948): 584
Bolling v. Sharpe, 347 U.S. 497 (1954): 586–87
Ex parte Bollman and Swartwout, 4 Cranch 75 (1807): 176
Booth v. Maryland, 107 S.Ct. 2529 (1987): 732
Bowen v. Gilliard, 107 S.Ct. 3008 (1987): 738
Bowen v. Kendrick, 108 S.Ct. 2562 (1988): 737
Bowers v. Hardwick, 106 S.Ct. 2841 (1986): 741–42
Bowsher v. Synar, 106 S.Ct. 3181 (1986): 751
Boynton v. Virginia, 364 U.S. 454 (1960): 592
Braden v. U.S., 365 U.S. 431 (1961): 577
Bradwell v. Illinois, 16 Wallace 131 (1873): 690
Brandenburg v. Ohio, 393 U.S. 948 (1969): 576, 579–80
Branzburg v. Hayes, 408 U.S. 665 (1972): 701
Breard v. Alexandria, 341 U.S. 622 (1951): 528
Breedlove v. Suttles, 302 U.S. 277 (1937): 596
Breithaupt v. Abram, 352 U.S. 432 (1957): 621

Bridges v. California, 314 U.S. 252 (1941): 531
Briscoe v. Bank of Kentucky, 11 Peters 257 (1837): 223–24
Bronson v. Kinzie, 1 Howard 311 (1843): 228
Brown v. Board of Education of Topeka 349 U.S. 294 (1954): 586–89, 591
Brown v. Board of Education of Topeka, 349 U.S. 294 (1955): 588–89
Brown v. Maryland, 12 Wheaton 419 (1827): 197, 232
Brown v. Mississippi, 297 U.S. 278 (1936): 619, 622
Brown v. Williams, 430 U.S. 387 (1977): 730
Browning-Ferris Industries v. Kelco Disposal Inc., 109 S.Ct. 2909 (1989): 748
Buchanan v. Warley, 245 U.S. 60 (1917): 359, 581, 583
Buckley v. Valeo, 424 U.S. 1 (1976): 697
Bunting v. Oregon, 243 U.S. 426 (1917): 444
Burch v. Louisiana, 99 Supreme Court Reporter 1623 (1979): 695
Burstyn v. Wilson, 343 U.S. 195 (1952): 528–29
Burton v. Wilmington Parking Authority, 365 U.S. 17 (1961): 592
Buttfield v. Stranahan, 92 U.S. 470 (1904): 413

Cady v. Dombrowski, 413 U.S. 433 (1973): 693
Calder v. Bull, 3 Dallas 386 (1798): 187
Califano v. Goldfarb, 430 U.S. 199 (1977): 691
California v. Cohen, 403 U.S. 15 (1971): 697
California v. Thompson, 313 U.S. 109 (1941): 494
Calvin's Case, 7 Co. Rep. 14 (1608): 53
Cantwell v. Connecticut, 310 U.S. 296 (1940): 527
Cargill v. Monfort, 107 S.Ct. 484 (1986): 746
Carpenters and Joiners Union v. Ritter's Cafe, 315 U.S. 772 (1942): 524
Carroll v. U.S., 267 U.S. 132 (1925): 464
Carter v. Carter Coal Co., 298 U.S. 238 (1936): 479
Central Hudson Gas and Electric Corp. v. Public Service Commission, 447 U.S.
    557 (1980): 732
Central Transportation Co. v. Pullman's Palace Car Co., 139 U.S. 24 (1890): 377
Champion v. Ames, 188 U.S. 321 (1903): 417
Chaplinsky v. New Hampshire, 315 U.S. 568 (1942): 525–26, 629, 697
Charles River Bridge v. Warren Bridge, 11 Peters 420 (1837): 224–27
Cherokee Nation v. Georgia, 5 Peters 1 (1831): 204, 381
Chicago, Burlington, and Quincy Railroad Co. v. Chicago, 166 U.S. 226 (1897):
    517, 518
Chicago, Milwaukee, and St. Paul Railway Co. v. Minnesota, 134 U.S. 418 (1890):
    395–96
Chisholm v. Georgia, 2 Dallas 419 (1793): 160–61
Cincinnati, New Orleans, and Texas Pacific Railway Co. v. Interstate Commerce
    Commission, 162 U.S. 184 (1896): 375
City of Akron v. Akron Center for Reproductive Health Services, 462 U.S. 416
    (1983): 740
City of Cleburne v. Cleburne Living Center Inc., 473 U.S. 432 (1985): 739
City of Mobile v. Bolden, 446 U.S. 55 (1980): 745
City of Renton v. Playtime Theatres, 106 S.Ct. 925 (1986): 734
City of Richmond v. Croson, 102 L.Ed. 2d 854 (1989): 744

Civil Rights Cases, 109 U.S. 3 (1883): 357, 583, 592, 600
Clark v. Community for Creative Non-Violence, 104 S.Ct. 3065 (1984): 733
Ex parte Clark, 100 U.S. 399 (1880): 358
Cleveland Board of Education v. LeFleur, 414 U.S. 632 (1974): 691
Cohens v. Virginia, 6 Wheaton 264 (1821): 181–82
Coker v. Georgia, 433 U.S. 583 (1977): 695
Cole v. Young, 351 U.S. 536 (1956): 573
Colgate v. Harvey, 296 U.S. 404 (1936): 495
Colegrove v. Green, 328 U.S. 549 (1946): 615
Coleman v. McLennan, 98 P. 281 (1908): 625
Collector v. Day, 11 Wallace 113 (1871): 387
Colorado v. Connelly, 107 S.Ct. 515 (1986): 730
Committee for Public Education and Religious Liberty v. Regan, 444 U.S. 646
    (1980): 736
Commonwealth v. Aves, 18 Pick. 193 (1836): 246
Commonwealth v. Hunt, 4 Metc. 111 (1842): 398
Communist Party of Indiana v. Whitcomb, 414 U.S. 441 (1974): 579
Communist Party v. Subversive Activities Control Board, 351 U.S. 115 (1956): 576
Communist Party v. Subversive Activities Control Board, 367 U.S. 1 (1961): 576
Connecticut General Life Insurance Co. v. Johnson, 303 U.S. 77 (1938): 495
Consolidated Edison Co. v. National Labor Relations Board, 305 U.S. 197 (1938):
    490
Consolidated Edison Co. v. Public Service Commission, 447 U.S. 530 (1980): 732
Continental T.V., Inc. v. GTE Sylvania, Inc., 97 S.Ct. 2549 (1977): 746
Cooley v. Pennsylvania Board of Wardens, 12 Howard 299 (1851): 233–34, 237
Cooper v. Aaron, 358 U.S. 1 (1958): 590
Coppage v. Kansas, 236 U.S. 1 (1915): 447
Corning Glass Works v. Brennan, 417 U.S. 188 (1974): 690
Corrigan v. Buckly, 271 U.S. 323 (1926): 583
Cousins v. Wigoda, 419 U.S. 477 (1975): 652
County of Allegheny v. American Civil Liberties Union Greater Pittsburgh
    Chapter, 109 S.Ct. 3086 (1989): 737
Craig v. Boren, 429 U.S. 190 (1976): 691–92
Craig v. Missouri, 4 Peters 410 (1830): 224
Cramer v. U.S., 325 U.S. 1 (1945): 549–50
Cramp v. Board of Public Instruction of Orange County, 368 U.S. 278 (1961): 578
Crandall v. Nevada, 6 Wallace 35 (1868): 633
Ex parte Crow Dog, 109 U.S. 556 (1883): 382
Crutcher v. Kentucky, 141 U.S. 47 (1891): 633
Cumming v. Richmond County Board of Education, 175 U.S. 528 (1899): 585
Cummings v. Missouri, 4 Wallace 277 (1867): 352
Curtis Publishing Co. v. Butts, 388 U.S. 130 (1967): 626–27

Dandridge v. Williams, 397 U.S. 471 (1970): 681
Dartmouth College v. Woodward, 4 Wheaton 518 (1819): 191–92, 224, 226
Davis v. Bandemer, 106 U.S. S.Ct. 2797 (1986): 707
Davidson v. New Orleans, 96 U.S. 97 (1878): 394
Dayton Board of Education v. Brinkman, 433 U.S. 406 (1979): 685

Dayton-Goose Creek Railway Cop. v. U.S., 263 U.S. 456 (1924): 445

Debs v. U.S., 249 U.S. 211 (1919): 513

In re Debs, 158 U.S. 564 (1895): 399–400

DeJonge v. Oregon, 299 U.S. 353 (1937): 529–30

DeLima v. Bidwell, 182 U.S. 1 (1901): 383

Dennis v. U.S., 341 U.S. 494 (1951): 560–61, 570–72

Derrington v. Plummer, 353 U.S. 924 (1957): 591

DeShaney v. Winnebago County Department of Social Services, 109 S.Ct. 998 (1989): 739

Doe v. Bolton, 410 U.S. 179 (1973): 696

Dombroski v. Pfister, 380 U.S. 479 (1965): 576

Dr. Bonaham's Case, King's Bench (1610): 61–62

Dorr v. U.S., 195 U.S. 138 (1904): 385

Dothard v. Rawlinson, 433 U.S. 321 (1977): 690

Dowdell v. U.S., 221 U.S. 325 (1911): 385

Downes v. Bidwell, 182 U.S. 244 (1901): 384

Dred Scott v. Sanford, 19 Howard 393 (1857): 235, 257, 268–75, 277–78, 282, 287, 289, 330, 332, 385, 388

Dun and Bradstreet v. Greenmoss Builders, 472 U.S. 749 (1985): 732

Duncan v. Kahanamoku, 327 U.S. 304 (1946): 547

Duncan v. Louisiana, 391 U.S. 145 (1968): 623, 694

Duplex Printing Press Co. v. Deering, 254 U.S. 443 (1921): 449

Edwards v. Aguillard, 107 S.Ct. 2573 (1987): 736

Edwards v. California, 314 U.S. 160 (1941): 494, 633

Equal Employment Opportunity Commission v. Wyoming, 460 U.S. 226 (1983): 749

Electric Bond and Share Co. v. Securities and Exchange Commission, 303 U.S. 419 (1938): 492

Elfbrandt v. Russell, 384 U.S. 11 (1966): 578

Elk v. Wilkins, 112 U.S. 94 (1884): 382

Elkison v. Deliesseline, Federal Cases No. 4366 (1823): 250

Ex parte Endo, 323 U.S. 284 (1944): 546

Engel v. Vitale, 370 U.S. 421 (1962): 631

Erie Railroad Co. v. Tompkins, 304 U.S. 64 (1938): 506–507

Escobedo v. Illinois, 378 U.S. 478 (1964): 622, 635

Euclid v. Ambler Realty Co., 272 U.S. 365 (1926): 747

Evers v. Dwyer, 358 U.S. 202 (1958): 592

Everson v. Board of Education, 330 U.S. 1 (1947): 630

Fallbrook Irrigation District v. Bradley, 164 U.S. 112 (1896): 445

Matter of Farber: State of New Jersey v. Mario E. Jascalelevich, 394 A. 2d 330 (1978): 701

Federal Trade Commission v. Curtis Publishing Co., 260 U.S. 568 (1923): 461

Federal Trade Commission v. Gratz, 253 U.S. 421 (1920): 461

Feiner v. New York, 340 U.S. 315 (1951): 528

FERC v. Mississippi, 456 U.S. 742 (1982): 749

Field v. Clark, 143 U.S. 649 (1892): 413

Firefighters Local Union No. 1784 v. Stotts, 467 U.S. 561 (1984): 744
First English Evangelical Lutheran Church of Glendale v. County of Los Angeles,
    482 U.S. 304 (1987): 747
First National Bank v. Bellotti, 435 U.S. 765 (1978): 697
Flast v. Cohen, 392 U.S. 83 (1968): 632, 703
Fletcher v. Peck, 6 Cranch 87 (1810): 179, 188
Follett v. McCormick, 321 U.S. 573 (1944): 527
Ford v. Wainwright, 106 U.S. 2595 (1986): 731
Frohwerk v. U.S., 249 U.S. 204 (1919): 513
Frontiero v. Richardson, 411 U.S. 677 (1973): 691
Frothingham v. Mellon, 262 U.S. 447 (1923): 632
Fullilove v. Klutznick, 100 Supreme Court Reporter 2758 (1980): 688–89
Furman v. Georgia, 408 U.S. 238 (1972): 695

Gannett Co. v. DePasquale, 443 U.S. 368 (1979): 700
Garcia v. San Antonio Metropolitan Transit Authority, 105 S.Ct. 1005 (1985): 749
Ex parte Garland, 4 Wallace 333 (1867): 353
Garner v. Board of Public Works of Los Angeles, 341 U.S. 716 (1951): 573
Garner v. Louisiana, 368 U.S. 157 (1961): 593
Gaston Co. v. U.S., 395 U.S. 285 (1969): 607–08
Gayle v. Browder, 352 U.S. 903 (1956): 592
Geduldig v. Aiello, 417 U.S. 484 (1974): 691
Gelpcke v. Dubuque, 1 Wallace 175 (1864): 228, 362
General Electric Co. v. Gilbert, 429 U.S. 126 (1976): 691
Georgia v. Stanton, 6 Wallace 50 (1867): 352
Gerende v. Election Board, 341 U.S. 56 (1951): 573
Gertz v. Robert Welch, Inc., 418 U.S. 323 (1974): 699
Gibbons v. Ogden, 9 Wheaton 1 (1824): 195–96, 231
Giboney v. Empire Storage and Ice Co., 336 U.S. 490 (1949): 525
Gibson v. Florida Legislative Investigating Committee, 372 U.S. 539 (1963): 577
Gideon v. Wainwright, 372 U.S. 335 (1963): 621–22, 694
Gilbert v. Minnesota, 254 U.S. 325 (1920): 517
Ginsberg v. New York, 390 U.S. 629 (1968): 630
Ginzburg v. U.S., 383 U.S. 463 (1966): 629
Gitlow v. New York, 268 U.S. 652 (1925): 515–16, 517–18, 571
Gojack v. U.S., 369 U.S. 749 (1966): 577
Gold Cases, 294 U.S. 240 (1935), 294 U.S. 317 (1935): 475–76
Goldberg v. Kelly, 397 U.S. 254 (1970): 680
Goldman v. Weinberger, 475 U.S. 503 (1986): 738
Gomillion v. Lightfoot, 364 U.S. 339 (1960): 596, 615
Gong Lum v. Rice, 275 U.S. 78 (1927): 585
Gooding, Warding v. Wilson, 405 U.S. 518 (1972): 697
Grand Rapids School District v. Ball, 105 S.Ct. 3216(1985): 736
Granger Cases, 94 U.S. 113 (1877): 389, 391
Gray v. Sanders, 372 U.S. 368 (1963): 617
Green v. Biddle, 8 Wheaton 1 (1823): 189
Green v. County Board of New Kent Co., 391 U.S. 430 (1968): 606
Green v. Frazier, 253 U.S. 233 (1920): 445

Greene v. McElroy, 360 U.S. 474 (1959): 573

Gregg v. Georgia, 428 U.S. 153 (1976): 695

Griffin v. County Board of Prince Edward Co., 377 U.S. 218 (1964): 590

Griggs v. Duke Power Co., 401 U.S. 424 (1971): 609, 686

Griswold v. Connecticut, 381 U.S. 479 (1965): 627–28, 636, 740

Groves v. Slaughter, 15 Peters 449 (1841): 231–32

Grovey v. Townsend, 295 U.S. 45 (1935): 595

Guinn v. U.S., 238 U.S. 347 (1915): 359, 581

H.J., Inc. v. Northwestern Bell Telephone Co., 109 S.Ct. 2893 (1989): 748

H.L. v. Matheson, 450 U.S. 398 (1981): 740

Hague v. CIO, 307 U.S. 496 (1939): 525

Hale v. Bimco Trading Co., 306 U.S. 375 (1939): 494

Hammer v. Dagenhart, 247 U.S. 251 (1918): 419, 447, 490

Harlow v. Fitzgerald, 457 U.S. 800 (1982): 731

Harper v. Virginia Board of Elections, 383 U.S. 667 (1966): 602

Harris v. McRae, 100 Supreme Court Reporter 1832 (1980): 696

Harris v. New York, 401 U.S. 222 (1971): 694

Hartzel v. U.S., 322 U.S. 680 (1944): 551

Haupt v. U.S., 330 U.S. 631 (1947): 550

Hawaii v. Mankichi, 190 U.S. 197 (1903): 385

Hawaii Housing Authority v. Midkiff, 104 S.Ct. 2321 (1984): 747

Hawke v. Smith, 253 U.S. 221 (1920): 463

Hayburn's Case, 2 Dallas 409 (1792): 159–60

Hazelwood School District v. Kuhlmeier, 108 S.Ct. 562 (1988): 733

Heart of Atlanta Motel v. U.S., 379 U.S. 241 (1964): 600

Helvering v. Davis, 301 U.S. 619 (1937): 489

Henderson v. U.S., 339 U.S. 816 (1950): 584

Hensley v. Eckhart, 461 U.S. 424 (1983): 756

Henry G. Spallone v. U.S., 110 S.Ct. 625 (1990): 757

Hepburn v. Griswold, 8 Wallace 603 (1870): 360, 388

Herbert v. Lando, 99 Supreme Court Reporter 1635 (1979): 701

Herndon v. Lowry, 301 U.S. 242 (1937): 530

Hess v. Indiana, 414 U.S. 105 (1973): 697

Hirabayashi v. U.S., 320 U.S. 81 (1943): 544–45

Hitchman Coal and Coke Co. v. Mitchell, 245 U.S. 229 (1917): 449

Hodel v. Virginia Surface Mining and Reclamation Association Inc., 452 U.S. 264
   (1981): 749

Hoke v. U.S., 227 U.S. 308 (1913): 418

Holden v. Hardy, 169 U.S. 366 (1898): 443–44, 447

Holmes v. City of Atlanta, 350 U.S. 879 (1955): 592

Holmes v. Walton, New Jersey (1780): 86

Holtzman v. Schlesinger, 414 U.S. 1304 (1973): 661

Home Building and Loan Association v. Blaisdell, 290 U.S. 398 (1934): 475, 539

Hood v. U.S., 307 U.S. 588 (1939): 491

Hudgens v. National Labor Relations Board, 424 U.S. 507 (1976): 698

Humphrey's Executor v. U.S., 295 U.S. 602 (1935): 497, 752

Hurd v. Hodge, 334 U.S. 24 (1948): 583–84

Hurtado v. California, 110 U.S. 516 (1884): 511, 516–17, 518

Hutcheson v. U.S., 365 U.S. 599 (1962): 577
Hutchinson v. Proxmire, 99 Supreme Court Reporter 2675 (1979): 700
Hylton v. U.S., 3 Dallas 171 (1796): 171, 401

Immigration and Naturalization Service v. Chadha, 103 S.Ct. 2764 (1983): 718, 750–51
Industrial Union Department, AFL-CIO v. American Petroleum Institute, 448 U.S. 607 (1980): 716, 746
International Brotherhood of Teamsters v. Hanke, 339 U.S. 470 (1950): 525
Interstate Commerce Commission v. Alabama Midland Railway Co., 168 U.S. 144 (1897): 375
Interstate Commerce Commission v. Cincinnati, New Orleans, and Texas Pacific Railway Co., 167 U.S. 479 (1897): 375–76
Interstate Commerce Commission v. Illinois Central Railroad Co., 215 U.S. 452 (1910): 425

Jackson v. Virginia, 443 U.S. 307 (1979): 738
Jacobellis v. Ohio, 378 U.S. 184 (1964): 629, 698
In re Jacobs, 98 N.Y. 98 (1885): 394

James v. Valtierra, 402 U.S. 138 (1971): 681
Jay Burns Baking Co. v. Burns, 264 U.S. 504 (1924): 451
Jenkins v. Georgia, 418 U.S. 153 (1974): 733
Johnson v. Louisiana, 406 U.S. 356 (1972): 695
Johnson v. Transportation Agency of Santa Clara County, 107 S.Ct. 1442 (1987): 743
Johnson v. Virginia, 373 U.S. 61 (1963): 592
Joint Anti-Fascist Committee v. McGrath, 341 U.S. 123 (1951): 573
Jones v. Mayer, 392 U.S. 409 (1968): 601, 604
Jones v. Opelika, 316 U.S. 584 (1942): 528
Jones v. Portland, 245 U.S. 217 (1917): 445

Kadrmas v. Dickinson Public Schools, 108 S.Ct. 2481 (1988): 739
Kahn v. Shevin, 416 U.S. 351 (1974): 692
Katzenbach v. McClung, 379 U.S. 294 (1964): 600
Katzenbach v. Morgan, 384 U.S. 641 (1966): 602
Kawakita v. U.S., 343 U.S. 717 (1952): 550
Kendall v. U.S. ex rel. Stokes, 12 Peters 524 (1838): 216–17
Kent v. Dulles, 357 U.S. 116 (1958): 576
Keyes v. School District No. 1, Denver, Colo., 413 U.S. 189 (1973): 684
Keyishian v. Board of Regents of the University of the State of New York, 385 U.S. 589 (1967): 578
Keystone Bituminous Coal Association v. DeBenedictis, 480 U.S. 470 (1987): 748
Kidd v. Pearson, 128 U.S. 1 (1888): 393
Kilbourn v. Thompson, 103 U.S. 168 (1881): 565
Kirby v. Illinois, 406 U.S. 682 (1972): 694
Kirkpatrick v. Preisler, 394 U.S. 526 (1967): 618
Klopfer v. North Carolina, 386 U.S. 213 (1967): 623

Konigsberg v. State Bar of California, 353 U.S. 252 (1957): 574
Korematsu v. U.S., 323 U.S. 214 (1944): 545–46
Kovacs v. Cooper, 336 U.S. 77 (1949): 529

Lambert v. Yellowley, 46 Supreme Court Reporter 335 (1925): 464
Lauf v. Shinner and Co., 303 U.S. 323 (1938): 491
Lemon v. Kurtzman, 403 U.S. 602 (1971): 735–37
Lemmon v. The People, 20 N.Y. 562 (1860): 278
Lerner v. Casey, 357 U.S. 468 (1958): 574
Levitt v. Committee for Public Education and Religious Liberty, 413 U.S. 472
    (1973): 736
Lewis v. City of New Orleans, 415 U.S. 130 (1972): 697
License Cases, 5 Howard 504 (1847): 232–33, 238
Linkletter v. Walker, 381 U.S. 618 (1965): 634–35
Lloyd Corp., Ltd. v. Tanner, 407 U.S. 551 (1972): 698
Loan Association v. Topeka, 20 Wallace 655 (1875): 394
Local 28 Sheet Metal Workers v. E.E.O.C., 106 S.Ct. 3019 (1986): 743
Local 93 v. City of Cleveland, 106 S.Ct. 3063 (1986): 743
Lochner v. New York, 198 U.S. 45 (1905): 446–47, 453–54, 456, 628
Lockett v. Ohio, 438 U.S. 586 (1978): 695
Loewe v. Lawlor, 208 U.S. 274 (1908): 449
Logan v. U.S., 144 U.S. 263 (1892): 597
Lombard v. Louisiana, 373 U.S. 267 (1963): 593
Louisville Bank v. Radford, 295 U.S. 555 (1935): 477
Louisville, Cincinnati and Charleston Railroad Co. v. Letson, 2 Howard 497
    (1844): 230
Lovell v. Griffin, 303 U.S. 444 (1938): 526
Loving et ux. v. Virginia, 388 U.S. 1 (1967): 592
Lucas v. Forty-Fourth General Assembly of Colorado, 377 U.S. 713 (1964): 618
Luther v. Borden, 7 Howard 1 (1849): 220, 237–38, 355, 616
Lynch v. Donnelly, 104 S.Ct. 1355 (1984): 737
Lyng v. International Union UAW, 108 S.Ct. 1184 (1988): 739
Lyng v. Northwest Indian Cemetery Protective Association, 108 S.Ct. 1319 (1988):
    738

Ex parte McCardle, 7 Wallace 506 (1869): 353–54
McCray v. U.S., 195 U.S. 27 (1904): 417
McCulloch v. Maryland, 4 Wheaton 316 (1819): 127, 183–85, 198–99, 206, 309
McGowan v. Maryland, 366 U.S. 420 (1961): 631
McGrain v. Daugherty, 273 U.S. 135 (1927): 565
McLaughlin v. Florida, 379 U.S. 184 (1964): 592
McLaurin v. Oklahoma State Regents, 339 U.S. 637 (1950): 586
Madden v. Kentucky, 309 U.S. 83 (1940): 495
Maher v. Roe, 97 Supreme Court Reporter 2376 (1977): 696
Malloy v. Hogan, 378 U.S. 1 (1964): 622
Manuel Enterprises v. Day, 370 U.S. 478 (1962): 629
Maple Flooring Association v. U.S., 268 U.S. 563 (1925): 453
Mapp v. Ohio, 367 U.S. 643 (1961): 621, 634, 692, 730

Marbury v. Madison, 1 Cranch 137 (1803): 170, 172–75, 179, 199, 590
Marsh v. Alabama, 326 U.S. 501 (1946): 527
Marsh v. Chambers, 103 U.S. 3330 (1983): 737
Marshall v. Baltimore and Ohio Railroad Co., 16 Howard 314 (1854): 230
Marshall v. Barlow's, Inc., 436 U.S. 307 (1978): 694
Martin v. Hunter's Lessee, 1 Wheaton 304 (1816): 180
Martin v. Mott, 12 Wheaton 19 (1827): 304
Martin v. Struthers, 319 U.S. 141 (1943): 527
Martin v. Wilks, 109 S.Ct. 2180 (1989): 744
Maryland v. Wirtz, 192 U.S. 183 (1968): 683
Massachusetts v. Laird, 400 U.S. 886 (1970): 661
Massachusetts v. Mellon, 262 U.S. 447 (1923): 460, 478
Meek v. Pittenger, 421 U.S. 349 (1975): 736
Members of the City Council of Los Angeles v. Taxpayers for Vincent, 104 S.Ct.
    2118 (1984): 733
Memoirs v. Massachusetts, 383 U.S. 413 (1966): 629
Meritor Savings Bank v. Vinson, 106 S.Ct. 2399 (1986): 745
Ex parte Merryman, Fed. Cases No. 9487 (1861): 304
Meyer v. Nebraska, 262 U.S. 390 (1923): 516
Michael M. v. Superior Court of Sonoma County, 101 Supreme Court Reporter
    1200 (1981): 692
Michigan v. DeFillippo, 100 Supreme Court Reporter 2627 (1979): 693
Michigan v. Tucker, 417 U.S. 433 (1974): 694
Milk Board v. Eisenburg, 306 U.S. 346 (1939): 494
Milk Wagon Drivers Union v. Meadowmoor Dairies, 312 U.S. 287 (1941): 524
Miller v. California, 413 U.S. 15 (1973): 698, 733
Ex parte Milligan, 4 Wallace 2 (1866): 337, 352, 510
Milliken v. Bradley, 418 U.S. 717 (1974): 685
Minersville School District v. Gobitis, 310 U.S. 586 (1940): 530
Minnesota v. Barber, 136 U.S. 313 (1890): 392
Minnesota Rate Cases, 230 U.S. 352 (1913): 425, 445
Minor v. Happersett, 21 Wallace 163 (1875): 690
Miranda v. Arizona, 377 U.S. 201 (1966): 622, 635, 730
Mishkin v. New York, 383 U.S. 502 (1966): 629
Mississippi v. Johnson, 4 Wallace 475 (1867): 353
Missouri ex rel. Gaines v. Canada, 305 U.S. 337 (1938): 585
Missouri v. Holland, 252 U.S. 416 (1920): 558
Mistretta v. U.S., 109 U.S. 647 (1989): 753
Mitchell v. U.S., 313 U.S. 80 (1941): 584
Monsanto Co. v. Spray-Rite Service Corp., 104 S.Ct. 1464 (1984): 746
Moore v. City of East Cleveland, 431 U.S. 494 (1977): 742
Moore v. Illinois, 14 Howard 13 (1852): 248
Moran v. Burbine, 106 S.Ct. 1135 (1986): 730
Morehead v. New York ex rel. Tipaldo, 298 U.S. 587 (1936): 487
Morgan v. Virginia, 328 U.S. 373 (1946): 584
Morrison v. Olson, 108 S.Ct. 1135 (1986): 722, 751–53
Motor Vehicles Manufacturers Association v. State Farm Mutual, 103 S.Ct. 2856
    (1983): 716

Mountain Timber Co. v. Washington, 243 U.S. 219 (1917): 444
Mueller v. Allen, 103 S.Ct. 3062 (1983): 736
Mugler v. Kansas, 123 U.S. 623 (1887): 395
Muir v. Louisiana Park Theatrical Association, 347 U.S. 971 (1955): 592
Mulford v. Smith, 307 U.S. 38 (1939): 491
Muller v. Oregon, 208 U.S. 412 (1908): 444, 447, 452, 456
Munn v. Illinois, 94 U.S. 113 (1877): 389–91, 396, 451
Murdock v. Pennsylvania, 319 U.S. 105 (1943): 527
Murray v. Carrier, 106 S.Ct. 2639 (1986): 756
Myers v. U.S., 272 U.S. 52 (1926): 497, 670, 752

Nashville Gas v. Satty, 434 U.S. 137 (1978): 691
National Labor Relations Board v. Fainblatt, 306 U.S. 601 (1939): 490
National Labor Relations Board v. Friedman–Harry Marks Clothing Co., 301 U.S.
    58 (1937): 488
National Labor Relations Board v. Jones and Laughlin Steel Corp., 301 U.S. 1
    (1937): 488, 519
National League of Cities v. Usery, 426 U.S. 833 (1976): 683, 749
National Prohibition Cases, 253 U.S. 350 (1920): 463
National Treasury Employees v. Von Raab, 109 S.Ct. 1384 (1989): 731
Neal v. Delaware, 103 U.S. 370 (1880): 358
Near v. Minnesota, 283 U.S. 697 (1931): 518
Nebbia v. New York, 291 U.S. 502 (1934): 475
Nebraska Press Association v. Stuart, 427 U.S. 539 (1976): 700
Nelson and Globe v. City of Los Angeles, 362 U.S. 1 (1960): 574
New Jersey v. Wilson, 7 Cranch 164 (1812): 189
New State Ice Co. v. Liebmann, 285 U.S. 262 (1932): 451
New York v. Belton, 68 L. Ed 2d 222 (1981): 693
New York ex rel. Bryant v. Zimmerman, 278 U.S. 63 (1928): 567
New York v. Ferber, 458 U.S. 747 (1982): 733
New York v. Miln, 11 Peters 102 (1837): 231
New York Central Railroad Co. v. White, 243 U.S. 188 (1917): 444
New York Times v. Sullivan, 376 U.S. 254 (1964): 625–26, 628, 732
New York Times Co. v. U.S., 403 U.S. 713 (1971): 675, 699
Nixon v. Herndon, 273 U.S. 536 (1927): 595
Nixon v. Sirica, 487 F. 2d 700 (1973): 669
Nollan v. California Coastal Commission, 483 U.S. 825 (1987): 748
North American Co. v. Securities and Exchange Commission, 327 U.S. 686 (1946):
    492
Northern Pacific Railway Co. v. North Dakota, 236 U.S. 585 (1919): 436
Northern Pipeline Construction Co. v. Marathon Pipeline Co., 458 U.S. 50 (1981):
    750
Northern Securities Co. v. U.S., 193 U.S. 197 (1903): 420–21
Noto v. U.S., 367 U.S. 290 (1961): 575

Ogden v. Saunders, 12 Wheaton 213 (1827): 193
Okanagan Indians v. U.S., 279 U.S. 655 (1929): 664
Oklahoma ex rel. Phillips v. Atkinson, 313 U.S. 508 (1941): 493

In re Oliver, 333 U.S. 257 (1948): 620
Olmstead v. U.S., 279 U.S. 849 (1928): 464
Olsen v. Nebraska, 313 U.S. 236 (1941): 495
Oregon v. Mitchell, 400 U.S. 112 (1971): 652
Osborn v. Bank of United States, 9 Wheaton 738 (1824): 185–86
Oyama v. California, 322 U.S. 633 (1948): 558

Pacific Gas and Electric Co. v. Public Utilities Commission of California, 106 S.Ct. 903 (1986): 732
Palko v. Connecticut, 302 U.S. 319 (1937): 520–21, 522, 620, 623
Panama Refining Co. v. Ryan, 293 U.S. 388 (1935): 475
Parker v. Brown, 317 U.S. 341 (1943): 494–95
Pasadena Board of Education v. Spangler, 427 U.S. 424 (1976): 685
Passenger Cases, 7 Howard 283 (1849): 233
Patterson v. Colorado, 205 U.S. 454 (1907): 512
Paul v. Virginia, 8 Wallace 168 (1869): 492
Payton v. New York, 100 Supreme Court Reporter 1371 (1980): 693
Pennekamp v. Florida, 328 U.S. 331 (1946): 531
Pennsylvania v. Delaware Valley Citizens' Council for Clean Air, 107 S.Ct. 3078 (1987): 756
Pennsylvania v. Nelson, 350 U.S. 497 (1956): 575–76
Pennsylvania v. Wheeling Bridge Co., 13 Howard 518 (1851): 234, 237
Pennsylvania Coal Co. v. Mahon, 260 U.S. 393 (1922): 451, 747,–48
Penry v. Lynaugh, 109 S.Ct. 2934 (1989): 731
Pensacola Telegraph Co. v. Western Union Telegraph Co., 96 U.S. 1 (1877): 392
Peters v. Hobby, 349 U.S. 331 (1956): 573
Peterson v. Greenville, 373 U.S. 244 (1963): 594
Philadelphia and Reading Railroad Co. v. Pennsylvania, 15 Wallace 232 (1873): 391–92
Phillips v. Martin Marietta Corp., 400 U.S. 542 (1971): 690
Pierce v. Society of Sisters, 268 U.S. 510 (1925): 516
Pierce v. U.S., 252 U.S. 239 (1920): 514
Pinkus v. U.S., 436 U.S. 293 (1978): 733
Planned Parenthood of Central Missouri v. Danforth, 428 U.S. 52 (1976): 740
Plessy v. Ferguson, 163 U.S. 537 (1896): 359, 583
Plyler v. Doe, 457 U.S. 202 (1982): 739
Pointer v. Texas, 380 U.S. 400 (1965): 622
Polish National Alliance v. National Labor Relations Board, 322 U.S. 643 (1944): 492
Pollock v. Farmers' Loan and Trust Co., 157 U.S. 429 (1895): 401–402, 431
Pollock v. Farmers' Loan and Trust Co., 158 U.S. 601 (1895): 402–403, 431
Posadas de Puerto Rico Associates v. Tourism Co. of Puerto Rico, 106 S.Ct. 2968 (1986): 732
Powell v. Alabama, 287 U.S. 45 (1932): 518, 619, 621
Powell v. McCormack, 395 U.S. 486 (1969): 750
Presser v. Illinois, 116 U.S. 252 (1886): 623
Price Waterhouse v. Hopkins, 109 S.Ct. 1775 (1989): 745
Prigg v. Pennsylvania, 16 Peters 539 (1842): 247–49

Prize Cases, 2 Black 635 (1863): 296–98, 300–301
Propeller Genesee Chief v. Fitzhugh, 12 Howard 443 (1851): 237
Providence Bank v. Billings, 4 Peters 514 (1830): 222, 225
Public Utilities Commission v. Pollak, 343 U.S. 451 (1952): 529

Ex parte Quirin, 317 U.S. 1 (1942): 548

Railroad Commission of Wisconsin v. Chicago, Burlington, and Quincy, 257 U.S. 563 (1922): 445
Rasmussen v. U.S., 197 U.S. 516 (1905): 385
Reagan v. Farmers' Loan and Trust Co., 154 U.S. 362 (1894): 396
Reed v. Reed, 404 U.S. 71 (1971): 691
Reitman v. Mulkey, 387 U.S. 369 (1967): 604
Retirement Board v. Alton Railroad Co., 295 U.S. 330 (1935): 476
Reynolds v. Sims, 377 U.S. 533 (1964): 617–18
Ribnik v. McBride, 277 U.S. 350 (1928): 451
Richmond Newspapers, Inc. v. Virginia, 100 Supreme Court Reporter 204 (1980): 700
Rizzo v. Goode, 423 U.S. 362 (1976): 683
Robbins v. California, 68 L.Ed. 2d 236 (1981): 693
Robbins v. Shelby County Taxing District, 120 U.S. 489 (1887): 392
Roberts v. Louisiana, 428 U.S. 325 (1976): 695
Roberts v. Louisiana, 97 Supreme Court Reporter 1993 (1977): 695
Roberts v. United States Jaycees, 104 S.Ct. 3244 (1984): 745
Robinson v. California, 370 U.S. 660 (1962): 623
Rochin v. California, 342 U.S. 165 (1952): 621
Roe v. Wade, 410 U.S. 113 (1973): 696, 740
Rogers v. Lodge, 102 S.Ct. 3272 (1982): 745
Rosenblatt v. Baer, 383 U.S. 75 (1966): 626
Rosenboom v. Metromedia Inc., 403 U.S. 29 (1971): 699
Rosenfeld v. New Jersey, 408 U.S. 901 (1972): 697
Rostker v. Goldberg, 101 Supreme Court Reporter 1 (1981): 692
Roth v. U.S., 354 U.S. 476 (1957): 629
Runyon v. McCrary, 427 U.S. 160 (1976): 604–605
Rupert v. Caffey, 251 U.S. 264 (1920): 435
Russell v. U.S., 369 U.S. 749 (1962): 577

Saia v. New York, 334 U.S. 558 (1948): 529
San Antonio School District v. Rodriguez, 411 U.S. 1 (1973): 682, 738–39
Santa Cruz Fruit Packing Co. v. National Labor Relations Board, 303 U.S. 453 (1938): 489
Scales v. U.S., 367 U.S. 203 (1961): 575
Schechter v. U.S., 295 U.S. 495 (1935): 476–77, 497
Schenck v. U.S., 249 U.S. 47 (1919): 513
Schlesinger v. Ballard, 419 U.S. 498 (1975): 692
Schneckleth v. Bustamente, 412 U.S. 218 (1973): 693
Schneider v. Irvington, 308 U.S. 147 (1939): 526–27
Schneiderman v. U.S., 320 U.S. 118 (1943): 550–51

Schnell v. Davis, 336 U.S. 933 (1949): 595–96

School District of Abington Township v. Schempp, 374 U.S. 203 (1963): 631

Schware v. New Mexico Board of Bar Examiners, 353 U.S. 232 (1957): 574

Screws v. U.S., 325 U.S. 91 (1945): 597

Second Legal Tender Cases, 12 Wallace 457 (1871): 360

Sedima S.P.R.C. v. Inrex Co., 473 U.S. 479 (1985): 748

Selective Draft Law Cases, 245 U.S. 366 (1918): 435

Senn v. Tile Layers Union, 301 U.S. 468 (1937): 524

Sharp Electronics v. Business Electronics, 108 S.Ct. 1515 (1988): 746

Shapiro v. Thompson, 394 U.S. 618 (1969): 633, 680

Shelley v. Kraemer, 334 U.S. 1 (1948): 583, 593

Sherbert v. Verner, 374 U.S. 398 (1963): 631

Shreveport Rate Cases, 234 U.S. 342 (1914): 426, 445

Ex parte Siebold, 100 U.S. 371 (1880): 358

Sipuel v. Board of Regents, 332 U.S. 631 (1948): 585–86

Skinner v. Railway Labor Executives' Association, 109 S.Ct. 1402 (1989): 731

Slaughterhouse Cases, 16 Wallace 36 (1873): 355–56, 388–89, 394

Slochower v. Board of Education of the City of New York, 350 U.S. 551 (1956): 574

Smith v. Allwright, 321 U.S. 649 (1944): 595

Smith v. Board of School Commissioners of Mobile County (S. D. Ala. 1987): 737

Smith v. Goguen, 415 U.S. 566 (1974): 697

Smith v. Murray, 106 S.Ct. 2661 (1986): 756

Smith v. U.S., 431 U.S. 291 (1977): 733

Smyth v. Ames, 169 U.S. 466 (1898): 396

Snepp v. U.S., 100 Supreme Court Reporter 1668 (1980): 699

Somerset v. Stewart, 20 How. St. Tr. 1 (1772): 244, 246

South Carolina v. Baker, 108 S.Ct. 1355 (1988): 749

South Carolina v. Katzenbach, 383 U.S. 301 (1966): 602

Spence v. Washington, 418 U.S. 405 (1974): 697

Springer v. U.S., 102 U.S. 586 (1881): 400

Stafford v. Wallace, 258 U.S. 495 (1922): 445

Standard Oil Co. v. U.S., 221 U.S. 1 (1911): 422

Stanford v. Kentucky, 109 S.Ct. 2969 (1989): 731

Stanton v. Stanton, 421 U.S. 7 (1975): 691

State Athletic Commission v. Dorsey, 359 U.S. 533 (1959): 592

Steuart and Bros. v. Bowles, 322 U.S. 398 (1944): 542

Stewart Machine Co. v. Davis, 301 U.S. 548 (1937): 488

Stone v. Farmers' Loan and Trust Co., 116 U.S. 307 (1886): 394

Stone v. Powell, 428 U.S. 465 (1976): 693

Stovall v. Denno, 388 U.S. 293 (1967): 635

Strader v. Graham, 10 Howard 82 (1850): 269, 272, 274

Strauder v. West Virginia, 100 U.S. 303 (1880): 358

Stromberg v. California, 283 U.S. 359 (1931): 518

Stuart v. Laird, 1 Cranch 299 (1803): 175

Sturges v. Crowninshield, 4 Wheaton 122 (1819): 192–93

Sunshine Anthracite Coal Co. v. Adkins, 310 U.S. 381 (1940): 492

Swann v. Adams, 385 U.S. 440 (1964): 618

Swann v. Charlotte-Mecklenburg Board of Education, 402 U.S. 1 (1971): 607, 684
Sweatt v. Painter, 339 U.S. 629 (1950): 586
Sweezy v. New Hampshire, 354 U.S. 234 (1957): 577
Swift and Co. v. U.S., 196 U.S. 375 (1905): 420
Swift v. Tyson, 16 Peters 1 (1842): 236, 506–507

Taylor v. Louisiana, 419 U.S. 522 (1975): 691
Taylor v. Mississippi, 319 U.S. 583 (1943): 531
Teague v. Lane, 109 S.Ct. 1060 (1989): 756
Tennessee Electric Power Co. v. Tennessee Valley Authority, 306 U.S. 118 (1939): 493
Terminiello v. Chicago, 337 U.S. 1 (1949): 527
Terrett v. Taylor, 9 Cranch 43 (1815): 190
Terry v. Adams, 345 U.S. 461 (1953): 596
Texas v. Johnson, 105 L. Ed. 2d 342 (1989): 734
Texas v. White, 7 Wallace 700 (1869): 318, 339, 354–55
Thornburgh v. American College of Obstetricians and Gynecologists, 106 S.Ct. 2169 (1986): 740
Thomas v. Collins, 323 U.S. 516 (1945): 526
The Thomas Jefferson, 10 Wheaton 28 (1825): 237
Thornhill v. Alabama, 310 U.S. 88 (1940): 524
Time v. Hill, 385 U.S. 374 (1967): 628
Time Inc. v. Firestone, 424 U.S. 448 (1976): 700
Tinker v. Des Moines Independent Community School District, 393 U.S. 503 (1969): 733
Tison v. Arizona, 107 S.Ct. 1676 (1987): 731
Toledo, Ann Arbor and Northern Michigan Railway Co. v. Pennsylvania Co., 54 Fed. Cas. 730 (1893): 398
Torasco v. Watkins, 367 U.S. 488 (1961): 632
Train v. City of New York, 95 S.Ct. 839 (1975): 676
Trevett v. Weeden, Rhode Island (1786): 86
Truax v. Corrigan, 257 U.S. 312 (1921): 450, 523
Tucker v. Texas, 326 U.S. 517 (1946): 527
In re Turner, 24 Fed. Cases 337 (1867): 355
Turner v. Department of Employment, 423 U.S. 44 (1975): 691
Twining v. New Jersey, 211 U.S. 78 (1908): 511, 517, 622, 633
Tyson and Bros. v. Banton, 273 U.S. 418 (1927): 451

United Mine Workers v. Coronado Coal Co., 259 U.S. 344 (1922): 450
U.S. v. Appalachain Electric Power Co., 310 U.S. 377 (1940): 493
U.S. v. Brignoni-Ponce, 422 U.S. 873 (1975): 693
U.S. v. Butler, 297 U.S. 1 (1936): 478, 480, 489
U.S. v. Calandra, 414 U.S. 338 (1973): 693
U.S. v. Carolene Products Co., 304 U.S. 144 (1938): 522, 613, 634, 681
U.S. v. Classic, 313 U.S. 299 (1941): 595
U.S. v. Cruikshank, 25 Fed. Cases 707 (1874): 356
U.S. v. Cruikshank, 92 U.S. 542 (1876): 357
U.S. v. Curtiss-Wright Export Corp., 299 U.S. 304 (1936): 534, 537, 539

U.S. v. Darby, 312 U.S. 100 (1941): 490, 502
U.S. v. E. C. Knight Co., 156 U.S. 1 (1895): 379–80, 420, 447, 479
U.S. v. Eichman, 110 L.Ed. 2d 287 (1990): 735
U.S. v. Gale, 109 U.S. 65 (1883): 358
U.S. v. Grimaud, 220 U.S. 506 (1911): 413
U.S. v. Guest, 383 U.S. 745 (1966): 601
U.S. v. Harris, 106 U.S. 629 (1883): 357
U.S. v. Harris, 403 U.S. 924 (1971): 693
U.S. v. Hoxie, 26 Fed. Cases 397 (1808): 148
U.S. v. Hudson and Goodwin, 7 Cranch 32 (1812): 165–66, 235
U.S. v. Hutcheson, 312 U.S. 219 (1941): 491
U.S. v. Jefferson Co. Board of Education, 372 F. 2d 836 (1966): 606
U.S. v. King, 7 Howard 833 (1849): 235
U.S. v. L. Cohen Grocery Co., 255 U.S. 81 (1921): 436
U.S. v. Lanza, 260 U.S. 377 (1922): 464
U.S. v. Leon, 468 U.S. 897 (1984): 730–31
U.S. v. Louisiana, 364 U.S. 500 (1960): 590
U.S. v. Lovett, 328 U.S. 303 (1946): 531–32
U.S. v. Mandujano, 425 U.S. 564 (1976): 694
U.S. v. Miller, 307 U.S. 174 (1939): 623
U.S. v. Nixon, 418 U.S. 683 (1974): 671, 750
U.S. v. O'Brien, 391 U.S. 367 (1968): 650
U.S. v. Paradise, 107 S.Ct. 1053 (1987): 743
U.S. v. Peters, 5 Cranch 115 (1809): 179
U.S. v. Powell, 212 U.S. 564 (1909): 597
U.S. v. Reese, 92 U.S. 214 (1876): 357
U.S. v. Rhodes, 27 Fed. Cases 785 (1866): 355
U.S. v. Rock Royal Cooperative, 307 U.S. 533 (1939): 491
U.S. v. Salerno, 107 S.Ct. 2095 (1987): 730
U.S. v. Seeger, 380 U.S. 163 (1965): 632
U.S. v. Southeastern Underwriters Association, 322 U.S. 533 (1944): 492
U.S. v. Trans-Missouri Freight Association, 166 U.S. 290 (1897): 376, 420, 422
U.S. v. U.S. District Court, 407 U.S. 297 (1972): 675, 694
U.S. v. U.S. Steel, 251 U.S. 417 (1920): 452
U.S. v. Wade, 388 U.S. 218 (1967): 694
U.S. v. The William, 28 Fed. Cases 614 (1808): 147
U.S. v. Worrall, 2 Dallas 384 (1798): 164
U.S. v. Wrightwood Dairy, 315 U.S. 110 (1942): 491
United Steelworkers of America v. Weber, 99 Supreme Court Reporter 2855
    (1979): 687–88, 743
United Transportation Union v. Long Island Rail Road Co., 455 U.S. 678 (1982):
    749
University of California Regents v. Bakke, 438 U.S. 265 (1978): 686, 688

Ex parte Vallandigham, 1 Wallace 243 (1864): 307
Vanhorne's Lessee v. Dorrance, 2 Dallas 304 (1795): 187
Village of Belle Terre v. Boraas, 416 U.S. 1 (1974): 742
Ex parte Virginia, 100 U.S. 347 (1880): 358

Virginia v. Rives, 100 U.S. 339 (1880): 358
Virginia v. West Virginia, 11 Wallace 39 (1870): 309
Virginia State Board of Pharmacy v. Virginia Citizens Consumer Council, 425 U.S. 748 (1976): 697

Wallace v. Jaffree, 104 S.Ct. 1704 (1985): 736
Wabash, St. Louis, and Pacific Railway Co. v. Illinois, 118 U.S. 557 (1886): 373, 392
Wainwright v. Sykes, 97 S.Ct. 2497 (1977): 756
Walker v. Birmingham, 388 U.S. 307 (1967): 650
War Prohibition Cases, 251 U.S. 146 (1919): 435
Wards Cover Packing Co., Inc. v. Atonio, 109 S.Ct. 2115 (1989): 744
Ware v. Hylton, 3 Dallas 199 (1796): 160
Washington v. Davis, 426 U.S. 229 (1976): 686
Washington v. Texas, 388 U.S. 14 (1967): 622
Watkins v. U.S., 354 U.S. 178 (1957): 577
Watson v. Fort Worth Bank, 108 S.Ct. 2777 (1988): 744
Watson v. Memphis, 373 U.S. 526 (1963): 592
Weaver v. Palmer Bros. Co., 270 U.S. 402 (1926): 451
Webster v. Reproductive Health Services, 109 S.Ct. 3040 (1989): 740–41
Weeks v. U.S., 232 U.S. 383 (1912): 620
Weinberger v. Wiesenfeld, 420 U.S. 636 (1975): 691
Wells v. Rockefeller, 394 U.S. 542 (1967): 618
Welton v. Missouri, 91 U.S. 275 (1875): 392
Wesberry v. Sanders, 376 U.S. 1 (1964): 617
West Coast Hotel Co. v. Parrish, 300 U.S. 379 (1937): 487–88
West River Bridge Co. v. Dix, 6 Howard 507 (1848): 227
West Virginia State Board of Education v. Barnette, 319 U.S. 628 (1943): 530–31
Wheaton v. Peters, 8 Peters 591 (1834): 235
White v. Regester, 412 U.S. 755 (1973): 744
Whitney v. California, 274 U.S. 357 (1927): 518, 576
Wickard v. Filburn, 317 U.S. 111 (1942): 492
Wieman v. Updegraff, 344 U.S. 183 (1952): 573
Wilkinson v. U.S., 365 U.S. 399 (1961): 577
Williams v. Florida, 399 U.S. 78 (1970): 694
Williams v. Mississippi, 170 U.S. 213 (1898): 359
Williams v. Standard Oil Co., 278 U.S. 235 (1929): 451
Willson v. Black Bird Creek Marsh Co., 2 Peters 245 (1829): 197, 222
Wisconsin v. Yoder, 406 U.S. 205 (1972): 737
Witherspoon v. Illinois, 391 U.S. 510 (1968): 695
Wolf v. Colorado, 338 U.S. 25 (1949): 620
Wolff Packing Co. v. Kansas Court of Industrial Relations, 262 U.S. 522 (1923): 451
Wolman v. Walter, 433 U.S. 229 (1977): 736
Wolston v. Readers' Digest Association, Inc., 99 Supreme Court Reporter 2701 (1979): 700
Woodson v. North Carolina, 428 U.S. 280 (1976): 695
Worcester v. Georgia, 6 Peters 515 (1832): 204–205

Wright v. U.S., 302 U.S. 583 (1938): 664
Wygant v. Jackson Board of Education, 106 S.Ct. 1842 (1986): 744
Wynehamer v. New York, 13 New York 378 (1856): 388

In re Yamashita, 327 U.S. 1 (1946): 548
Ex parte Yarbrough, 110 U.S. 651 (1884): 358
Yates v. U.S., 355 U.S. 66 (1957): 574–75, 579
Ex parte Yerger, 8 Wallace 85 (1869): 354
Young v. American Mini-Theatres, 427 U.S. 50 (1976): 734
Youngstown Sheet and Tube Co. v. Sawyer, 343 U.S. 579 (1952): 537, 556–57

Zorach v. Clausen, 343 U.S. 306 (1952): 630
Zurcher v. Stanford Daily, 436 U.S. 547 (1978): 701

Index

Abortion cases, 695–96, 709, 740–41
Adams, John: on Parliament's authority over colonies, 54; in Continental Congress, 56–57; on committee to draft Declaration of Independence, 59; minister to England, 83; as vice-president, 120; and veto power, 122; and decline of executive power, 123; reads annual message to Congress, 141; appoints "midnight" judges, 162
Adams, John Quincy: as weak president, 142; supports mercantilist policy, 154–55; Indian policy, 204; protests gag rule, 252
Adams, Samuel: dominion theory of empire, 54; in Continental Congress, 56–57
Adamson Eight-Hour Act (1916), 419
Administration of Justice Act (1774), 52
Administrative agencies (federal): in progressive era, 414–16; World War I, 440; expansion in 1920s, 460–61; World War II, 540–43; in post-New Deal period, 643–48. See also Regulatory movement
Administrative Procedure Act (1946), 644
Administrative Reform Act (1950), 641
Admiralty: English admiralty law and courts in eighteenth century, 39–40; federal courts admiralty jurisdiction in Taney era, 236–37
Adolescent Family Life Act (1981), 737
Affirmative action: in 1980s cases, 742–45
Agnew, Spiro, 673; resigns as vice-president, 670
Agricultural Adjustment Act (1933), 471; invalidated, 478
Agricultural Adjustment Act (1938), 491–92
Agricultural Adjustment Administration, 471
Agricultural Marketing Act (1929), 465, 471

Agricultural Marketing Agreement Act (1937), 491
Aid to Families with Dependent Children, 711
Alabama: law concerning foreign corporations, 230; refuses to adopt reconstruction state constitution, 340; secession, 283; readmitted to Union, 340; massive resistance to desegregation in, 589; redistricting law to deny Negro voting rights, 596, 615; secular humanism case in, 737
Alien Act (1798), 131
Alien Enemies Act (1798), 131
Alien Registration (Smith) Act (1940), 561, 566, 567, 570, 571, 574, 575
American Revolution, 11; nature of constitutional issues in, 43; revolutionary constitutionalism, 65, 81; nature of as radical movement, 70–71; as conservative movement, 70–71; internal political consequences, 70–71. See also Constitutionalism; Declaration of Independence; Republicanism; States
American System, 150, 178, 201–2
Americans with Disabilities Act (1990), 716
Andros, Edmund: governor of Dominion of New England, 20–22
Annapolis Convention, 87
Antifederalists: in ratification struggle, 103–6, 109–14; constitutional ideas, 104–6; fear of unitary state, 117; contribute to Constitution worship in 1790s, 130
Antitrust: rule of reason, 452; policy after World War II, 642, 745–46
Antitrust Act of 1890 (Sherman Act), 363, 376–80, 415, 449; in relation to labor, 399–400; enforcement in progressive era, 419–23

Antitrust Act of 1914 (Clayton Act), 423, 449–50
Appropriations power: of Congress, 718–20
Arkansas: secession, 288–89; reconstruction government, 321; readmitted to Union, 340; resistance to desegregation, 589
Army Appropriation Act (1867), 341
Arnold, Thurman: on effect of government regulation, 423
Articles of Confederation, xix, 70, 772–79; affirm state equality, 55; framing, adoption, analysis of as system of government, 76–81; reforms proposed, 82; inadequacies of, 82–83; modification proposed in New Jersey Plan, 91–92
Attorney general: office created, 121; designation of subversive organizations, 562; enforces civil rights, 597, 599, 601–2
Australian (secret) ballot, 429
Automobile safety regulations, 716

Bacon's Rebellion (1676), 21–22
Bad-tendency test, 511–12
Bail Reform Act (1984), 730
Bailyn, Bernard: quoted on American constitutionalism, 63
Balanced Budget and Emergency Deficit Control Act (1985), 710–11, 713, 719, 751, 765
Balancing test, 523, 527
Bank of the United States: debate over incorporation of, 126–27; Second Bank of the United States, 152, 183; recharter bill and veto, 205–7
Bankruptcy: federal and state power asserted, 192–93
Bankruptcy courts, 750
Barbour, Philip B.: appointed to Supreme Court, 222; opinion on commerce power, 231
Bates, Edward: defends use of the war power, 304
Beard, Charles A.: *An Economic Interpretation of the Constitution of the United States*, 111; on growth of judicial power, 406
Bedford, Gunning: delegate from Delaware to Constitutional Convention, 91
Benzine case, 715–16, 746–47
Berkeley, John: proprietor of New Jersey, 16
Berkeley, William: governor of Virginia, 15, 21
Bicameralism: in Massachusetts Bay, 7–8, 13, 14; in Virginia, 15; in state constitutions of the Revolution, 71–72; in constitutional reform of 1780s, 85
Biden, Joseph H., 764
Bill of Rights: in state constitutions during Revolution, 76; in Constitutional Convention, 106; in Antifederalist critique of the Constitution, 106; in Federalist thought, 109; in ratification, 110; framing and adoption, 118–19; applicable only against federal government, 198; in relation to overseas colonialism, 385; during World War I, 512–16; effective against states, 511; nationalization of in twentieth century, 516–23, 619–24; applied to Indians on reservations, 604. *See also specific amendments;* Civil liberties; Civil rights
Bingham, John: framer of Fourteenth Amendment, 333
Bituminous Coal Act (1935), 479; Act of 1937, 492
Black, Charles L., Jr.: on contemporary judiciary, 704
Black, Hugo L.: appointed to Supreme Court, 489; concurs in California "Okie" case, 494; supports libertarian bloc, 520; incorporation of Bill of Rights, 521–22, 621–22; interprets picketing as free speech, 524; pamphlet peddling cases, 527; rejects group libel idea, 528; applies clear and present danger rule, 531; opinion in bill of attainder case, 532; opinion in *Korematsu* case, 545; invalidates military trials, 547; opinion in Steel Seizure Case, 556–57; affirms U.N. charter over state law, 558; libertarian outlook, 569; dissent in *Dennis* case, 572; forms libertarian majority, 574; affirms school desegregation, 591; maintains state-action distinction, 594; and libel law, 627; critical of *Griswold* case, 628; and free exercise of religion, 632; view of First Amendment, 636; opposes mob demonstrations, 650; opposes equal protection, 681; retirement, 679
Black codes, 326, 328, 331
Blackmun, Harry A.: appointed to Supreme Court, 679, 761; approves racial classification, 686; abortion opinion, 696, 741; as liberal, 730; on states' rights, 749
Blatchford, Samuel: appointed to Supreme Court, 393; opinion in *Chicago, Milwaukee* case, 395
Board of Economic Warfare (World War II), 541
Board of Trade, 24, 28
Boland amendments, 724, 725, 726
Bonus bill (1816), 152–53
Bork, Robert: attorney general, 66–70, 762; Supreme Court nomination of, 727, 730, 755, 761–64, 767
Boston Port Act (1774), 52

Bradley, Joseph P.: appointed to Supreme Court, 360; on Electoral Commission, 351; opinions on civil rights and Fourteenth Amendment, 356–57; *Slaughterhouse* dissent, 389, 394; dissent in *Chicago, Milwaukee* case, 396

Brandeis, Louis D.: affirms War Prohibition Act, 435–36; applies Sherman Act to labor, 460; dissent in antitrust case, 452; view of judicial function, 455–56; as liberal in 1930s, 474; voids Frazier-Lemke Act, 478; dissent in *Butler* case, 478; supports federal regulation of production, 480; connection with Frankfurter, 489; opinion in *Erie* case, 506; dissent in free speech cases, 514, 517; forms liberal bloc, 520; upholds picketing, 524; Brandeis brief, 444, 452

Brennan, William J.: appointed to Supreme Court, 569; joins libertarian bloc, 574; upholds Communists' rights, 579; opinion in Maryland sit-in case, 594; invalidates literacy tests, 602; and affirmative action, 606; opinion in *Baker v. Carr*, 616; reapportionment principle, 619; incorporation problem, 622; proposes *New York Times* rule, 626–27; and right of privacy, 628; upholds postal censorship, 629; supports egalitarianism, 623; approves racial classification, 686–87; opposes gender classification, 692; opposes capital punishment, 695; as liberal, 730; flag burning opinions of, 734–35; on Attorneys' Fees Act, 756; on state constitutions, 757; on original-intent, 760; resignation of, 764

Brewer, David J.: appointed to Supreme Court, 393; role in income tax case, 403

Bricker, John: Bricker amendment, 558–59

Brockenbrough, William: criticizes John Marshall, 185

Brown, Henry B.: appointed to Supreme Court, 393; opinion in insular cases, 384–85; income tax cases, 402; opinion in *Muller v. Oregon*, 444

Buchanan, James: role in *Dred Scott* case, 270; secession policy, 283

Budget and Accounting Act (1921), 364, 416, 496–97

Budget and Impoundment Control Act (1974), 676, 709, 719

Budget deficit, 706, 709, 713

Budget process, 718–19

Bureau of the Budget, 498–99, 641, 662; creation of, 718. *See also* Office of Management and Budget

Bureau of Corporations, 421–22

Burger, Warren E.: appointed to Supreme Court, 679; supports affirmative action, 606–7, 679, 684, 687–88; and employment discrimination, 609; opinion on executive privilege, 671–72; and sex discrimination cases, 691–92; definition of obscenity, 698; on press access to trials, 700; as conservative, 730; on legislative veto, 750; on separation of powers, 751; retirement of, 730

Burger Court: resists egalitarianism, 680–83; and women's rights, 689–92; criminal procedure, 692–95; and freedom of speech, 697–98; and freedom of the press, 698–701; judicial activism of, 680, 701–2; on civil liberties in 1980s, 729–35; religious exercise and, 735–38; on suspect classifications, fundamental rights, and government regulation, 738–42; and affirmative action, 742–45; on economic and property rights, 745–47; on separation of powers, 749–52; judicial restraint of, 754–57

Burr, Aaron: election of 1800, 143; role in Chase impeachment, 169; treason trial, 175–77

Burton, Harold H.: appointed to Supreme Court, 568; opinion in Steel Seizure Case, 557; desegregation decision, 606

Bush, George: election of, 706; pocket veto of bill extending Chinese students' residency issued by, 714*n*; Hatch Act amendment vetoed by, 500; military power used by, 727; Souter nominated by, 764

Bush administration: regulatory state maintained by, 716; flag burning issue and, 734–35

Butler, Pierce, 474

Byrnes, James F., 489

Calhoun, John C.: relation to Kentucky and Virginia Resolutions, 134–35; constitutional views, 150–54; supports Jacksonian coalition, 201; nullification crisis, 207–12; mail controversy, 253; state sovereignty theory, 253, 257–58

California: as territory, 259–60; admitted to Union, 261; Proposition 14 and Fourteenth Amendment, 603–4; tax revolt of, 709

Calvert, Cecilius: second Lord Baltimore, 11

Calvert, George: first Lord Baltimore, 10

Cambridge Agreement (1629), 6

Campbell, John A.: opposes corporation as citizen in diversity jurisdiction, 230; concurs in *Dred Scott* opinion, 274

Cannon, Joseph, 427–28

Capital punishment, 695, 731–32

Cardozo, Benjamin N.: on liberal bloc, 474, 520; dissent in *Butler* case, 478; supports federal regulation, 480; affirms Social Security Act, 489; on incorporation of Bill of Rights in Fourteenth Amendment, 520–21, 620

Carswell, G. Harrold, 679, 761

Carter, James E., 656

Carter administration, 721

Carteret, George, 16

Cass, Lewis, 259–60

Catron, John: appointed to Supreme Court, 222; affirms concurrent state power over interstate commerce, 232; concurs in *Dred Scott,* 274; death, 360

Chase, Salmon P.: presides over Johnson impeachment trial, 343; opinion in habeas corpus case, 354–55; upholds Civil Rights Act, 355

Chase, Samuel: impeachment trial, 168–70; vested rights, 187–88

Chayes, Abram, 758–59

Child Labor Act (1916), 418, 419; second Child Labor Act (1919), 448

Child pornography, 733–34

Church and state: separation of, 735

Circuit Court Act (1802), 167, 175

Circuit courts (federal): organization and jurisdiction of, 157, 161–63, 165, 359–60

Circular Letter of Massachusetts General Court, 62–63

Citizenship: in Confederation period, 77; problem of Negro citizenship, 270–72, 330; national and state as defined in Civil Rights Act of 1866 and Fourteenth Amendment, 330–31, 332; and Indians, 380–83; and inhabitants of overseas colonies, 383–85

Civil liberties: definition of civil liberty, 508–10; pre-World War I, 510–12; in twentieth century, xx, 508–32; and World War II, 543–47; and Communist problem, 559–80; and right of privacy, 627–29; Supreme Court's 1980s decisions on, 729–35. *See also specific amendments;* Bill of Rights; Libertarianism

Civil rights: defined, 508–10; nationalization of during reconstruction, 333–35, 358–61; enforcement of, 346–50, 355; in twentieth century, xx; and Japanese-Americans, 543–47; and Negroes in twentieth century, 581–611; legislation, 595–602; in school integration, 605–7; affirmative action approach toward, 602–11, 679–82, 684–89; women's rights, 689–92; Section 1983 (U.S. Code), 703; Con-

gress exempt from laws on, 712–13; lawyers' fees and, 756; civil rights acts: 1866, 329–32, 355, 359, 596, 601, 604; 1875, 350, 357, 599; 1957, 597–98; 1960, 598; 1964, 594–95, 598–602, 608, 687, 690, 742–45. *See also* Enforcement Acts

Civil Rights Attorneys' Fees Awards Act (1976), 756

Civil Service Act (1883), 369–70

Civil Service Commission, 369, 499–500, 582

Civil War: and emergency government, 292–98; legal nature of, 298–301; internal security measures, 301–7; expansion of federal power, 308–11, 708; conscription, 311–13; Union war aims, 313–15; emancipation, 315–17; constitutional significance of, 317–18

Civilian Conservation Corps, 470

Clark, Tom C.: appointed to Supreme Court, 568–69; and film censorship, 529; supports executive prerogative, 557; affirms state-action theory, 592; upholds Civil Rights Act of 1964, 600; concurs in reapportionment case, 617; and exclusionary rule, 621; school-prayers question, 631–32; retroactivity problem, 634–35

Clarke, John H., 514

Clay, Henry, 150; view of constitutional change, 154; supports land sales distribution bill, 203; Union theory, 212; and Compromise of 1850, 260

Clayton, John: Clayton Compromise, 259, 261

Clear and present danger rule, 513–16, 523; in Communist cases, 567, 570–72; repudiated, 580

Cleveland, Grover: conception of executive office, 363; and removal power, 365; Pullman strike, 398–99, 400, 410

Clifford, Nathan, 351

Coelho, Tony, 728

Coke, Edward, 61–62

Colonial agents, 28

Colonial constitution, xv; in seventeenth century, 12–26; in eighteenth century, 42; mixed government framework, 29–30; role of assembly, 24–26, 27–29; assembly struggles against governors, 38; assembly and local autonomy, 41–42, 49, 50–51; colonial governor, 29–35, 37–38; colonial council, 29, 33; colonial politics, nature of, 20–23, 33–38; colonial judiciary, 39–40; county courts, 41–42

Comity: comity clause in Articles of Confederation, 77, 80–81; in slavery conflicts among states, 245–46

Commerce Court, 425

Commerce power: in Constitutional Convention, 95; in ratification debate, 116; in embargo, 146–47; in Marshall era, 194–97; in Taney period, 230–34; Cooley rule, 233–34, 237; slaves as articles of commerce, 250–51; for national free trade area, 391–93; as basis of federal police power, 416–19; and New Deal legislation, 488–93; and state regulation in 1930s, 493–95

Commission on Executive, Legislative, and Judicial Salaries, 720

Commission on Sentencing Guidelines, 720

Committee on Public Information (World War I), 440

Committees of correspondence, 54–55

Common law, xx, 30, 39; reception in colonies, 39; seditious libel, 131; as part of federal law, 131–33, 156, 159, 163–66; federal common law under *Swift v. Tyson,* 236, 506

Communist Control Act (1954), 567

Community Relations Service, 599–600

Compromise of 1850, 257, 259–62

Comptroller general of the United States, 416, 497, 710n, 751

Concessions and Agreement (1665), 17

Confederate States of America, 285–86, 299–301

Confederation, *see* Articles of Confederation

Confiscation Act (1861), 315–16; Act of 1862, 302–3, 314

Congress: formation of in Constitutional Convention, 93–96; passes organic legislation, 119–22; resists executive domination, 123; committee development, 123; ascendancy in early nineteenth century, 142; and emergency government during Civil War, 295–97; adopts dual-status theory, 300–301; asserts Union war aims, 313–17; forms reconstruction policy, 325–35; impeachment of Johnson, 340–46; control of administration in late nineteenth century, 363–65; coercion by riders, 364; House of Representatives reform of internal organization, 370–71; delegation of power to executive, 436–41, 472–74, 476, 537, 539–40; war-powers legislation during World War II, 539–40; concedes warmaking power to executive, 554–55; investigations, 563–65, 577; Nixon impeachment inquiry, 670–73; legislation restricting executive, 675–77; Democratic control of, 705–8; budget deficit and, 710–11, 713; civil rights laws not applied to, 712–13; regulatory struggle between executive and, 713–17; Chinese

students residency bill and, 714n; legislative supremacy and, 717–20; as people's representatives, 718; unconstitutionality of legislative veto of, 718, 750–51; budget process and, 718; appropriations power of, 718–20; omnibus continuing resolution passed by, 719; outside commissions created by, 720; Iran-Contra affair and, 723–27; flag burning issue and, 734–35; separation of powers and, 749–53

Congressional Budget Office, 676, 751

Connecticut: founding, 8, 9–10, 11; charter of 1662, 19; under Dominion of New England, 20, 23; government restored, 24; charter as revolutionary constitution, 69, 72; ratifies Constitution, 110; welfare residence law, 633

Conscription: in Civil War, 311–13; in World War I, 435; in World War II, 540

Constitution of the United States, xxii–xxiv, 780–800; formation of, 87–102; ratification, 103–16; 1780s judicial view of, 86–87; embodies republican principle, 87; relationship to American Revolution, 109, 113–16; and political parties, 129–30; worship of, 130; disputes concerning meaning of, 117, 134; nature of constitutional politics, 145; adequacy of during Civil War, 291–92; during World War II, 551–52; Article V convention process, 765–66; politicization of, 754–55; amendment vs. change of, 764–67. *See also specific amendments;* Bill of Rights; Constitutional Convention

Constitutional Convention (1787), xxiii; Virginia Plan, 87–92; New Jersey Plan, 91–93; Great Compromise, 93–96; formation of executive branch, 96–98; judiciary, 98–100; locus of sovereignty, 101–2; negative over state legislation, 88–89, 98–99; supremacy clause, 92, 99; view of judicial power, 157–59

Constitutionalism, xix–xxiv; Roman, xx; English conception of, 27, 44, 61–62, 68, 116; American, central themes of, 1, 11, 12, 28, 100–101, 140, 156, 363; American, seventeenth-century development of, 25–26; in eighteenth century, 30; in revolutionary era, 43, 61–64; in ratification debate, 115–16; Marshall's contribution to, 197–99; threatened by slavery, 263; threatened by secession, 289–300; in Civil War, 301, 317–18; relation to overseas imperialism and Indian policy, 380–85; reformist approach to in New Deal era, 481; impact of New

Constitutionalism *(continued)*
Deal on, 503–7; in World War II, 551–52; effect of civil rights movement on, 609–11; attacked in 1960s, 648–53; effect of Watergate on, 673–77; effect of politicization on, 654–56; limited government and, 708–13; positive vs. negative liberty in, 711; minority rights and, 755; original-intent debate and, 757–61; divided government and, 705–8, 712–17, 727–28
Continental Association, 57
Continental Congress: first, 56–57, 68, 76–81; second, 58–63
Contract clause (Article I, Section 10): in Marshall era, 186–90, 192–93; in Taney era, 228–29, 387
Contract law: in state courts, 235–36
Contras, 723–27, 767
Cooley, Thomas, 375
Coolidge, Calvin: advocates laissez-faire principles, 456–57; vetoes McNary-Haugen bill, 461–62; and executive reorganization, 497
Corporation: in English history, 2; as basis of government in Virginia and Massachusetts, 4–8, 11; congressional power to create, 126–27; in Marshall Court decisions, 190–92; Jacksonian policy toward, 223–24; in Taney Court, 229–30; regulation by states, 376, 391; and Antitrust Act, 376–80; as person under the Constitution, 394; regulation under antitrust laws in progressive period, 419–23
Corwin, Edward S.: view of Constitution as law, 99; on vested-rights doctrine, 186; on New Deal impact on Constitution, 481; assessment of Supreme Court, 507; on executive power, 536, 539
Cotton dust case, 716
Covenant: as basis for colonization, 6–7, 11, 63
Cox, Archibald: Watergate special prosecutor, 667–68, 669–70, 721, 762
Crittenden, John J.: Crittenden Compromise Resolutions, 284; Crittenden-Johnson Resolutions on war aims, 313–15
Croly, Herbert: view of public administration, 414–15
Cumberland (National) Road, 152–53; Cumberland Road veto, 153
Cummings, Homer: attorney general, role in Court-packing plan, 482
Curtis, Benjamin R.: opinion in *Cooley* case, 233–34; dissent in *Dred Scott* case, 274

Dallas, Alexander James: view of federal common law, 164–65

Daniel, Peter V.: upholds state eminent domain power, 227; opposes corporations, 230; concurs in *Dred Scott,* 274
Davenport, John, 9
Davis, David: on Electoral Commission, 351
Davis, Henry Winter: theory of reconstruction, 323; reconstruction bill, 321–22, 324
Davis, Jefferson: asserts rights of slave property in territories, 258; secession theory, 281–82; on Committee of 33 (1861), 284; treason trial, 303
Davis, John: upholds embargo, 147
Davis, John W., 586
Dawes Severalty Act (1887), 382
Day, William R.: opinion in *Hammer v. Dagenhart,* 447–48
Declaration and Resolves of First Continental Congress, 56–57
Declaration of Causes and Necessity of Taking Up Arms, 58
Declaration of Independence, xxii, 59–61, 67–69, 764, 768–71
Declarative jurisprudence, 453–54, 480–81
Declaratory Act (1766), 50
Defense Plant Corporation (World War II), 542
Defense spending, by Reagan administration, 706, 710
Defense Supplies Corporation (World War II), 542
Delaware: revolutionary government in, 55; revolutionary constitution, 69, 72; ratifies Constitution, 110
Democratic party: Jacksonian origins, 212–14; and Compromise of 1850, 261; in realignment of 1850s, 264–65; and popular sovereignty, 267–68, 275; and election of 1860, 280; and election of 1876, 350–52; and election of 1896, 406–7; Congress controlled by, 705–8; budget deficit and, 709–10, 713; Bork nomination and, 761–64
Desegregation: *see* Civil rights
Dickinson, John: federal theory of empire, 47–48; defends colonial assembly, 51–52; in first Continental Congress, 56, 58; and American conception of constitutionalism, 63; draft of Articles of Confederation, 78–79, 80; supports state election of senators, 90; favors weak executive, 96
District courts (federal): under Judiciary Act of 1789, 157; under Judiciary Act of 1801, 162; flag burning case and, 734–35; in Yonkers housing discrimination case, 756–57
District of Columbia: slavery and slave trade in, 251–53; abolition of slavery in, 315

District of Columbia Circuit Court of Appeals, 721

Diversity jurisdiction: under Judiciary Acts of 1789 and 1801, 163; available for corporations, 229–30; relation to state courts, 235–36, 506–7

Divided government: as constitutional problem in 1980s, 705–8, 712–17, 727–28; political sources of, 705–8; budget deficit and, 709–13; foreign policy and, 723–27; Supreme Court and Constitution under, 729–53; legislative veto and, 750–51

Domestic Council (Nixon administration), 662

Dominion of New England, 20–24, 44

Dorr, Thomas Wilson, 220; Dorr Rebellion, 219–20, 237

Douglas, Stephen A.: and Compromise of 1850, 259–62; Kansas-Nebraska Act, 265–68; debates Lincoln, 275–78; candidate in election of 1860, 280

Douglas, William O.: appointed to Supreme Court, 489; concurs in California "Okie" case, 494; view of rationality test, 495; supports libertarian bloc, 520, 574; endorses total incorporation theory, 521; supports preferred freedoms doctrine, 522; rejects group libel theory, 528; upholds war power, 542; upholds Japanese-American relocation policy, 546; dissent in treason case, 549–50; affirms U.N. charter over state law, 558; libertarian outlook, 569; dissent in *Dennis* case, 572; and freedom of speech, 579–80; view of state action in civil rights cases, 593, 594, 597; upholds Civil Rights Act of 1964, 600; asserts one man, one vote rule, 617; and libel law, 627; asserts right to privacy, 628, 636; on separation of church and state, 630–31; opposes death penalty, 695

Drug testing, 731

Dual federalism: Jacksonian origins, 200–203, 205–7, 209–12; and Taney Court, 223; in commerce cases of Taney era, 230–34; affirmed by Taney, 279; after Civil War, 387; revived in *Hammer v. Dagenhart*, 447–48; in anti-New Deal decisions, 480; extinction of, 502

Duane, William, 216

Due process: Fourteenth Amendment, procedural view, 387–88; substantive view, 388–91, 404–5. *See also* Fourteenth Amendment; Judicial review

Dulany, Daniel: asserts federal theory of empire, 47

Durham, Palatinate: powers of government, 11, 16

Duval, Gabriel: appointed to Supreme Court, 177

Eaton, Theophilus, 9

Economic Opportunity Act (1964), 647

Economic Stabilization Act (1970), 653

Eighteenth Amendment, 462–64

Eighth Amendment: incorporated in Fourteenth Amendment, 623; and death-penalty cases, 695, 731–32; excessive fines prohibited by, 748

Eisenhower, Dwight D.: and war-making power, 555; loyalty review policy, 562–63; exercise of executive power, 641

Electoral college: 718; in Constitutional Convention, 97; operation 1788–89, 119–20; amended, 143

Electoral Commission (1877), 350–52

Eleventh Amendment, 181–82, 186

Ellsworth, Oliver, 92: author of Judiciary Act of 1789, 157

Emancipation: during Civil War, 315–17; proposed by Lincoln, 315; Proclamation of, 316–17; result of Civil War, 318; in reconstruction policy, 320

Embargo, 146–48

Emergency Banking Act (1933), 470

Emergency Fleet Corporation (World War I), 440

Emergency Price Control Act (1942), 541

Eminent domain: and Taney Court, 227; and Justice Field, 391

Employer's Liability Act (1906), 418–19; second Employer's Liability Act, 419

Employment Act (1946), 641

Enforcement Acts: 1870, 348, 596; February 1871, 349, 359; April 1871 (Ku Klux Act), 348–49

England: constitution, 28–29, 34, 37, 65–66; British Empire, xxii, 12–15, 18–21, 23–28, 44–45, 65, 717; reception of common law in empire, 39; federal theory of empire, 46–50, 56–57; dominion theory of empire, 53–55, 61

Environmental Protection Agency, 653, 654, 716

Equal Employment Opportunity Commission, 599, 608, 690

Equal Pay Act (1963): amendment to Fair Labor Standards Act, 690

Equal protection of the law: *see* Civil rights; Fourteenth Amendment

Equity: in English law, 39–40

Equity jurisdiction: in labor disputes, 398

Erdman Act (1898): prohibits yellow-dog contracts, 418, 447

Espionage Act (1917), 512–14

Essex Result, 85

Establishment clause: and exercise of religion, 735–38
Ethics in Government Act (1978), 713, 721–22, 752
Exclusionary rule, 620–21, 692–93
Executive: in revolutionary state constitutions, 72–74; in Constitutional Convention, 96–98; effect of Washington on, 121–23; cabinet development, 123; power over foreign affairs, 124–25; effect of Jefferson on, 141–48; Jackson's exercise of executive power, 200–201, 214–17; executive veto, 215; Lincoln's exercise of power, 291–95; weakness of in late nineteenth century, 363–65; strengthened in early twentieth century, 409–16; expanded during World War I, 436–41; Franklin D. Roosevelt's effect on, 469–70, 504–5; FDR and foreign policy power, 533–39; FDR and World War II, 539–43; executive war-making power in cold war, 553–55; post-New Deal executive, 640–41; imperial presidency post-World War II, 658–60; effect of Nixon on, 660–67; toward plebiscitary presidency, 664–67; post-Watergate restrictions on, 675–77; Republican control of, 705–8; regulatory struggle between Congress and, 713–17; and legislative supremacy of Congress, 717–20; republicanist fear of tyranny by, 717; as elected by electoral college, 718; budget process and, 718; Iran-Contra affair and, 723–27; Reagan's strengthening of, 727; separation of powers and, 749–53; democratization of, 766. See also Impoundment; Removal power; War power
Executive Office of the President, 498, 499, 714
Executive Order No. 12291, 714–15
Executive Order No. 12498, 715
Executive privilege, 668–69, 671–72, 750
Executive reorganization, 416; in 1930s, 486; and New Deal, 496–500
Executive Reorganization Act (1939), 498–99
Export Trade Board (World War I), 440

Fair Employment Practices Commission (1941), 582, 597
Fair Labor Standards Act (1938), 490, 749
Farm Mortgage Act (1935), 484
Federal block grants, 647–48
Federal Bureau of Investigation, 659, 666, 731
Federal Election Campaign Act (1974), 697
Federal Farm Board, 465
Federal Farm Loan Board, 415

Federal grant-in-aid, 459, 501, 502, 647
Federal police power, 416–19
Federal Power Commission, 460
Federal Radio Commission, 460
Federal Reserve Board, 415
Federal Road Act (1916), 459
Federal Surplus Deposit Act (1836), 203
Federal Test Act (1865), 353
Federal Trade Commission: in 1920s, 461
Federal Trade Commission Act (1914), 415, 423
Federalism: defined, 13, 27, 43, 46; in imperial-constitution controversy, 49; in Articles of Confederation, 79–81; in Constitutional Convention, 101–2; in ratification debates, 108–9, 116; as issue in constitutional politics, 140; role of Supreme Court in maintaining, 158, 160; Marshall's theory of, 197; Calhoun's theory of, 208–9; effect of Civil War on, 308–11; effect of Thirteenth Amendment on, 326–27; effect of Fourteenth Amendment on, 333–34, 358; effect of reconstruction on, 360–61; weakened federal administration, 365–66; in progressive reform, 431; federal power extended in twentieth century, 456–64; in New Deal era, xxiii–xxiv, 489–93, 500–503, 708–9; impact of United Nations treaties on, 558; cooperative federalism, 647; revival of concern for by Burger Court, 683; spending limits and, 710; separation of powers and, 749–53; judicial restraint and, 759. See also Dual federalism; State sovereignty; Union
Federalist No. 1, 115
Federalist No. 10, 106–7
Federalist No. 39, 108
Federalist No. 51, 712, 721
Federalist No. 73, 719
Federalist party: in ratification, 104, 109–13; constitutional principles, 106–9, 117–23, 129
Fess-Kenyon Act (1920): disabled veterans' rehabilitation, 459–60
Feudal patent: see Proprietary grant
Field, Stephen J.: on electoral commission, 351; attitude toward business, 389; dissent in Munn v. Illinois, 391; opinion against state taxing power, 392; Slaughterhouse dissent, 394
Fifteenth Amendment, xxiii; framing and adoption, 347–50; application and enforcement, 357–58; See also Civil rights
Fifth Amendment: as restriction on federal government, 198; in slavery controversy, 252, 257, 273, 278; in Adair case, 447; in Adkins case, 448; and Four-

teenth Amendment due process clause, 516–17, 621–23, 739–41; and criminal procedure in Burger Court, 694, 730; North and, 725, 726*n*; takings clause of, 747

First Amendment: defined as no prior restraint, 131–32, 512; in World War I cases, 513–14; incorporated in Fourteenth Amendment, 517–18, 520, 619; and preferred freedoms doctrine, 522; and picketing, 523–25; in free speech problems 1930s and 1940s, 525–29; and freedom of expression, 623–27; right of privacy, 628; obscenity as unprotected speech, 629–30; and establishment of religion question, 630–32; and free exercise of religion, 632; in free speech issues in Burger Court, 697–98; problems of press freedom, Burger Court, 698–701; in 1980s cases, 730, 732–35; religious exercise and, 736–38. *See also* Freedom of the press; Freedom of speech

Flag burning, 734–35

Flag Protection Act (1989), 734

Florida: secession, 283; readmitted to Union, 340; cohabitation law, 592

Force Act (1833), 210–11

Ford, Gerald R.: elected vice-president by Congress, 670; and War Powers Act, 676

Ford, Henry Jones: quoted on presidential power, 410

Fortas, Abe: appointed to Supreme Court, 574; nominated for chief justice, 678; resigns, 679, 761

Fourteenth Amendment: framing and original intention, 332–35; state-action theory of congressional power under, 333; in relation to Civil Rights Act of 1866, 333–34; ratified by Tennessee, 334; and Reconstruction Act of 1867, 337–38; and Negro civil rights, 355–57; economic application, 386–87; procedural and substantive due process, 387–91; interpreted in Slaughterhouse Cases, 388–91; liberty of contract, 403, 446–48; interpretation in late nineteenth century, 404–5; substantive due process in 1920s, 450–51; revival of privileges and immunities clause, 495; due process in *Meyer v. Nebraska*, 516; interpreted to include Bill of Rights, 516–19; procedural due process in Burger Court, 681–83; equal protection clause and the Burger Court, 602, 684–89, 744; source of right of privacy, 696; as individual right, 623; in *Davis v. Bandemer*, 707*n*; social issues regulated through, 709; due process clause of in 1980s, 739–41;

drug testing and, 731; takings clause of, 747

Fourth Amendment: in embargo cases, 147; incorporated in Fourteenth Amendment, 619–21; and exclusionary rule, 621, 692–93, 730–31

Frankfurter, Felix: appointed to Supreme Court, 489; advocates judicial restraint, 495–96, 520; votes with libertarian bloc, 520; and incorporation doctrine, 521; restricts picketing, 524–25; warns against judicial usurpation, 527; asserts group libel idea, 528; flag-salute case, 530; dissent in *Scheidermann* case, 551; concurs in Steel Seizure case, 557; as leader of Court in 1940s, 568; concurs in *Douds* case, 570; opposes reapportionment decision in *Baker v. Carr,* 616; interprets Fourth Amendment, 620; resigns, 574

Franklin, Benjamin. on internal and external taxes, 47, 50; on committee to draft Declaration of Independence, 59

Frazier-Lemke Farm Bankruptcy Act (1934), 478

Freedmen's Bureau Act (1865), 328; Act of 1866, 329

Freedom of the press: English view, 131; in Sedition Act crisis, 135–37; in World War I, 511; protected under Fourteenth Amendment, 517–18; in Warren Court, 624–27; in 1980s cases, 732

Freedom of speech: in Sedition Act crisis, 135–37; in World War I, 511; protected under Fourteenth Amendment, 517–18; in 1930s and 1940s, 525–32; in Warren era, 624–27; as freedom of expression, 629–30; for business, 732, 735

Freeport doctrine, 277–78

Free-Soil party, 256–57

Fugitive slaves: fugitive slave clause in Constitution, 95; Fugitive Slave Act of 1793, 246–48; Fugitive Slave Act of 1850, 238, 249, 279, 284, 334

Fuller, Melville W.: appointed to Supreme Court, 393; opinion in *Knight* case, 379; opinion in income tax cases, 401–2; dissent in oleo and lottery cases, 417–18

Fundamental Constitutions of Carolina, 17

Fundamental law: in English constitution, xxi, 61–64. *See also* Constitutionalism

Fundamental Orders of Connecticut, 9–10

Gag rule, 252–53

Gallatin, Albert: liaison with Congress as secretary of the Treasury, 141–42; internal improvement plan, 152

Galloway, Joseph; in Continental Congress, 56; plan of union, 56
Garfield, James A.: conception of executive office, 363; defends executive prerogative, 364–65; assassinated, 369
General Accounting Office, 710n, 720
General Orders No. 100 (1863), 297
General Survey Act (1824), 153
Georgia: revolutionary government in, 55; constitution of 1777, 69, 72: ratification, 110; policy toward Indian tribes, 198, 203–5; secession, 283; readmitted to Union, 340; opposes desegregation, 589
Gerry, Elbridge, 94
Ginsburg, Douglas, 730, 764
Glorious Revolution: in England, xx, 21, 26, 29, 35; in America, 21–27
Goldberg, Arthur J.: appointed to Supreme Court, 574; view of state-action theory, 594; upholds Civil Rights Act of 1964, 600
Goodnow, Frank J.: view of public administration, 414
Gramm, Phil, 710
Gramm-Rudman-Hollings bill (1985), 710–11, 713, 719, 751, 765
Grant, Ulysses S.: appointed secretary of war, 342; seeks to curtail southern violence, 348; conception of executive office, 363
Gray, Horace: appointed to Supreme Court, 393; role in income-tax cases, 403
Grier, Robert C.: opinion in Prize Cases, 296–97, 300
Guarantee of republican government: Article IV, Section 4, origin of, 84; in Dorr Rebellion, 220; in reconstruction, 320, 332–34, 338
Guild, 2–3; medieval guild merchant, 3

Habeas corpus: operation of writ under Judiciary Act of 1789, 210; in personal liberty laws, 245; in slavery controversy, 279; suspended during Civil War, 297–98, 303–4; Habeas Corpus Act of 1863, 298, 305–7, 359; Habeas Corpus Act of 1867, 353–54, 360
Hale, Matthew, 390
Hamilton, Alexander: proposes reforms in Confederation, 82; calls for Constitutional Convention, 87; favors proportional representation in Senate, 91; favors strong executive, 96; on committee on style, 102; author of the Federalist, 106, 115; as secretary of the Treasury, 122; theory of executive power, 124; constitutional doctrines, bank argument, 125–28; economic policies, 125–26; theory of implied powers, 128, 184; mercantilist outlook, 139; prediction about Jefferson as president, 146; view of judiciary, 156; theory of commerce power, 194
Hand, Learned: defines clear and present danger rule, 571
Harlan, John Marshall (1877–1911): appointed to Supreme Court, 393; on substantive due process, 395; income tax cases, 402; on executive ordinance power, 413; opinion in lottery case, 417; opinion in Northern Securities case, 420–21; opinion in Adair v. United States, 447; asserts color-blind Constitution, 583
Harlan, John Marshall (1955–1971): appointed to Supreme Court, 569; Yates opinion, 574–75; upholds congressional power of investigation, 577; sit-in decisions, 593; maintains state-action distinction, 594; invalidates North Carolina literacy test, 608; criticizes reapportionment decisions, 616–17; and libel law, 626–27; and right of privacy, 628; on obscenity problem, 629; opposes judicial activism, 633–34; retirement, 679
Harrington, James, 36, 67
Harrison, William Henry, 214
Harrison Antinarcotic Act (1914), 418
Hartford Convention, 149–50
Hat Act (1733), 47
Hatch Act (1939), 499–500
Hawaii: land reform case in, 747
Hayes, Rutherford B.: election of 1876, 350–52; conception of executive office, 363; resists coercion by riders, 364; controls patronage, 364–65
Haynesworth, Clement, 679, 761
Henry, Patrick: opposes Stamp Act, 46; calls for provincial congress, 55–56; in Continental Congress, 56
Hepburn Act (1906), 425
Hollings, Ernest, 710
Holmes, Oliver Wendell: opinion in Swift case, 421; dissent in Lochner case, 453; view of judicial function, 455–56; and free-speech problems, 513–16
Holt, Joseph: judge advocate general enforces Habeas Corpus Act, 306
Home Owners Loan Corporation, 470
Homestead Act (1862), 365
Homosexuals, 738, 741, 762
Hooker, Thomas, 36
Hoover, Herbert C.: as secretary of commerce, 442, 457–58; supports trade-association movement, 453; vetoes Muscle Shoals bill, 462; policies toward depression,

464–66; and the regulatory movement, 464–66; and executive reorganization, 497

Hoover, J. Edgar, 659; and Nixon security plan, 666

Hopkins, Stephen: asserts federal theory of empire, 47; in Continental Congress, 56

House Judiciary Committee, 751

House of Representatives: Democratic control of, 706; power of Speaker of, 717

Howard, Jacob: on congressional war power, 296; role in framing Fourteenth Amendment, 333

Howard, Oliver Otis, 328

Hughes, Charles Evans: appointed chief justice, 474; opinion in Minnesota moratorium case, 475; opinion in Gold Cases, 476; invalidates NIRA, 476–77; supports New Deal measures, 487–89; upholds National Labor Relations Act, 490; in free-speech cases, 518, 526, 530; desegregation opinion, 584

Immigration and Nationality Act (1968), 750

Impeachment: of federal judges, 167–70; Andrew Johnson, 340–46; Richard Nixon inquiry, 670–73; independent counsel as substitute for, 722, 723, 725

Imperialism: constitutional problems, 383–85

Impoundment, 662–63, 676, 709, 718–19

Income tax law (1894), 397; invalidated, 400–403

Incorporation: Bill of Rights included in Fourteenth Amendment, 516–18, 520–22, 619–24; doctrine of incorporation of overseas possessions in American constitutional system, 383–85

Independent counsel: creation of, 720–23; Iran-Contra affair and, 720, 725; separation of powers and, 750–51

Indian Removal Act (1830), 204

Indian Reorganization Act (1934), 601n

Indiana Territory, 145

Indians: Georgia conflict with Cherokees, 203–5; constitutional status of, 203; removal policy, 204; citizenship of, 381–82; federal policy toward in late nineteenth century, 380–83; federal policy since 1930s, 610; Bill of Rights applied to, 604, 738

Injunction: in labor disputes, 397–400, 449–50, 490–91

Insular cases, 383–84

Interest groups: conflict in eighteenth-century American politics, 34–35, 74–76; in ratification debate and 1790s, 103, 107; in late nineteenth century, 370–71; in progressive era, 430–31; interest-group liberalism in New Deal, xxiv, 468, 504; in post-New Deal era, 639–48; attacks on interest-group liberalism in, 1960s, 648–53; persistence of in 1970s, 653–56

Intergovernmental tax immunity, 432

Interior Department, U.S., 719

Internal improvements: as issue in Republican mercantilism, 152–53; Jackson's Maysville veto, 202; during Civil War, 310

Internal security: Union policy during Civil War, 301–8; and cold war Communist problem, 559–80; federal loyalty program, 561–63; congressional investigations, 563–65; national legislation, 565–68; state loyalty programs, 573–75

Interstate Commerce Act (1887), 363, 373–76, 415, 584; and labor disputes, 398

Interstate Commerce Commission: original powers, 373–76; in progressive era, 424–26; in 1920s, 445, 460–61

Intolerable Acts (1774), 52, 54–55

Iran-Contra affair, 723–27, 767

Iredell, James: affirms state power against vested rights, 187

Iron Act (1750), 47

Jackson, Andrew: exercise of executive power, 200–201; Maysville veto, 202; Indian policy, 203–5; bank veto, 205–7, 215; nullification crisis, 209–12; constitutional legacy, 221; removal power, 216–17, 341; Supreme Court appointments, 222; supports federal mail censorship, 251

Jackson, Howell E.: role in income tax case, 402

Jackson, Robert H.: view of Court-packing crisis, 484; appointed to Supreme Court, 489; upholds Agricultural Adjustment Act, 492; concurs in Edwards v. California, 494; rejects group libel theory, 528; opinion in second flag-salute case, 530; as attorney general and foreign-policy crisis, 535; dissent in Korematsu case, 545; and Nazi treason cases, 549, 550; dissent in denaturalization and espionage cases, 551; opinion in Steel Seizure case, 557; moderate outlook, 568; concurs in Douds case, 570

Jacksonian Democracy, xxiii; states' rights outlook, 155; constitutional-political ideology, 200–203, 205–7

James II (duke of York), 16–17, 19–20, 23

Javits, Jacob: opposes Nixon pocket veto, 664; supports War Powers Act, 675

Jaworski, Leon, 671

Jay, John: in Continental Congress, 56; author of *The Federalist,* 106; Jay Treaty, 125; as chief justice, 160–61

Jefferson, Thomas: calls for provincial congress, 55; author of Declaration of Causes and Necessity, 58; and Declaration of Independence, 59–61; on executive veto, 122; view of executive power, 124–25; argument against bank, 126–27; author of Kentucky Resolutions, 132–37; argument against federal common law, 134, 165; election of 1800, 137; inaugural address, 139; as chief executive, 141–43; and Louisiana Purchase, 144; embargo policy, 146–48; supports internal improvements constitutional amendment, 152; attitude toward judiciary, 166; conduct in Burr trial, 176–77; criticizes John Marshall, 182, 194; view of importation and migration clause, 250; and executive privilege, 668

Johnson, Andrew: and reconstruction, 320, 322–26; vetoes Freedmen's Bureau bill, 329; vetoes Civil Rights Act, 331; reconstruction policy, 334–35; opposes congressional reconstruction, 336–37; impeachment trial, 340–46; vetoes repeal of Habeas Corpus Act, 354

Johnson, Hugh S., 473

Johnson, Lyndon B.: supports interest-group liberal policies, 646; and war in Vietnam, 646, 660; use of executive war power, 658, 723; use of FBI, 658; and impoundment, 662, 718–19; Fortas nominated by, 678, 761

Johnson, William: appointed to Supreme Court, 177; circuit court opinion in embargo case, 147; rejects federal common law, 165–66; on contract clause, 193; invalidates South Carolina Negro seamen's law, 250

Johnson, William Samuel, 102

Joint Committee on the Conduct of the War, 296

Joint Committee on Reconstruction, 326, 331–35

Joint-stock company, 2–4, 16, 63

Judicial Repeal Act (1802), 166–67, 175

Judicial review: in 1780s in states, 86; in Constitutional Convention, 99–100; place in constitutional system, 156; in Marshall era, 170–75; in Taney period, 235–38; in late nineteenth century, 386–87; traditional judicial restraint outlook, 390–91; new activist review, 396–97, 403–6, 443–44; in progressive era, 450–52; in relation to theories of jurisprudence,

453–56; and Court-packing crisis, 485; judicial restraint outlook, 498; in New Deal era, 505–7; retroactivity problem, 635; liberal activist outlook of Warren Court, 634–38; revival of restraint in 1960s, 637–38; double standard-strict scrutiny review in Burger Court, 682; activism in Burger Court, 701–2; rationality test, 395–96, 404, 495; constitutionalism and, 754–67

Judiciary: power in colonial period, 30; in constitutional reform of 1780s, 85–87; reform in 1790s, 159–61; expansion of power in Taney era, 235–38; organization and jurisdiction of federal courts in reconstruction, 360; role in late nineteenth century, 386–406; equity jurisdiction, federal, 398; policy-making function, 404–5; attacked in progressive era, 451–52; effect of New Deal on, 504–7; expanding power 1970s, 701–4; restraint vs. activism of, 754–57; minority rights and, 755, 767

Judiciary Act (1789), 157–59, 162, 164, 172, 205; Section 25, 158, 180–81, 198; Section 34, 159, 236, 507*n*

Judiciary Act (1801), 161–63, 165–67, 175

Judiciary Reform Act (1937), 484

Jurisdiction and Removal Act (1875), 359

Justice Department, U.S., 721, 744

Kansas: popular sovereignty and slavery, 268–69; Lecompton constitution, 275; prohibition law, 395; law forbidding yellow-dog contracts, 447; libel case, 625

Kansas-Nebraska Act (1854), 265–68

Kendall, Amos, 212–17

Kennedy, Anthony: Supreme Court appointment of, 730, 764; flag burning concurrence of, 734

Kennedy, Edward: on Bork, 762–63

Kennedy, John F.: and war-making power, 555, 658; supports civil rights legislation, 598–99; New Frontier liberalism, 645–47; and impoundment, 662

Kent, James, 195

Kentucky: land-titles controversy, 189–90; neutrality attempted in Civil War, 308–9

King, Rufus: favors proportional representation, 91; on committee on style, 102

Ku Klux Act (1871), 348

Labor unions: legal status and rights, 397–400; in Supreme Court decisions early twentieth century, 449–50; picketing protected, 523–25

La Follette, Robert M., 452
La Follette, Robert M., Jr., 519
Laissez faire: approach to constitutionalism, xxiii, 70; in Jeffersonian Republican party, 141; constitutional doctrines in late nineteenth century, 393–94; in early twentieth century, 442–43; rejected in New Deal, 495
Lamar, Joseph R., 414
Lamar, L. Q. C., 393
Lansing, John, 91
Lawyers' fees, 756
Lecompton constitution, 275–76
Lee, Richard Henry: in Continental Congress, 56; resolution for American independence, 59; arguments against the Constitution, 104–5
Legal positivism, 63
Legal realism, 455
Legislative supremacy: Congress and, 717–20
Legislative veto, 718, 720, 750
Leisler, Jacob, 22, 24
Letters from a Pennsylvania Farmer, 47, 51, 63
Lever Act (1917), 434, 436–38, 463
Levy, Leonard: view of Warren Court, 637; on judicial activism, 758
Libel law, 624–27
Liberal Republican party, 349
Liberalism: tension between Republicanism and, 708; balance and equilibrium in, 711; rationality test and, 738; minority rights and, 755
Libertarianism: in World War I era, 510, 512; in 1930s, 515, 519–20; in New Deal, 522–23, 532; in World War II, 550–51; during cold war, 559–61
Liberty: positive vs. negative, 711–12
Liberty of contract, 403, 447
Lieber, Francis: author of General Orders No. 100, 297; expresses states' rights nationalism, 318
Limited government: in Constitution, 708; budget deficit and, 709–13
Lincoln, Abraham: Springfield Lyceum address, 221; debates with Douglas, 275–78; election 1860, 288; secession policy, 286–90; exercise of executive power, 291–95; and emergency government, 296–98; suspends habeas corpus, 304–5; and internal security policy, 306–7; on conscription, 311–13; war aims, 313–15; and emancipation policy, 315–17; reconstruction policy, 319–22
Lippmann, Walter: describes Hoover's constitutional significance, 466
Livingston, H. Brockholst: appointed to Supreme Court, 177; decides embargo case, 148

Livingston, Philip, 56
Livingston, Robert, 59
Llewellyn, Karl, 481
Lobby groups, 707
Locke, John, 36, 60
Lords of Trade, 24
Lottery Act (1895), 417
Louisiana: territorial act (1804), 250; secession, 283; reconstruction government, 321; readmitted to Union, 340; massive resistance to desegregation in, 589; sit-in conflict, 590, 593
Louisiana Purchase: constitutional issues in, 143–45, 150, 152

McCarran Internal Security Act (1950), 565–68, 576–77, 579
McFarlane, Robert, 725
McKenna, Joseph: upholds Mann Act, 418; opinion in *Gilbert v. Minnesota,* 517
McKinley, John: appointed to Supreme Court, 222
McKinley, William: election of 1896, 407; influence over Congress, 410; antitrust policy, 419–20
McLane, Louis, 216
McLean, John: appointed to Supreme Court, 222; opinion in Kentucky bank case, 224; view of state power over slavery, 232; on federal commerce power, 233–34; on slaves as beyond commerce power, 251; dissent in *Dred Scott* case, 274
McNary-Haugen bill (1927), 461, 465
McReynolds, James C.: dissent in antitrust case, 453; member of conservative bloc, 474; and proposal for retirement of federal judges, 482; opinion in *Meyer v. Nebraska,* 516
Madison, James: on parliamentary authority, 54; on weakness of Confederation, 81; supports constitutional reform, 87; proposes congressional negative, 88–89; favors proportional representation, 90; favors centralization, 92; favors strong executive, 96; supports negative on state legislation, 98; and judicial review, 100; author of *The Federalist,* 106–7, 712; theory of extended republic, 107; theory of federalism, 108; proposes Bill of Rights, 118; bill to create Department of State, 120; fears Hamilton and executive power, 124; opposes Hamiltonian policy, 126; author of Virginia Resolutions, 132–37; opposes federal common law, 133–34; as weak president, 142; vetoes bank bill, 151; Bonus Bill, 152–

Madison *(continued)*
53; opinion on internal improvements,
153; withholds commission of William
Marbury, 172–73; refrains from attacking John Marshall, 182; on protection of
minorities, 207–8; resolution against
congressional interference with slavery,
243; view of importation and migration
clause, 250
Maine: comes under Massachusetts control,
14; admitted to Union, 255
Mann Act (1910), 415, 418
Mann-Elkins Act (1910), 425
Marshall, John: prediction about Jefferson as
president, 142; and judicial review, 170,
172–75; and Burr trial, 176–77; general
political outlook, 178; defense of federal
judiciary, 179–82; Federalist theory of,
183–86; asserts national supremacy,
181–82; and corporations, 190–92; con-
tract-clause cases, 186–90, 192–93; theory of federalism, 183–86, 196–97, 206;
commerce clause, 194–97; significance
in American constitutionalism, 197–98;
Indian cases, 204–5, 381; on state taxing
power, 225; on role of judiciary, 237–38;
activism of, 758–59; death, 222
Marshall, Thurgood: racist objections to nomination of, 761; argues school desegregation case, 586; approves racial classification, 686, 688; opposes capital
punishment, 695; as liberal, 730
Martial law, *see* Habeas corpus
Martin, Luther: favors small states, 91; favors
weak executive, 96; introduces supremacy clause, 99
Maryland: in seventeenth century, 10–12, 15,
19, 21, 22–25; revolutionary government, 55; revolutionary constitution,
69, 72; ratifies Constitution, 110; taxes
Bank of U.S., 183; constitutional reform
in 1830s, 219; interferes with Union war
effort, 308–9; sit-in case, 594
Massachusetts: early history, 5–8, 12–13; charter, 5–7, 10; General Court, 13–14; position in empire, 14–15; under Dominion
of New England, 19–20; Revolution of
1689, 22; second charter, 24; revolutionary government, 55; constitution of
1780, 69, 72, 74, 85; ratifies Constitution, 110; calls Hartford Convention,
149; liquor regulations, 232; passenger
tax, 233; sojourner slave case, 246
Massachusetts Bay Company, *see* Massachusetts
Massachusetts Government Act (1774), 52
Mayflower Compact, 8–9
Mayhew, Jonathan: natural law theory, 36

Meat Inspection Act (1906), 418
Meese, Edwin, III, 760
Mellon, Andrew W., 456
Mercantilism, 35, 44, 67; in Federalist policy,
139; in Jeffersonian era, 148–55; in
states, 196–97, 239–40
Mexican War, 256
Michigan: territorial government, 219; civil
rights act, 584
Military tribunals: use in Civil War, 306–7; in
World War II, 547–49
Militia: federal power under the Constitution,
149
Militia Act (1792), 128; Act of 1862, 311
Miller, Samuel F.: on Electoral Commission,
351; Slaughterhouse opinion, 355–56,
388
Minton, Sherman: appointed to Supreme
Court, 569; dissent in Steel Seizure case,
557
Mississippi: constitutional provision concerning slaves, 231–32; secession, 283; readmitted to Union, 340; massive resistance to desegregation in, 589; sit-in
protests, 590; Negro officials in, 607
Missouri: slave territory, 201; admitted to
Union, 254–55; Missouri Compromise,
254–55, 257; Compromise line repealed,
266–67; Negro citizenship question,
271–72; Compromise restriction on
slavery invalidated by Supreme Court,
273–74; license tax, 392; segregation
policy, 585
Mitchell, John, 668
Mixed government, xxi, 28–30, 61, 66; as basis
of colonial constitution, 39, 41; in constitutional reform 1780s, 85
Molasses Act (1733), 45
Monroe, James: presidency, 142; proposes constitutional amendment for internal improvements, 153; Cumberland Road
veto, 153
Montesquieu, Charles: *Spirit of the Laws,* 38
Morris, Gouverneur: supports strong central
government, 89; hostile to western region, 94; on judicial review, 100; committee on style, 102
Morris, Robert: favors reform of Articles of
Confederation, 82
Morrison, Alexia, 751–52
Municipal reform: in progressive era, 430–31
Murphy, Frank: appointed to Supreme Court,
489; concurs in California "Okie" case,
494; supports libertarian bloc, 520; favors total incorporation, 521; on picketing as free speech, 524; obscenity decision, 525–26, 629; as attorney general
on executive power in foreign affairs,

536; dissent in *Korematsu* case, 545; Communist naturalization case, 551; on U.N. charter and state law, 558; as attorney general, view of executive emergency power, 536
Muscle Shoals bills, 462

National Bituminous Coal Conservation Act (1935), 477
National Economic Commission, 720
National Emergencies Act (1976), 676
National Industrial Recovery Act (1933), 471–74, 476–77
National Labor Relations Act (1935), 477, 484, 488–90, 519–20; Taft-Hartley amendments, 565, 569
National Recovery Administration, 472–73
National Republican party, 203, 206, 213
National Security Act, 724
National Security Council, 724, 725, 727
Natural law, xx, 35–37, 60, 63; natural rights theory and the Constitution, 114–16
Naturalization Act (1798), 131
Navigation Acts, 18–19, 21, 24, 40, 44, 51
Navy Department, 121
Nebraska, 737
Negroes: as American citizens, 230, 269–72, 273–74; suffrage and Fourteenth Amendment, 332; suffrage under reconstruction policies, 337, 339–40, 347–50. *See also* Civil rights
Nelson, Samuel: state power over interstate commerce, 232; role in *Dred Scott* case, 269–70; concurrence in *Dred Scott*, 274, 277; minority opinion in *Prize Cases*, 297
New Deal: constitutional strategy, 468–70; economic policy, 471–74; and Supreme Court, 474–80; proposed judiciary reform, 480–86; policies approved by Supreme Court, 487–95; effect on federalism, 500–503; constitutional significance, xxiii–xxiv, 503–7
New Hampshire: proprietary grant, 14; under Dominion of New England, 20; as royal colony, 23; revolutionary government, 55; revolutionary constitution, 69, 72; ratifies Constitution, 110; liquor regulations, 232; obscenity statute, 525
New Haven, 8–10, 11, 19
New Jersey: in seventeenth century, 16, 20, 23; East and West Jersey as single colony, 23; revolutionary government, 55; revolutionary constitution, 69, 72; plan in Constitutional Convention, 91–93; ratifies Constitution, 110; policy toward corporations, 377, 380

New York: as royal colony, 16, 20, 23; Charter of Liberties, 17, 23, 24; under Dominion of New England, 20; revolt, 22; receives royal charter, 23; assembly, 24–25; revolutionary government, 55; revolutionary constitution, 69, 72; ratification, 110; passenger tax, 233; ten-hour law, 446; criminal syndicalism law, 515, 517–18; Ku Klux Klan registration law, 567; English literacy requirement, 602
Nicaragua, 724
Nineteenth Amendment, 428
Ninth Amendment, 119, 628
Nixon, Richard M.: seeks strict constructionist judges, 635; supports reforms of 1970s, 649; creates EPA, 653; exercise of presidential power, 660–67; impoundment, 662–63, 709, 719; uses pocket veto, 664; and plebiscitary presidency, 664–67; Vietnam War and, 723; and Watergate, 667–75, 713, 721
Nonimportation agreements, 48, 51, 54
Norris-La Guardia Anti-Injunction Act (1932), 490–91
North, Oliver, 725–26
North Carolina: in seventeenth century, 16–17, 19, 22; revolutionary government, 55; revolutionary constitution, 69, 72; ratifies Constitution, 110; secession, 288; readmitted to Union, 340
Northwest Ordinance, 94, 243, 254
Nullification: in Kentucky Resolution, 135; in South Carolina, 201–2, 205, 207–12; in fugitive slave case, 279

Obscenity, 733–34, 735
Occupational Safety and Health Administration, 653, 655, 715–16, 746
O'Connor, Sandra Day: Supreme Court appointment of, 730, 761; on abortion, 741
Office of Civilian Defense (World War II), 541
Office of Contract Compliance, 608–9
Office of Economic Opportunity, 664
Office of Emergency Management (World War II), 541
Office of Food Administration (World War I), 440
Office of Fuel Administration (World War I), 440
Office of Management and Budget, 662, 714–15, 720, 751
Office of Price Administration (World War II), 541
Office of Production Management (World War II), 541
Office of War Censorship (World War II), 541–42

Office of War Information (World War II), 541
Ohio: admitted to Union, 152; tax on Bank of United States, 185–86; ratification of Eighteenth Amendment, 463; criminal syndicalism law, 576
Oklahoma: territory enters Union, 382; segregation policy, 586
Oleomargarine Excise Act (1902), 417
Olney, Richard: attorney general, role in Pullman strike, 399
Olson, Theodore, 751
Omnibus continuing resolution, 719
Opposition ideology: in colonial period, 33, 35–38, 50–51, 69–76, 138–39
Oregon: territorial organization, 259; ten-hour law for women, 444
Otis, James: argument in writs of assistance case, 62
Overman Act (1918), 439–40
Owen-Keating Child Labor Act (1916), 447

Packers and Stockyards Act (1921), 445, 459
Paine, Thomas: Common Sense, 58
Parliament, xx–xxi, 28, 29, 39; power of taxation, 45; in imperial constitution, 46–50; claim to sovereignty, 61–62
Paterson, William: defends state sovereignty, 90; on vested rights, 187
Peace Conference (1861), 285
Peckham, Rufus W.: appointed to Supreme Court, 393; opinion in Lochner case, 446; on judicial function, 453–54
Penn, William, 16, 17, 22
Pennsylvania: in seventeenth century, 16–18, 22–23; Charter of Privileges, 25; revolutionary government, 55; revolutionary constitution, 69, 72; ratification, 110; resists federal judiciary, 179; Buckshot war, 219; sedition prosecution, 575; welfare residence requirement, 633; parochial school aid law of, 735–36
Personal liberty laws, 248–49, 278–79
Pickering, John: impeachment trial, 168, 342
Picketing, 450, 523–25, 735
Pierce, Franklin, 265
Pinckney, Henry: proposes gag rule, 252
Pitney, Mahlon: approves workmen's compensation law, 444; opinion in Duplex case, 450
Plantation Duties Act (1673), 18
Plymouth Colony, 8–10, 12; under Dominion of New England, 20; absorbed by Massachusetts Bay, 23
Pocket veto, 664, 714n
Poindexter, John, 725, 726
Political parties: in 1790s, 129–30; in constitutional system, 136; second party system,

200, 212–14; and slavery controversy, 263–65; in Civil War, 317; constitutional function, 365; during Gilded Age, 365–68; third-party movements, 370; in late nineteenth century, 404; reform in progressive era, 427–32; initiative and referendum as reform techniques, 429; decline of, 706–7; bipartisanship action by, 713, 716; as popular representatives, 767
Politicization: in 1970s, 654–56
Polk, James K.: vetoes rivers and harbors bill, 203; view of Oregon territorial act, 259–60
Popular sovereignty: in Declaration of Independence, 60; in Confederation era, 84; in Constitutional Convention, 101; in Federalist thought, 109; in Jacksonian era, 218–21; in slavery question, 258–62; in Kansas-Nebraska Act, 265–68; after Dred Scott case, 275; in Lincoln-Douglas debates, 276–78
Pornography, 733–34, 735
Post Office Department, 121
Pound, Roscoe: on declarative jurisprudence, 454
Powell, Lewis F.: appointed to Supreme Court, 679, 761; on school financing, 682; on judicial power, 702; as centrist, 730; retirement of, 730, 762
Preferred freedoms doctrine, 521–22. See also Civil liberties
Presidency, see Executive
President's Committee on Administrative Management (Brownlow Committee), 498
Privacy: right of, 739–40
Privileges and immunities clause (Article IV, Section 2), 230. See also Fourteenth Amendment
Privy Council, 28, 40
Proclamation of Rebellion (1775), 58
Proclamation of 1763, 45, 53
Progressivism: nature and purpose of movement, 408–9; and regulatory movement, 408–9; and executive power, 409–14; and public administration, 414–16; and federal police power, 416–19; and antitrust, 419–23; and railroads, 424–26; and reform of politics, 427–44
Prohibition, 462–64; Webb-Kenyon Act, 462–63; Lever Act, 463; Eighteenth Amendment, 463–64
Prohibitory Act (1775), 58
Property Claims Act (1948), 547
Proprietary grant: as colonizing instrument, 2, 10–11, 16–18, 63
Public-interest lobby groups, 707

Public Utility Holding Company Act (1935), 492
Pullman strike, 397–99
Pure Food and Drug Act (1906), 415, 418

Quartering Act (1765), 51; Act of 1774, 52–53
Quebec Act (1774), 53

Racketeer Influenced and Corrupt Organizations Act (RICO) (1970), 748
Radio Act (1927), 460
Railroad regulation, 373–76, 424–26
Railway Labor Act (1934), 484
Railway Labor Board, 416
Ramsay, David: on state constitutions, 68
Randolph, Edmund, 89
Randolph, Edward, 19
Randolph, John, 155
Ratification of the Constitution, 103–16; economic interpretation, 111–13
Rationality test, 731
Reagan, John H., 374
Reagan, Ronald. election of, 705, 706; Washington establishment criticized by, 656, 714; regulatory struggle between Congress and, 713–15; media effectively used by, 714; executive orders of, 714–15; and legislative supremacy of Congress, 717, 719; Iran-Contra affair and, 725; presidency strengthened by, 727; Supreme Court nominations of, 761–62
Reagan administration: private sector stimulated by, 706; defense spending by, 706, 710; regulatory struggle between Congress and, 713–17; discretionary rule-making authority claimed by, 714; Iran-Contra affair and, 723–27; affirmative action opposed by, 744; legislative veto and, 750–51; original-intent debate and, 760; judicial restraint debate and, 754–55
Reapportionment: in constitutional law, 614–19, 765
Recaption, 245
Reconstruction: during Civil War, 319–22; congressional role during wartime, 320–22; Lincoln's policy, 320; theories of, 322–24; Military Reconstruction Act, 324; Johnson's policy, 324–26; and freedmen's policy, 326–28; and Thirteenth Amendment, 326–27; moderate policy in Congress, 328–35; effect of Fourteenth Amendment on, 332–35; congressional policy, 336–40; radical aims, 337–39; moderate aims, 337–39; reconstruction legislation: act of March

2, 1867, 337–38; act of March 23, 1867, 338–39, 340; act of July 1867, 339, 341; act of March 1868, 340; restoration of southern white rule, 349–50; constitutional significance of reconstruction, 360–61
Reconstruction Finance Corporation, 465
Reed, Stanley F.: appointed to Supreme Court, 489; upholds federal regulation of agriculture, 491; defends picketing as free speech, 524; rejects group libel idea, 528; sound-truck cases, 529; applies clear and present danger rule, 531; moderate outlook in 1940s, 568
Reed, Thomas B.: strengthens power of Speaker of the House, 371, 427
Regulatory movement: in late nineteenth century, 363; in relation to railroads, 373–76; rationale of, 371–72; and state railroad commissions, 373; nature and purpose, 408–9; in constitutional law, 416–26; in relation to trusts, 419–23; railroads, 424–26; in early twentieth century, 442–43, 456–62; in New Deal era, 467–74; post-New Deal movement, 641–48, 653–56, 708–9
Rehnquist, William H.: as attorney general, on impoundment, 663; appointed to Supreme Court, 679; Usery opinion, 683; in Bakke majority, 686; on independent counsels, 752; as conservative, 730, 761; as chief justice, 730; flag burning dissent of, 734; on due-process clause, 739; on abortion, 740–41
Rehnquist Court: on civil liberties in 1980s, 729–35; on suspect classifications, fundamental rights, and government regulation, 738–42; on economic and property rights, 745–48; religious exercise and, 735–38; on separation of powers, 749, 752–53; judicial restraint of, 754–57
Religion: free exercise of, 735–38
Removal power: controversy in 1789, 120; in Jacksonian era, 216–17; during reconstruction, 340–45; and Franklin D. Roosevelt, 497; over independent counsels, 751–53
Representation: American character as actual, 34, 46; in revolutionary era, 74–76; virtual representation, 34; in Constitutional Convention, 87–96; reapportionment reforms nineteenth century, 217; reapportionment twentieth century, 614–19
Republican party: formation and ideology, 129; opposition to Sedition Act, 132–37; constitutional ideas, 138–41; and execu-

Republican party *(continued)*
tive power, 141–43; territorial expansion, 143–45; embargo, 146–48; mercantile policy, 148–53; constitutional outlook, 154–55; impeachment trials, 167–70; policy toward judiciary, 166–70; reconstruction policy, 328–49; in election of 1896, 406–7; executive controlled by, 705–8; budget deficit and, 709–10, 713; Bork nomination and, 761–64

Republicanism: as constitutional ideology, in Revolution, 65–66; revisions in 1780s, 98; conflicting views during ratification, 103–10; Federalist theory of extended republic, 106–8; and Jacksonian Democracy, 200–203; in relation to imperialism, 380–85; in colonies, 38; tension between liberalism and, 708; executive tyranny feared by, 717

Restraining Act (1767), 51

Rhode Island: founding, 8–10, 11; charter, 19; and Dominion of New England, 20, 23, 24; charter as constitution, 69, 72; refuses to consider federal Constitution, 102; ratifies Constitution, 110; Dorr Rebellion, 219–20, 237; liquor regulations, 232; rejects Eighteenth Amendment, 463

Richardson, Elliott, 669–70; nativity scene case in, 737

Roane, Spencer: and Virginia states' rights, 180–82; criticizes John Marshall, 185

Roberts, Owen J.: appointed to Supreme Court, 474; opinion in *Nebbia* case, 475; *Retirement Board* opinion, 476; *Butler* opinion, 478, 480; conception of judicial review, 480; reverses view of *Adkins* precedent, 488; upholds anti-injunction act, 491; upholds second Agricultural Adjustment Act, 491; opinion in *Herndon v. Lowry,* 530; applies clear and present danger rule, 531; dissent in *Korematsu* case, 545–46

Roosevelt, Franklin D.: impact on presidency, xxiii–xxiv, 467–68; and analogue of war, 468–70; and regulatory movement, 469–74; and Court-packing plan, 480–86; and executive reorganization, 496–500; and foreign-policy crisis, 533–39; wartime presidency, 539–43; loyalty-review program, 561; establishes Fair Employment Practices Commission, 582, 597; and executive war making, 658–59; uses FBI for political intelligence, 659

Roosevelt, Theodore: as chief executive, 410–11, 412; and trust problem, 420–21; and administrative reform, 496

Rubber Reserve Corporation (World War II), 542

Rudman, Warren, 710

Rule of law, 708, 726

Rule of reason, 717, 746

Rutledge, John, 56

Rutledge, Wiley B.: appointment to Supreme Court, 489; joins libertarian bloc, 520; supports total incorporation, 521; opinion in labor free-speech case, 526; affirms U.N. charter over state law, 558; invalidates state segregation law, 584

Sanford, Edward T.: opinion in *Gitlow* case, 517–18

Sawyer, Charles, 556

Scalia, Antonin: Supreme Court appointment of, 730, 762; flag burning concurrence of, 734; on abortion, 741; *Morrison* dissent of, 753

Schlesinger, Arthur M., Jr.: on Franklin D. Roosevelt's constitutional concerns, 658

Secession: at Hartford Convention, 149; southern states, 278–90; reasons for, 280–82; northern resistance to, 289–90

Second Amendment, states'-rights view of, 623–24

Sedition Act (1798), 131–32, 135–36, 165; Act of 1918, 512–14

Seditious Conspiracy Act (1861), 302

Selective Service Act (1917), 435, 438

Selective Service System (World War II), 541

Senate: as advisory council, 123; impeachment trials, 167–70, 340–46; direct election of senators, 428, 718; Republican control of, 706; Democratic control of, 706; balanced-budget constitutional amendment approved by, 710; and approval power over presidential appointments, 720, 727, 761–64; Bork nomination rejected by, 727, 761–64

Senate Judiciary Committee, 763

Sentencing Commission, 753

Sentencing Reform Act (1984), 753

Separate-but-equal rule, 359, 684–95

Separation of powers, xxi, 28, 66, 81; advanced by opposition writers, 37; in state constitutions, 71–74, 76; in revolutionary era, 83–87; and federal Constitution, 114–16; in Republican party ideology, 138–39; asserted by Congress during Civil War, 295–96; divided government under, 705, 713; limited government under, 708, 710*n*, 712–13, 727; Congressional regulatory function under, 715; Congressional legislative suprem-

acy under, 718; conflict of interest under, 721; Iran-Contra affair and, 726; federalism and, 749–53; judicial restraint and, 759
Separatists, 8
Seventeenth Amendment, 718
Seward, William H., 283
Shaw, Lemuel: opinion in sojourner slave case, 246
Sheppard-Towner Maternity Aid Act (1921), 460
Sherman, John: on congressional war power, 296; proposes antitrust bill, 377–78
Sherman, Roger: in Continental Congress, 56; committee to draft Declaration of Independence, 59; view of executive power, 96; opposes congressional negative, 99
Sherman Act, *see* Antitrust
Shiras, George: role in income tax case, 403
Sidney, Algernon, 36, 67
Sirica, John: in Watergate, 667, 669
Sixteenth Amendment, 431–32
Sixth Amendment: and due process clause of Fourteenth Amendment, 519–20, 621–22; in burger era, 694
Slavery: in Constitutional Convention, 95, 242–43; federal neutrality toward, 243–44; and Jacksonian Democracy, 200; as political issue, 241–42, 249–53; and American nationality, 241–42; in relation to republican government, 242–46; and conflict of laws, 245–46; fugitive slaves, 246–49; migration or importation question, 249–51; and postal censorship, 251; slave trade in District of Columbia, 251–53; and gag rule, 252–53; in territories, 254–62; nationalization of, 262–63, 274–75; proposed amendment to protect, 285; philosophical rejection of, 712. *See also* Emancipation
Smith-Lever Act (1914), 459–60
Social compact: in New England colonies, 8–9; theory, 11; in Declaration of Independence, 60; in states, 69–70; in federal Constitution, 114–15
Social Security Act (1935), 484, 488–89, 493, 502–3, 738
Sociological jurisprudence, 454–55
Soil Conservation Act (1935), 479
Somerset doctrine, 244–46
Sons of Liberty, 51
Souter, David H.: Supreme Court nomination of, 764
South Carolina: as separate colony, 23; revolutionary government, 55; revolutionary constitution, 69, 72; ratifies Constitution, 110; Negro seamen's act, 250; nul-

lification crisis, 201–2, 205, 207–12; secession, 283; repeal of secession ordinance, 325; readmitted to Union, 340; massive resistance to desegregation in, 589; opposes Voting Rights Act, 602
Sovereignty: in English constitution, xx–xxi; in imperial constitution, 48–50, 53–54, 57; under Articles of Confederation, 76–81, 83–84; limited nature of federal, 100, 708; in Constitution, 87, 101–2; Antifederalist unitary theory, 105; Marshall's conception of, 183–84, 197–99; Calhoun's theory, 208–9. *See also* Popular sovereignty; State sovereignty
Speaker of the House, 717
Special Division, 721
Special prosecutor: Watergate investigation, 667–68, 669–70, 721; in Ethics in Government Act, 713. *See also* Independent counsel
Stamp Act (1765), 45–48, 50–51, 54; Stamp Act Congress, 45–46
Stanbery, Henry: enforces reconstruction policy, 339; argues in reconstruction case, 353
Stanton, Edwin M., 342
State-action theory: Fourteenth Amendment, 333–34, 357, 583, 591–95, 600–601
State and church: separation of, 735
State Department: establishment of, 121
States: revolutionary constitutions, xix–xx, 68–76; legislative ascendancy in, 71–74; excessive power in Confederation, 83–87; limitations imposed by federal Constitution, 87–100; state court jurisdiction under Judiciary Act of 1789, 158–59; constitutional change in nineteenth century, 217–18; doctrine of police power, 224–27; mercantilist policies of, 239–40; role in mobilization during Civil War, 308–9; taxation and interstate commerce policy in late nineteenth century, 391–93; constitutional reform in progressive era, 429; attempts to tax in New Deal period, 493–94; loss of power during New Deal, 500–503; loyalty programs during cold war, 573–74; resistance to desegregation, 589; legislative excesses by, 717; federal spending limit sought by, 710; budgetary restriction laws of, 710; constitutions of, 757; constitutional convention sought by, 765–66. *See also* Bill of Rights; Fourteenth Amendment; State sovereignty
State sovereignty: in Confederation, 79–81; in federal Constitution, 101–2; in Hartford Convention, 149–50; in Jacksonian era, 200–201; Calhoun's theory, 211, 253, 258; and Taney Court, 223, 234, 238; in

State sovereignty *(continued)*
  fugitive slave case, 278–79; repudiated during Civil War, 317–18; Blackmun on, 749
Stevens, John Paul: position in *Bakke* case, 686; Supreme Court appointment of, 761; as centrist, 730
Stevens, Thaddeus, 323
Stewart, Potter: concurs in reapportionment decision, 617; libel law, 627; dissent in *Griswold* case, 628; opposes egalitarianism, 681; in majority in *Bakke* case, 686; opposes capital punishment, 695
Stone, Harlan F.: as liberal in 1930s, 474, 520; dissent in *Butler* case, 478; upholds federal regulation of production, 480; affirms Fair Labor Standards Act, 490; advances preferred freedoms doctrine, 522; upholds government in Japanese-American relocation policy, 545; and trial of enemy war criminals, 548–49; dissent in *Schneidermann* case, 551
Story, Joseph: appointed to Supreme Court, 177; upholds federal appellate jurisdiction, 180; on public and private corporations, 190–91; dissent in Kentucky bank case, 224; dissent in Charles River Bridge case, 226–27; on federal commercial common law, 235–36; fugitive slave law upheld, 247–49
Strong, William: appointed to Supreme Court, 360; on Electoral Commission, 351; upholds federal civil rights protection, 355
Substantive due process, 386, 388–91, 405; rejected in New Deal, 495. *See also* Fourteenth Amendment; Judicial review
Subtreasury system, 206–7
Subversive Activities Control Board, 566–67, 576
Suffolk Resolves, 56
Suffrage: in Massachusetts Bay colony, 7; in colonial policies, 34; in New England town meeting, 41; reforms during Revolution, 74–75; reforms in Jacksonian era, 217; reform attempted in Rhode Island, 220; Negro suffrage, 322, 337–38; disenfranchisement under reconstruction policy, 339–40; Fifteenth Amendment, framing and adoption, 347–49, 357–58; black disenfranchisement, 359; direct election of senators, 427–28; secret ballot reform, 429; primary election reform, 429; women's suffrage, 428; "grandfather" laws struck down, 581; Negro voting enforced, 595–97; voting rights legislation, 597–98, 600–602, 607–8, 651–52
Sugar Act (1764), 45

Sugar Equalization Board (World War I), 440
Sumner, Charles: reconstruction theory, 323; proposes equal rights amendment, 327; and Civil Rights Act of 1875, 350
Sumners, Hatton: opposes Court-packing plan, 483
Supreme Court: in Constitutional Convention, 99–100; appellate jurisdiction, 157–59; size reduced, 163; sessions set by Congress, 167; appellate jurisdiction challenged, 180–82; proposed legislation restricting Court, 198; and slavery in territories, 268; and *Dred Scott* case, 268–75; reaction to Civil War emergency government, 296–98; on dual-status theory, 300–301; critical of military government, 337; and reconstruction, 352–60; size reduced, 360; decisions affecting ICC, 375–76; in late nineteenth century, 386–407; on commerce clause, 391–93; in defense of property and corporations, 393–403; policy-making role, 397; expanded power of judicial review, 403–6; and trust question, rule of reason, 422; and ICC, 425–26; and World War I legislation, 434–36; policy-making role, 455; and laissez-faire revival, 445–53; approves regulatory legislation, 444–45; decisions affecting labor unions, 449–50; activist role, 450–52; trust question in 1920s, 452–53; and New Deal, 474–80; and Court-packing crisis, 480–86; approves New Deal measures, 485–96; evaluation of role in New Deal era, 505–7; and civil liberties, 523–42; and Japanese-American relocation policy, 543–47; checks executive emergency power, 556–57; on internal security problems, 568–78; and school desegregation, 584–95; and equal protection law, 612–14; criminal procedure reform, 619–24; expands freedom of speech and press, 624–27; liberal activism of Warren era, 634–38; and civic disorders, 649–51; on executive privilege, 671–72; and wire-tapping, 675; resists egalitarian trend, 680–89; and women's rights, 689–92; criminal procedure, 692–95; and abortion, 695–96; freedom of speech and press, 697–701; activism of Burger Court, 701–4; Congress-executive regulatory struggle and, 715–16; on Congressional legislative veto, 718, 750; independent counsel act upheld by, 722; and civil liberty issues in 1980s, 729–35; ideological camps of, 730; suspect classifications, fundamental rights, and government regulations and, 738–42; on affirmative action in

1980s, 742–45; on economic and property rights, 745–47; restraint vs. activism of, 754–57; Yonkers housing discrimination case and, 756–57; original-intent debates and, 757–61

Sutherland, George: opinion in *Adkins* case, 448; opinion in *Massachusetts v. Mellon*, 460; member of conservative bloc, 474; invalidates New Deal regulation, 479–80; on Sixth Amendment and states, 518–19; asserts executive power in foreign affairs, 534, 539

Swayne, Noah: upholds federal civil rights law, 355

Swisher, Carl B.: quoted on *Cooley* rule, 234

Taft, William Howard: view of executive power, 411; and trust question, 422; role in framing Sixteenth Amendment, 431–32; interprets commerce power in 1920s, 445; invalidates second child labor law, 448; upholds labor injunction, 450; applies public interest doctrine, 451; and administrative reform, 496–97; interprets removal power, 512*n*–13*n*

Taft-Hartley Act (1947): Communist registration, 569

Taney, Roger B.: removal of deposits, 216; appointed chief justice, 222; dual-federalism outlook, 223; Charles River Bridge case, 224–27; attitude toward corporations, 229–30; commerce power cases, 230–34; and judicial power, 235–38; and admiralty jurisdiction, 236–37; and judicial restraint, 237; concurs in *Prigg* case, 248; on slavery in territories, 257; *Dred Scott* opinion, 269–74, 278, 385; and state sovereignty, 279; habeas corpus suspension, 304; on conscription, 312–13; on citizenship in *Dred Scott* case, 330; status of Negroes, 385

Tariff: South Carolina opposition, 207–12

Taxation: parliamentary power over disputed, 46–48; excise and Whiskey Rebellion, 128; and federal police power, 416–19; child labor tax, 448; in Agricultural Adjustment Act, 471, 478; state taxes in 1930s, 593–95. *See also* Income tax law; Sixteenth Amendment

Taylor, Zachary: and Compromise of 1850, 260, 262

Tea Act (1773), 52

Tennessee: reconstruction government, 321; secession, 288–89; readmitted to Union, 334; apportionment law, 615–16

Tennessee Valley Authority, 470, 479

Tenth Amendment: framing, 119; invoked by Jefferson in bank argument, 126–27; federal price controls in World War I, 434; in child labor case, 448; in *Butler* case, 478; and Agricultural Adjustment Act, 506; in *Usery* case, 683; state power protected by, 749. *See also* Dual federalism; State sovereignty

Tenure of Office Act (1867), 341, 344–45; repealed, 365

Territorial policy: under Articles of Confederation, 80–81; Northwest Ordinance, 94; Louisiana Purchase, 142–45; slavery in territories, 254–62; overseas colonial administration, 383–85

Texas: annexation, 255–56; secession, 283; readmitted to Union, 340; white primary law, 595; school desegregation, 586

Thirteenth Amendment: framing and adoption, 316–17, 324–27; congressional power under, 331; as basis for Civil Rights Act of 1866, 332; interpreted during reconstruction, 355; and peonage cases, 581; in *Jones v. Mayer*, 604; in *Runyon v. McCrary*, 604–5

Three-fifths clause: in Constitutional Convention, 95–96; and Hartford Convention, 149

Todd, Thomas: appointed to Supreme Court, 177

Tower, John, 727

Townshend Acts, 50–51

Trade associations, 452–53

Trading with the Enemy Act (1917), 438, 470

Transportation Act (1920), 426, 445, 458–59, 460–61

Transportation Department, U.S., 716

Treason: defined in Constitution, 176; Burr trial, 175–77; during Civil War, 301–5; World War II cases, 549–50

Treasury Department: established, 121; as executive department, 718

Truman, Harry S.: and exercise of executive power, 640–41; war-making power, 554–55; Steel Seizure case, 556–57; establishes loyalty review program, 561–62; vetoes McCarran Act, 566; appoints Committee on Civil Rights, 582; supports civil rights, 597; and impoundment, 662; and executive privilege, 668

Trumbull, Lyman: introduces Freedmen's Bureau bill, 329; view of Thirteenth Amendment and congressional power, 329; and Civil Rights Act of 1866, 330–31

Twelfth Amendment, 143

Twenty-fifth Amendment, 670

Twenty-first Amendment, 464

Twenty-fourth Amendment, 596

Twenty-sixth Amendment, 652
Tyler, John: opposes U.S. bank, 207; Peace Conference 1861, 285

Union: republican character, 70–71; expresses American nationality, 76; in Articles of Confederation, 76–81; structure as determined by Constitutional Convention, 101–2; nature of debated during ratification struggle, 113–14; identified with republicanism, 114–15; assertion of compact theory, 134–36, 138, 140, 145; Marshall's theory, 184–86; Jackson's theory, 210–12; theories asserted in nullification crisis, 209–12; Calhoun's theory, 253; repudiation of compact theory in Civil War, 317–18; states'-rights nationalist conception, 318, 328–29, 358. *See also* Dual federalism; Federalism; State sovereignty
United States Food Administration (World War I), 440
United States Shipping Board (World War I), 415–16, 440

Vallandigham, Clement L., 307
Van Buren, Martin: forms Jacksonian party, 165, 201; constitutional view of subtreasury system, 207; election 1836, 214; makes Supreme Court appointments, 222
Van Devanter, Willis: member of conservative bloc, 474; retirement, 489
Vested rights doctrine, 186–88, 387; in slavery controversy, 250
Veterans Administration, 716
Vice-admiralty courts, 24, 51
Vietnam war, 660–61, 709, 713, 718, 723
Vinson, Fred M.: appointed to Supreme Court, 568; upholds restrictions on speech, 527–28; dissent in Steel Seizure case, 557; Communist cases, 569–71; opinion in desegregation case, 583, 586
Virginia: founding, 4–5; charters, 4–5; House of Burgesses created, 5; as royal colony, 5–8; in seventeenth century, 10–12, 14–15, 19; Bacon's Rebellion, 21–22; revolutionary government, 55; revolutionary constitution, 69, 72; plan in Constitutional Convention, 87–91, 96, 99; ratification, 110; opposes assumption of state debts, 126; Virginia Resolutions, 132–35, 211; challenges appellate jurisdiction of Supreme Court, 180–82; land-title conflict with Kentucky, 189–90; secession, 288–89; partitioned in

Civil War, 309; loyal government during Civil War, 321; readmitted to Union, 340; resistance to desegregation, 590
Virginia Company of London, 4–5, 8
Virginia Company of Plymouth, 4
Volstead Act (1919), 463
Voting Rights Act (1965), 601–3, 742, 744

Wade, Benjamin F.: on Committee of 33 (1861), 284; and Johnson impeachment trial, 345; Wade-Davis bill, 321, 324
Waite, Morrison R.: asserts state-action theory, 357; opinion in *Munn* case, 389–92; view of due process, 394
War Department: established, 120
War of 1812, 148–49, 152
War Industries Board (World War I), 440
War Labor Board (World War II), 541
War Manpower Commission (World War II), 541
War power: in Civil War, 292–95; and Congress, 295–97; in World War I, 433–36; in World War II, 539–43; post-World War II, 554–55
War Powers Act (1973), 675, 676, 724, 727; post-Vietnam War, 713; Act of 1941, 540; Act of 1942, 540
War Production Board (World War II), 541
War Prohibition Act (1918), 434–35
Warren, Earl: Japanese-Americans and, 547; appointed to Supreme Court, 569; and substantive due process, 405–6; loyalty review cases, 573–74; opinion in *Pennsylvania v. Nelson*, 575; McCarran Act decisions, 576; restricts congressional investigations, 577; desegregation decision, 587–89; on state-action theory, 594; affirms Voting Rights Act, 602; reapportionment decision, 617–18; criminal procedure reform, 622; and libel law, 627; establishment and free exercise of religion, 630–32; resigns, 678
Warren Court: liberalism of, 634–38, 754, 756; right of privacy established by, 739–40; antitrust policy of, 746; on separation of powers, 750
War Shipping Administration (World War II), 541
Washington, Bushrod, 189
Washington, George: in Continental Congress, 56; source of legitimacy for new government, 121–22; elected president, 120; executive leadership, 121–23; in foreign affairs, 124–25; annual message to Congress, 141; asks judiciary for advice, 160; executive privilege, 668

Watergate affair, 667–75; constitutional significance, 673–75, 721; origin of, 713
Water Power Act (1920), 460
Wayne, James M.: appointed to Supreme Court, 222; view of commerce power, 233; role in *Dred Scott* case, 270; concurs in *Dred Scott,* 274; opinion in *Ex parte Vallandigham,* 307
Webb-Kenyon Act (1913), 462–63
Webster, Daniel: Union theory, 212
Weeks Act (1911), 459
Welfare: hostility toward, 709–10
West Jersey Concessions and Agreement (1677), 17
West Virginia: created during Civil War, 309
Whig party, 203, 206, 213–14; demise, 264
Whiskey Rebellion, 128
White, Byron R.: and state-action theory, 594; invalidates California Proposition 14, 604; on reapportionment, 618; and libel law, 627; approves racial classification, 686; against death penalty, 695; rejects journalistic privilege, 701; as centrist, 730; on privacy, 741
White, Edward D.: appointed to Supreme Court, 393; opinion in insular case, 384; minority in income tax cases, 402; and oleomargarine tax case, 417; rule of reason, 422; upholds war power, 436
Whittaker, Charles E.: appointed to Supreme Court, 569; resigns, 574
Williams, Roger, 9; natural law theory, 36
Wilmot Proviso, 256, 259
Wilson, James: favors proportional representation, 90–91; supports three-fifths clause, 96; favors strong executive, 96; opinion in *Chisholm* case, 161
Wilson, James F.: on scope of Civil Rights Act of 1866, 331; on Johnson impeachment
Wilson, Woodrow: on congressional government, 363; on civil service reform, 370; on regulation of economy, 371; approves executive leadership, 410; as chief executive, 411–12; on public administration, 414; agencies created under, 415–16; antitrust policy, 422–23; war dictatorship, 436–41
Winthrop, John, 7; natural law theory, 36
Wisconsin: territorial government, 268; resists fugitive slave law, 278–79
Wisdom, John Minor: affirmative action opinion, 606
Wise, John: natural law theory, 36
Women's rights: suffrage, 428; women's rights upheld by Supreme Court, 689–92; Equal Rights Amendment, 745
Woodbury, Levi: view of commerce power, 232
Woods, William B.: affirms federal civil rights power, 355; asserts state-action theory, 357
Woolen Act (1699), 47
Wright, J. Skelly: desegregation case, 590; as judicial activist, 636
Wright, Jim, 717, 728
Writs of assistance, 51, 62

Yates, Abraham, 104
Yazoo land fraud, 188–89
Yellow-dog labor contracts, 418–19, 447
Yonkers, N.Y., housing discrimination case in, 756–57